D1568733

SOCIODYNAMICS

A Systematic Approach to Mathematical
Modelling in the Social Sciences

SOCIODYNAMICS

A Systematic Approach to Mathematical Modelling in the Social Sciences

Wolfgang Weidlich

DOVER PUBLICATIONS, INC.
Mineola, New York

Bibliographical Note

This Dover edition, first published in 2006, is an unabridged republication
of the edition published by the Taylor & Francis Group, London, in 2002.
The work was originally published by The Gordon and Breach Publishing
Group, London, in 2000.

International Standard Book Number: 0-486-45027-9

Manufactured in the United States of America
Dover Publications, Inc., 31 East 2nd Street, Mineola, N.Y. 11501

Contents

Part III Mathematical Methods

Preface

The purpose of this book is to give an account of the present 'state of the art' of an interdisciplinary project named 'Sociodynamics' which has been developed over three decades.

The intention of sociodynamics is to develop – by combining appropriate mathematical methods with concepts from social science – a systematic approach to setting up and evaluating mathematical models for a broad class of collective dynamic social processes in different sectors of society.

The interested reader can trace the evolution of sociodynamics – besides various articles in journals – in some previous books: The early results of the seventies have been presented in I [28] (1983). In II.1 [21] (1988) the concrete application to interregional migration has been worked out and the books and review articles II.4 [19] (1989), I [32] (1991) and I [33] (1995) give an account of the results of sociodynamic modelling in the eighties, whereas this book presents in detail the method of sociodynamics together with various models most of which have been set up and analyzed in the nineties.

Its first part considers general system structures, social systems in particular, with their characteristic properties. In Chapter 3 the modelling strategy of sociodynamics is exhibited in general terms.

The second and main part contains six concrete models applying the modelling procedure of sociodynamics to problems of population dynamics, sociology, economics and regional science.

The last part provides a self-contained presentation of the mathematical concepts and methods utilized in sociodynamics.

Several coinciding and fortunate circumstances were helpful and even indispensible for the development of sociodynamics:

Some of its ideas originated in *physics*. Here, the theory of new objects, in particular the LASER, necessitated the exhaustive use of methods of statistical physics and nonlinear dynamics in order to treat such non-equilibrium systems. Out of physics thereupon developed *synergetics*, a new interdisciplinary branch of science, and the long term cooperation and discussion with my friend and colleague Hermann Haken, the founder of synergetics, was a permanent source of inspiration and encouragement to me. It turned out that one of the main mathematical instruments for the description of physical dynamic stochastic systems, the master equation, proved to also be an appropriate central tool for formulating the concepts of *sociodynamics*.

However, the whole project would not have been possible without the endeavour of my research fellows, the diplomands, doctorands and habilitands of our Institute, cooperating with me over the years. Their ideas have influenced the models exhibited here and in other publications.

I am very grateful to all of them for their cooperation and want to thank here explicitly those who contributed by their PhD-dissertations and by collaborative publications to the evolution of the project, namely K. Brandt, M. Braun, T. Brenner, N. Empacher, P. Frankhauser, G. Haag, T. Hagel, D. Helbing, M. Hilliges, J. Hugo, N. Koch, P. Molnàr, M. Munz, R. Reiner, T. Sigg, J. Starke and K. Teichmann.

Special thanks go to M. Braun, T. Brenner, M. Mikuletz, R. Reiner, S. Rupp and S. Stöckle, whose computer simulations of the models are presented in the chapters of this book.

In particular I want to thank G. Haag, my partner over the years in developing sociodynamics, who now demonstrates its applicability to 'hard' real world problems in his firm STASA, and D. Helbing, who continues to go forcefully beyond physics in his interdisciplinary contributions to sociodynamics and traffic dynamics.

The interdisciplinary project of sociodynamics has also led to a very fruitful *international cooperation*. This internationalism proved to be of particular value in a comparative analysis of interregional migration (see II.1 [21] and Chapter 4). It was very fortunate – and not self-evident – that we (i.e. G. Haag and the author) found friendly acceptance among scientists (economists, geographers, physicists, regional scientists, sociologists, system scientists) who were willing to cooperate with us and from whom we have learned much! We are grateful for this cooperation in discussions, joint-investigations and -publications to Å. E. Andersson, D. S. Dendrinos, W. Ebeling, F. Englmann, M. Fischer, I. Holmberg, J. A. Holyst, J. Hubert, A. Kujawski, J. Ledent, S. Lombardo, G. O. Mensch, E. Mosekilde, K. Müller, Y. Y. Papageorgiou, Y. S. Popkov, D. Pumain, T. Puu, G. Rabino, N. Sarafoglou, L. Sanders, T. Saint-Julien, F. Schweitzer, V. Shvetsov, M. Sonis and U. Witt, and we are pleased that with some of them the communication, cooperation, and friendship continues over the years!

Last but not least I thank the Volkswagen-Stiftung, the Deutsche Forschungsgemeinschaft and the German–Israeli Foundation who generously furnished us with funds over the years for the project.

It was my intention to embed the selected sociodynamic models of this book into some broader qualitative considerations about the social sector to which they belong. In the cases of migration and multiculturality (Chapter 4) and of totalitarian political systems (Chapter 6) this was not an easy task for me, because the considerations inevitably have led to deep and difficult problems faced by societies, which include the catastrophies having haunted mankind in this century in which Germany was the prime cause.

Nevertheless I felt that I should not evade mentioning these problems. Concerning the relevant historical problems I gratefully acknowledge the advice given to me by Y. S. Popkov, H. Shoolman, M. Sonis, P. Tarnesby, and in particular by the historians E. Jäckel and A. Rödder.

The target audience of this book consists of two groups: firstly *social scientists* interested in strategies for the mathematical modelling of dynamic social phenomena and in an introduction to the mathematics of stochastic dynamic systems, and secondly of *natural scientists, computer scientists and mathematicians* searching for new applications of their mathematical and computational methods in the broad field of the social sciences.

It remains to thank those who helped me in the preparation of the manuscript. Thus, I am very grateful to Harvey Shoolman, who not only converted my 'broken English of scientists' into readable English prose, but also critically supervised and discussed the text giving me much valuable advice.

Special thanks go to Mrs A. Steinhauser who tirelessly typed the complex text with high precision and to M. Mikuletz, S. Rupp and S. Stöckle who managed the many figures of the text.

Finally I thank Harwood Academic Publishers, an imprint of the Gordon and Breach Publishing Group, for perfectly managing the publication of the book with their customary high standards.

Wolfgang Weidlich

Biographical Notes About the Author

Born 1931 in Dresden, Wolfgang Weidlich attended the Kreuzgymnasium and simultaneously was a member of the prestigious Dresdner Kreuzchor. On February 13th, 1945, he narrowly survived the destruction of Dresden. After his Abitur in 1949 he left the communist 'Deutsche Demokratische Republik' together with his family and studied physics and mathematics at the Free University of West-Berlin. There he took a diploma in 1954 (MSc), a doctorate in 1957 and habilitation in physics in 1963.

Since 1966 he has been professor of theoretical physics at the University of Stuttgart. A honorary doctorate of the University of Umea (Sweden) was awarded to him 1985 for merits in interdisciplinary research.

His research areas include quantum physics, quantum optics, statistical physics and the foundation of sociodynamics.

Introduction

This book introduces the results of a project we have called "*Sociodynamics*".

The approach of sociodynamics provides a general strategy, or set of theoretical concepts, for designing mathematical models for the quantitative description of a rather broad class of collective dynamical phenomena within human society.

The concepts of sociodynamics have an *interdisciplinary* character in two main respects:

Firstly, the modelling concepts of sociodynamics should be applicable to phenomena of *different sectors* of human society which are conventionally investigated in separate social sciences such as demography, sociology, political science, economics and regional science.

Secondly, sociodynamics utilizes mathematical concepts applicable to a very general class of systems in both natural and social science. These concepts belong to the mathematical theory of stochastic (probabilistic) systems and the theory of nonlinear dynamics.

Since these mathematical methods have already found a rich field of application in statistical physics and other natural sciences, it seems understandable that natural scientists – like the author of this book – have taken advantage of the possibility of also applying these successful mathematical methods *mutatis mutandis* to problems of social science. We stress, however, that no form of *physicalism* is implied in sociodynamics. Apart from the universal mathematical methods employed only concepts strictly applicable to human behaviour enter its modelling approach. The laws of physics are therefore not relevant and are excluded. (The problem, whether and to which extent there can arise interdisciplinary insights into structural analogies between phenomena in nature and society will be discussed in more detail below.)

The organisation of the chapters of this book is, more or less, a consequence of the intention of sociodynamics to provide a set of interdisciplinary general concepts for the construction of quantitative models in the social sciences:

Part I provides the general framework into which sociodynamical concepts should be embedded. It begins in Chapter 1 with a short global survey about the stratified layer structure of reality focussing on a comparison of the systems of nature and society with respect to their form and degree of complexity (Section 1.1).

1

The problem of exactly how this stratification is generated and how the "bottom up" and "top down" interaction between layers must be interpreted leads to a short discussion of the philosophical concepts of *reductionism* and *holism* (Section 1.2).

There already exist sciences of interdisciplinary relevance, namely *General System Theory* and *Synergetics* which have contributed much to the understanding of qualitative and quantitative properties of complex systems. Their conceptual framework and their relation to each other and to *Sociodynamics* is discussed in some detail in Section 1.3.

Chapter 2 inquires into the general problem of *quantitative modelling in social science*. Since social systems are in general much richer than those found in natural science a *qualitative characterization* and demarcation of the system properties and the relevant key variables must always precede the *quantitative treatment* (Section 2.1) in order to determine the scope of the subsequent quantitative model (Section 2.2). However, in successful cases of quantitative modelling we believe there will always develop an interplay, a *feedback loop between qualitative and quantitative argumentation* (Section 2.3) leading to deeper insights.

Nevertheless, certain critical arguments against the use of quantitative methods in social science have been raised. Some aspects of these arguments are justified and should be reconsidered whereas others are misleading and can be refuted. The discussion of this issue is taken up in Section 2.4.

We then focus upon the general modelling concept of sociodynamics in Chapter 3. This concentrates in the quantitative description of the *dynamics of social processes* by cyclically relating the microlevel with the macrolevel of the social system. The *microlevel* consists of considerations, decisions and actions of individuals and the *macrolevel* consists of relevant collective macrovariables of the system and their evolution. The general purposes of the modelling concept are exhibited in Section 3.1 and the steps of the modelling procedure which finally lead to evolution equations for the macrovariables are developed in Section 3.2.

Part II is devoted to the demonstration of the applicability of the sociodynamic concept to different sectors of the society. Four principal sectors are considered:

(II.1)   *population dynamics* (Chapter 4 Migration of Interacting Populations);

(II.2)   *sociology* (Chapter 5: Group Dynamics: The Rise and Fall of Interacting Social Groups, and Chapter 6: Opinion Formation on the Verge of Political Phase-Transitions);

(II.3)   *economics* (Chapter 7: Quality Competition between High Tech Firms and Chapter 8: Dynamics of Conventional and Fashion Demand);

(II.4)   *regional science* (Chapter 9: Urban Evolution and Population Pressure).

The general modelling concepts of Chapter 3 are *necessary* but *not sufficient* requisites for designing concrete models in these sectors. Instead, the social environment into which the modelled process is embedded must first be considered in qualitative terms (see Chapter 2). Only afterwards the constituents of the concrete model, i.e. the variables, the trendparameters, the motivation potentials and the transition rates, can be chosen appropriately.

Therefore the Chapters 4 to 9 typically begin with a *qualitative consideration* of the general social structures within which the dynamic process to be described by the quantitative model takes place.

Thereupon the relevant variables can be chosen, plausible assumptions about the form of motivation potentials and transition rates can be made, from which follows the form of evolution equations, either on the stochastic level or on the approximate deterministic level. *These design elements constitute the quantitative model.* Finally, in most cases specific sets of trendparameters can be chosen in order to make numerical simulations of characteristic scenarios which can be sociologically interpreted according to the meaning given to those trendparameters and dynamic variables.

The purpose of Part III is to give a more or less selfcontained introduction to the mathematical methods utilized in this book for the quantitative modelling of social processes.

Starting with the derivation of the *master equation* for the probability distribution over the states of an ensemble of stochastically evolving systems and the explanation of its main properties in Chapter 10, the exact and approximate form of *meanvalue- and variance-equations* is derived from the master equation in Chapter 11. At last the concept of *stochastic trajectories* is introduced in Chapter 12 and its relation to the probability distribution is explained. It can be shown that the mean evolution of partial ensembles of stochastic trajectories can be described by *quasi-meanvalue equations*. These equations are often used in the models of Part II.

We conclude this introduction with a

Guide to the reader

Readers primarily interested in general interdisciplinary relations between sciences of complex systems are referred to Part I, Chapters 1, 2 and 3. Chapter 3 of Part I exhibits the general modelling strategy of sociodynamics.

Readers only interested in a specific model out of one of the fields populations dynamics, sociology, economics, or regional science, are advised to read first Chapter 3 about the general modelling concepts and then to jump to the corresponding chapter of Part II. Each of the chapters of Part II makes use of the general concepts of Chapter 3, applying and combining them with specific modelling concepts developed in selfcontained form.

Readers wanting to be informed in more detail about the mathematical methods utilized in sociodynamics are referred to Part III, Chapters 10, 11 and 12. In these chapters the main tools of sociodynamics, the master equation, meanvalue- and quasi-meanvalue-equations, stochastic trajectories and their interrelations are derived in concise selfcontained manner.

Part I
Structures and Modelling Concepts

1. The Structure of Reality Under Interdisciplinary Perspective

In this chapter we consider the structure of reality under very global points of view which however allow a comparison of systems in nature and society with respect to such general questions as the relation between the whole and its part, the kind of interactions within systems and their degree of complexity.

The first section gives a short *description* of such system properties and the second section introduces to some considerations potentially leading to *explanations* of the stratification of reality into layers of subsystems. The third section relates the contributions of more recently arisen interdisciplinary branches of science, namely *Synergetics* and *Sociodynamics*, to the conceptual framework of *General System Theory*.

1.1 Systems and their Parts: The Stratification of Reality

It seems obvious that the reality, including the inanimate and the animate worlds, is stratified into sequences of layers of varying organisational complexity. The higher, more macroscopic layers are composed of and in this sense "rest upon" the lower, more microscopic layers. We leave open at the moment the kind of causal interrelation between the layers. Nicolai Hartmann was one of the first philosophers basing his ontology on this layer-structure of the world; see [1], [2].

We define a layer to be a stratum of reality of a certain self-contained internal organisation. If the organisational structure between the parts and the whole of the stratum leads to the emergence of new characteristic qualities which cannot be found in lower strata, we denote the stratum as *system*. A system "is more than the sum of its parts" because it possesses properties which cannot be attributed to the parts but only to the system as a whole. It should be mentioned that the definition of a system applied in this chapter is a very general one. It comprises systems of the inanimate and the animate world, that means physical, chemical, biological or social systems, being in a static state or stationary equilibrium as well as systems exhibiting a specific dynamic behaviour.

7

Examples are easily found: A gas in a box is a thermodynamic *system*, because its temperature and pressure are properties which can only be attributed to the *gas as a whole*, but not to its atoms. An animal is a system composed of organs whose life activities can only be attributed to the *whole animal* and not to the organs or the simple sum of organs.

Let us next consider the *relation between systems*. In the simpler case of the inanimate world this relation is usually a *hierarchical* one in the sense of the following vertical sequence of "being constituent of":

The constituent parts of a given system may themselves be systems constituted of more elementary parts, and the given system may on the other hand be the constituent part of a higher system.

As a simple example from physics take a molecule to be the given system. A molecule is composed of nuclei and electrons and has system properties not found in nuclei and electrons. But nuclei themselves are not structureless but are systems composed of protons and neutrons which again are composed of quarks and gluons. On the other hand molecules are usually parts of higher systems, for instance of a gas or a molecular crystal. Each system level has characteristic properties of its own.

In biology or social science the system architecture is more complex. Take the society with the human individual as its elementary constituent part. Here there exist many subsystems, like families, schools, firms, political parties etc., that means social groups forming organisational units. These subsystems have an overlapping structure since the same individual can simultaneously be the member of several groups. Near the *"vertical"* system hierarchy "individual – group – society" there exist also *"horizontal"* relations and interactions between groups of comparable size, e.g. between firms or political parties.

Since the stratification of *reality* into sequences of systems is such a dominant fact, it is only natural that *sciences* – where each science is defined as having a certain domain of objects – will also more or less be structured sequentially according to the organisational layers of the inanimate and animate world.

The Figures 1.1 and 1.2 depict – in a rather global form – how the sequence of systems of reality bring about an arrangement of sciences. The part-whole interaction within the architecture of systems leads to a corresponding overlap of the domains of sciences.

Natural scientists [3], [4], [5] as well as modern philosophers [6], [7] develop global views on the world as a whole which fit in this hierarchically ordered scheme of objects and sciences.

The complexity of systems and system architectures is of course intimately connected with the *nature of the constituent parts* which will now be considered. We compare the cases of *physical thermodynamic systems* like gases or solids with *social systems*.

In the first case the potential system elements – electrons, atoms, molecules – are *relatively poorly structured* in the following sense: If these elements are integrated into a system and become its constituent parts, only relatively few states or "degrees of freedom" are excitable in these elements. For example, consider the vibrations of atoms around their normal position in a solid or vibrations and rotations of molecules of a gas according to the temperature of the thermodynamic system.

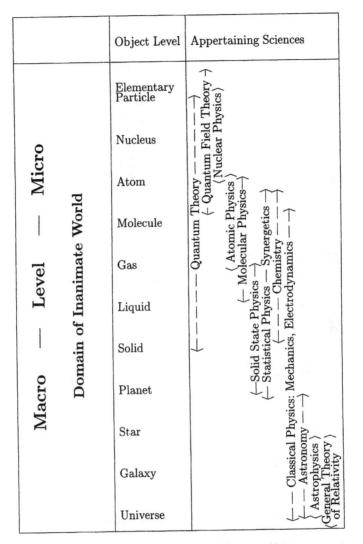

Figure 1.1   Sciences of the inanimate world.

In the second case the constituents of the system, the individuals, are *themselves highly complex units*. These individuals possess a manifold of potential modes of behaviour. It depends on the situation in all subsystems in which the individual simultaneously plays its role, which mode of his/her behaviour or action is *excited* and in the process of *surfacing* and which on the other hand remains *latent* and *dormant*. That means that the nature and behaviour of complex units like human individuals is *not* fixed once for all, *but depends on the system into which it is integrated*. (The latter fact is an example of a whole ⇒ part, i.e. top ⇒ down interaction.)

Finally we shortly discuss the most important question with respect to the structure of a system: the question of the *kind of interactions between the parts* of a system and

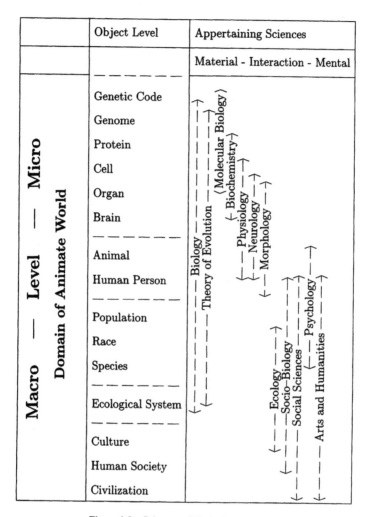

Figure 1.2   Sciences of the animate world.

between the *parts* and the *whole*. The *pairwise interaction* between parts is denoted as *direct* interaction whereas the *part-whole* and *whole-part* interaction is denoted as *indirect interaction*. The part-whole together with the whole-part interaction creates an *indirect interdependence* of all parts since they all are coupled to the same whole.

First we discuss the *pairwise direct* interaction and compare the cases of *simple* and of *complex elements of a system*.

For *simple elements* – for instance for particles in physics – the interaction mechanism is usually an *immediate* (not mediated) one: Interaction forces (e.g. gravitational or electromagnetic or nuclear forces) between the interacting elements (*a*) and (*b*) change their states (namely the trajectory and the inner state) of (*a*) and (*b*) *gradually or abruptly* (the latter case happens e.g. in collisions of particles). Typical *quantum interactions* produce *discrete changes* of the states of the interacting elements (e.g. creation- and annihilation processes of particles, absorption and emission of photons, excitations of internal degrees of freedom like electronic, vibrational and rotational excitations of molecules). The result of the pairwise interaction of the elements (a) and (b) is always a change of their states $i(a)$ and $j(b)$ into $i'(a)$ and $j'(b)$. (In quantum processes this may even include creation and annihilation.)

For *complex elements* – like human individuals – the direct pairwise interaction mechanism e.g. at meetings or encounters is a *mediated* one: The exchange of *information* between the meeting partners (a) and (b) leads to thoughts and emotions worked out in a *complex inner process* in the mind of each partner. These *intermediate mental processes* finally give rise to a change of the states $i(a)$ and $j(b)$ of the elements before the meeting into states $i'(a)$ and $j'(b)$ after the meeting.

Even more important for the *system character of a system* than the *direct interactions* between its parts are the *indirect interactions*. Because indirect interactions couple each part of the system to the whole, i.e. to the collective global system structure, they provide the *inner coherence of the system* by bringing all parts indirectly together in a system-specific manner.

Let us again compare indirect part-whole and whole-part interactions in the cases of simple physical and complex social systems.

In the case of *physical systems* the introduction of the *field concept* proved to be most important for the deeper understanding of their systemic character. Take the characteristic example of electromagnetic interaction: Particles, the elements of the physical system, possess – besides other properties – both mass and electric charge, and generate in their environment a gravitational as well as an electromagnetic field. The field contributions of many particles are *superposed* and form a *collective field*. Together with other composite quantities the collective field characterizes the macro-level of the many-particle system. It has been established by the *"bottom-up"* inter-action from the microlevel of particles to the macrolevel of collective system properties.

But now the *"top-down"* interaction from macrolevel to microlevel sets in: The collective field *acts back* on the single particles by *exerting forces* on each of them and thus determining its motion. In this way the indirect interaction of each particle with each other via the collective field has been established. Simultaneously the collective field proves to be a typical property of the *system as a whole*.

Now we consider the *social system* and its elements, the individuals. Although the interactions and activities of individuals are cognitively mediated and are therefore not so immediate effects as physical interactions, the principal aspects of the part-whole and whole-part interaction between the microlevel and macrolevel of the system remain the same:

Individuals with all their intellectual qualifications, their readiness to show emo-tions and their ability to develop behavioural repertoires contribute in the form of cultural and economic activities – via a *bottom-up interaction* – to the generation of a general "field" of civilisation consisting of cultural, religious, political, social and economic components. In particular, all institutions of state, religion, economy, law and political ideology belong to this *collective civilisatory field* which deter-mines the socio-political climate as well as the cultural and economic situation of a society.

It is on this macrolevel that the new system qualities of the society emerge.

It is important to stress that the systemic qualities of social systems cannot be sufficiently characterized by pure *structure* only as previously mentioned. Since the parts of the social system, the individuals, are full of wishes, intentions, purposes and goals, their system building activities via bottom-up, i.e. part-whole interaction lead to the generation of systemic qualities carrying certain *functions* purposefully constructed to satisfy these wishes. Furthermore the individuals possess a set of *values* and derive from them *ethical principles* of behaviour, or a morality. The question arises how these normative principles influence the structure of the social system. It seems that values lead to a *vision* of an *ideal structure* of the system able to incorporate the *functions* for the *realization* of these *values*. The morality of individuals leads to *selection rules* used to create functionally optimal system structures and norms. Organisations and institutions maintaining the norms may then be seen as "materialized" moral selection rules.

These efficacious system qualities now lead to a strong *top-down* or *whole-part interaction*, because the collective civilisatory field strongly influences the range of possible activities of an individual, by offering orientation and yielding integration into cultural traditions, by extending and also restricting the scope of available information, of thought and of action, by partially removing decision-making about issues already predetermined by the structure of the society from individuals and by activating or perhaps frustrating the individuals' latent aptitudes.

Evidently the "systemicity" of a system is particularly strengthened by the *cyclical character* of the indirect bottom-up and top-down interactions: On the one side the parts of the system are indispensable to building up the macroproperties of the

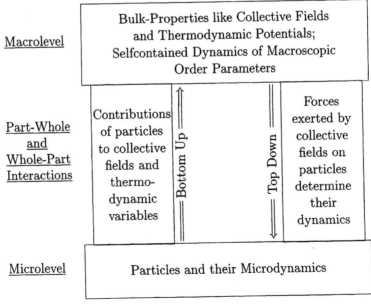

Figure 1.3 Part-whole and whole-part interaction between microlevel and macrolevel of physical systems.

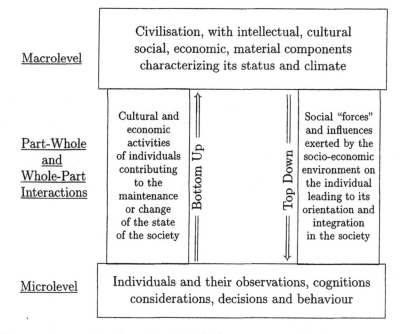

Figure 1.4   Part-whole and whole-part interaction between microlevel and macrolevel of social systems.

system. On the other side the new system qualities emerge on this macrolevel, and not on the level of parts. Finally, the parts are no more independent, because of the top-down influence restricting or even determining their dynamic behaviour. In Figures 1.3 and 1.4 the part-whole and whole-part interactions of physical and social systems are represented schematically.

1.2   Towards Explanations of System Structure: Reductionism versus Holism

The system structure which appears to be such a dominant phenomenon of nature is now seen as a problem raising several questions and demanding further explanations.

The questions are concerned with the deeper meaning and the ontological status of the "whole". The efforts to give explanations are concerned with the operationalisation of the system concept, involving the setting up of concepts clarifying the universal nature of systemic organisation.

We begin with the formulation of two opposite philosophical standpoints with respect to the nature of systems. Later we will attempt to reconcile both standpoints by a process of partial justification and relativisation.

The first standpoint is *Reductionism*. According to reductionism all properties of a system including the newly emerging qualities at the macrolevel must and can be reduced to – and therefore explained by – the properties and qualities of the lower (micro) level consisting of the components of the system.

The second and opposite standpoint is *Holism*. According to Holism the newly emergent properties and qualities of a system define its wholeness and make it an *entity of its own right*. Thus the hierarchy of systems, each taken holistically, is considered as an absolute non-decomposable and non-reducible structure, which is *ontologically individuated*.

It seems that physicists and most natural scientists are more inclined to adopt the reductionist standpoint, whereas psychologists and scholars of the arts seem to prefer holism. These preferences appear at least understandable for the following reasons:

In physics there already exist successful examples of the reductionist procedure. The most prominent example is the derivation of the laws of *phenomenological thermodynamics* from the microlevel, namely from the fundamental laws of *statistical mechanics*. In particular it turns out that new qualities, the concepts characterizing thermodynamic equilibrium, which are only definable at the system level, are consistently explainable starting from the microlevel of interacting particles. More recent generalisations of these concepts in *Synergetics* are discussed below (see Section 1.3).

On the other hand, psychologists, scholars and social scientists have to work with the human mind and its individual and collective interactions. They are unavoidably confronted with the most complex system hitherto created in nature: the *human brain*. And here they are led to the as yet unsettled *psycho-physical* problem, namely the problem how the physico-chemical and neurological structures and properties of the brain are related to the newly emerging qualities of mind, i.e. its cognitive and emotional abilities.

Although the mental capacity of the brain must somehow be carried by its neurological structure, the bottom-up and top-down interaction between both layers of qualities seems to be extremely complex:

Firstly, psychological introspection and logical regression lead to more archetypical emotions and to more fundamentally evident ideas, but never lead directly back to underlying *neurological* structures. On the other hand neurologically static or dynamic structures *isomorphic* to the structure of emotions and ideas have not yet been identified.

Secondly, it may turn out that the limitations of reductionism show up here for the following *principal reasons*: Evidently the mind possesses degrees of freedom which can be utilized to represent thoughts about theories, ideas about art and literature, and to carry emotions. These activities of mind have *their own internal structure and logic*. Their representation in the brain would be *impossible* if its neurophysiological structures could fix all possible varieties of brain state. Instead, the perhaps reductionistically explainable "hardware" of the brain must leave enough free scope for the "software" of mental activities to follow their own *autonomous* rules and programmes.

From the research about systems of very different nature and complexity it has turned out that neither the standpoint of extreme holism nor of extreme reductionism can be maintained.

On the *side of holism* it becomes more and more clear that the independence of levels exhibiting different qualities in complex systems cannot be an *absolute* one but only a *relative* one. Indeed, since these complex organisational levels are produced by the contributions of units at lower levels, the emergent qualities of the higher level have somehow to be the collective resultant of cooperative effects on the more elementary level, even if degrees of freedom leave space for the arisal of new qualities which have their own immanent structure.

On the *side of reductionism* the close inspection of the kind of interaction in multi-component systems has, perhaps surprisingly, led to some universal insights into the way how *almost selfcontained substructures* organize themselves in such systems.

Two such principles of general importance for the formation of systems will now be considered.

(a) *The Self-Consistency Principle*

We have already seen that in physics the *field concept* has a powerful ability to account for the formation of systems since it explains the part-whole interaction between particles and a collective field. It is however not yet clear whether this part-whole interaction produces a *persistently stabilizing system*. Therefore the field concept must be complemented by the *self-consistency principle*:

If each particle contributes to the generation of a collective field and if conversely each particle moves under the influence of this collective field, then this cyclic relation between causes and effects is *self-consistent* if causes and effects are *mutually reproduced* and thus *stabilized*.

As an example let us take the case of electrons around the nucleus of an atom. The electrons are in stationary quantum states of motion (determined by the Schroedinger equation) and contribute to a collective electric field, which depends on these electronic quantum states. Vice versa, the quantum states depend on the collective field because it enters the Schroedinger equation for electronic states. *Self-consistency* is fulfilled, if the electronic quantum states are chosen in such manner that they together create a collective field which *reproduces* these quantum states. Then the whole system is in a stable self-reproducing state.

The self-consistency principle can (*mutatis mutandis*) be easily transferred to social systems. Take a democratic political system as an example. Its democratic institutions are created and sustained by the activity of people. Conversely, the democratic rules and institutions provide the possibilities for people to develop their political activities. Self-consistency holds if individual activities and democratic institutions fit together by mutual reproduction so that the system persists in stability. This stability does not necessarily mean stationarity. There may exist many forms of non-stationary evolution in which the properties defining the identity of the democratic system are preserved and reproduced.

The democratic system may however be destroyed if self-consistency does not hold, for instance if sworn enemies of democracy abuse the free democratic institutions to seize power and to destroy them. (This is the theorem of the philosopher Karl Popper regarding the instability of absolute unrestricted freedom against abuse by its enemies.) The phase transitions between political systems which then may take place will be discussed in detail in Chapter 6.

(b) *The "Slaving" or "Entrainment" Principle*

The slaving principle in its general mathematical form was set up by H. Haken [8]. It is able to *explain* (and not only to take as a given) the rather universal fact that in most systems of nature, even in systems of high complexity, there exist only a few "*order parameters*" on the macroscopic level which dominate the whole dynamics of the system in the sense that the many other variables of the system are essentially compelled, drawn along and entrained, or "slaved" to follow the order parameters.

The essence of the algorithm developed by H. Haken can be described as follows: It is presumed that a set of fundamental in general nonlinear equations of motion for the system variables exists. (In natural science such equations are available or derivable from the fundamental laws of nature.) One starts from the stationary solution of these equations. After changing some exogenous control parameters it appears that in general only a few variables $\xi_u(t)$ become unstable and begin slowly to grow, whereas the motion of the great majority of the variables $\xi_s(t)$ around their stationary values is quickly dampened out. It turns out that the further temporal evolution of the majority of variables $\xi_s(t)$ is "entrained" or "slaved" by the $\xi_u(t)$, since the fast variables $\xi_s(t)$ hastily adapt to the (slow) motion of the ruling variables $\xi_u(t)$. Hence the $\xi_s(t)$ can be expressed by the $\xi_u(t)$ and "adiabatically" *eliminated*. As a result the dynamics of the whole system can be expressed solely by equations of motion for the few "order parameters" $\xi_u(t)$ which dominate the whole system.

This algorithm (for more details see Section 1.3) not only explains the appearance of a *quasi self-contained autonomous subdynamics* for a few macroscopic order parameters which often characterize *new emergent qualities* of the system, but also explains how this fact relates to characteristic *timescales* separating the *slow dominant order parameters* from the majority of *fast but "slaved"* variables. Thus the slaving principle contributes to the solution of the problem of how new system properties can arise: The autonomous subdynamics of order parameters can be explained by the dynamic interaction of *all* system variables but it emerges as a characteristic feature of the system as a whole.

In social systems the connection between the time-scale of evolution and separation between dominant and adaptive variables is also often taken for granted. However the rigour of a mathematical algorithm is absent here, because fundamental "microscopic" equations of motion for social systems are not available.

At the end of this section we discuss the old but still not obsolete question of the *ontological primacy* of single objects or of universal categories, concepts and laws. Here we find the two opposite standpoints of *nominalism* and *universalism* which were already formulated in ancient and medieval philosophy but can be transformed into standpoints about modern problems in natural and social science.

The *nominalism* in its Aristotelian definition asserts the *ontological primacy of single real objects* so that universal categories and concepts, are *ontologically secondary* simple classifications, merely summaries and synopses of the properties of single objects.

Instead, the *universalism* in its Platonic definition asserts the *ontological primacy of universal categories* of ideal perfect prototypes. They are the "ontological source" from which the real, but imperfect and ontologically secondary objects derive their properties.

A modern version of these classical standpoints could be constructed as follows:

On the one side there exist the *phenomena*, either simple or composite and complex ones. On the other side there exists a – more or less – logically coherent set of universally valid *laws of nature*. All individual phenomena obey these laws of nature and are – apart from contingent facts – in their structure and dynamics to a large extent dominated and determined by the full and universal interrelated set of laws of nature.

The problem of ontological rank arises for this version, too: Is the ontological primacy due to the individual (simple or complex) phenomena or to the background-framework of universal abstract laws of nature governing the structure and evolution of the phenomena?

The *modern version of nominalism* would attribute the ontological primacy to the *foreground of phenomena* and would consider the background of theorems and laws to be obeyed by the phenomena as an ontologically secondary mere synopsis and summary of the structure and the dynamics of the individual phenomena.

In contrast to this, the *modern version of universalism* would assign the ontological primacy to the *background of universal laws* of nature and would consider the phenomena as ontologically secondary mere examples, realisations, and partial fulfillers of the governing universal principal laws.

Let us now – in a somewhat speculative manner – put into analogy the relation between the individual phenomena and the overarching universal laws of nature with the relation between the parts and the transindividual whole of a system.

In this view the modern versions of *nominalism* and *universalism* correspond to the standpoints of *reductionism* and *holism* in the discussion of system structure: Reductionism attributes priority to the parts and tries to reduce the emergent structures of a system as a mere result of properties of parts, whereas holism attributes priority to the wholeness structures of a system whereas its parts are entrained and governed by the whole.

However, we have learned that the controversy between the standpoints of reductionism and holism loses its acuteness, because of the *cyclic interdependence* of the parts and the whole of a system. It seems, therefore, that in view of the analogy mentioned above, the consideration of system structure may also shed new light on the problem of the ontological primacy of individual phenomena or, alternatively, of universal frameworks of laws of nature.

Indeed, also here a *cyclical ontological conditionality* between phenomena and laws seems to substitute the absolute standpoints of a nominalistic primacy of phenomena or universalistic primacy of frameworks of laws:

On the one hand, single objects and phenomena which would *not belong* to universal categories, including lawlike properties and would *not obey* any general laws of interaction and evolution, would be *fully contingent and isolated*. Because of the lack of definable interactions their ontological status as identifyable individual objects and phenomena would become *questionable*.

On the other hand, universal categories, and the whole framwork of universal laws of nature would become empty, without meaning and therefore *ontologically vacuous* if no objects exist which could be realisations of such universal categories and fulfillers of universal laws.

Summarizing, It seems that system structures like the *cyclical interdependence* between parts and the whole have a *generic meaning* shedding light on other fundamental problems of science and philosophy.

1.3   General System Theory, Synergetics and Sociodynamics

In this section we shall briefly consider the conceptual frameworks developed in General System Theory, Synergetics, and Sociodynamics, with the intention of clarifying their relationship to each other. One should however keep in mind that at least the first two branches of interdisciplinary science, viz. General System Theory and Synergetics, together comprise a huge literature, so that only some main definitions and positions, achievements and problems can be mentioned.

General System Theory

With respect to *General System Theory* (G.S.T.) we follow the lines of two eminent authors, L. von Bertalanffy [9] and A. Rapoport [10] who are the main founders and developers of the frame of G.S.T. It should however be mentioned that System Theory is a rapidly developing field. Nowadays it comprises systems of Physics [11], [12], [13] and Biology [14], [15] as well, and recent surveys [16], [17], [18] show how quantitative methods, particularly the methods of nonlinear dynamics, more and more penetrate into this field.

General System Theory begins with the general definition of a "system" as a complex of components endowed with interactions forming an *organized complex whole*. In G.S.T. no principal barrier exists between physical (inorganic), biological (organic) and behavioral (social) systems. However, the inner dynamics and embedding in the environment presumed to obtain for the systems considered in G.S.T. is defined in such a way as to lead to a type of organisation which makes this class of systems highly interesting but somewhat less general than the very broadly characterized class of systems used in Sections 1.1 and 1.2.

The guideline along which system properties are recognized and classified in G.S.T. can perhaps best be seen in the *organismic paradigm*, although the conceptual framework of G.S.T. extends far beyond biological systems and leads to the discovery of comparable structures in physical systems on the simpler level and in social systems on the more complex level.

The starting point of the definition of systems given in G.S.T. is the astonishing observation that biological systems, i.e. organisms and individual organs, *preserve their identity*, which means that these systems maintain a certain *constancy amid a changing environment* although they are *open systems*, interacting with and having *input–output exchanges* (e.g. of energy and matter) with the environment. Obviously several questions present themselves, for instance: Which properties are preserved? What are the identity preserving mechanisms?

Because an exchange of matter (of system elements) takes place between an open system and its environment, the *elements* of such systems *cannot be conserved*, however the *relations between the elements* and the *system structure* which consists of the whole set of relations between the elements. A higher kind of identity preservation takes place if the organisation of the system leads to a *reproduction of structures* if these are perturbed by exterior influences, and a still higher kind of maintenance of the wholeness of the system is the *production* and *reproduction* of its internal organisation by *self-organisation and self-reproduction*.

In simpler cases of "constancy amid change" the conserved or approached property of the system is a *steady* or *stationary state*, for instance a kind of equilibrium (fluxequilibrium) to which the system strives after independently of its initial conditions (*equifinality*). In organisms the preservation or re-establishment of a steady state is termed as *homeostasis* and the *mechanism of attaining homeostasis* can often be explained by a *feedback loop* so that deviations from the steady state lead to chains of events eliciting "restoring forces" re-establishing the original steady state.

This kind of pre-established feedback loops belongs to the *cybernetic concept of selfregulation* which also finds many applications in *engineering*. It is related to the classical stimulus–response-mechanism but the decisive difference is that the feedback loop relates causes and effects *cyclically*.

An alternative scheme of restoring the stationary state is the *dynamic restoration scheme*, where it is not a specific feedback mechanism but instead the *free dynamic interplay of interactions* within the multicomponent system which lead to a "blind" unsteered selfregulation of the system.

For the highly complex system of the *human individual* the preservation of identity denotes the "maintenance of individual autonomy and of an integrated personality". The interaction and exchange of this "open system" with its environment takes place by communication and exchange of information, knowledge and emotion. The selection within this exchange process here leads to a hierarchy of acception–rejection rules, even to the exclusion of any kind of information that threatens to clash with previously formed (e.g. ideological or religious) ideas which would otherwise result in cognitive dissonance. The form of this exchange process evidently contributes decisively to the shaping of the structure of personality.

Because a system consists of the organized whole of the totality of all relations between its elements, the problem of its *boundaries*, of its *delimitation* inevitably arises. In many cases the delimitation problem is solved rather unambiguously because one can clearly distinguish on the one hand between the *strongly interacting* system components with a cyclically coupled dynamics exhibiting a certain *selfcontainedness* and on the other hand the *weaker* and *unspecific* interaction between system components and the *environment* external to the system.

However, the individuation of a system from its environment simultaneously leading to a classification of the strength and kind of interaction between system- and environment-components, is *not an absolute* but a *relative one*: Systems and their environments may always be considered as subsystems composing an *integrated system* of hierarchical order and of higher complexity.

In more general cases of open systems surrounded by an environment the systems do not *strictly preserve their identity* under changing environmental conditions but they react to the changes by *structure-conserving dynamic adaptation*. Here "adaptation" means that the inner relations between the system elements may continuously change without losing their principal quality as long as the environmental changes remain in a certain domain. (However, if the environmental changes cross certain *thresholds*, the system can become *unstable* and perform a *transition to another phase* of inner relations and global dynamics. *Equifinality* is then replaced by *instability* and *phase-transition*.)

Identity preserving and dynamically adaptive properties amid changing environments in the broad class of systems considered in G.S.T. inevitably lead to the fundamental question of whether the system is teleologically oriented and goal-directed.

The ancient Greek philosopher Aristotle long ago introduced different causation principles, namely a "*causa efficiens*" (efficient cause) and a "*causa finalis*" (final cause). By a causa efficiens he understood a force producing effects by "pushing from behind" and by a causa finalis a striving after a purpose "beckoning from ahead". He considered both kinds of causes as being independent and having the same ontological status.

In G.S.T. we find a modern formulation of the old problem which is now connected with either holism or reductionism (see Section 1.2).

Teleological concepts expressed in *functional* and *goal-directed* terms stress the *wholeness* of a system and are therefore considered as *fundamental and underivable* principles by *holists* who claim the epistemological primacy of teleological functionality and purposefulness at least for biological systems. This is the standpoint of *vitalism* whose proponents reject "mechanistic" explanations of functionality.

Conversely, *reductionism* asserts that teleological concepts like purposefulness, goaldirectedness and the underlying functionality, even if they have high *heuristic* and *pragmatic value* in detecting interdependences in complex systems, are *not independent causes* in their own right. Instead it is asserted that the realisation and implementation of purposes and goals and of all functions assisting in their realisation must be carried into effect and maintained by underlying *structures* which provide a network of *efficient causes* ("Wirkursachen") for the fulfilment of these purposes.

Indeed, many results of modern science can be seen as the implementation of a *de-teleologising programme*, which means that *functions* are step by step "*explained*" i.e. "reduced to" complex networks of *efficient causes*. This takes place in particular in biology where the strict vitalist standpoint is on a steady retreat. (For instance, random mutations of the genome and Darwinian natural selection are *non-teleological* concepts to explain evolution.)

Nevertheless, even if all purposes and functions are carried by structures, teleological system properties retain their value as *emergent properties* instead of being *causation principles*. In particular they provide insight into the *cyclical nature* of *causes and effects* in selfsustaining systems.

To illustrate this let us consider the emergent goal of "*survival*" of animals in connection with the definition of "fitness". The following statements are unquestioned:

"Fitness leads to the survival of animals."
"Only those animals survive which are fit."

A shortcut conclusion from these two statements could be that "the fitness" of surviving animals is "nothing but" a *pure tautology* because those and only those animals survive which are fit. This conclusion is however misleading. It rests on the (mis-)interpretation of fitness as a *global causa finalis* which is assumed to be already sufficient to explain survival. Instead, fitness is an *emergent property*, namely the result of a cyclically intertwined network of (efficient) causes and effects which together lead to the self-maintenance of the animal.

Now we briefly consider, under a comparative point of view, the role of "*structure*" and "*function*" and their relation in systems of different degrees of complexity, namely in physical, biological and social systems.

Physical Systems

We begin with *physical systems*. Their *structure* can often be derived in quantitative detail with rather general mathematical algorithms (see below the formalism of Synergetics) derived from laws of nature at the micro-level. As to the question which *functions* are carried by the structures one must distinguish between two kinds of physical systems:

(1) Systems *without* intentionally designed and constructed function-carrying structures. If such systems have a certain persistence exhibiting dynamic stability and/or adaptivity to their environment which could be interpreted as *wholeness*, then this wholeness is a "*blindly*" emerging system property which is *an end in itself*. Nevertheless one can say about such systems that their structures carry the (emergent) function of "self-preservation of the whole".

(2) The huge class of *technical systems* intentionally designed by humans and endowed with specific structures carrying specific functions *instrumentalized* for some purposes intended by their maker. Here the purposes are not "ends in themselves" but are derived from *intentions in the mind of human engineers and end users*. The technical systems endowed with specific adaptive regulation devices could be defined as belonging to the subclass of *cybernetic* systems.

The essential difference between both kinds of physical systems lies in the construction and *instrumentalisation of system functions* by human designers in the second kind, and the *undirected emergence of wholeness-patterns* in the first kind.

Biological Systems

Secondly we consider *biological systems* with their evidently function-carrying organ-structures. The functional meaning of the interdependences of substructures of an organism is here so obvious that one may denote it as *ratiomorphic*. This means that the interplay of structures behaves *as if it were constructed and directed by rational design* with respect to the fulfilment of some system-benefitting purposes.

However, even the intense function-directedness of structures in biological organisms can to an increasing extent be explained by the long term effects of *evolution*. The question remains open whether the evolutionary standard scheme "*mutation plus selection*" is already sufficient to explain all aptitudes of organisms or whether higher proficiencies which are not explicable by "fitness maximization through selection" need new explanatory schemes, e.g. as yet undetected causal relations between phenotype and genotype generating a "creative surplus" beyond pure adaptation. Here, new insights on regulatory circuits and morphogenesis, making use of the conceptional frame of nonlinear dynamics, will soon complement and lead beyond the pure Darwinian scheme, as comprehensively elaborated in the book of S. A. Kauffman [14].

Social Systems

Thirdly let us consider *social systems*, i.e. societies and their short term and long term history. Human individuals endowed with *rationality, emotionality* and *intentionality* are the elementary components of these most complex systems. The socio-cultural system is established by a universe of *symbols* comprised in the language and by social relations. Interactions now have the new quality of *communication of messages*, i.e. *information exchange*. The functions carried by the structures of the social system are no longer "ratiomorphic" results of evolution as in biology, but the results of intentionally and consciously operating *rational* actors who have anticipated in their mind which structures might carry the functions producing the intended purposes. The complete set of consciously formulated goals, purposes and achievements of a society establishes its *meaning and cultural identity* in the understanding of its members.

Thus, comparing physical, biological and social systems, one starts from the "blind" emergence of wholeness-patterns by the undirected effect of natural laws in *physics* or their intentionally directed effect in *technology* and proceeds to the *ratiomorphic behaviour* by function-carrying structures generated *via evolution* in biology, and finally arrives at the *meaning*-carrying functions introduced by human individuals *via intentional activity* into their socio-cultural systems.

Although *rational intentionality* seems to be a higher quality than *ratiomorphic functionality*, social systems exhibit a much looser, more flexible and also more unstable inner coherence than biological organisms. The reason is simple: The members of a society possess, at least in principle, a much higher degree of freedom in relation to the social system than organs (e.g. cells) in relation to the whole organism. In particular *conflicts of goals and purposes* arise normally between different groups of individuals. These can destabilize the whole social system; hence a substantial part of political theory is concerned with the question of the stability of a given socio-political system.

Because of this higher flexibility and openness of the possible evolution of a society most historians reject a *life cycle theory of civilisations* (e.g. worked out by O. Spengler [19]) in analogy to the stages of childhood, adolescence, maturity, and old age of an organism. However, it must be admitted that quasi-cyclical sequences of historical events (describable in terms of rise, maturity, and decline) of different periodicities can be observed in almost all societies. On the other hand, since *unidirectional irreversible processes* like population explosion, technological innovations, exhaustion of resources etc. are always *superimposed* on perhaps existing cyclical processes, pure cyclicity is never to be expected in historical events; more feasible is a kind of "helical" evolution resulting from the *superposition* of quasi-cyclical and irreversible processes.

The long term trajectory of a large social system like a nation or even a civilisation will – due to large changes amongst internal variables or environmental parameters – traverse not only steadily evolving states but also *critical situations* (e.g. catastrophe cusps) leading to *social phase transitions*, i.e. dramatic global events like wars, revolutions and changes of the socio-political system.

General system-theoretical insights retain their value even with respect to the *structure* of such grand events of history. However the system-theoretical power of making historical long-term *forecasts* is *rather weak* because the exact course of dramatic *macro-events* depends sensitively on critical micro-conditions and -decisions which are not included in global system-theoretical structural considerations. Therefore the *nomothetic* point of view of G.S.T. does not aim at substituting the *ideographic* point of view of the historian insisting on the value of the detailed retrospective description and analysis of events in any given individual historical system.

After this short discussion of some aspects of the framework of General System Theory it may be useful to classify the *kind of insight* which can be won from such general theoretical frameworks like G.S.T., Synergetics and Sociodynamics. The line towards deeper insight and understanding seems to lead from *observation* and *recognition* to *operationalism* and finally to *explanation*.

We begin with the conceptual classification and descriptive delineation of the properties of the systems under consideration by *observation* and *recognition*. One of the great merits of G.S.T. is to have recognized that there exist structural and dynamical similarities (and not only accidental and superficial analogies) between otherwise very different physical, biological and social systems. Without this kind of recognition any further investigation of common properties and their reasons by overlapping concepts would be impossible.

However, recognition and verbal description of comparable structures and dynamics in different systems is not enough. The important and difficult next step is *operationalism*. This means the introduction of a *formal algorithm* leading to a precise formulation of the form and extent of the structural comparability of different systems. *Quantitative formalisms* are preferable here, even if they are more abstract and less colourful than verbal descriptions, because the criteria for the verification (or falsification) of quantitative statements are *much sharper* and *less contentious* than those for qualitative characterisations (even if the latter must always stand at the beginning of an analysis). The higher degree of abstraction inherent in any mathematical formalism appropriate for the measurement and comparison of system properties can in fact be an *advantage* because it *automatically* disregards the irrelevancies and focusses on the essentials.

The last step in system-theoretical considerations is *explanation*. One can speak of "explanation" of system properties, if and only if the following relation between theory and realisation of a system exists:

(1)   There must exist a *verification* (and *falsification*) *procedure* with sharp (if pos-
      sible quantitive) criteria able to distinguish between correct and incorrect
      theoretical statements about the considered system. The *value* of a theory is *high*
      if it is proved true with respect to many independent criteria and if as many
      alternative theories as possible *had to be sorted out* by the same criteria because
      they proved fallacious. (On the other hand a theory has a *low value* if its
      concepts are so over-flexible, trite and hackneyed that they can be adapted so as
      to fulfill every criterion. Such theories which are "always true" (like astrology)
      and never falsifiable are therefore necessarily shallow and trivial, whereas
      valuable theories make statements precise enough to be exposable to possible
      falsification.)

(2)   The *truth content* of a theory then consists in the *isomorphism* (to be empirically
      verified by crucial experiments) between at least some strata of the existing real
      system(s) and the conceptual framework of the theory. Such a theory acquires
      explanatory power if its internal conceptual structure can be proved to be a
      necessary consequence of logical and/or mathematical deductions. In this case
      the *logically deduced interrelation* between the theoretical concepts corresponds
      (via verified isomorphy) to the *structural and dynamic relations* within the real
      system. The main prerequisite for the validity of the explanatory power of the
      theory is the verification of its isomorphism with the real systems by a set of
      strategically chosen reproducible experiments of generic character leading to
      general insights about the nature of the real system.
         In this sense the latter structures of reality are then *"explained"* by the inner
      logic of the theory. Since this *"explanation"* presumes *recognition* of properties
      of the real system and their theoretical *operationalism* by *formal algorithms* one
      must conclude that the explanation so defined is the deepest kind of insight
      attainable by human thought.

Synergetics

In the last three decades a new interdisciplinary branch of science rapidly developed
which was called *Synergetics* by its founder H. Haken (see [8], [20], [21]). (The main
achievements of Synergetics are represented in the Springer Series in Synergetics
which now (December 1998) comprises 67 volumes.)

   H. Haken defines *Synergetics* as the general theory of collective spatial, temporal
or functional macrostructures (i.e. global structures) of multi-component systems.

   It is clear that between the definitions of the fields of General System Theory and
of Synergetics there exists a strong overlap. Nevertheless the origins of the two
interdisciplinarily defined fields were somewhat different (biology and cybernetics
in the case of G.S.T. and physics in the case of Synergetics). However, we shall not
focus on considerations merging or demarcating the two fields; rather we want to
stress that Synergetics has made remarkable contributions to the *operationalism* and
explanation of general system properties.

   The physical system which proved to be the *trailblazer of Synergetics* was the
LASER, because in the physical theory of this remarkable open system all concepts

could be concretely formulated and tested which later by grand generalisation have led to the conceptual framework of Synergetics (see [22]).

Let us therefore go into some detail in explaining this physical system: The LASER consists of a cavity with parallel mirrors at the two opposite sides and a number of, say, 10^{18} of laser-active atoms in the cavity. These atoms can be excited from their groundstate to an energetically excited state by some external "pumping" procedure. Normally the atoms thereupon make transitions to the ground state by *spontaneous emission* of photons in random directions. But if the number of the excited atomic states passes a certain *threshold* a dramatic process amounting to a *dynamic phase transition* sets in: The photons propagating back and forth between the mirrors remain longer in the cavity than those in the other directions. They interact with the atoms by *stimulating the excited ones* to emit their photon (belonging to the same frequency and wavelength) in the *same direction*. Finally there is produced an *avalanche of photons of macroscopic order* in that direction, namely the LASER-beam, created through Light Amplification by Stimulated Emission of Radiation.

A closer inspection of this mechanism, the equations of motion of which were first derived from the *microscopically valid* equations of quantum electrodynamics by H. Haken [23], shows the following: After the appearance of the macroscopic amplitude of the LASER light mode the laser-active atoms no longer behave stochastically and independently but instead exhibit a *well-ordered and cooperative light emission behaviour* which is fully determined and steered by the LASER light mode. In other words: The LASER light mode has adopted the role of an *"order parameter"* and *"slaves"* the dynamic behaviour of the other components of the system, i.e. of the atoms. The whole system has then made a *phase-transition* to a *globally different* dynamic behaviour, because the external conditions (the growing pump rate) and the internal interactions (the stimulated emission of photons) have lead to a new *self-organized dynamics* of the system.

An immense descriptive simplification has taken place: Instead of dealing with more than 10^{18} equations for all atoms and all kinds of photons it is now sufficient to treat the equations for a few *macro-variables* or *order-parameters* characterizing the LASER light mode and a few collective atomic variables, whereas the dynamics of all other variables is "slaved", that means fully determined by that of the order-parameters.

Synergetics now consists in the far-reaching generalisation of the insights obtained in the special case of the LASER not only verbally, but by developing a *general mathematical formalism* applicable to a broad class of physical and nonphysical systems for which *fundamental microscopic equations of motion for the components of the systems exist*. One of the main objectives of Synergetics is to *explain* (in the sense introduced above) by this mathematical formalism the remarkable fact that complex multicomponent systems can on the macrolevel be characterized by only *a few order parameters* (i.e. relevant macrovariables), which obey a *selfcontained autonomous dynamics among themselves*, whereas the dynamics of the vast majority of microvariables in such systems is dominated ("slaved" or "entrained") by these few order parameters.

We shall now sketch the formalism of Synergetics. (A full presentation of this formalism including many applications can be found in H. Haken [8], [20].)

Let us assume that a vector of time-dependent state variables

$$\mathbf{q}(t) = \{q_1(t), q_2(t), \ldots, q_n(t)\} \tag{1.1}$$

exists which describe the state of the system on a detailed "microscopic" level. We also presume that the variables $\mathbf{q}(t)$ satisfy a set of known *microscopic evolution equations* which are assumed to have the following general form:

$$\frac{d\mathbf{q}}{dt} = \mathbf{N}(\mathbf{q}; \boldsymbol{\alpha}) + \mathbf{F}(t) \tag{1.2a}$$

or in components

$$\frac{dq_i}{dt} = N_i(\mathbf{q}; \boldsymbol{\alpha}) + F_i(t) \quad i = 1, 2, \ldots, n. \tag{1.2b}$$

Here, the set of functions $\mathbf{N}$ represents *nonlinear functions* of the *state variables* $\mathbf{q}$ and of external (environmental) *control parameters* $\boldsymbol{\alpha}$. The set $\mathbf{F}(t)$ represents *small stochastic forces* describing additional exogenous accidental effects on the system which will be ignored in the following. The dynamic behaviour of the system is now considered in the *vicinity of an instability*, a very interesting domain, because here there may emerge new system properties.

One starts from a known solution $\mathbf{q}_{00}$ of (1.2) for given constant control parameters $\boldsymbol{\alpha}_0$. In the simplest cases $\mathbf{q}_{00}$ is a constant vector which is a stable solution of $\mathbf{N}(\mathbf{q}_{00}; \boldsymbol{\alpha}_0) = 0$. If the value of the external control parameter is now shifted from $\boldsymbol{\alpha}_0$ to $\boldsymbol{\alpha}$, the system variable will thereupon assume the form

$$\mathbf{q}(t) = \mathbf{q}_0 + \mathbf{w}(t), \tag{1.3}$$

where $\mathbf{q}_0$ is the – stable or unstable – stationary solution of (1.2), i.e. of $\mathbf{N}(\mathbf{q}_0; \boldsymbol{\alpha}) = 0$, and where $\mathbf{w}(t)$ is a small deviation from this stationary solution $\mathbf{q}_0$.

In order to analyze the question of whether $\mathbf{q}_0$ remains a stable solution of (1.2) or whether there evolves another (emergent) dynamics after the shift $\boldsymbol{\alpha}_0 \to \boldsymbol{\alpha}$, one may insert (1.3) into equation (1.2) (with $\mathbf{F}(t) = 0$) and expand the r.h.s. of equation (1.2) into a Taylor series with respect to $\mathbf{w}(t)$, obtaining

$$\frac{d\mathbf{w}}{dt} = \mathbf{L}(\mathbf{q}_0, \boldsymbol{\alpha})\mathbf{w} + \mathbf{M}(\mathbf{q}_0, \boldsymbol{\alpha}; \mathbf{w}) \tag{1.4a}$$

or in components

$$\frac{dw_i}{dt} = \sum_{j=1}^{n} L_{ij}(\mathbf{q}_0, \boldsymbol{\alpha})w_j + M_i(\mathbf{q}_0, \boldsymbol{\alpha}; \mathbf{w}) \quad i = 1, 2, \ldots, n. \tag{1.4b}$$

Here the first term on the r.h.s. of (1.4) with

$$\mathbf{L} = ((L_{ij})) = \left(\left(\frac{\partial N_i}{\partial q_j}\Big|_{\mathbf{q}=\mathbf{q}_0} \right) \right) \tag{1.5}$$

contains the linear terms in $\mathbf{w}$ of the Taylor expansion and the second term contains all higher expansion terms. The quadratic and cubic expansion terms for instance read in components:

$$M_i(\mathbf{q}_0, \boldsymbol{\alpha}; \mathbf{w}) = \sum_{a,b} M_{i,ab}^{(2)} w_a w_b + \sum_{a,b,c} M_{i,abc}^{(3)} w_a w_b w_c + \cdots \tag{1.6}$$

As long as the deviations $\mathbf{w}(t)$ are small one can neglect the higher terms in (1.4) and – for the first – only analyze the approximate linearized equation

$$\frac{d\mathbf{w}}{dt} = \mathbf{L}(\mathbf{q}_0, \boldsymbol{\alpha})\mathbf{w}. \tag{1.7}$$

Its solutions can be decomposed into eigensolutions $\mathbf{w}^{(k)}(t)$ by

$$\mathbf{w}(t) = \sum_k c_k \mathbf{w}^{(k)}(t), \tag{1.8}$$

where the eigensolutions have the form

$$\mathbf{w}^{(k)}(t) = \exp(\lambda^{(k)} t)\mathbf{v}^{(k)}. \tag{1.9}$$

The eigenvalues $\lambda^{(k)}$ and the eigenvectors $\mathbf{v}^{(k)}$ appearing in equation (1.9) and their adjoint eigenvectors $\tilde{\mathbf{v}}^{(k)+}$ have to satisfy the following equations:

$$\mathbf{L}(\mathbf{q}_0, \boldsymbol{\alpha})\mathbf{v}^{(k)} = \lambda^{(k)}\mathbf{v}^{(k)} \tag{1.10a}$$

or in components:

$$\sum_{j=1}^n L_{ij} v_j^{(k)} = \lambda^{(k)} v_i^{(k)} \tag{1.10b}$$

and

$$\tilde{\mathbf{v}}^{(l)+}\mathbf{L}(\mathbf{q}_0, \boldsymbol{\alpha}) = \lambda^{(l)}\tilde{\mathbf{v}}^{(l)+} \tag{1.11a}$$

or in components:

$$\sum_{i=1}^n \tilde{v}_i^{(l)*} L_{ij} = \lambda^{(l)} \tilde{v}_j^{(l)*}. \tag{1.11b}$$

It is easy to see that with respect to the scalar product (where u_j^* is the conjugate complex of u_j)

$$(\mathbf{u}\,|\,\mathbf{v}) = \sum_{j=1}^n u_j^* \cdot v_j = \mathbf{u}^+ \cdot \mathbf{v} \tag{1.12}$$

the eigenvectors $\mathbf{v}^{(k)}$ and the adjoint eigenvectors $\tilde{\mathbf{v}}_j^{(l)}$ of $\mathbf{L}$ obeying (1.10) and (1.11), respectively, form a *bi-orthogonal system* fulfilling

$$\left(\tilde{\mathbf{v}}^{(l)} \mid \mathbf{v}^{(k)}\right) = \delta_{lk}. \tag{1.13}$$

Proof For the expression $(\tilde{\mathbf{v}}^{(l)} \mid \mathbf{L}\mathbf{v}^{(k)})$ one obtains, making use of (1.10) and (1.11):

$$\left(\tilde{\mathbf{v}}^{(l)} \mid \mathbf{L}\mathbf{v}^{(k)}\right) \equiv \sum_{i,j}^{n} \tilde{v}_i^{(l)*} L_{ij} v_j^{(k)} = \lambda^{(k)} \left(\tilde{\mathbf{v}}^{(l)} \mid \mathbf{v}^{(k)}\right) = \lambda^{(l)} \left(\tilde{\mathbf{v}}^{(l)} \mid \mathbf{v}^{(k)}\right). \tag{1.14}$$

For $\lambda^{(l)} \neq \lambda^{(k)}$, a contradiction in equation (1.14) can only be avoided if $(\tilde{\mathbf{v}}^{(l)} \mid \mathbf{v}^{(k)}) = 0$ holds, i.e. if equation (1.13) is satisfied.

The stability of the solution (1.3) now depends on the eigenvalues $\lambda^{(k)}$ which are in general complex numbers $\lambda^{(k)} = \lambda'^{(k)} + i\lambda''^{(k)}$. One must now distinguish the cases

$$\lambda'^{(s)} = \text{Re}(\lambda^{(s)}) < 0 \tag{1.15}$$

and

$$\lambda'^{(u)} = \text{Re}(\lambda^{(u)}) > 0. \tag{1.16}$$

If only eigenvalues $\lambda^{(s)}$ with negative real parts exist, the corresponding deviations $\mathbf{w}^{(s)}(t) = \exp(\lambda^{(s)}t)\mathbf{v}^{(s)}$ will remain small with time so that the linearized equation (1.7) is sufficient for all times and the system remains stable and essentially in the vicinity of $\mathbf{q}_0$ after the controlparameter shift $\alpha_0 \Rightarrow \alpha$.

If, instead, a few eigenvalues $\lambda^{(u)}$ with positive real part also exist, the corresponding eigensolutions $\mathbf{w}^{(u)}(t) = \exp(\lambda^{(u)}t)\mathbf{v}^{(u)}$ will grow exponentially with time so that the linearized equation (1.7) becomes invalid. The stationary solution of (1.2) then becomes unstable and the expansion (1.8) has to be substituted by

$$\mathbf{w}(t) = \sum_u \xi_u(t)\mathbf{v}^{(u)} + \sum_s \xi_s(t)\mathbf{v}^{(s)} \tag{1.17}$$

with as yet unknown amplitudes $\xi_u(t)$ for the unstable modes and $\xi_s(t)$ for the stable modes. The $\xi_u(t)$ and $\xi_s(t)$ must be determined by inserting (1.17) into the *exact nonlinear equations of motion* (1.4). These equations can be transformed into equations for $\xi_u(t)$ and $\xi_s(t)$ by taking the scalar products with the adjoint eigenvectors $\tilde{\mathbf{v}}^{(u)}$ and $\tilde{\mathbf{v}}^{(s)}$:

$$\frac{d}{dt}(\tilde{\mathbf{v}}^{(u)} \mid \mathbf{w}(t)) = \left(\tilde{\mathbf{v}}^{(u)} \mid \mathbf{L}\mathbf{w}(t)\right) + \left(\tilde{\mathbf{v}}^{(u)} \mid \mathbf{M}[\mathbf{w}(t)]\right);$$

$$\frac{d}{dt}(\tilde{\mathbf{v}}^{(s)} \mid \mathbf{w}(t)) = \left(\tilde{\mathbf{v}}^{(s)} \mid \mathbf{L}\mathbf{w}(t)\right) + \left(\tilde{\mathbf{v}}^{(s)} \mid \mathbf{M}[\mathbf{w}(t)]\right) \tag{1.18}$$

and by making use of the eigenvector equations (1.10) and the bi-orthogonality relation (1.13). This procedure yields:

$$\frac{d\xi_u(t)}{dt} = \lambda^{(u)}\xi_u(t) + M_u(\boldsymbol{\xi}_u,\boldsymbol{\xi}_s); \tag{1.19}$$

$$\frac{d\xi_s(t)}{dt} = \lambda^{(s)}\xi_s(t) + M_s(\boldsymbol{\xi}_u,\boldsymbol{\xi}_s). \tag{1.20}$$

The expressions M_u and M_s arise from $(\tilde{\mathbf{v}}^{(u)} \mid \mathbf{M}[\mathbf{w}(t)])$ and $(\tilde{\mathbf{v}}^{(s)} \mid \mathbf{M}[\mathbf{w}(t)])$, respectively, by inserting the decomposition (1.17) of $\mathbf{w}(t)$ in unstable and stable modes into $\mathbf{M}(\mathbf{w})$. The quadratic and cubic expansion terms of (1.6) then give rise to bilinear and trilinear expressions in $\boldsymbol{\xi}_u, \boldsymbol{\xi}_s$ of the form

$$M_u(\boldsymbol{\xi}_u,\boldsymbol{\xi}_s) = \sum_{r,r'} m^{(2)}_{u,rr'}\xi_r\xi_{r'} + \sum_{r,r',r''} m^{(3)}_{u,rr'r''}\xi_r\xi_{r'}\xi_{r''};$$

$$M_s(\boldsymbol{\xi}_u,\boldsymbol{\xi}_s) = \sum_{r,r'} m^{(2)}_{s,rr'}\xi_r\xi_{r'} + \sum_{r,r',r''} m^{(3)}_{s,rr'r''}\xi_r\xi_{r'}\xi_{r''}, \tag{1.21}$$

where the sums over r, r', r'' extend over all stable and unstable modes s and u.

The coupled nonlinear equations (1.19) and (1.20) for the amplitudes $\xi_u(t)$ and $\xi_s(t)$ of the unstable and stable modes, which are still equivalent to the original equations (1.2) for $\mathbf{F}(t) = 0$, have now very interesting properties due to the different kind of the eigenvalues $\lambda^{(u)}$ and $\lambda^{(s)}$ (see (1.15) and (1.16)) which lead to a *dramatically different dynamic behaviour* of the $\xi_u(t)$ as compared to that of the $\xi_s(t)$:

In a whole class of important cases (including the LASER and many other physico-chemical systems such as chemical diffusion-reaction systems) there exist for a given control parameter set $\boldsymbol{\alpha}$ only *one* or *very few* eigenvalue(s) $\lambda^{(u)}$ with *a small but positive real part* whereas the *bulk* of eigenvalues $\lambda^{(s)}$ retain *large negative real parts*. Due to the structure of equations (1.19) and (1.20) the $\xi_u(t)$ will then begin to *increase* exponentially whereas the $\xi_s(t)$ will begin to *decrease* exponentially. The nonlinear terms in equations (1.19) and (1.20) do however modify this initial behaviour.

A close further inspection of equations (1.19) and (1.20) shows that in the further evolution the $\xi_s(t)$ *adapt* their dynamics to that of the $\xi_u(t)$ which grow to *macroscopic order* and thus become *order parameters of the system*. The adaptation behaviour of the $\xi_s(t)$ can in first (but often very good) approximation be described by "*adiabatic elimination*", i.e. by neglecting the time derivative in (1.20), yielding the approximate equations:

$$\xi_s \approx -\frac{1}{\lambda^{(s)}} M_s(\boldsymbol{\xi}_u,\boldsymbol{\xi}_s). \tag{1.22}$$

These equations can be used to express the ξ_s in terms of the unstable amplitudes $\boldsymbol{\xi}_u$ and to *eliminate* $\boldsymbol{\xi}_s$ in this manner; this means one obtains from equation (1.22):

$$\xi_s = f_s(\boldsymbol{\xi}_u) \quad \text{for all } \xi_s. \tag{1.23}$$

Since the dynamics of the ξ_s is via equation (1.23) fully determined by that of the "dominant" order parameters $\boldsymbol{\xi}_u$ one can, following a proposal of H. Haken, illustratively say that the mode amplitudes $\xi_s(t)$ are "slaved" by the order parameters.

It remains to set up the *selfcontained dynamics* of the (often small number of) *order parameters* $\xi_u(t)$. These *order parameter equations* follow by inserting (1.23) into equation (1.19) with the result

$$\frac{d\xi_u(t)}{dt} = \lambda^{(u)}\xi_u(t) + M_u\big(\boldsymbol{\xi}_u(t), \mathbf{f}_s(\boldsymbol{\xi}_u(t))\big). \tag{1.24}$$

In some cases it happens that the equations (1.24) can be written in the form

$$\frac{d\boldsymbol{\xi}_u}{dt} = -\frac{\partial V(\boldsymbol{\xi}_u)}{\partial \boldsymbol{\xi}_u}. \tag{1.25}$$

This equation has the interpretation that the order parameters $\boldsymbol{\xi}_u = (\xi_{u_1}, \xi_{u_2}, \ldots, \xi_U)$ move in their U-dimensional space following a "driving force" which is given by the gradient of the potential $V(\boldsymbol{\xi}_u)$. The potential may possess one or several stationary points characterized by

$$\frac{\partial V}{\partial \xi_u} = 0; \quad u = u_1, u_2, \ldots, U \tag{1.26}$$

and the $\xi_u(t)$ approach one of the minima of $V(\boldsymbol{\xi}_u)$ which coincide with the stable stationary solutions of (1.25).

From (1.24) and (1.25) it is evident that the $\boldsymbol{\xi}_u(t)$ dominate the dynamics of the system because the $\boldsymbol{\xi}_u(t)$ are dynamically coupled *only among themselves* through equations (1.24) whereas the dynamics of the many variables $\xi_s(t)$ *follows that of the* $\boldsymbol{\xi}_u(t)$ because of (1.23).

The evolution of the original state vector $\mathbf{q}(t)$ is then described by

$$\mathbf{q}(t) = \mathbf{q}_0 + \sum_u \xi_u(t)\mathbf{v}^{(u)} + \sum_s \xi_s(t)\mathbf{v}^{(s)}, \tag{1.27}$$

where $\xi_u(t)$ and $\xi_s(t)$ obey (1.24) and (1.23), respectively. The original state $\mathbf{q}_0$ is destabilized if unstable modes exist whose amplitudes $\xi_u(t)$ grow to macroscopic orders of magnitude and determine the new dynamical order of the system.

Let us now discuss the achievements of the formalism of Synergetics with respect to some general system-theoretical aspects. For all systems for which fundamental "microscopic" equations of type (1.2) exist, the synergetic formalism is certainly an essential step forward in the *operationalism* of the description of system properties. Beyond that it gives a rather general *explanation* of the remarkable fact that relatively few macrovariables can dominate the dynamics of a whole system. The explanation consists in the mathematical insight that the *dominance* – or conversely *adaptivity* – of system variables is intimately linked to an inherent growth- or decline-trend of the variables on a corresponding time scale and that this trend becomes decisive and determines *situations of instability*.

The systematic derivation of (approximately) selfcontained, i.e. autonomous non-linear equations of motion for the relevant macrovariables, i.e. the order parameters, has also explanatory relevance: It explains on the one hand that the global system dynamics remains stable, adaptive and "good-natured" in a large domain of changes of environmental control-parameters or boundary conditions, and that on the other hand the global system dynamics may be destabilized if the control parameters pass certain critical values. Only a *nonlinear dynamic formalism* like that developed in Synergetics is able to comprise simultaneously system aspects such as adaptation, stabilisation, saturation and on the other hand escalation, destabilisation, enhancement and phase-transitions.

Even in cases where – because of lacking fundamental equations – the synergetic formalism cannot be worked out in the manner sketched above, it can serve as a guideline towards the operationalism of system concepts, including the partial accomplishment and carrying out of the framework developed by G.S.T.

Sociodynamics

The purpose, the procedure and the applications of Sociodynamics are the main subject of this book. Therefore we shall here only briefly discuss its relation to General System Theory and Synergetics.

A human society, whose collective dynamics is to be quantitatively modelled by an overarching formalism in Sociodynamics, is certainly included in the broad conceptual frame of General System Theory as we have already discussed above. Therefore the question can only be "how far is Sociodynamics able, at least partially to fill out, to implement and to operationalize *quantitatively* some statements of G.S.T. which are normally formulated in *qualitative* and *verbal* terms?".

In its quantitative procedure Sociodynamics makes use of a microlevel and a macrolevel of the society. Furthermore it considers the society as governed by relatively few economical, social, cultural, political and religious *macroscopic key-variables* or *order parameters* and it is its main goal to derive from relatively general principles *dynamic equations* for these *order parameters*.

Since the definition of all these concepts is the same as in Synergetics, one can therefore consider Sociodynamics as that part of Synergetics which is devoted to social systems.

On the other hand it seems justified to give the name "Sociodynamics" to this endeavour of modelling social systems, because it differs in some essential respects from the formalism of Synergetics described above:

(1) In contrast to physical, chemical and several physiological systems *no equations of motion on the microlevel* (i.e. on the level of human individuals) are available as yet for social systems. Therefore an *alternative formalism* has to be found in Sociodynamics which gets along *without micro-equations* but nevertheless takes into account the decisions and actions of individuals and derives from them

dynamic equations for the *relevant macrovariables* (i.e. order parameters) of the social system.

(2) Simultaneously the alternative formalism must make use of general motivations and manners of behaviour which are characteristic of the members of social systems and interpretable in sociological terms.

This alternative formalism of Sociodynamics is introduced in detail in Chapter 3. Its starting point is the presumed existence of individual motivations which on the one hand *depend* on the macro-situation and on the other lead to individual decisions and actions *influencing* the macro-situation.

Although no micro-equations are necessary in this formalism it is nevertheless tempting to develop a *vision* of how a *future* microscopic theory could give a deeper foundation to it in terms of synergetic equations for the "brain dynamics of decision making".

Let us consider in this somewhat speculative sense the subsystem of the brain of an individual engaged in deliberations leading to decisions between a set of alternative choices. The different lines of argumentation comprised in these deliberations are generated by the cooperation of a multitude of neurological micro-processes and they dominate and guide these processes. Therefore the components of argumentation seem to represent (or to be the mental resultant of) a *set of neurological order parameters*. Due to the nature of deliberations which can lead to different possible decisions these order parameters will *in general not* be in a stationary state. The subsystem of the brain must therefore be in a state *allowing for destabilisation and phase-transitions*. Therefore it is plausible to assume that the set of order parameters $\xi_u = \{\xi_1, \xi_2, \ldots, \xi_U\}$ corresponding to the argumentation lines included in a deliberation satisfy equations of motion of the type (1.24). For simplicity let us assume that even a potential $V(\xi_u)$ exists so that the equations are of the form (1.25). The shape of this potential which then determines the evolution of the "deliberation state" ξ_u will have to depend on *motivations*. These motivations will in their turn depend on a combination of *inherent properties* of the individual (e.g. inherited reaction patterns) and time-dependent inputs from the *social environment*. The state ξ_u will then, according to equation (1.25), fulfill a highly complicated motion in the – in general time-dependent – multidimensional potential-landscape and will approach one of the potential minima where it will come to (preliminary) rest. The *set of potential minima* will then correspond to the *set of choices*, in which the deliberation has reached a stationary state. However, due to the time-dependence of the potential a stable stationary state can be destabilized in the course of time. This would lead to a new deliberation process ending in a new (preliminarily stable) stationary state.

It should be mentioned that ideas of brain dynamics of the kind outlined here for the general decision process have already been worked out in detail and applied to the problem of *pattern recognition* by H. Haken and his school [21].

On the other hand it is clear that a brain-dynamical description of the *decision process in each individual* on the lines envisioned here would be too complex to serve as the basis of a general model design procedure for collective social processes. The reason is that too many details of individual circumstances would enter such a formalisation of individual decision processes.

Therefore the formalism of Sociodynamics to be developed in Chapter 3 gets along without brain-dynamical equations for individual decision processes by employing a *short cut*: It only takes into account the trend forming influence of the social macro-variables (and not all individual circumstances) on the decision making of individuals. However a price has to be paid for the neglect of the individual details by going over to a *probabilistic description* of the individual decision process.

2. Quantitative Modelling in Social Science

Although in some sectors of social science, in particular in economics, quantitative theory has already a rather long and successful tradition, there exist other sectors of social science where the applicability and usefulness of quantitative modelling is still controversial.

This situation contrasts with that in natural sciences like physics and chemistry where a throughgoing mathematical formulation of a theory and reproducible experiments with quantitative results which have to coincide *quantitatively* with the theory are seen as the ultimate and best level of description attainable.

The deeper reasons for this difference will be discussed in this chapter in order to obtain not only a better understanding of the possibilities but also in order to appreciate the limitations of quantitative procedures in the social sciences.

In Section 2.1 it is argued that *qualitative* (verbal) characterisations of social systems are *indispensible* and must *precede* every quantitative model design in a more intense manner than in natural sciences. In Section 2.2 the scope and the role, but also the limitations of quantitative models are discussed. It turns out that they are *complementary* and *not substitutable* for qualitative conceptualisations of social phenomena. These arguments lead in Section 2.3 to the conclusion that the ideal procedure of research in social sciences could consist of a *feedback loop between qualitative and quantitative thought*. In the light of these arguments some criticism of quantitative models in the social sciences is reconsidered and partially accepted, partially refuted in Section 2.4. The possibilities of this feedback loop have always been a challenge to natural scientists to apply quantitative thought to social phenomena; see e.g. [24].

2.1 The Necessity of Qualitative Characterisations of Social Systems

The fact that the "elementary" components of the social system, the individuals, are themselves highly complex subsystems, makes a *qualitative* investigation of a social system indispensable before any quantitative model is designed.

The qualitative analysis has to find out which trends and which modes of individual behaviour are *activated* and *relevant*, and which are *dormant* and *irrelevant* in

35

a *given situation*. This analysis is the *necessary background* for the choice of variables on the micro-, meso- and macro-level and for the delimitation of relevant trends and motivations from irrelevant ones in the design of quantitative models. (In contrast to this the variables in a sector of physics are usually welldefined and in the dynamical equations there appear constants of nature or material constants which do not vary dependent on the external situation as do trends and motivations.)

This situation-dependent analysis of the relevant trends and variables is connected with another difficulty which leads to differences between social and natural sciences: In social science usually only *one or at most a few samples* of the kind of investigated systems are empirically available. If only one series of events in one sample (e.g. a nation or an economy) is given it is extremely difficult to draw conclusions about the underlying causes of the – in general multicausally conditioned – events in retrospective analysis. Nevertheless it is the *normal situation* of social scientists or historians to have at their disposal for analysis *one* or at best *a few comparable systems*, whereas in natural sciences many experiments under controllable, reproducible boundary conditions with a great number of similarly prepared systems can be made. Under these circumstances one must admire how much information social scientists extract by an ingenious combination of methods from analysis of *one* system only.

2.2   The Scope and the Limitations of Quantitative Models

Quantitative models can never comprise the full richness of qualitatively different properties in a social system. On the contrary: Only models which are parsimoniously designed with respect to the number of variables and trendparameters are sufficiently transparent to yield possible insights into the structure and dynamics of a social system.

However it must first be shown why quantitative models with a few variables, which have been appropriately chosen from a preceding qualitative analysis, can in principle *depict the central dynamic behaviour* of a complex social system.

This justification comes from a generalized application of the *order parameter concept* to social systems. Even if the algorithm of Synergetics (see Section 1.3 and [8]) cannot be explicitly applied to social systems, because micro-equations of motion are not available, it is obvious that the "slaving principle" works *mutatis mutandis* for social systems, too:

The global situation and its evolution, which is on the one hand characterizable by a few order parameters or relevant macrovariables is on the other hand the resultant of very many micro-actions on the part of individuals. However the individuals are not fully free in their decisions and actions but are in turn *partially* guided and coordinated by the global situation. They generate the global situation but are simultaneously envolved and entrained into it. This cyclical relation sustains the global situation which therefore can be considered as the dominant structure of the social system. (It should however be mentioned that the relative extent of partial involvement and partial independence of the individuals within the global social system may vary considerably from system to system. The "slaving principle", if applied to social systems *does not mean* that the collective system *deterministically compels*, but means that it *more or less strongly orients* the decisions and actions of individuals.)

A reasonably constructed quantitative model of a sector of the society should therefore comprise relatively few well-chosen key-variables and relatively few (controllable or immanent) trendparameters but not the bulk of (partially entrained) microvariables. The structure of such models will then determine their *scope and value* and simultaneously their *limitations*.

Their *value* consists in the fact that such models have properties which are *complementary* to verbal qualitative analyses of single social systems:

Due to its simple structure it is possible to investigate with *one model* a *whole manifold of numerically calculable scenarios* by varying the set of trendparameters and of initial conditions. (This corresponds to the procedure in simulations of complex systems in natural science, for instance the global climate under varying parameter sets like CO_2 concentration.) The *empirically realized* system should then be *embedded* into this manifold of *imaginary* systems and should belong to the corresponding *realized* set of trendparameters and of initial conditions.

Even if the quantitative model is *oversimplified* and can therefore only be considered as a *semiquantitative*, somehow *stylized* and *idealized* approach to reality, the insights won by mathematical analysis of the manifold of its solutions remain valuable if the model turns out to be *generic* and *robust*. This means that the simplified model still describes the "generic" essentials of the dynamics and that these essentials have survived even under the neglections made in the model design.

Some of the most important insights won from generic and robust semiquantitative models fitted out with *nonlinear dynamics* are *not quantitative* in the narrow sense, but *qualitative*: Such models show under which circumstances with respect to the trendparameters *social phasetransitions* (this means *global changes* of the mode of dynamic behaviour of the whole system) may occur and which signals are indicators of such imminent revolutionary events.

On the other side the simple and transparent form of parsimonious mathematical models is the reason for their *limitations*. Such models always imply a *reduction by projecting* the immense colourful variety of the micro-behaviour of individuals to the dynamics of a few key-variables or order-parameters. This means a far-reaching *information-compression* in which the colours and qualities of detailed individual behaviours are lost. One might say that mathematical models describe the skeleton and its dynamics but not the flesh of social systems. This fact makes indispensible now as ever the detailed qualitative analysis of the microlevel.

Even more important for the indispensibility of qualitative analysis and interpretation at the microlevel is the fact that a *whole equivalence class* of *microbehaviours* may lead to the *same* dynamics of macrovariables, or in other words: Even if the macrodynamics is fully known there remains ambiguity concerning the question by which aggregated microbehaviour it has been generated. The reason for this micro-ambiguity is that many different modes of microbehaviour may lead to the *same* values of the composite trendparameters and macrovariables which determine the macrodynamics.

An example should illustrate this important fact: In totalitarian political systems there exist strong opinion pressures which are taken into account in mathematical models (see Chapter 6) by a trendparameter being a measure for the readiness of individuals to adapt to the prevailing political opinion. The same degree of adaptiveness may however come about by very different causes and motivations at the level of individuals, for instance (a) by coerced adaptation, (b) by opportunistic adaptation and (c) by voluntary adaptation. Only a micro-analysis of individuals and not the theoretical description or empiric observation of the macro-effect can differentiate between these motivations.

Having discussed the scope of mathematical models of social systems which turn out to have a *complementary and not substitutable* relation to qualitative analysis we summarize the requirements for a useful quantitative modelling of social systems:

(1)   In view of the order parameter concept which also holds for social systems, a quantitative model should be *parsimonious* in the number of key-variables and trendparameters it employs so that the *interpretative transparency* is preserved, and simultaneously it should be *generic* and *robust*.

(2)   Since the system structure, namely the relation between the whole and its parts, is so fundamental, a model should relate at least the main levels of a social system, namely the level of individual behaviour and the level of global macro-variables. (The treatment of intermediate levels, e.g. groups and their relations, should of course be included if indicated.)

(3)   The model structure should be open to "*horizontal*" and "*vertical*" extensions: Here, "horizontal" extension means that it should be possible to combine models for neighboring sectors of the society in integrated models. "Vertical" extension means that the model should allow for the inclusion of a possible (slow) dynamics of trendparameters, because the latter are not "constants of nature" but are also slowly varying (psychological or situational or environmental) variables.

(4)   It should be possible to calibrate the parameters of a model and evaluate it numerically in comparison with empirical data if the latter are available.

2.3   The Feedback-Loop of Qualitative and Quantitative Thought

The relation between qualitative and quantitative thought in the process of model design should now be discussed in more detail.

We have already argued that qualitative analysis of a social system must precede quantitative model design and that the quantitative approach is complementary to the qualitative one. Now we will argue that the gap between qualitative and quantitative thought is not a principal one but that there exists a considerable, although sometimes disguised and tacit overlap.

On the one hand the analysis of a *qualitatively arguing* social scientist will be excellent if he selects at most a few dozen relevant key-characteristics of the social system under consideration and if he makes a qualitative estimate of the interactions of these characteristic features. If he can make estimates concerning the *order of magnitude* of these features and their mutual influence then he can come to certain conclusions about the dynamics of the system, namely the growth or the decay of some characteristics, interactions and influences. This means that a *qualitative* description of a system and its evolution over time tacitly implies estimates about the *amount* or *magnitude, strength* or *intensity* of the relevant characteristics. However, this is already the essential first step towards a *quantified* description.

On the other hand we have already seen that the explanatory potential of quantitative or semiquantitative models also includes *qualitative changes* in the nature of a system in terms of social phase transitions. Such conclusions about the *qualitative* structure or system behaviour by *quantitative models* becomes the more important when less exact estimates of the trendparameters are all that is available.

The overlap discussed above now makes possible a fruitful interaction between both forms of thought which can in the optimal case lead to a mutual improvement and sharpening of argumentation in the process of model design. We denote this form of interaction as the *feedback loop of qualitative and quantitative thought*. It consists of the following steps:

(1) Qualitative thought leads to the delimitation of the social sector, to the selection of relevant key-variables, and to the identification of the trends, motivations and ensuing activities of the social actors.

(2) The model design thereupon leads to quantitative measures for all variables, interactions, trends and activities. Finally the dynamics of the system must be formulated quantitatively, e.g. in terms of coupled differential equations.

(3) After the calibration of trendparameters and choice of initial conditions, "scenario simulations" can be implemented and compared with empirical cases which have to be embedded into the manifold of simulated cases.

(4) The evaluation leads either to a substantiation of the model design or demands a correction.

(5) At this stage the feedback loop comes into action. The correction may consist in a re-calibration of trendparameters. More generally, the introduction of additional or alternative interaction terms or even new variables might be necessary. Their introduction must be justified by *qualitative argumentation and interpretation*. The augmented model must be compared with the empirical cases until the latter can be successfully embedded and interpreted within the scenario-manifold.

(6) The trial and error procedure which consists in *iteratively passing through steps 1 to 5* leads to an improvement of the quantitative model as well as to increased precision of the qualitative analysis. Both effects are the result of the feedback loop.

2.4 Discussion of Critical Arguments about Quantitative Modelling in Social Science

During the evolution of quantitative modelling in social science criticisms have been made against the adequacy of this procedure. Some of this criticism has to be accepted, some is refutable. In any case the discussion is valuable because it leads to deeper insights about the nature of quantitative research in and beyond social science. Our presentation of the arguments is incomplete. For a more comprehensive recent discussion of these problems see e.g. [25].

The Argument of Physicalism

The reproach that quantitative models are inadequate for capturing social systems because they use methods only applicable to physics and are therefore *"physicalistic"* or *"materialistic"* must be accepted for certain forms of quantitative description but can be refuted for most of the modern quantitative approaches.

Some early attempts to formalize social behaviour made *direct use of physical laws* and re-interpreted them in application to social systems. We illustrate this by an example: The equation of state for an ideal gas states that (at constant temperature) the pressure increases if the volume is compressed. A social re-interpretation would be that the "social pressure" – however it may be defined and measured – increases if the available space for life is diminished. This "application" of physical laws to social systems would of course be *inadmissible* and physicalistic because laws of nature valid for physical objects cannot be directly applied to social systems and their elements, even if some analogies between both sorts of systems may be found.

However in the case of other quantificational procedures, the reproach of physicalism does *definitely not apply*. Such procedures start from *universally* valid and applicable *mathematical formalisms and algorithms* and apply them to the quantified description of social phenomena after adding concepts *characteristic of social systems*.

Here the reproach of physicalism is *refutable* due to the simple reason that universal mathematical formalisms have nothing to do with physical laws of nature. The refutation remains valid, if the same universal mathematics can on the other hand also be utilized for the formulation of physical laws which have nothing to do with social science. (This is so in the case of Sociodynamics where we utilize the universal mathematical formalism for stochastic dynamic systems and combine it with concepts about social behaviour. The same mathematical formalism has on the other hand found widespread application to the formulation of physico-chemical laws, a fact which does not affect the nonphysical nature of its application in Sociodynamics.)

The "No Isomorphism" Argument

This argument is related to the physicalist criticism and can be seen as a more precise formulation of it (see [26]). It says that comparisons between the structures of social and physical systems are misleading and at best superficial because between the elements and interactions of physical and of social systems there *does not exist any isomorphism*. In particular, human individuals do *not* exhibit the same spatial and temporal *invariance of properties and interactions* as for instance physical particles; therefore the reproducibility of theoretical statements about social systems does not hold true in the same manner as for physical systems.

The lack of isomorphy between the elements of social and physical systems can indeed be confirmed. It is the underlying reason why a direct application or re-interpretation of physical laws for social systems is *inadmissible*.

However the more general conclusion that because of this lack of isomorphism on the level of elements, comparisons between structures of social and physical systems are not allowed at all cannot be accepted, for the following reasons:

Universal mathematical methods valid for *all* multicomponent systems lead to *general conclusions* with respect to the structure of the dynamic behaviour of multi-component systems on the *macrolevel* (for instance conclusions about the manifolds of solutions of systems of nonlinearly coupled differential equations for the macro-variables).

On this macrolevel, a considerable *information-compression* has taken place which has *wiped out* differences and non-isomorphisms on the *microlevel*, which continue to be rather different in social and physical systems: It turns out that nevertheless there exist *structural analogies* on the *macrolevel* of the otherwise very differently composed systems.

The comparison of these macrostructures which have *survived* the information-compression is evidently *justified* and also *valuable* because it highlights a system behaviour which only depends on the very general properties of the components and their system, but *not* on all details of the nature and interaction of those components.

However, this fact has also a *seamy side* which leads back to the limitations of the quantitative macro-description: Just because in the general macro-scenario the detailed behaviour of the components is *wiped out to a great extent* it is not possible to make detailed conclusions about the micro-behaviour of components starting from the observation and calculation of the macro-structure only.

The *non-invariance* of human interactions in contrast to the always equal interaction forces between physical particles is also a valid observation which can be traced back to the complexity of human nature and its mediated – and not immediate – interaction with the environment. However this non-invariance does not prevent its systematic inclusion in quantitative treatments:

In such formulations the probabilistic decision- and action-behaviour of individuals is expressed in terms of a set of trendparameters. Often these trendparameters can be considered as *constant for the time interval under interest*. However, since such trendparameters are no "constants of nature" but are instead conditioned by talents, education, tradition and the social environment, they also exhibit a *slow and sometimes even relatively fast dynamics* which can be cast in the form of equations in extended models. Such equations contain coefficients denoted as "trend parameters of second order" which again might be slowly variable with time, and so on. Finally, the *"hierarchy of trendparameter dynamics"* must be cut off appropriately in order to close the formalism. (Of course, in verbal qualitative formulations of social theory the same is done by tacit assumptions about the quasi-invariance of certain modes of human behaviour.)

The Argument of Naturalism

This argument imputes that quantitative models necessarily lead to a natural-istic misunderstanding of social phenomena because they describe the social order as a phenomenon which simply occurs, happens, takes place – like phenomena in nature – but not as an intentional construction which can be actively organized and framed according to the will of humans.

This argument can be rejected because correctly designed quantitative models of social systems do not only comprise "blindly occurring" natural construction elements but also incorporate the *strength and direction of human attempts* to conserve or, alternatively, to change a given social situation. The model will therefore describe objectively the *resultant* of naturally occurring *and* intentionally effected events in the social system so far as they can be modelled.

The Argument of Instrumentalism

This argument imputes that quantitative models are appropriate to be (ab)used as an *instrument* for controlling, manipulating and engineering the structure of society.

At first it must be remarked that the positions of naturalism and instrumentalism are mutually exclusive, because a model could only *either* describe blindly occurring events *or* have the capacity to encroach upon and manipulate human behaviour.

However, *neither* the argument of *naturalism nor* the argument of *instrumentalism* prove true. A correctly designed quantitative model can never be per se an instrument of manipulation because it describes in a quantified, objective and neutral form the possible results of trends and activities of individuals for the global evolution of their society. Although quantitative models describe the *effects of tendencies* and are therefore not naturalistic, they are on the other hand *not instrumentalist* because they give a *neutral overview* of the effects of tendencies. Therefore quantitative models clearly belong to the *cognitive domain of social theory* and may rather contribute to objective, i.e. nonideologic, verbal and qualitative theory.

However there exists a *metatheoretical level* of evaluation and differentiation between politically, economically and morally desirable or undesirable directions of social evolution; and of course different value systems lead to controversial opinions about the most desirable ways of reaching them. At this level any quantitative model as well as any verbal theory can be used to draw conclusions about how to utilize some influences (e.g. political propaganda) in order to reach specific social aims. Even abuse by extremists cannot be excluded. It seems, however, that the seductive potential and the danger for abuse of verbally formulated ideologies exceeds by far that of quantitative models.

3. The General Modelling Concept of Sociodynamics

3.1 The Modelling Purposes of Sociodynamics

In view of the discussion of the general structure of social systems in Chapter 1 and of the problems arising in their quantitative description in Chapter 2 we shall now try to develop a general approach to mathematical model design. The concept should be applicable to a whole class of phenomena as they appear in different social sciences such as population dynamics, sociology, economics and regional science.

From the very beginning the modelling concept should meet the following demands, which were already discussed in Chapter 2:

(a) Only universally applicable mathematical methods should be used. That means the mathematics should not be restricted to applications to a small class of objects.

(b) In a decisive step the modelling procedure should *integrate* into the mathematical method concepts which refer to the *typical structure of social systems* and therefore should differ from concepts applying to natural systems. However, these concepts must be general enough to apply in an overarching manner to *all* social sectors.

(c) According to the structure of social systems the model design should *connect* the *microlevel* of decisions and actions of individuals which are intentionally driven and the *macrolevel* of the evolution dynamics of the material, spatial and abstract macrostructures of the system. (It should also be possible to include the dynamics of *intermediate* levels like *groups, organisations and institutions.*) The *cyclic relation* between micro- and macrolevel is in this construction.

 The *main purpose* is then to derive in a consistent manner *dynamic equations for the evolution of relevant variables* ("key-variables" or "order-parameters") *at the macrolevel of the system.*

(d) A difficulty specific for social systems which has already been mentioned in Chapter 1.3 must be overcome here: *No "equations of motion" are available* at the microlevel of individual behaviour. The standard formalism of Synergetics

43

(see Section 1.3) is therefore not applicable because it presumes the existence of a set of micro-equations from which the order-parameter equations can be derived.

This difficulty leads to an *alternative treatment* of the behaviour of individuals which simultaneously fulfills the *purpose of describing correctly* the fact that the decisions and actions of individuals are *partially free and independent* and *partially entrained* into and *guided* by the social *system as a whole*. This description will make use of *probabilistic concepts* which by their definition comprise the partially free and contingent and partially entrained nature of individual decision making. (We can leave open here the question of whether the partial contingency of human decisions can be traced back to a more fundamental description of brain dynamics as it was indicated in Section 1.3. In our context it is only essential that the probabilistic treatment of individual decisions lead to their *partial freedom and non-determination* by the variables at the *collective macrolevel* of the system.)

(e) From the probabilistic description of the behaviour of individuals (which will be implemented in terms of probabilistic transition rates between different attitudes and actions in Section 3.2.2) there necessarily follows the stochastic nature of the dynamics of the macrovariables at the collective level. The central equation for this *probabilistic macrodynamics* will then be the *master equation for the probability distribution of macrovariables* derived in Section 3.2.3. For its mathematical properties see Chapter 10.

This equation still contains the macro-effects of the partially contingent random behaviour of individuals. However, these effects are normally *small* for *large numbers* of individuals because the random fluctuations of individual decisions cancel each other out at the collective level. The only exception to this rule are *social phase transitions*. In these cases the *"critical fluctuations"*, i.e. the unpredictable probabilistic decision behaviour of a few or even one individual could trigger global change.

(f) The master equation can be interpreted as the equation for the evolution of the macrovariables of an ensemble of systems traversing sequentially and probabilistically different macrostates. Considering the *mean evolution* of bundles (partial ensembles) of such "stochastic trajectories" one arrives at *"quasi-meanvalue-equations"* which are closely related to the master equation formalism (see Chapter 12).

The quasi-meanvalue-equations form a set of in general nonlinear differential equations for the mean evolution of the macrovariables. Normally they suffice for describing the essentials of social macrodynamics.

The derivation and evaluation of the *probabilistic master equation* and the *deterministic quasi-meanvalue-equations* are the main purpose of the modelling procedure which will now be described in some detail.

Readers who want to trace back the development of Sociodynamics are referred to [27], [28], [29], [30], [31], [32], [33] and [34]. A qualitative survey of methods and results is given in [35].

3.2 The Steps of the Modelling Procedure

In setting up the steps of the modelling design in general terms we proceed in three steps. The *first step* consists of finding *appropriate variables* for the social sector to be considered; the *second step* is the crucial one because it introduces the *elementary dynamic processes* taking into account their specifically *social nature*, and the *third step* makes use of the mathematics of stochastic systems to derive *equations for the global evolution* of the key-variables of the system. In each step the specific problems which arise for *social systems* as distinct from natural systems are explicitly considered.

3.2.1 The Configuration Space of Macrovariables

Firstly we must briefly characterize the framework of the *fundamental aspects of life* into which the human individual with its activities is embedded. Here we follow the view of J. Burckhardt [36]. According to him, *political institutions* respond to the need for the protection of rights and of individual safety by organizing a system of participation and of "law and order". The *economy* provides structures satisfying the demands for material needs. The *culture* allows the free expression of the activities of the human mind and soul, and *religion* responds to the human need for transcendence.

The appropriate choice of relevant macrovariables (= key-variables or order parameters) for a subsector of this total social system is not as obvious as is usually the case in natural systems.

Whereas in natural systems (e.g. physics and chemistry) the micro- and macro-level are relatively well-defined and well-separated, we find in social systems, due to their higher complexity, a rather dense architecture of subsectors, including substructures and subprocesses, of a *relatively integrated selfcontainedness*, between which however more or less strong interactions take place which *soften and weaken* this integrity. The sectors of politics, economy and science are examples of subsectors of partial *independence* but also partial *interdependence*.

The choice of a sector and its relevant variables (and the division of a university into faculties treating separately such sectors) *implies* that the *delimitation* of one sector from other sectors is approximately possible and that the comparatively weak interaction *between* sectors and processes can be taken into account in terms of boundary conditions and exogenous parameters. The main assumption implied in the anticipated delimitation of a sector is that its *descriptive key-variables should obey a quasi-autonomous selfcontained dynamics of their own*.

Given that qualitative analysis of the nature of the system has led to an implied delimitation of a subsector (which must be substantiated later), we may now distinguish and classify different kinds of key-variables for the sector under consideration:

(a) *Collective Material Variables*
Macrovariables of this material aggregated kind are wellknown and have for long been used in particular in economics. One may distinguish, as in thermodynamics, between *extensive* variables which are proportional to the system size, and *intensive* variables which are independent of the size of the system.

Examples for *extensive material* variables are stock and flow variables such as the following: the capital stock; the total inventory of the industry; the total number of buildings in a city; production (total amount of goods turned out per period); investment (invested capital assets per period); capacity (potential output of goods per period of the industry); gross national product (GNP); gross income.

Examples for *intensive material* variables are the price and the quality of a commodity, the productivity (production per worker), the capacity utilization rate, the salary (income per worker). *Intensive* variables are often *densities* of *extensive* variables, that means extensive variables divided through another extensive variable like area, number of people, labour force, etc.

It is characteristic of material macrovariables $m_1, \ldots m_k, \ldots$ appearing in a sector of the society that their amount (in the case of extensive variables) or intensity (in the case of intensive variables) can be influenced by individual actors or groups of actors (e.g. the management of firms), but that this influence is an *indirect* one. This means that the activity of individuals *behind* the evolution of material macrovariables *does not show up explicitly* but nevertheless must always be kept in mind when modelling their dynamics.

The set of material macrovariables

$$\mathbf{m} = \{m_1, \ldots, m_k, \ldots, m_M\} \tag{3.1}$$

necessary to be included into the description of the social sector under consideration is denoted as the *material configuration*.

(b) *Extensive Personal Variables*
Material variables alone, which are the traditional basis of quantitative theoretical economics, are *necessary but not sufficient* if more general sociological phenomena are to be described such as the interactions between individuals *beyond* their being rational producers and consumers producing and consuming according to the rule of optimized efficiency.

According to the characterization of the fundamental aspects of life the individual will then participate in the society in his or her role as homo politicus, homo oeconomicus, homo sapiens, homo ludens, homo religiosus and quite generally as homo socialis. With respect to each of these aspects there exist several possible modes of activity, or of opinions assumable by an individual in view of the problems and issues in the actual social situation. We denote these possible opinions or modes of activity at the disposal of individuals in their social environment as *attitudes*.

The notion of "*attitudes*" is a very general and flexible concept, applying for instance to political opinions or actions, to roles in economic life as a producer or consumer of commodities, to choices of living- and working-place, to scientific and cultural views and activities, to forms of religious faith and denomination.

We assume that to each individual there can be assigned an *attitudinal index* "i", where i runs through C values, $i = 1, 2, \ldots, C$, if C is the number of different possible attitudes with respect to the set of issues of the considered social sector. In other words: the attitudes $i = 1, 2, \ldots, C$ are the *choice set* available to the individual.

Whereas the individual is free to choose attitudes, other properties of him or her cannot be changed. Biographical, genetical, and educational backgrounds belong to these *practically unchangeable properties*. Individuals characterizable by the same constant background "α" of such unchangeable properties do by definition belong to the same subpopulation $\mathcal{P}^\alpha$ of the society. In the general case we assume that P subpopulations $\mathcal{P}^\alpha, \alpha = 1, 2, \ldots, P$ exist. (It depends on the focus and the purpose of a model whether one needs a fine or a coarse distinction between subpopulations or no distinction at all.) An attitudinal index "i" and a background index "α" can be assigned to each member of the society. Therefore these indices have nothing to do with the size and extent of the society. But now let us construct a set of *extensive variables* belonging to the indices $i = 1, 2, \ldots, C$, and $\alpha = 1, 2, \ldots, P$.

For this we introduce the number n_i^α of members of the subpopulation $\mathcal{P}^\alpha$ who have the attitude i. In most cases the n_i^α are large integers, i.e. $n_i^\alpha \gg 1$. If we are not interested in the social state of *each individual* but instead in the *distribution of attitudes* (= opinions or actions) among the members of all subpopulations on the *macroscopic level*, then the "*socioconfiguration*", i.e. the multiple of integers

$$\mathbf{n} = \{n_1^1, \ldots, n_C^1; \ldots; n_1^\alpha, \ldots, n_i^\alpha, \ldots, n_C^\alpha; \ldots; n_1^P, \ldots, n_C^P\} \qquad (3.2)$$

is the appropriate *set of extensive personal macrovariables* yielding this information.

Some obvious relations hold, if the socioconfiguration $\mathbf{n}$ is given. If N^α is the number of members of subpopulation $\mathcal{P}^\alpha$, and N_i the number of all members of the society with attitude i, and N the total number of members of the society, one obtains:

$$N^\alpha = \sum_{i=1}^{C} n_i^\alpha; \quad N_i = \sum_{\alpha=1}^{P} n_i^\alpha \qquad (3.3)$$

and

$$N = \sum_{\alpha=1}^{P} N^\alpha = \sum_{i=1}^{C} N_i. \qquad (3.4)$$

(c) *Intensive Personal Variables*

The attitudes i are visible and openly exhibited opinions and activities of individuals, in other words they are "*extrovert*" properties. However there also exist *inner intellectual and emotional states* of the individual which are not openly shown. If such inner states are "introvert" properties, more or less *isolated* from social life they cannot and should not be included in the design of models of social processes. In cases however, where the inner hidden state of the individuals is in *strong interaction* with the external social situation one cannot avoid including its dynamics in the modelling design, even if it may be not easy to measure such inner variables. Otherwise the conclusions of the model would become error prone because of the neglection of possibly decisive key-variables.

Evidently inner state variables are *intensive* variables because they describe the amplitude or intensity of a psychological reaction on the part of each single individual to a social situation. This reaction has effects on the global state of the society, if many individuals possess the same inner state. Nevertheless such variables evidently cannot be aggregated to an *extensive* macrovariable by merely taking their sum!

Let us now formulate in principle the *procedure of quantifying inner states*. At first one must identify the field to which the tacit inner state belongs. This is a matter of qualitative analysis. Secondly, the quantitative intensity of the variable assigned to the corresponding component of the inner state must be defined. Normally it will range between different (positive) degrees of *tacit approval* and different (negative) degrees of *tacit aversion* with respect to relevant aspects of the realized social situation.

To each individual there can be assigned in principle several of such inner state variables. It depends on the scope and detailedness of the model just how many are needed. Let us write down one *representative variable* of this kind. In the general case its amplitude (and its dynamics) will depend on the subpopulation $\mathcal{P}^\alpha$ and the attitude i of the individuals to which it is assigned. Thus:

$$\vartheta = \{\vartheta_1^1, \ldots, \vartheta_C^1; \ldots; \vartheta_1^\alpha, \ldots, \vartheta_i^\alpha, \ldots, \vartheta_C^\alpha; \vartheta_1^P, \ldots, \vartheta_C^P\} \tag{3.5}$$

with

$$-\Theta \leq \vartheta_i^\alpha \leq +\Theta \tag{3.6}$$

describes the *configuration of intense personal variables* with respect to one field. For instance the ϑ_i^α may describe the degree of inner approval and favour or inner disapproval and disfavour with regard to a political situation. (For an application of this concept see Chapter 6.) In equation (3.6) an upper limit $+\Theta$ and a lower limit $-\Theta$ has been attributed to the inner state variable, which seems psychologically plausible.

(d)   *Trend- and Control-Parameters*
Finally the individuals belonging to a subpopulation $\mathcal{P}^\alpha$ are – in their stationary and dynamic behaviours – characterized by a set of *inherent trendparameters*. These trendparameters are considered as *constants* because they belong to the deeply rooted *inherent properties* of the members of $\mathcal{P}^\alpha$ being quantitative expressions of the biographical, genetical, and cultural backgrounds which define the subpopulation $\mathcal{P}^\alpha$. They enter the framework of dynamic equations as *constant coefficients*. Because the inherent trendparameters are assigned to each individual they must be considered as *intensive quantities*. Normally they are not at our disposal. That means their values must be considered as given.

Another kind of parameter which also may enter the framework of dynamic equations as constant coefficients are defined by certain (geographical, political, economical, environmental) *boundary conditions*. Such parameters may in principle be at our disposal and *controllable* by exogenous interference into the sector under consideration. Therefore they are denoted as *controlparameters*.

Because trendparameters as well as controlparameters enter the dynamic equations not as *variables* but as *coefficients*, we shall group them in one set of parameters κ.

It depends on the sector and the focus of the model how many trend- and control-parameters are needed for each subpopulation $\mathcal{P}^\alpha$. Writing down one representative parameter κ^α for each $\mathcal{P}^\alpha$ we arrive at the *trend and control parameter-configuration*

$$\kappa = \{\kappa^1, \ldots, \kappa^\alpha, \ldots, \kappa^P\}. \tag{3.7}$$

The *total configuration of variables and parameters* of a sectorial model then consists of the material variables, the extensive and intensive personal variables, and the trend- and/or control-parameters, i.e. we have the

$$\text{total configuration} = \{\mathbf{m}, \mathbf{n}, \vartheta; \kappa\}. \tag{3.8}$$

Some general remarks about the problems of the choice of an appropriate set of variables and parameters for a sectorial model should conclude this section.

The most important aim for quantifying the macrodynamics of a sector is to find an *approximately selfcontained and complete set of macrovariables and assisting trend- and control-parameters* in the following sense: In order to calculate the probability of the values of a set of macrovariables at a later time it should be sufficient to know the probability distribution for the values of the *same set of macrovariables* at a former time. In other words: For given constant values of trend- and control-parameters the selected set of macrovariables should be "complete" in so far as it obeys an *autonomous selfcontained probabilistic subdynamics*.

This dynamic process will be described as a *probabilistic Markov process* in the next sections. (By definition of a *Markov process* it is sufficient to know the probability distribution over a set of variables *at present* in order to calculate the same distribution for *any future time*.) In order to have a Markov process the influence of *past events* (history, tradition, biography) have to be included in the *momentary set of variables* in terms of appropriately chosen *memory variables* representing the presently stored accumulated experience of the past and in terms of trendparameters incorporating the momentary effect of traditions and of biography. Only if the memory of the past is included in terms of such memory-storing variables and parameters can the set of *momentary* variables and trends be considered as complete and selfcontained in the sense discussed above.

The aim of finding a "complete" set of variables obeying a selfcontained subdynamics may also include the problem of quantifying indispensible but "fuzzy" variables. As examples of fuzzy variables we mention the "quality" of a commodity, the extent of officialdom or inner state variables like the personal intensity of approval or disapproval of a political situation.

In principle a quantitative measure of such fuzzy variables can be found by taking a weighted meanvalue of a set of appropriate indicators assigned to the variable which can e.g. take the values "very positive", "positive", "neutral", "negative", "very negative". Even if such a direct quantification method is not (yet) available it may suffice to determine the role and influence of a fuzzy variable by positioning it appropriately within the framework of the dynamic equations. If then its dynamical influence on the directly accessible and measurable variables proves to be correct whereas its exclusion leads to errors, the necessary role of the fuzzy variable has been substantiated.

A final remark concerns the relation between the personal intensive inner state variables and the trendparameters. The first ones are considered as *variables* and the latter ones as *constants*, although both characterize behavioural properties of the individual. Indeed, both kinds of quantities only differ with respect to the time period in which they significantly vary or, alternatively, vary so slowly that they can be treated as constants. Nevertheless, quasi-constant trendparameters are no "constants of nature" like the Planck constant h or the velocity of light c in physics.

If one wants to include in terms of equations of evolution the slow time dependence of trendparameters one arrives at the *hierarchy of trendparameter dynamics* where new equations require new coefficients, i.e. trendparameters of higher order. This hierarchy must however be cut off after a finite number of model extensions in order to obtain a finite and manageable model structure.

In models which are designed to depict explicitly social learning processes or secular shifts of the system of moral values the corresponding slow change of trendparameters will have to be included in terms of such equations of evolution.

3.2.2 The Elementary Dynamics

If all key-variables $\{\mathbf{m}, \mathbf{n}, \vartheta\}$ remain constant with time the considered sector of the society is in a macroscopically stationary equilibrium, which may in some respects and mutatis mutandis be compared to thermodynamic equilibrium.

It is however our main purpose to describe the *dynamics of the macrovariables*. Since global evolutions are composed of elementary steps we shall in this section consider these steps which we will treat in a standardized manner.

At first the elementary steps as such are introduced. Without restriction of generality we may always choose appropriate units such that the elementary step of change consists of the increase or descrease of one component of the – extensive or intensive – macrovariables by one unit.

Assume for instance, that the component m_k of the material configuration $\mathbf{m}$ increases or decreases by one unit. Then the *material configuration* makes the elementary transition

$$\mathbf{m} \Rightarrow \mathbf{m}_{k\pm} = \{m_1, \ldots, (m_k \pm 1), \ldots, m_M\} \tag{3.9}$$

to the neighbouring material configuration $\mathbf{m}_{k\pm}$.

The elementary change of the *socioconfiguration* $\mathbf{n}$ takes place if one individual of subpopulation $\mathcal{P}^\alpha$ changes his/her attitude (= opinion or action) from i to j. This "generalized elementary migration process" leads to the elementary transition

$$\mathbf{n} \Rightarrow \mathbf{n}_{ji}^\alpha = \{n_1^1, \ldots, n_C^1; \ldots; n_1^\alpha, \ldots, (n_j^\alpha + 1), \ldots, (n_i^\alpha - 1), \ldots, n_C^\alpha; \ldots; n_1^P, \ldots, n_C^P\}$$

$$\tag{3.10}$$

from $\mathbf{n}$ to the neighbouring socioconfiguration $\mathbf{n}_{ji}^\alpha$.

Finally, if the component ϑ_i^α of the intensive personal variable changes by one unit, the configuration of the intensive personal variables makes the transition

$$\boldsymbol{\vartheta} \to \boldsymbol{\vartheta}_{i\pm}^\alpha = \{\vartheta_1^1, \ldots, \vartheta_C^1; \ldots; \vartheta_1^\alpha, \ldots, (\vartheta_i^\alpha \pm 1), \ldots, \vartheta_C^\alpha; \ldots; \vartheta_1^P, \ldots, \vartheta_C^P\} \qquad (3.11)$$

to the neighbouring intensive configuration $\boldsymbol{\vartheta}_{i\pm}^\alpha$.

Now the decisive dynamic quantities must be introduced which put into effect the elementary transitions between the macroconfiguration $\{\mathbf{m}, \mathbf{n}, \boldsymbol{\vartheta}\}$ and its neighbours $\{\mathbf{m}_{k\pm}, \mathbf{n}, \boldsymbol{\vartheta}\}$, $\{\mathbf{m}, \mathbf{n}_{ji}^\alpha, \boldsymbol{\vartheta}\}$ and $\{\mathbf{m}, \mathbf{n}, \boldsymbol{\vartheta}_{i\pm}^\alpha\}$. At this crucial step many modelling requirements must simultaneously find their expression:

(1) *No microscopic equations of motion* of the individual can be utilized because they are not available.

(2) The transitions which are effected by individuals should be described by a *probabilistic process* which may or may not happen, so that the individual "freedom of decision and action" is not restricted. That means the elementary process cannot be a deterministic one!

(3) Nevertheless this probabilistic process must be oriented and guided by the *social driving forces* behind it, namely, by *decision- and action-generating motivations*.

(4) This description of the elementary process must simultaneously provide the circular coupling between the microlevel of individual activity and the macrolevel of the society so far as this can be expressed by the introduced macrovariables.

The four requirements are satisfied by introducing *probabilistic transition rates per unit of time* for the transitions (3.9), (3.10) and (3.11).

Such transition rates are by definition probabilities generated per unit of time for the occupation of a new state into which the system may go (see Chapter 10 for further mathematical details). Therefore they are by definition positive (semi)definite quantities. Such quantities can be written in exponential form (since the exponential function of real variables is always positive) on whatsoever variables they may depend.

Let us begin with the transition (3.9) $\mathbf{m} \Rightarrow \mathbf{m}_{k\pm}$ and the inverse transition $\mathbf{m}_{k\pm} \Rightarrow \mathbf{m}$. For these two transitions we introduce probabilistic transition rates of the following form:

$$w_k(\mathbf{m}_{k\pm}, \mathbf{m}; \mathbf{n}; \boldsymbol{\vartheta}; \boldsymbol{\kappa}) \equiv w_k^\pm(\mathbf{m}; \mathbf{n}; \boldsymbol{\vartheta}; \boldsymbol{\kappa}); = \mu_0 \exp\{M_k(\mathbf{m}_{k\pm}, \mathbf{m}; \mathbf{n}; \boldsymbol{\vartheta}; \boldsymbol{\kappa})\}$$
$$\text{for the transition } \mathbf{m} \Rightarrow \mathbf{m}_{k\pm}; \qquad (3.12a)$$

$$w_k(\mathbf{m}, \mathbf{m}_{k\pm}; \mathbf{n}; \boldsymbol{\vartheta}; \boldsymbol{\kappa}) \equiv w_k^\mp(\mathbf{m}_{k\pm}; \mathbf{n}; \boldsymbol{\vartheta}; \boldsymbol{\kappa}) = \mu_0 \exp\{M_k(\mathbf{m}, \mathbf{m}_{k\pm}; \mathbf{n}; \boldsymbol{\vartheta}; \boldsymbol{\kappa})\}$$
$$\text{for the transition } \mathbf{m}_{k\pm} \Rightarrow \mathbf{m}. \qquad (3.12b)$$

Here we have introduced *motivation potentials* $M_k(\mathbf{m}_{k\pm}, \mathbf{m}; \mathbf{n}; \boldsymbol{\vartheta}; \boldsymbol{\kappa})$ being measures of the intensity of the transition from the *initial state* $\mathbf{m}$ to the *final state* $\mathbf{m}_{k\pm}$ in case (3.12a), and $M_k(\mathbf{m}, \mathbf{m}_{k\pm}; \mathbf{n}; \boldsymbol{\vartheta}; \boldsymbol{\kappa})$ for the inverse transition from initial state $\mathbf{m}_{k\pm}$ to the final state $\mathbf{m}$ in case (3.12b). They are functions of the initial and final macroconfigurations because these are compared and judged by the decision makers giving rise to that transition. Furthermore they are also functions of the set κ of constant trendparameters characterizing the trends of the decision makers. With respect to notation we point out that in $w_k(\mathbf{m}', \mathbf{m}; \mathbf{n}; \vartheta; \kappa)$ and $M_k(\mathbf{m}', \mathbf{m}; \mathbf{n}; \vartheta; \kappa)$ and the following transition rates and motivation potentials the *final* configuration always stands left of the *initial* configuration.

Similarly, the transition rate for the transition from socioconfiguration $\mathbf{n}$ to $\mathbf{n}_{ji}^\alpha$, that means for generalized migration of individuals of $\mathcal{P}^\alpha$ from state i to state j, reads

$$w_{ji}^\alpha(\mathbf{m}; \mathbf{n}_{ji}^\alpha, \mathbf{n}; \vartheta; \kappa) = \nu_0 n_i^\alpha p_{ji}^\alpha(\mathbf{m}; \mathbf{n}_{ji}^\alpha, \mathbf{n}; \vartheta; \kappa)$$
$$= \nu_0 n_i^\alpha \exp\{M_{ji}^\alpha(\mathbf{m}; \mathbf{n}_{ji}^\alpha, \mathbf{n}; \vartheta; \kappa)\} \quad (3.13a)$$

and the corresponding transition rate for the inverse transition from $\mathbf{n}_{ji}^\alpha$ to $\mathbf{n}$ reads

$$w_{ij}^\alpha(\mathbf{m}; \mathbf{n}, \mathbf{n}_{ji}^\alpha; \vartheta; \kappa) = \nu_0(n_j^\alpha + 1) p_{ij}^\alpha(\mathbf{m}; \mathbf{n}, \mathbf{n}_{ji}^\alpha; \vartheta; \kappa)$$
$$= \nu_0(n_j^\alpha + 1) \exp\{M_{ij}^\alpha(\mathbf{m}; \mathbf{n}, \mathbf{n}_{ji}^\alpha; \vartheta; \kappa)\}. \quad (3.13b)$$

Here, the p_{ji}^α and p_{ij}^α are *individual transition rates* from state i to j and state j to i, respectively. The factors n_i^α and $(n_j^\alpha + 1)$ on the r.h.s. of (3.13a) and (3.13b), respectively, appear because one has to take into account that the transition from $\mathbf{n}$ to $\mathbf{n}_{ji}^\alpha$ can be executed by n_i^α individuals starting from state i, and the transition from $\mathbf{n}_{ji}^\alpha$ to $\mathbf{n}$ by $(n_j^\alpha + 1)$ individuals starting from state j.

Since in the case of transitions between socioconfigurations the motivations do not only depend on the initial and final macrovariables but also on the initial and final state of the individual executing that transition, the motivation potentials $M_{ji}^\alpha(\mathbf{m}; \mathbf{n}_{ji}^\alpha, \mathbf{n}; \vartheta; \kappa)$ and $M_{ij}^\alpha(\mathbf{m}; \mathbf{n}, \mathbf{n}_{ji}^\alpha; \vartheta; \kappa)$ now explicitly depend on the initial state and final state of the transition making individual.

We omit here birth–death-rates which could easily be introduced, too, but play no role in the examples of part II.

Finally we introduce the transition rates from the intensive configuration ϑ to $\vartheta_{i\pm}^\alpha$

$$w_{i,\vartheta}^\alpha(\mathbf{m}; \mathbf{n}; \vartheta_{i\pm}^\alpha, \vartheta; \kappa) \equiv w_{i,\vartheta}^{\alpha\pm}(\mathbf{m}; \mathbf{n}; \vartheta; \kappa)$$
$$= \rho_0 \exp\{M_{i\vartheta}^\alpha(\mathbf{m}; \mathbf{n}; \vartheta_{i\pm}^\alpha, \vartheta; \kappa)\} \quad (3.14a)$$

and the corresponding transition rates for the inverse transition from $\vartheta_{i\pm}^\alpha$ to ϑ:

$$w_{i,\vartheta}^\alpha(\mathbf{m}; \mathbf{n}; \vartheta, \vartheta_{i\pm}^\alpha; \kappa) \equiv w_{i,\vartheta}^{\alpha\mp}(\mathbf{m}; \mathbf{n}; \vartheta_{i\pm}^\alpha; \kappa)$$
$$= \rho_0 \exp\{M_{i\vartheta}^\alpha(\mathbf{m}; \mathbf{n}; \vartheta, \vartheta_{i\pm}^\alpha; \kappa)\}. \quad (3.14b)$$

The probabilistic transition rates (3.12), (3.13) and (3.14) *only* depend on the macrovariables where the system point is just before and after the transition which takes place at a given moment t. In particular this means that the transition rates do *not depend* on the history of the considered sample of the stochastic ensemble. Instead, the past history of the members of the ensemble must be taken into account by *momentary memory variables* as already indicated in Section 3.2.1. By this device we are able to ensure that the probabilistic evolution process can *in any case* be treated as a *Markov process*!

Furthermore, the very fact that the transition rates depend on the macrovariables $\{\mathbf{m}, \mathbf{n}, \vartheta\}$ provides *the link between the microlevel of individual decisions and the macrolevel of collective macrovariables*: On the one hand *individual decisions* give rise to the transition rates which lead to elementary changes of the macrovariables and in turn to their full interconnected macrodynamics treated in the next section. On the other, the motivations on which the transition rates depend *are functions of the momentary configuration of macrovariables*. This cyclical relation between microlevel and macrolevel will finally lead to a selfcontained, though probabilistic, subdynamics of the macrovariables among themselves!

Before setting up this macrodynamics it is for interpretational purposes convenient to decompose the motivation potentials for the transitions $\mathbf{m} \Rightarrow \mathbf{m}_{k\pm}$; $\mathbf{n} \Rightarrow \mathbf{n}_{ji}^{\alpha}$; $\vartheta \Rightarrow \vartheta_{i\pm}^{\alpha}$ and the inverse transitions $\mathbf{m}_{k\pm} \Rightarrow \mathbf{m}$; $\mathbf{n}_{ji}^{\alpha} \Rightarrow \mathbf{n}$; $\vartheta_{i\pm}^{\alpha} \Rightarrow \vartheta$ into their symmetrical and antisymmetrical part.

For the case of transitions between *material variables* we introduce

$$M_k^{(s)}(\mathbf{m}_{k\pm}, \mathbf{m}; \mathbf{n}; \vartheta; \kappa) = \frac{1}{2}\{M_k(\mathbf{m}_{k\pm}, \mathbf{m}; \mathbf{n}; \vartheta; \kappa) + M_k(\mathbf{m}, \mathbf{m}_{k\pm}; \mathbf{n}; \vartheta; \kappa)\} \qquad (3.15a)$$

and

$$M_k^{(as)}(\mathbf{m}_{k\pm}, \mathbf{m}; \mathbf{n}; \vartheta; \kappa) = \frac{1}{2}\{M_k(\mathbf{m}_{k\pm}, \mathbf{m}; \mathbf{n}; \vartheta; \kappa) - M_k(\mathbf{m}, \mathbf{m}_{k\pm}; \mathbf{n}; \vartheta; \kappa)\} \qquad (3.15b)$$

so that the motivation potentials for the forward process $\mathbf{m} \Rightarrow \mathbf{m}_{k\pm}$ and backward process $\mathbf{m}_{k\pm} \Rightarrow \mathbf{m}$ appear in the form:

$$M_k(\mathbf{m}_{k\pm}, \mathbf{m}; \mathbf{n}; \vartheta; \kappa) = M_k^{(s)}(\mathbf{m}_{k\pm}, \mathbf{m}; \mathbf{n}; \vartheta; \kappa) + M_k^{(as)}(\mathbf{m}_{k\pm}, \mathbf{m}; \mathbf{n}; \vartheta; \kappa) \qquad (3.16a)$$

and

$$M_k(\mathbf{m}, \mathbf{m}_{k\pm}; \mathbf{n}; \vartheta; \kappa) = M_k^{(s)}(\mathbf{m}_{k\pm}, \mathbf{m}; \mathbf{n}; \vartheta; \kappa) - M_k^{(as)}(\mathbf{m}_{k\pm}, \mathbf{m}; \mathbf{n}; \vartheta; \kappa)\}. \qquad (3.16b)$$

In the case of transitions between *extensive personal macrovariables*, i.e. transitions within the socioconfiguration, the symmetric and antisymmetric part of the motivation potentials for the process $\mathbf{n} \Rightarrow \mathbf{n}_{ji}^{\alpha}$ and $\mathbf{n}_{ji}^{\alpha} \Rightarrow \mathbf{n}$ read

$$M_{ji}^{\alpha(s)}(\mathbf{m}; \mathbf{n}_{ji}^{\alpha}, \mathbf{n}; \vartheta; \kappa) = \frac{1}{2}\{M_{ji}^{\alpha}(\mathbf{m}; \mathbf{n}_{ji}^{\alpha}, \mathbf{n}; \vartheta; \kappa) + M_{ij}^{\alpha}(\mathbf{m}; \mathbf{n}, \mathbf{n}_{ji}^{\alpha}; \vartheta; \kappa)\}; \qquad (3.17a)$$

$$M_{ji}^{\alpha(as)}(\mathbf{m}; \mathbf{n}_{ji}^{\alpha}, \mathbf{n}; \vartheta; \kappa) = \frac{1}{2}\{M_{ji}^{\alpha}(\mathbf{m}; \mathbf{n}_{ji}^{\alpha}, \mathbf{n}; \vartheta; \kappa) - M_{ij}^{\alpha}(\mathbf{m}; \mathbf{n}, \mathbf{n}_{ji}^{\alpha}; \vartheta; \kappa)\} \qquad (3.17b)$$

so that the motivation potentials for the forward process $\mathbf{n} \Rightarrow \mathbf{n}_{ji}^{\alpha}$ and backward process $\mathbf{n}_{ji}^{\alpha} \Rightarrow \mathbf{n}$ can be decomposed into

$$M_{ji}^{\alpha}(\mathbf{m}; \mathbf{n}_{ji}^{\alpha}, \mathbf{n}; \vartheta; \kappa) = M_{ji}^{\alpha(s)}(\mathbf{m}; \mathbf{n}_{ji}^{\alpha}, \mathbf{n}; \vartheta; \kappa) + M_{ij}^{\alpha(as)}(\mathbf{m}; \mathbf{n}_{ji}^{\alpha}, \mathbf{n}; \vartheta; \kappa) \qquad (3.18a)$$

and

$$M_{ij}^{\alpha}(\mathbf{m}; \mathbf{n}, \mathbf{n}_{ji}^{\alpha}; \vartheta; \kappa) = M_{ji}^{\alpha(s)}(\mathbf{m}; \mathbf{n}_{ji}^{\alpha}, \mathbf{n}; \vartheta; \kappa) - M_{ji}^{\alpha(as)}(\mathbf{m}; \mathbf{n}_{ji}^{\alpha}, \mathbf{n}; \vartheta; \kappa). \qquad (3.18b)$$

Finally for transitions between *intensive personal variables* the symmetric and antisymmetric part of the motivation potentials for the processes $\vartheta \Rightarrow \vartheta_{i\pm}^{\alpha}$ and $\vartheta_{i\pm}^{\alpha} \Rightarrow \vartheta$ are introduced by

$$M_{i\vartheta}^{\alpha(s)}(\mathbf{m}; \mathbf{n}; \vartheta_{i\pm}^{\alpha}, \vartheta; \kappa) = \frac{1}{2}\{M_{i\vartheta}^{\alpha}(\mathbf{m}; \mathbf{n}; \vartheta_{i\pm}^{\alpha}, \vartheta; \kappa) + M_{i\vartheta}^{\alpha}(\mathbf{m}; \mathbf{n}; \vartheta, \vartheta_{i\pm}^{\alpha}; \kappa)\}; \qquad (3.19a)$$

$$M_{i\vartheta}^{\alpha(as)}(\mathbf{m}; \mathbf{n}; \vartheta_{i\pm}^{\alpha}, \vartheta; \kappa) = \frac{1}{2}\{M_{i\vartheta}^{\alpha}(\mathbf{m}; \mathbf{n}; \vartheta_{i\pm}^{\alpha}, \vartheta; \kappa) - M_{i\vartheta}^{\alpha}(\mathbf{m}; \mathbf{n}; \vartheta, \vartheta_{i\pm}^{\alpha}; \kappa)\} \qquad (3.19b)$$

so that the motivation potentials for the forward process $\vartheta \Rightarrow \vartheta_{i\pm}^{\alpha}$ and the backward process $\vartheta_{i\pm}^{\alpha} \Rightarrow \vartheta$ appear in the form

$$M_{i\vartheta}^{\alpha}(\mathbf{m}; \mathbf{n}; \vartheta_{i\pm}^{\alpha}, \vartheta; \kappa) = M_{i\vartheta}^{\alpha(s)}(\mathbf{m}; \mathbf{n}; \vartheta_{i\pm}^{\alpha}, \vartheta; \kappa) + M_{i\vartheta}^{\alpha(as)}(\mathbf{m}; \mathbf{n}; \vartheta_{i\pm}^{\alpha}, \vartheta; \kappa) \qquad (3.20a)$$

and

$$M_{i\vartheta}^{\alpha}(\mathbf{m}; \mathbf{n}; \vartheta, \vartheta_{i\pm}^{\alpha}; \kappa) = M_{i\vartheta}^{\alpha(s)}(\mathbf{m}; \mathbf{n}; \vartheta_{i\pm}^{\alpha}, \vartheta; \kappa) - M_{i\vartheta}^{\alpha(as)}(\mathbf{m}; \mathbf{n}; \vartheta_{i\pm}^{\alpha}, \vartheta; \kappa). \qquad (3.20b)$$

The decompositions (3.16), (3.18) and (3.20) may now be inserted into the formulas (3.12), (3.13) and (3.14) for the transition rates, respectively. One observes that these rates now factorize into two terms, where the one factor contains the symmetrized, and the other the antisymmetrized motivation potential.

We now introduce another notation for the symmetrical factors in (3.12), (3.13) and (3.14):

$$\mu_0 \exp\{M_k^{(s)}(\mathbf{m}_{k\pm}, \mathbf{m}; \mathbf{n}; \vartheta; \kappa)\} = \mu_k(\mathbf{m}_{k\pm}, \mathbf{m}; \mathbf{n}; \vartheta; \kappa) \equiv \mu_k(\mathbf{m}, \mathbf{m}_{k\pm}; \mathbf{n}; \vartheta; \kappa) \qquad (3.21)$$

and

$$\nu_0 \exp\{M_{ji}^{(s)}(\mathbf{m}; \mathbf{n}_{ji}^{\alpha}, \mathbf{n}; \vartheta; \kappa)\} = \nu_{ji}^{\alpha}(\mathbf{m}; \mathbf{n}_{ji}^{\alpha}, \mathbf{n}; \vartheta; \kappa) \equiv \nu_{ij}^{\alpha}(\mathbf{m}; \mathbf{n}, \mathbf{n}_{ji}^{\alpha}; \vartheta; \kappa) \qquad (3.22)$$

and

$$\rho_0 \exp\{M_{i\vartheta}^{\alpha(s)}(\mathbf{m}; \mathbf{n}; \vartheta_{i\pm}^{\alpha}, \vartheta; \kappa)\} = \rho_{i\vartheta}^{\alpha}(\mathbf{m}; \mathbf{n}; \vartheta_{i\pm}^{\alpha}, \vartheta; \kappa) \equiv \rho_{i\vartheta}^{\alpha}(\mathbf{m}; \mathbf{n}; \vartheta, \vartheta_{i\pm}^{\alpha}; \kappa). \qquad (3.23)$$

Furthermore we assume a slightly specialized form for the antisymmetrical parts of the motivation potentials

$$M_k^{(as)}(\mathbf{m}_{k\pm}, \mathbf{m}; \mathbf{n}; \vartheta; \kappa) = u_k(\mathbf{m}_{k\pm}; \mathbf{n}; \vartheta; \kappa) - u_k(\mathbf{m}; \mathbf{n}; \vartheta; \kappa) \qquad (3.24)$$

and

$$M_{ji}^{\alpha(as)}(\mathbf{m}; \mathbf{n}_{ji}^{\alpha}, \mathbf{n}; \vartheta; \kappa) = u_j^{\alpha}(\mathbf{m}; \mathbf{n}_{ji}^{\alpha}; \vartheta; \kappa) - u_i^{\alpha}(\mathbf{m}; \mathbf{n}; \vartheta; \kappa) \qquad (3.25)$$

and

$$M_{j\vartheta}^{\alpha(as)}(\mathbf{m}; \mathbf{n}; \vartheta_{j\pm}^{\alpha}, \vartheta; \kappa) = v_j^{\alpha}(\mathbf{m}; \mathbf{n}; \vartheta_{j\pm}^{\alpha}; \kappa) - v_j^{\alpha}(\mathbf{m}; \mathbf{n}; \vartheta; \kappa). \qquad (3.26)$$

Making use of the notations (3.21), (3.22) and (3.23) and the form (3.24), (3.25) and (3.26) of the antisymmetrical parts of the motivation potentials, one obtains the final form of the transition rates (3.12), (3.13) and (3.14). The transition rates within the material configuration now read

$$w_k(\mathbf{m}_{k\pm}, \mathbf{m}; \mathbf{n}; \vartheta; \kappa) = \mu_k(\mathbf{m}_{k\pm}, \mathbf{m}; \mathbf{n}; \vartheta; \kappa) \exp\{u_k(\mathbf{m}_{k\pm}; \mathbf{n}; \vartheta; \kappa) - u_k(\mathbf{m}; \mathbf{n}; \vartheta; \kappa)\};$$
$$(3.27a)$$

$$w_k(\mathbf{m}, \mathbf{m}_{k\pm}; \mathbf{n}; \vartheta; \kappa) = \mu_k(\mathbf{m}, \mathbf{m}_{k\pm}; \mathbf{n}; \vartheta; \kappa) \exp\{u_k(\mathbf{m}; \mathbf{n}; \vartheta; \kappa) - u_k(\mathbf{m}_{k\pm}; \mathbf{n}; \vartheta; \kappa)\}$$
$$(3.27b)$$

the transition rates within the socioconfiguration now assume the form:

$$w_{ji}^{\alpha}(\mathbf{m}; \mathbf{n}_{ji}^{\alpha}, \mathbf{n}; \vartheta; \kappa) = n_i^{\alpha} \nu_{ji}^{\alpha}(\mathbf{m}; \mathbf{n}_{ji}^{\alpha}, \mathbf{n}; \vartheta; \kappa) \exp\left\{u_j^{\alpha}(\mathbf{m}; \mathbf{n}_{ji}^{\alpha}; \vartheta; \kappa) - u_i^{\alpha}(\mathbf{m}; \mathbf{n}; \vartheta; \kappa)\right\};$$
$$(3.28a)$$

$$w_{ij}^{\alpha}(\mathbf{m}; \mathbf{n}, \mathbf{n}_{ji}^{\alpha}; \vartheta; \kappa) = (n_j^{\alpha} + 1) \nu_{ij}^{\alpha}(\mathbf{m}; \mathbf{n}, \mathbf{n}_{ji}^{\alpha}; \vartheta; \kappa) \exp\left\{u_i^{\alpha}(\mathbf{m}; \mathbf{n}; \vartheta; \kappa) - u_j^{\alpha}(\mathbf{m}; \mathbf{n}_{ji}^{\alpha}; \vartheta; \kappa)\right\}$$
$$(3.28b)$$

and the transition rates within the configuration of intense personal variables now read:

$$w_{i,\vartheta}^{\alpha}(\mathbf{m}; \mathbf{n}; \vartheta_{i\pm}^{\alpha}, \vartheta; \kappa) = \rho_{i\vartheta}^{\alpha}(\mathbf{m}; \mathbf{n}; \vartheta_{i\pm}^{\alpha}, \vartheta; \kappa) \exp\left\{v_i^{\alpha}(\mathbf{m}; \mathbf{n}; \vartheta_{i\pm}^{\alpha}; \kappa) - v_i^{\alpha}(\mathbf{m}; \mathbf{n}; \vartheta; \kappa)\right\};$$
$$(3.29a)$$

$$w_{i,\vartheta}^{\alpha}(\mathbf{m}; \mathbf{n}; \vartheta, \vartheta_{i\pm}^{\alpha}; \kappa) = \rho_{i\vartheta}^{\alpha}(\mathbf{m}; \mathbf{n}; \vartheta, \vartheta_{i\pm}^{\alpha}; \kappa) \exp\left\{v_i^{\alpha}(\mathbf{m}; \mathbf{n}; \vartheta; \kappa) - v_i^{\alpha}(\mathbf{m}; \mathbf{n}; \vartheta_{i\pm}^{\alpha}; \kappa)\right\}.$$
$$(3.29b)$$

Interpretation of the transition rates

The mathematical transformation of the transition rates into their form (3.27), (3.28) and (3.29) is in one respect fully general, apart from the slight specialisation of the antisymmetrical part of the motivation potentials. In another respect the form (3.27), (3.28) and (3.29) lends itself to a plausible interpretation:

The first factors μ_k, ν_{ji}^α and $\rho_{i\vartheta}^\alpha$ are by definition *symmetrical* in the initial and final variables and states of the individual at the respective transition. They describe the *flexibility* or *mobility* of the change and give rise to the frequency by which the transitions take place. Because of the symmetry of these factors the mobility is the same for forward and backward transitions.

The second factors depend exponentially on the difference of a function u depending on the variables and the state of the individual *after* the transition and the same function u depending on variables and individual state *before* the transition.

Therefore it seems highly plausible to interpret the functions u as measures for the "utility" of the given configuration of variables and the state of the transition-making individual. In more detail:

$u_k(\mathbf{m}; \mathbf{n}; \vartheta; \kappa)$ is the measure for the utility of the material configuration $\mathbf{m}$ (*ceteris paribus*, i.e. for constant $\mathbf{n}, \vartheta; \kappa$) seen by the decision makers in view of a transition $\mathbf{m} \Rightarrow \mathbf{m}_{k\pm}$.

Similarly, $u_i^\alpha(\mathbf{m}; \mathbf{n}; \vartheta; \kappa)$ can be interpreted as a measure for the utility of the socioconfiguration $\mathbf{n}$ (*ceteris paribus*, i.e. for constant $\mathbf{m}, \vartheta; \kappa$) estimated by a member of subpopulation $\mathcal{P}^\alpha$ who is in state i. If this member of $\mathcal{P}^\alpha$ considers a transition to another state j, this transition would not only lead to the new socioconfiguration $\mathbf{n}_{ji}^\alpha$ but also to a new utility $u_j^\alpha(\mathbf{m}; \mathbf{n}_{ji}^\alpha; \vartheta; \kappa)$ for him/her.

Finally, $v_i^\alpha(\mathbf{m}; \mathbf{n}; \vartheta; \kappa)$ can be interpreted as a measure for the utility (the inner satisfaction) of the intense personal variables ϑ (*ceteris paribus*, i.e. for constant $\mathbf{m}, \mathbf{n}, \kappa$) being estimated by a member of subpopulation $\mathcal{P}^\alpha$ in state i in view of a change $\vartheta \Rightarrow \vartheta_{i\pm}^\alpha$ which would lead to the new utility (or inner satisfaction) $v_i^\alpha(\mathbf{m}; \mathbf{n}; \vartheta_{i\pm}^\alpha; \kappa)$.

With these interpretations of the terms in the exponential factors in mind it is now evident that due to these factors in the transition rates (3.27), (3.28) and (3.29) a transition is favoured (disfavoured), if the utility of the configuration and individual state *before the transition* is lower (higher) than the utility of the configuration and individual state *after the transition*.

The case (3.28) which refers to a member of subpopulation $\mathcal{P}^\alpha$ who changes from attitude i to attitude j or vice versa can be considered as a *generalized migration process*. This case includes *real* migration processes between regions (to be treated in Chapter 4) if "attitude i" is identified with "living in region i".

In view of this true migratory process, related but equivalent interpretations can be given to the mobility and utility terms of the transition rates (3.28). Thus one may write the mobility $\nu_{ji}^\alpha = \nu_{ij}^\alpha$ in the form

$$\nu_{ji}^\alpha(\mathbf{m}; \mathbf{n}_{ji}^\alpha, \mathbf{n}; \vartheta; \kappa) = \nu_0 \exp\{-d_{ij}^\alpha(\mathbf{m}; \mathbf{n}_{ji}^\alpha, \mathbf{n}; \vartheta; \kappa)\} \qquad (3.30)$$

and interpret d_{ij}^α as a measure for the (generalized) distance between states i and j to be overcome in the intended transition from i to j or vice versa. (A large distance diminishes the mobility and the probability rate of a transition.)

Furthermore, the exponential term in (3.28a) (and analogously in (3.28b)) may be factorized into

$$\mathrm{pull}_j^\alpha(\mathbf{m}; \mathbf{n}_{ji}^\alpha; \vartheta; \kappa) = \exp\{u_j^\alpha(\mathbf{m}; \mathbf{n}_{ji}^\alpha; \vartheta; \kappa)\} \qquad (3.31)$$

and

$$\text{push}_i^\alpha(\mathbf{m};\mathbf{n};\vartheta;\kappa) = \exp\{-u_i^\alpha(\mathbf{m};\mathbf{n};\vartheta;\kappa)\}, \tag{3.32}$$

where evidently the pull-term (3.31) pulls (in case of large u_j^α) the individual into the new state j and the push-term (3.32) pushes (in case of small or even negative u_i^α) the individual away from the old state i.

Whereas we have now given some general interpretations of the terms appearing in the transition rates it is not possible to "derive" the explicit form of mobilities and utilities as functions of the set of variables and parameters $\{(\mathbf{m};\mathbf{n};\vartheta;\kappa)\}$. Rather it is the case that appropriate functional forms for mobilities and utilities can only be found for special models describing special sectors of the society taking into account the trends of the individuals. Such models will be introduced and discussed in detail in part II of this book.

3.2.3 Equations of Evolution for the Macrovariables

The transition rates introduced in Section 3.2.2 will now be used as constitutive elements for setting up the equation of motion for the probabilistic evolution of the set of macrovariables $\{(\mathbf{m},\mathbf{n},\vartheta)\}$. (In the following we omit the trend- and control-parameters κ in order to simplify the notation and because they are given constants.)

The Master Equation

The central evolution equation for sociodynamics is the so-called *master equation*. It is the evolution equation for the *probability distribution function over the macrovariables* $\{(\mathbf{m},\mathbf{n},\vartheta)\}$:

$$P(\mathbf{m},\mathbf{n},\vartheta;t) \geq 0 \tag{3.33}$$

which is normalized by

$$\sum_{\mathbf{m};\mathbf{n};\vartheta} P(\mathbf{m},\mathbf{n},\vartheta;t) = 1 \tag{3.34}$$

and is interpreted as the probability of finding a social system with macrovariables $\{(\mathbf{m},\mathbf{n},\vartheta)\}$ at time t. (This probability is measured as "relative frequency of realization" in a very large ensemble of systems underlying the same evolution laws.)

The form of the master equation is derived in Chapter 10 and the reader is referred to this chapter for details. But even without these details the master equation is easily understandable and interpretable and for the first it is sufficient to set it up and to introduce this interpretation. This will be done now.

Let us assume that the only nonvanishing transition rates in the space of variables $\{(\mathbf{m},\mathbf{n},\vartheta)\}$ are the rates (3.27), (3.28) and (3.29) introduced above. The corresponding transitions take place between the configuration $\{\mathbf{m},\mathbf{n},\vartheta\}$ and the neighboring configurations $\{\mathbf{m}_{k\pm},\mathbf{n},\vartheta\}$, $\{\mathbf{m},\mathbf{n}_{ji}^\alpha,\vartheta\}$ and $\{\mathbf{m},\mathbf{n},\vartheta_{i\pm}^\alpha\}$.

With the probability $P(\mathbf{m}, \mathbf{n}, \vartheta; t)$ and the specific rates we can now construct probability flows from the configuration $\{\mathbf{m}, \mathbf{n}, \vartheta\}$ to the neighboring configurations. For instance, $w_k(\mathbf{m}_{k+}, \mathbf{m}; \mathbf{n}; \vartheta)P(\mathbf{m}, \mathbf{n}, \vartheta; t)$ is the flow of probability, namely the probability transferred per unit of time, from the origin configuration $\{\mathbf{m}, \mathbf{n}, \vartheta\}$ to the destination configuration $\{\mathbf{m}_{k+}, \mathbf{n}, \vartheta\}$ at time t; and $w_{ji}^\alpha(\mathbf{m}; \mathbf{n}_{ji}^\alpha, \mathbf{n}; \vartheta)P(\mathbf{m}, \mathbf{n}, \vartheta; t)$ is the flow of probability from the origin configuration $\{\mathbf{m}, \mathbf{n}, \vartheta\}$ to the destination configuration $\{\mathbf{m}, \mathbf{n}_{ji}^\alpha, \vartheta\}$ at time t. Simultaneously there exist the inverse flows $w_k(\mathbf{m}, \mathbf{m}_{k+}; \mathbf{n}; \vartheta)P(\mathbf{m}_{k+}, \mathbf{n}, \vartheta; t)$ from the origin $\{\mathbf{m}_{k+}, \mathbf{n}, \vartheta\}$ to the destination $\{\mathbf{m}, \mathbf{n}, \vartheta\}$ and $w_{ij}^\alpha(\mathbf{m}; \mathbf{n}, \mathbf{n}_{ji}^\alpha; \vartheta)P(\mathbf{m}, \mathbf{n}_{ji}^\alpha, \vartheta; t)$ from the origin $\{\mathbf{m}, \mathbf{n}_{ji}^\alpha, \vartheta\}$ to the destination $\{\mathbf{m}, \mathbf{n}, \vartheta\}$, and so on.

The master equation is now nothing but a dynamical balance equation for the probability of each configuration, for instance the arbitrarily selected configuration $\{\mathbf{m}, \mathbf{n}, \vartheta\}$.

Evidently, an *increase* per unit of time of the probability of configuration $\{\mathbf{m}, \mathbf{n}, \vartheta\}$ comes about by summing *all probability flows from neighboring configurations into the configuration* $\{\mathbf{m}, \mathbf{n}, \vartheta\}$, and simultaneously a *decrease* per unit of time of the probability of the same configuration $\{\mathbf{m}, \mathbf{n}, \vartheta\}$ comes about by summing the probability flows *from the configuration* $\{\mathbf{m}, \mathbf{n}, \vartheta\}$ *into all neighboring* configurations. Thus, the total time derivative of the probability $P(\mathbf{m}, \mathbf{n}, \vartheta; t)$ of configuration $\{\mathbf{m}, \mathbf{n}, \vartheta\}$ is equal to the *total probability inflow* into configuration $\{\mathbf{m}, \mathbf{n}, \vartheta\}$ minus the *total probability outflow* from configuration $\{\mathbf{m}, \mathbf{n}, \vartheta\}$. This consideration leads to the master equation, i.e. the following equation for $P(\mathbf{m}, \mathbf{n}, \vartheta; t)$:

$$\frac{dP(\mathbf{m}, \mathbf{n}, \vartheta; t)}{dt} =$$

$$+ \sum_k \{w_k(\mathbf{m}, \mathbf{m}_{k+}; \mathbf{n}; \vartheta)P(\mathbf{m}_{k+}, \mathbf{n}, \vartheta; t) + w_k(\mathbf{m}, \mathbf{m}_{k-}; \mathbf{n}; \vartheta)P(\mathbf{m}_{k-}, \mathbf{n}, \vartheta; t)\}$$

$$- \sum_k \{w_k(\mathbf{m}_{k+}, \mathbf{m}; \mathbf{n}; \vartheta)P(\mathbf{m}, \mathbf{n}, \vartheta; t) + w_k(\mathbf{m}_{k-}, \mathbf{m}; \mathbf{n}; \vartheta)P(\mathbf{m}, \mathbf{n}, \vartheta; t)\}$$

$$+ \sum_{i,j,\alpha} \left\{w_{ij}^\alpha(\mathbf{m}; \mathbf{n}, \mathbf{n}_{ji}^\alpha; \vartheta)P(\mathbf{m}, \mathbf{n}_{ji}^\alpha, \vartheta; t)\right\}$$

$$- \sum_{i,j,\alpha} \left\{w_{ji}^\alpha(\mathbf{m}; \mathbf{n}_{ji}^\alpha, \mathbf{n}; \vartheta)P(\mathbf{m}, \mathbf{n}, \vartheta; t)\right\}$$

$$+ \sum_{i,\alpha} \{w_{i\vartheta}^\alpha(\mathbf{m}; \mathbf{n}; \vartheta, \vartheta_{i+}^\alpha)P(\mathbf{m}, \mathbf{n}, \vartheta_{i+}^\alpha; t) + w_{i\vartheta}^\alpha(\mathbf{m}; \mathbf{n}; \vartheta, \vartheta_{i-}^\alpha)P(\mathbf{m}, \mathbf{n}, \vartheta_{i-}^\alpha; t)\}$$

$$- \sum_{i,\alpha} \{w_{i\vartheta}^\alpha(\mathbf{m}; \mathbf{n}; \vartheta_{i+}^\alpha, \vartheta)P(\mathbf{m}, \mathbf{n}, \vartheta; t) + w_{i\vartheta}^\alpha(\mathbf{m}; \mathbf{n}; \vartheta_{i-}^\alpha, \vartheta)P(\mathbf{m}, \mathbf{n}, \vartheta; t)\}.$$

$$(3.35)$$

The first, third and fifth line on the r.h.s. of equation (3.35) describe the probability *inflows* into the configuration $\{\mathbf{m}, \mathbf{n}, \vartheta\}$ from neighboring material configurations, socioconfigurations and intense personal configurations, respectively; the second, fourth and sixth line on the r.h.s. of equation (3.35) describe the probability *outflows* from the configuration $\{\mathbf{m}, \mathbf{n}, \vartheta\}$ into the corresponding neighboring configurations.

Equation (3.35) represents the most general form of the master equation for a whole class of sociodynamic systems. In specialized models not all variables and not all kinds of transition rates need to appear. Then the master equation may become much simpler.

The master equation gives the most detailed description available on the macro-level of systems. Its solution, i.e. the explicit form of the probability distribution $P(\mathbf{m}, \mathbf{n}, \vartheta; t)$, does of course imply the evolution with time of the most probable values $\{\mathbf{m}_{\max}(t), \mathbf{n}_{\max}(t), \vartheta_{\max}(t)\}$, i.e. those values of the macrovariables $\{\mathbf{m}, \mathbf{n}, \vartheta\}$ for which $P(\mathbf{m}, \mathbf{n}, \vartheta; t)$ attains its absolute maximum, or relative maxima, at time t. Furthermore, the more or less sharply peaked unimodal or in the general case multimodal distribution $P(\mathbf{m}, \mathbf{n}, \vartheta; t)$ includes full information about the probability of *deviations* from the most probable values $\{\mathbf{m}_{\max}(t), \mathbf{n}_{\max}(t), \vartheta_{\max}(t)\}$.

A case of particular importance is that of a *social phase transition*, i.e. a destabil-isation of the most probable path $\{\mathbf{m}_{\max}(t), \mathbf{n}_{\max}(t), \vartheta_{\max}(t)\}$ of the sector of the society under consideration. In that case a socalled *bifurcation* can take place, which means that an originally *unimodal* probability distribution evolves into a *bimodal* or even *multimodal* distribution over the space of macrovariables with two or even more than two relative maxima. (Examples are discussed in part II of this book.) Since during this transient evolution the distribution always continues to be a smooth function of the macrovariables it is intuitively clear that the *deviations from the maxima* obtain a higher relative weight at phase transitions. For the individual system belonging to the ensemble described by $P(\mathbf{m}, \mathbf{n}, \vartheta; t)$ this means that its macrovariables undergo *critical fluctuations* during the *phase transition* until they practically stabilize around one of the newly arising maxima. Conversely, the *occurrence of critical fluctuations* of large amplitude can be taken as an *infallible indicator* and *criterion* for the social system coming into the vicinity of an imminent destabil-isation and ensuing phase transition.

Equations for Meanvalues

Although the master equation has a central role in the modelling concept presented here because it correctly reflects the fact that the probabilistic description of indi-vidual activities (in terms of probabilistic transition rates) can only lead to a probab-ilistic description of the dynamics at the macrolevel, this description also has disadvantages. Firstly, only numerical solutions of the master equations are in general available, and secondly, the probability distribution $P(\mathbf{m}, \mathbf{n}, \vartheta; t)$ contains too much information in comparison to the available empirical data. In order to exhaust fully the information implied in the probability distribution one would need a *large ensemble of social systems* evolving stochastically under the same boundary conditions, i.e. the same trend- and control-parameters. However, in reality only one or at most a few comparable systems are empirically at hand.

Therefore it must be the intention to derive from the master equation simpler equations of motion for simpler quantities. Their result should contain the main information of the model and should be comparable to the evolution of a *single real social system*. A suggestive proposal for quantities appropriate for this purpose are the *meanvalues* $\{\bar{\mathbf{m}}(t), \bar{\mathbf{n}}(t), \bar{\vartheta}(t)\}$ of the macrovariables, and perhaps of functions of mean values. The meanvalues are defined by

$$\bar{m}_k(t) = \sum_{\mathbf{m},\mathbf{n},\vartheta} m_k P(\mathbf{m}, \mathbf{n}, \vartheta; t); \qquad (3.36a)$$

$$\bar{n}_i^\alpha(t) = \sum_{\mathbf{m},\mathbf{n},\vartheta} n_i^\alpha P(\mathbf{m}, \mathbf{n}, \vartheta; t); \qquad (3.36b)$$

$$\bar{\vartheta}_i^\alpha(t) = \sum_{\mathbf{m},\mathbf{n},\vartheta} \vartheta_i^\alpha P(\mathbf{m}, \mathbf{n}, \vartheta; t). \qquad (3.36c)$$

The exact and approximate evolution equations for the meanvalues have been derived in Chapter 11. The exact equations read

$$\frac{d\bar{m}_k(t)}{dt} = \overline{w_k(\mathbf{m}_{k+}, \mathbf{m}; \mathbf{n}; \vartheta)} - \overline{w_k(\mathbf{m}_{k-}, \mathbf{m}; \mathbf{n}; \vartheta)}; \qquad (3.37a)$$

$$\frac{d\bar{n}_i^\alpha(t)}{dt} = \sum_j \overline{w_{ij}^\alpha(\mathbf{m}; \mathbf{n}_{ij}^\alpha, \mathbf{n}; \vartheta)} - \sum_j \overline{w_{ji}^\alpha(\mathbf{m}; \mathbf{n}_{ji}^\alpha, \mathbf{n}; \vartheta)}; \qquad (3.37b)$$

$$\frac{d\bar{\vartheta}_i^\alpha(t)}{dt} = \overline{w_{i\vartheta}^\alpha(\mathbf{m}; \mathbf{n}; \vartheta_{i+}^\alpha, \vartheta)} - \overline{w_{i\vartheta}^\alpha(\mathbf{m}; \mathbf{n}; \vartheta_{i-}^\alpha, \vartheta)}. \qquad (3.37c)$$

However, these equations do not yet lead to simplifications for the following reason: In order to calculate the r.h.s. of equations (3.37), i.e. the meanvalues over certain transition rates, one would need the full probability distribution $P(\mathbf{m}, \mathbf{n}, \vartheta; t)$ which is only known after solving the master equation (3.35).

Only under one assumption and approximation can the equations (3.37) lead to a considerably simplified description of the system dynamics: If it can be presumed that the probability distribution – without knowing its exact form – remains *unimodal* and *sharply peaked* for the period of time under consideration, we can say that "*the meanvalue over a function $f(\mathbf{m}, \mathbf{n}, \vartheta)$ of the variables is approximately equal to the function over the meanvalues*", or in formal terms:

$$\overline{f(\mathbf{m}, \mathbf{n}, \vartheta)}\Big|_t \approx f(\bar{\mathbf{m}}(t), \bar{\mathbf{n}}(t), \bar{\vartheta}(t)). \qquad (3.38)$$

Making use of (3.38) on the r.h.s. of (3.37) one obtains the *approximate meanvalue equations*:

$$\frac{d\bar{m}_k(t)}{dt} = w_k(\bar{\mathbf{m}}_{k+}, \bar{\mathbf{m}}; \bar{\mathbf{n}}; \bar{\vartheta}) - w_k(\bar{\mathbf{m}}_{k-}, \bar{\mathbf{m}}; \bar{\mathbf{n}}; \bar{\vartheta}); \qquad (3.39a)$$

$$\frac{d\bar{n}_i^\alpha(t)}{dt} = \sum_j w_{ij}^\alpha(\bar{\mathbf{m}}; \bar{\mathbf{n}}_{ij}^\alpha, \bar{\mathbf{n}}; \bar{\vartheta}) - \sum_j w_{ji}^\alpha(\bar{\mathbf{m}}; \bar{\mathbf{n}}_{ji}^\alpha, \bar{\mathbf{n}}; \bar{\vartheta}); \qquad (3.39b)$$

$$\frac{d\bar{\vartheta}_i^\alpha(t)}{dt} = w_{i\vartheta}^\alpha(\bar{\mathbf{m}}; \bar{\mathbf{n}}; \bar{\vartheta}_{i+}^\alpha, \bar{\vartheta}) - w_{i\vartheta}^\alpha(\bar{\mathbf{m}}; \bar{\mathbf{n}}; \bar{\vartheta}_{i-}^\alpha, \bar{\vartheta}). \qquad (3.39c)$$

In order to obtain their fully explicit form one must insert the transition rates (3.27), (3.28) and (3.29). For instance, the explicit form of equation (3.39b) reads

$$\frac{d\bar{n}_i^\alpha(t)}{dt} = \sum_j \bar{n}_j^\alpha \nu_{ji}^\alpha(\bar{\mathbf{m}}; \bar{\mathbf{n}}_{ij}, \bar{\mathbf{n}}; \bar{\vartheta}) \exp\left\{ u_i^\alpha(\bar{\mathbf{m}}; \bar{\mathbf{n}}_{ij}; \bar{\vartheta}) - u_j^\alpha(\bar{\mathbf{m}}; \bar{\mathbf{n}}; \bar{\vartheta}) \right\}$$

$$- \sum_j \bar{n}_i^\alpha \nu_{ij}^\alpha(\bar{\mathbf{m}}; \bar{\mathbf{n}}_{ji}, \bar{\mathbf{n}}; \bar{\vartheta}) \exp\left\{ u_j^\alpha(\bar{\mathbf{m}}; \bar{\mathbf{n}}_{ji}; \bar{\vartheta}) - u_i^\alpha(\bar{\mathbf{m}}; \bar{\mathbf{n}}; \bar{\vartheta}) \right\}. \quad (3.40)$$

The approximate equations (3.39) are now a *closed system* of coupled, autonomous, in general nonlinear differential equations for the meanvalues $\bar{\mathbf{m}}(t)$, $\bar{\mathbf{n}}(t)$ and $\bar{\vartheta}(t)$.

In addition to the meanvalue equations (3.37) and (3.39) there can also be derived from the master equation a set of exact and approximate equations for the *variances*. (For their derivation and discussion of the limits of their applicability see Chapter 11.) In the case of the personal variables of the socioconfiguration they are defined by

$$v_{ij}^{\alpha\beta}(t) = \overline{(n_i^\alpha - \bar{n}_i^\alpha)(n_j^\beta - \bar{n}_j^\beta)} = \overline{n_i^\alpha n_j^\beta} - \bar{n}_i^\alpha \cdot \bar{n}_j^\beta. \quad (3.41)$$

The variance matrix (3.41) provides a measure for the width and shape of the distribution function. The equations have been omitted here because they are rather complicated and seldom used. The utilization of true meanvalues defined by (3.36) and their approximate equations of motion (3.39) however leads to a disappointing conclusion; namely, it is just in those interesting cases of social phase transitions that the true meanvalues become *irrelevant* and simultaneously the approximation (3.38) leading to their approximate equations (3.39) becomes *invalid*!

If the unimodal probability distribution develops under a phase transition into a bi- or multimodal distribution the true meanvalue point $\{\bar{\mathbf{m}}(t), \bar{\mathbf{n}}(t), \bar{\vartheta}(t)\}$ defined by (3.36) becomes *irrelevant*, because it lies *between the maxima* of the distribution. Thus it is not at all characteristic of the stochastic trajectories of the individual systems belonging to the ensemble.

On the other hand the nonlinear approximate equations (3.39) which accompany the multimodal probability distribution do in general have more than one stationary solution. This clearly shows that they *can in such cases no more be valid equations* for the motion of the true meanvalue, because the true meanvalue $\{\bar{\mathbf{m}}(t), \bar{\mathbf{n}}(t), \bar{\vartheta}(t)\}$ belonging to $P(\mathbf{m}, \mathbf{n}, \vartheta; t)$ is always a *uniquely defined quantity*. (For details see Chapter 11.)

Equations for Quasi-Meanvalues

The search for quantities more adequately characterizing the mean behaviour of the stochastic trajectories of the ensemble than the true meanvalues (3.36) now leads to the concept of *quasi-meanvalues*.

The stochastic trajectory of an individual social system executes a stochastic hopping process from a given point $\{\mathbf{m}, \mathbf{n}, \vartheta\}$ in configuration space to neighboring points like $\{\mathbf{m}_{k\pm}, \mathbf{n}, \vartheta\}$, $\{\mathbf{m}, \mathbf{n}_{ji}^\alpha, \vartheta\}$ and $\{\mathbf{m}, \mathbf{n}, \vartheta_i^\alpha\}$. The hopping into different directions takes place with different probabilities which are determined by the transition rates. Taking the weighted mean over the hopping processes of a bundle of stochastic trajectories starting from a given point $\{\mathbf{m}, \mathbf{n}, \boldsymbol{\vartheta}\}$ leads to equations for the *preferential mean direction* and *mean velocity* by which the trajectory-bundle proceeds. The *quasi-meanvalues* $\{\hat{\mathbf{m}}(t), \hat{\mathbf{n}}(t), \hat{\boldsymbol{\vartheta}}(t)\}$ by definition describe *the mean path of the stochastic trajectories on each point of the configuration space*. Their equations have been derived in Chapter 12.

Remarkably, it turns out that they just fulfil the same equations as those obtained as approximate equations for true meanvalues in the case of unimodal probability distributions. But the derived equations are *exact equations of motion* for the so defined quasi-meanvalues which are associated with the probability distribution for the ensemble in *all cases*. Although they have the same form as equations (3.39) they obviously have a different meaning and interpretation. (For details see Chapter 12.) They read:

$$\frac{d\hat{m}_k(t)}{dt} = w_k(\hat{\mathbf{m}}_{k+}, \hat{\mathbf{m}}; \hat{\mathbf{n}}; \hat{\boldsymbol{\vartheta}}) - w_k(\hat{\mathbf{m}}_{k-}, \hat{\mathbf{m}}; \hat{\mathbf{n}}; \hat{\boldsymbol{\vartheta}}); \qquad (3.42a)$$

$$\frac{d\hat{n}_i^\alpha(t)}{dt} = \sum_j w_{ij}^\alpha(\hat{\mathbf{m}}; \hat{\mathbf{n}}_{ij}^\alpha, \hat{\mathbf{n}}; \hat{\boldsymbol{\vartheta}}) - \sum_j w_{ji}^\alpha(\hat{\mathbf{m}}; \hat{\mathbf{n}}_{ji}^\alpha, \hat{\mathbf{n}}; \hat{\boldsymbol{\vartheta}}); \qquad (3.42b)$$

$$\frac{d\hat{\vartheta}_i^\alpha(t)}{dt} = w_{i\vartheta}^\alpha(\hat{\mathbf{m}}; \hat{\mathbf{n}}; \hat{\boldsymbol{\vartheta}}_{i+}^\alpha, \hat{\boldsymbol{\vartheta}}) - w_{i\vartheta}^\alpha(\hat{\mathbf{m}}; \hat{\mathbf{n}}; \hat{\boldsymbol{\vartheta}}_{i-}^\alpha, \hat{\boldsymbol{\vartheta}}). \qquad (3.42c)$$

Since the quasi-meanvalues are more closely associated with the evolution of a *single social system* (in contrast to the true meanvalues which are associated with the distribution over the whole ensemble of systems) they will be utilized as the main instrument of analysis in the concrete models of Part II.

Part II
Selected Applications

II.1 Application to Population Dynamics

Introductory remarks

Our selection of models designed according to the construction principles of socio-dynamics begins with a model for the migration of interacting populations. The modelling of this sector of social phenomena is relatively easy, but also important because of the following positive aspects:

- The configuration of variables consists of extensive personal variables only (see §3.2.1), namely the regional population numbers of the interacting subpopulations.

- There exist easily interpretable transition rates describing the migration of individuals from one region to another.

- The collective effect of migration is directly visible and empirically ascertainable in terms of the spatial structure of the evolving population distribution.

- Migration of populations of different cultural and/or ethnical backgrounds is not only of academic interest but also of great political relevance: Interregional and international migration may turn out to become one of the most important problems of the next century.

4. Migration of Interacting Populations

Before treating quantitatively of the migration of populations we must inevitably consider in *qualitative terms* the much more general phenomenon of *multiculturality*, because the tendency of members of subpopulations to migrate is very often connected with their affiliation and commitment to one culture. (Multiculturality on its turn is a part of the wider category of multiple diversity. Multiple diversity includes also demographical (age/sex) diversity, socio-biological diversity, professional diversity etc. not connected with culture.) Therefore we begin our consideration with the section

4.1   Multiculturality and Migration

Our view on the phenomena of multiculturality and the implied processes of migration will be primarily a structural and system-theoretical one, because the following mathematical models as such can only answer certain questions about the *structure* and *dynamics* of migratory processes, whereas they are value-*neutral* with respect to political and moral issues.

In a preliminary qualitative analysis it is however our intention to *include aspects of valuation*, too, because the inevitable questions will arise, which migratory processes are *desirable* or *unwanted*, and whether or not they can be *influenced*. Therefore we begin with a general view of:

4.1.1   Forms of Multiculturality and their Valuation

We understand by "*culture*" that complex of attainments, beliefs, customs and traditions, which forms the cognitive background of a particular group of people, for instance the members of a subpopulation $\mathcal{P}^\alpha$, which distinguishes them from other people or groups and gives their particular civilization its peculiar quality or character. The word "*civilisation*" is then reserved for the historical growth of common traditions and group-cultural achievements leading to feelings of affiliation, unity and partnership within *large groups* of nations or races. Thus *civilisation* in our usage appears as the more broad concept to which more specific cultural subunits may belong.

67

The author agrees with the view of S. P. Huntington [1] that civilisational and cultural identities are important social trend parameters guiding the orientation- and decision-behaviour of individuals belonging to that civilisation and culture. Thus, cultural traditions give rise to deeply rooted inherent trends predicated of the members of a cultural group and it seems justified to consider *culturally conditioned trends* as either constant or very slowly variable over time. (This implies that the short term influence of politicians on them is rather limited.)

There exists another kind of important behavioural trend which is ideologically motivated, examples being the macro-ideologies of this century, namely *nationalism, racism* and *communism*. However, history tells us, that such *ideological trends* which are induced in the mind of their adherents by the intense propaganda of political ideologies are (fortunately) not so long-lived and obey other trendparameter-dynamics than the *culturally conditioned trends*. (In Chapter 6 the problem of trends and variables influenced by political ideology is discussed in more detail.)

Let us now characterize briefly and in general terms the forms and problems of multicultural societies from a *structural* and from a *valuational* standpoint as well.

In terms of *structure* we consider a multicultural society as a highly complex system consisting of hierarchically ordered interacting layers, substructures or levels. The *micro-level* is that of individuals. Then there is the *meso-level* of interacting groups of different kinds. Each individual may simultaneously be a member of and play its role in more than one of the overlapping groups. The multicultural society comprises among other social groups *cultural and/or ethnical minorities* which can be embedded in several ways (to be discussed below) within the *cultural majority*. Finally, the *civilisation* with its socio-political institutions and economic standards forms the *overarching macro-level* to which all individuals and groups belong.

Due to the general structure of *systems* there exists a complex *feedback loop* between all levels:

The manner in which individuals as members of the majority or a minority maintain their rights, fulfill their duties and define their allegiance to the whole, and the way in which the majority and the minorities as groups develop their relation to the other groups are phenomena that can either stabilize or, conversely, destabilize the structure and coherence of the whole system.

On the other hand, the structure of the whole socio-political system can either safeguard and enable or, conversely, impair and frustrate the realisation and evolution of rights of the cultural groups and their members.

Coming now to the *valuation* of multiculturality we must first define the *principles of valuation*. Because the human individual as such, and culture and civilisation as the most complex achievement of mankind, are both *values in themselves*, the principles of valuation must comprise *both* the *individual* and the *collective* level.

On the *individual level* the principle of valuation can only consist in humanity which implies the *acknowledgement* of an indispensible core of *universally valid human rights* applicable to any individual combined with his/her right to be affiliated to a cultural group and to submit to its rules and habits.

On the *collective level* the principle of valuation can only consist in the acknowledgement of the intrinsic value of cultures which implies the preservation and maintenance of those existing cultures and global civilisation in any given society.

Evidently, indifference to the existing civilisation and negligent cultural relativism is not allowed by this principle. However, the principle presumes what Popper would call an "open society", i.e. a state in which different cultural ideas and forms of life can coexist, but also be exchanged and communicated. This requires an experienced government based on the rule of law and able to provide the reliable framework for the rights and duties of all cultural groups.

These valuation principles seem to be easily reconcilable at first sight. But a closer inspection shows that between the different aspects of valuation and the ensuing political intentions there may arise *conflicts of goals* even if good will can be presumed on all sides. Indeed, it turns out that different civilisations attribute different relative weights to the value of rights of the individuals and the value of demands of the collectives. If violence and political crime instead of good will is involved even relatively harmless latent conflicts of multiculturality can escalate so as to end in human tragedy. History unfortunately provides rich material about this fact. We shall discuss this case later.

We will now discuss the structure and valuation of multicultural societies, mainly in general terms, making use of a variety of thought experiments allowing us to refine our concepts. Examples illustrating the general considerations could also be found but are beyond the space available for this section. Our interest will focus on the *order of magnitude* and the *evolution* of cultural frameworks and in particular on the *types of interaction* between partial cultures.

We begin with the imaginary scenario of a *universal worldwide civilisation or monoculture*. Assuming theoretically that a global monoculture could be established the problems of multiculturality would cease to exist and Fukujama's vision of "the end of history" [2] would become a reality. However, the question arises whether such a universal monoculture would be *stable* and if so whether it would be *desirable*.

Concerning the *stability* of such a globally homogeneous civilisation one could argue that *science* with its universally valid findings and *technology* with its universally applicable procedures would be sufficient to generate and sustain this homogeneity. However, the universal cover of science and technology is *broad but thin* and does not meet the deeper needs and desires of humans who search for affiliation with people of *similar background* in a smaller environment easy to survey. A universal monoculture is too anonymous and too vast to satisfy such needs. Therefore it is to be expected that it becomes *unstable* and sooner or later decays into separate smaller cultural forms.

Concerning the *valuation* of a monoculture the latter would have some advantages – for instance the globally unquestioned definition and observance of universal human rights – but also many disadvantages, because it would mean the loss of independent cultural forms, leading to an impoverishment and monotony of the whole cultural system, which could be compared to the shrinkage of the variety of biological species.

Let us now consider the *opposite imaginary scenario* of a mankind being partitioned into a *conglomerate of partial mini-cultures*. Such a conglomerate could arise, e.g. in the economically and politically attractive countries of the USA and Western Europe under (imaginary) conditions of completely free and unrestricted admission of all migrants from all countries of the world with their different cultures.

Again we consider the questions of *stability* and *desirability* of this scenario. The answers to these questions are *ambivalent*: If the partial cultures have a tendency to cooperation, integration and cultural synthesis and full participation with fair rights and duties in the global society the whole system can be *stable*. If, conversely, the partial cultures neutralize and paralyze each other or even fight against each other (where n partial cultures could lead to $n(n-1)/2$ possibilities of friction and conflict) the whole system *becomes unstable and decomposes* either into the precarious equilibrium of a mosaic of partial mini-cultures situated in ghettos without much cultural interaction, or it ends in even worse situations of violence between the partial cultures.

The answer to the question of the *desirability* of a system of many mixed mini-partial-cultures follows from the following structural considerations.

An *approvable situation* can only arise if a true *synthesis of partial cultures* towards an *integrated culture* takes place in which the contributions of the original cultures find a new role appreciated by all members of the society. It is to be expected that the creation of such an integrated culture is a *slow process*, because, as already mentioned, culturally conditioned trends are slow variables.

The *nondesirable situation* would consist in a segregation into small isolated subunits (ghettos) which are *incapable of higher cultural achievement* and whose members are *alienated* from the broad culture. Such segregation processes do also exist in reality, where presently they convert their direction from ghettoization to fundamentalism, i.e. from still socio-culturally open ghettos to fundamentalistically closed culturally and religiously separated spatial districts.

The problems arising in the scenarios of "monoculture" and "conglomerate of partial mini-cultures" considered above lead to the suggestion that the optimal combination of form, composition and consistency of a civilisation will lie *between* these extremes!

Indeed, the higher forms and products of a civilisation like a *religion* with theological traditions, an *art* with interacting styles, a *science* and higher education with universities and academies, a *technology* developing in competent industries, a humane and efficient *administration* – all require a certain *magnitude, coherence* and *homogeneity* of the *civilisational framework*. In a mixture of partial mini-cultures these properties are in danger of becoming lost. On the other hand a worldwide monoculture would be in danger of becoming sterile because of its very uniformity.

Since societies and their cultural frameworks are not stationary but show a dynamic evolution, the *driving forces of this evolution* should now briefly be discussed.

One of the driving forces is of course the international emigration and immigration or the interregional migration of populations of different cultural backgrounds. The dynamics of such migratory processes will be the subject of the mathematical model in the next sections.

Beyond that there exists an *internal dynamics of selforganisation within cultural groups* which may lead to newly arising cultural substructures within the society. Generally speaking, two *antagonistic trends* can be identified: That of *universal participation* in the global civilisation on the one hand, and on the other the trend to *self-isolation and -separation*. The first trend is desirable because it leads to integrative processes stabilizing and developing the cultural framework. The second, opposite trend is precarious because it may lead to the formation of political or religious sects and subcultures with closed ideologies denying cultural or social cooperation with the rest of the society. Evidently such trends promote the decomposition of the society into subcultures.

From this consideration we see, that the fate and the evolution of a whole civilisation composed of cultural groups depends essentially on the *kind of interaction between these groups*, in particular between the *majority* and the *minorities*.

Since the whole civilisation and the cultures of its groups are both *values in themselves*, there evidently exist *natural rights* and *duties* applicable to *all formations*, i.e. the minorities, the majority and the whole political civilisatory system.

Beginning with the *rights* of a *minority*, there evidently belong to these rights the individual human rights of its members and beyond these the right to pursue the language, culture, religion, and way of life which define the identity of that minority. However there also exist *duties* specific to minorities which begin where the rights of individuals, other groups, or of the whole political and cultural system become involved.

Conflicts between competing rights can arise if a group exerts internal coercion and pressure on its members or urges in unfair manner non-members to join the group (as is often observed in the case of religious or political sects). Even more problematic – and having the potential to deny and destroy the rights of the majority and of the liberal political system as such – are minorities with a totalitarian ideology and the subversive intention of undermining and removing the existing (pluralistic) system. Fanatical political and fundamentalist religious groups belong to this kind of minority. Their activities should be restricted or not tolerated at all, because they violate their duty of loyalty to all other groups and because a liberal system which grants rights to all loyal groups has the moral right to maintain its structure and to prevent its destabilisation.

The rights and duties of the *majority* are even heavier because their correct and responsible fulfilment decides the fate of the whole system. It is the *right* of the majority to establish a legal and just political structure including a legislature, executive and judicature, and it is its *duty* to defend this structure against its foes. An important part of the *legitimation* of this political structure will then depend on the extent to which it grants rights to and demands duties from both minorities and majority in a well-balanced and fair manner.

Whenever the majority in a cultural-political community or nation fails to protect the legitimate system – for instance against fanatical political forces – by giving them the chance to seize power, the situation of cultural, political, and ethnic minorities in natural opposition to the then ruling ideology may become extremely dangerous, even tragic.

The largest multicultural catastrophy of the 20th century, the holocaust, (i.e. the systematic murder of the Jews by the Nazis during the second world war) must of course be mentioned in this context, even though the consideration of the holocaust is somewhat beyond the scope of this book.

An event of the order of magnitude of the holocaust of course cannot be explained by a *single cause*. Instead, one must expect a complex superposition of *multiple causes*. In order to disentangle these causes it is appropriate to classify them into (a) *long-term causes* of historical, cultural and perhaps even genetic origin, and (b) *short-term causes* of political and ideological origin.

The *long-term causes* consist of an *antisemitism* thriving in Germany (and elsewhere), rooted in certain cultural and also christian traditions, furthermore certain specifically German traditions of *authoritarianism*, i.e. a predisposition to obey and comply with and to be subservient to given authorities, whether legitimized or not.

The *short-term causes* consist in the fact that after the seizure of power by Hitler, he and his Nazi-fellows utilized all the facilities of a modern totalitarian state, i.e. propaganda, supervision and suppression, to influence in disastrous manner the political psyche of the German population. This intense agitation seduced, after all, in the short span of a few years some part of the German population into holding the absurd opinion that "the Jews are internally their misfortune and externally their enemies".

Another discussion among historians crosscutting the classification into short-term and long-term causes concerns the controversy between *intentionalism*, i.e. the thesis that *one driving force*, namely the intention of Hitler, was the main cause, and the thesis that an *accumulative radicalisation*, namely a selforganizing and escalating negative cooperative process was the main cause of the holocaust (see [3]).

Although there can be no doubt that all kinds of causes have contributed in disastrous way to the coming about of the holocaust, the *interpretational question of the relative weight of the different causal components is still contentious*.

This interpretation does not become easier, if the following facts and arguments (about which there seems to exist agreement among most historians) are also taken into account:

It can be substantiated that *before* the Nazis, antisemitism existed in Germany as in other European countries but was *even less pronounced* than for instance in Poland or Austria with large Jewish ghettos in their capitals. Simultaneously the long-term process of *the cultural integration of the Jews* has been rather successful in Germany before Hitler, and the German Jews contributed much to German culture. (Tragically, for this reason many German Jews underestimated the imminent danger of the Nazis and missed the chance to emigrate until it was too late.) Therefore Goldhagen's thesis [4] of a long-term continuity of a *specifically German "eliminationist antisemitism"* finds no basis in the history of Germany and Europe.

Nevertheless, it is a fact, that the Nazis found among their fanatized adherents *some tens of thousands of "willing executioners"* [4] who were ready to organize and perpetrate this atrocious crime. However, it is also true that the number of these willing executioners amounted to about one millesimal of the German population and that the Nazis *took extreme measures to conceal the crime of the holocaust* from the eyes of the bulk of the German population because they feared that it would not be approved. (The BBC, to which many Germans listened during the war, did not broadcast about the holocaust until the end of 1944.) The ordinary Germans, on the other hand, were apart from a few exceptions no heroes; they faced the death penalty if caught helping or hiding Jews and so preferred to muddle through in the confusions of war instead of risking their lives. The situation of the infamously oppressed Jews has been described by the German Jew Victor Klemperer [5], originally a German patriot, who survived Nazism in the home-town of the author.

Looking now at the different explanations given for the holocaust, which arise by giving different weight and relevance to the partial causes, it seems, that *two main patterns of interpretation and lines of valuation* have predominated:

The first line of argument, which can be denoted as "*the uniqueness thesis*", asserts that the holocaust is a *specific singular event* which in this way could *only have occurred in Germany*, due to the specific national characteristics and historical and cultural (and perhaps even genetical?) predispositions of the Germans, which also include an "*eliminatory antisemitism*" [4]. This argument has the consequence that comparable disastrous deeds – whether in war or peace – could never be perpetrated by the Americans, the English, the French, or the Russians, because only German cultural soil was long prepared to receive such a bacillus as Nazism.

The second line of argument, which may be denoted as "*the universality thesis*", asserts that human catastrophies such as the holocaust are *rare but nevertheless universal phenomena* which are *accidents beyond design of civilisation* and can eventually occur in the course of a *phase-transition* of the respective society towards a *collective malignant state beyond civilisation*.

The asserted *universal possibility* of such catastrophies *does not imply* that they are fully predictable events. Instead, historical phase-transition phenomena as such do always include "critical events" occurring in unpredictable, singular and non-repetitive manner.

In the case of Nazism the specific and indeed singular driving force was Hitler with his *obsession* to liquidate the Jewish "race", his *instinct* for arousing malevolent emotions among his adherents, and, after having unleashed the world war, having the *scope and frame* for realizing his intentions [6].

Given that such driving forces exist – singular and unpredictable in each individual case – the asserted universal nature of the catastrophy means that under such global destructive circumstances *metamorphoses of human behaviour* take place in which there rise to the surface negative human attitudes never observed under normal conditions which *then reinforce the malignant status quo*.

And the universal possibility of such sequences of events would have the consequence that *in principle no society could be exempted* from the danger of such catastrophic phenomena.

Before discussing the general consequences of the alternative interpretations, their meaning for the Germans, in whose society the crime of the holocaust occurred, must be considered first. The result is, that *neither of these interpretations brings moral relief for Germans*, for the following reasons:

If the *specific German national character and history* are the necessary condition for the holocaust it would have for long been the responsibility of the Germans to critically revise certain aspects of this character and to give their historical evolution another direction.

If, alternatively, the holocaust is *the outstanding example of rare phenomena occurring "beyond civilisation"* by specific driving forces and a negative cooperative effect arising under extreme political conditions it would have been the responsibility of the German cultural and religious elites to foresee and to prevent by active action the imminent danger of the Nazi regime before it was too late. (Thus, Hitler's plans laid down in his book "Mein Kampf" (My Struggle) (1925) should not have been ignored and should have provoked sharp unanimous reactions among the political elites.)

Since the Germans failed to fulfil their responsibility under both interpretations of the event, in spite of possessing high moral, educational and cultural standards, it remains the shame of the German people that this secular crime of the holocaust *could be perpetrated at all by members of their nation.* It is therefore *their inevitable moral obligation to remember that due to essential failures occurring in their history* this crime happened in their own society.

Let us now discuss the consequences of the two alternative explanations of the holocaust *for other societies.*

The first thesis, asserting the unique and completely incommensurable behaviour of the Germans, would lead to an *optimistic perspective* for the non-German world: *Only the Germans* – among the about 200 nations of the world – would then need supervision entailing the highest precautions for their own and their neighbours benefit, in order to exclude the recurrence of the disaster.

The second thesis, asserting that the holocaust is the extreme example of a disastrous social trajectory under extreme circumstances, implies the *pessimistic conclusion* that an event of this kind can *in principle happen in any society if it falls into the trap of totalitarianism,* and that therefore the whole of mankind – the Germans of course included – urgently needs pre-warning- and supervisory measures in order to prevent the recurrence of this kind of cultural disaster.

The author is, unfortunately, led to the conclusion that the *pessimistic second thesis is the more realistic and cautious one.* In order to substantiate this conclusion it would of course be possible to refer to other catastrophies of comparable magnitude in other totalitarian systems. (Such events have recently been documented for the communist system by the French authors Stephane Courtois *et al.* in their "livre noir du communisme" [7].) Instead, the author wants to use another argument, which only refers to the Germans and in which the pessimistic and optimistic aspects are intertwined:

In order to introduce the argument, we begin with an attempt to capture the concept of *"normality"* of a society in a sufficiently broad manner as to be able to imply the diversity of cultural traits among civilisations.

According to our definition, *normality* prevails in a society, if the minds of the politically decisive part of its members are *not distorted, biased and fanatized by an internalized ideology of extreme, one-sided and prejudiced contents and intentions.* (This definition implies, that *normal people* of whatsoever nation or culture will condemn crimes such as the holocaust.)

It is then evident that the Nazis, with Hitler at the top, succeeded in seducing during their rule the minds of their adherents – and in addition a part of the ordinary German population – into a *non-normal ideologized state* according to this definition (see Chapter 6.1.4, where this process is described in more detail.)

On the other hand it seems also evident – and has been substantiated by several sociological and political field inquiries – that the great majority of the German population is *nowadays normal* according to the same definition. As Saul Friedländer, the Israeli historian, has recently formulated it (in his address of thanks on the occasion of the Geschwister Scholl price awarded to him 1998): "The Germans are now a normal people, an ordinary society like other societies". This normality not only includes the private and civilian sphere but also that of political life in a pluralistic democratic society.

This has a very positive aspect: It shows that recovery from deep political and moral breakdowns and return to constructive political behaviour is possible in a relatively short time. However, this fact also has its reverse: In the case of the Germans we *know* that they now belong to the community of democratic countries; but we *also know* that about six decades before, the Germans were assailed by a political totalitarian infection bringing them into the deepest crisis of their history. These historical facts *show*, that in the German case normal political behaviour of people under normal circumstances *does not exclude* the *same people* (certainly genetically unaltered during only two generations) tumbling into an extremely ideo-logized state leading to political disaster.

Therefore it seems *implausible*, that in the case of all other nations their normal, democratic and constructive behaviour under *normal* circumstances *is a sufficient guarantee* for *possessing immunity* against the threat of totalitarian political infection, which of course would not need to assume exactly the same form as Nazism.

Paradoxically, however, this pessimistic view which takes *the malign potential of human nature in its individual and collective behavioural aspects as a universal given*, bears an optimistic perspective: If all people of the world become aware of the dormant, but universal dangers of totalitarianism, the chances of avoiding or at least confining these grand political disasters can be optimized!

Let us now come back to some conclusions about multiculturality: If multicultural-ity already exists or is admitted (for instance by immigration), the *cultural trend-parameters* and corresponding identity formations thereupon develop at a slow pace and are practically impermeable to outside influence. In contrast, the *control para-meters* of the *political system* develop at a relatively fast pace. They provide the boundary conditions for the evolution of the multi-cultural system which can be a prosperous one or in other cases an endangered or even disastrous one. Evidently the responsibility of the political system is to find differentiated and balanced forms and laws granting rights and demanding duties from the majority as well as the minority with respect to their relations. Here, the right of preservation of cultural identity must be reconciled with the duty of allegiance of all cultural groups to the global political system which grants and safeguards their rights and duties. All members of the society, in particular the majority, are responsible for defending this system against totalitarian (e.g. racist, nationalistic or fundamentalist) forces which are otherwise able to destroy a well-functioning multicultural system.

4.1.2 Migratory Trends and their Multicultural and Socio-Economic Reasons

Interregional and international migration and its effects on the population distribu-tion is the *spatially visible signature* of economic, social and in particular multi-cultural processes in the society. Migration and the spatial visibility of multicultural, social and economical trends only sets in if such trends have passed certain *thresholds* so that they result in a spatial differentiation of the population(s).

In general, *many motivations* merge in *relatively few migratory trends* and processes. That means, the migratory process only reflects the *superposition* of all individual motivations (as far as they show up at all in migration). A quantitative determination of the differential relevance of influences on migration is only possible by a detailed factor analysis (see e.g. Section 4.5.2).

Therefore, we firstly begin with a short (and incomplete) *classification of the main motivations and trends* giving rise to migration and secondly we delineate the *main effects* of these trends. Analyses of the reason of migration and of socio-spatial dynamics have been given at several places, of which we only mention a few [8], [9], [10].

Motivations for migration may have *cultural reasons* in a multicultural society: Cultural and/or ethnic *propinquity* and *proximity* may lead to an *agglomeration trend*, i.e. the wish to live together with people of similar kind and background, and on the other hand cultural and/or ethnic *distance* and *remoteness* may lead to a *segregation trend*, i.e. the wish to live in other places than the people of different kind and background. [Here we restrict our consideration to *voluntary* trends in a liberal political system and exclude *enforced* processes like "ethnic cleansing" occurring in totalitarian systems.] The segregation trend because of cultural and/or ethnical reasons is usually a *reciprocal* one because the corresponding distance is felt on both sides.

The *interregional* agglomeration and segregation processes *within* a multicultural society are nowadays often superposed by *international migration* processes taking place because of the unfavourable economic and/or political situation in the country of origin. Of course these migration flows also create a new and sometimes quickly developing multicultural situation.

The more traditional reasons and motivations for migration are *socio-economic*. The migration flows will be attracted to locations with prospering industry because of the employment offered there. (Indeed, the inhomogeneity of settlement and population distribution at all seems to be essentially generated by this effect. For this see also [11] and [12].) The different standard of life afforded by different social classes, the solidarity among members of the same class, but also the wish for prestige and style of life then lead to differentiated trends to migrate into quarters where the corresponding social requirements are satisfied best. It is worth noting that the migratory trends of different *social classes* need not to be reciprocal ones. For instance the socially "better off" classes may prefer to live among themselves in their quarters whereas the upwardly mobile may try to move to and penetrate the privileged quarters.

Finally, the natural preferences of a location, its beauty and its climate, will also contribute to migratory trends, in particular for those people (e.g. retired ones) who can afford a free selection of residence and for whom multicultural and socio-economic reasons play a minor role.

The migratory motivations discussed so far may be classified into those derived from *exogenous* and those derived from *endogenous* reasons: *Exogenous influences* on decisions to migrate are the regional economical situation and the natural attractiveness of the city or the landscape; *Endogenous influences*, on the other hand, depend on the existing population configuration. In particular agglomeration- and segregation-trends lead to migratory decisions taking into account the spatial distribution of the different subpopulations.

The main *effects* of the various migratory trends can now easily be guessed and anticipated:

If the exogenous trends prevail, the mixture of subpopulations of different cultural and/or ethnical background will remain a practically homogeneous one and spatial density agglomerations will develop in an area according to its economic, or leisure attractions.

If, on the other hand, endogenous intercultural agglomeration- and segregation-trends play a strong role, a spatial disintegration and separation of the different subpopulations is to be expected. In the extreme case a mosaic of different quarters or ghettos can arise, each of them preferentially populated by people of *one* cultural and/or ethnic background. Whether or not this pattern is influencable and desirable should be judged in view of the structure- and valuation-principles discussed above.

4.2   The General Interregional Migratory Model

In setting up a general migratory model for interacting populations we strictly proceed along the lines of Chapter 3. Parts of the model described here in general form have been presented in several articles: [13], [14], [15], [16].

The *first step* of the modelling procedure consists in the introduction of an appropriate *configuration space of variables*. The macrovariables of the model only consist of *extensive personal variables*.

At first we assume that there exist P different subpopulations $\mathcal{P}^\alpha$, with $\alpha = 1, 2, \ldots, P$, of different cultural, ethnic or social background. Their total numbers be N^α. We neglect birth/death-processes, so that the N^α remain constant with time.

Second, we have to identify the possible "attitudes" which the members of all subpopulations $\mathcal{P}^\alpha$ can assume. These attitudes refer to a spatial system of C regions i, where $i = 1, 2, \ldots, C$. Depending on the scale of the spatial system, regions can for instance be districts or counties of a state or quarters of a city. Then, "attitude i" is identified with "living in region i".

Let now n_i^α be the number of members of subpopulation $\mathcal{P}^\alpha$ who have attitude i, that means who live in region i. The multiple of integers

$$\mathbf{n} = \{n_1^1, \ldots, n_C^1; \ldots; n_1^\alpha, \ldots, n_i^\alpha, \ldots, n_C^\alpha; \ldots; n_1^P, \ldots, n_C^P\} \tag{4.1}$$

is then denoted as *socioconfiguration* and represents the set of macrovariables of the model. They fulfil the simple relations already mentioned in Chapter 3:

$$N^\alpha = \sum_{i=1}^{C} n_i^\alpha; \quad N_i = \sum_{\alpha=1}^{P} n_i^\alpha \tag{4.2}$$

and

$$N = \sum_{\alpha=1}^{P} N^\alpha = \sum_{i=1}^{C} N_i \tag{4.3}$$

where N^α is the number of members of $\mathcal{P}^\alpha$, N_i is the number of all people in region i and N is the number of members of the total population.

The *second step* is the introduction of the elementary dynamics. The elementary migration process consists in the migration of one individual of subpopulation $\mathcal{P}^\alpha$ from region i to region j. (The "circulation" of migrants within the same region is not taken into account.) This amounts to the following change of the socioconfiguration:

$$\mathbf{n} \Rightarrow \mathbf{n}_{ji}^\alpha = \{n_1^1,\ldots,n_C^1;\ldots;n_1^\alpha,\ldots,(n_j^\alpha+1),\ldots,(n_i^\alpha-1),\ldots,n_C^\alpha;\ldots;n_1^P\ldots n_C^P\}. \tag{4.4}$$

The transition rates effecting the transition from $\mathbf{n}$ to $\mathbf{n}_{ji}^\alpha$ and the inverse transition from $\mathbf{n}_{ji}^\alpha$ to $\mathbf{n}$ read (compare (3.13)):

$$w_{ji}^\alpha(\mathbf{n}_{ji}^\alpha,\mathbf{n};\kappa^\alpha) = n_i^\alpha p_{ji}^\alpha(\mathbf{n}_{ji}^\alpha,\mathbf{n};\kappa^\alpha)$$
$$= n_i^\alpha \nu_0 \exp\{M_{ji}^\alpha(\mathbf{n}_{ji}^\alpha,\mathbf{n};\kappa^\alpha)\}. \tag{4.5a}$$

and

$$w_{ij}^\alpha(\mathbf{n},\mathbf{n}_{ji}^\alpha;\kappa^\alpha) = (n_j^\alpha+1)p_{ij}^\alpha(\mathbf{n},\mathbf{n}_{ji}^\alpha;\kappa^\alpha)$$
$$= (n_j^\alpha+1)\nu_0 \exp\{M_{ij}^\alpha(\mathbf{n},\mathbf{n}_{ji}^\alpha;\kappa^\alpha)\}. \tag{4.5b}$$

Here, the p_{ji}^α and p_{ij}^α are *individual probabilistic transition rates* from i to j and j to i, respectively, of each individual out of subpopulation $\mathcal{P}^\alpha$. (It is assumed, that people of the same subpopulation exhibit the same probabilistic transition behaviour.) The numbers n_i^α and $(n_j^\alpha+1)$, respectively, are the number of people who can independently execute the respective transition. The individual transition rates, being positive definite quantities by definition, can be written in terms of *motivation potentials* $M_{ji}^\alpha(\mathbf{n}_{ji}^\alpha,\mathbf{n};\kappa^\alpha)$ and $M_{ij}^\alpha(\mathbf{n},\mathbf{n}_{ji}^\alpha;\kappa^\alpha)$, respectively, which depend on the initial and final state of the individual executing the transition and the initial and final state of the socioconfiguration which are compared and valued by the individuals, and on trendparameters κ^α of the subpopulation $\mathcal{P}^\alpha$. The motivation potentials are quantitative formulations of the push- and pull-"forces" between origin and destination.

After a decomposition of the motivation potentials into their symmetric and antisymmetric part with respect to the forward and backward transition which is explicitly implemented in Chapter 3, the transition rates (4.5) can be rewritten as follows:

$$w_{ji}^\alpha(\mathbf{n}_{ji}^\alpha,\mathbf{n};\kappa^\alpha) = n_i^\alpha \nu_{ji}^\alpha(\mathbf{n}_{ji}^\alpha,\mathbf{n};\kappa^\alpha)\exp\left\{u_j^\alpha(\mathbf{n}_{ji}^\alpha;\kappa^\alpha)-u_i^\alpha(\mathbf{n};\kappa^\alpha)\right\} \tag{4.6a}$$

and

$$w_{ij}^\alpha(\mathbf{n},\mathbf{n}_{ji}^\alpha;\kappa^\alpha) = (n_j^\alpha+1)\nu_{ij}^\alpha(\mathbf{n},\mathbf{n}_{ji}^\alpha;\kappa^\alpha)\exp\left\{u_i^\alpha(\mathbf{n};\kappa^\alpha)-u_j^\alpha(\mathbf{n}_{ji}^\alpha;\kappa^\alpha)\right\}. \tag{4.6b}$$

The prefactors are symmetrical:

$$\nu_{ij}^\alpha(\mathbf{n},\mathbf{n}_{ji}^\alpha;\kappa^\alpha) = \nu_{ji}^\alpha(\mathbf{n}_{ji}^\alpha,\mathbf{n};\kappa^\alpha) \tag{4.7}$$

and can be interpreted as the (forward as well as backward) *mobility* of people of $\mathcal{P}^\alpha$ at their transitions between regions i and j, and the term $u_i^\alpha(\mathbf{n}; \boldsymbol{\kappa}^\alpha)$ can be interpreted as the *utility* (or *attractiveness*) which a member of $\mathcal{P}^\alpha$ sees in living in region i, given that the momentary socioconfiguration is $\mathbf{n}$. (After migrating from i to j the same individual sees the utility $u_j^\alpha(\mathbf{n}_{ji}^\alpha; \boldsymbol{\kappa}^\alpha)$ of living in region j at then existing socioconfiguration $\mathbf{n}_{ji}^\alpha$.) The reason for interpreting the u_i^α as "utilities" is the following: According to (4.6), migratory transitions are favoured (disfavoured), if the utility of the destination region exceeds (falls short of) the utility of the origin regions.

In order to make the model explicit, a *concrete choice* of the form of the mobilities and utilities must be made. This choice should on the one side reflect in general terms social experience, but should on the other side include a whole variety of possible behavioural cases (e.g. by giving different numerical values to the trendparameters $\boldsymbol{\kappa}^\alpha$).

We begin with the mobility factors. A careful investigation of the empirical facts (see Section 4.5) has shown that the mobilities do *not* practically depend on the configuration $\mathbf{n}$, but that instead the following formula can be confirmed:

$$\nu_{ij}^\alpha = \nu_{ji}^\alpha = \nu_0^\alpha(t) \exp(-d_{ij}^\alpha), \tag{4.8}$$

where $\nu_0^\alpha(t)$ is a (sometimes explicitly time-dependent) global mobility factor and $d_{ij}^\alpha = d_{ji}^\alpha$ is a measure for the "distance" between region i and j as seen by members of $\mathcal{P}^\alpha$. This "distance" measures in general not only the geographical distance, but includes the informational distance and other distance effects like intervening obstacles between region i and j for population $\mathcal{P}^\alpha$.

Of crucial importance is the socially interpretable and plausible choice of the *utility functions* u_i^α. They should comprise the valuation of the region i by members of population $\mathcal{P}^\alpha$ concerning its exogenous and endogenous (i.e. population dependent) qualities as well. The simplest nontrivial form fulfilling these requirements is the following:

$$u_i^\alpha(\mathbf{n}; \boldsymbol{\kappa}^\alpha) = \frac{1}{2}\left(\delta_i^\alpha + \sum_{\beta=1}^{P} \kappa^{\alpha\beta} n_i^\beta\right). \tag{4.9}$$

Here, the δ_i^α comprise the attractiveness of all qualities and facilities, i.e. the *physical* push/pull factors of region i for members of $\mathcal{P}^\alpha$ (e.g. working places, traffic connections, landscape etc.) which are *independent* of the population composition in i.

The second term of the r.h.s. of (4.9) describes the valuation of region i by members of $\mathcal{P}^\alpha$ concerning its *population-composition*. It comprizes the *social* push/ pull factors. Only linear dependences on the n_i^β, which can be seen as the first terms of a Taylor expansion, are taken into account, but the inclusion of further terms would not lead to principal difficulties. The term with $\beta = \alpha$, and $\kappa^{\alpha\alpha} > 0$, can be interpreted as the effect of an *agglomeration trend* within the population $\mathcal{P}^\alpha$, because it leads to a more and more positive u_i^α, the higher the value of the trendparameter $\kappa^{\alpha\alpha}$ and of the number n_i^α is. Analogously, the terms $\kappa^{\alpha\beta} n_i^\beta$ for $\beta \neq \alpha$ describe the effect of agglomeration trends (for $\kappa^{\alpha\beta} > 0$) or segregation trends (for $\kappa^{\alpha\beta} < 0$) of population $\mathcal{P}^\alpha$ concerning the population $\mathcal{P}^\beta$. For *positive* trendparameter $\kappa^{\alpha\beta}$ the utility u_i^α

of region i estimated by members of $\mathcal{P}^\alpha$ *grows* with growing numbers n_i^β, whereas it *sinks*, if the trendparameter $\kappa^{\alpha\beta}$ is *negative*. It is clear, that the values and signs of the trendparameters $\kappa^{\alpha\beta}$ reflect the cultural and/or socio-economic proximity or distance between subpopulations $\mathcal{P}^\alpha$ and $\mathcal{P}^\beta$, in so far as they determine the intensity of the wishes of members of $\mathcal{P}^\mu$ to live together with those of $\mathcal{P}^\beta$ (if $\kappa^{\alpha\beta} > 0$) or to live separate from those of $\mathcal{P}^\beta$ (if $\kappa^{\alpha\beta} < 0$). The model as such *neither determines nor valuates* these trends; instead it takes them for given and allows of the calculation of their consequences in scenario simulations.

The *third step* of model construction consists in setting up the *equations of evolution* for the socioconfiguration. The evolution equation for the (appropriately normalized) *probability distribution function,* to find the socioconfiguration $\mathbf{n}$ at time t, namely

$$P(\mathbf{n}; t) \geq 0 \quad \text{with} \quad \sum_{\mathbf{n}} P(\mathbf{n}; t) = 1 \tag{4.10}$$

is the *master equation.* It is a special case of the general master equation (3.35) and making use of the abbreviations (writing out only the initial configuration in the transition rates)

$$
\begin{aligned}
w_{ji}^\alpha(\mathbf{n}_{ji}^\alpha, \mathbf{n}; \boldsymbol{\kappa}^\alpha) &\Rightarrow w_{ji}^\alpha(\mathbf{n}); \\
w_{ij}^\alpha(\mathbf{n}, \mathbf{n}_{ji}^\alpha; \boldsymbol{\kappa}^\alpha) &\Rightarrow w_{ij}^\alpha(\mathbf{n}_{ji}^\alpha)
\end{aligned}
\tag{4.11}
$$

it reads

$$\frac{dP(\mathbf{n}; t)}{dt} = \sum_{i,j,\alpha} \left\{ w_{ij}^\alpha(\mathbf{n}_{ji}^\alpha) P(\mathbf{n}_{ji}^\alpha; t) - w_{ji}^\alpha(\mathbf{n}) P(\mathbf{n}; t) \right\}. \tag{4.12}$$

Here, the explicit forms of the transition rates (4.6) with (4.8) and (4.9) must be inserted.

From the master equation there can be derived equations for the meanvalues $\bar{n}_i^\alpha(t)$ which are defined by

$$\bar{n}_i^\alpha(t) = \sum_{\mathbf{n}} n_i^\alpha P(\mathbf{n}; t). \tag{4.13}$$

Their exact form reads (compare (3.37b)):

$$\frac{d\bar{n}_i^\alpha(t)}{dt} = \sum_j \overline{w_{ij}^\alpha(\mathbf{n})} - \sum_j \overline{w_{ji}^\alpha(\mathbf{n})}. \tag{4.14}$$

However, these equations are not selfcontained and closed. Instead, the quasi-mean-values $\hat{n}_i^\alpha(t)$, which describe the mean path of the stochastic trajectories on each point of the space of socioconfigurations, satisfy the equations (compare (3.42b)):

$$\frac{d\hat{n}_i^\alpha(t)}{dt} = \sum_j w_{ij}^\alpha(\hat{\mathbf{n}}) - \sum_j w_{ji}^\alpha(\hat{\mathbf{n}}). \tag{4.15}$$

The equations (4.15) are selfcontained. By inserting the explicit form of the transition rates they assume the form:

$$\frac{d\hat{n}_i^\alpha(t)}{dt} = \sum_j \hat{n}_j^\alpha \cdot \nu_{ij}^\alpha \exp\left[u_i^\alpha(\hat{\mathbf{n}}, \boldsymbol{\kappa}^\alpha) - u_j^\alpha(\hat{\mathbf{n}}, \boldsymbol{\kappa}^\alpha)\right]$$

$$- \sum_j \hat{n}_i^\alpha \cdot \nu_{ji}^\alpha \exp\left[u_j^\alpha(\hat{\mathbf{n}}, \boldsymbol{\kappa}^\alpha) - u_i^\alpha(\hat{\mathbf{n}}, \boldsymbol{\kappa}^\alpha)\right] \quad (4.16)$$

which shows that they are in general a set of *coupled nonlinear differential equations* for the $\hat{n}_i^\alpha$. Only in the special case, if the $u_i^\alpha(\hat{\mathbf{n}}, \boldsymbol{\kappa}^\alpha)$ contains exogenous terms but no endogenous terms, i.e. if all trendparameters $\kappa^{\alpha\beta}$ are equal to zero, the equations (4.16) reduce to a set of *linear equations* which can be solved easily.

The equations (4.12), (4.15) and (4.16) represent the mathematical form of the general interregional migratory model.

4.3 The Case of Two Interacting Populations in Two Regions

In spite of the compact form of equations (4.12) and (4.15) they comprise complex migratory phenomena. Fortunately, however, already the simplest nontrivial case, namely the migration of two interacting subpopulations, say $\mathcal{P}^\mu$ and $\mathcal{P}^\nu$, in two districts or regions 1 and 2, is of generic nature in so far as some elementary migratory phenomena can be studied in its frame and as simple interpretations can be given to the trendparameters.

4.3.1 The Specialized Form of the Evolution Equations

Evidently, for this case the *socioconfiguration* consists of four integers only:

$$\mathbf{n} = \{n_1^\mu, n_2^\mu; n_1^\nu, n_2^\nu\}. \quad (4.17)$$

Because we neglect birth- and death-processes in the two populations $\mathcal{P}^\mu$ and $\mathcal{P}^\nu$, the total population numbers

$$2M = n_1^\mu + n_2^\mu \quad (4.18)$$

and

$$2N = n_1^\nu + n_2^\nu \quad (4.19)$$

of the populations $\mathcal{P}^\mu$ and $\mathcal{P}^\nu$ are *constant with time*, so that the only *relevant variables* within the system are

$$m = \frac{(n_1^\mu - n_2^\mu)}{2} \quad \text{with} \quad -M \le m \le +M \quad (4.20)$$

and

$$n = \frac{(n_1^\nu - n_2^\nu)}{2} \quad \text{with} \quad -N \le n \le +N \tag{4.21}$$

so that

$$n_1^\mu = M + m; \quad n_2^\mu = M - m \tag{4.22}$$

and

$$n_1^\nu = N + n; \quad n_2^\nu = N - n. \tag{4.23}$$

The *utility functions* for members of population $\mathcal{P}^\alpha$, $\alpha = \mu, \nu$, in district $i = 1, 2$ are special cases of (4.9) and read:

$$u_i^\alpha(n_i^\mu, n_i^\nu) = \frac{1}{2}(\delta_i^\alpha + \kappa^{\alpha\mu} n_i^\mu + \kappa^{\alpha\nu} n_i^\nu). \tag{4.24}$$

Since the *individual transition rates* p_{ji}^α have the general form

$$p_{ji}^\mu = \tilde{\nu}_\mu \exp\left[u_j^\mu(n_j^\mu + 1, n_j^\nu) - u_i^\mu(n_i^\mu, n_i^\nu)\right] \tag{4.25}$$

and

$$p_{ji}^\nu = \tilde{\nu}_\nu \exp\left[u_j^\nu(n_j^\mu, n_j^\nu + 1) - u_i^\nu(n_i^\mu, n_i^\nu)\right] \tag{4.26}$$

there follows by inserting (4.24) and making use of the variables (4.20) and (4.21):

$$p_{12}^\mu(m, n) = \nu_\mu \exp[\Delta u^\mu(m, n)]; \tag{4.27a}$$
$$p_{21}^\mu(m, n) = \nu_\mu \exp[-\Delta u^\mu(m, n)]; \tag{4.27b}$$
$$p_{12}^\nu(m, n) = \nu_\nu \exp[\Delta u^\nu(m, n)]; \tag{4.27c}$$
$$p_{21}^\nu(m, n) = \nu_\nu \exp[-\Delta u^\nu(m, n)] \tag{4.27d}$$

with

$$\Delta u^\mu(m, n) = (\delta^\mu + \kappa^{\mu\mu} m + \kappa^{\mu\nu} n); \tag{4.28a}$$
$$\Delta u^\nu(m, n) = (\delta^\nu + \kappa^{\nu\mu} m + \kappa^{\nu\nu} n), \tag{4.28b}$$

where

$$\delta^\alpha = \frac{1}{2}(\delta_1^\alpha - \delta_2^\alpha) \quad \alpha = \mu, \nu \tag{4.29}$$

and

$$\nu_\alpha = \tilde{\nu}_\alpha \exp\left(\frac{1}{2}\kappa^{\alpha\alpha}\right) \quad \alpha = \mu, \nu. \tag{4.30}$$

The *configurational transition rates* then follow from (4.5):

$$w_{12}^\mu \equiv w_\uparrow^\mu(m, n) = p_{12}^\mu n_2^\mu = \nu_\mu(M - m) \exp[\Delta u^\mu(m, n)]; \tag{4.31a}$$
$$w_{21}^\mu \equiv w_\downarrow^\mu(m, n) = p_{21}^\mu n_1^\mu = \nu_\mu(M + m) \exp[-\Delta u^\mu(m, n)]; \tag{4.31b}$$
$$w_{12}^\nu \equiv w_\uparrow^\nu(m, n) = p_{12}^\nu n_2^\nu = \nu_\nu(N - n) \exp[\Delta u^\nu(m, n)]; \tag{4.31c}$$
$$w_{21}^\nu \equiv w_\downarrow^\nu(m, n) = p_{21}^\nu n_1^\nu = \nu_\nu(N + n) \exp[-\Delta u^\nu(m, n)]. \tag{4.31d}$$

The transition rates $w_\uparrow^\nu(m,n)$, $w_\downarrow^\mu(m,n)$, $w_\uparrow^\nu(m,n)$ and $w_\downarrow^\nu(m,n)$ induce the transition from (m,n) to $(m+1,n)$, $(m-1,n)$, $(m,n+1)$ and $(m,n-1)$, respectively.

The Master Equation

The *master equation* now follows immediately as a special case of equation (4.12). However, for given constant M and N we let the probability distribution $P(m,n;t)$ only depend on the relevant variables m and n, and obtain its explicit form

$$\frac{dP(m,n;t)}{dt} = -\left\{\left[w_\uparrow^\mu(m,n) + w_\downarrow^\mu(m,n) + w_\uparrow^\nu(m,n) + w_\downarrow^\nu(m,n)\right]P(m,n;t)\right\}$$
$$+ \left\{w_\uparrow^\mu(m-1,n)P(m-1,n;t) + w_\downarrow^\mu(m+1,n)P(m+1,n;t)\right.$$
$$\left. + w_\uparrow^\nu(m,n-1)P(m,n-1;t) + w_\downarrow^\nu(m,n+1)P(m,n+1;t)\right\}. \quad (4.32)$$

The first term on the r.h.s. of (4.32) describes the probability flow *out of the configuration* (m,n) into the neighboring configurations $(m+1,n)$, $(m-1,n)$, $(m,n+1)$ and $(m,n-1)$ and the second term describes the probability flows from the neighboring configurations $(m-1,n)$, $(m+1,n)$, $(m,n-1)$ and $(m,n+1)$ *into the configuration* (m,n).

The master equation (4.32) is a good example to which the general considerations of Section 12.5 about *detailed balance* and the possibility of the analytic *construction of the stationary solution* of (4.32) can be applied:

Under certain conditions for the transition rates (4.31) the stationary solution $P_{st}(m,n)$ of (4.32) fulfils "detailed balance", reading for all (m,n):

$$w_\downarrow^\mu(m+1,n)P_{st}(m+1,n) = w_\uparrow^\mu(m,n)P_{st}(m,n); \quad (4.33a)$$
$$w_\downarrow^\nu(m,n+1)P_{st}(m,n+1) = w_\uparrow^\nu(m,n)P_{st}(m,n) \quad (4.33b)$$

which means that the stationary probability outflows and backward inflows in m-direction and analogously in n-direction are individually in balanced equilibrium so that they cancel each other pairwise.

In order that detailed balance (4.33) be fulfilled, the transition rates must satisfy certain conditions which in our case reduce to the following one:

$$\frac{w_\downarrow^\nu(m,n+1)}{w_\uparrow^\nu(m,n)} \cdot \frac{w_\downarrow^\mu(m+1,n+1)}{w_\uparrow^\mu(m,n+1)} \cdot \frac{w_\uparrow^\mu(m+1,n)}{w_\downarrow^\nu(m+1,n+1)} \cdot \frac{w_\uparrow^\mu(m,n)}{w_\downarrow^\mu(m+1,n)} \stackrel{!}{=} 1. \quad (4.34)$$

By inserting the rates (4.31) into the condition (4.34) one easily checks that the condition (4.34) is satisfied if and only if

$$\kappa^{\mu\nu} = \kappa^{\nu\mu} \equiv \sigma \quad (4.35)$$

holds, whereas no restrictions are required for the parameters $\kappa^{\mu\mu}$, $\kappa^{\nu\nu}$, δ^μ and δ^ν. The meaning of (4.35) is that the "public opinion" of the population $\mathcal{P}^\nu$ about the "attractiveness" of population $\mathcal{P}^\mu$ is the same as that of population $\mathcal{P}^\mu$ about $\mathcal{P}^\nu$.

Assuming now, that (4.35) holds and (4.34) is satisfied, one can explicitly construct the stationary solution $P_{st}(m, n)$ of the master equation (4.32) applying the method derived in Section 12.5.

Choosing the path from $(0, 0)$ over $(m, 0)$ to (m, n) one obtains:

$$P_{st}(m, n) = \prod_{b=0}^{n-1} \frac{w_\uparrow^\nu(m, b)}{w_\downarrow^\nu(m, b+1)} \cdot \prod_{a=0}^{m-1} \frac{w_\uparrow^\mu(a, 0)}{w_\downarrow^\mu(a+1, 0)} \cdot P_{st}(0, 0)$$

and by insertion of the transition rates (4.31) there follows explicitly:

$$P_{st}(m, n) = \binom{2M}{M}^{-1} \binom{2M}{M+m} \binom{2N}{N}^{-1} \binom{2N}{N+n}$$
$$\cdot \exp\{2\delta^\mu m + 2\delta^\nu n + \kappa^{\mu\mu} m^2 + 2\sigma m n + \kappa^{\nu\nu} n^2\} P_{st}(0, 0), \qquad (4.36)$$

where

$$\binom{A}{B} = \frac{A!}{B!(A-B)!} \qquad (4.37)$$

and where $P_{st}(0, 0)$ is to be determined by the normalisation of the probability to

$$\sum_{m=-M}^{+M} \sum_{n=-N}^{+N} P_{st}(m, n) \overset{!}{=} 1. \qquad (4.38)$$

If detailed balance is not fulfilled, the stationary solution of the master equation does of course exist, too, but it can only be determined numerically.

The Quasi-Meanvalue Equations

Let us now consider the *quasi-meanvalue equations*. After transition to the variables m, n there follows by specialisation of the equations (4.15):

$$\frac{d\hat{m}(t)}{dt} = 2\nu_\mu\{M \sinh[\Delta u^\mu(\hat{m}, \hat{n})] - \hat{m} \cosh[\Delta u^\mu(\hat{m}, \hat{n})]\} \qquad (4.39)$$

and

$$\frac{d\hat{n}(t)}{dt} = 2\nu_\nu\{N \sinh[\Delta u^\nu(\hat{m}, \hat{n})] - \hat{n} \cosh[\Delta u^\nu(\hat{m}, \hat{n})]\}. \qquad (4.40)$$

For the further evaluation and interpretation of the model we specify its parameters in the following manner:

$$M = N; \qquad (4.41)$$
$$\delta_i^\mu = \delta_i^\nu = 0 \quad i = 1, 2; \qquad (4.42)$$
$$\kappa^{\mu\mu} = \kappa^{\nu\nu} = \kappa; \qquad (4.43)$$
$$\nu_\mu = \nu_\nu = \nu. \qquad (4.44)$$

This means that we treat the symmetrical case of *equal population numbers* of $\mathcal{P}^\mu$ and $\mathcal{P}^\nu$ and that we assume "*no natural preferences*" between the two districts $i = 1, 2$. Furthermore the internal agglomeration trends of both populations $\mathcal{P}^\mu$ and $\mathcal{P}^\nu$ are set to be equal, as well as the migration speed parameters ν_μ and ν_ν. Finally, it is convenient to introduce *scaled variables*

$$x = \frac{\hat{m}}{N}; \quad -1 \le x \le +1; \quad y = \frac{\hat{n}}{N}; \quad -1 \le y \le +1; \tag{4.45}$$

$$\tilde{\kappa}^{\alpha\beta} = \kappa^{\alpha\beta} N; \quad \tau = 2\nu t. \tag{4.46}$$

The quasi-meanvalue equations then assume the form

$$\frac{dx}{d\tau} = \sinh(\tilde{\kappa}x + \tilde{\kappa}^{\mu\nu}y) - x \cosh(\tilde{\kappa}x + \tilde{\kappa}^{\mu\nu}y); \tag{4.47}$$

$$\frac{dy}{d\tau} = \sinh(\tilde{\kappa}^{\nu\mu}x + \tilde{\kappa}y) - y \cosh(\tilde{\kappa}^{\nu\mu}x + \tilde{\kappa}y). \tag{4.48}$$

The quasi-meanvalue-equations (4.47) and (4.48) and the master equation (4.32) with the correspondingly specialized transition rates are the starting point for the following analysis of the two population–two region model.

4.3.2   Linear Stability Analysis

Evidently, the origin $(x, y) = (0, 0)$ which describes the equi-distribution of $\mathcal{P}^\mu$ and $\mathcal{P}^\nu$ in both regions 1 and 2, is a stationary solution of equations (4.47) and (4.48). However the question arises whether this point is a *stable* or *unstable* stationary point. The precise meaning of this question is: Will a system point $(x(\tau), y(\tau))$ in the vicinity of the origin $(0, 0)$ which obeys equations (4.47) and (4.48) *move away from* $(0, 0)$ or *converge to* $(0, 0)$? The first case means instability of $(0, 0)$, and the second case means stability of $(0, 0)$.

In order to answer the question we make a Taylor expansion of the r.h.s. of (4.47) and (4.48) with respect to the (small) deviations $(x(\tau), y(\tau))$ from the stationary point $(0, 0)$ and take into account the linear terms in $(x(\tau), y(\tau))$ only. This standard procedure of linear stability analysis leads to the linear differential equations:

$$\frac{dx}{d\tau} = (\tilde{\kappa} - 1)x + \tilde{\kappa}^{\mu\nu}y; \tag{4.49}$$

$$\frac{dy}{d\tau} = \tilde{\kappa}^{\nu\mu}x + (\tilde{\kappa} - 1)y \tag{4.50}$$

which can be solved by

$$x(\tau) = x_0 \exp(\lambda\tau); \quad y(\tau) = y_0 \exp(\lambda\tau). \tag{4.51}$$

By inserting (4.51) into the equations (4.49) and (4.50) one obtains two homogeneous linear equations for x_0 and y_0. A nontrivial solution of these equations does only exist, if the determinant of the coefficient vanishes, i.e. if

$$\begin{vmatrix} (\tilde{\kappa} - 1) - \lambda & ; & \tilde{\kappa}^{\mu\nu} \\ \tilde{\kappa}^{\nu\mu} & ; & (\tilde{\kappa} - 1) - \lambda \end{vmatrix} \overset{!}{=} 0 \qquad (4.52)$$

holds. Equation (4.52) is a condition for the "eigenvalues" λ which lead to true solutions of (4.49) and (4.50). Equation (4.52) can easily be solved and leads to the two eigenvalues:

$$\lambda_\pm = (\tilde{\kappa} - 1) \pm \sqrt{\tilde{\rho}} \quad \text{with} \quad \tilde{\rho} = \tilde{\kappa}^{\mu\nu} \tilde{\kappa}^{\nu\mu}. \qquad (4.53)$$

From the form of the solutions (4.51) with $\lambda = \lambda_+$ and $\lambda = \lambda_-$ it follows that the origin $(0,0)$ will be a *stable* stationary point, if and only if the real part of both eigenvalues λ_+ and λ_- is negative:

Condition for *stability* of $(0,0)$:

$$\text{re}(\lambda_+) < 0 \quad \text{and} \quad \text{re}(\lambda_-) < 0. \qquad (4.54a)$$

Complementary to (4.54) is the

Condition for *instability* of $(0,0)$:

$$\text{re}(\lambda_+) > 0 \quad \text{and/or} \quad \text{re}(\lambda_-) > 0. \qquad (4.55a)$$

In view of (4.53) the conditions (4.54) and (4.55) read in terms of trendparameters $\tilde{\kappa}$ and $\tilde{\rho}$:

Condition for *stability* of $(0,0)$:

$$\tilde{\kappa} < 1 \quad \text{and} \quad \tilde{\rho} < (\tilde{\kappa} - 1)^2 \qquad (4.54b)$$

and

Condition for *instability* of $(0,0)$:

$$\tilde{\kappa} > 1 \quad \text{and/or} \quad \tilde{\rho} > (\tilde{\kappa} - 1)^2 \qquad (4.55b)$$

These conditions have a *plausible sociological interpretation*:

If the agglomeration trend $\tilde{\kappa}$ *within* $\mathcal{P}^\mu$ and $\mathcal{P}^\nu$ is below the threshold value 1 and if simultaneously the agglomeration/segregation trends *between* $\mathcal{P}^\mu$ and $\mathcal{P}^\nu$ have either *different sign* (so that $\tilde{\rho} = \tilde{\kappa}^{\mu\nu} \tilde{\kappa}^{\nu\mu} < 0$) or are *sufficiently weak* (so that $\tilde{\rho} < (\tilde{\kappa} - 1)^2$), the homogeneous distribution and population mixture of $\mathcal{P}^\mu$ and $\mathcal{P}^\nu$ in both regions 1 and 2 is a stable migratory state. The small values of $\tilde{\kappa}$ and $\tilde{\rho}$ below the thresholds (4.54b) are indicators of small socio-cultural distances between $\mathcal{P}^\mu$ and $\mathcal{P}^\nu$ so that the homogeneous mixture of both populations is a stable state without problems.

If, on the other hand, the internal *agglomeration trend* $\tilde{\kappa}$ *within* $\mathcal{P}^\mu$ and $\mathcal{P}^\nu$ is strong and above the threshold value 1 or if, for instance, strong *reciprocal segregation trends* $\tilde{\kappa}^{\mu\nu} < 0$, $\tilde{\kappa}^{\nu\mu} < 0$ exist (so that $\tilde{\rho} = \tilde{\kappa}^{\mu\nu} \tilde{\kappa}^{\nu\mu} > (\tilde{\kappa} - 1)^2$), the homogeneous mixture of $\mathcal{P}^\mu$ and $\mathcal{P}^\nu$ becomes *unstable* and a *segregation process* sets in. Evidently, the large values of $\tilde{\kappa}$ and/or $\tilde{\rho}$ necessary for this case are indicators of a high socio-cultural profile and propinquity *within* $\mathcal{P}^\mu$ and $\mathcal{P}^\nu$ and/or a high sociocultural distance *between* $\mathcal{P}^\mu$ and $\mathcal{P}^\nu$ being the reason for this process.

4.3.3 Scenario-Simulations

The stability analysis is not sufficient for a more comprehensive insight into the behaviour of the migratory system. Therefore we present a few characteristic scenario simulations. Each simulation corresponds to a set of parameters $\{\tilde{\kappa}^{\mu\mu} = \tilde{\kappa}^{\nu\nu} = \tilde{\kappa}; \tilde{\kappa}^{\mu\nu}, \tilde{\kappa}^{\nu\mu}\}$, and to each simulation belong two Figures a and b: Figure a represents the fluxlines of the quasi-meanvalue-equations and Figure b represents the stationary solution of the master equation. For the last scenario we add a Figure c showing a typical stochastic trajectory.

For the first two scenarios we have chosen a *symmetrical and segregative reciprocal interaction between* $\mathcal{P}^\mu$ and $\mathcal{P}^\nu$

$$\tilde{\kappa}^{\mu\nu} = \tilde{\kappa}^{\nu\mu} = -\tilde{\sigma} \quad \text{where} \quad \tilde{\sigma} > 0. \tag{4.56}$$

The trendparameters of the first scenario fulfil the condition (4.54b) so that the homogeneous population mixture $(x_{st}, y_{st}) = (0,0)$ is *stable*, whereas the trend-parameters of the second scenario fulfil (4.55b) for which $(x_{st}, y_{st}) = (0,0)$ is *unstable*. The symmetrical cases (4.56) satisfy the condition of detailed balance, so that the stationary solution of the master equation has the analytical form (4.36).

For scenarios 3 and 4 we have chosen an *antisymmetrical reciprocal interaction between* $\mathcal{P}^\mu$ and $\mathcal{P}^\nu$

$$
\begin{aligned}
\tilde{\kappa}^{\mu\nu} &= -\tilde{\sigma} \quad \text{(segregative)} \\
\tilde{\kappa}^{\nu\mu} &= +\tilde{\sigma} \quad \text{(agglomerative)}
\end{aligned}
\quad \text{with} \quad \tilde{\sigma} > 0. \tag{4.57}
$$

The trendparameters of the third scenario fulfil (4.54b) so that $(x_{st}, y_{st}) = (0,0)$ is *stable*, whereas those of the fourth scenario fulfil (4.55b) so that $(x_{st}, y_{st}) = (0,0)$ is *unstable*. The choice (4.57) violates detailed balance, so that no analytical form of the stationary solution of the master equation can be constructed in this case.

The strictly symmetrical or strictly antisymmetrical choice of the reciprocal trend-parameters is of course only one out of many possible choices. We have chosen them for mathematical convenience, because in these cases the master equation and the quasimeanvalue-equations satisfy certain symmetry relations which simplify the form of their solutions.

Let us discuss these symmetry relations before going over to the concrete scenarios.

In the *symmetrical cases* (i.e. scenarios 1 and 2) with trendparameters obeying (4.56) we have the transition rates

$$w_\uparrow^\mu(m,n) = \nu(N-m)\exp[(\kappa m - \sigma n)]; \tag{4.58a}$$

$$w_\downarrow^\mu(m,n) = \nu(N+m)\exp[-(\kappa m - \sigma n)]; \tag{4.58b}$$

$$w_\uparrow^\nu(m,n) = \nu(N-n)\exp[(-\sigma m + \kappa n)]; \tag{4.58c}$$

$$w_\downarrow^\nu(m,n) = \nu(N+n)\exp[-(-\sigma m + \kappa n)] \tag{4.58d}$$

which obey the additional relations

$$w_\uparrow^\mu(-m, -n) = w_\downarrow^\mu(m, n);$$ (4.59a)

$$w_\uparrow^\nu(-m, -n) = w_\downarrow^\nu(m, n).$$ (4.59b)

Because of (4.59), the master equation (4.32) remains invariant (that means is transformed into itself) under the substitution $(m, n) \rightarrow (m'', n'') = (-m, -n)$. This means that

$$\tilde{P}(m, n; t) = P(-m, -n; t)$$ (4.60)

fulfills the same master equation as $P(m, n; t)$. Since both solutions $P(m, n; t)$ of the same master equation approach one and the same *unique stationary solution* $P_{st}(m, n)$ for $t \Rightarrow \infty$, the latter must satisfy the symmetry relation

$$P_{st}(-m, -n) = P_{st}(m, n).$$ (4.61)

Similarly one shows that to each solution $(\hat{m}(t), \hat{n}(t))$ of the quasi-meanvalue-equations (4.47) and (4.48) with trendparameters (4.56) there belongs another solution:

$$(\hat{m}''(t), \hat{n}''(t)) = (-\hat{m}(t), -\hat{n}(t)).$$ (4.62)

In the antisymmetrical cases (i.e. scenarios 3 and 4) with trendparameters obeying (4.57) we have the transition rates

$$w_\uparrow^\mu(m, n) = \nu(N - m) \exp[(\kappa m - \sigma n)];$$ (4.63a)

$$w_\downarrow^\mu(m, n) = \nu(N + m) \exp[-(\kappa m - \sigma n)];$$ (4.63b)

$$w_\uparrow^\nu(m, n) = \nu(N - n) \exp[(\sigma m + \kappa n)];$$ (4.63c)

$$w_\downarrow^\nu(m, n) = \nu(N + n) \exp[-(\sigma m + \kappa n)].$$ (4.63d)

They fulfil not only (4.59) but in addition also

$$w_\uparrow^\mu(n, -m) = w_\uparrow^\nu(m, n);$$ (4.64a)

$$w_\downarrow^\mu(n, -m) = w_\downarrow^\nu(m, n);$$ (4.64b)

$$w_\uparrow^\nu(n, -m) = w_\downarrow^\mu(m, n);$$ (4.64c)

$$w_\downarrow^\nu(n, -m) = w_\uparrow^\mu(m, n)$$ (4.64d)

so that the master equation now remains invariant under the two substitutions $(m, n) \rightarrow (m', n') = (n, -m)$ and $(m, n) \rightarrow (m'', n'') = (-m, -n)$. Consequently, the stationary solution $P_{st}(m, n)$ must now fulfil the symmetry relation

$$P_{st}(n, -m) = P_{st}(-m, -n) = P_{st}(-n, m) = P_{st}(m, n).$$ (4.65)

Similarly, to each solution $(\hat{m}(t), \hat{n}(t))$ of the quasi-meanvalue-equations now belong the other solutions

$$(\hat{m}'(t), \hat{n}'(t)) = (\hat{n}(t), -\hat{m}(t)); \qquad (4.66a)$$

$$(\hat{m}''(t), \hat{n}''(t)) = (-\hat{m}(t), -\hat{n}(t)); \qquad (4.66b)$$

$$(\hat{m}'''(t), \hat{n}'''(t)) = (-\hat{n}(t), \hat{m}(t)). \qquad (4.66c)$$

Concrete Scenarios and their Interpretation

We begin with a *preremark*:

The fluxline figures of all scenarios do not depend on the number $2N = 2M$ of members of population $\mathcal{P}^\nu$ or $\mathcal{P}^\mu$, if the scaled trendparameters $\tilde{\kappa}^{\mu\mu}, \tilde{\kappa}^{\nu\nu}, \tilde{\kappa}^{\mu\nu}, \tilde{\kappa}^{\nu\mu}$ are given. In contrast to this the stationary probability distributions *depend* on the number $2N = 2M$. The *higher* $2N$ the more shrinks the relative width of the probability peaks, and it would be extremely small for realistic population numbers of several thousands. We use the relatively small number $2N = 2M = 80$ and do this for *illustrative purposes* because then the structure of the distributions is more visible. An even more important reason for using the small number $2N = 2M = 80$ is the following: the transition rates do in reality only depend on a number of members of the own and the other population with whom a more or less *direct contact* exists. Therefore it is reasonable to restrict the consideration for the first to such smaller subgroups of $\mathcal{P}^\mu$ and $\mathcal{P}^\nu$. In these subgroups the fluctuations around the quasi-meanvalues are indeed much larger than in the total populations.

Scenario 1

Trendparameters: $\tilde{\kappa}^{\mu\mu} = \tilde{\kappa}^{\nu\nu} = \tilde{\kappa} = 0.2$ and $\tilde{\kappa}^{\mu\nu} = \tilde{\kappa}^{\nu\mu} = -\tilde{\sigma} = -0.5$.

$$(\tilde{\kappa} - 1) = -0.8 < 0; \quad \tilde{\rho} = \tilde{\sigma}^2 = 0.25 < (\tilde{\kappa} - 1)^2 = 0.64. \qquad (4.67)$$

Because of (4.67), the origin $(0,0)$ must be according to condition (4.54b) a stable stationary point which is confirmed by Figure 4.1(a). The eigenvalues λ_+ and λ_- are real.

Interpretation of Scenario 1

Figure 4.1(a) shows the evolution of the quasi-meanvalues $(x(\tau), y(\tau))$ in terms of the fluxlines of equations (4.47), (4.48). The origin $(0,0)$ describes the homogeneous mixture of both populations $\mathcal{P}^\mu$ and $\mathcal{P}^\nu$ in both regions 1 and 2, and all fluxlines converge to this point. We conclude that under low internal agglomeration trends and low reciprocal segregation trends the homogeneous mixture is approached and remains stable.

Figure 4.1(b) shows for the same parameters the stationary probability distribution which has a maximum at the point $(m, n) = (0, 0)$. However, population distributions with $(m, n) \neq (0, 0)$ are also possible, but with lower probability. The width of the distribution depends on the chosen number $2N = 2M = 80$ as already mentioned.

(a)

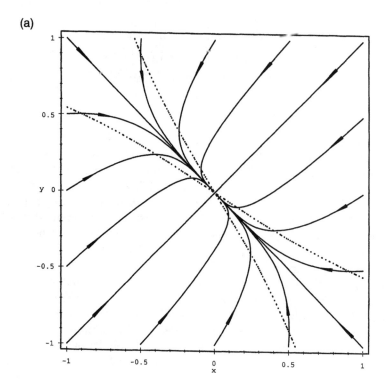

(b)

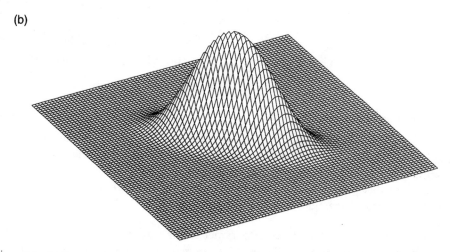

Figure 4.1 (a) Parameters $\tilde{\kappa} = 0.2$ and $\tilde{\sigma} = 0.5$. Weak internal agglomeration trend and weak symmetrical reciprocal segregation trend. All fluxlines approach the origin $(0,0)$ which describes the homogeneous mixture of populations $\mathcal{P}^{\mu}$ and $\mathcal{P}^{\nu}$ and is the only stable stationary point; (b) Parameters as in Figure 4.1(a). $2N = 80$; Unimodal stationary probability distribution peaked around the stable origin $(0,0)$.

Scenario 2

Trendparameters $\tilde{\kappa}^{\mu\mu} = \tilde{\kappa}^{\nu\nu} = \tilde{\kappa} = 0.5$ and $\tilde{\kappa}^{\mu\nu} = \tilde{\kappa}^{\nu\mu} = -\tilde{\sigma} = -1.0$.

$$(\tilde{\kappa} - 1) = -0.5 < 0; \quad \tilde{\rho} = \tilde{\sigma}^2 = 1 > (\tilde{\kappa} - 1)^2 = 0.25. \tag{4.68}$$

Because of (4.68) the origin $(0, 0)$ must be according to condition (5.55b) an unstable stationary point. This is confirmed by Figure 4.2(a). The eigenvalues λ_+ and λ_- are real.

Interpretation of Scenario 2

Figure 4.2(a) shows that the quasi-meanvalue-equations now possess two stable stationary states in the second and fourth quadrant and that the origin has become an unstable point. All fluxlines now converge to the stable stationary points. The latter describe a "ghetto situation" where the majority of one population agglomerates in one district and the majority of the other population in the other district.

Figure 4.2(b) shows that fluctuations around the stationary points of maximal probability take place and that the origin, i.e. the point of homogeneous population mixture is now a saddle point of very low probability.

Scenario 3

Trendparameters $\tilde{\kappa}^{\mu\mu} = \tilde{\kappa}^{\nu\nu} = \tilde{\kappa} = 0.5$ and $\tilde{\kappa}^{\nu\mu} = -\tilde{\kappa}^{\mu\nu} = \tilde{\sigma} = 1.0$.

$$(\tilde{\kappa} - 1) = -0.5 < 0; \quad \tilde{\rho} = -\tilde{\sigma}^2 = -1 < (\tilde{\kappa} - 1)^2 = 0.25. \tag{4.69}$$

Because of (4.69) the origin $(0, 0)$ must be according to (4.54b) a stable stationary point, which is confirmed by Figure 4.3(a). The eigenvalues λ_+ and λ_- are complex.

Interpretation of Scenario 3

Figure 4.3(a) The strong asymmetrical interaction parameters $\tilde{\kappa}^{\mu\nu} = -\tilde{\kappa}^{\nu\mu}$ between population $\mathcal{P}^\mu$ and $\mathcal{P}^\nu$ mean that $\mathcal{P}^\mu$ tries to live *apart from* population $\mathcal{P}^\nu$, whereas $\mathcal{P}^\nu$ tries to live *together with* population $\mathcal{P}^\mu$, for whatsoever socio-cultural reasons. The agglomeration trend $\tilde{\kappa}^{\mu\mu} = \tilde{\kappa}^{\nu\nu} = \tilde{\kappa}$ *within* $\mathcal{P}^\mu$ and $\mathcal{P}^\nu$ is *moderate only*. Therefore the origin $(0, 0)$, in Figure 4.3(a), i.e. the homogeneous population mixture, is still stable. The fluxlines *spiral* into the focus $(0, 0)$ because the eigenvalues are now *complex*.

Figure 4.3(b) shows the unimodal stationary probability distribution with fluctuations around the stable focus $(0, 0)$.

Scenario 4

Trendparameters $\tilde{\kappa}^{\mu\mu} = \tilde{\kappa}^{\nu\nu} = \tilde{\kappa} = 1.2$ and $\tilde{\kappa}^{\nu\mu} = -\tilde{\kappa}^{\mu\nu} = \tilde{\sigma} = 1.0$.

$$(\tilde{\kappa} - 1) = 0.2 > 0; \quad \tilde{\rho} = -\tilde{\sigma}^2 = -1 < (\tilde{\kappa} - 1)^2 = 0.04. \tag{4.70}$$

Because of (4.70) the origin $(0, 0)$ must be according to (4.55b) an unstable stationary point, which is confirmed by Figure 4.4(a). The eigenvalues λ_+ and λ_- are complex.

(a)

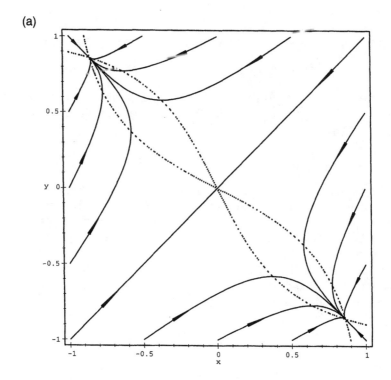

(b)

Figure 4.2 (a) Moderate internal agglomeration trend $\tilde{\kappa} = 0.5$ and strong reciprocal segregation trend $\tilde{\sigma} = 1.0$. The two stable stationary points in the second and fourth quadrant describe stable segregation of populations $\mathcal{P}^\mu$ and $\mathcal{P}^\nu$ in separate "ghettos". The fluxlines approach one of these stable equilibrium points; (b) Parameters as in Figure 4.2(a), $2N = 80$. The bimodal stationary probability distribution is peaked around the stationary points.

(a)

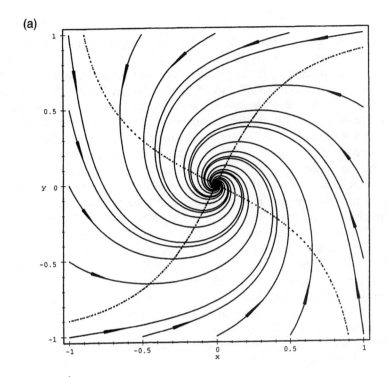

(b)

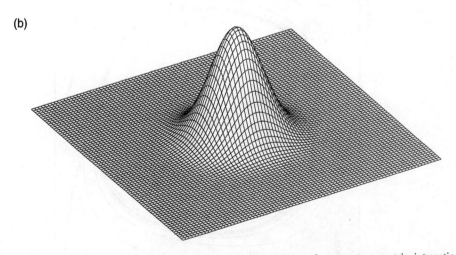

Figure 4.3 (a) Moderate internal agglomeration trend $\bar{\kappa} = 0.5$ and strong asymmetric interaction $\bar{\kappa}^{\mu\nu} = -1.0$ and $\bar{\kappa}^{\nu\mu} = +1.0$. There exists one stable focus, the origin $(0,0)$ into which all fluxlines spiral; (b) Parameters as in Figures 4.3(a), $2N = 80$. The unimodal stationary probability distributions is peaked around the stable focus $(0,0)$.

Interpretation of Scenario 4

Figure 4.4(a) describes in terms of the fluxlines of the quasi-meanvalues a migratory process which never comes to end and instead approaches a *limit cycle* which traverses all four quadrants. If the process starts, for instance, in quadrant 1, i.e. a situation where the majority of $\mathcal{P}^\mu$ and $\mathcal{P}^\nu$ lives in district 1, then $\mathcal{P}^\mu$ wishes to *evade* into the district 2 void of $\mathcal{P}^\nu$ because of its segregation trend, and to agglomerate there because of its internal agglomeration trend. This means that the quasi-mean-value trajectory traverses into quadrant 2. However, now the population $\mathcal{P}^\nu$ wishes to *invade* into the district 2 where $\mathcal{P}^\mu$ lives, because of its agglomeration trend with $\mathcal{P}^\mu$. Finally, the majority of $\mathcal{P}^\nu$ settles in district 2, too, also because of its internal agglomeration trend. This means that the trajectory has reached quadrant 3. Here the evasion–invasion process repeats so that the trajectory wanders to quadrant 4, then to quadrant 1 and so on. Either both populations live together (quadrants 1 and 3); then $\mathcal{P}^\mu$ wishes to *evade* into the region void of $\mathcal{P}^\nu$; or both populations live separately (quadrants 2 and 4); then $\mathcal{P}^\nu$ wishes to *invade* into the region where $\mathcal{P}^\mu$ lives. This migratory process describes in oversimplified manner the rather unpleasant general process observed in several multi-cultural metropoles all over the world: the sequential erosion of one district after another by asymmetric evasion–invasion interaction of populations of different cultural, religious, social, ethnic or economic background and origin.

The Figure 4.4(b) contains additional information. The quadrumodal stationary probability distribution has peaks between all four quadrants. This means that

(a)

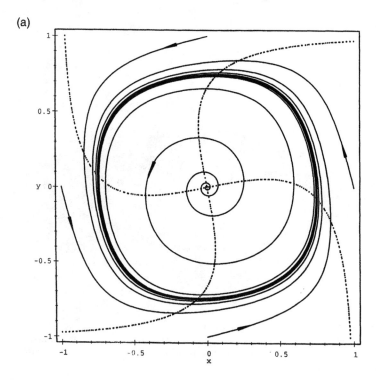

(b)

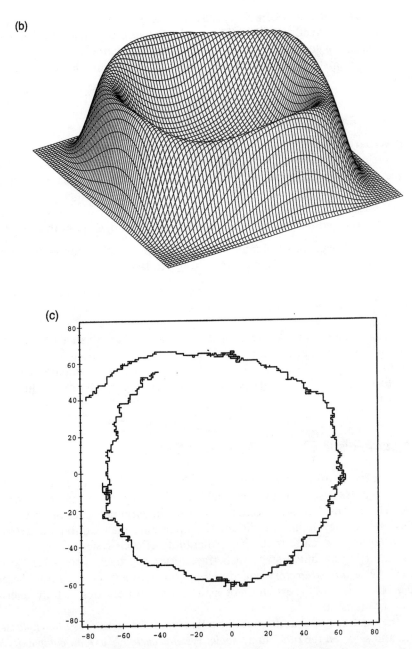

Figure 4.4 (a) Very strong internal agglomeration trend $\tilde{\kappa} = 1.2$ and strong asymmetric interaction $\tilde{\kappa}^{\mu\nu} = -1.0$ and $\tilde{\kappa}^{\nu\mu} = +10$. The origin $(0,0)$ is an unstable focus. All fluxlines approach a limit cycle; (b) Parameters as in Figure 4.4(a), $2N = 80$. The quadrumodal stationary probability has four maxima corresponding to metastable situations and ridges between the maxima along the limit cycle; (c) Parameters as in Figure 4.4(a) and 4.4(b). Example of a stochastic trajectory belonging to the transition rates (4.63). The trajectory abides around the metastable points of maximal probability and traverses at fast pace the states between the metastable situations.

there the abiding-probability of a stochastic trajectory is somewhat higher than on the ridges within the quadrants. In other words: Between the quadrants there exist *metastable states* of a somewhat longer lifetime than the *transient states* in between. Figure 4.4(c) exhibits a typical stochastic trajectory of a form which confirms this statement.

Summary

The four scenarios discussed above which have been generated in the two population – two region model by choice of different sets of trendparameters show that at least three principally different global migratory situations or "phases" can arise here:

(1)   The *homogeneous mixture* of both populations $\mathcal{P}^\mu$ and $\mathcal{P}^\nu$ in both districts.

(2)   The *ghetto-formation*, i.e. the more or less complete separation of the populations $\mathcal{P}^\mu$ and $\mathcal{P}^\nu$ by reciprocal segregation trends.

(3)   The never-ending *"invasion–evasion-migration"* in the case of asymmetrical mutual agglomeration–segregation trends.

If one considers the trendparameters $\tilde{\kappa}^{\mu\mu}, \tilde{\kappa}^{\nu\nu}, \tilde{\kappa}^{\mu\nu}, \tilde{\kappa}^{\nu\mu}$ not as constants but as *slowly changing variables*, for instance by socio-cultural accomodation- or, conversely, disintegration-processes between $\mathcal{P}^\mu$ and $\mathcal{P}^\nu$, and if then the trendparameters pass *critical values*, the migratory system will follow and undergo the corresponding *global phase transition*.

4.4   Deterministic Chaos in Migratory System

An intense research during the last decades in natural and social science has shown that many complex systems in different fields exhibit the phenomenon of *deterministic chaos*. This means that the trajectories in a low-dimensional space of a few system variables which obey nonlinear differential equations may exhibit an *extremely complex behaviour*, which restricts the predictibility of such systems:

After traversing an initial stage such trajectories approach a so-called *"strange attractor"*, i.e. a *limit-trajectory* which never returns to any point and is therefore *a-periodic*. Nevertheless the evolution of such "chaotic trajectories" is fully deterministic at every moment.

Since the existence of chaotic trajectories is one of the *signatures of complexity* of a system and since on the other hand *social systems certainly exhibit complexity*, it is a natural question whether differential equations for social processes – like our migratory equations (4.16) – are able to capture at least a part of this social complexity by leading to *chaotic solutions* or *strange attractors*. For the present model this question has been investigated in several articles [17], [18], [19], [20].

In this section we will show that the migratory equations indeed have chaotic solutions if the number of variables is larger than 3. (As it is well known, for one or two dynamic variables continuous in time, such as $m(t)$ and $n(t)$ in Section 4.3, deterministic chaos cannot exist.)

We write the equations (4.16) in the form

$$\frac{dn_i^\alpha(t)}{dt} = F_i^\alpha(\mathbf{n}) \quad \alpha = 1, 2, \ldots, P; \quad i = 1, 2, \ldots, C \tag{4.71}$$

with

$$F_i^\alpha(\mathbf{n}) = \sum_{j=1}^{C} \nu \left\{ n_j^\alpha \exp\left[u_i^\alpha(\mathbf{n}) - u_j^\alpha(\mathbf{n})\right] - n_i^\alpha \exp\left[u_j^\alpha(\mathbf{n}) - u_i^\alpha(\mathbf{n})\right] \right\}, \tag{4.72}$$

where we have slightly changed the notation by $\hat{n}_i^\alpha \Rightarrow n_i^\alpha$ and chosen the mobility factors

$$\nu_{ij}^\alpha = \nu_{ji}^\alpha = \nu. \tag{4.73}$$

For later use we introduce appropriately scaled variables

$$x_i^\alpha = C \frac{n_i^\alpha}{N^\alpha} \quad \text{with} \quad N^\alpha = \sum_{i=1}^{C} n_i^\alpha = \text{const.} \tag{4.74}$$

and write now the utility functions in the form

$$u_i^\alpha(\mathbf{n}) = \sum_{\beta=1}^{P} \kappa^{\alpha\beta} x_i^\beta + \delta_i^\alpha. \tag{4.75}$$

Evidently, for equivalent regions without preferences, i.e. for

$$\delta_i^\alpha = 0 \tag{4.76}$$

the homogeneous distribution of each of the P populations $\mathcal{P}^\alpha$ over all C regions $i = 1, 2, \ldots, C$, which amounts to

$$\tilde{n}_i^\alpha = \frac{N^\alpha}{C}; \quad \tilde{x}_i^\alpha = 1; \quad F_i^\alpha(\tilde{\mathbf{n}}) = 0 \tag{4.77}$$

is a stationary solution of (4.71), which will be the starting point of our analysis.

Before beginning with this analysis we must introduce some concepts necessary to characterize deterministic chaos.

Let us first consider an infinitesimal volume element ΔV in the $P \cdot C$-dimensional configuration space around the moving system point $n_i^\alpha(t)$. It is easy to prove that the time evolution of ΔV is given by

$$\frac{1}{\Delta V} \frac{d\Delta V}{dt} = \text{Div} \, F \equiv \sum_{\alpha=1}^{P} \sum_{i=1}^{C} \frac{\partial F_i^\alpha}{\partial n_i^\alpha}. \tag{4.78}$$

If

$$Div\, F < 0 \tag{4.79}$$

holds in a domain D of variables, the system is denoted as *dissipative in D*. In this case the original set of points contained in the volume $\Delta V(t=0)$ contracts for $t \to \infty$ asymptotically to a set within configuration space of volume zero. This asymptotic set is denoted as *the attractor*.

The migratory system turns out to be a dissipative system for the interpretable values of the trendparameters.

The *kind of the attractor* may be further specified by choosing for ΔV an infinitesimal $P \cdot C$-dimensional sphere of radius $\epsilon(0)$ which in the course of time deforms to an infinitesimal ellipsoid. Its principal axes $\epsilon_i(t)$ evolve according to

$$\epsilon_i(t) = \epsilon(0)e^{\lambda_i t}. \tag{4.80}$$

In the limit $\epsilon(0) \to 0$, this formula holds for arbitrarily long times, so that the λ_i, denoted as *Lyapunov exponents*, can be defined by:

$$\lambda_i = \lim_{t\to\infty} \lim_{\epsilon(0)\to 0} \left[\frac{1}{t} \ln \frac{\epsilon_i(t)}{\epsilon(0)} \right]. \tag{4.81}$$

Because of the contraction of the volume ΔV in dissipative systems there must always hold the relation

$$\sum_i \lambda_i < 0. \tag{4.82}$$

Different cases of Lyapunov exponents now allow a *distinction between different kinds of attractors*:

(a) If all $\lambda_i < 0$, the attractor is a *stable fixed point*, because all principal axes of the ellipsoid are simultaneously contracted.

(b) If $\lambda_1 = 0; \lambda_i < 0$ for $i = 2, 3, \ldots, PC$, one obtains a *limit cycle* as an attractor. The principal axis along the limit cycle remains uncontracted whereas all other principal axes contract.

(c) If $\lambda_1 = \lambda_2 = 0; \lambda_i < 0$ for $i = 3, 4, \ldots, PC$, then the attractor is a *torus*.

(d) If $\lambda_1 > 0$ holds for at least one, namely the largest, Lyapunov coefficient, then there exists a "*strange attractor*". Although the volume of the ellipsoid will be shrinking to zero for $t \to \infty$, at least one of its main axes will be exponentially *increasing*. This means that the distance of two originally infinitesimally neighboring points will in general be diverging over time.

We come now back to the migratory system (4.71) and follow R. Reiner [20] in his analysis of the case of two populations $\alpha = \mu, \nu$ and three regions $i = 1, 2, 3$, where because of

$$n_1^\mu + n_2^\mu + n_3^\mu = N^\mu; \quad n_1^\nu + n_2^\nu + n_3^\nu = N^\nu \tag{4.83}$$

only four relevant dynamic variables exist.

Nevertheless all kinds of attractors including strange attractors turn out to appear in this case after appropriate choice of the four trendparameters

$$((\kappa^{\alpha\beta})) = \begin{pmatrix} \kappa^{\mu\mu} & \kappa^{\mu\nu} \\ \kappa^{\nu\mu} & \kappa^{\nu\nu} \end{pmatrix} \tag{4.84}$$

in the utility functions (4.75).

At first a *linear stability analysis* shows for which trendparameter-sets the homogeneous distribution of both populations over the three regions

$$\tilde{x}_i^\alpha = 1 \quad \text{with} \quad \alpha = \mu, \nu \text{ and } i = 1, 2, 3 \tag{4.85}$$

remains *stable*. Proceeding in standard manner by putting

$$x_i^\alpha(t) = \tilde{x}_i^\alpha + \xi_i^\alpha(t) \quad \text{with} \quad \xi_i^\alpha(t) = \xi_i^\alpha(0) \exp(\lambda t) \tag{4.86}$$

in the vicinity of $\tilde{x}_i^\alpha$ and inserting (4.86) into the linearized equations (4.71) one obtains for the eigenvalues λ two two-fold degenerate values:

$$\lambda_\pm = 3 \left\{ (\kappa^{\mu\mu} + \kappa^{\nu\nu} - 1) \pm \left[(\kappa^{\mu\mu} + \kappa^{\nu\nu} - 1)^2 - ((2\kappa^{\mu\mu} - 1)(2\kappa^{\nu\nu} - 1) - 4\kappa^{\mu\nu}\kappa^{\nu\mu}) \right]^{\frac{1}{2}} \right\}. \tag{4.87}$$

The stationary solution (4.85) is stable, if the real part of λ_+ and λ_- is negative. This leads to the conditions for the parameters $\kappa^{\alpha\beta}$:

$$(\kappa^{\mu\mu} + \kappa^{\nu\nu} - 1) < 0 \tag{4.88}$$

and

$$\left[(2\kappa^{\mu\mu} - 1)(2\kappa^{\nu\nu} - 1) - 4\kappa^{\mu\nu}\kappa^{\nu\mu} \right] > 0. \tag{4.89}$$

The conditions (4.88) and (4.89) are illustrated by Figures 4.5(a) and 4.5(b) for given products $\kappa^{\mu\nu}\kappa^{\nu\mu} = 1/16$ and $\kappa^{\mu\nu}\kappa^{\nu\mu} = -1/16$, respectively, corresponding to a symmetrical or antisymmetrical interaction between the populations $\mathcal{P}^\mu$ and $\mathcal{P}^\nu$.

Secondly, the migratory system is investigated in domains of trendparameters, for which the homogeneous solution (4.85) is *unstable*. For this aim we choose the following path through the trendparameter space:

$$((\kappa^{\alpha\beta})) = \left(\begin{pmatrix} 1.0 & -1.5 \\ \kappa^{\nu\mu} & 1.0 \end{pmatrix} \right). \tag{4.90}$$

Since (4.88) is not fulfilled for sets of the kind (4.90), the homogeneous solution is *unstable* on the whole trendparameter path (4.90).

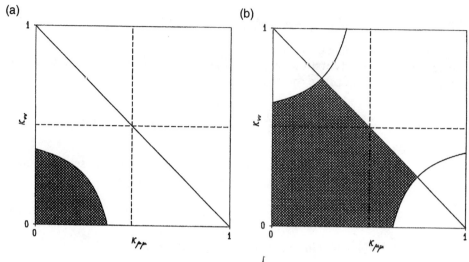

Figure 4.5 (a) Stable domain (hatched) of the homogeneous population distribution $\tilde{x}_i^\alpha = 1$ in the $\kappa^{\mu\mu}/\kappa^{\nu\nu}$- space for $\kappa^{\mu\nu} \cdot \kappa^{\nu\mu} = 1/16$; (b) Stable domain (hatched) of the homogeneous population distribution $\tilde{x}_i^\alpha = 1$ in the $\kappa^{\mu\mu}/\kappa^{\nu\nu}$- space for $\kappa^{\mu\nu} \cdot \kappa^{\nu\mu} = -1/16$.

For selected values of $\kappa^{\nu\mu}$ from $\kappa^{\nu\mu} = 0.6$ to $\kappa^{\nu\mu} = 3.0$, namely for (a) $\kappa^{\nu\mu} = 0.6$, (b) $\kappa^{\nu\mu} = 1.5$, (c) $\kappa^{\nu\mu} = 1.6$, (d) $\kappa^{\nu\mu} = 2.7$, (e) $\kappa^{\nu\mu} = 2.8$, (f) $\kappa^{\nu\mu} = 2.87$, (g) $\kappa^{\nu\mu} = 2.895$, (h) $\kappa^{\nu\mu} = 2.9$, (i) $\kappa^{\nu\mu} = 3.0$, one finds an alternating sequence of limit cycles and strange attractors. The Figures 4.6(a) to 4.6(i) depict the projections of the trajectories onto the x_1^μ/x_1^ν-plane (left hand side) and the Fourier-spectra of $\ln[x_1^\mu(\omega)]$ for this sequence of characteristic $\kappa^{\nu\mu}$-values (right hand side).

From Figure 4.6(a) to Figure 4.6(i) the following migratory phases have been traversed: From (a) to (b) there occurs a transition from a *limit cycle* to a *strange attractor*. And for the $\kappa^{\nu\mu}$-values belonging to Figures 4.6(c) through Figure 4.6(h) the system has returned to regular limit cycle behaviour. However, the transitions from (d) to (e), from (e) to (f), from (f) to (g) and from (g) to (h) each involve a *period*

(a)

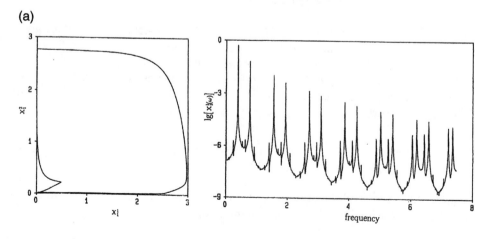

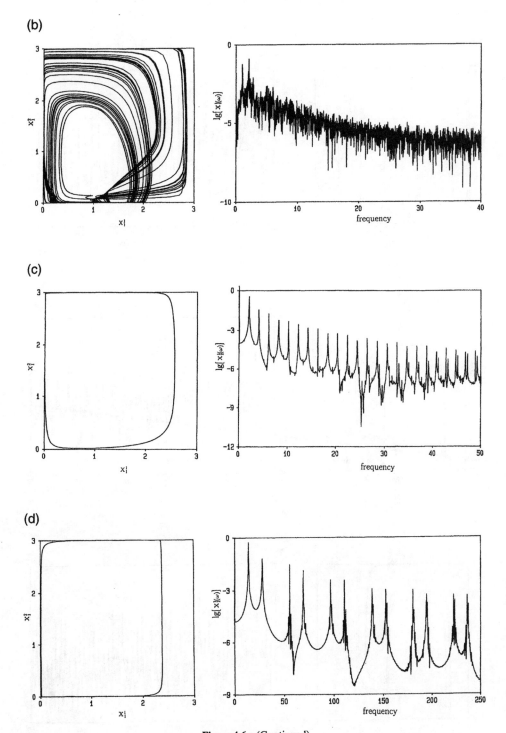

Figure 4.6 (Continued)

Figure 4.6   (Continued)

(e)

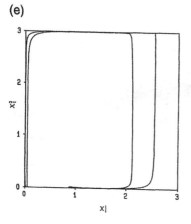
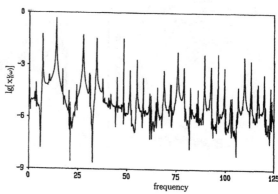

(f)

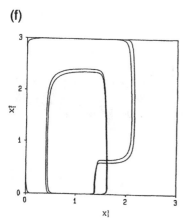
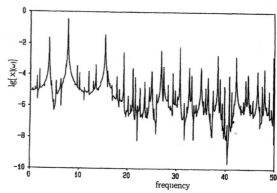

(g)

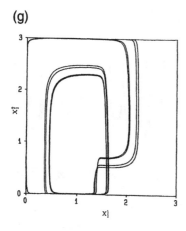
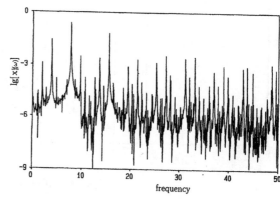

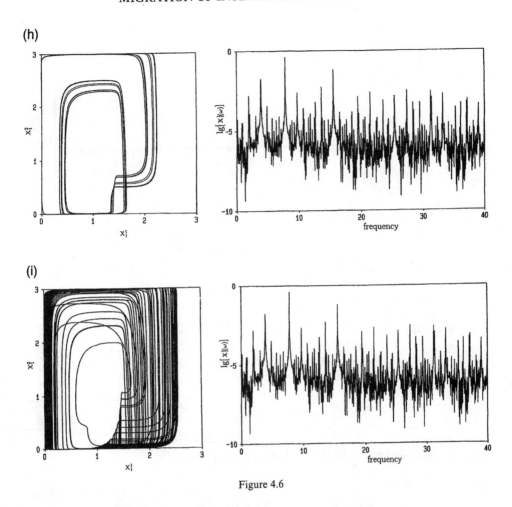

Figure 4.6

doubling of the limit cycle and a corresponding transition to a more complex Fourier-spectrum containing the half frequency and combination frequencies. After this series of period doubling processes, the transition from (h) to (i) again leads from a regular limit cycle behaviour to the *chaotic motion* of a *strange attractor* with the corresponding dense Fourier-spectrum.

The evaluation of the two largest Lyapunov exponents λ_1 and λ_2 for $0 \leq \kappa^{\nu\mu} \leq 7$ presented in Figure 4.7 confirms this picture. The intermittent alternation between regular and chaotic behaviour can be easily read off here. The limit cycle behaviour is given, if $\lambda_1 = 0, \lambda_2 < 0$, and a strange attractor exists for $\lambda_1 > 0$ and $\lambda_2 = 0$. The case $\lambda_1 = \lambda_2 = 0$ does not appear, so that the chaos is not evolving via a torus.

Summary

The result of the investigation of migratory chaos in this section shows that even relatively easily interpretable interactions between two populations, like the

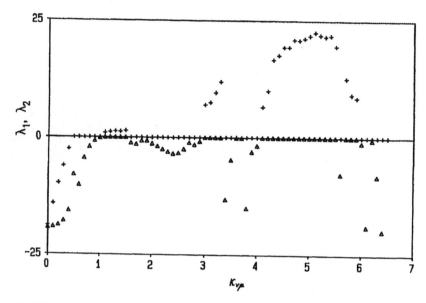

Figure 4.7 The two largest Lyapunov exponents λ_1 and λ_2 in the domain $0 \leq \kappa^{\nu\mu} \leq 7$ of the trendparameter path (4.90).

agglomeration- and segregation-trends between them, may lead in the case of three (or more) regions to a highly complex dynamic behaviour of the migratory system which also restricts its predictibility as soon as the domain of stability-providing trendparameters has been left.

4.5   Concrete Applications of Migration Theory

The preceding Sections 4.3 and 4.4 of this chapter were devoted to the description and model-based semi-quantitative explanation of some migratory phenomena of *principal interest*.

Now we will apply the general model of Section 4.2, in particular the quasi-mean-value equations (4.16), to the *empirical interregional migration*. Here we follow the main lines of argumentation of a comprehensive comparative analysis of interregional migration in the respective countries in cooperation with experts of six countries (Canada, France, Israel, Italy, Sweden, Germany) on the basis of this model [21]. Related concrete model-based evaluations are given in [22], [23].

In the application of the model to empirical case studies the procedure is in some sense *inverted*: Whereas in the scenario simulations of Sections 4.3 and 4.4 the region- and population-dependent utilities and mobilities were considered as *given functions* of population numbers and trendparameters, their numerical value and their functional form is now *to be determined from the empirical data by an appropriate regression analysis*! (Such procedures have of course also been applied to other migratory models, for instance the so called gravitation model. For a comparison of both models see Denise Pumain, Section 6.7, pp. 148–153 in [21].)

Our specific procedure consists in a *two-step regression analysis*:

In the *first step* the yearly numerical values of the regional utilities $u_i^\alpha(t)$ and interregional mobilities $\nu_{ji}^\alpha(t) = \nu_{ij}^\alpha(t)$ are determined from the yearly empirical migration data for some period in the past. (Simultaneously it can be checked whether the form of the transition rates is suitable.)

In a *second step* the utilities and mobilities are correlated with the yearly regional socio-economic key-factors, i.e. they are represented as functions of these key-factors and their weight-coefficients are determined by a specific sequential regression analysis.

If such a representation of utilities and mobilities has been found by correlating them with socio-economic key-factors in a *past period*, it is in principle possible to extrapolate the found form of the transition rates – *ceteris paribus* – into the *future* and thus to make at least a medium term forecast of the forthcoming interregional migration.

4.5.1 Determination of Regional Utilities and Interregional Mobilities from Empirical Data

At first we list in the Table 4.1 the empirical data concerning interregional migration between C regions and regional birth–death-processes, which under optimal circumstances are registered in a country at the usual time intervals ΔT of one year (or $\Delta \tau = 1$, if τ is measured in years). Since usually different subpopulations $\mathcal{P}^\alpha$ are not distinguished in such a registration we omit the index α.

By definition of the quantities in Table 4.1, $w_{ji}^{(e)}(\tau)$ coincides with the empirical migration rate from region i to region j, and $w_{j+}^{(e)}(\tau)$, $w_{j-}^{(e)}(\tau)$ coincide with the empirical birth- and death-rates, respectively, in region j, if τ is measured in *units of years*. Therefore the following relation between $n_j^{(e)}(\tau)$ and $n_j^{(e)}(\tau + \Delta \tau)$ with $\Delta \tau = 1$ must hold:

$$\frac{n_i^{(e)}(\tau + \Delta \tau) - n_i^{(e)}(\tau)}{\Delta \tau} \equiv \frac{n_i^{(e)}(\tau + 1) - n_i^{(e)}(\tau)}{1}$$

$$= \sum_{j=1}^{C}{}' w_{ij}^{(e)}(\tau) - \sum_{j=1}^{C}{}' w_{ji}^{(e)}(\tau) + w_{i+}^{(e)}(\tau) - w_{i-}^{(e)}(\tau). \quad (4.91)$$

One easily recognizes that (4.91) corresponds to the quasi-meanvalue equations (4.15), if only one homogeneous population is considered, if additional birth–death-rates are taken into account in (4.91) which have been omitted in (4.15), if the time derivative on the l.h.s. of (4.15) is approximately substituted by the difference quotient in (4.91), and if time is measured in units of years.

In particular one recognizes that the *theoretical transition rates*, which here assume the form

$$w_{ji}(\tau) = \hat{n}_i(\tau) p_{ji}(\tau) = \hat{n}_i(\tau) \cdot \nu_{ji}(\tau) \cdot \exp[u_j(\tau) - u_i(\tau)] \quad (4.92)$$

106 SOCIODYNAMICS

Table 4.1 Yearly registered data of interregional migration and regional births and deaths of one homogeneous population in C regions

Destination region	Destination population	Number of migrations in time interval $[\tau, \tau+1]$ from origin region i to destination region j					Births in$[\tau, \tau+1]$ in region j	Deaths in $[\tau, \tau+1]$ in region j
1	$n_1^e(\tau)$	—	$w_{12}^{(e)}(\tau)$	... $w_{1i}^{(e)}(\tau)$	...	$w_{1C}^{(e)}(\tau)$	$w_{1+}^e(\tau)$	$w_{1-}^e(\tau)$
2	$n_2^e(\tau)$	$w_{21}^{(e)}(\tau)$	—	... $w_{2i}^{(e)}(\tau)$	...	$w_{2C}^{(e)}(\tau)$	$w_{2+}^e(\tau)$	$w_{2-}^e(\tau)$
$\vdots$	$\vdots$	$\vdots$	$\vdots$	$\vdots$		$\vdots$	$\vdots$	$\vdots$
j	$n_j^e(\tau)$	$w_{j1}^{(e)}(\tau)$	$w_{j2}^{(e)}(\tau)$	... $w_{ji}^{(e)}(\tau)$ ...		$w_{jC}^{(e)}(\tau)$	$w_{j+}^e(\tau)$	$w_{j-}^e(\tau)$
$\vdots$	$\vdots$	$\vdots$	$\vdots$	$\vdots$		$\vdots$	$\vdots$	$\vdots$
C	$n_C^e(\tau)$	$w_{C1}^{(e)}(\tau)$	$w_{C2}^{(e)}(\tau)$	... $w_{Ci}^{(e)}(\tau)$ ...		—	$w_{C+}^e(\tau)$	$w_{C-}^e(\tau)$
origin population		$n_1^e(\tau)$	$n_2^e(\tau)$	... $n_i^e(\tau)$	...	$n_C^e(\tau)$		
origin region		1	2	... i	...	C		

have to agree with the *empirical migration rates* $w_{ji}^{(e)}(\tau)$ if the theoretical form (4.92) is fully correct, and if $\hat{n}_i(\tau)$ is identified with $n_i^{(e)}(\tau)$.

It is however not self-evident, that the empirical rates $w_{ji}^{(e)}(\tau)$ can be represented at all in the theoretical form (4.92), because in the latter form there enters the (though plausible) assumption, that it should only depend on the utilities of the origin and destination region and not on the whole system of all other regions.

This can also be seen by counting the number of empirical rates $w_{ji}^{(e)}(\tau)$ and the number of independent theoretical quantities $\nu_{ji}(\tau) = \nu_{ij}(\tau)$ and $[u_j(\tau) - u_i(\tau)]$ for C regions and T years: There exist $C(C-1) \cdot T$ empirical rates $w_{ji}^{(e)}(\tau)$, $C(C-1)/2 \cdot T$ mobilities $\nu_{ji}(\tau) = \nu_{ij}(\tau)$ and $(C-1) \cdot T$ utility differences $[u_j(\tau) - u_i(\tau)]$. The difference between the number of empirical quantities and the number of available theoretical quantities is

$$C(C-1) \cdot T - \frac{(C+2)(C-1)}{2} \cdot T = \frac{1}{2}(C-2)(C-1) \cdot T \tag{4.93}$$

which is > 0 for $C > 2$ and $T \geq 1$.

Therefore it will be a good test for the validity of the form (4.92) to make a *best fit* of the theoretical rates $w_{ji}(\tau)$ to the empirical ones $w_{ji}^{(e)}(\tau)$ by choosing optimal $\nu_{ji}(\tau)$ and $u_j(\tau)$ and to check how well they coincide with the empirical $w_{ji}^{(e)}(\tau)$.

A very convenient and in our case *analytically tractable estimation procedure* for finding the optimal yearly utilities and mobilities $u_i(\tau)$ and $\nu_{ji}(\tau)$ for the C regions and for the period of T years $(\tau = 1, 2, \ldots, T)$ in which $w_{ji}^{(e)}(\tau)$ is available consists in a *"log-linear" least square method*. It determines the optimal $u_i(\tau)$ and $\nu_{ji}(\tau)$ by minimizing the expression (where the prime $'$ at the sum over k and l excludes the values $k = l$):

$$F(\mathbf{v},\mathbf{u}) = \sum_{\tau=1}^{T}\sum_{k,l=1}^{C}{}'\left\{\ln\left[w_{kl}^{(e)}(\tau)\right] - \ln\left[n_{l}^{(e)}(\tau)\nu_{kl}(\tau)\exp(u_{k}(\tau) - u_{l}(\tau))\right]\right\}^{2} \quad (4.94)$$

under the additional constraints, that the mobilities are symmetrical:

$$\nu_{kl}(\tau) = \nu_{lk}(\tau) \quad (4.95)$$

and that the utilities can be normalized to

$$\sum_{i=1}^{C} u_{i}(\tau) = 0 \quad \text{for} \quad \tau = 1, 2, \ldots, T \quad (4.96)$$

(The constraint (4.96) can always be imposed on the $u_{i}(\tau), i = 1, \ldots, C$, because only the differences of the utilities enter the transition rates (4.92).) The minimisation of $F(\mathbf{v},\mathbf{u})$ under constraints (4.94) and (4.95) leads to the condition that its variation vanishes:

$$\delta F = \sum_{\tau=1}^{T}\left\{\sum_{i=1}^{C}\left[\frac{\partial F}{\partial u_{i}(\tau)} + \lambda(\tau)\right]\delta u_{i}(\tau) + \sum_{i,j}{}'\frac{1}{2}\left[\frac{\partial F}{\partial \nu_{ij}(\tau)} + \frac{\partial F}{\partial \nu_{ji}(\tau)}\right]\delta \nu_{ji}(\tau)\right\} \overset{!}{=} 0. \quad (4.97)$$

Here, the constraints (4.94) and (4.95) have been taken into account by the Lagrangian parameter $\lambda(\tau)$ and by $\delta \nu_{ji}(\tau) = \delta \nu_{ij}(\tau)$. Otherwise the variations $\delta u_{i}(\tau)$ and $\delta \nu_{ji}(\tau)$ are independent. Therefore, (4.97) is only fulfilled, if holds:

$$\frac{\partial F}{\partial u_{i}(\tau)} + \lambda(\tau) = 0 \quad \text{for} \quad i = 1, 2, \ldots, C; \text{ and } \tau = 1, 2, \ldots, T \quad (4.98)$$

and

$$\frac{\partial F}{\partial \nu_{ji}(\tau)} + \frac{\partial F}{\partial \nu_{ij}(\tau)} = 0 \quad \text{for} \quad i,j = 1, 2, \ldots, C; \text{ where } i \neq j \text{ and } \tau = 1, 2, \ldots, T. \quad (4.99)$$

Making use of (4.94) one obtains

$$\frac{\partial F}{\partial u_{i}(\tau)} = \sum_{k=1}^{C}{}'2\left\{\ln[\nu_{ik}(\tau)] + [u_{i}(\tau) - u_{k}(\tau)] - \ln\left[p_{ik}^{(e)}(\tau)\right]\right.$$
$$\left. - \ln[\nu_{ki}(\tau)] + [u_{i}(\tau) - u_{k}(\tau)] + \ln\left[p_{ki}^{(e)}(\tau)\right]\right\}$$
$$= \sum_{k=1}^{C}{}'4\left\{[u_{i}(\tau) - u_{k}(\tau)] - \frac{1}{2}\ln\left[\frac{p_{ik}^{(e)}(\tau)}{p_{ki}^{(e)}(\tau)}\right]\right\} \quad (4.100)$$

and

$$\frac{\partial F}{\partial u_{ji}(\tau)} = \frac{2}{v_{ji}(\tau)} \left\{ \ln[v_{ji}(\tau)] + [u_j(\tau) - u_i(\tau)] - \ln\left[p_{ji}^{(e)}(\tau)\right] \right\}, \tag{4.101}$$

where we have introduced the empirical individual transition rate

$$p_{ji}^{(e)}(\tau) = \frac{w_{ji}^{(e)}(\tau)}{n_i^{(e)}(\tau)} \tag{4.102}$$

and have used $v_{ik}(\tau) = v_{ki}(\tau)$. The conditions (4.98) and (4.99) for the optimal $u_i(\tau)$ and $v_{ji}(\tau)$ now take the form:

$$\sum_{k=1}^{C}{}' 4\left\{ [u_i(\tau) - u_k(\tau)] - \frac{1}{2}\ln\left[\frac{p_{ik}^{(e)}(\tau)}{p_{ki}^{(e)}(\tau)}\right] \right\} + \lambda(\tau) = 0 \tag{4.103}$$

and, again using $v_{ik}(\tau) = v_{ki}(\tau)$:

$$\left\{ \ln\left[v_{ji}^2(\tau)\right] - \ln\left[p_{ji}^{(e)}(\tau)p_{ij}^{(e)}(\tau)\right] \right\} = 0. \tag{4.104}$$

Evidently, equations (4.103) and (4.104) are uncoupled equations for the determination of $u_i(\tau)$ and $v_{ji}(\tau) = v_{ij}(\tau)$, respectively. At first we determine the value of the Lagrangian parameter $\lambda(\tau)$: Taking the sum over $i = 1, 2, \ldots, C$ of (4.103) one obtains:

$$\lambda(\tau) = \frac{2}{C}\sum_{i,k}{}' \ln\left[\frac{p_{ik}^{(e)}(\tau)}{p_{ki}^{(e)}(\tau)}\right] = 0. \tag{4.105}$$

Thereupon $u_i(\tau)$ can be determined uniquely, if the constraint (4.96) is utilized in equation (4.103). The result is:

$$u_i(\tau) = \frac{1}{2C}\sum_{k=1}^{C}{}' \ln\left[\frac{p_{ik}^{(e)}(\tau)}{p_{ki}^{(e)}(\tau)}\right] \quad \text{for} \quad i = 1, 2, \ldots, C \text{ and } \tau = 1, 2, \ldots, T. \tag{4.106}$$

Finally, (4.104) yields:

$$v_{ji}(\tau) = v_{ij}(\tau) = \left[p_{ji}^{(e)}(\tau)p_{ij}^{(e)}(\tau)\right]^{\frac{1}{2}}$$
$$\text{for} \quad j, i = 1, 2, \ldots, C, \text{ where } j \neq i, \text{ and } \tau = 1, 2, \ldots, T. \tag{4.107}$$

The quality of the fitted theoretical expressions $w_{ji}(\tau)$ of (4.92) in comparison to the empirical transition rates $w_{ji}^{(e)}(\tau)$ can now be checked in concrete cases. In the

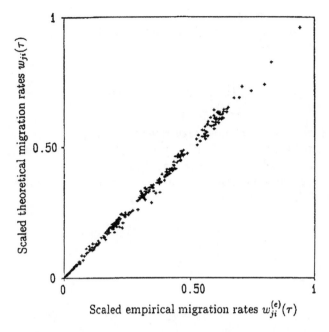

Figure 4.8 Theoretical least square fitted migration rates $w_{ji}(\tau)$ plotted against empirical migration rates $w_{ji}^{(e)}(\tau)$ in a concrete example.

book [21] the Federal Republic of Germany (FRG) was among other countries investigated in this way. It consisted (before reuniting with East Germany) of $C = 11$ Federal States and the registration of interregional migration between them was considered for a period of $T = 27$ years. This led to $C(C - 1) \cdot T = 2970$ empirical migration rates $w_{ji}^{(e)}(\tau)$ to which the $\frac{1}{2}(C + 2)(C - 1) \cdot T = 1782$ mobilities and utilities had to be fitted according to the formulas (4.107) and (4.106). In the Figure 4.8 the 2970 *theoretical* migration rates (4.92) (variable y) are depicted in comparison to the corresponding *empirical* migration rates (variable x). For perfect coincidence between theoretical and empirical rates all points should lie on the line $y = x$. The Figure 4.8 shows that this is fulfilled in very good approximation.

4.5.2 The Dependence of Regional Utilities on Socio-Economic Key-Factors

In a second step we now correlate the empirically determined utilities (see formula (4.106)) to regional socio-economic variables. For this aim we make use of a "ranking regression formalism" (see [19] and [21]) yielding a ranking of socio-economic variables with respect to the degree of their correlation to the just estimated regional utilities. The utilized mathematical method can be seen as a Schmidt orthogonalisation procedure in a vector space of finite dimension, combined with a selection principle making the sequential choice of base vectors unambiguous.

Henceforth we consider the regional utilities $u_i(\tau) \equiv u(i, \tau)$, with $i = 1, 2, \ldots, C$ and $\tau = 1, 2, \ldots, T$ as elements $|\mathbf{u}\rangle$ (in Dirac notation) of a $C \cdot T$-dimensional vector space $\mathcal{V}$ with the (real) scalar product

$$\langle h \,|\, g \rangle = \sum_{i=1}^{C} \sum_{\tau=1}^{T} h(i, \tau) g(i, \tau). \tag{4.108}$$

Vectors for which $\langle h \,|\, g \rangle = 0$ holds are denoted as "orthogonal". Furthermore, we go over from arbitrary positive definite region- and time-dependent socio-economic variables $\tilde{\Omega}^\alpha(i, \tau)$ (of which we guess that they may have some relevance for the interregional migratory process) to scaled dimensionless variables of vanishing regional mean-value (like the utilities because of (4.96))

$$\Omega^\alpha(i, \tau) = \frac{\tilde{\Omega}^\alpha(i, \tau) - \bar{\tilde{\Omega}}^\alpha(\tau)}{\bar{\tilde{\Omega}}^\alpha(\tau)} \tag{4.109}$$

with

$$\bar{\tilde{\Omega}}^\alpha(\tau) = \frac{1}{C} \sum_{i=1}^{C} \tilde{\Omega}^\alpha(i, \tau). \tag{4.110}$$

The $\Omega^\alpha(i, \tau)$ are also considered as vectors $|\Omega^\alpha\rangle \in \mathcal{V}$. Vectors with norm $\|\Omega^\alpha\| = \langle \Omega^\alpha \,|\, \Omega^\alpha \rangle^{\frac{1}{2}} = 1$ are denoted by $|\hat{\Omega}^\alpha\rangle$.

Now we try to represent the utility vector $|u\rangle$ in successive approximation *as a linear combination of those socio-economic variables $|\Omega^\alpha\rangle$ which correlate best with $|u\rangle$. This is achieved by an iterative procedure. The first two steps of it are illustrated here.*

The first iteration step

Among the normalized $|\hat{\Omega}^\alpha\rangle$ one has to find the "optimal" one, henceforth named $|\hat{\Omega}^1\rangle$, leading to a decomposition of $|u\rangle$ as

$$|u\rangle = a_1 |\hat{\Omega}^1\rangle + |u_{\perp 1}\rangle \tag{4.111}$$

with a rest term $|u_{\perp 1}\rangle$ of minimal norm. That means, $|\hat{\Omega}^1\rangle$ must be the vector "most parallel" to $|u\rangle$ among all $|\Omega^\alpha\rangle$. The minimal norm of $|u_{\perp 1}\rangle$ is obtained for

$$a_1 = \langle \hat{\Omega}^1 \,|\, u \rangle \quad \text{hence} \quad \langle \hat{\Omega}^1 \,|\, u_{\perp 1} \rangle = 0. \tag{4.112}$$

The second iteration step

Each of the remaining socio-economic variables $|\Omega^\alpha\rangle$, $(\alpha \neq 1)$ can now be decomposed into a component parallel to $|\hat{\Omega}^1\rangle$ and a remaining term which is orthogonal to $|\hat{\Omega}_1\rangle$ and is henceforth named as $|\Omega^\alpha_{\perp 1}\rangle$, by the formula:

$$|\Omega^\alpha\rangle = c_{1\alpha}|\hat{\Omega}^1\rangle + |\Omega^\alpha_{\perp 1}\rangle \quad \text{for} \quad \alpha = 2, 3, \ldots$$
$$\text{with} \quad c_{1\alpha} = \langle\hat{\Omega}^1|\Omega^\alpha\rangle \quad \text{and} \quad \langle\hat{\Omega}^1|\Omega^\alpha_{\perp 1}\rangle = 0. \tag{4.113}$$

Among the normalized $|\hat{\Omega}^\alpha_{\perp 1}\rangle$, namely those components of $|\Omega^\alpha\rangle$ which are not *parallel* but *orthogonal* to $|\hat{\Omega}^1\rangle$, one has again to find the optimal one, enumerated as $|\hat{\Omega}^2_{\perp 1}\rangle$, which is "most parallel to $|u_{\perp 1}\rangle$", that means which leads to a rest term $|u_{\perp 2}\rangle$ of minimal norm in the decomposition as

$$|u_{\perp 1}\rangle = a_2|\hat{\Omega}^2_{\perp 1}\rangle + |u_{\perp 2}\rangle$$
$$\text{with} \quad a_2 = \langle\hat{\Omega}^2_{\perp 1}|u_{\perp 1}\rangle \quad \text{hence} \quad \langle\hat{\Omega}^2_{\perp 1}|u_{\perp 2}\rangle = 0. \tag{4.114}$$

After the second iteration step the representation of $|u\rangle$ reads

$$|u\rangle = a_1|\hat{\Omega}^1\rangle + a_2|\hat{\Omega}^2_{\perp 1}\rangle + |u_{\perp 2}\rangle. \tag{4.115}$$

Evidently this iteration can be continued until a rest term $|u_{\perp\gamma}\rangle$ of sufficiently small norm is obtained in step γ, and the representation of $|u\rangle$ reads:

$$|u\rangle = a_1|\hat{\Omega}^1\rangle + a_2|\hat{\Omega}^2_{\perp 1}\rangle + \cdots + a_\gamma|\hat{\Omega}^\gamma_{\perp(\gamma-1)}\rangle + |u_{\perp\gamma}\rangle$$
$$\text{with} \quad \langle\hat{\Omega}^\beta_{\perp(\beta-1)}|u_{\perp\gamma}\rangle = 0 \quad \text{for} \quad \beta = 1, 2, \ldots, \gamma. \tag{4.116}$$

Neglecting the rest term $|u_{\perp\gamma}\rangle$ and going back to the original, non-normalized and non-orthogonal socio-economic variables (4.109) one finally obtains the representation of $|u\rangle$ in the form:

$$|u\rangle = \sum_{\alpha=1}^{\gamma} b_\alpha|\Omega^\alpha\rangle, \tag{4.117}$$

where the weight coefficients b_α, $\alpha = 1, 2, \ldots, \gamma$ have been determined by the iteration procedure and an automatic selection of the γ "most important" socio-economic variables, i.e. the "key-factors", has taken place.

In the application to the question of interregional migration in six countries (see [21]) it turned out that the two most important socio-economic variables (in the definition of the iteration scheme!) were the *regional personal variables*:

$$\tilde{\Omega}_1(i, \tau) = n_i(\tau); \quad \tilde{\Omega}_2(i, \tau) = n_i^2(\tau) \tag{4.118}$$

with the corresponding scaled dimensionless variables

$$\Omega_1(i, \tau) = \frac{n_i(\tau) - \bar{n}(\tau)}{\bar{n}(\tau)}; \quad \Omega_2(i, \tau) = \frac{n_i^2(\tau) - \overline{n^2}(\tau)}{\overline{n^2}(\tau)}. \tag{4.119}$$

Therefore, the regional utilities could always be decomposed as follows:

$$u_i(\tau) = s_i(\tau) + \delta_i(\tau) \qquad (4.120)$$

with a population- or size-dependent term

$$s_i(\tau) = \kappa\Omega_1(i,\tau) + \sigma\Omega_2(i,\tau) \qquad (4.121)$$

and a term $\delta_i(\tau)$ describing the regional preferences being composed of other socio-economic factors.

It turned out that $\kappa > 0$ and $\sigma < 0$, so that the first term of $s_i(\tau)$, describes the agglomeration in regions of high $n_i(\tau)$, whereas the second term of $s_i(\tau)$ leads to a saturation of this agglomeration for very high values of $n_i(\tau)$.

Concerning the composition of $\delta_i(\tau)$, the iteration procedure selected in the case of Germany – out of many other socio-economic variables at disposal – only four regional variables of "migratory relevance":

$$\begin{aligned}
OS_i &= \text{overnight stays per capita in region } i\\
EI_i &= \text{export structure index in region } i\\
UR_i &= \text{unemployment rate in region } i\\
TS_i &= \text{quota of employment in tertiary sector in region } i
\end{aligned} \qquad (4.122)$$

The explicit representation of $|u\rangle$ in terms of socio-economic key-factors then reads:

$$\begin{aligned}
u_i(\tau) = &\, 1.037\Omega_1(i,\tau) - 0.180\Omega_2(i,\tau) + 0.156OS_i(\tau) + 0.474EI_i(\tau-2)\\
&- 0.083UR_i(\tau) + 0.193TS_i(\tau). \qquad (4.123)
\end{aligned}$$

Further details of the analysis and its interpretation can be found in [21].

A final remark should be made concerning the question whether the key-factors have a *causal* meaning or not. It is of course tempting to guess that variables which have a strong spatio-temporal *correlation* to the regional utilities or attractiveness $u_i(\tau)$, do also have a *causative influence* on the migratory process. The answer is, that this *can be so* but *needs not to be so!* Evidently, the overnight stays per capita in region i are not the *cause* for regional attractiveness but they may well be an *indicator* for it, because many businessmen and many tourists staying overnight in a region are an indication that this region is a prosperous one; and this fact may then be the cause of attracting migrants.

II.2 Applications to Sociology

Introductory Remarks

In the applications of the modelling concepts of sociodynamics to problems of *sociology* the *personal variables* describing the status, the attitude and the behaviour of persons in their different roles are in the foreground. However, the observed effects are in general *not spatial* – as in population dynamics – but concern different aspects of mental relations between people and the corresponding structure of the society.

In Chapters 5 and 6 two such aspects will be treated. In Chapter 5 one of the major problems of sociology, the formation and evolution of social groups, is considered from the formalized standpoint of a mathematical model. The model tries to capture those interactions *between* groups, which are present within their specific intentions and purposes. Chapter 6 is devoted to a problem of political sociology of dramatic global effect: the behaviour of citizens in the vicinity of a phase-transition from a liberal to a totalitarian political system, or vice versa.

In the Chapters 5 and 6 somewhat different "windows of perception" will be utilized: Chapter 5 uses a "mesoscopic" scale of perception and goes into some detail concerning the role of and the relation between members of a group. Instead, Chapter 6 uses a rather global coarse grained scale of perception neglecting many finer details within the citizenry. However, such an oversimplification finds a partial justification in the fact that in politically revolutionary situations and their pre- and post-phases certain psycho-political alignments and mergence-processes take place which allow a less differentiated and more global treatment.

5. Group Dynamics: The Rise and Fall of Interacting Social Groups

5.1 Introduction

The dynamics of social groups can be considered to be one of the most general and fundamental problems of sociology. The society, being the main subject of sociology, is constituted by interacting human individuals. However, they are not an amorphous crowd. The interaction-"forces" between the individuals generated by material, emotional and mental needs and desires concerning different aspects of life lead to a *selforganization of structures* within the society. These structures take the form of *groups* (i.e. ensembles of individuals with certain common goals and objectives). Each individual will in general *simultaneously* belong to *several groups* assuming the role of a nominal or leading member in each of them. These groups will belong to different "dimensions" or sectors of social life, for instance to the religious, cultural, political, economical or leisure sector. Nevertheless there exist common structures and a common kind of dynamics within and between all sorts of groups. The model presented here will focus on this common structure and dynamics and leave out the differences.

Many verbal or formal investigations of social groups consider their static structure and *stationary equilibrium state*. However, the restriction to the stationary state has one disadvantage: Many "forces" and causes constituting a group mutually *compensate* in the equilibrium situation. Only the full *dynamics* of group evolution reveals the relevance of certain partial structures and causes whereas *their effect may be concealed in the equilibrium state*. Therefore our interest will be mainly in the *dynamics of groups*, in particular if they influence each other.

The "*window of perception*" of the model will be on a *mesoscale* or *differentiated macroscale*.

The *extensive* personal variables (scaling proportional to group size) will describe in some detail the *hierarchical structure* of a group. Furthermore it will prove important to introduce at least one *intensive* personal variable (scaling independently of group size), namely the *solidarity variable* which is responsible for the formation of an *internalized consciousness of group identity* in each member of the group.

115

On the other hand, *network-variables* belonging to the *microscale* and describing in detail the interrelations between group members which generate the status of each member, are *not included* in the model. This can be justified by invoking the "*slaving principle*" according to which the microvariables can be *eliminated* if one is only interested in the *resultant dynamics of the macrovariables*.

Because of the importance of the phenomenon of group formation there does of course exist an extensive literature about it. Our brief remarks only refer to the *embedding* of our model design into some strains of argumentation in this literature.

We begin with mentioning the book of *Burt* [1] giving a survey about network models which give the background on the microscale to our mesoscopic model. He distinguishes between *relational approaches* focussing on the relationship between a pair of actors and *positional approaches* focussing on the pattern of relations which defines the position (status) of an actor in a system of actors. The hierarchical status level structure of a group which will be used in our model indeed depends on underlying network relations, because, according to Burt, "all statuses are network positions in the sense of being defined by patterns of relations linking status occupants with other actors in the system".

Homans [2], [3] analyses small groups with preferentially direct interaction between their members. After structuring the inter-individual relations by a few micro-sociological variables like sentiments and pair-interactions he goes beyond them by including *emergent group customs, norms and practices* and thus is aware of the elements of group dynamics. His qualitative investigation shows how *internalized intensive personal variables* like customs and norms emerge from *inter-individual interactions* and form a background for the introduction of the solidarity variable in our model.

Between the mathematical models of *Coleman* [4] and our model one can find several parallels but also differences. The core of his model consists of adaptation processes, namely adjustment processes of values of certain goods, and an exchange process of goods between agents. His equations are *linear exchange equations*, the solutions of which approach a unique equilibrium state, whereas our model leads to *nonlinear* generalized migration between status levels with more complex solutions.

Durkheim [5], [6], [7] has contributed much to the understanding of the role of solidarity in groups and in the modern society at all. For its explanation he invokes *rational necessities* (e.g. interdependence by division of labour in differentiated societies) as well as *emotional bonds* (cults, quasi-religious bonds). Thus, intensive personal variables with a transpersonal effect like the solidarity may have *rational as well as emotional* causes.

Parsons [8], [9], who generalizes the ideas of Durkheim, stresses the *normative character* of the sources of solidarity. According to him, any social structure is defined by *roles* and *collectivities, norms* and *values*. In view of our model one could say that the *roles* and *collectivities* are captured by the *extensive personal variables* (the group configuration) whereas *norms* and *values* belong to the kind of internalized intensive variables (with transpersonal effect), of which the solidarity is a representative.

Collins [10], [11] also starting from Durkheim, does not follow the structuralistic–functionalistic line but focusses on the *emotional* and *ideological* causes of solidarity within groups. His concepts do already imply the process character, e.g. when speaking about mutual amplification effects. Essentially his arguments amount to explaining the emergence of solidarity and group dynamics as a selforganisation process via a feedback loop of mutually enhancing components.

Any formalisation of group dynamics, including our model, must take into account the *free rider problem*. An advanced and more recent treatment of this problem is that of *Glance and Huberman* [12]. They introduce the plausible aspect that cooperating people expect that their decision will positively influence other agents to do the same in the future. However, this effect depends on the *size of the group* and becomes effective for smaller groups only where "outbreaks of cooperation" can occur. After all, the conclusion derivable from their article is that under appropriate conditions (not too large groups) cooperation (i.e. voluntary compliance with obligations) is maintainable against abuse even without coercion. Another approach to the micro-foundation of cooperation within a society has been developed by Axelrod [13] using the concept of *prisoner's dilemma* in repeated contracting processes between individuals.

In a macro-sociological model like ours the free-rider effect can only be taken into account in a lump manner: The evolution equation for solidarity will contain the solidarity-reducing influence of free-riders.

Hechter's approach in his book about the principles of group solidarity [14] is a macro-sociological one and therefore of particular relevance for our formal modelling approach. After a concise comparative consideration of *normativistic, functionalistic* and *structuralistic* approaches he prefers concepts of *rational choice* theory because they lend themselves better to *operationalisation*. The pure rationalists' operational concept of solidarity (dropping internalization of norms, emotional satisfaction, voluntary insight in group functions) then is to define solidarity as a function of the extent of corporate obligations and the probability of compliance with these obligations.

It seems, however, that the concept of "rationality" in the decision making of individuals must be *generalized*: It is a fact of social psychology that norms and ideologies of a group *are* to some extent internalized by its members. However, this implies that the personal estimation of benefits and costs also takes place from a *new perspective*.

In our formalization of group dynamics we have implicitly used such a *generalized concept of rational choice* because the motivation potentials of our model do not only depend on individual gains and losses in a narrow sense but also on personal satisfactions or frustrations depending on the global state of the group including its level of solidarity.

Very recently, a new effort was undertaken by the authors *Farraro and Doreian* and further authors to capture and formalize the *problem of solidarity* [15]. This author (together with D. Helbing) has also contributed to that book where the present model is exhibited with other scenario simulations so that both presentations are complementary. In particular the relation between group formation and the role of solidarity is stressed there.

Finally we mention that the formation and persistence of social groups of a specific identity is a *great example of General System Theory*, where its concepts can be tested.

In particular, a *cyclical relationship* can be observed between different causative factors establishing a group and comprising the concepts of (generalized) rational choice, structure, function and norm. All these elements are embedded into a *feedback loop* which makes it impossible to isolate one element and to construct a "linear" causal nexus.

Let us suggest in *qualitative* terms such a stylized cyclic causation scheme for the formation of groups, which however is certainly incomplete.

(1)   Individuals coalesce in nascent groups by virtue of sharing common (material or immaterial) interests.

(2)   Simple collective structures are built up under individual rational aspects.

(3)   The simple group structures bring along and carry simple functions facilitating the pursuit of the common interests.

(4)   Compliance with obligations is still fully voluntary and needs no norms because of the close direct interaction between the few members of the small group.

(5)   It is observed by the members of the growing group that its stabilizing structure can carry extended functions leading to power and influence of the group as a whole, and thereby also of its individual members. However, also the individual obligations are transforming and going beyond the original extent.

(6)   Feelings of group identity and solidarity as entities of their own begin to emerge and manifest formulations of group objectives begin to develop. Rules consolidating to norms begin to be practised and entrained.

(7)   A transition takes place from inter-individual cooperation and rationality to "transpersonal" solidarity and formulations of group ideology. This facilitates further growth and efficiency of the group because *direct* interactions are no longer indispensable but partially substitutable by the *indirect* bond of group-solidarity and -ideology.

(8)   The loss of direct inter-individuality on the one side favours free-riders but on the other side simultaneously stabilizes norms which, if necessary, can justify sanctions and enforce the compliance with obligations.

(9)   The now fully stabilizing structures include hierarchical levels and lead to an efficient performance of functions secured by fully consolidated norms.

(10) The stabilized structural, functional and normative system of the group acts back on the members of the group by psychological internalisation processes. The personal identification with the transpersonal "superego" of the group leads to a transformation of the perspectives of estimation of benefits and costs, of satisfaction and frustration in the sense that *group ideals* are now partially taken over as *personal desires*. The subsequent personal decisions and/or actions take place in terms of *generalized rational choice*.

(11) Equipped with the transformed mentality of "ideologically modified rationalists" there begins a new round of organizing new levels of structure, of emergence

of new functions and the "bottom up" and "top down" interactions within the group may lead to a slow inherent transformation of the shape and the objective of the group.

(12)   The inner slow change of structure, function and ideology within a group together with the interfering or even undermining influence of competing groups does not always lead to a consolidation of a given group but may also lead to erosion, decline and even complete breakdown of that group. Only if the original purposes and ideas survive they can in such cases become the germ of a renewed group.

5.2   The Design of the Model

A mathematical model of group dynamics can only be a *projection* of the full qualitative conceptualisation of this process to the character and the evolution of a few variables. In our case they characterize the group on the *meso-level*.

Although group-purposes and group-ideology are the driving forces behind group-evolution they *do not show up explicitly* but are hidden in the formalisation of the motivations and decisions of the group members. Thus the model captures just those features of group evolution which *independently of the concrete purpose and ideology* are always existent and comparable.

The design of the model takes place along the lines of Chapter 3 by filling out the modelling steps by concrete proposals for the choice of variables, the transition rates, and the form of the motivation potentials, and thereupon by setting up the equations of evolution.

5.2.1   The Key-Variables

We restrict the model to *one* sector or *one* dimension of social life (for instance only to political or only to the cultural sector). In *one sector* it can be assumed that the groups are *non-overlapping*, because individuals will normally be members of at most *one group* in each sector. For instance, memberships in political parties are mutually exclusive. The same holds for the parishs of different religious denominations.

Extensive Personal Variables

Let us under this restriction consider G non-overlapping groups $G_i, G_j, \ldots$, with $i, j = 1, 2, \ldots, G$, belonging to *one sector of social life*. We want to describe the fact that each group develops a *hierarchy* of organisational *sublevels* so that the members of them possess *different degrees of influence, responsibility and obligation*. Therefore we introduce in each group G_i a *hierarchy of status levels* $h, k = 0, 1, 2, \ldots, H_i$ reaching from nominal membership $h = 0$ over staff levels up to the leading level $h = H_i$, where each level has benefits and advantages but also charges and obligations of its own. In each group G_i the total number of its members N_i is distributed over the status levels h in a characteristic manner. If N_i^h denotes the *number of members of G_i occupying the status level h*, one obtains the obvious relation

$$N_i = \sum_{h=0}^{H_i} N_i^h. \tag{5.1}$$

A member of group G_i with status h will be said to be in state (ih). Furthermore we introduce the number N_0^0 of individuals being involved in *none* of the groups and refer to these as to the *crowd of individuals*. For these individuals we do not distinguish any status levels, i.e. $N_0^0 \equiv N_0$.

Since double memberships in one and the same social sector are excluded by assumption, we have the relation

$$N_0^0 + \sum_{i=1}^{G} N_i = N_0^0 + \sum_{i=1}^{G} \sum_{h=0}^{H_i} N_i^h = N \tag{5.2}$$

where N is the total number of individuals in the social system under consideration. The set of numbers

$$\begin{aligned}
\mathbf{N} &= \{N_0^0; N_1^0, \ldots, N_1^{H_1}; \ldots; N_i^0, \ldots, N_i^h, \ldots, N_i^{H_i}; \ldots; N_G^0, \ldots, N_G^{H_G}\} \\
&= \{N_0^0; \mathbf{N}_1; \ldots; \mathbf{N}_i; \ldots; \mathbf{N}_G\}
\end{aligned} \tag{5.3}$$

is denoted as (one out of many possible) *group configuration*, where $\mathbf{N}_i = \{N_i^0, \ldots, N_i^{H_i}\}$ is the *group configuration* of G_i.

Furthermore we introduce the *shifted group configuration*

$$\begin{aligned}
\mathbf{N}_{ji}^{kh} =\Big\{& N_0^0; N_1^0, \ldots, N_1^{H_1}; \ldots; N_j^0, \ldots, (N_j^k + 1), \ldots, N_j^{H_j}; \ldots; \\
& N_i^0, \ldots, (N_i^h - 1), \ldots, N_i^{H_i}; \ldots; N_G^0, \ldots, N_G^{H_G}\Big\}
\end{aligned} \tag{5.4}$$

arising from $\mathbf{N}$ after the transition of one individual from state (ih) into state (jk).

From the group configuration further variables can immediately be derived. Evidently

$$\sum_{k=0}^{h-1} N_i^k = \text{personnel below status } h \tag{5.5}$$

is the number of all subordinates of the status level h in group G_i and the *average number of subordinates of one member with status h in G_i* is given by

$$n_i^h = \sum_{k=0}^{h-1} \frac{N_i^k}{N_i^h}. \tag{5.6}$$

It is plausible to assume that the potential *influence and power* of a staff member of G_i with status h is more or less proportional to the number of members subordinate to him plus himself. Therefore we introduce the *potential influence in state (i, h)* as

$$i_i^h(\mathbf{N}_i) = n_i^h + 1 = \sum_{k=0}^{h} \frac{N_i^k}{N_i^h} \quad i = 1, 2, \ldots, G. \tag{5.7}$$

An indicator of the *total* (internal as well as external) *potential influence* and power of group G_i can be defined as the sum of the i_i^h of all its members:

$$i_i(\mathbf{N}_i) = \sum_{h=0}^{H_i} N_i^h i_i^h = \sum_{h=0}^{H_i} \sum_{k=0}^{h} N_i^k \quad i = 1, 2, \ldots, G. \tag{5.8}$$

However, a deeper consideration leads to taking into account *saturation effects*: In large groups the potential influence i_i^h will not really grow proportionally to the number of subordinates because the intensity of direct personal interactions with these subordinates can not be maintained if their number increases. Therefore, we introduce instead of N_i^h saturated numbers $\tilde{N}_i^h$:

$$N_i^h \rightarrow \tilde{N}_i^h = N_{\max} \cdot \frac{N_i^h}{(N_{\max} - 1) + N_i^h} = N_{\max} \cdot y_i^h \tag{5.9}$$

with

$$N_{\max} > 1 \quad \text{and} \quad 0 \le y_i^h = \frac{x_i^h}{1 + x_i^h} \le 1 \quad \text{where} \quad x_i = \frac{N_i^h}{(N_{\max} - 1)} = \frac{y_i^h}{1 - y_i^h}. \tag{5.10}$$

Evidently, the *saturated numbers* $\tilde{N}_i^h$ have the following properties:

$$\tilde{N}_i^h = N_{\max} \cdot y_i^h = \begin{cases} 0 & \text{for } N_i^h = 0 \\ 1 & \text{for } N_i^h = 1 \\ \tilde{N}_i^h \Rightarrow N_{\max} & \text{for } N_i^h \Rightarrow \infty \\ \tilde{N}_i^h \Rightarrow N_i^h & \text{for } N_{\max} \Rightarrow \infty \end{cases} \tag{5.11}$$

It is now easy to take into account the saturation effect in (5.7) and (5.8) by going over to the *saturated potential influence in state* (ih):

$$\tilde{i}_i^h(\mathbf{N}_i) = \sum_{k=0}^{h} \frac{\tilde{N}_i^k}{N_i^h} \le (h + 1) \frac{N_{\max}}{N_i^h} \tag{5.12}$$

and to the *total saturated potential influence of* G_i

$$\tilde{i}_i(\mathbf{N}_i) = \sum_{h=0}^{H_i} N_i^h \tilde{i}_i^h = \sum_{h=0}^{H_i} \sum_{k=0}^{h} \tilde{N}_i^k \le \frac{(H_i + 1)(H_i + 2)}{2} N_{\max}. \tag{5.13}$$

The number $N_{\max}$ appearing in $\tilde{N}_i^h$ has to be calibrated carefully because it limits the range of influence of higher status levels. It may be different in different social sectors, e.g. different for political parties and for sport clubs.

Intensive Personal Variables: The Group-Solidarities S_i

The *"groupness of a group"* is only partially captured by the variables of the group configuration (5.3). A group is led by ideas and visions of its members which sometimes even form a *coherent ideology* with respect to the common purposes and objectives of the group. We are *not* interested in the concrete content of these ideas and visions, but we *are* interested in the fact that they provide a kind of *glue* keeping the group together and establishing the feeling of *identification with the group* among its members. The *intensity* of this sentiment may reach from "feeling at home in the group" up to enthusiasm and fanatism.

The ideology of a group is, on the one hand, established and sustained by all individual members. On the other hand it acts back on all members by inspiring them and urging them to *internalize* the ideology and to consider it as part of their own.

Just by being supported by all and, vice versa, by inspiring all members, the group ideology is *internalized in each member* and simultaneously takes on a *transpersonal quality* since it cannot be attributed and allocated to particular persons only but belongs to the group as a whole. Due to this transpersonal quality the group ideology and related mental structures create a *climate* and an *atmosphere* within the group and thus provide an *indirect cohesion* and *togetherness* between its members.

Therefore it is adequate to treat variables like group-*ideology*, group-*norms* and -*customs*, which simultaneously have been *internalized* and have adopted a *transpersonal quality*, as *intensive personal variables* being *entities of their own* and obeying a *dynamics of their own*.

In a parsimonious model like the present one it is indicated to introduce only *one* intensive personal variable of this kind (with simultaneously transpersonal character) for each group. This variable should be a measure for the intensity of the emotional affection and adherence produced by the group ideology among the group members, but it should abstract from the content and colour of that specific ideology. This *central intensive personal variable* (being simultaneously transpersonal and internalized in each group member) is denoted as *group solidarity* S_i.

We are free to choose the domain of variation of S_i by an appropriate scaling and thus confine $S_i(t)$ to a domain which it must not leave in the course of time. We choose

$$0 \le S_i(t) \le 1 \quad i = 1, 2, \ldots, G. \tag{5.14}$$

All key-variables can now be comprised in the *total key-variable configuration*:

$$\mathbf{C} = \{N_0^0; S_1, \mathbf{N}_1; \ldots; S_i, \mathbf{N}_i; \ldots; S_G, \mathbf{N}_G\} = \{N_0^0; \mathbf{S}, \mathbf{N}\}$$
$$= \{N_0^0; \mathbf{C}_1; \ldots; \mathbf{C}_i; \ldots; \mathbf{C}_G\}, \tag{5.15}$$
$$\text{where} \quad \mathbf{S} = \{S_1, \ldots, S_i, \ldots, S_G\} \quad \text{and} \quad \mathbf{C}_i = \{S_i, \mathbf{N}_i\}$$

is the *key-variable configuration of group* G_i. Correspondingly to (5.4) we also introduce the *shifted total key-variable configuration*

$$\mathbf{C}_{ji}^{kh} = \left\{ N_0^0; \mathbf{S}; \mathbf{N}_{ji}^{kh} \right\}. \tag{5.16}$$

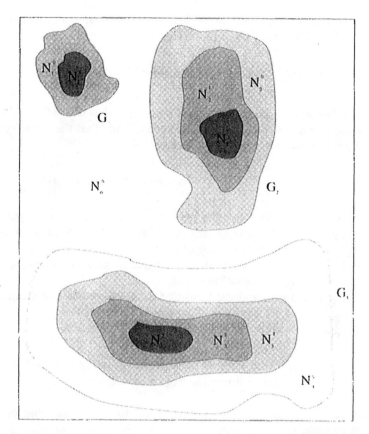

Figure 5.1 The picture illustrates one social sector (dimension) with three non-overlapping groups G_1, G_2, G_3. The points of the plane represent the individuals of the total population. Their position in this abstract space has nothing to do with their location in real space. The space between the groups represents the crowd of N_0^0 non-members. G_1 has two, G_2 three, and G_3 four hierarchical subgroups corresponding to nominal up to leading members of the groups. The components $\{N_1^0, N_1^1; N_2^0, N_2^1, N_2^2; N_3^0, N_3^1, N_3^2, N_3^3\}$ of the group configuration are assigned to these subgroups. The grade of obligations and influence of the subgroups are indicated by hatchings of different densities.

For illustrative purposes we show in Figure 5.1 a system of non-overlapping groups belonging to one social dimension and possessing internal hierarchical level structures.

5.2.2   The Transition Rates

The elements of the dynamics of a group are its transition rates. At first we introduce the

Transition Rates for Extensive Personal Variables

They belong to the transition steps $(ih) \rightarrow (jk)$ and $\mathbf{C} \Rightarrow \mathbf{C}_{ji}^{kh}$. Since the numerical value of the transition rate will in general depend on the configuration $\mathbf{C}$ and on the state (ih) of the transition making individual *before* the transition, and the configuration $\mathbf{C}_{ji}^{kh}$ and his/her state (jk) *after* the transition we write

$$\nu(jk; \mathbf{C}_{ji}^{kh} \mid ih; \mathbf{C}) = \text{total individual transition rate} \qquad (5.17)$$

which is, by definition, the probability per unit of time that *one individual* arrives at state (jk), given that he/she was originally in state (ih) and that the group system was originally in configuration $\mathbf{C}$. From (5.17) there follows:

$$\nu(jk; \mathbf{C}_{ji}^{kh} \mid ih; \mathbf{C})N_i^h = \text{configurational transition rate} \qquad (5.18)$$

which is, by definition, the probability per unit of time that the configuration has shifted to $\mathbf{C}_{ji}^{kh}$, given that it was originally in $\mathbf{C}$. Because N_i^h individuals in the origin state (ih) can independently by their individual transitions from (ih) to (jk) contribute to the shift $\mathbf{C} \Rightarrow \mathbf{C}_{ji}^{kh}$, the configurational transition rate is connected with the individual transition rate via equation (5.18).

The relation between probabilistic transition rates and changes of meanvalues $\bar{N}_i^h$ and quasi-meanvalues $\hat{N}_i^h$ discussed in Chapters 3, 11 and 12, leads to a less abstract and directly utilizable meaning of the configurational transition rate:

$$\nu(jk; \hat{\mathbf{C}}_{ji}^{kh} \mid ih; \hat{\mathbf{C}})\hat{N}_i^h = \begin{array}{l}\text{mean number of persons who make a transition} \\ \text{per unit of time from state } (ih) \text{ to state } (jk).\end{array} \qquad (5.19)$$

(Exactly speaking we use quasi-meanvalues here, the exact meaning of which is explained in Chapter 12.)

We now assume that two different processes contribute to the total (individual and hence also configurational) transition rate: On the one hand, there exist transitions from (ih) to (jk) which are *indirectly* motivated by the general mood of the individuals in state (ih) originating in the global situation. On the other hand, there exist transitions from (ih) to (jk) which are *directly* induced by persuasive activities of the members of group G_j.

Hence it is plain to decompose the total (individual) transition rate into contributions arising from *indirect* and *direct* interactions:

$$\nu(jk; \mathbf{C}_{ji}^{kh} \mid ih; \mathbf{C}) = \nu_I(jk; \mathbf{C}_{ji}^{kh} \mid ih; \mathbf{C}) + \nu_D(jk; \mathbf{C}_{ji}^{kh} \mid ih; \mathbf{C}), \qquad (5.20)$$

where the partial rates $\nu_I(\ldots \mid \ldots)$ and $\nu_D(\ldots \mid \ldots)$ stem from indirect and direct influences on the individuals in the initial states (ih), respectively. Since both rates are positive definite quantities by definition we can put them both proportional to an exponential expression:

$$\nu_I(jk; \mathbf{C}_{ji}^{kh} \mid ih; \mathbf{C}) = \nu_0 \exp[m(jk; \mathbf{C}_{ji}^{kh} \mid ih; \mathbf{C})]; \qquad (5.21a)$$

$$\nu_D(jk; \mathbf{C}_{ji}^{kh} \mid ih; \mathbf{C}) = \nu_0 e_j \tilde{i}_j \exp[m(jk; \mathbf{C}_{ji}^{kh} \mid ih; \mathbf{C})]. \qquad (5.21b)$$

Here, the *global rate* ν_0 calibrates the transition speed, i.e. the time scale on which the whole transition process will take place. The function in the exponent,

$$-\infty < m(jk; \mathbf{C}_{ji}^{kh} \mid ih; \mathbf{C}) < +\infty \qquad (5.22)$$

is denoted as the *conditional motivation potential*. It decides about whether the transition from (ih) to (jk) – and correspondingly from $\mathbf{C}$ to $\mathbf{C}_{ji}^{kh}$ – will be a frequent one (happening at short intervals).

If the final state (jk) is more attractive for an individual than its initial state (ih), then $m(\ldots \mid \ldots)$ will be positive. In the opposite case $m(\ldots \mid \ldots)$ will be negative. Furthermore, $m(\ldots \mid \ldots)$ will *increase* monotonously with growing attractiveness of the final state (jk). $m(\ldots \mid \ldots)$ will also depend on the transaction costs from (ih) to (jk). The form of $m(\ldots \mid \ldots)$ will be introduced in detail in the next Section.

The direct transition rate (5.21b) takes into account – in addition to the bias in favour of either the final state (jk) or the initial state (ih) – the special effect of direct persuasion activities of members of the envisaged group G_j urging the person in state (ih) to make the transition $(ih) \rightarrow (jk)$. This influence is taken in consideration by the factor

$$e_j \sum_{k=0}^{H_j} N_j^k \tilde{i}_j^k = e_j \tilde{i}_j = persuasion\ activity\ of\ G_j, \qquad (5.23)$$

where e_j calibrates the *individual persuasion activity*.

Combining both partial rates (5.21a,b) one obtains according to (5.20) the total rate:

$$\begin{aligned} \nu(jk; \mathbf{C}_{ji}^{kh} \mid ih; \mathbf{C}) &= \nu_0 (1 + e_j \tilde{i}_j) \exp[m(jk; \mathbf{C}_{ji}^{kh} \mid ih; \mathbf{C})] \\ &= \nu_0 \exp[m'(jk; \mathbf{C}_{ji}^{kh} \mid ih; \mathbf{C})] \end{aligned} \qquad (5.24)$$

with the *effective conditional motivation potential*

$$m'(jk; \mathbf{C}_{ji}^{kh} \mid ih; \mathbf{C}) = m(jk; \mathbf{C}_{ji}^{kh} \mid ih; \mathbf{C}) + \ln(1 + e_j \tilde{i}_j). \qquad (5.25)$$

A simple mathematical transformation can now be made (see also Chapter 3) which later will lead to a better interpretability of the transition rate. For this purpose we simplify the notation of $m'(\ldots \mid \ldots)$ by writing $m'(jk \mid ih)$ into its *symmetrical* and *antisymmetrical* part with respect to the original and final state:

$$m'(jk \mid ih) = m'_s(jk \mid ih) + m'_a(jk \mid ih) \qquad (5.26)$$

with

$$m'_s(jk \mid ih) = m'_s(ih \mid jk) = \frac{1}{2}\{m'(jk \mid ih) + m'(ih \mid jk)\}; \qquad (5.27a)$$

$$m'_a(jk \mid ih) = -m'_a(ih \mid jk) = \frac{1}{2}\{m'(jk \mid ih) - m'(ih \mid jk)\}. \qquad (5.27b)$$

Introducing the symmetrical mobility

$$\mu(jk \mid ih) = \mu(ih \mid jk) = \nu_0 \exp[m'_s(jk \mid ih)] \qquad (5.28)$$

the total rate (5.24) now assumes the form

$$\nu(jk \mid ih) = \mu(jk \mid ih) \exp[m'_a(jk \mid ih)]. \qquad (5.29)$$

The final form of the total rate will follow after we have found an explicit representation of the conditional motivation potential in the next Section (see equation (5.50)).

Transition Rates for the Solidarity Variables S_i

We must now make plausible assumptions in agreement with the meaning of the solidarity variables S_i about the rate-terms which contribute to the quantity:

$$\frac{1}{S_i}\frac{dS_i}{dt} = \text{relative rate of change of } S_i(t) = \alpha'_i - \sigma'_i \qquad (5.30)$$

Our fundamental assumption is, that the relative rate of change of $S_i(t)$ *is composed of two counteractive rate terms*:
The first term α'_i is a *growth rate* which is mainly due to the collective activities of the members of G_i to enhance their solidarity, and the second (counteractive) term σ'_i is a *saturation rate* limiting the unrestricted growth of S_i due to frustration effects, a limited receptivity for group ideology, and in particular to the free rider effect. The *growth rate* has obtained the form

$$\alpha'_i = \alpha'_i(\mathbf{C}_i) = (\alpha_{0i} + \alpha_{1i}N_i)(1 - S_i) \equiv \alpha_i(1 - S_i) \qquad (5.31)$$

and is substantiated as follows: The term α_{0i} comprises solidarity creation processes (perhaps of ideological nature) which enhance the sentiments of identity within G_i *independently* of the size of the group, and the term $\alpha_{1i}N_i$ which is *proportional to the number of members* of G_i comprises all activities of members of G_i enhancing their feeling of commonness. However, as solidarity S_i approaches its maximum value 1, the growth rate is reduced. This is accounted for by the factor $(1 - S_i)$. The *saturation rate* has obtained the form

$$\sigma'_i = \sigma'_i(\mathbf{C}_i) = \sigma_{0i}S_i + \sigma_{1i}N_i^2 S_i \equiv \sigma_i S_i \qquad (5.32)$$

for the following reasons:
The term $\sigma_{0i}S_i$ takes into account those saturation effects of S_i which are independent of the size of G_i (for instance a limited receptivity of each member in the group for too much ideology and solidarity).
The term $\sigma_{1i}N_i^2 S_i$ takes into account the free-rider effect. Its form can be justified as follows: A single individual is the more tempted to behave in an uncooperative

way the less apparent it will be (i.e. the easier he/she can hide in the crowd of members) and the less necessary it is to cooperate (i.e. the higher the level of solidarity S_i already is). That means the individual temptation is proportional to $N_i S_i$; since this temptation effect concerns every member, the total free-rider effect must be proportional to $N_i \cdot N_i S_i = N_i^2 S_i$.

At the end of this Section we illustrate the transition rates for the persons in different states (ih) for the case of two groups, each with three status levels.

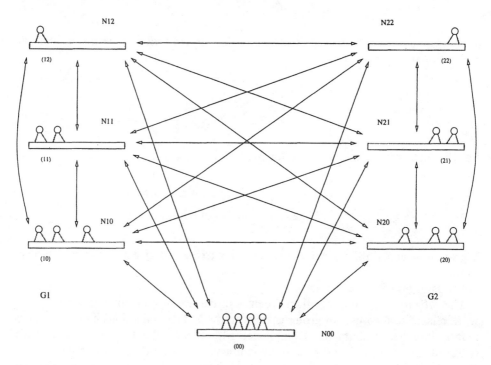

Figure 5.2   The transitions within and between groups described by transition rates (5.29) in the case of two groups G_1 and G_2, each with three status levels.

5.2.3   The Structure of the Motivation Potentials

The form of the conditional motivation potentials (5.22) must now be determined in more detail! The following decomposition of $m(jk; \mathbf{C}_{ji}^{kh} \mid ih; \mathbf{C})$ is suggestive and will be substantiated:

$$m(jk; \mathbf{C}_{ji}^{kh} \mid ih; \mathbf{C}) = u_j^k(\mathbf{C}_{jk}^{kh}) - u_i^h(\mathbf{C}) - t_{ji}^{kh}. \qquad (5.33)$$

Here, $u_j^k(\mathbf{C}_{jk}^{kh})$ and $u_i^h(\mathbf{C})$ can be interpreted as the *net utilities* of the state (jk) after the transition and of the state (ih) before it, respectively, and the term t_{ji}^{kh} represents the *transaction costs* (i.e. economic costs as well as the effect of psychological inhibition) related to the transition from (ih) to (jk).

Let us now further *decompose* the *net-utilities* and the *transaction costs*.

The net utility of a state (ih) – and analogously of any other state (jk) – is a measure of the attractiveness of this state (ih). It can vary from $-\infty$ to $+\infty$ and contains positive and negative terms. The positive terms are *benefits* b_i^h (i.e. satisfactory, gratifying aspects) and the negative ones are *costs* c_i^h (frustrating, disappointing aspects) connected with the state (ih). Therefore, u_i^h will assume the form

$$u_i^h = b_i^h - c_i^h, \tag{5.34}$$

where benefits and costs can in their turn be decomposed into sub-terms of different motivational origin:

$$b_i^h = p_i^h + f_i; \tag{5.35}$$
$$c_i^h = o_i^h + q_i. \tag{5.36}$$

For the subterms we choose the following terminology

$$p_i^h = \text{payoff}; \quad f_i = \text{faith confirmation};$$
$$o_i^h = \text{obligations}; \quad q_i = \text{contributions}.$$

We will now explain the meaning of these four terms and give a mathematical form to them.

Let us begin with the *cost terms*:

The *obligations* o_i^h comprise the burden of duties and responsibilities as well as the work related to members of group G_i with status h. The obligations have a predominantly immaterial character. Compliance with these obligations can be partially enforced (by sanctions) and partially voluntary. The following form of the term o_i^h seems persuasive:

$$o_i^h = o_i \cdot h^{d_i} \quad \text{with} \quad d_i \geq 0. \tag{5.37}$$

That means, for nominal members with status $h = 0$ the obligations are zero; for members with higher status $h = 1, 2, \ldots, H_i$ they grow with a certain power $d_i \geq 0$ of the status level. We denote d_i as the *exponent of obligations*; the prefactor o_i is a *global calibrating factor of the obligations* in G_i.

The *contributions* q_i have material as well as immaterial character and consist of regular payments (e.g. membership fees and grants providing the financial support of the group), but also of personal initiatives. We assume here, that q_i is independent of the status level and of the size of the group.

Now we turn to the *benefit terms*.

The *payoff-term* p_i^h consists of partially material, partially immaterial satisfactions. It comprises material rewards (status-dependent remunerations) as well as status-, influence- and solidarity-dependent advantages, and honours.

In order to capture these components, the following formula seems adequate:

$$p_i^h(\mathbf{C}) = N_i q_i S_i (g_0 + g_1 \tilde{i}_i S_i) \cdot \frac{r_i^h}{\sum_{k=0}^{H_i} r_i^k N_i^k} \tag{5.38}$$

with

$$r_i^h = q_i + r_i o_i^h. \tag{5.39}$$

The formula (5.38) looks complicated at first sight, but has a simple meaning: The factor $N_i q_i$ is the sum of all (material and immaterial) contributions available for group G_i. The solidarity factor $S_i \leq 1$ provides a measure for the reliability with which the members make their contributions. The next factor $(g_0 + g_1 \tilde{i}_i S_i)$ contains modifications of a pure redistribution of the contributions. The first term $g_0 < 1$ expresses the *diminution of the payoff* by administration costs. The second term represents an immaterial or material increase of the payoff by group activities. This term is proportional to the potential (saturated) total influence $\tilde{i}_i$ and to the solidarity S_i putting this influence into effect. The coefficient g_1 calibrates the *effective total influence* $\tilde{i}_i S_i$. The last factor, namely the fraction containing the *payoff-share coefficients* r_i^h, r_i^k, is denoted as the *payoff-distribution*. It determines the share received by a member of the group G_i with status h. The *share coefficient* r_i^h itself consists of the status-independent term q_i and a term proportional to the obligations, $r_i o_i^h$, where r_i is a *reward coefficient*.

The payoff formula (5.38) has the following obvious implications:

$$p_i^h / p_i^k = r_i^h / r_i^k \tag{5.40}$$

and the total payoff for all members of G_i is:

$$\sum_{h=0}^{H_i} N_i^h p_i^h = N_i q_i S_i (g_0 + g_1 \tilde{i}_i S_i). \tag{5.41}$$

Furthermore, the *faith confirmation term* f_i describes the immaterial satisfaction by receiving a reconfirmation of the own ideas and beliefs due to being a member of group G_i. This term is assumed to have the form

$$f_i = f_i(\mathbf{C}) = \sum_{j=1}^{G} w_{ij} \tilde{i}_j S_j \tag{5.42}$$

which can be validated as follows:

The *faith feedback coefficients* w_{ij} represent the effect of the total effective influence $\tilde{i}_i S_i$ of group G_j on the faith in the values of group G_i. The term $w_{ii} \tilde{i}_i S_i$ with $j = i$ and $w_{ii} > 0$ describes a *positive feedback effect* of the total effective influence $\tilde{i}_i$ of group G_i

on the belief of its members in the values of their own group G_i. This *reconfirmed belief* is, according to (5.34) with (5.35), considered as a positive term of the utility of state (ih). The influence of *competing groups* G_j on the faith within G_i can be *constructive* (if $w_{ij} > 0$) but also destructive (if $w_{ij} < 0$). In the latter case f_i is diminished. In this way a competing group can have a positive or negative influence on the utilities of another group.

The final form of the utility (5.34) is now:

$$u_i^h(\mathbf{C}) = [p_i^h(\mathbf{C}) + f_i(\mathbf{C})] - [o_i^h + q_i], \tag{5.43}$$

where (5.38), (5.42) and (5.37) must be inserted. In this way the utilities u_i^h have become functions not only of the state (ih) but also of the whole group configuration $\mathbf{C}$.

Finally, also the *transaction costs* can be decomposed in plausible manner:

$$t_{ji}^{kh} = a_j^k + l_i^h, \tag{5.44}$$

where l_i^h are the *"leaving costs"* and a_j^k the *"admission costs"*.

The *leaving costs* are often primarily immaterial losses and consist of losing and breaking off old contacts when withdrawing from a previously joined group G_i. The *admission costs* consist of an entrance fee and of the efforts necessary to be accepted in a new group G_j. Both terms together diminish the motivation to change from the previous state (ih) to a new state (jk) even if the utility of (jk) is higher than the utility of (ih).

Inserting (5.33), (5.43) and (5.44) into the formula (5.25) for the effective conditional motivation potential, this quantity now appears in decompsed form so that each term has a definite mathematical form with definite interpretation:

$$
\begin{aligned}
m'(jk; \mathbf{C}_{ji}^{kh} \mid ih; \mathbf{C}) &= m(jk; \mathbf{C}_{ji}^{kh} \mid ih; \mathbf{C}) + \ln\left(1 + e_j \tilde{i}_j\right) \\
&= u_j^k\left(\mathbf{C}_{ji}^{kh}\right) - u_i^h(\mathbf{C}) - t_{ji}^{kh} + \ln\left(1 + e_j \tilde{i}_j\right) \\
&= \left[p_j^k\left(\mathbf{C}_{ji}^{kh}\right) + f_j\left(\mathbf{C}_{ji}^{kh}\right) - o_j^k - q_j\right] \\
&\quad - \left[p_i^h(\mathbf{C}) + f_i(\mathbf{C}) - o_i^h - q_i\right] \\
&\quad - \left[a_j^k + l_i^h\right] + \ln\left(1 + e_j \tilde{i}_j\right).
\end{aligned}
\tag{5.45}
$$

The decomposition of $m'(jk; \mathbf{C}_{ji}^{kh} \mid ih; \mathbf{C})$ into its symmetrical and antisymmetrical part according to (5.26) and (5.27) now yields the explicit expressions:

$$
\begin{aligned}
m_s'(jk \mid ih) &= -\frac{1}{2}\left(a_j^k + a_i^h + l_j^k + l_i^h\right) + \frac{1}{2}\ln\left[(1 + e_i \tilde{i}_i)(1 + e_j \tilde{i}_j)\right] \\
&= -\ln d_{ji}^{kh}
\end{aligned}
\tag{5.46}
$$

with

$$d_{ji}^{kh} = d_{ij}^{hk} = \frac{\exp\left\{\frac{1}{2}\left(a_j^k + a_i^h + l_j^k + l_i^h\right)\right\}}{\sqrt{(1 + e_j \tilde{i}_j)\cdot(1 + e_i \tilde{i}_i)}} \tag{5.47}$$

and

$$m'_a(jk \mid ih) = v(jk) - v(ih) \qquad (5.48)$$

with the *effective utilities* $v(jk)$ and $v(ih)$ of states (jk) and (ih), respectively:

$$v(jk) = u_j^k + \frac{1}{2}(l_j^k - a_j^k) + \frac{1}{2}\ln(1 + e_j \tilde{i}_j); \qquad (5.49a)$$

$$v(ih) = u_i^h + \frac{1}{2}(l_i^h - a_i^h) + \frac{1}{2}\ln(1 + e_i \tilde{i}_i). \qquad (5.49b)$$

Inserting (5.46) and (5.48) into the formula (5.24) one obtains the *final form of the transition rates*:

$$\nu(jk; \mathbf{C}_{ji}^{kh} \mid ih; \mathbf{C}) = \nu_0 \frac{\exp[v(jk) - v(ih)]}{d_{ji}^{kh}} \qquad (5.50)$$

which easily lends itself to a *sociological interpretation*:

Firstly, the transition is *favoured*, i.e. the transition rate becomes increasingly large, the more the effective utility $v(jk)$ of the destination state (jk) exceeds the effective utility $v(ih)$ of the origin state (ih). *Secondly*, the transition is *disfavoured*, the larger the denominator d_{ji}^{kh} is in equation (5.50). Therefore, d_{ji}^{kh} can be interpreted as a "*generalized sociological distance*" between the two states (ih) and (jk). (According to (5.47) this distance *increases* the higher the leaving costs and admission costs in (ih) and (jk) are, but it *decreases* the higher the persuasion activities are, to come to the other group.)

Table 5.1 Key-variables

Variable	Name and meaning	Defining equation
N_i	total number of members of group G_i	(5.1)
N_i^h	number of members of group G_i with status level h	(5.1)
N_0^0	number of the crowd of individuals belonging to no group	(5.2)
N	total number of individuals in the social system	(5.2)
$\bar{N}_i^h$	saturated number of members of group G_i in status level h	(5.9)
$\hat{N}_{max}$	limit of saturated numbers $\bar{N}_i^h$	(5.9), (5.11)
$\hat{N}_i^h$	quasi-meanvalue of N_i^h	(5.19)
S_i	solidarity variable of group G_i	(5.14)
$\mathbf{N}_i$	group configuration of G_i = set of numbers $\{N_i^0, \ldots, N_i^{H_i}\}$	(5.3)
$\mathbf{N}$	group configuration = $\{\mathbf{N}_1; \ldots \mathbf{N}_i; \ldots \mathbf{N}_G\}$	(5.3)
$\mathbf{N}_{ji}^{kh}$	shifted group configuration after transition of one individual from state (ih) to state (jk)	(5.4)
$\mathbf{S}$	set of solidarity variables $\{S_1, \ldots, S_G\}$	(5.15)
$\mathbf{C}_i$	key-variable configuration of group G_i: $\{S_i, \mathbf{N}_i\}$	(5.15)
$\mathbf{C}$	total key-variable configuration = $\{N_0^0; \mathbf{C}_1; \ldots; \mathbf{C}_G\} = \{N_0^0; \mathbf{S}; \mathbf{N}\}$	(5.15)
$\mathbf{C}_{ji}^{kh}$	shifted total key-variable configuration = $\{N_0^0; \mathbf{S}; \mathbf{N}_{ji}^{kh}\}$	(5.16)

Table 5.2 Trend-functions

Trend-function	Name and meaning	Defining equation
n_i^h	number of subordinates per member of status h in group G_i	(5.6)
$t_i^h = n_i^h + 1$	potential influence in state (ih)	(5.7)
$\tilde{t}_i^h$	saturated potential influence in state (ih)	(5.12)
i_i	total potential influence of group G_i	(5.8)
$\tilde{i}_i$	saturated total potential influence of group G_i	(5.13)
$\tilde{i}_i S_i$	effective total influence of group G_i	(5.38)
$e_i \tilde{i}_i$	persuasion activity of G_i	(5.23)
$\nu(jk; \mathbf{C}_{ji}^{kh} \mid ih; \mathbf{C})$	total individual transition rate from $(ih; \mathbf{C})$ to $(jk; \mathbf{C}_{ji}^{kh})$	(5.17), (5.50)
$\nu_I(jk; \mathbf{C}_{ji}^{kh} \mid ih; \mathbf{C})$	indirect individual transition rate	(5.20), (5.21a)
$\nu_D(jk; \mathbf{C}_{ji}^{kh} \mid ih; \mathbf{C})$	direct individual transition rate	(5.20), (5.21b)
$\nu(jk; \mathbf{C}_{ji}^{kh} \mid ih; \mathbf{C}) N_i^h$	configurational transition rate from $\mathbf{C}$ to $\mathbf{C}_{ji}^{kh}$	(5.18), (5.19)
$m(jk; \mathbf{C}_{ji}^{kh} \mid ih; \mathbf{C})$	conditional motivation potential for transition from $(ih; \mathbf{C})$ to $(jk; \mathbf{C}_{ji}^{kh})$	(5.22)
$m'(jk; \mathbf{C}_{ji}^{kh} \mid ih; \mathbf{C})$	effective conditional motivation potential	(5.25)
$m_s'(jk; \mathbf{C}_{ji}^{kh} \mid ih; \mathbf{C})$	symmetrical part of $m'(jk; \mathbf{C}_{ji}^{kh} \mid ih; \mathbf{C})$	(5.26), (5.27a)
$m_a'(jk; \mathbf{C}_{ji}^{kh} \mid ih; \mathbf{C})$	antisymmetrical part of $m'(jk; \mathbf{C}_{ji}^{kh} \mid ih; \mathbf{C})$	(5.26), (5.27b)
$\alpha_i'(\mathbf{C}_i)$	growth rate of solidarity S_i	(5.31)
$\sigma_i'(\mathbf{C}_i)$	saturation rate of solidarity S_i	(5.32)
$u_i^h(\mathbf{C})$	net utility of state (ih)	(5.33), (5.34), (5.43)
$b_i^h(\mathbf{C})$	benefits of state (ih)	(5.34), (5.35)
$c_i^h(\mathbf{C})$	costs of state (ih)	(5.34), (5.36)
$p_i^h(\mathbf{C})$	payoff of state (ih)	(5.35), (5.38)
$f_i(\mathbf{C})$	faith confirmation for members of G_i	(5.35), (5.42)
o_i^h	obligations in state (ih)	(5.36), (5.37)
q_i	contributions of members of G_i	(5.36)
t_{ji}^{kh}	transaction costs of transition from state (ih) to state (jk)	(5.33), (5.44)
l_i^h	leaving costs when leaving state (ih)	(5.44)
a_j^k	admission costs when entering state (jk)	(5.44)
d_{ji}^{kh}	generalized sociological distance between the states (ih) and (jk)	(5.47)
$v(ih)$	effective utility of state (ih)	(5.48), (5.49b)

For convenience of the reader we summarize at the end of this Section all mathematical variables, functions and coefficients introduced so far in three tables for the *key-variables*, the *trend functions* and the *trend coefficients*, respectively. The notation is the following: key variables are latin capitals; multiples of them are bold face capitals; trend coefficients and trend functions are small latin letters; rates of the dimension [1/*time*] are denoted by greek letters.

Table 5.3 Trend-coefficients

Trend-coefficient	Name and meaning	Defining equation
ν_0	global rate calibrating the transition speed	(5.21)
e_i	individual persuasion activity	(5.23)
d_i	exponent of obligations	(5.37)
o_i	global factor of obligations	(5.37)
r_i^h	payoff-share coefficient	(5.38), (5.39)
r_i	reward coefficient	(5.39)
g_0	factor of influence-independent payoff	(5.38)
g_1	factor of influence-dependent payoff	(5.38)
w_{ij}	faith feedback coefficients	(5.42)
α_{0i}	constant term of the growth rate of solidarity	(5.31)
α_{1i}	coefficient of the term linear in N_i of the growth rate of solidarity	(5.31)
σ_{0i}	constant term of the saturation rate of solidarity	(5.32)
σ_{1i}	coefficient of the free rider term in the saturation rate of solidarity	(5.32)

5.2.4 The Quasi-Meanvalue Equations

In principle we now have all prerequisites to set up the master equation as well as the quasi-meanvalue equations. Because of the relatively complex structure of the model and because the main information will come from scenario-simulations of the latter, we omit the master equation and set up the *selfcontained quasi-meanvalue equations* only. They consist of the evolution equations of the $\hat{N}_i^h(t)$, which are generalized migratory equations, and the evolution equations of the solidarity variables $\hat{S}_i(t)$.

The equations for the extensive personal variables $\hat{N}_i^h(t)$ take a form which is nothing but a transcription of the general equation (3.42b) to the present model. They read:

$$\frac{d\hat{N}_j^k(t)}{dt} = \sum_{i,h} \nu(jk; \hat{C}_{ji}^{kh} \mid ih; \hat{C})\hat{N}_i^h - \sum_{i,h} \nu(ih; \hat{C}_{ij}^{hk} \mid jk; \hat{C})\hat{N}_j^k \tag{5.51}$$

$$\text{for} \quad j = 1, \ldots, G; \quad k = 0, \ldots, H_j$$

and

$$\frac{d\hat{N}_0^0(t)}{dt} = \sum_{i,h} \nu(00; \hat{C}_{0i}^{oh} \mid ih; \hat{C})\hat{N}_i^h - \sum_{i,h} \nu(ih; \hat{C}_{i0}^{h0} \mid 00; \hat{C})\hat{N}_0^0 \tag{5.52}$$

with $\hat{C} = \{N_0^0; S; N\}$. The sums on the right hand sides of (5.51) and (5.52) extend over the states $(ih) = (00)$ and (ih) with $h = 0, 1, \ldots, H_i$ and $i = 1, 2, \ldots, G$.

The mathematical meaning of equations (5.51) is easily comprehensible: The *first term on the r.h.s.* describes the mean number of individuals *arriving* per unit of time in state (jk) and coming from one of the states (ih), each of them with the individual mean transition rate $\nu(jk; \hat{C}_{ji}^{kh} \mid ih; \hat{C})$. This term leads to an *increase* of $\hat{N}_j^k$ with time. The *second term on the r.h.s.* describes the mean number of individuals *leaving* the state (jk) per unit of time and performing transitions into any of the states (ih), including $(0,0)$, each of them with the individual mean transition rate $\nu(ih; \hat{C}_{ij}^{hk} \mid jk; \hat{C})$. This term leads to a *decrease* of $\hat{N}_j^k$ with time. Hence, the total change of $\hat{N}_j^k$ with time comes about by the counter-active effect of transition *into* state (jk) and transitions *out of* state (jk). The analogous holds for (5.52), the evolution equation for the crowd of nonmembers.

From (5.51) and (5.52) there follows:

$$\frac{d}{dt}\left(\hat{N}_0^0 + \sum_{j=1}^{G}\sum_{k=0}^{H_j} \hat{N}_j^k\right) = \sum_{jk}\sum_{ih} \nu(jk; \hat{C}_{ji}^{kh} \mid ih; \hat{C})\hat{N}_i^h - \sum_{jk}\sum_{ih} \nu(ih; \hat{C}_{ij}^{hk} \mid jk; \hat{C})\hat{N}_j^k$$

$$= 0 \qquad\qquad\qquad (5.53)$$

so that the total number N of individuals remains constant with time, which was already anticipated in equation (5.2). Note, that on the r.h.s. of (5.53) the sums over (ih) and (jk) extend over $i, j = 1, \ldots, G$, $h = 0, 1, \ldots, H_i$; $k = 0, 1, \ldots, H_j$; and $(ih) = (0,0)$, $(jk) = (0,0)$.

The equations for the solidarity variables $\hat{S}(t)$ follow immediately from our proposition that their relative rate of change is composed of two counter-active terms, namely the growth rate α_i' and the saturation rate σ_i'. This leads to

$$\frac{1}{\hat{S}_i}\frac{d\hat{S}_i}{dt} = \alpha_i' - \sigma_i' \quad \text{with} \quad i = 1, 2, \ldots, G \qquad (5.54)$$

or, inserting (5.31) and (5.32):

$$\frac{d\hat{S}_i}{dt} = \alpha_i(\hat{N}_i)\hat{S}_i - [\alpha_i(\hat{N}_i) + \sigma_i(\hat{N}_i)]\hat{S}_i^2 \quad \text{for} \quad i = 1, 2, \ldots, G, \qquad (5.55)$$

where

$$\alpha_i(\hat{N}_i) = (\alpha_{0i} + \alpha_{1i}\hat{N}_i); \quad \sigma_i(\hat{N}_i) = (\sigma_{0i} + \sigma_{1i}\hat{N}_i^2). \qquad (5.56)$$

The equations of evolution for the $\hat{S}_i(t)$ turn out to be *generalized logistic equations*, where however the coefficients are functions of $\hat{N}_i$, which are themselves variables.

The equations (5.51), (5.52) *and* (5.55) *establish the mathematical form of our group-dynamic model.* Because of the conservation law (5.53), the equation (5.52) is redundant and can be left away. The remaining set consists of G equations for the solidarity variables $\hat{S}_i(t)$, and $(H_i + 1)$ equations for the quasi-meanvalues $\hat{N}_i^h$, with $h = 0, \ldots, H_i$, of each group G_i, where $i = 1, 2, \ldots, G$. Hence one obtains:

$$\sum_{i=1}^{G} H_i + 2G = \text{number of independent evolution equations.} \qquad (5.57)$$

Remarks about stationary solutions

Before discussing in the next Section *dynamic solutions* of the equations, we make some simple remarks about their *stationary solutions* $\bar{N}_i^h, \bar{S}_i$ which obey the equations (5.51) and (5.55) with vanishing time-derivatives, i.e. with vanishing left hand sides.

The stationary solidarity equations can immediately be solved with the result:

$$\bar{S}_i = \frac{\alpha_i(\bar{N}_i)}{\alpha_i(\bar{N}_i) + \sigma_i(\bar{N}_i)} < 1. \tag{5.58}$$

The dependence of the stationary solidarity $\bar{S}_i$ within a group on the (stationary) number $\bar{N}_i$ of its members is depicted for different values of the trend coefficients $(\alpha_{0i}, \alpha_{1i}, \sigma_{0i}, \sigma_{1i})$ in Figures 5.3(a),(b),(c).

If the set of equations

$$\bar{N}_i^h = C \exp[2v(ih; \bar{\mathbf{N}})], \tag{5.59}$$

where $i = 1, \ldots, G$, $h = 0, \ldots, H_i$, or $(ih) = (0,0)$ and where C is determined from the normalisation condition

$$\bar{N}_0^0 + \sum_{i=1}^{G} \sum_{h=0}^{H_i} \bar{N}_i^h = N \tag{5.60}$$

has one or more solution, then this solution is simultaneously a solution of the stationary equations (5.51). This can be seen, if the form (5.50) of the transition rates is taken into account and if (5.59) is inserted in the stationary equations (5.51). Because of

$$\{\exp[v(jk, \bar{\mathbf{N}}) - v(ih, \bar{\mathbf{N}})]\bar{N}_i^h - \exp[v(ih, \bar{\mathbf{N}}) - v(jk, \bar{\mathbf{N}})]\bar{N}_j^k\}$$
$$= C\{\exp[v(jk, \bar{\mathbf{N}}) + v(ih, \bar{\mathbf{N}})] - \exp[v(ih, \bar{\mathbf{N}}) + v(jk, \bar{\mathbf{N}})]\} \equiv 0, \tag{5.61}$$

the terms on the r.h.s. of (5.51) vanish individually so that the stationary equation (5.51) is fulfilled. Simultaneously this means that then the stationary quasi-mean-values satisfy the condition of *detailed balance*

$$v(jk \mid ih; \bar{\mathbf{N}})\bar{N}_i^h = v(ih \mid jk; \bar{\mathbf{N}})\bar{N}_j^k \tag{5.62}$$

which means that the stationary flow of individuals from state (ih) to state (jk) is the same as the stationary flow from state (jk) to state (ih) *for each pair* of states (ih) and (jk). In complex cases, however, there can exist stationary solutions of (5.51) which do not fulfil (5.59). Then the stationary flows between the status levels are not in detailed balance and complicated ring-flows can arise.

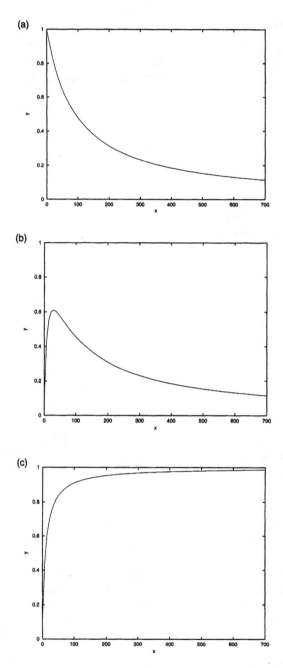

Figure 5.3 (a) Trend-Coefficients: $\alpha_{0i} = 0.01; \alpha_{1i} = 0.01; \sigma_{0i} = 0.0; \sigma_{1i} = 1.1 \cdot 10^{-4}$. No size-independent saturation, but free-rider effect. The solidarity decreases with growing number of members; (b) Trend-Coefficients: $\alpha_{0i} = 0.01; \alpha_{1i} = 0.01; \sigma_{0i} = 0.1; \sigma_{1i} = 1.1 \cdot 10^{-4}$. Size-independent saturation plus free-rider effect. The solidarity assumes a maximum for an optimal number of members; (c) Trend-Coefficients: $\alpha_{0i} = 0.01; \alpha_{1i} = 0.01; \sigma_{0i} = 0.1; \sigma_{1i} = 0$. Without free-rider effect the solidarity increases monotonously with group-size and approaches asymptotically the maximal value 1.

5.3   Simulation and Interpretation of Selected Scenarios

Each scenario-simulation begins with the following procedure:

- A complete set of trend-coefficients must be specified so that all trend-functions are explicitly defined functions of the key-variables.

- The initial values of all key-variables must be determined.

Because of the relatively large number of coefficients and variables one must expect an immense variety of scenarios and it is an "art" to select the most interesting ones.

In our selection of scenarios we follow M. Mikuletz [16] who has made a thorough analysis of the solution manifold of the model and has found very interesting and even unexpected cases of which some will be presented here.

Among these scenarios we leave out those focussing in the evolution of the status-hierarchy within the groups, because this topic has already been investigated in detail in [15], based on the same model. (Nevertheless the model equations in all simulations always comprise the full configuration of interacting variables.) In order to facilitate the survey the following procedure is introduced:

(a)   We always restrict the scenarios to *two interacting groups*.

(b)   In proceeding from one to the next scenario in a *sequence of scenarios* only one trend-coefficient is switched to a new value whereas all others keep their value.

(c)   The initial values of the key-variables are appropriately chosen for the *first scenario* of a sequence. For *all following scenarios* their initial values coincide with the values at the end of the preceding scenario.

The prescriptions (b) and (c) mean that we "switch over" one trend-coefficient only when passing from one scenario to the next.

5.3.1   Competitively Interacting Groups

In this first sequence of scenarios we investigate the fate of two competing groups, G_1 and G_2, each with three internal hierarchy levels (simple members, staff, leading staff) in a "closed society" of $N = 750$. Whereas group G_1 keeps on the same behaviour in all scenarios, group G_2 changes its "strategy" from scenario to scenario with the insinuated intention to defend its interests and to gain a competitive advantage over group G_1. One could think of two firms of middle size having comparable organisational structures (with most trend-coefficients being equal) and competing in hiring their members out of a restricted pool of labour-force. (Of course, the economic situation of the "firms" is not considered here; in so far the model can only yield restricted insights for such a case.)

In the Tables 5.4(a) and 5.4(b) the trend-coefficients and the initial values of the variables of the first scenario are listed for the sequence of scenarios depicted in the series of Figures 5.4(a)–(h). The values in braces can change proceeding in the sequence of scenarios of Figures 5.4(a)–(h).

Table 5.4 (a) Trend-coefficients for scenarios of Figures 5.4(a)–(h)

Coefficient	Name and meaning	Group G_1	Group G_2
α_{0i}	constant term of growth rate of solidarity	0.1	0.1
α_{1i}	coefficient of the term linear in N_i of the growth rate of solidarity	0.5	0.5
σ_{0i}	constant term of the saturation rate of solidarity	1.0	1.0
σ_{1i}	coefficient of the free-rider term in saturation rate of solidarity	0.0005	(0.0005)
e_i	individual persuasion activity	0.0	(0.0)
N_{max}	limit of saturated numbers $\bar{N}_i^h$	100	100
o_i	global factor of obligations	3.0	3.0
d_i	exponent of obligations	1.0	1.0
g_0	factor of influence-independent payoff	0.7	0.7
g_1	factor of influence-dependent payoff	0.004	0.004
r_i	reward coefficient	0.7	0.7
a_i^k	admission costs	0.0	(0.0)
l_i^h	leaving costs	0.0	0.0
w_{1i}	faith feedback to G_1 from G_i	0.0	(0.0)
w_{2i}	faith feedback to G_2 from G_i	0.0	0.0
w_{0i}	faith feedback to nonmembers from G_i	0.0	(0.0)

(b) Initial values of key-variables of scenario Figure 5.4(a)

Variable	Group G_1	Group G_2	Crowd in no group
Simple members N_i^0	125	73	500
Staff members N_i^1	30	7	–
Leading staff members N_i^2	15	0	–
Total number N_i	170	80	500
Solidarity S_i	0.80	0.90	–

Explanations to the Scenario-Sequence of Figures 5.4(a)–(h)

In each scenario of Figure 5.4 the evolution of the number of members $N_0(t)$, $N_1(t)$, $N_2(t)$ of the crowd and the groups G_1 and G_2, and of their solidarities $S_1(t)$ and $S_2(t)$ are depicted. The hierarchy level numbers $N_i^h(t)$ are left out.

Scenario (a) begins with the initial values of Table 5.4(b). The trend-coefficients are those of Table 5.4(a). Due to the high initial values of the solidarities both groups grow and reach an equal equilibrium state $N_1 = N_2$; $S_1 = S_2$ in Figure 5.4(a). This is very plausible, since all trend-coefficients of G_1 and G_2 coincide.

Scenario (b) Switch of trend-coefficients: $e_2 = 0.0 \Rightarrow e_2 = 0.01$. Members of G_2 now develop persuasion activities (i.e. they entice members from G_1 and the crowd to come to their group). The result can be seen in Figure 5.4(b): N_2 has increased, and N_1 and N_0 have decreased. The solidarities go to the corresponding new equilibrium values.

Scenario (c) Switch of trend-coefficients: $a_2^k = 0.0 \Rightarrow a_2^k = 2.0$. The group G_2 now impedes admission to G_2 by levying admission fees. This results in an increase of the crowd and even of the competing group G_1 (see Figure 5.4(c)) so that the positive effect of persuasion activities is over-compensated.

Scenario (d)   Switch of trend-coefficients: $w_{12} = 0.0 \Rightarrow w_{12} = -0.003$. The subversive activity of G_2 now undermines the faith in their own success among the members of G_1. The result, which can be seen in Figure 5.4(d), is a decrease of N_1, because the less motivated members of G_1 now wander partially to the crowd and partially to G_2. The solidarity variables essentially follow the group size. Here this means, that to *higher* group numbers there belongs a *lower* solidarity (because of the free-rider effect).

Scenario (e)   Switch of trend-coefficients: $w_{02} = 0.0 \Rightarrow w_{02} = +0.003$. Group G_2 develops an additional activity: It convinces the crowd of nonmembers of the value (the utility) of their independence. The effect is dramatical, because the relative attractivity of group G_1 for members of the crowd has now decreased. Figure 5.4(e) shows that this even leads to the breakdown of G_1 and the strong increase of the crowd, whereas G_2 remains almost unchanged under its "unfair" competitive strategy. Only the solidarity S_1 of the remaining rest of G_1 survives for a long time before it collapses, too.

Scenario (f)   Switch of trend-coefficients: $\sigma_{12} = 5.0 \cdot 10^{-4} \Rightarrow \sigma_{12} = 3.2 \cdot 10^{-3}$. The members of G_2 now develop a free-rider mentality: their free-rider coefficient has increased by almost one order of magnitude. This leads to the breakdown of G_2, too, as can be seen in Figure 5.4(f). Apart from some lagging behind sentiments of solidarity the group structures have disappeared and only the crowd survives: On the one hand, membership in G_1 was blocked by the activity of G_2, and on the other hand the engagement in G_2 was spoiled by an excessive increase of the free-rider effect, so that finally both groups collapsed.

Scenario (g)   Switch of trend-coefficients: $\sigma_{12} = 5.0 \cdot 10^{-4} \Rightarrow \sigma_{12} = 3.2 \cdot 10^{-3}$. The only difference between scenario (e) and (g) is, that the change to a high free-rider coefficient in group G_2 sets in already at the time-point 2.8 of scenario (e) instead of 3.0.

Scenario (h)   The same trend-coefficients as in (g).   The somewhat earlier appearance of the free-rider effect in scenario (g) compared to scenario (f) has dramatic consequences: The earlier breakdown of G_2 sets free many of its members who are now in the crowd. The almost broken down group G_1 (which is however fitted out with a high solidarity) is now able to recover, to recruit members, and finally to revive fully.

Comparing the transitions (e) $\rightarrow$ (f) and (g) $\rightarrow$ (h) with their very different outcome in spite of equal sets of trend-coefficients it becomes obvious that tiny differences of initial conditions of the variables may lead to dramatically different evolution paths even if all trend-parameters are the same.

5.3.2   Political Parties with Reciprocal Undermining Activity

Whereas the scenario-sequence of Section 5.3.1 depicts the fate of two interacting groups, where one of them develops different forms of *"interest-dominated"*

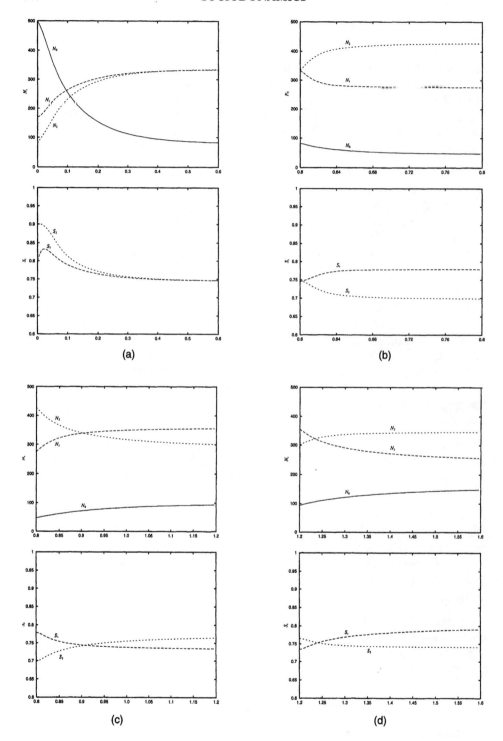

(a)

(b)

(c)

(d)

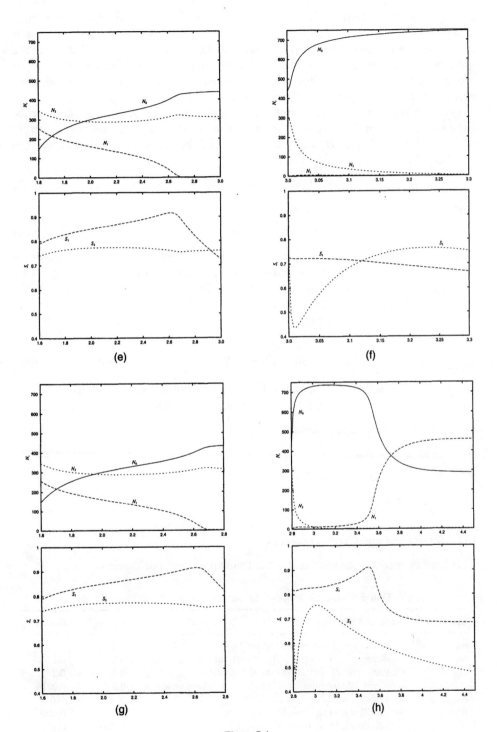

Figure 5.4

strategies, we now consider the dynamics of two in all trendparameters symmetrical groups which exhibits a *strong reciprocal "subversive" undermining activity*. This is expressed by strong *negative* faith-feedback coefficients $w_{12} = w_{21} < 0$ disturbing the faith of each group in its own identity by the destructive interference of the other group. Such a reciprocal strategy can be interpreted as the activity of opposing, or even hostile, political parties with antagonistic ideologies.

The following scenarios are simplified by neglecting those structures which prove to be not essential in this context. That means we neglect the hierarchy-level structure of G_1 and G_2 and put $H_1 = H_2 = 0$. The total key-variable configuration then consists of

$$C = \{N_0; N_1, S_1; N_2, S_2\}, \tag{5.63}$$

where

$$N_0 + N_1 + N_2 = N = \text{const.} \tag{5.64}$$

The set of trend-coefficients is then considerably smaller and only consists of $\{\alpha_{0i}, \alpha_{1i}, \sigma_{0i}, \sigma_{1i}, N_{max}, w_{11}, w_{12}, w_{21}, w_{22}\}$. They are chosen in symmetrical way for G_1 and G_2, so that the groups are fully symmetrical in this respect. Asymmetries in the dynamics of G_1 and G_2 then can only evolve starting from different initial conditions of the key-variables. We choose the latter in all following scenarios as follows:

Initial conditions:

$$N_0 = 350; \quad N_1 = 50; \quad N_2 = 250; \quad S_1 = 0.45; \quad S_2 = 0.25. \tag{5.65}$$

We shall now see that somewhat different (symmetrical) sets of trend-coefficients will lead to structurally different sorts of dynamics, namely to scenarios of

(A) *Bifurcation and Cyclic Dynamics*

(B) *Chaotic Dynamics*

(C) *Delusive Longterm-Stability*

At first we consider:

(A) Bifurcation and Cyclic Dynamics

This kind of scenario appears under the following trend-coefficients:

Table 5.5 Trend-coefficients for scenarios A of Figures 5.5(a)–(e)

Coefficient	Name and meaning		Group G_1	Group G_2
α_{0i}	constant term of growth rate of solidarity	0.0	0.0	
α_{1i}	coefficient of linear term of the growth rate of solidarity		0.1	0.1
σ_{0i}	constant term of saturation rate of solidarity		0.2	0.2
σ_{1i}	coefficient of free-rider term in saturation rate of solidarity		0.0013	0.0013
N_{max}	limit of saturated numbers $\tilde{N}_i$		500	500
w_{1i}	faith feedback to G_1 from G_i		(x)	$(-2x)$
w_{2i}	faith feedback to G_2 from G_i		$(-2x)$	(x)

Explanations to Scenarios A with Figures 5.5(a)–(e)

Scenario A(a)   Figure 5.5(a) *Trend-Coefficients of Table 5.5 with* $x = 0.00181$. The faith parameter x which determines the faith-confirming coefficients $w_{11} = w_{22}$ as well as the faith-undermining coefficients $w_{12} = w_{21} = -2w_{11}$, is small. A symmetrical stationary endstate of both groups is reached, which seems natural, because all trend-coefficients are symmetrical.

Scenario A(b)   Figure 5.5(b) *Trend-Coefficients of Table 5.5 with* $x = 0.0187$. The amplitude of the faith-confirming and faith-undermining coefficients is now larger. Again a stationary endstate is reached, but remarkably, the *symmetry between G_1 and G_2 is now broken in spite of symmetrical trend-coefficients*. One observes a *bifurcation* and a dependence of the endstates on the initial states. Such an unsymmetrical endstate can arise if in the larger group the members have a smaller motivation. This means a large group of lethargic members can be in equilibrium with a small group of energetic members. Indeed, under the parameters of Table 5.5, the stationary solidarity decreases with increasing number of members.

Scenario A(c)   Figure 5.5(c) *Trend-Coefficients of Table 5.5 with* $x = 0.0190$. The slight increase of x and of the corresponding coefficients $w_{11} = w_{22} = x$; $w_{12} = w_{21} = -2x$ once more leads to a change of group dynamics: Cyclic changes of the membership of G_1 and G_2 set in, where however G_1 always prevails over G_2 after an initial swing-in process.

Scenario A(d)   Figure 5.5(d) *Trend-Coefficients of Table 5.5 with* $x = 0.02$. A second slight increase of x and of the amplitudes of the corresponding faith-confirming and -undermining coefficients w_{ij} leads to a breakdown of the permanent superiority of G_1 over G_2: A great cyclic motion sets in, where G_1 and G_2 alternate in having large or small memberships.

Phase-Portrait of Scenarios A(a)–(d)   Figure 5.5(e). A summary and comparison of scenarios A(a)–(e) is given in Figure 5.5(e) where the phase-portrait of the stationary states (a) and (b) and of the limit cycles (c) and (d) is exhibited.

Secondly, we turn to the case of

(B)   Chaotic Dynamics

In Table 5.6 we choose a set of symmetrical trend-coefficients leading to chaotic dynamics

Table 5.6 Trend-coefficients for scenario B, Figures 5.6(a)–(b)

Coefficient	Name and meaning	Group G_1	Group G_2
α_{0i}	constant term of growth rate of solidarity	0.0	0.0
α_{1i}	coefficient of linear term of growth rate of solidarity	0.01	0.01
σ_{0i}	constant term of saturation rate of solidarity	0.0	0.0
σ_{1i}	coefficient of free-rider term in saturation rate of solidarity	$0.3 \cdot 10^{-4}$	$0.3 \cdot 10^{-4}$
N_{max}	limit of saturated numbers $\tilde{N}_i$	85	85
w_{1i}	faith feedback to G_1 from G_i	0.016	-0.040
w_{2i}	faith feedback to G_2 from G_i	-0.040	0.016

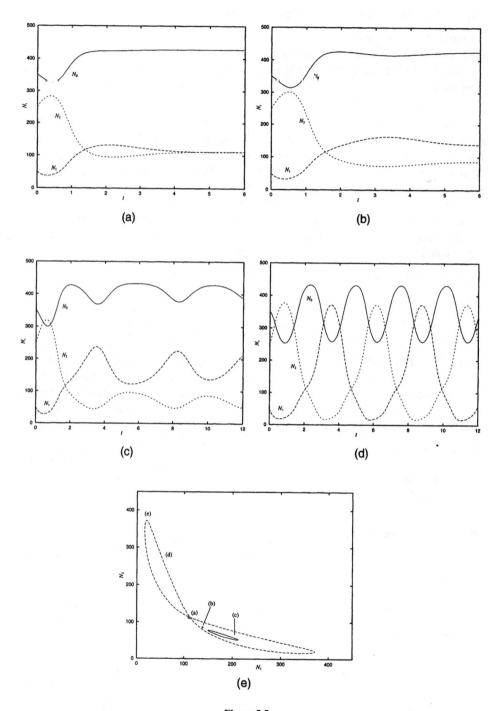

Figure 5.5

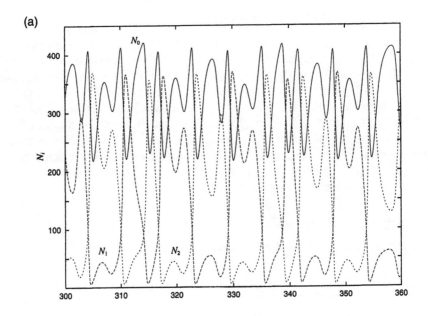

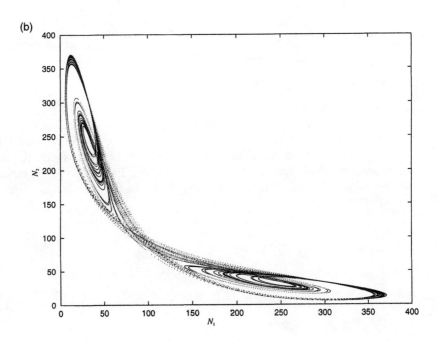

Explanation to Scenario B with Figures 5.6(a) and (b)

The *non-periodic, irregular* and *chaotic evolution* with time of the population numbers $N_1(t), N_2(t), N_0(t)$ of G_1, G_2 and the crowd, respectively, is exhibited in Figure 5.6(a). An even better insight into the chaotic character of this evolution yields the phase-portrait of the trajectory in the N_1/N_2 plane exhibited in Figure 5.6(b). Both figures show that even in a fully deterministic case with fully known (symmetric) strategy and behavioural trends in both groups and without exogenous influences the predictability of the system becomes low, because it never returns exactly to an initial state and because its further evolution depends sensitively on tiny differences of the values $N_0(t_0), N_1(t_0), N_2(t_0)$ at a given reference time t_0.

Finally we consider the scenario of

(C) Delusive Long-Term Stability

which belongs to a set of trend-coefficients listed in Table 5.7.

Table 5.7 Trend-coefficients for scenario C, Figures 5.7(a)–(b)

Coefficient	Name and meaning	Group G_1	Group G_2
α_{0i}	constant term of growth rate of solidarity	0.0	0.0
α_{1i}	coefficient of linear term of growth rate of solidarity	0.01	0.01
σ_{0i}	constant term of saturation rate of solidarity	0.0	0.0
σ_{1i}	coefficient of free-rider term in saturation rate of solidarity	$0.24 \cdot 10^{-4}$	$0.24 \cdot 10^{-4}$
N_{max}	limit of saturated numbers $\tilde{N}_i$	100	100
w_{1i}	faith feedback to G_1 from G_i	0.020	−0.040
w_{2i}	faith feedback to G_2 from G_i	−0.040	0.020

Explanation to Scenario C with Figures 5.7(a) and (b)

After the time $t = 30$ a (delusive) stationary state of the variables $N_1(t)$, $N_2(t)$, $S_1(t)$, $S_2(t)$ seems to have stabilized. However the persistently high solidarity in the subdued group G_2 and the creeping stagnation in the dominant group G_1 finally lead after $t = 60$ to a rather sudden breakdown of G_1, and rise of G_2. Afterwards, the same evolution takes place with exchanged roles of G_1 and G_2. Evidently the dynamics is decisively influenced by the delicate interplay between the population- and the solidarity-variables.

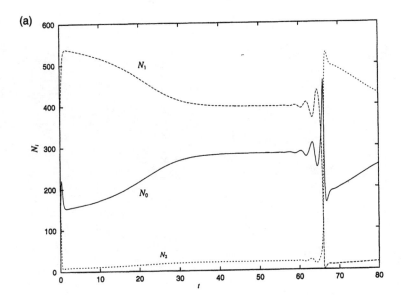

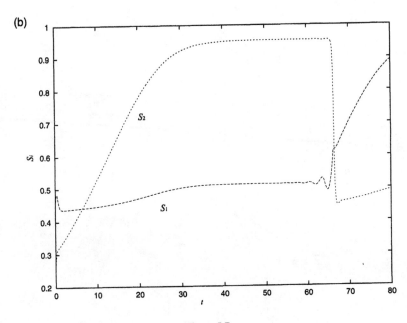

Figure 5.7

6. Opinion Formation on the Verge of Political Phase-Transitions

This chapter is a difficult and in some respects even a disquieting one!

On the one side it deals with the *complex problems of political phase-transitions*, from liberal to totalitarian political systems or vice versa. These large scale events in societies are mostly of a tragic nature. They include the breakdown of a whole political system, the liquidation of its established institutions etc, and for the people involved as witnesses and/or active or passive participants it means a break in their personal biography, and in the worst case of the arisal of a violent totalitarian regime it can mean concentration camp and death for its victims.

Each of such large scale phase-transitions is of course a unique event in so far as it will never recur in exactly the same form. However, in each event of this kind there appear *universal structures* of human character and social behaviour which play an essential role in enabling political phase-transitions.

We will focus in this chapter on the analysis of these *universal features of such phase-transitions*. (Of course our procedure implies the thesis that such universal features do exist at all; this thesis *rejects the contrary thesis*, that, for instance, the seizure of power of the Nazis in Germany (see Section 6.1.4) is to be seen as a completely unique event which could only have occurred in Germany due to its specific history and due to the specific character of the Germans.)

On the other side it will turn out in the course of this analysis that a certain *reduction of complexity* takes place in the transition to a *totalitarian system*. This will enable us to set up in Section 6.2 an *oversimplified model* which nevertheless yields some insight into such systems. (The difference between the complexity of a pluralistic democracy and the relative simplicity of a totalitarian state is well illustrated by an old joke of journalists comparing Italy and the Soviet Union: "In Italy we know everything but understand nothing, whereas in the Soviet Union we know nothing but understand everything".)

The chapter is organised as follows: In Section 6.1 we make the attempt of briefly mentioning (in Section 6.1.1) some *characteristic structure elements* of open liberal and, by contrast, of totalitarian political systems. In Section 6.1.2 we discuss the question whether at transitions between both systems the *phase-transition concept* or the *continuity hypothesis* proves to be the more adequate descriptive frame. We shall give arguments favouring the phase-transition concept. The *political psychology* of the active and passive participants on the verge of a phase-transition is then discussed in Section 6.1.3 so far as this is possible in general terms, i.e. without reference to the specific case. Section 6.1.4 gives a short account of the *seizure of power by Hitler*, seen as a paradigm of a political phase-transition.

The estimations made in Section 6.1.3 are not based on retro-spective field-inquiries but partially rest on the personal experience of the author who was in a position to witness as a teenager examples of the behaviour of people under two totalitarian regimes (the Nazi-regime and the postwar communist regime in East-Germany) before escaping to West-Berlin and living in the democracy of West-Germany since 1950. The valuation of Hitler's seizure of power as a *"worst case accident"* of the Weimar-democracy in Section 6.1.4 is due to the internationally renowned historian Eberhard Jäckel [17]. His thesis is further substantiated by the recent very comprehensive biography of Hitler by Jan Kershaw [18].

After the qualitative analysis of the macro-phenomenon of a political phase-transition in Section 6.1 the modelling procedure of sociodynamics is applied in Section 6.2 to the case of totalitarian systems after their arisal by a phase-transition. A justification of the choice of a minimal model is given and the equations of evolution are set up. These equations are to some extent mathematically analyzed in Section 6.3. In Section 6.4 selected scenarios and their interpretation in the light of Section 6.1 yield some insight into the "mechanisms" of stabilisation and collapse of totalitarian regimes.

6.1   Remarks about Phase-Transitions between Liberal and Totalitarian Political Systems

In this section we do of course *not* intend to develop a detailed theory of liberal and totalitarian political systems. This can be found in textbooks of political science. Rather we want to accentuate some essential constituents of both sorts of systems in their developed stage and stress the fundamental differences between them.

6.1.1   Some Features of Developed Liberal and Totalitarian Systems

The Liberal System

In the developed stage of a liberal society the dominant political conviction is that a *space of freedom* is indispensible for the individuals to realize their different styles of life, to activate their different talents and to express their different ideas. It turns out, however, that on all levels there exist *conflicts* between the activities and intentions of individuals or groups of them. Therefore the extent of their freedom finds its *necessary limitation* in the *interfering* activities and intentions of other individuals and groups. In order to avoid chaotic circumstances *rules for the coexistence of conflicting activities* must be developed. In a well-ordered liberal society endowed with adequate institutions this takes place according to principles of *justice* creating *laws* for the order within the society and yielding *rights* to individuals and groups for their free space of evolution.

In modern liberal societies this frame of freedom and justice includes the principle that *all humans are equal with respect to their fundamental human rights*, so that specific rights can only be acquired by acknowledged achievements and merits. The combination of the principles of *liberty, justice* and *equality* of humans in their fundamental rights leads in an almost deductive manner to an *open liberal society with a democratic constitution*.

Given the framework of these principles there still exist *many possibilities* for the detailed formation of the society, and consequently there may evolve *many political ideologies* for shaping and organising it. Under these circumstances the adequate form of political participation in a liberal democratic system is the formation of *competing political parties with different socio-political concepts but principal equality of status*. Within this *plurality of political ideologies* a single ideology *cannot claim* to have an *absolute value* or to represent the *absolute truth*. (This holds in contradistinction to *mathematical truth* provable by logical deduction, and also in contradistinction to the *empirical truth of natural laws* verifiable in principle by always and everywhere reproducible experiments.)

However, the *relative value and consistency* of a political ideology becomes apparent if it is *approved temporally* in elections by a majority of the people and if the government formed succeeds in organizing a *relatively optimal* society of members with competing goals, until a change of power by system-conforming elections leads to the realization of another relatively optimal structure gaining a broader approval.

The socio-political dynamics of such a pluralistic liberal democratic system is so complex that only very partial aspects of it can be depicted in terms of mathematical models, as we have seen in the simple cases of competing groups of Chapter 5.

The more so must it be appreciated that modern liberal democratic political systems have succeeded in organizing a differentiated framework of *checks and balances* – among them the division of power in *legislative, executive* and *judicature* – guaranting (at least if prudent foresight always rules) the dynamic stability of this complex, but at last most satisfactory system.

The Totalitarian System

Let us now describe some essentials of an established totalitarian political system, which are in full contrast to those of a liberal system.

The big totalitarian ideologies dominating their political systems in this century were and are *nationalism, racism* and *communism* or combinations of them. (For instance the Nazi-ideology was a combination of nationalism and racism; some post-communist systems after the failure of communism are combinations of totalitarian socialism with nationalism.) The imminent threat of the next century may be *cultural and religious fundamentalism*. One must be grateful to S. Huntington [19] who did not keep silent about this new threat.

Observing the pervasive agitation and propaganda by which the leaders of a totalitarian system proclaim the "absolute truth" of their ideology to their adherents and trimmers, one might think that it is the *content* of this specific ideology that is of the highest importance.

Comparing however the *inner structure of totalitarian systems*, in particular their effect on the political psychology of the people under their control, one becomes aware of the *farreaching structural similarity* of all totalitarian regimes *independently of the otherwise very different contents of their specific ideologies*.

We are above all interested in these *content-invariant structural features of totalitarian systems*. (It should be mentioned that fervent adherents of totalitarian ideologies will *contest* the existence of such structural similarities between totalitarian systems. For instance it will be difficult for admirers of Stalin who perhaps fought against the Nazi-aggressors, to admit that nevertheless there existed strong structural analogies between the Soviet "Archipelago Gulag" and the Nazi concentration camps.)

In the center of totalitarian systems there stands a *totalitarian ideology* ("Weltanschauung"). Compared to the ideologies, i.e. the sociopolitical programs competing in liberal systems a totalitarian ideology can be denoted as a *degenerate political philosophy* with the following features (see also M. Sonis, who has given a concise formulation of totalitarian attitudes in terms of "ten commandments of aggressive intolerance" in [20]):

(1)   A totalitarian ideology presents itself as a *dogma* expressing an *unquestionable ultimate truth*. Analysis, dialogue or discussion of this "truth" is neither welcome nor allowed.

(2)   The *propaganda and agitation* for this ideology is intended to lead to a *global emotionalisation* of the people accompanied by a shrinking of their horizon of thought. These emotions can be escalated to *fanaticism* by a *cult of personality* and on the other hand by a character and status-based *defamation* of the political foes.

(3)   The totalitarian ideology is *protected* by its adherents *against objective comparison with reality* by several restrictive methods circumventing free information and free expression of opinion. In the fully developed totalitarian system its ideology is further stabilized by *coercion* and by *sanctions* creating *permanent fear* among the people, in particular among the remaining dissidents.

(4)   Within the totalitarian system finally a strong *mental decomplexification* sets in: The *complexity of causes* and the *diversity of intentions* are reduced to *monocausality* and *monofinality*. This means, that practically all aspects of life are now entrained into the totalitarian ideology, are viewed under its perspective and instrumentalized for its purposes. ("Thanks to the teachings and the wise foresight of our great leader our system will win through! Whatsoever our personal activities are, we are fighting for you, our beloved leader, and for your victorious system!" Such are the expected acclamations at official celebrations.)

The *political psychology* of the population under the strong pressure of an established totalitarian system with an unpredictable future differs substantially from that in a liberal system. Strong psychological distortions are to be expected! In this sense the people living in a totalitarian system are not in a "normal" psychological state.

For the *leaders and their fanatical adherents* who are sworn enemies of an open liberal society the situation is simple: fully seduced, trapped and even intoxicated by their own ideology and simultaneously strongly priviledged by the system one must expect *everything* from them; including suppression and even liquidation of their foes inside the system, and in the worst case aggression against the enemies outside the system if their resistence is not determined enough.

For the *determined dissidents* – a relatively small number – the situation is also clear: They know that after the irreversible establishment of the totalitarian system it is too late to achieve political change by *regular methods*, because the system *denies* such democratic opportunities to its population. Therefore only different *"illegal"* activities – which nevertheless can be *legitimate* by a higher natural right beyond the ideological boundaries of the system – are possible. It depends on the degree of rigidity and coercion in the system whether the strategy of the dissident is successful and whether he risks or forfeits his life.

The *majority of the population* will neither consist of fanatical adherents nor of determined dissidents. This holds independently of their attitude towards the ruling ideology before it became totalitarian. This majority is rather apolitical and wants to find *a method enabling them to muddle through* in difficult times.

The totalitarian regime requires a strict adaptation to its rules in all sectors of the society and a public collectively and personally expressed approval of its ideology by all individuals. Otherwise everybody is threatened with sanctions concerning his profession and/or career. Open and direct opposition is forbidden and punished by prison.

Therefore a remarkable and rather universal *fissionary process* sets in within the mind of the average member of a totalitarian society:

On the one side he/she knuckles under and complies with the situation by *openly exhibiting a political opinion conforming to the official doctrine*. In this way he/she protects his/her career and family.

On the other side he/she builds up his/her *true opinion and attitude* which is *strictly disguised and hidden from the public* and reserved for a few trustworthy friends and family members only.

Thus the political life of this individual takes place on two levels: the level of *official conformation to the party-line* in the environment of its professional life, and the level of *isolation, alienation and inner emigration* concerning its true attitude towards the regime. Between the externally exhibited and hidden true opinion there develops in his/her mind a complicated dialectic between affirmative internalisation and fierce rejection of the official doctrine.

This fundamental *"level splitting"* is the *reaction of the individual* against the massive opinion pressure exerted by the totalitarian regime. It will be the basis of the model set up in Section 6.2.

A short remark about a highly important but also very difficult problem should follow here: How is *moral guilt* and *moral merit* to be measured concerning deeds under totalitarian conditions? Three points must be taken into account here:

(1) A core of absolute, intangible human rights must remain the *invariant basis* for valuation and judgement of deeds in whatever situation.

(2) Merit and guilt are *personal* and *not collective categories* of moral judgement under all conditions.

(3) The main problem consists in the fact that the range and the impact of personal decisions and actions are *dramatically deformed and distorted* under the conditions of a totalitarian system as compared to those in a normal open liberal society. Because the system of checks and balances and of institutions protecting individual rights have been abolished, rescinded and substituted by a conformist judicature under the totalitarian regime, the whole coordinate-system for moral or immoral activities has changed fundamentally. A fair judgement of personal merits and guilts must on the one side take into account the range of personal facilities in that coordinate system and on the other side judge how this range was used or abused in applying or violating principles of humanism.

It is a consequence of this shift of coordinates that hitherto latent virtues (but also depravities) become relevant whereas other hitherto prominent human qualities may change their value and their effect may even *be inverted*. Consider for instance "primary" virtues like humanity, justice and compassion. Applying these virtues to the foes of the system may now mean threat and danger for their defenders. The effects of "secondary" though hitherto highly estimated virtues like discipline and diligence may even be converted to their contrary through their systematic abuse by the totalitarian regime.

An adequate philosophy of morale and jurisdiction which systematically attributes merit and guilt under conditions of totalitarian regimes is still in a rudimentary stage and should be further worked out!

6.1.2 The Phase-Transition Concept versus the Continuity-Hypothesis

Before going into some detail in the analysis of the political psychology at the transition between so different systems as the liberal and the totalitarian society we discuss the more general question of the *interpretation* of such a transition.

Two alternative theses are under discussion among historians: the *continuity thesis* and the *discontinuity- or phase-transition thesis*.

The *continuity-thesis* asserts that every historical event or sequence of events is *in principle explainable* from the previously known continuous stream of historical events. Even the persons and their actions in extraordinary political events are *under this interpretation* the in principle exchangeable executioners of previously visible historical longterm-processes and trends.

In contrast to this, the *discontinuity or phase-transition thesis* asserts that in history there exist relatively infrequent *revolutionary events* where *historical discontinuities* occur which are *not fully explainable* and understandable on the basis of previously known historical facts. One could say that in these cases there occurs an "*accident beyond design*" because of an unpredictable *coincidence of accidental factors* which is as such highly improbable.

Considering from a system-theoretical standpoint the question which of the two controversial theses is to be preferred we come to the conclusion that the discontinuity thesis is the better founded one.

The argument for this conclusion is the following: Historical and/or social phase-transitions are by definition revolutionary events in which the macrovariables of the system *change their whole dynamical mode*. A *necessary concomitant circumstance* of such a phase-transition is the appearance of *critical fluctuations*. These critical fluctuations are crucial for deciding the question *which direction* the path of the system will take at the *cross-roads*. In our case they are decisive for the question whether the political system will remain a liberal democratic one or whether it tumbles into the new totalitarian phase.

However – and this is the essential argument – the critical fluctuations are of *random nature* and are *neither* predictable by the research of historians, *nor* by the macroequations of any mathematical model! At best the *full set* of macrovariables and (not predictable) fluctuating microvariables which *both together* are causative for the concrete course of historical events at a phase-transition can be recognized by historians *only retrospectively*.

Therefore the general conclusion must be: In the rare cases of historical phase-transitions *fluctuations* become decisive (in contrast to smoothly and continuously evolving situations). These fluctuations consist of thoughts, decisions and activities of one or a few persons in key-positions in a global situation on the verge of a possible phase-transition.

This does of course not mean, that the continuous – to a high degree "calculable" and therefore predictable – macrovariables would be unimportant. In the contrary! They lead to the "revolutionary situation", i.e. into the vicinity of a destabilizable situation where "*everything can happen*". However, *at* the phase-transition these macrovariables are *insufficient* to make the further course of events predictable!

6.1.3 Political Psychology at a Phase-Transition

In this section we focus on the transition from a liberal democratic society to a totalitarian one. According to the arguments of Section 6.1.2 we interpret this transition as a *political phase-transition*.

In view of the merits of liberal democratic systems and the disastrous structure of totalitarian systems discussed in Section 6.1.1 one may wonder *why* the lib → tot phase-transition *is possible at all*. However, it is our thesis that political phase-transitions (including the lib-tot-transition) are *rare but nevertheless universal phenomena* and that their appearance can be embedded within the framework of system-theoretical concepts. If this thesis is correct it must be possible to explain, at least in general terms, which political psychology brings a liberal system into the vicinity of a possible phase-transition, and what is the nature of the steps engendering the transition. (Due to the accidental, casual nature of these steps it is nevertheless *impossible to predict* them and their result in the individual historical event, as already discussed in Section 6.1.2.)

In order to systematize the following considerations we distinguish between the role of the *active promoters* of the phase-transition just before, during, and just after its occurrence, and the role of the *affected participants* of the phase-transition in the same critical time-interval.

The *active promoters* of a phase-transition are fanatical adherents of an extreme totalitarian ideology. Because this political or religious ideology has no chance of finding the approval of a majority of the population under conditions of openly competing ideas in a liberal democratic society, their intention can only be to *overthrow the whole liberal system*. In other words: these active promoters are *necessarily sworn enemies of the liberal system*.

Their origins are political or religious groups of authoritarian organisation in which extremistic political or fundamentalist religious doctrines are thriving. If such groups do not only exert strong opinion pressure against their own members but also *infiltrate* the society either tacitly or by aggressive propaganda they may – and have – become dangerous to the whole society. Because of the deviant nature of their extreme ideology the promoters of the overthrow are often *underestimated* concerning their instinct for the critical situation and their talent to engender the transition.

In *abstract terms* their strategy consists of three steps: (a) to bring the existing liberal system into a *disorienting* and *destabilizing* situation, (b) to *magnify* and *escalate those critical fluctuations* at the phase-transition which go in *the direction desired by them*, and (c) to make the phase-transition *irreversible* by *cutting off* all still existing fluctuations which could re-establish the old phase.

In *concrete terms* this can for instance mean (a) propaganda, arousal of emotions, defamation of political foes; (b) corruption, tricky negotiations, "strategic" lies, and (c) revoking of rights, abolishment of "old" institutions, creation of fear.

Let us now consider the role of the *affected participants*. They are the majority, but a diverse one, consisting of defenders of the liberal system and of many apolitical indifferent people, active and passive citizens, moral and opportunistic ones, etc. If they would react against the active promoters of the phase-transition in a *determined manner*, then a lib $\rightarrow$ tot transition would be impossible. However there may exist structural deficiencies, exogenous effects, faulty behaviour of key-persons and the misguided reactions of an unconcerned and inconsiderate part of the population which together with the decidedness of the transition-promoters may engender a *coincidence of factors* leading to the *"accident beyond design"*, i.e. the collapse of the system into a totalitarian phase.

In this process the structural deficiencies, exogenous effects, the general political psychology in the society and the decidedness of the extremists are to some extent predictable, whereas the decisions, the failure and the success of key-persons on both sides belong to the unpredictable accidental and casual factors.

We now indicate a few *possible structural deficiencies* of a liberal system and some *elements of a common political psychology* among people which may favour the lib-tot-transition.

One possible deficiency and weakness of a liberal system is connected with *Popper's paradox* which states that a liberal democracy granting unrestricted absolute freedom of activity to the sworn enemies of freedom is *potentially unstable*.

Indeed, a liberal democracy is more safe if it provides certain "boundary conditions", i.e. legal measures protecting it against ideologists determined to destroy the whole system of liberty at all. Without such protective measures a democracy must trust in the hoped for probability that a critical situation on the verge of a phase-transition never occurs.

Another possible deficiency could consist in built-in institutional structures allowing of *self-paralysis*, e.g. in terms of unsolvable stalemate situations. The consequential inefficiency of democratic procedures ("Problemstau") could then lead to frustration concerning the liberal system as such which is a destabilizing factor.

Let us now consider factors of common political psychology *before* an imminent lib-tot-transition, i.e. in a situation where it still can be avoided.

The first main factor is a *lack of readiness* of the citizen *to defend the liberal system* which grants his own freedom. It is clear that a widespread renunciation of public responsibilities and commitments and a withdrawal from public life *weakens the democracy* which depends on broad participation.

The second main factor is the fact that in times of exogenous difficulties, e.g. economical crises or international tension, the *demagogic agitation of totalitarian parties*, working with delusive promises and denunciations of their foes is able *to exert a seductive attraction* on politically naive minds who thereupon begin to internalize parts of the totalitarian ideology. Also intellectuals are not immune against this propaganda, in particular if expressed in *grand yet vague phrases*. The reason is that some of them are overcharged by the complex diversity of competing ideas and views in a pluralistic world, and begin to long for a simple, strong and seemingly unambiguous political ideology expressed by a strong man, i.e. the potential dictator.

The third main factor is the politically immoral attitude of *anticipatory opportunism*. In this case people betray their true political opinion by an early opportunistic change to the ideology of the impending totalitarian system because they expect to be privileged after the turnover. It is clear that this attitude if occurring in relevant numbers is particularly destructive and destabilizing for the existing liberal system and that it helps to engender the phase-transition.

After the lib → tot phase-transition the psycho-political situation has dramatically changed and has become both fatal and crystal clear for most citizens: To the first measures of the promoters of the overthrow it belongs that a fear of sanctions is generated for all who do not want to align to the demands of the just established totalitarian system. The results of these measures have already been described in Section 6.1.1.

Finally let us make some remarks about the *inverse transition*, namely that from a totalitarian to a liberal system. Even if one sympathizes, like the author, with this kind of transition – because it is more adequate to the nature and dignity of humans to prove their worth in the complexity of the world than to be coerced into a predetermined ideology – there nevertheless exist difficult problems with the tot-lib-transition, too.

Firstly, there will inevitably arise *critical fluctuations* in this transition and these can comprise *violent actions and measures*, which are even inherent in the nature of the totalitarian system, when it defends its status.

Secondly, the tot-lib-transition dismisses the former members of the totalitarian system from what is in many respects a *predetermined and prescribed style of life* into the *diversity of a pluralistic system*. It will be difficult and need time to cope with this new diversity, to build up adequate new institutions etc. Help from outside should be granted in order to alleviate and to facilitate this process, so that the new phase does not degenerate into chaos!

However, with a rising level of complexity in the world, with new means of communication etc. it seems *almost inevitable*, if desired or not, that the tot → lib transition will take place sooner or later wherever totalitarian regimes exist. If so, the question arises whether it will be a *hard transition*, with disastrous violent fluctuations, or whether a *soft transition*, with mild fluctuations, is conceivable.

The answer depends in precarious manner on the interplay between those who defend and those who want to get rid of the system. If the proponents of the state-doctrine yield more flexibility and openness *within* the frame, and finally *beyond* the frame of their ideology, and if their foes are ready to participate in this opening process, there exists a certain chance for a soft transition: This soft variant will however occur only if it is *fast enough* to satisfy those waiting impatiently for the liberalisation, and simultaneously *slow enough* to allow of a sufficient learning process among the ideologists.

6.1.4 The Seizure of Power by Hitler as a Paradigm of a Political Phase-Transition

In this section the author follows – in very condensed and abridged form – the description and interpretation of Hitler's seizure of power by the internationally renowned historian Eberhard Jäckel in his book "Das deutsche Jahrhundert" [17]. There he uses the word "Der grösste anzunehmende Unfall", i.e. "the worst case accident" for this event, in analogy to the "accident beyond design" in a nuclear power station. The author owes to Eberhard Jäckel the insight, that Hitler's seizure of power can in practically all respects be taken as the *paradigm* of a (big and disastrous) *political phase-transition*.

In Section 6.1.3 we have tried to characterize in general terms the role of the active promoters of a phase-transition *just before, during* and *just after* its occurrence. Of course, Hitler and his acolytes *were determined* to overthrow the Weimar democracy and to substitute it with the totalitarian "Third Reich". Therefore let us follow the sequence of events in the stages "the way to power", "the seizure of power", and "the liquidation of the democracy", restricting our condensed presentation to the time from 1928 to 1938.

The Way to Power

The Weimar democracy, established after the first world war, was moderately successful in spite of many internal and external difficulties, so that Hitler's extremist party, the NSDAP ("national socialist german workers party") was at first completely irrelevant and won only 2.6% votes in the elections of 1928. However, in 1929, parallel to the economic world crisis beginning in October 1929, the NSDAP began to *grow*. Simultaneously, after the death of the successful foreign minister Stresemann in 1929, the Weimar democracy began to *destabilize*.

After the resignation of the last parliamentary coalition government president Hindenburg nominated on March 30th, 1930, Heinrich Brüning as chancellor, now governing by decree (Verordnungen) and no longer by parliamentary majority. This was according to the wishes of right-wing conservativists who wanted back the old system of a constitutional monarchy instead of a parliamentary democracy. Brüning dissolved the Reichstag (The Imperial parliament) and in the new elections on September 14th, 1930, the NSDAP won 18.3% votes. After the re-election of Hindenburg on April 10th, 1932, for his second term in office as president he dismissed Brüning and nominated Franz von Papen, a reactionary conservativist politician, as chancellor on June 1st, 1932.

The Seizure of Power

Von Papen's plans were restaurative ones and he intended to realize them with the help of Hitler in his cabinet and his strengthening NSDAP behind him. Hitler however, being aware of the destabilizing effects of the economic crisis and trusting in the alluring effect of his demagogy, required new elections, which took place on July 31st, 1932. Indeed, he won 37.3% of the votes, more than one third of the electorate, but nevertheless not the majority. Hitler now insisted on becoming chancellor, but Hindenburg, distrusting him, denied this office to him. On the other hand, the newly elected Reichstag gave on September 12th, 1932, a vote of non-confidence against van Papen. New elections followed on November 6th, 1932, in which the number of votes for Hitler sank, in spite of his massive agitation, from 37.3% to 33.1%. Again Hitler required to become chancellor, and again Hindenburg denied it. The world felt relief and believed that the threat by Hitler was now averted.

However, von Papen now negotiated with Hitler, who insidiously stipulated for becoming the chancellor, but offered to form a cabinet with eight conservatives, von Papen included, and only three NSDAP-members, and to govern via an "emergency power act" ("Ermächtigungsgesetz"). Von Papen, in his short-sightedness, believed that in this way the influence of the conservativists could be permanently secured (in spite of the small minority behind them) and that Hitler could be "tamed" by this construction, whereas Hitler of course already knew that he would easily manoeuvre out the conservative members of the government. Finally, von Papen and his colleague Schleicher convinced Hindenburg to nominate Hitler as chancellor of Germany on January 30th, 1933.

The Liquidation of the Democracy

After the seizure of power Hitler liquidated, destroyed and abolished in a breathtaking speed all laws, orders, and institutions of the democracy whose too lenient and generous freedom he had abused in order to come to power.

Taking the setting on fire of the Reichstag-building by a confused criminal as pretext, he rescinded on February 28th, 1933, "for the time being" *all rights of the constitution of the Weimar democracy*, including the rights of free opinion, free press and the right of public meetings. Here, "for the time being" meant until 1945.

After the dissolution of the Reichstag on February 1st, 1933, new elections under the new conditions took place on March 5th, 1933. In spite of the hindrance and obstruction of the still existing old parties, the NSDAP reached 43.9% only, so that even now a majority of the Germans did *not vote* for Hitler.

The newly elected Reichstag now passed (against the votes of the SPD only) the decisive *Ermächtigungsgesetz* (emergency power act) which empowered the government to enact laws on its own authority. The labour unions were dissolved on May 2nd, 1933, and since July 14th, 1933, the NSDAP was the only permitted party. The formation of new parties was forbidden. Henceforth no legal avenue was left for the opposition to express its opinion.

The next fundamental liquidation law was the *"law on the reconstruction of the Reich"* of January 30th, 1934, in which the old federal structure of Germany was annulled: The parliaments of the countries of Germany were dissolved and the sovereign rights of the countries abolished. The central national government even usurped the right to change the constitution (although Hitler governed without a constitution).

In the meantime Hitler also took the office of the Reichspräsident after Hindenburg's death in August 1934.

Although the central government was simultaneously executive and legislative by the Ermächtigungsgesetz, it was finally rendered powerless and inert by Hitler. The last session of the cabinet took place on December 9th, 1937, and the last consultation of ministers on February 5th, 1938.

The Reichstag now consisted of the NSDAP only and had a merely propagandistic role.

This means that in all decisive respects Hitler alone decided about the policy of Germany, only advised by individuals of his own choice. In all respects estimated important by Hitler the Nazi-state did not function by laws and norms any more, but by "measures" ordered by the "Führer". By uniting the power over executive, legislative and judicature in his hands, Hitler had reached the climax of his power. The time was now ripe for the obsessional perpetrator to unleash the next phase-transition, the second world war!

It needs no further emphasis to state, that in the history of this phase-transition all its elements, namely the *destabilization* of the old phase, the unpredictable *random fluctuations during the transition* and the radical measures to make the new phase *irreversible*, are present in dramatic completeness.

6.2   The Minimal Quantitative Model

We shall now try to set up a minimal model in order to capture in *semiquantitative manner* at least some main processes within the lib-tot transition. (The model has been worked out in [21], [22] and [23]. Earlier and simpler versions of the model can be found in [24] and [25].) It needs however some justification that such a "minimal model" is possible at all.

6.2.1   The Justification of a "Minimal Model"

In view of the complex sequence of events in a lib-tot phase-transition, which was verbally indicated in Section 6.1 it seems unwise to design a model comprising the full complexity of the liberal phase and the details of the fluctuations of the transient phase before the setting in of the totalitarian phase.

However, in view of the *dramatic shrinkage of complexity* it seems possible to focus on the generation and the initially stabilizing and finally destabilizing processes of the totalitarian phase. The following simplifying structures of the nascent totalitarian system must then be taken into account:

(1) Practically all members of the totalitarian system underlie a *strong alignment* ("Gleichschaltung") *pressure*. The system e.g. demands that the citizens publicly express approval of the now ruling ideology. The consequence is a rather sudden change of the trends (and the corresponding trend-parameters) determining the political decision behaviour of the citizens under the new situation.

(2) The former differentiated political opinion of the citizens *plays no role any more*. Instead, the plurality of the (openly exhibited) political opinions has been reduced to two possibilities only: approval of, or dissidence from, the official political doctrine of the totalitarian state.

(3) While all citizens are *collectivated* concerning the required open "confession of allegiance", they are *isolated* concerning their *true opinion*, because it can mean a danger or at least a personal disadvantage to mention this true opinion openly.

Therfore a *new characteristic of the political psychology* in totalitarian states begins to evolve its own dynamics: The inner (hidden and disguised) political attitude concerning the situation in the totalitarian system. Due to its very nature this *inner attitude* cannot be revealed by naive field surveys. (Naive positivistic behaviourists would even tend to cancel this "hidden variable" because it cannot be directly measured.) Nevertheless this characteristic plays a decisive role in the dynamics of a totalitarian system and cannot be dismissed in the construction of a quantitative model.

The design of any model should capture at least points 1, 2 and 3.

6.2.2 The Variables, Transition Rates, and Utility Functions

Personal Variables

Let us now introduce the extensive and intense personal variables of the model. At first we make the drastically simplifying assumption of *one homogeneous population* whose members react in the same manner to the situation. This means we omit the index α distinguishing between different subpopulations. The oversimplification can be partially justified because in a system of "state-slavery" not only the normal citizens but even the members of the administration (the "nomenclatura") underlie comparable pressures and show eventually comparable reactions. (Detailed information about this pressure in another totalitarian system, the communist system, has e.g. been given in [26].)

We have already stated, that under totalitarian conditions only *two contrasting publicly exhibited political opinions* exist: the opinion $i = $ "+" of the *ruling ideology*, and the opinion $i = $ "−" of *dissidence from that ideology*.

We now assume that each individual exhibits exactly one of these two opinions. (This includes that indifference is not tolerated.) If n_+ and n_- are the numbers of people with opinion + and −, respectively, the *configuration of openly exhibited political opinions* consists of the two extensive personal variables only:

$$n = \{n_+, n_-\}. \tag{6.1}$$

If $2N$ is the number of the total population (for convenience assumed to be an *even* integer), one has the evident relations

$$n_+ + n_- = 2N \tag{6.2}$$

and

$$n_+ = N + n; \quad n_- = N - n \tag{6.3}$$

after introducing the *majority variable*

$$n = \frac{1}{2}(n_+ - n_-) \tag{6.4}$$

which is an integer varying in the domain

$$-N \leq n \leq +N. \tag{6.5}$$

Birth–death processes are neglected, so that $2N$ remains constant with time.

In order to take into account point 3 of Section 6.2.1 we now introduce a hidden, i.e. not externally exhibited *intense personal variable* characterizing the *internal inclination and estimation* of each person concerning his/her own publicly exhibited opinion $i = +$ or $-$. (The introduction of this kind of variable does of course correspond to the already mentioned splitting of the political psychology into a public and a hidden level for individuals living in totalitarian systems.)

This *inner inclination* of an individual to its own publicly expressed "official" opinion i is described by a variable ϑ_i assuming discrete integer values for simplicity. The *inner inclination variable* ϑ_i is introduced as a *measure for the different degrees* of inner approval, inner neutrality or inner disapproval of the externally pronounced opinion i. This measure is chosen so, that

values $\vartheta_i > 0$ describe inner approval of opinion i;

value $\vartheta_i = 0$ describes inner neutrality to opinion i;

values $\vartheta_i < 0$ describe inner disapproval of opinion i.

We assume that ϑ_i varies between the limits $\pm\Theta$, so that

$$-\Theta \leq \vartheta_i \leq +\Theta. \tag{6.6}$$

Whereas the ruling ideology "+", but also the opposing dissident ideology "−" in totalitarian systems have often a tendency to lose contact with reality and to give a biased, distorted or even perverted interpretation of facts, the inner inclination variables ϑ_+ and ϑ_- do represent the still persisting realism and common sense in the minds of the adherents to ideology "+" and "−", respectively. Therefore there exists a *strong correlation* between ϑ_+ and ϑ_-, which can be seen as follows:

If, say, the ruling ideology "+" gives by its propaganda a strongly distorted account of the situation, the variable ϑ_+ will go − perhaps after some relaxation time − into a state of inner disapproval $\vartheta_+ < 0$. Simultaneously, the dissident ideology "−" will strongly reproach this distorted picture given by ideology "+" and will therefore find inner approval $\vartheta_- > 0$ among the adherents of ideology "−".

This antagonistic behaviour of the variables ϑ_+ and ϑ_- can be generalized, and it is highly plausible to postulate the general relation between them

$$\vartheta_- = -\vartheta_+ \quad \text{or} \quad \vartheta_+ + \vartheta_- = 0 \tag{6.7}$$

which simultaneously reduces the number of independent variables. Of course, the dynamics of ϑ_+ and ϑ_- will have to be introduced in a manner compatible with (6.7).

Concomitant Variables

There can be no doubt about the fact that further macrovariables − in particular economic and legislative ones − determine the way of life in any system, whether liberal or totalitarian. However, in a totalitarian system with a comprehensive ideology claiming to be "the truth" the structure and evolution of *all macrovariables* are dominated, if not fully determined, by the ruling ideology. (For instance, this holds definitely for the structure and evolution of the whole economy in communist regimes.) Under such circumstances it is a plausible, albeit only approximately valid assumption that all further macrovariables are *functions of the majority variable n* which stands proxy for the degree of penetration of the state-ideology into all aspects of life. The consequence of this assumption is a *dramatic simplification of the macrodynamics of the system*: If all other macrovariables are (approximately) concomitant functions of n, it is sufficient for a minimal model of a totalitarian system to consider only the dynamics of the variables $\{n_+, n_-\}$ interacting with $\{\vartheta_+, \vartheta_-\}$, because all other macrovariables accompany and are resulting functions of these key-variables. Therefore we consider the *socioconfiguration*

$$\{n_+, n_-; \vartheta_+, \vartheta_-\} \tag{6.8}$$

consisting of the extensive personal variables $\{n_+, n_-\}$ and the intense personal variables $\{\vartheta_+, \vartheta_-\}$ as the set of relevant variables of the minimal model.

Trend-Parameters

The trend-parameters describe behavioural trends and are *measures for the political psychology* of the citizens. In our model they are treated as *exogenously given constants* (see Section 6.4.1) or given simple functions of time co-evolving with the variables of the system (see Section 6.4.2). We remark that an extended model would have to take into account that such trend-parameters are neither "constants of nature" nor simple "concomitant functions of time" but will satisfy a (usually slow, but under extreme circumstances even fast) coupled dynamics which could be endogenized by setting up equations of evolution for them, too.

Here we summarize the trend-parameters used in the minimal model and give a short explanation of their meaning. Their explicit meaning follows from their role in the transition rates set up below.

List of trendparameters

$$\kappa = \text{opinion pressure parameter}$$
$$\gamma = \text{inclination influence parameter}$$
$$\beta > 0 = \text{affirmation propensity parameter}$$
$$\beta < 0 = \text{dissidence propensity parameter}$$
$$\nu = \text{opinion evolution speed parameter}$$
$$\mu = \text{inclination evolution speed parameter}$$

Short explanation of their meaning:

A positive κ measures the readiness of a representative citizen to adapt to and to align oneself publicly with the majority opinion, the more pronounced this majority is. (This readiness has nothing to do with the true conviction of the citizen.)

A positive γ measures the strength of the amplification (diminution) of the adaptation readiness by an approving (disapproving) inner inclination. (Here, the inner inclination ϑ_i is an expression of the true attitude of the citizen.)

A positive β measures a principally affirmative evolution trend of the inner inclination. It leads – sooner or later – to the evolution of a *positive* inner inclination ϑ_i, if "i" is the majority opinion.

A negative β measures a principally dissident evolution trend of the inner inclination. It leads – sooner or later – to the evolution of a *negative* inner inclination ϑ_i, if "i" is the majority opinion.

ν and μ measure the time scale on which the evolution of the majority variable and the inclination variables, respectively, take place.

Transition Rates

The elementary transitions of the political socioconfiguration (6.8) are the following:

$$
\begin{aligned}
\{n_+, n_-; \vartheta_+, \vartheta_-\} &\Rightarrow \{n_+ + 1, n_- - 1; \vartheta_+, \vartheta_-\} \quad \text{(a)} \\
\{n_+, n_-; \vartheta_+, \vartheta_-\} &\Rightarrow \{n_+ - 1, n_- + 1; \vartheta_+, \vartheta_-\} \quad \text{(b)} \\
\{n_+, n_-; \vartheta_+, \vartheta_-\} &\Rightarrow \{n_+, n_-; \vartheta_+ + 1, \vartheta_- - 1\} \quad \text{(c)} \\
\{n_+, n_-; \vartheta_+, \vartheta_-\} &\Rightarrow \{n_+, n_-; \vartheta_+ - 1, \vartheta_- + 1\} \quad \text{(d)}
\end{aligned}
\qquad (6.9)
$$

The transitions (a) and (b) describe generalized migration processes, namely the transition of one citizen from (publicly exhibited) opinion "$-$" to opinion "$+$", and vice versa. The transitions (c) and (d) describe a transition step of the inner attitude ϑ_+ towards a higher (lower) value and simultaneously of ϑ_- towards a lower (higher) value. Taking into account, that because of (6.2) and (6.7) the variables n (see (6.4)) and

$$\vartheta = \frac{1}{2}(\vartheta_+ - \vartheta_-) = \vartheta_+ = -\vartheta_- \qquad (6.10)$$

are the only relevant variables, the transitions (6.9) may also be characterized by

$$\begin{aligned} \{n, \vartheta\} &\Rightarrow \{n+1, \vartheta\} \quad &\text{(a)} \\ \{n, \vartheta\} &\Rightarrow \{n-1, \vartheta\} \quad &\text{(b)} \\ \{n, \vartheta\} &\Rightarrow \{n, \vartheta+1\} \quad &\text{(c)} \\ \{n, \vartheta\} &\Rightarrow \{n, \vartheta-1\} \quad &\text{(d)} \end{aligned} \qquad (6.11)$$

We have now to set up the transition rates by which the transitions (6.9), or equivalently (6.11) take place. Here we follow the general rules of Chapter 3.

The generalized migratory rates have, according to equation (3.28) the form

$$\begin{aligned} w_{+-}(\mathbf{n}_{+-}, \mathbf{n}; \vartheta) &= n_- p_{+-}(\mathbf{n}_{+-}, \mathbf{n}; \vartheta) \quad &\text{(a)} \\ w_{-+}(\mathbf{n}, \mathbf{n}_{+-}; \vartheta) &= (n_+ + 1) p_{-+}(\mathbf{n}, \mathbf{n}_{+-}; \vartheta) \quad &\text{(b)} \end{aligned} \qquad (6.12)$$

with the individual transition rates between the opinions

$$\begin{aligned} p_{+-}(\mathbf{n}_{+-}, \mathbf{n}; \vartheta) &= \nu_{+-}(\mathbf{n}_{+-}, \mathbf{n}; \vartheta) \exp\{u_+(\mathbf{n}_{+-}; \vartheta) - u_-(\mathbf{n}; \vartheta)\}; \\ p_{-+}(\mathbf{n}, \mathbf{n}_{+-}; \vartheta) &= \nu_{-+}(\mathbf{n}, \mathbf{n}_{+-}; \vartheta) \exp\{u_-(\mathbf{n}; \vartheta) - u_+(\mathbf{n}_{+-}; \vartheta)\}. \end{aligned} \qquad (6.13)$$

Here,

$$\nu_{+-}(\mathbf{n}_{+-}, \mathbf{n}; \vartheta) = \nu_{-+}(\mathbf{n}, \mathbf{n}_{+-}; \vartheta) = \tilde{\nu} \qquad (6.14)$$

is chosen as a constant mobility factor for the transition and

$$u_i(\mathbf{n}; \vartheta) = u_i(n_i; \vartheta_i) \qquad (6.15)$$

is the "utility" felt by adherents of opinion "i" to express publicly that opinion.

Similarly, the rates for the changes (c), (d) of the inner inclination $\vartheta = \vartheta_+ = -\vartheta_-$ assume for all citizens (regardless whether having opinion "+" or "−") the form:

$$\begin{aligned} w_\vartheta^\uparrow(n, \vartheta) &= \rho_\vartheta^\uparrow(n, \vartheta) \exp\{v(n, \vartheta+1) - v(n, \vartheta)\} \quad &\text{(c)} \\ w_\vartheta^\downarrow(n, \vartheta) &= \rho_\vartheta^\downarrow(n, \vartheta) \exp\{v(n, \vartheta-1) - v(n, \vartheta)\} \quad &\text{(d)} \end{aligned} \qquad (6.16)$$

Here,

$$v(n, \vartheta) = v_+(n_+, \vartheta_+) = v_-(n_-, \vartheta_-) \qquad (6.17)$$

is the degree of satisfaction of a citizen with his/her inner inclination ϑ_+ or ϑ_- (where $\vartheta_+ = \vartheta$; $\vartheta_- = -\vartheta$), and the mobilities $\rho_\vartheta^\uparrow(n, \vartheta)$, $\rho_\vartheta^\downarrow(n, \vartheta)$ are chosen to take into account the *saturation effect* if ϑ approaches its maximal or minimal amplitude Θ or $(-\Theta)$, respectively. A simple and plausible choice for $\rho_\vartheta^\uparrow$ and $\rho_\vartheta^\downarrow$ is

$$\rho_\vartheta^\uparrow(n,\vartheta) = \mu(\Theta - \vartheta) \equiv \mu(\Theta - \vartheta_+) \equiv \mu(\Theta + \vartheta_-);$$
$$\rho_\vartheta^\downarrow(n,\vartheta) = \mu(\Theta + \vartheta) \equiv \mu(\Theta + \vartheta_+) \equiv \mu(\Theta - \vartheta_-). \tag{6.18}$$

Utility Functions

The utility functions (6.15) and (6.17) must now be explicitly chosen. They are expressions of the political psychology of the citizens in the given situation described by $\{n_+, n_-, \vartheta_+, \vartheta_-\}$ or equivalently by $\{n, \vartheta\}$. The trend-parameters κ, γ, β listed above appear in them. We make the following choices:

$$u_+(n_+, \vartheta_+) = \frac{1}{2}(\kappa n_+ + \gamma \vartheta_+);$$
$$u_-(n_-, \vartheta_-) = \frac{1}{2}(\kappa n_- + \gamma \vartheta_-), \tag{6.19}$$

and

$$v_+(n_+, \vartheta_+) = \beta(n_+ - N)\vartheta_+;$$
$$v_-(n_-, \vartheta_-) = \beta(n_- - N)\vartheta_-, \tag{6.20}$$

so that

$$v(n,\vartheta) = \beta n\vartheta = v_+(n_+, \vartheta_+) = v_-(n_-, \vartheta_-) \tag{6.21}$$

with the following meaning:

For given positive opinion pressure κ and inclination influence γ the *utility* $u_i(n_i, \vartheta_i)$ *of pronouncing publicly opinion "i"* is the higher, the more people do already align to that opinion "i". This utility is increased (diminished) if the inner inclination ϑ_i approves (disapproves) the opinion "i".

The satisfaction $v_i(n_i, \vartheta_i)$ with the inner inclination ϑ_i depends on the sign of the trend-parameter β. For $\beta > 0$ (i.e. affirmation propensity), $v(n,\vartheta) = \beta n\vartheta$ is positive for given majority variable $n > 0$, if ϑ is *positive* (approving). For $\beta < 0$ (i.e. dissidence propensity), $v(n,\vartheta)$ is positive for given majority variable $n > 0$, if ϑ is *negative* (disapproving).

The final form of the transition rates (6.11(a)–(d)) now follows if the utility functions (6.19) and (6.21) as well as the mobility factors (6.14) and (6.18) are inserted into the formulas (6.12) and (6.16). One easily obtains:

$$
\begin{aligned}
w_{+-}(\mathbf{n_{+-}}, \mathbf{n}; \boldsymbol{\vartheta}) \equiv w_{+-}(n, \vartheta) &= \nu(N - n)\exp[\kappa n + \gamma\vartheta] && \text{(a)}\\
w_{-+}(\mathbf{n_{-+}}, \mathbf{n}; \boldsymbol{\vartheta}) \equiv w_{-+}(n, \vartheta) &= \nu(N + n)\exp[-(\kappa n + \gamma\vartheta)] && \text{(b)}\\
w_\vartheta^\uparrow(\mathbf{n}; \boldsymbol{\vartheta}) \equiv w_\vartheta^\uparrow(n, \vartheta) &= \mu(\Theta - \vartheta)\exp[\beta n] && \text{(c)}\\
w_\vartheta^\downarrow(\mathbf{n}; \boldsymbol{\vartheta}) \equiv w_\vartheta^\downarrow(n, \vartheta) &= \mu(\Theta + \vartheta)\exp[-\beta n] && \text{(d)}
\end{aligned}
\tag{6.22}
$$

with $\nu = \tilde{\nu}\exp[\kappa/2]$.

The role of the trend-parameters κ, γ and β in the transition rates (6.22) is the reason for their interpretation given above, which can now be repeated with more quantitative precision:

Let us assume a positive κ. Then a positive n, which means an existing majority of opinion "+" leads to a favouring of transitions (6.22a) from $-$ to $+$, and simultaneously to a disfavouring of transitions (6.22b) from $+$ to $-$. A negative n, that means a majority of opinion "$-$", conversely leads to a higher individual transition rate from "+" to "$-$" and a lower one from "$-$" to "+". That means: a positive κ always leads to a trend of the individual to adapt its own (publicly exhibited) opinion to the opinion of the *majority*. The degree of this trend therefore measures the amount of "opinion pressure" in the society.

However, the transition rates (6.22a,b) also depend on the values of $\vartheta = \vartheta_+ = -\vartheta_-$. Let us assume a *positive* γ. If $\vartheta = \vartheta_+$ is positive (that means inner approval of opinion "+") and if $n > 0$, the terms κn and $\gamma \vartheta$ in (6.22a,b) have the *same sign* and the transition "$-$" $\Rightarrow$ "+" is further favoured against the inverse transition "+" $\Rightarrow$ "$-$". If, on the other hand, $\vartheta = \vartheta_+$ is negative (that means inner disapproval of opinion "+") and if $n > 0$, the terms κn and $\gamma \vartheta$ in (6.22a,b) have *opposite sign*. This means that the disapproving inner inclination ($\vartheta_+ < 0$) diminishes the effect of the opinion pressure term κn in the transition rates. As we shall see this effect may become dramatic and may eventually lead to the destabilisation of the totalitarian system.

The parameter β governs the evolution of the inner inclination via the transition rates (6.22c,d). If β is positive (describing an affirmation propensity), then a positive n (majority of opinion "+") eventually leads to the evolution of a positive ϑ_+ (approval of opinion "+") which further stabilizes opinion "+". If, on the other hand, β is negative (describing a dissident propensity) then a positive n will eventually lead to the evolution of a negative ϑ_+ (inner disapproval of opinion "+") which may finally destabilize the majority for opinion "+".

6.2.3   The Evolution Equations of the Minimal Model

The evolution equations of the model, namely the *master equation* for the probability distribution over the relevant variables $\{n, \vartheta\}$ and the *quasi-meanvalue equations* for the mean evolution of the stochastic trajectories, can now be set up in straight forward manner.

The Master Equation

Let $P(n, \vartheta; t)$ be the probability distribution over the integer variables $\{n, \vartheta\}$ which vary in the domain

$$-N \leq n \leq +N;$$
$$-\Theta \leq \vartheta \leq +\Theta. \tag{6.23}$$

Since the probability of the system to be in anyone of the states $\{n, \vartheta\}$ is equal to 1, the probability function $P(n, \vartheta; t) \geq 0$ must be normalized to

$$\sum_{n=-N}^{+N} \sum_{\vartheta=-\Theta}^{+\Theta} P(n, \vartheta; t) = 1. \tag{6.24}$$

Specializing the general form (3.35) of the master equation to the present model one obtains:

$$\frac{dP(n,\vartheta;t)}{dt} = \left[w_{+-}(n-1,\vartheta)P(n-1,\vartheta;t) + w_{-+}(n+1,\vartheta)P(n+1,\vartheta;t)\right]$$
$$- \left[w_{+-}(n,\vartheta)P(n,\vartheta;t) + w_{-+}(n,\vartheta)P(n,\vartheta;t)\right]$$
$$+ \left[w_\vartheta^\uparrow(n,\vartheta-1)P(n,\vartheta-1;t) + w_\vartheta^\downarrow(n,\vartheta+1)P(n,\vartheta+1;t)\right]$$
$$- \left[w_\vartheta^\uparrow(n,\vartheta)P(n,\vartheta;t) + w_\vartheta^\downarrow(n,\vartheta)P(n,\vartheta;t)\right], \tag{6.25}$$

where of course the explicit transition rates (6.22) must be inserted.

The Quasi-Meanvalue Equations

The quasi-meanvalue equations follow by specialisation of equations (3.42) to the present case. They read, after going over from $\{\hat{n}_+, \hat{n}_-, \hat{\vartheta}_+, \hat{\vartheta}_-\}$ to the relevant variables $\{\hat{n}, \hat{\vartheta}\}$:

$$\frac{d\hat{n}(t)}{dt} = w_{+-}(\hat{n}(t),\hat{\vartheta}(t)) - w_{-+}(\hat{n}(t),\hat{\vartheta}(t))$$
$$= 2\nu\{N\sinh(\kappa\hat{n} + \gamma\hat{\vartheta}) - \hat{n}\cosh(\kappa\hat{n} + \gamma\hat{\vartheta})\} \tag{6.26}$$

and

$$\frac{d\hat{\vartheta}(t)}{dt} = w_\vartheta^\uparrow(\hat{n}(t),\hat{\vartheta}(t)) - w_\vartheta^\downarrow(\hat{n}(t),\hat{\vartheta}(t))$$
$$= \mu\{(\Theta - \hat{\vartheta})\exp(\beta\hat{n}) - (\Theta + \hat{\vartheta})\exp(-\beta\hat{n})\}$$
$$= 2\mu\{\Theta\sinh(\beta\hat{n}) - \hat{\vartheta}\cosh(\beta\hat{n})\}. \tag{6.27}$$

Under the assumption of constant trendparameters $\kappa, \gamma, \beta, \nu, \mu$ they are autonomous nonlinear coupled differential equations for $\hat{n}(t)$ and $\hat{\vartheta}(t)$.

From the equations (6.26) and (6.27) one may go over to their *scaled form* by introducing:

$$x = \frac{\hat{\vartheta}}{\Theta} \quad \text{where} \quad -1 \le x \le +1; \quad y = \frac{\hat{n}}{N} \quad \text{where} \quad -1 \le y \le +1 \tag{6.28}$$

and

$$\tau = 2\nu t; \quad \tilde{\mu} = \frac{\mu}{\nu} > 0; \quad \tilde{\kappa} = N\kappa; \quad \tilde{\gamma} = \Theta\gamma; \quad \tilde{\beta} = N\beta. \tag{6.29}$$

The dynamic variables are now the *scaled majority variable* $y(\tau)$ and the *scaled inner inclination variable* $x(\tau)$ depending on the dimensionless time $\tau = 2\nu t$. The scaled quasi-meanvalue equations read:

$$\frac{dy}{d\tau} = \{\sinh(\tilde{\kappa}y + \tilde{\gamma}x) - y\cosh(\tilde{\kappa}y + \tilde{\gamma}x)\}; \tag{6.30}$$

$$\frac{dx}{d\tau} = \tilde{\mu}\{\sinh(\tilde{\beta}y) - x\cosh(\tilde{\beta}y)\}. \tag{6.31}$$

The master equation (6.25) and the scaled quasi-meanvalue equations (6.30), (6.31) are the basis for simulations of characteristic scenarios in Section 6.4.

6.3 Analytical Considerations

Before the *numerical* solution of the evolution equations we draw some *analytical* conclusions which directly follow from the structure of these equations.

6.3.1 Symmetry of the Evolution Equations

At first we show that the master equation (6.25) and the quasi-meanvalue equations (6.26) and (6.27) exhibit a *simple symmetry* which is due to the fact that the transition rates (6.22) satisfy the symmetry relations

$$w_{-+}(n, \vartheta) = w_{+-}(-n, -\vartheta) \tag{6.32}$$

and

$$w_{\vartheta}^{\downarrow}(n, \vartheta) = w_{\vartheta}^{\uparrow}(-n, -\vartheta). \tag{6.33}$$

After the substitution

$$n \Rightarrow n' = (-n); \quad \vartheta \Rightarrow \vartheta' = (-\vartheta) \tag{6.34}$$

and after making use of (6.32) and (6.33) one observes that

$$\tilde{P}(n, \vartheta; t) \equiv P(-n, -\vartheta; t) \tag{6.35}$$

fulfills exactly the same master equation as $P(n, \vartheta; t)$. In other words: The master equation is invariant under the substitution (6.34). This invariance has the consequence that to each distribution $P(n, \vartheta; t)$ which is a solution of the master equation, there belongs another distribution $\tilde{P}(n, \vartheta; t)$ (defined by (6.35)) being *also a solution* of the same master equation. Since all time dependent solutions of (6.25) converge with $t \to \infty$ into the same *unique* stationary solution $P_{st}(n, \vartheta)$, this solution must therefore fulfill the symmetry relation:

$$P_{st}(n, \vartheta) = P_{st}(-n, -\vartheta). \tag{6.36}$$

The analogous holds for the quasi-meanvalue equations (6.26) and (6.27). These are invariant under the substitution

$$\hat{n}(t) \Rightarrow \hat{n}'(t) = -\hat{n}(t);$$
$$\hat{\vartheta}(t) \Rightarrow \hat{\vartheta}'(t) = -\hat{\vartheta}(t). \tag{6.37}$$

Therefore to each solution $\{\hat{n}(t), \hat{\vartheta}(t)\}$ of the equations (6.26) and (6.27) there belongs another solution $\{\hat{n}'(t) = -\hat{n}(t); \hat{\vartheta}'(t) = -\hat{\vartheta}(t)\}$ of the same equations.

6.3.2 A Special Stationary Solution of the Master Equation

In Chapter 10 it was demonstrated that the stationary solution of the master equation can be constructed *analytically*, if the *condition of detailed balance* holds for the transition rates. In the present case this condition reads

$$w_{-+}(n+1,\vartheta)P_{st}(n+1,\vartheta) = w_{+-}(n,\vartheta)P_{st}(n,\vartheta);$$
$$w_{\vartheta}^{\downarrow}(n,\vartheta+1)P_{st}(n,\vartheta+1) = w_{\vartheta}^{\uparrow}(n,\vartheta)P_{st}(n,\vartheta) \tag{6.38}$$

or equivalently, after elimination of $P_{st}(n,\vartheta)$

$$\frac{w_{\vartheta}^{\downarrow}(n,\vartheta+1)}{w_{\vartheta}^{\uparrow}(n,\vartheta)} \cdot \frac{w_{-+}(n+1,\vartheta+1)}{w_{+-}(n,\vartheta+1)} \cdot \frac{w_{\vartheta}^{\uparrow}(n+1,\vartheta)}{w_{\vartheta}^{\downarrow}(n+1,\vartheta+1)} \cdot \frac{w_{+-}(n,\vartheta)}{w_{-+}(n+1,\vartheta)} = 1. \tag{6.39}$$

After inserting the transition rates (6.22) it turns out, that detailed balance is only fulfilled for the special trendparameter case:

$$\beta = \gamma \tag{6.40}$$

which describes, because of $\gamma > 0$, the case of a *special affirmative* β only.

The stationary $P_{st}(n,\vartheta)$ can then be found making use of the construction formula (see (10.108)).

$$P_{st}(n,\vartheta) = \prod_{\tau=0}^{\vartheta-1} \frac{w_{\vartheta}^{\uparrow}(n,\tau)}{w_{\vartheta}^{\downarrow}(n,\tau+1)} \cdot \prod_{\nu=0}^{n-1} \frac{w_{+-}(\nu,0)}{w_{-+}(\nu+1,0)} P_{st}(0,0) \tag{6.41}$$

which yields, after inserting (6.22) and (6.40):

$$P_{st}(n,\vartheta) = \binom{2N}{N-n}\binom{2N}{N}^{-1}\binom{2\Theta}{\Theta-\vartheta}\binom{2\Theta}{\Theta}^{-1}\exp\left[2\gamma\vartheta n + \kappa n^2\right]P_{st}(0,0) \tag{6.42}$$

with the binomial factor

$$\binom{N}{M} \equiv \frac{N!}{(N-M)!M!}. \tag{6.43}$$

The value of $P_{st}(0,0)$ is finally determined by the normalisation (6.24) of the stationary probability distribution.

It is interesting to note how in this case the extrema, in particular the maxima of the stationary probability distribution are related to the stationary solutions of the corresponding quasi-meanvalue equations:

Rewriting $P_{st}(n,\vartheta)$ by making use of the Stirling formula:

$$n! \approx n^n \exp(-n) \tag{6.44}$$

one obtains the form

$$P_{st}(n,\vartheta) \approx c\exp[F(n,\vartheta)] \tag{6.45}$$

with

$$F(n,\vartheta) = 2\gamma\vartheta n + \kappa n^2 - [(N+n)\ln(N+n) + (N-n)\ln(N-n)] \\ - [(\Theta+\vartheta)\ln(\Theta+\vartheta) + (\Theta-\vartheta)\ln(\Theta-\vartheta)]. \tag{6.46}$$

The *extrema* $\{\tilde{n}, \tilde{\vartheta}\}$ of $P_{st}(n, \vartheta)$ are then determined by

$$\left.\frac{\partial F(n, \vartheta)}{\partial n}\right|_{\tilde{n}, \tilde{\vartheta}} = 0; \quad \left.\frac{\partial F(n, \vartheta)}{\partial \vartheta}\right|_{\tilde{n}, \tilde{\vartheta}} = 0 \tag{6.47}$$

which leads to the transcendental equations for $\{\tilde{n}, \tilde{\vartheta}\}$:

$$\tilde{n} = N \tanh[\kappa\tilde{n} + \gamma\tilde{\vartheta}] \tag{6.48}$$

and

$$\tilde{\vartheta} = \Theta \tanh[\gamma\tilde{n}]. \tag{6.49}$$

On the other hand the *stationary solutions* $\{\hat{n}_{st}, \hat{\vartheta}_{st}\}$ of the quasi-meanvalue equations (6.26) and (6.27) have to satisfy the equations

$$0 = N \sinh(\kappa\hat{n}_{st} + \gamma\hat{\vartheta}_{st}) - \hat{n}_{st} \cosh(\kappa\hat{n}_{st} + \gamma\hat{\vartheta}_{st}); \tag{6.50}$$

$$0 = \Theta \sinh(\gamma\hat{n}_{st}) - \hat{\vartheta}_{st} \cosh(\gamma\hat{n}_{st}) \tag{6.51}$$

which obviously coincide with (6.48) and (6.49), respectively.

A more detailed analysis shows, that the maxima (minima) of $P_{st}(n, \vartheta)$ coincide with the stable (unstable) stationary solutions of the quasi-meanvalue equations.

6.3.3 Stability Analysis of the Stationary Point $\{\hat{y}, \hat{x}\} = \{0, 0\}$

The point $\{\hat{y}, \hat{x}\} = \{0, 0\}$ or $\{\hat{n}, \hat{\vartheta}\} = \{0, 0\}$ is always a stationary point of the quasi-meanvalue equations. Politically interpreted it means (in terms of the oversimplified minimal model) a balanced opinion distribution $\{\hat{n}_+ = \hat{n}_-\}$ with a neutral inner inclination $\{\hat{\vartheta}_+ = \hat{\vartheta}_- = 0\}$ which could describe in oversimplified form *a liberal system in opinion equilibrium* between "+" and "−". However, this state could also be the initial state of a *nascent totalitarian system*. Which case is realized will depend on the question whether $\{\hat{y}, \hat{x}\} = \{0, 0\}$ is a *stable* or *unstable* stationary state.

To decide this question we make a *linear stability analysis* around this point. It will turn out that this analysis also decides about the *global behaviour* of the system.

For *small* $y(\tau)$ and $x(\tau)$ the quasi-meanvalue equations (6.30) and (6.31) read in linearized form:

$$\frac{dy}{d\tau} = \tilde{\gamma}x + \tilde{\rho}y; \tag{6.52}$$

$$\frac{dx}{d\tau} = -\tilde{\mu}x + \tilde{\mu}\tilde{\beta}y, \tag{6.53}$$

where

$$\tilde{\rho} = (\tilde{\kappa} - 1). \tag{6.54}$$

These linear differential equations are solved by the "eigensolutions"

$$y(\tau) = y_0 \exp(\lambda\tau); \quad x(\tau) = x_0 \exp(\lambda\tau), \tag{6.55}$$

where λ must fulfill the eigenvalue condition:

$$\begin{vmatrix} (-\tilde{\mu} - \lambda) & ; & \tilde{\mu}\tilde{\beta} \\ \tilde{\gamma} & ; & (\tilde{\rho} - \lambda) \end{vmatrix} \overset{!}{=} 0 \tag{6.56}$$

which has the solutions:

$$\lambda_{\pm} = -\frac{1}{2}(\tilde{\mu} - \tilde{\rho}) \pm \frac{1}{2}\sqrt{(\tilde{\mu} - \tilde{\rho})^2 + 4\tilde{\mu}(\tilde{\rho} + \tilde{\gamma}\tilde{\beta})}. \tag{6.57}$$

The general solutions of (6.52) and (6.53) can now be represented as a linear combination of two eigensolutions (6.55) with $\lambda = \lambda_+$ and $\lambda = \lambda_-$.

The stationary point $(y, x) = (0, 0)$ will be *stable* only, if any one small deviation $(y(\tau), x(\tau))$ from it converges to zero. This is only fulfilled if both eigenvalues are real and negative or if they are conjugate complex and have negative real parts. Conversely, the stationary point $(y, x) = (0, 0)$ is *unstable*, if at least one eigenvalue is positive or if they are conjugate complex with positive real part.

Hence we read off from the form (6.57) of $\lambda_{\pm}$, that the point $(0, 0)$ is *stable* if the trendparameters are in the domain

$$(\tilde{\mu} - \tilde{\rho}) > 0 \quad \text{and} \quad (\tilde{\rho} + \tilde{\gamma}\tilde{\beta}) < 0 \tag{6.58a}$$

or equivalently

$$\tilde{\kappa} < (1 + \tilde{\mu}) \quad \text{and} \quad \tilde{\beta} < \frac{1 - \tilde{\kappa}}{\tilde{\gamma}}. \tag{6.58b}$$

Conversely, the point $(0, 0)$ is *unstable*, if at least one of the conditions

$$(\tilde{\mu} - \tilde{\rho}) < 0 \quad \text{and/or} \quad (\tilde{\rho} + \tilde{\gamma}\tilde{\beta}) > 0 \tag{6.59a}$$

or equivalently

$$\tilde{\kappa} > (1 + \tilde{\mu}) \quad \text{and/or} \quad \tilde{\beta} > \frac{1 - \tilde{\kappa}}{\tilde{\gamma}} \tag{6.59b}$$

is satisfied.

The eigenvalues are *conjugate complex* if

$$(\tilde{\mu} - \tilde{\rho})^2 + 4\tilde{\mu}(\tilde{\rho} + \tilde{\gamma}\tilde{\beta}) < 0 \tag{6.60a}$$

or equivalently

$$\tilde{\beta} < -\frac{(\tilde{\mu} + \tilde{\rho})^2}{4\tilde{\mu}\tilde{\gamma}} < 0. \tag{6.60b}$$

A limit cycle solution of the full (non-linearized) quasi-meanvalue equations can be expected, if the origin $(0, 0)$ is unstable and if the eigenvalues are complex, that means if (6.59) and (6.60) are simultaneously fulfilled.

Interpretation

The conditions (6.58) for stability and, conversely, (6.59) for instability of point $(0, 0)$, i.e. of the balanced opinion distribution with neutral inner inclination are rather plausible:

If $(0, 0)$ is to remain stable, the opinion pressure parameter $\tilde{\kappa}$ must not exceed a certain threshold and simultaneously the propensity parameter $\tilde{\beta}$ must not be too affirmative, so that both conditions (6.58) are satisfied. If, on the other hand, one of the conditions (6.59) is fulfilled, the balanced opinion situation does not remain stable. This situation occurs if the opinion pressure $\tilde{\kappa}$ exceeds a certain threshold and/or the propensity $\tilde{\beta}$ is sufficiently positive. Indeed, a nascent totalitarian system can be characterized by such trends.

In the next section we will investigate numerically the dynamics of $\{y(\tau), x(\tau)\}$ not only in the vicinity of $\{\hat{y}, \hat{x}\} = \{0, 0\}$ under the conditions of a stable or unstable origin.

6.4   Simulation and Interpretation of Selected Scenarios

The simulations of scenarios have to begin with a remark about the limitations of the model. Apart from its oversimplification it assumes that the trend-parameters $\kappa, \gamma, \beta, \mu, \nu$ listed in Section 6.2.2 are constants during the investigated period of time. This means that we presume a *stable political psychology* in this period. This presumption seems plausible for a stationary liberal system, which is however not in the focus of interest, because the model cannot capture its complexity.

However, for totalitarian systems the assumption needs some further comments: Whereas there is no reason to assume that the speed parameters μ, ν and the influence parameter γ change much at the lib $\rightarrow$ tot phase-transition, it is highly probable that the *opinion pressure parameter* κ and the *propensity parameter* β (determining the dynamics of the inner inclination) have changed their values during the revolutionary events of the lib-tot phase-transition.

This holds in particular for the rather sudden increase of the value of κ due to a mixture of opportunism and fear at the beginning of the totalitarian regime. It is realistic to assume that thereupon this high value of κ persists during the existence of the totalitarian system.

Concerning β it is plausible to assume that a *nascent totalitarian regime* begins with an affirmative propensity β which drives the inner inclination ϑ to positive values of inner approval. The strong deficiencies and violations of the established totalitarian system will however sooner or later drive the propensity β from an affirmative $(\beta > 0)$ to a dissident political psychology $(\beta < 0)$ dragging the inner inclination to values of inner disapproval.

Thus it will be realistic to assume a parameter β *co-evolving* from positive to negative values during the consolidation of the totalitarian regime. As we will see this kind of inner dynamics can finally lead to the *collapse* of the totalitarian system! After this rather sudden event of collapse the parameters κ and β could once more change their values depending on the dramatically changing global political circumstances. In Section 6.4.2 we will try to approach reality by scenario simulations under such quasi-realistic assumptions about κ and β.

It will however be very instructive to investigate first a series of *imaginary scenarios*, each of them being a solution of the model with a *set of constant trend-parameters*. This will be done in Section 6.4.1. The figures and the interpretations of the scenarios with constant trend-parameters will more clearly exhibit the effect of each political trend than the "quasi-realistic approach" with time-dependent trend-parameters where all effects are superimposed.

6.4.1 Scenarios with Constant Trend-Parameters

The presentation of some characteristic scenario simulations of the model equations (6.25) and (6.30), (6.31) is organized according to the following scheme:

Firstly the parameters belonging to each one scenario are fixed and it is decided whether the origin $\{\hat{y}, \hat{x}\} = \{0, 0\}$ is stable or unstable. For illustrative purposes a relatively small number $2N = 80$ of people interacting in a representative subgroup of the society has been chosen, which leads to a reasonable width of the probability distributions.

Secondly each scenario is interpreted in terms of the fluxlines of the quasi-mean-value equations and the solution of the stationary master equation.

Thirdly the Figures (a) depicting the fluxlines and the Figures (b) depicting the stationary probability distribution are exhibited. In some cases also the equipotential lines of the evolution speed parameter and some characteristic stochastic trajectories are represented and discussed.

Since it turns out that societies with an affirmative propensity $\beta > 0$ and those with a dissident propensity $\beta < 0$ behave differently in many mathematical and interpretational aspects we intend to divide the scenarios of this section in two series for (A) "affirmative" societies and (B) "dissident" societies.

(A) Scenarios of Affirmative Societies

Scenario A1

Parameters $N = \Theta = 40$; $\tilde{\mu} = \mu/\nu = 2$; $\tilde{\kappa} = 0$; $\tilde{\beta} = 0.5$; $\tilde{\gamma} = 0.5$.

Stability of Origin Because of $\tilde{\kappa} = 0 < (1 + \tilde{\mu}) = 3$ and $\tilde{\beta} = 0.5 < (1 - \tilde{\kappa})/\tilde{\gamma} = 1/0.5$, the condition (6.58) is fulfilled and the origin is a *stable stationary state*. The eigenvalues λ_+, λ_- are real, because $\tilde{\beta}$ is positive (see (6.60b)).

Interpretation of Scenario A1   Because there exists no opinion pressure ($\tilde{\kappa} = 0$) and the propensity parameter ($\tilde{\beta} = 0.5$) is only weakly affirmative, the fluxlines of the quasi-meanvalues shown in Figure 6.1(a) approach the *balanced opinion situation* $(\hat{y}, \hat{x}) = (0, 0)$ of a *neutral inner inclination* $\hat{\vartheta} = 0$, and an *equal number* $\hat{n}_+ = \hat{n}_-$ of people avowing opinion "+" or "−".

(a)

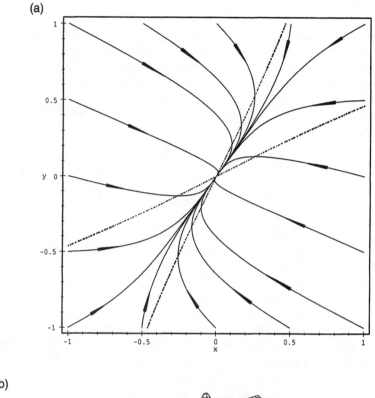

(b)

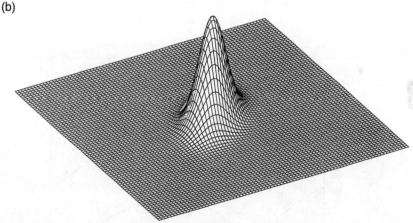

Figure 6.1 (a) (Scenario A1): The fluxlines of the quasi-meanvalues (y, x) approach the balanced opinion situation $(\hat{y}, \hat{x}) = (0, 0)$ which is a stable stationary state; (b) (Scenario A1): The unimodal stationary probability distribution depicts the stochastic fluctuations around the origin $(\hat{y}, \hat{x}) = (0, 0)$.

Although we have stated that the model is too simple to describe a liberal society realistically, the scenario A1 could nevertheless be taken as an *indicator of a liberal political situation* in which two main political parties (e.g. the "conservatives" and the "progressionists") compete. Since for $\tilde{\kappa} = 0$ there is no need to hide one's opinion, the political alternatives are discussed publicly and no one-sided ideology can stabilize internally and publicly. Therefore the stationary inner inclination has no bias and the two political directions gain about equal shares of public approval.

The corresponding stationary probability distribution exhibited in Figure 6.1(b) is unimodal and peaked around the origin $(\hat{y}, \hat{x}) = (0,0)$. It shows that there occur deviations from the exact equality $\hat{n}_+ = \hat{n}_-$ and the exact neutrality $\hat{\vartheta} = 0$ for probabilitstic reasons without any predeterminate bias, because opinion formation is a stochastic process.

Scenario A2

Parameters $N = \Theta = 40; \tilde{\mu} = \mu/\nu = 2; \tilde{\kappa} = 0; \tilde{\beta} = 1.2; \tilde{\gamma} = 1.2.$

Stability of Origin   Because of $\tilde{\kappa} = 0 < (1 + \tilde{\mu}) = 3$, and $\tilde{\beta} = 1.2 > (1 - \tilde{\kappa})/\tilde{\gamma} = 1/1.2$, the condition (6.59) is fulfilled and the origin is an *unstable stationary state*. The eigenvalues λ_+, λ_- are real, because $\tilde{\beta}$ is positive (see (6.60b)).

Interpretation of Scenario A2   This case still corresponds to the situation in a liberal society without opinion pressure, since $\tilde{\kappa} = 0$. However there exists by assumption a rather strong affirmative propensity $\tilde{\beta} = 1.2$, which leads eventually to the "selfinduced" stabilisation of an inner inclination $\vartheta > 0$ for opinion "+", as soon as accidentially a majority $n_+ > n_-$ has formed. (The same holds for the inner inclination $\vartheta < 0$ for opinion "−" as soon as by chance a majority $n_- > n_+$ has arisen.) Since $\vartheta > 0$ (respectively $\vartheta < 0$) favours further transitions from "−" to "+"

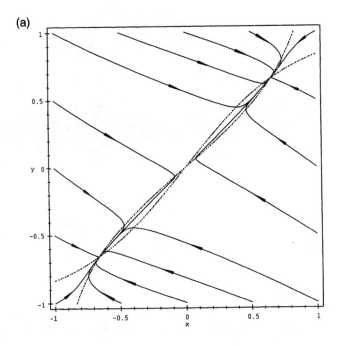

(a)

(b)

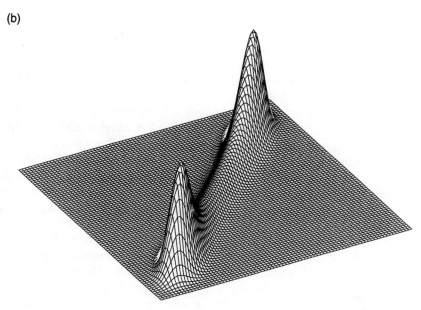

Figure 6.2 (a) (Scenario A2): The fluxlines of the quasi-meanvalues approach stable unbalanced opinion majority situations maintained by inner inclination. The balanced opinion situation $(\hat{y}, \hat{x}) = (0, 0)$ is unstable; (b) (Scenario A2): The bimodal stationary probability distribution is peaked around the stable opinion majority situations.

(respectively from "+" to "−") we obtain instead of a balanced opinion situation $n_+ = n_-$, which is now unstable, two possibilities of selforganized stable situations: either a stable majority $n_+ > n_-$, maintained by a stable inner inclination $\vartheta > 0$, or a stable majority $n_- > n_+$, maintained by a stable inner inclination $\vartheta < 0$. In each of these cases the society has a biased opinion situation (for "+" or for "−") but lives in "inner harmony", because the bias is not induced through an opinion pressure exerted by the majority but by inner inclination of the population.

Figures 6.2(a) and (b) illustrate this situation: Figure 6.2(a) shows that the fluxlines of the quasi-meanvalues approach *stable stationary states* in the first or third quadrant, each describing a stable majority $n_+ > n_-$ (respectively $n_- < n_+$) maintained by a stable inner inclination $\vartheta > 0$ (or $\vartheta < 0$). Figure 6.2(b) shows the corresponding bimodal stationary probability distribution peaked around the stable stationary opinion states.

Scenario A3

Parameters $N = \Theta = 40$; $\tilde{\mu} = \mu/\nu = 2$; $\tilde{\kappa} = 1.0$; $\tilde{\beta} = 0.8$; $\tilde{\gamma} = 0.8$.

Stability of Origin   Because of $\tilde{\kappa} = 1 < (1 + \tilde{\mu}) = 3$ and $\tilde{\beta} = 0.8 > (1 - \tilde{\kappa})/\tilde{\gamma}$ $= (1 - 1)/0.8$, the condition (6.59) is fulfilled and the origin is an *unstable stationary state*. The eigenvalues λ_+, λ_- are real, because $\tilde{\beta}$ is positive (see (6.60b)).

Interpretation of Scenario A3   This case describes a society with considerable opinion pressure $\tilde{\kappa} = 1$, that means with totalitarian tendencies, and with moderate affirmative propensity $\tilde{\beta} = 0.8$. We find a similar global situation as in scenario A2. Again the global situation, depicted in Figures 6.3(a) and (b) shows that the balanced opinion situation $(\hat{y}, \hat{x}) = (0, 0)$ is unstable and that under this political psychology two stable majority situations (either $n_+ > n_-$ or $n_- > n_+$) are approached by the quasi-meanvalues (Figure 6.3(a)) and that the bimodal probability distribution is peaked around them (Figure 6.3(b)).

In spite of the global similarity to scenario A2 the scenario A3 comes about in different manner: The affirmative propensity $\tilde{\beta} = 0.8$ *alone* would not suffice to create a self-maintained stable opinion majority. (Indeed, $\tilde{\beta} = 0.8$ and $\tilde{\kappa} = 0$ would lead to the stability of the origin $(\hat{y}, \hat{x}) = (0, 0)$.) However the considerable opinion pressure $\tilde{\kappa} = 1.0$ *together* with the moderate affirmative propensity $\tilde{\beta} = 0.8$ *cooperate* in stabilizing majority situations ($n_+ > n_-$ or $n_- > n_+$), together with accompanying inner inclinations ($\vartheta > 0$ or $\vartheta < 0$). The latter are however less pronounced than in scenario A2.

The global situation as such illustrated by Figures 6.2(a), 6.3(a) and 6.2(b), 6.3(b) is therefore not sufficient to distinguish unambiguously between scenario A2 and scenario A3. In A2 the society is an unburdened one living without opinion pressure in accordance with the inner inclinations of its members. Instead, in A3 the majority situation is mainly stabilized by the effect of opinion pressure and only partially by the inner inclination of the people. Here, the society is an appeased and reassured one living under considerable opinion pressure.

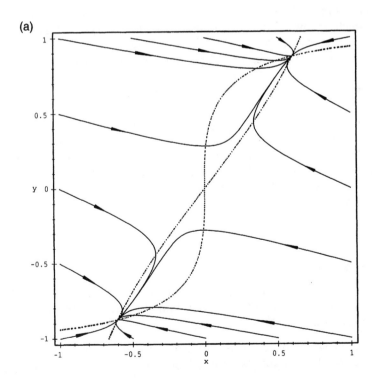

(a)

(b)

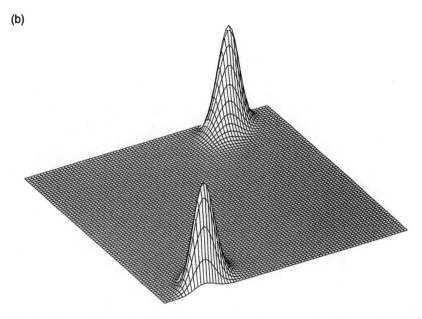

Figure 6.3 (a) (Scenario A3): The fluxlines of the quasi-meanvalues approach stable unbalanced opinion majority situations, which are partially stabilized by an affirmative propensity and partially by opinion pressure. The balanced opinion situation $(\hat{y}, \hat{x}) = (0,0)$ is unstable; (b) (Scenario A3): The bimodal stationary probability distribution is peaked around the stable opinion majority situations.

(B)   Scenarios of Dissident Societies

Scenario B1

Parameters $N = \Theta = 40; \; \tilde{\mu} = \mu/\nu = 2; \; \tilde{\kappa} = 0; \; \tilde{\beta} = -2; \; \tilde{\gamma} = 1.$

Stability of Origin   Because of $\tilde{\kappa} = 0 < (1 + \tilde{\mu}) = 3$ and $\tilde{\beta} = -2 < (1 - \tilde{\kappa})/\tilde{\gamma} = 1$, the condition (6.58) is fulfilled and the origin $(\hat{y}, \hat{x}) = (0,0)$ is a *stable stationary state*. Because of $\tilde{\beta} = -2 < -(\tilde{\mu} + \tilde{\rho})^2/4\tilde{\mu}\tilde{\gamma} = -(2 - 1)^2/4 \cdot 2 \cdot 1 = -1/8$ the eigenvalues λ_+ and λ_- are conjugate complex (see (6.60)).

Interpretation of Scenario B1   This case corresponds, despite of its oversimplification, to a society in a liberal state without opinion pressure ($\tilde{\kappa} = 0$) but a strong dissidence propensity $\tilde{\beta} = -2$ which drags the inner inclination ϑ to amplitudes opposing the just existing majority (and the incumbent administration). Therefore, any existing majority opinion is soon impaired by an inner inclination among the people going into inner reservation and opposition. One could characterize such societies as somewhat cavilling, distrustful, and relatively ungovernable.

The Figures 6.4(a) and (b) illustrate this case. Figure 6.4(a) shows that the fluxlines of the quasi-meanvalues now spiral (because of the complex eigenvalues) into the origin $(\hat{y}, \hat{x}) = (0,0)$, which is a stable state. An accidental majority will soon be levelled down and removed by the counteractive inner inclination. Figure 6.4(b) shows the probabilistic deviations from the balanced opinion situation $(\hat{y}, \hat{x}) = (0,0)$.

(a)

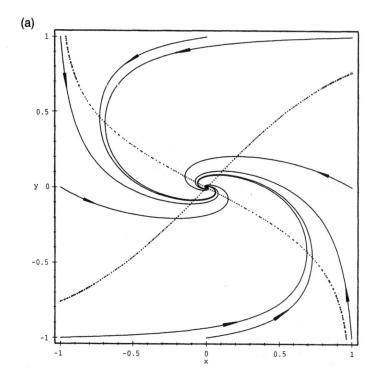

(b)

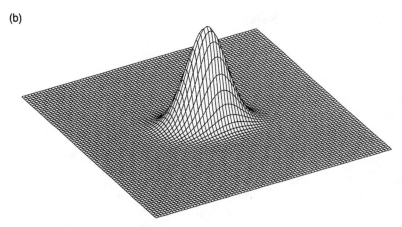

Figure 6.4 (a) (Scenario B1): The fluxlines of the quasi-meanvalues spiralling into the stable origin $(\hat{y}, \hat{x}) = (0, 0)$; (b) (Scenario B1): The unimodal stationary probability distribution peaked around the balanced opinion situation $(\hat{y}, \hat{x}) = (0, 0)$.

Apart from the different sign of the propensity parameter $\tilde{\beta}$ the scenarios A1 and B1, both without opinion pressure, exhibit strong similarities. They both characterize liberal situations with a balanced stationary situation for avowed opinions and inner inclincations, apart from stochastic fluctuations.

Scenario B2

Parameters $N = \Theta = 40$; $\tilde{\mu} = \mu/\nu = 2$; $\tilde{\kappa} = 1$; $\tilde{\beta} = -0.25$; $\tilde{\gamma} = 1$.

Stability of Origin   Because of $\tilde{\kappa} < (1 + \tilde{\mu}) = 3$ and $\tilde{\beta} = -0.25 < (1 - \tilde{\kappa})/\tilde{\gamma} = 0$, the condition (6.58) is fulfilled and the origin $(\hat{y}, \hat{x}) = (0, 0)$ is a *stable stationary state*. Because of $\tilde{\beta} = -0.25 > -(\tilde{\mu} + \tilde{\rho})^2/4\tilde{\mu}\tilde{\gamma} = -(2 + 0)^2/4 \cdot 2 \cdot 1 = -1/2$ the eigenvalues λ_+ and λ_- are real (see (6.60)).

Interpretation of Scenario B2   This case corresponds to a society with totalitarian tendencies, i.e. a considerable opinion pressure $\tilde{\kappa} = 1$, and a weak dissidence propensity $\tilde{\beta} = -0.25$. It turns out that the situation of balanced opinions and neutral inner inclination, i.e. the origin $(\hat{y}, \hat{x}) = (0, 0)$, is still a stable stationary state. However, opinion majorities ($n_+ > n_-$, or $n_- > n_+$), once established, have a long life-time.

This is demonstrated by Figures 6.5(a) and (b). Figure 6.5(a) depicts the fluxlines of the quasi-meanvalues. Because of the relatively strong opinion pressure, a majority for one opinion ("+" or "−") builds up in almost selfstabilizing manner. However, the relatively weak dissidence propensity thereupon induces a counteractive inner inclination which eventually leads to the breakdown of the opinion-majority. The large amplitudes of the arising opinion majorities and their subsequent breakdown lead to large deviations from the balanced opinion situation $(\hat{y}, \hat{x}) = (0, 0)$. These are exhibited in Figure 6.5(b) which shows the broad stationary probability distribution.

(a)

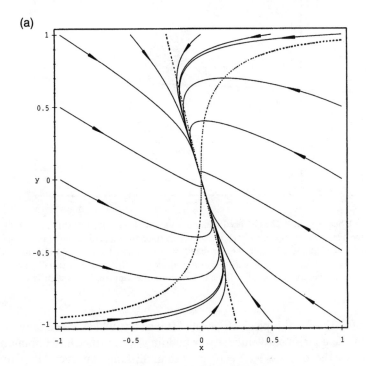

Figure 6.5   (Continued)

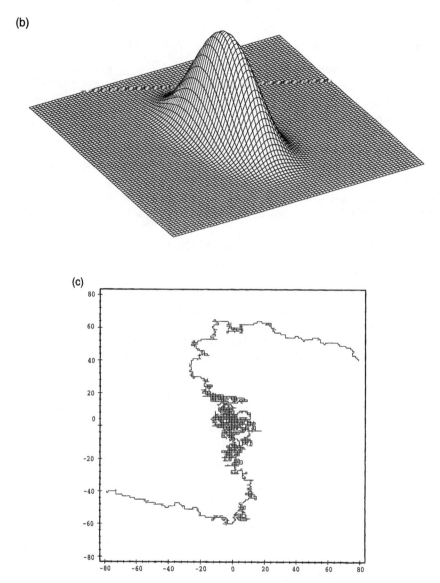

Figure 6.5 (a) (Scenario B2): The balanced opinion situation $(\hat{y}, \hat{x}) = (0, 0)$ is still (marginally) stable. The fluxlines of the quasi-meanvalues approach the origin via strongly unbalanced opinion states; (b) (Scenario B2): Broad but still unimodal stationary probability distribution with large width around the origin $(\hat{y}, \hat{x}) = (0, 0)$; (c) (Scenario B2): Typical stochastic trajectories. They move essentially along the fluxlines of the quasi-meanvalues and accomplish large fluctuations after approaching the origin.

Figure 6.5(c) shows a typical stochastic trajectory which essentially follows the fluxlines of the quasi-meanvalues. After building up a rather large opinion majority it approaches the origin $(\hat{y}, \hat{x}) = (0, 0)$, accomplishing however large fluctuations around it which correspond to the large width of the probability distribution.

Scenario B3

Parameters $N = \Theta = 40$; $\tilde{\mu} = \mu/\nu = 2$; $\tilde{\kappa} = 1.5$; $\tilde{\beta} = -0.25$; $\tilde{\gamma} = 1$.

Stability of Origin   Because of $\tilde{\kappa} = 1.5 < (1 + \tilde{\mu}) = 3$ and $\tilde{\beta} = -0.25 > (1 - \tilde{\kappa})/\tilde{\gamma} = -0.5/1 = -0.5$, the condition (6.59) is fulfilled and the origin is an *unstable stationary point*. Because of $\tilde{\beta} = -0.25 > -(\tilde{\mu} + \tilde{\rho})^2/4\tilde{\mu}\tilde{\gamma} = -(2.5)^2/4 \cdot 2 \cdot 1 \approx -0.78$ the eigenvalues λ_+ and λ_- are real (see (6.60)).

Interpretation of Scenario B3   This case describes a society in a totalitarian state possessing a political psychology of strongly developed opinion pressure ($\tilde{\kappa} = 1.5$) and only weak (dissident) propensity $\tilde{\beta} = -0.25$ to engender an opposing inner inclination. It turns out that this society stabilizes in a state of a high majority for one of the (publicly expressed) opinions "+" or "−" which is maintained purely by opinion pressure.

Simultaneously the inner inclination ϑ goes to a stationary value of inner opposition which is however not strong enough to destabilize the once established stationary totalitarian state. Hence this scenario is "the dictator's dream", since the small value of the dissidence propensity $\tilde{\beta}$ is not sufficient to arouse amplitudes of inclination ϑ of inner opposition and disapproval strong enough to destabilize his totalitarian system.

The Figures 6.6(a)–(d) confirm this picture. Figure 6.6(a) shows the fluxlines of the quasi-meanvalues. They end in one of the stationary states describing an established stationary totalitarian political system. Such a stationary state is characterized by a very high (publicly avowed) majority for one political opinion (the official doctrine) and simultaneously by a value of the inner inclination which is in dissidence to the public doctrine but of moderate amplitude. Figure 6.6(b) shows the bimodal stationary probability distribution with modes centered on the stationary states. We complement these figures by two further figures yielding additional information.

At first we introduce the evolution speed:

$$s(y, x) = (\dot{y}^2 + \dot{x}^2)^{\frac{1}{2}} \geq 0, \tag{6.61}$$

where on the r.h.s. of (6.61) the expressions (6.30) and (6.31) for $\dot{y} \equiv dy/d\tau$ and $\dot{x} \equiv dx/d\tau$ must be inserted. The quantity $s(y, x)$ is a measure for the speed of evolution of quasi-meanvalues at any given system point. In general terms this measure is introduced in Chapter 12 (see equation (12.18)).

At *stationary states* the evolution speed takes the value $s = 0$, which is simultaneously its *absolute minimum*. System points (y_{stg}, x_{stg}) which are not stationary points, where however $s(y, x)$ has a relative minimum, are denoted as *stagnation points*.

In Figure 6.6(c) the equi-potential lines of the evolution speed ($s(y, x)$) are depicted. As expected, the function has three absolute minima, one at the origin, the unstable stationary point, and two at the states of "totalitarian stability".

In Figure 6.6(d) the area around one state of totalitarian stability is enlarged and a typical stochastic trajectory wandering into this area and fluctuating around that stable stationary state is exhibited.

(a)

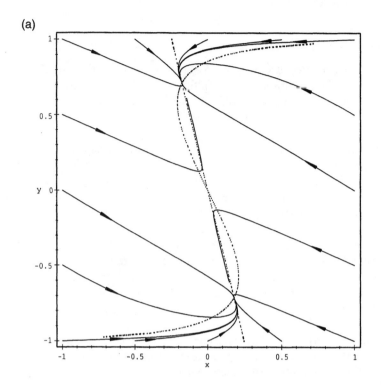

(b)

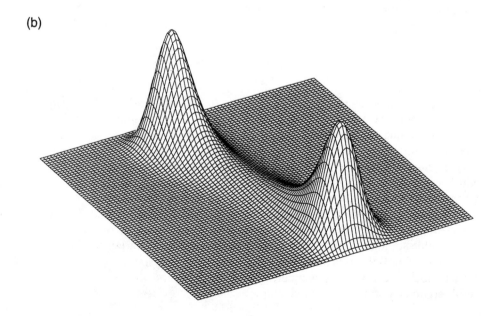

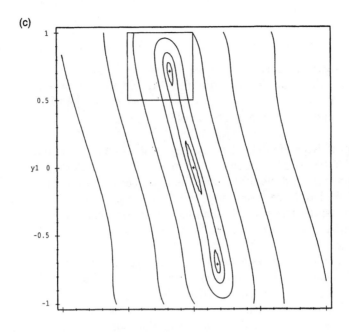

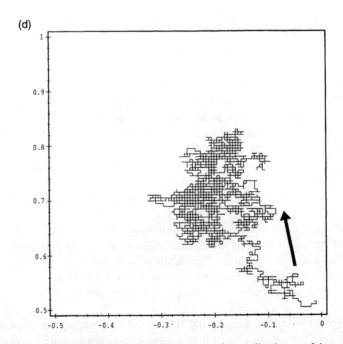

Figure 6.6 (a) Scenario B3): The fluxlines of the quasi-meanvalues ending in one of the stationary states; (b) (Scenario B3): The bimodal stationary probability distribution. Its modes are centered on the two stable stationary states; (c) (Scenario B3): The equipotential lines of the evolution speed $s(y, x)$; it has three absolute minima $s(y, x) = 0$ at the origin and the two stable stationary states; (d) (Scenario B3): A typical stochastic trajectory approaching and fluctuating around one of the stable stationary states.

Scenario B4

Parameters $N = \Theta = 40$; $\tilde{\mu} = \mu/\nu = 2$; $\tilde{\kappa} = 3.5$; $\tilde{\beta} = -2$; $\tilde{\gamma} = 2$.

Stability of Origin   Because of $\tilde{\kappa} = 3.5 > (1 + \tilde{\mu}) = 3$ and $\tilde{\beta} = -2 < (1 - \tilde{\kappa})/\tilde{\gamma} = -2.5/2 = -1.25$, the condition (6.59) is fulfilled and the origin is an *unstable stationary point*. Because of $\tilde{\beta} = -2 < -(\tilde{\mu} + \tilde{\rho})^2/4\tilde{\mu}\tilde{\gamma} = -4.5^2/4 \cdot 2 \cdot 2 \approx -1.266$ the eigenvalues λ_+ and λ_- are conjugate complex.

Interpretation of Scenario B4   This is the most dramatical scenario among the selected ones! The very high value $\tilde{\kappa} = 3.5$ means that there exists a strong totalitarian opinion pressure. On the other hand there has been assumed the highly negative value $\tilde{\beta} = -2$ of dissidence propensity, which can be seen as the counter-reaction to the opinion pressure exerted within the totalitarian regime. Sooner or later the trend $\tilde{\beta} = -2$ will drive the inner inclination variable ϑ, respectively x, to high amplitudes of *inner disapproval*.

Let us now see how this system evolves! We start from a system point in the *first quadrant* with small positive y (moderate majority for opinion "+") and relatively high positive value of x (relatively strong inner approval of opinion "+"). The opinion pressure thereupon engenders a steep increase of the majority variable y parallel to firmly establishing the totalitarian situation with its characteristic high values of y. Simultaneously, however, due to $\tilde{\beta} = -2$, the originally approving inner inclination ($x > 0$) turns over to very negative values of x, i.e. to a strongly disapproving inner inclination ($x < 0$).

The system point thus approaches the left upper corner of the *second quadrant*. In this stage each member of the society is in an extremely torn condition: On the one hand he/she is exposed in his environment to the majority of people publicly avowing the official doctrine "+" and urging him to join them or to remain in their community of followers. On the other hand he feels a very strong moral and rational inner disapproval of the established regime and its doctrine and thinks of outing himself and exposing himself to the risk of losing his status in this society. It turns out (see Figures 6.7(c)–(e)) that this tragic state of the society is a metastable and long-lived one. However, in contrast to scenario B3 this situation is not a stable one because the counteractive inner anger (i.e. the negative inner inclination) is now too strong.

Finally the society overcomes this stage of stagnation: The mood of inner disapproval in the members of the totalitarian system leaves its isolation, becomes a collective effect and wins through. This leads to a rather sudden breakdown of the totalitarian opinion majority, which now turns into a transient revolutionary process towards an opposite majority. The quasi-meanvalue trajectory thus traverses the *third quadrant*.

At this stage we should keep in mind that we have assumed persistently constant trendparameters, in particular constant $\tilde{\kappa}$ and $\tilde{\beta}$. Under these assumptions of political psychology there builds up under persisting strong opinion pressure a strong majority of public avowers of the opposite ideology "−". However, this leads, under persisting dissidence propensity $\tilde{\beta}$, very soon to an equally strong inner disapproval of the newly established regime, which has the opposite ideology but exhibits the same totalitarian mechanisms. Therefore the system again approaches in the *fourth quadrant* a tragic stagnation point of extreme public opinion pressure and simultaneous extreme inner disapproval which is structurally equivalent to that in the second quadrant, independently of the differences between the ideologies "+" and "−". Again a revolutionary breakdown can follow, and so on.

Mathematically, this tragic wandering process between totalitarian regimes of different doctrines is represented by the *limit cycle*, being the asymptotic attractor for the model solutions in this case of model parameters (see Figures 6.7(a) and (b)).

One might argue that the scenario B4 is only a purely fictitious one since the trendparameters will in general change during the evolution, in particular at revolutionary events. This is indeed true in general, and in Section 6.4.2 we will consider cases with co-evolving trendparameters.

Nevertheless there exist political phase-transitions in history, namely transitions from one to the next totalitarian regime, where the assumption of constant political psychology under changing totalitarian doctrines seems to be realized at least approximately. The most prominent example seems to be the Shah-Ajatollah-transition in Iran, i.e. the transition from an authoritarian monarchistic regime to a fundamentalist religious Mullah regime, both exhibiting strongly totalitarian structures.

The Figures 6.7(a)–(e) of the model solutions confirm and consolidate the interpretations given above.

The Figure 6.7(a) represents the fluxlines of the quasi-meanvalues. In contrast to all other scenarios presented so far the fluxlines here approach a limit cycle, wherever they start. This limit cycle traverses with varying speed all four quadrants which belong to different evolution stages of the totalitarian system.

In Figure 6.7(b) the limit cycle is compared with a representative stochastic trajectory. It is satisfactory that such stochastic trajectories, although they traverse a sequence of probabilistic hopping processes, essentially follow the limit cycle solution of the quasi-meanvalue equations. This confirms the usefulness of the latter in investigating stochastically evolving dynamic systems.

Figure 6.7(c) shows the stationary probability distribution. It exhibits remarkably high peaks in the second and fourth quadrant. Since the stationary probability at a system point is proportional to the mean staying time of a stochastic trajectory at this point (see equation (12.11)), it must be concluded that the states of high stationary probability are *points of stagnation*. In our case they could be denoted as *totalitarian traps*.

Figure 6.7(d) confirms this supposition: The equipotential lines of the evolution speed $s(x, y)$ exhibit relative minima at points of maximal stationary probability. Therefore these points are indeed *stagnation points*, where $s(x, y)$ does not vanish but has a minimal value.

Figure 6.7(e) shows a representative stochastic trajectory fluctuating around the stagnation point before it eventually leaves the area of the totalitarian trap.

6.4.2 Scenarios with Co-Evolving Trend-Parameters

In the previous section the values of $\tilde{\kappa}$ and $\tilde{\beta}$ were fixed for each scenario. Since the value of $\tilde{\kappa}$ decides about the liberal or totalitarian political atmosphere, the scenarios

(a)

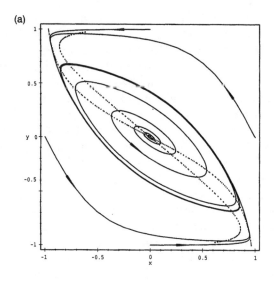

(b)

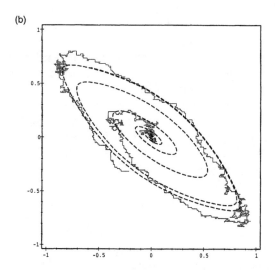

(c)

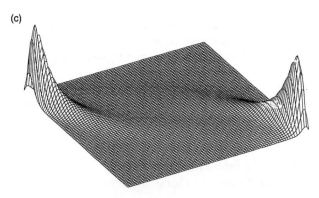

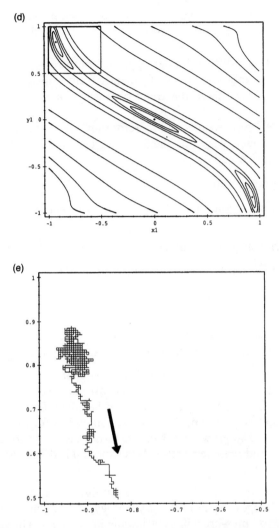

Figure 6.7 (a) (Scenario B4): The fluxlines of the quasi-meanvalues approaching a limit cycle; (b) (Scenario B4): Comparison of a representative stochastic trajectory with the limit cycle, i.e. the attractor of the quasi-meanvalue equations;   (c) (Scenario B4): The stationary probability distribution, i.e. the solution of the stationary master equation; (d) (Scenario B4): The equipotential lines of the evolution speed $s(x, y)$ exhibiting three minima at one stationary point (the origin) and two stagnation points; (e) (Scenario B4): A representative stochastic trajectory fluctuating around a stagnation point and eventually leaving it.

described *either* a liberal *or* a totalitarian system and the evolution *within it*, but *not the transition between them.*

Instead, in this section we take into account, that the trend-parameters, in particular $\tilde{\kappa}$ and $\tilde{\beta}$, are in general not constant with time.

In a fully sophisticated approach they would even have to obey dynamic evolution equations. However, such an approach would lead to new problems, because in the evolution equations for trend-parameters certain parameters would have to be introduced. These "trend-parameters of second order" would need a socio-political interpretation, too.

In order to avoid such difficulties our approach of introducing co-evolving trend-parameters is not so ambitious. Instead we start from some plausible assumptions about how and in which stage the trend-parameters $\tilde{\kappa}$ and $\tilde{\beta}$ may change their numerical values.

It is certainly a relatively weak – and therefore sufficiently general – assumption to distinguish the following stages in the rise and eventual endogenously produced collapse of a totalitarian regime:

(1) The pre-totalitarian stage;

(2) The (short-term) revolutionary stage of seizure of power by the totalitarian forces;

(3) The (long-term) stage of consolidation and persistence of the totalitarian regime;

(4) The critical meta-stable stage of destabilisation, if it exists;

(5) The post-totalitarian stage.

We now consider three scenarios C, D, E. They coincide concerning the stages 1, 2 and 3, but they differ with respect to the stages 4 and 5. Let us first introduce the assumptions common to all three scenarios for stages 1, 2 and 3.

Stage 1   This *pre-totalitarian, still liberal stage* is characterized by a low opinion pressure (the chosen value is $\tilde{\kappa} = 0.1$) but a high affirmative propensity $\tilde{\beta}$: (the chosen value is $\tilde{\beta} = 3.0$). The mood produced by this $\tilde{\beta}$ has the effect of drawing the inner inclination ϑ (respectively x) to positive, approving values for the impending totalitarian ideology "+". The growing ϑ wins in turn adherents avowing this ideology publicly (and more and more fervently). This situation is the necessary condition for the success of the next stage.

Stage 2   The *seizure of power by the totalitarian forces* is a revolutionary act which rather suddenly changes the political psychology, hence the trend-parameters. In particular the opinion pressure will now assume high values. The smooth but short-term change of $\tilde{\kappa}$ is here approximated by a sudden jump from $\tilde{\kappa} = 0.1$ to $\tilde{\kappa} = 3.2$ at point $P1$ (see Figures 6.8, 6.9 and 6.10). The new value corresponds to a fully totalitarian situation. Simultaneously the propensity parameter $\tilde{\beta}$ becomes less affirmative because now the negative effect of the majority $y(P1) > 0$ becomes visible. It is assumed that $\tilde{\beta}$ jumps from $\tilde{\beta} = 3.0$ to $\tilde{\beta} = 3.0 - 5y(P1)$.

Stage 3   The *consolidated persistence of the totalitarian regime* is a long-term stage. Since opinion pressure is indispensible for such a regime it will take all available measures to maintain it. Therefore it is plausible that $\tilde{\kappa}$ keeps its high value (here: $\tilde{\kappa} = 3.2$).

On the other hand the regime does not dispose of the propensity $\tilde{\beta}$ which is a factor of political psychology steering the hidden inner inclination. With increasing consolidation of the totalitarian system and growing deprivation effects the propensity $\tilde{\beta}$ of the individuals will turn from affirmative to dissident values. Since on the

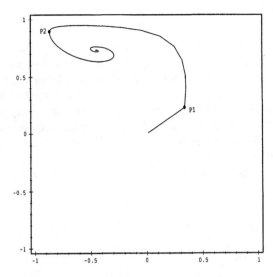

Figure 6.8 (Scenario C): Fluxlines of the quasi-meanvalues with trend-parameters $\tilde{\kappa} = 2.5$ and $\tilde{\beta}(t) = 3.0 - 5y(t)$ after point $P2$. A re-stabilisation of the totalitarian system takes place.

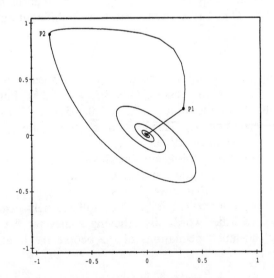

Figure 6.9 (Scenario D): Fluxlines of the quasi-meanvalues with trend-parameters $\tilde{\kappa} = 2.5$ and $\tilde{\beta} = -1.4875$ after point $P2$. A full breakdown of $y(t)$ and an oscillatory approach of the balanced situation $(x, y) = (0, 0)$ takes place.

other hand the growing majority variable $y(t)$ sustained by opinion pressure can be seen as a *proxy* for the consolidating totalitarianism, it is plausible to assume that $\tilde{\beta}(t) = 3.0 - 5y(t)$. This $\tilde{\beta}(t)$ will turn to negative values if $y(t)$ approaches values $\lesssim 1$.

Let us now discuss different possibilities of

Stage 4 and Stage 5 *Endogenous destabilisation of the totalitarian system and post-totalitarian situation* Under the assumptions for $\tilde{\kappa}$ and $\tilde{\beta}$ in stages 1, 2 and 3 the totalitarian system eventually reaches the point of destabilisation $P2$ (see Figures 6.8, 6.9 and 6.10), where $y(t)$ begins to break down due to the massive disapproving inner inclination (here $x(t) = -0.8975$). This is again a revolutionary situation in which also sudden changes of $\tilde{\kappa}$ and $\tilde{\beta}$ can be expected. It depends however sensitively on the circumstances *which changes* of $\tilde{\kappa}$ and $\tilde{\beta}$ can be expected at the critical point $P2$ and for the subsequent evolution.

We make three scenario-assumptions for $\tilde{\kappa}$ and $\tilde{\beta}$ at $P2$ and afterwards:

Scenario C: $\tilde{\kappa} = 2.5$ and $\tilde{\beta}(t) = 3.0 - 5 \cdot y(t)$;

Scenario D: $\tilde{\kappa} = 2.5$ and $\tilde{\beta}(t) = 3.0 - 5 \cdot 0.8975 = -1.4875$;

Scenario E: $\tilde{\kappa} = 0.5$ and $\tilde{\beta}(t) = 3.0 - 5 \cdot 0.8975 = -1.4875$.

Although in all three scenarios the general tendency consists in a decrease of opinion pressure $\tilde{\kappa}$ (because the beginning decrease of $y(t)$ encourages people no longer to back down under the regime) and in a persistence of a *negative* $\tilde{\beta}(t)$ (because the distrust still survives in a dissident propensity), the differences between the parameters of scenarios C, D and E suffice to lead to very different outcomes:

Scenario C

Here the beginning destabilisation process at point $P2$ leads only to a relatively small decrease of the opinion pressure ($\tilde{\kappa} = 3.2 \Rightarrow \tilde{\kappa} = 2.5$). Furthermore, $\tilde{\beta}(t) = 3.0 - 5 \cdot y(t)$, starting from the value $\tilde{\beta}(P2) = 3.0 - 5 \cdot 0.8975 = -1.4875$ becomes less negative with decreasing $y(t)$. This leads to a less definite inner disapproval of the (still existing) totalitarian situation.

Figure 6.8 represents the quasi-meanvalue fluxlines of the corresponding evolution. It shows that the totalitarian system under these circumstances is able to *re-stabilize itself* at a somewhat lower but still very high value $y = 0.74$ of the majority variable and a somewhat milder but still strongly negative disapproval level of $x = -0.46$. In other words: By relieving somewhat the opinion pressure and by appeasing the inner inclinations of the people the totalitarian system as such is able to survive.

Scenario D

In this scenario the opinion pressure at the critical point $P2$ is, as in scenario C, assumed to decrease from $\tilde{\kappa} = 3.2$ to the still high value $\tilde{\kappa} = 2.5$ only. However the people retain here by assumption their highly negative dissidence propensity $\tilde{\beta} = 3.0 - 5 \cdot 0.8975 = -1.4875$ which they had at the point $P2$ of beginning destabilisation. Therefore the inner inclination also retains strongly negative (non-appeased) disapproving amplitudes which now engenders a full breakdown of the majority variable $y(t)$.

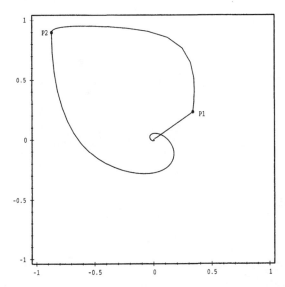

Figure 6.10 (Scenario E): Fluxlines of the quasi-meanvalues with trend-parameters $\tilde{\kappa} = 0.5$ and $\tilde{\beta} = -1.4875$ after point P2. A full breakdown of $y(t)$ and a direct approach of the balanced situation $(x, y) = (0.0)$ takes place.

Figure 6.9 exhibits this breakdown of $y(t)$, and that now even an opposite opinion majority $y(t) < 0$ builds up which however breaks down, too, due to the counter-active inner inclination. After some oscillations the majority- and inclination variable end up in a balanced value, the origin. However, the opinion pressure $\tilde{\kappa} = 2.5$ would still be high enough to destabilize the balanced situation, if the strongly negative $\tilde{\beta}$ would relax to lower amplitudes (see e.g. scenario B3).

Scenario E

In this scenario it has been assumed that the opinion pressure is dramatically decreasing at the critical point P2 from $\tilde{\kappa} = 3.2$ to $\tilde{\kappa} = 0.5$, whereas the dissidence propensity retains its strictly negative value which was reached at P2, namely $\tilde{\beta} = 3.0 - 5 \cdot 0.8975 = -1.4875$.

Figure 6.10 shows that under these conditions the breakdown of the majority $y(t)$ takes place even more directly, and the system stabilizes without large oscillations in the situation of balance. Because of the low value of $\tilde{\kappa}$ this liberal situation would thereupon remain stable (in contrast to scenario D) even if the strongly negative $\tilde{\beta}$ would relax to lower amplitudes.

Remark   It is evident that the stages 3, 4 and 5 described in scenarios C, D and E cannot be compared with the fate of the totalitarian Nazi-regime. After seizure of power and a few years of seeming consolidation Hitler led his regime toward a second, even more frightening phase-transition by unleashing the second world war. The latter phase-transition is evidently beyond the scope of the model presented here.

II.3 Applications to Economics

II.3.1 Introductory Remarks

Economics is a social science with well developed, rather appealing and stringent quantitative formalism. The reason for this fact seems to be that the material variables, playing the main role in this field, are relatively easily to measure, hence amenable to quantitative treatment, and that economic motivations, decisions and actions can be well demarcated from other deliberations and activities.

The question therefore arises as to what Sociodynamics can contribute to formalized theoretical economics and how it relates to the standard neoclassical formalism and to more recent developments in economic theory, namely Evolutionary Economics. Before coming to concrete models we will discuss this question in some detail. We begin with

II.3.1.1 Remarks on the Simplest (Neo)-Classical Approach of Economics

Let us briefly illustrate the principles of the neo-classical approach by means of its simplest case, the market equilibrium under the assumption of perfect competition, a case which is treated in standard textbooks of Economics [1], [2], [3], [4].

A perfectly competitive commodity market is defined by the following properties:

(a) Homogeneous commodities are produced by all firms, and consumers are identical from the seller's point of view in that there are no advantages or disadvantages associated with selling to a particular consumer.

(b) Producers and consumers are numerous; therefore sellers and buyers are "price takers": Buyers adjust quantities purchased and sellers adjust quantities sold to the given price without considering that their purchases or sales may affect the price.

(c) Producers and consumers possess complete information about prices and current bids. They take advantage of every opportunity to increase their profits or their utility, respectively.

The main theoretical problem then consists in determining the values of all variables in the *stationary market equilibrium*. The neo-classical formalism solves this problem by introducing the *principle of utility maximisation* (for consumers) and *profit maximisation* (for producers), and by a contracting and recontracting procedure between producers and consumers leading to a levelling off of all prices to their equilibrium values. The quantitative formulation of these principles proceeds as follows:

The consumer side

Let us assume that there are s commodities $Q_1, Q_2, \ldots, Q_s$ on the market with prices per unit $\{p_1, p_2, \ldots, p_s\} = \mathbf{p}$. Each of the C consumers $k = 1, 2, \ldots, C$ has a budget $y^{(k)}$ available for buying, say, the quantities, i.e. number of units, $q_1, q_2, \ldots, q_s$ of commodities $Q_1, Q_2, \ldots, Q_s$ in a given period of time. His budget constraint (also denoted as a budget equation) is then expressed by

$$y^{(k)} - \sum_{i=1}^{s} p_i q_i = 0 \tag{II.3.1}$$

if the households are assumed not to save. Furthermore one assumes that each of the C consumers has a *utility function*

$$u^{(k)} = f^{(k)}(q_1 \ldots q_s) > 0 \tag{II.3.2}$$

which is a quantitative measure of the usefulness of the batch or vector of commodities $\mathbf{q} = \{q_1 \ldots q_s\}$ for him. The utility $u^{(k)}$ is considered as a *cardinal function* of the amounts $q_1, \ldots, q_s$.

The question, *which* batch $\{q_1 \ldots q_s\}$ is bought by the consumer k is then answered by assuming that he is *maximizing* his utility (II.3.2) under his *budget constraint* (II.3.1). This amounts mathematically to determining the maximum of the Lagrangian function

$$V^{(k)} = f^{(k)}(q_1 \ldots q_s) + \lambda \left(y^{(k)} - \sum_{i=1}^{s} p_i q_i \right) \tag{II.3.3}$$

by setting its partial derivatives with respect to the q_i and to λ equal to zero

$$\frac{\partial V^{(k)}}{\partial q_i} = \frac{\partial f^{(k)}}{\partial q_i}(q_1 \ldots q_s) - \lambda p_i \overset{!}{=} 0;$$

$$\frac{\partial V^{(k)}}{\partial \lambda} = \left(y^{(k)} - \sum_{i=1}^{s} p_i q_i \right) \overset{!}{=} 0 \tag{II.3.4}$$

and by determining $\mathbf{q} = \{q_1 \ldots q_s\}$ and the Lagrangian parameter λ such as to satisfy eqution (II.3.4). (We omit the second order conditions deciding about whether the extremum determined by (II.3.4) is a true maximum; we assume that these conditions are fulfilled for the given utility function.)

By solving (II.3.4) for the q_i and λ, one obtains the demand of consumer k for the good Q_i at given prices $\{p_1, \ldots, p_i, \ldots p_s\}$ and given budget $y^{(k)}$:

$$q_i^{(k)} = D_{ki}(p_1, \ldots, p_i, \ldots p_s; \, y^{(k)}), \tag{II.3.5}$$

or

$$q_i^{(k)} = D_{ki}[p_i]. \tag{II.3.6}$$

In (II.3.6) we consider the demand for Q_i as a function of its price p_i only and treat the prices $p_l (l \neq i)$ and the budget $y^{(k)}$ as given constant parameters.

Going over from the microlevel of individual consumers $k = 1, \ldots, C$ to the market-level, the *aggregate demand* for the good Q_i at any price p_i (for constant $y^{(k)}$ and constant prices $p_l (l \neq i)$) is given by

$$q_i = \sum_{k=1}^{C} q_i^{(k)} = \sum_{k=1}^{C} D_{ki}(p_i) = D_i[p_i]. \tag{II.3.7}$$

The individual demand functions (II.3.5) as well as the aggregate demand functions (II.3.7) are – in the standard textbook case – *monotonically decreasing functions* of the price p_i of the good Q_i.

The producer side

The formal analysis of producers or firms is similar to the formal analysis of the consumer in many respects: The consumer purchases commodities with which he produces "satisfaction" (utility). The producer purchases inputs with which he produces commodities. The consumer's preferences can be represented by a utility function (see (II.3.2)), and the firm's technologies by production functions (see (II.3.8)). The consumers budget equation (II.3.1) is a linear function of the amounts of the commodities he purchases; the firm's cost equation (II.3.9) is a linear function of the amounts of inputs it purchases.

However, there also exist differences between the consumer and the producer: A firm may produce more than one output. The optimisation process of the producer (the firm) comprizes more possibilities than that of the consumer. The analogous action of the firm to the consumer's maximisation of utility for a given budget would be to maximize the quantity of its output for a given cost level. But the firm may also consider its cost level as *variable* and desire to minimize the cost of producing a given output level in order to maximize the profit it obtains from the production and sale of a batch of commodities.

Let us consider one version of this optimization procedure with the aim of constructing the individual and aggregate supply-functions of producers.

We assume F firms $f = 1, 2, \ldots, F$, each of them making use of n inputs $\{x_1, \ldots, x_n\} = \mathbf{x}$ in order to produce s outputs $\{q_1 \ldots q_s\} = \mathbf{q}$. The production takes place under conditions of technical efficiency so that always optimal output vectors $\mathbf{q} = \{q_1 \ldots q_s\}$ are obtained from the possible input vectors $\mathbf{x} = \{x_1 \ldots x_n\}$.

The *production function* of firm f is formulated in implicit form and reads

$$F^{(f)}(q_1 \ldots q_s; x_1 \ldots x_n) \equiv F^{(f)}(\mathbf{q}; \mathbf{x}) = 0. \tag{II.3.8}$$

It describes *technological constraints* and means that for a given input vector $\mathbf{x}$ the firm f may produce (in the general case) different output vectors $\mathbf{q}$, i.e. different combinations of commodities, but only those for which (II.3.8) is fulfilled. (We assume for simplicity that only *one* technological constraint, namely (II.3.8), exists.)

In order to describe how the firm f optimizes its production we proceed in *two steps*:

In a *first step* we determine for a given assumed output vector $\mathbf{q}$ the optimal input vector $\mathbf{x}$ with which $\mathbf{q}$ can be produced by choosing that input $\mathbf{x}$ which *minimizes its costs*. If the input unit X_j has the price r_j, the costs c of the input vector $\mathbf{x} = \{x_1 \ldots x_n\}$ are given by the *cost equation*

$$c = \sum_{j=1}^{n} r_j x_j. \tag{II.3.9}$$

These costs must be minimized at given prices $\{r_1 \ldots r_n\} = \mathbf{r}$ under the technological constraint (II.3.8). This amounts to taking the minimum of the Lagrangian

$$K^{(f)}(\mathbf{x}; \mathbf{r}, \mathbf{q}, \lambda) = \sum_{j=1}^{n} r_j x_j + \lambda F^{(f)}(\mathbf{q}; \mathbf{x}) \tag{II.3.10}$$

with respect to $\mathbf{x}$ for given constant vectors $\mathbf{q}$ and $\mathbf{r}$.

Introducing the notation for any function $G(\mathbf{q}; \mathbf{x})$:

$$\frac{\partial G}{\partial x_j} \equiv G_{\|j} \quad j = 1, \ldots, n \quad \text{and} \quad \frac{\partial G}{\partial q_i} \equiv G_{|i} \quad i = 1, \ldots, s \tag{II.3.11}$$

the first order conditions for a minimum of $K^{(f)}$ read

$$K^{(f)}_{\|j}(\mathbf{x}; \mathbf{r}, \mathbf{q}, \lambda) = r_j + \lambda F^{(f)}_{\|j}(\mathbf{q}; \mathbf{x}) = 0; \tag{II.3.11a}$$

$$K^{(f)}_{|\lambda}(\mathbf{x}; \mathbf{r}, \mathbf{q}, \lambda) = F^{(f)}(\mathbf{q}; \mathbf{x}) = 0 \tag{II.3.11b}$$

and we assume that the second order conditions for $K^{(f)}$ respectively $F^{(f)}$ warranting a true minimum are also fulfilled. Solving the n equations (II.3.11a) for $\{x_1 \ldots x_n\} = \mathbf{x}$ one obtains the optimal x_k in terms of $\mathbf{q}, \mathbf{r}$ and λ:

$$x_k = g_k^{(f)}(\mathbf{q}; \mathbf{r}; \lambda) \quad \text{or} \quad \mathbf{x} = \mathbf{g}^{(f)}(\mathbf{q}; \mathbf{r}; \lambda). \tag{II.3.12}$$

Inserting of (II.3.12) into (II.3.11b) yields

$$F^{(f)}(\mathbf{q}; \mathbf{g}^{(f)}(\mathbf{q}; \mathbf{r}; \lambda)) = 0, \tag{II.3.13}$$

a relation from which λ can be obtained as a function of $\mathbf{q}$ and $\mathbf{r}$:

$$\lambda = \lambda(\mathbf{q}; \mathbf{r}). \tag{II.3.14}$$

Finally one can insert (II.3.14) into (II.3.12) in order to express the optimal input vector $\mathbf{x}$, which leads to a constrained minimum of costs, in terms of the given prices $\mathbf{r}$ and the output vector $\mathbf{q}$ to be produced:

$$\mathbf{x} = \mathbf{g}^{(f)}(\mathbf{q}; \mathbf{r}; \lambda(\mathbf{q}; \mathbf{r})) \equiv \mathbf{g}^{(f)}[\mathbf{q}; \mathbf{r}]. \tag{II.3.15}$$

This result can now be used to express the minimal costs in terms of the input prices $\mathbf{r}$ and the output vector $\mathbf{q}$. The so obtained *cost function* of firm f reads:

$$c^{(f)} = \sum_{j=1}^{n} r_j x_j = \sum_{j=1}^{n} r_j g_j^{(f)}[\mathbf{q}; \mathbf{r}] = \phi^{(f)}(\mathbf{q}; \mathbf{r}). \tag{II.3.16}$$

In a *second step*, the firm f is assumed to choose its output vector $\mathbf{q} = \{q_1 \ldots q_s\}$ such as to *maximize its profit*. The profit is defined as the difference between the total revenue from the sale of all outputs and the expenditure upon all inputs.

Making use of (II.3.16), i.e. assuming cost-minimizing inputs, the profit can be expressed as a function of the input prices, the output vector $\mathbf{q}$ and the output prices $\mathbf{p}$

$$\pi^{(f)}(\mathbf{q}; \mathbf{p}; \mathbf{r}) = \sum_{i=1}^{s} p_i q_i - \sum_{j=1}^{n} r_j x_j$$

$$= \sum_{i=1}^{s} p_i q_i - \phi^{(f)}(\mathbf{q}; \mathbf{r}). \tag{II.3.17}$$

The first order *conditions for profit maximisation* (at given input and output prices) reads:

$$\pi_{|i}^{(f)}(\mathbf{q}; \mathbf{p}; \mathbf{r}) = p_i - \phi_{|i}^{(f)}(\mathbf{q}; \mathbf{r}) = 0 \quad i = 1, \ldots, s. \tag{II.3.18}$$

This means that the profit-maximizing output vector is obtained, if the *marginal cost* $\phi_{|i}^{(f)}(\mathbf{q}; \mathbf{r})$ of producing Q_i equals the price p_i of Q_i.

Solving the equations (II.3.18) for the $q_i \equiv q_i^{(f)}$ one obtains the *supply of the commodity* Q_i of the firm f as a function of $\mathbf{p}$ and $\mathbf{r}$ delivered under conditions of *input cost minimisation* and *profit maximisation*:

$$q_i^{(f)} = S_i^{(f)}(p_1 \ldots, p_i, \ldots p_s; \mathbf{r}). \tag{II.3.19}$$

Considering the prices $p_k(k \neq i)$ of the other outputs as well as the input prices $\mathbf{r}$ as constant, one may write the supply of Q_i as a sole function of its price p_i:

$$q_i^{(f)} = S_i^{(f)}[p_i]. \tag{II.3.20}$$

The aggregate supply of commodity Q_i is now easily obtained by taking the sum over the supplies of all firms:

$$q_i = \sum_{f=1}^{F} q_i^{(f)} = \sum_{f=1}^{F} S_i^{(f)}[p_i] = S_i[p_i]. \qquad (II.3.21)$$

The second-order conditions for maximum profit ensure that the firm's supply function (II.3.20), hence the aggregate supply function (II.3.21), are monotonically increasing with p_i.

The market equilibrium

Consumers and producers meet at the market. The consumers demand the quantity $D_i[p_i]$ (see (II.3.7)) of good Q_i, and the producers supply the quantity $S_i[p_i]$ (see (II.3.21)) of good Q_i at the given market price p_i. *Market equilibrium* exists if, for each commodity Q_i, the demand and the supply for Q_i coincide, i.e. if

$$D_i(p_i^*) = S_i(p_i^*) \qquad (II.3.22)$$

holds. Under standard conditions a unique equilibrium price p_i^* exists, where the monotonically decreasing demand function intersects with the monotonically increasing supply function (see [1], [2]).

The question arises whether this market equilibrium is stable. Introducing the *excess demand* at price p_i

$$E_i(p_i) = D_i(p_i) - S_i(p_i), \qquad (II.3.23)$$

the *Walrasian condition for stability* at $p_i = p_i^*$ reads

$$\frac{dE_i}{dp_i}(p_i^*) = \frac{dD_i(p_i^*)}{dp_i} - \frac{dS_i(p_i^*)}{dp_i} < 0. \qquad (II.3.24)$$

The condition means that excess demand will become negative (positive) if the price exceeds (falls below) the equilibrium price p_i^*. Since buyers tend to raise their bids if excess demand is positive and sellers to lower their prices if excess demand is negative, this behaviour drives the deviating price back to its equilibrium value p_i^*, if (II.3.24) is fulfilled.

The market equilibrium, the simplest case of which we have just discussed, is a *central theme of neo-classical economic theory*. In the next Section we shall see that this case describes an *over-idealized situation* which is often violated. Nevertheless this idealized conceptual framework of equilibrium-economics will retain its value because economic stationarity can be seen as a special case embedded into a more general flow of evolutionary economic processes.

II.3.1.2   The Necessity of an Extended Framework: The Approach of Evolutionary Economics

The basic principle of neo-classical economics is the *maximisation of utility and profit* of the economic actors. It leads to mutual coordination and adaptation processes such as arbitrage, adjustment of prices and amounts of produced goods via contracting and recontracting processes, i.e. to the coordination of individual plans in the economy until they have merged in the global equilibrium state.

However, this basic principle *alone* seems to be *insufficient* to describe and explain discoordination-, disruption- and destabilisation-effects which lead to the often observed varieties of *economic dynamics beyond equilibrium*. "Why", one could ask, "should there be any motivation in the neoclassical equilibrium to come up with a destabilizing novelty, once everyone is, within the equilibrium state, at an optimum?"(U. Witt [5]).

Evidently, a *more general conceptual framework* is needed which not only allows of the explanation of economic equilibrium, but provides a theory of growth and beyond that a framework with "the interest in economic change and its causes, in processes in which change materializes, and their consequences" [5]. We call this extended framework "*Evolutionary Economics*".

A fully worked out coherent theoretical conceptualisation of Evolutionary Dynamics, let alone a full quantitative framework, does not yet exist. This is not surprising, because the challenge of understanding all processes of economic evolution is of *another "order of magnitude"* than merely understanding the equilibrium state. Reasons for this increased order of difficulties are (a) that the interacting dynamic processes occurring at very different time-scales – which *do not show up at all* in the stationary state, because they have equilibrated – must now be explicitly treated, and (b) that the understanding of this dynamics in general requires us to give up the *isolated* consideration of the economy.

Nevertheless there do already exist valuable investigations devoted to Evolutionary Economics [6], [7] and successful endeavours to systematize the present "state of art" in Evolutionary Economics [5]. In these remarks the author draws from the lucid survey of U. Witt [5] about the present lines of thought in this quickly developing field.

In order to *classify* the different lines of thought we make use of two *complementary guidelines*:

The *first guideline* is a *system-theoretical classification scheme*: If the economy is *one* subsystem among several intertwined subsystems constituting the society and if a specific mode of behaviour of this partial system – namely the market equilibrium – destabilizes and is transformed into other dynamic modes, the reason can be the following:

(a)   The constituent parts of the partial system (i.e. the economic agents) can introduce a new and destabilizing kind of activity. This is the *personalistic or individualistic* creation of economic dynamics.

(b) The partial system itself has, due to its systemic organisation or structure, the ability to develop new dynamic modes. This is the *perspective of endogenously selforganizing economic dynamics*.

(c) The partial system interacts with other partial systems (such as the political or cultural subsystem). This is *the perspective of exogenously generated economic dynamics* due to being embedded in the global system. (This aspect is taken into account in the so-called "New classical theory of business cycles".)

In short, the destabilization of economic stationarity can be engendered (a) from *below*, i.e. from the microlevel, (b) from *within*, and (c) from *outside* at the macro-level.

The *second guideline* is a classification scheme by analogy: Here the analogy between *economic processes* and corresponding processes in *biological evolution* is employed. The deeper reason to trust in the relevance of this analogy seems to be the presumed *principle of the "repetitive similarity of organisational rules"* stating that "on the level of more complex systems – such as society – *organisational rules reappear in modified form* which did already appear mutatis mutandis in less complex systems – such as the biosphere. Thus the principle originates in the idea of a *"parsimony of generic organizing rules"*.

Let us now enumerate some concepts of evolutionary economics – each of them leading beyond the pure market equilibrium – along these classification lines.

Schumpeter [8], the first economist to provide a consistent evolutionary interpretation of economic change, stressed the role of the *entrepreneur*, whose pioneering personality and motivation gives rise to an *incessant competitive restructuring of the economy*. Business cycles are interpreted by Schumpeter as cyclical patterns in entrepreneurial innovative activities, including the "swarm-like" appearance of them. (An attempt to formalize this concept was given in [9]). This explanation scheme of creative innovations by entrepreneurs evidently belongs to the "personalistic perspective" (a) of economic dynamics.

However, one of the central themes of Evolutionary Economics, the *appearance of innovations*, has not only the aspect of personal creativity when an invention is introduced, but also leads to new production techniques, to changes of the nature and quality of commodities and thus to the opening of new ways of consumption, and finally to *dissemination* of the innovation by a process of diffusion and simultaneously competitive selection in the whole economy. Thus, an innovative idea is eventually *entrained* into the economic system according to its endogenous rules, i.e. according to (b) [10], [11].

The market has thereupon endogenously assumed another more dynamic quality: The incessant arisal of innovative events disrupts the equilibration in the old sense; instead, the market proves to be a *novelty generating, testing and selecting institution or mechanism*. A new dynamics is generated in which de-coordinating and coordinating activities are simultaneously at work. Phases of instability, phase-transitions to another dynamic behaviour do now obtain another explanatory background. Even the long-term economic cycles (Kondradieff) with their phases "prosperity, recession, depression and recovery" must be seen in the context of an intensifying or attenuating flow of mutually interacting innovations [12]. These explanatory schemes belong to category (b).

Exogenous reasons of type (c) for the destabilisation of economic equilibrium are also obvious: The exhaustion of natural resources, e.g. of fossile energy resources, stimulates and drives the innovation process. The most prominent example of an interaction between the economic and political subsystem of the society is communism, whose arisal was promoted by the deficiencies of early capitalism and whose breakdown was ironically favoured by the malfunction of its economy which was due to its construction according to communist ideology.

A grand vision of the embedding of the economic system into the global system of the society is given by Hayek [13], [14], who assumes three levels of evolution: The *first one* is that of *genetic evolution*; the *second one* is the evolution of the *products of human intelligence and knowledge*, which include the products of the economy; the third one is the level of *cultural evolution* which includes a selection process between rules of social interactions.

The second above mentioned classification guideline, the *search for analogies between economic and biologic evolution*, was utilized by several authors (see e.g. [15], [16]), in particular by Nelson and Winter [17].

Indeed, the biosphere provides a rich field of dynamic processes which reappear mutatis mutandis in the economy.

One of the central paradigms of biological evolution is the (Neo-)Darwinian *mutation-selection scheme*: The inherited *genotype* of a species leads to its – for the first stationary – *phenotype*. However, the genome can be changed by exogenous influences (chemicals, radiation) leading to *spontaneous mutations* providing a diversification of phenotypes within the species. In a *competitive selection process* on the phenotypic macrolevel the unsuccessful mutations die out whereas the fittest mutants win through and survive.

Similarly, in the economy there exists an *inherited set* of approved and successful production technologies and organisational routines within the firms leading to a stationarily supplied batch of commodities. However, improved organisational structures and exogenous influence such as new discoveries and insights, the appearance of inventions, learning processes and the acquisition of new knowledge lead to *mutations* in terms of new technologies and a modified batch of commodities containing innovations. The market now proves to be the testing and selection institution where *competitive selection* takes place. Successful innovations survive whereas the unsuccessful ones die out [18]. In the nascent phase of innovations there appear *critical fluctuations* deciding about the survival or the elimination of a novelty. The role of these probabilistic fluctuations has been treated in detail by Ebeling and his school with master equation methods closely related to Sociodynamics [19]. Also G. Haag and G. Erdmann have utilized the sociodynamic master equation method to formulate a theory of economic decision making [20] and an evolutionary theory of innovations [21].

Biological and economic evolution as well implies in the long run the phenomenon of *path-dependency*. Self-reinforcing tendencies resulting from an inter-dependency of agents' decisions lead to mutually exclusive coordination equilibria or dynamic modes denoted as "attractors" in nonlinear dynamics. "The future time path describing the historical development of a system then depends on which of the alternative "*basins of attraction*" has already been visited, or will be entered. In a more imaginative metaphor one may speak of a (multidimensional) "adaptive landscape" on which evolution proceeds, with a multiplicity of basins of attraction" (see also [22], [23], [24] and [25] where the consequences of nonlinear economic dynamics are investigated). For biological evolution this conceptual framework has been extensively employed by S. A. Kauffman [26].

The path-dependency of the long-term evolution of an economic system – as well as of a biological system – makes clear that *within the interplay between chance and necessity* in the long run the role of chance prevails more and more and is less and less eliminable. In other words: In the long run *predictibility must decrease* independently of the utilized modelling formalism. The reason is – as already generally stated in part I – that *transitions between basins of attraction in an adaptive landscape* have an unavoidable concomitant: *critical probabilistic fluctuations* deciding at each crossroad, into which of alternative directions the path of the economy will proceed.

II.3.1.3   Contributions of Sociodynamics to Evolutionary Economics

Now we try to demonstrate that Sociodynamics could provide a bridge from the neo-classical formalism towards a formalism treating at least some of the problems of Evolutionary Economics.

Comparison of Utility Concepts

In neo-classical as well as in sociodynamic formalisms *utility functions* are used as measures for the usefulness or attractiveness of a certain configuration of variables. However, the conceptual context in which the utility functions are embedded is a different one in the two formalisms.

In Neo-classical Textbook-Economics the context is a *static* or better *stationary* one, or one of "comparative statics". As we have seen above in the case of perfectly competitive market equilibrium, each of the economic agents disposes of a certain subset of the economic variables in order to *maximize his objective function* (i.e. consumers utility or producers profit, respectively).

Instead, in Sociodynamics "dynamic utility functions" and in addition "mobility functions" are introduced as *constituent terms of probabilistic transition rates* (see Chapter 3.2), i.e. in a *conceptualisation of dynamics*.

Thereupon stochastic and quasi-deterministic *evolutionary equations* can be derived (see Chapter 3.3 and Chapters 10, 11 and 12). These dynamic equations describe – either in probabilistic form (master equation) or in quasi-deterministic form (quasimeanvalue equations) – the struggle of interacting groups of economic agents (e.g. producers and consumers) for improving, at least in the ensemble average, the usefulness or attractiveness of their economic situation. In this process, the *differences* between the utility of an origin state and a state strived for serve as "driving forces" within the set of dynamic equations.

A "maximisation of utilities" is *not* the necessary consequence of the dynamic process described in this manner. Instead, the set of nonlinear dynamic quasimean-value equations may possess one or several stable and/or instable stationary states or more general attractors such as limit cycles or even strange attractors (describing deterministic chaos). However, in *special cases* the dynamic equations may possess *exactly one stable stationary state* which *then* corresponds to an *unambiguous market equilibrium*. (Examples for all cases are given in the models of Chapters 7 and 8.)

(Since probabilistic transition rates are *cardinal* quantities, the *dynamic utilities* of Sociodynamics are *by definition cardinal quantities*, too. This means the dispute of Neoclassical Economics as to whether utilities are cardinal or ordinal quantities does not arise here.)

The Descriptive Potential of Sociodynamics

In trying to give an estimate of the possibilities of sociodynamic modelling we begin with a remark about the relation between probabilistic and deterministic modelling.

The master equation is the central equation of Sociodynamics; it yields the evolution of a *probability distribution*. Such a distribution describes the *relative frequency* with which samples out of an *ensemble of equally prepared economic systems* (having equal trend parameters and equal initial conditions) reach certain states at a given time. However, such an *ensemble* of economic systems is practivally *never available*. The way out of this difficulty is to compare only the *mean trajectory* (as described by quasimeanvalue equations) or a *representative stochastic trajectory* with the one and only realized "sample".

On the other hand it is just this probabilistic description frame of Sociodynamics, which does not suppress – in contrast to purely deterministic description frames – the unavoidable amount of uncertainty inherent in all socio-economic processes, because they trace back to the decision making of actors, which always contains a contingent element of spontaneity. In particular the critical fluctuations at economical phase-transitions are included in the probabilistic frame.

Secondly, we remark that the *configuration of variables* in Sociodynamics is *an extended one*. As explained in Chapter 3, not only *material* variables but also intensive and extensive *personal* variables are included in the descriptive frame. This leads to the possibility of modelling collective interactions within and between groups of economic agents. Such interactions may consist in self-reinforcing tendencies such as network-externalities, lock in effects, cooperative and imitative, or, on the other hand, antagonistic and rivalling group behaviour. The effects of such collective interactions typically result in *nonlinear* quasi-meanvalue equations, the solutions of which may include – in the often realized case of slowly varying control- and trend-parameters – the possibility of *economic phase-transitions* such as transitions to another stationary state or another dynamic mode.

One may summarize in schematic manner the three levels participating in the dynamic interaction which can be captured – at least in partial models – by the sociodynamic formalism:

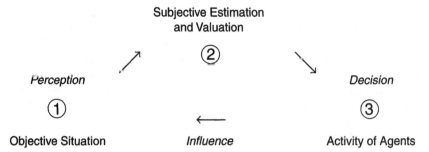

In detail the components ①, ②, ③ of the interaction-scheme mean:

① The *objective (economic) situation* is described in terms of the "economic con-figuration" consisting of material and personal variables.

② *The subjective estimation and valuation* of the objective (economic) situation is formalized by "dynamic utilities" being functions of the economic configuration and of control- and trend-parameters.

③ The *activity of (economic) agents* influences – by producing economic dynamics – the objective situation. The influence is described in terms of transition rates with mobilities and utility differences as constituent "driving forces". The transition rates are the construction elements for the (probabilistic or deter-ministic) evolution equations.

A final remark refers to the *possibilities and limitations of modelling the evolutionary long-term perspective.* The restriction of the sociodynamic interaction scheme to the economic sector does of course presume that the interaction of this sector with other sectors of the social system is relatively weak. This will in general work for short-term and medium-term processes, but not for evolutionary long-term processes.

In the long run the global path of the society will – as already mentioned – also traverse historical stages of *strong interaction* between the economic, political and cultural sector, for instance in cases of economic emergency and political and/or cultural revolutions. In this long-term perspective the term "economic" must be cancelled in the interaction scheme set up above.

That means one must resort to *integrated models*

(1) by extending the configuration of variables to include e.g. collective variables of political and cultural behaviour;

(2) by the setting up of dynamic utility functions depending on the extended set of variables and including – beyond measuring pure economic usefulness – the effects of political ideology and cultural trends, and

(3) by the setting up of a corresponding extended set of evolutionary equations now comprising the interacting dynamics of all partial systems of economy, politics and culture.

Thus there arises in principle the grand vision of an expansive modelling procedure finally "integrating everything", the long-term evolution of the economy, the rise and fall of nations, the birth and death of ideologies, the phase-transitions between peace and war, the formation and the clash of religions and civilisations.

However, against this euphoric vision there exist reservations due to principal reasons which are independent of the utilized modelling formalism. The grand historical perspective necessarily contains, if modelled quantitatively, several small-size and large-size phase-transitions along the trajectory of the society. As already mentioned, each of them represents a cross-road with open issues decided by critical fluctuations, i.e. by chance and not by necessity. This means, that in the historical perspective contingency prevails and the system's fate turns out to be *an open one* which is not predictable by an integrated model.

If, on the other hand, a grand integrative model would at best comprise *probabilistically* all grand alternatives of historic evolution (for instance, whether or not Christianity had a chance to appear, or whether or not the third world war will take place), it would become *the less useful the more divergent alternatives* it includes. Since *only one* of these potential alternatives was realized in the past and will be realized in the future, it is only on *this realized* eventuality on which human interest eventually focusses.

The following two models which have first been published in [27], [28] and [29] and which are constructed according to sociodynamic concepts will *not* be concerned with such grand perspectives. Instead they will treat the dynamics of concrete economic subsystems. Nevertheless both subsystems exhibit a nonlinear dynamics transgressing the standard neoclassical modelling. However, since equilibrium cases are also included as special model solutions, the relation between the formalisms can be studied.

7. Quality Competition between High-Tech Firms

7.1 Lines of Model Design

We have seen in the introduction that innovations are basic events in causing economic dynamics beyond the equilibrium state and which therefore belong to the field of Evolutionary Economics.

It is however not easy to *formalize* the role of product innovations, or a sequence of such innovations, in *direct* and simultaneously *general* form, since each innovation is a *novelty*. Its acceptance and success on the market can therefore not easily be theoretically anticipated.

Nevertheless the model studied in this chapter is designed to describe a dynamic process among competing firms in which innovations play at least an *indirect* role. In order to capture indirectly the role of a sequence of innovations in a newly appearing and developing high-tech-product manufactured by competing firms we will introduce as a central variable the *"quality of a given product"*, or better the qualities of a given set of functionally equivalent (substitutable) high-tech-commodities (such as, for instance, video-recorders). The product quality can of course be influenced by the innovative effort of the producing firm.

Again, the variable of "quality" is a complex and composite one, because it consists of *objective properties* such as technological perfection and *subjective properties* such as aesthetic appeal.

However, we will *only* be interested in how the variable "quality" enters the expressions for dynamic utilities and transition rates which thereupon constitute the dynamic equations. In other words: The *variable "quality of a product"* needs not to be traced back to the sequence of innovations creating this quality but *is implicitly defined by the role it plays within the dynamics of the considered economic sector*.

Another element of model design will be the introduction of personal variables, namely a *consumer's configuration* of non-owners and owners of different types of the substitutable high-tech-commodity. For such high-tech-products it is plausible to assume that each consumer is only interested in buying *at most one unit* of the product. This means that the total number of customers and the mean lifetime of the products will lead to a *saturation limit of the aggregate demand* independently of the prices of the products.

209

Finally the conventional rules of production and consumption, namely that (a) firms produce in order to make profit, and (b) consumers have a demand decreasing with product-price, are of course not ruled out and must be implied in the construc- tion of the model. They have however to be *reformuluted* to fit into the *conceptional frame of a dynumlc* model.

The result of these elements of design will be a *nonlinear dynamics of interacting producers and consumers*, formulated in terms of quasimeanvalue-equations. The firms compete by enhancing the quality of their products, if they are encouraged to do this by the demand of customers, and the customers react in their demand not only to the *price*, but first of all to the *quality* of the innovative product. This leads to a (positive or negative) feedback loop structure: Higher (lower) quality leads to higher (lower) demand, which enables (prevents) the firm of enhancing the product quality. As we will see, this "mechanism" can lead to a bifurcation process, i.e. to a destabilisation of an existing equilibrium between the firms participating in the market.

7.2   The General Model of L Competing Firms

In setting up the model we proceed as outlined in Chapter 3. In contrast to the population-dynamic and sociological models of II.1 and II.2 we have now to take into account both personal *and* material variables.

7.2.1   Variables and Transition Rates

Let us consider L competing firms $F_j, j = 1, 2, \ldots, L$, and assume that each firm F_j produces one version c_j of a durable high-tech commodity. The c_j are assumed to be functionally equivalent and substitutable. (For instance, all firms produce video- recorders and F_j produces the type c_j.)

The Variables

At first we have to introduce the *variables* of the "*economic configuration*", among which the dynamics of the considered system takes place.

On the *demand or consumption side* we introduce a *set of extensive personal vari- ables* describing the consumers.

For simplicity we assume a homogeneous consumer population $\mathcal{P}$ neglecting possible social subspecifications (α). Furthermore we assume that each consumer may own either *none* or *one* of the high-tech-commodities c_j. Let n_0 be the momentary number of nonowners and n_j the momentary number of consumers owning one unit c_j. Then the demand side is described by the set of integer variables:

$$\mathbf{n} = \{n_0, n_1, \ldots, n_L\}. \tag{7.1}$$

If N is the total number of $\mathcal{P}$ and if birth/death processes are neglected, the follow- ing conservation law must be fulfilled during the evolution:

$$n_0 + \sum_{j=1}^{L} n_j = N \tag{7.2}$$

On the *supply or production side* we introduce *material variables* which are only *indirectly* coupled to the decision makers in the firms F_j.

Let S_j be the (momentary) number of units c_j supplied per unit of time by firm F_j. Furthermore, let P_j be the (momentary) price of one unit c_j. For the high-tech-products c_j another quantitative measure will play a decisive role in the dynamics between competing firms F_j and consumers: The quality Q_j of the product c_j. We assume that such a one-dimensional (perhaps composite) quality measure Q_j for c_j exists and assumes positive discrete values $0, 1, 2, \ldots$, such that higher values of Q_j mean higher quality of c_j. (As already indicated, we are *not* interested in explaining how the quality Q_j is technologically brought about; instead we *are* interested in the evolution of Q_j with time, that means how Q_j is entrained into the endogeneous dynamics of the considered economic system.)

Summarizing, we describe the production side by the following set of variables:

$$\mathbf{m} = \{S_1 \ldots S_L; P_1 \ldots P_L; Q_1 \ldots Q_L\} \tag{7.3}$$

so that the *total economic configuration* $\mathbf{E}$ is given by

$$\{\mathbf{E}\} = \{\mathbf{n}, \mathbf{m}\} = \{n_0, n_1, \ldots n_L; S_1 \ldots S_L; P_1 \ldots P_L; Q_1 \ldots Q_L\}. \tag{7.4}$$

The Transition Rates

The core of the model consists in the choice of transition rates for the variables of the economic configuration $\mathbf{E}$.

On the *demand side* the elementary dynamic processes are the following: A non-owner may buy one unit c_j and become an owner. An owner of c_j may abandon c_j and become a nonowner. We assume that a change from c_i to c_j takes place via $i \Rightarrow 0 \Rightarrow j$. Thus the transitions on the demand side are *generalized migration processes between nonownership and ownership.*

Accordingly, we postulate in applying the general form of transition rates for migratory processes deduced in Chapter 3, that the transition rate for $\mathbf{n} = \{n_0, \ldots n_j, \ldots, n_L\} \Rightarrow \mathbf{n}_{j0} = \{(n_0 - 1), \ldots, (n_j + 1), \ldots, n_L\}$ has the form (the index c stands for "consumers"):

$$w_{j0}^c = \tilde{\nu} \exp[u_j - u_0] \cdot n_0, \tag{7.5}$$

where u_j is the (dynamic) utility associated with possessing one unit c_j, and u_0 the utility associated with nonownership. The parameter $\tilde{\nu}$ is a global measure for the frequency of buying the commodities.

Since the transition rate (7.5) only depends on the *difference* of u_j and u_0, the latter utilities are not uniquely defined but may be re-gauged by

$$u_0' = u_0 - c; \quad u_j' = u_j - c \quad j = 1, 2, \dots, L. \tag{7.6}$$

It is convenient to choose the gauge such that

$$u_0' = 0. \tag{7.7}$$

Furthermore, it seems plausible to choose for the dynamic utility u_j' a simple *trade-off* between the quality and the price of the commodity c_j, that means, omitting henceforth the prime $'$:

$$u_j \equiv u_j(Q_j, P_j) = \kappa Q_j^b - \sigma P_j \quad j = 1, 2, \dots, L. \tag{7.8}$$

A simple interpretation can now be given of the parameters κ, σ and b: $\kappa (\geq 0)$ is a measure for the *quality-sensitivity*, and $\sigma (\geq 0)$ a measure for the *price-sensitivity* of the consumers. The parameter $b > 0$ describes a possible *saturation of the effect of growing quality*, if a value $0 < b < 1$ is chosen. In the following we put $b = 1$, because it turns out that a choice $b < 1$ does not change the principal structure of the model.

The inverse transition $\mathbf{n} = \{n_0, \dots n_j \dots n_L\} \Rightarrow \mathbf{n}_{0j} = \{(n_0 + 1), \dots, (n_j - 1), \dots, n_L\}$ has to do not with the *utility* of c_j but rather with its *lifetime*. We assume that the mean lifetime $\tilde{\rho}^{-1}$ of all products c_j is the same. Hence the transition rate w_{0j}^c reads

$$w_{0j}^c = \tilde{\rho} n_j. \tag{7.9}$$

The value of the transition rate w_{j0}^c given by (7.5) is equal to the *realized demand* D_j. That means the number of units c_j bought per unit of time is

$$D_j = w_{j0}^c = \tilde{\nu} \exp[u_j(Q_j, P_j)] \cdot n_0. \tag{7.10}$$

Evidently the quantity

$$\Delta_j = D_j / n_0 = \tilde{\nu} \exp[u_j(Q_j, P_j)] \tag{7.11}$$

has the properties of an individual income-compensated demand function which include:

$$\frac{\partial \Delta_j}{\partial P_j} < 0; \quad \frac{\partial \Delta_j}{\partial Q_j} > 0. \tag{7.12}$$

Now we discuss the *supply side*. The elementary changes of the variables S_j, P_j and $Q_j, j = 1, 2, \dots, L$ are modelled by transition rates $w_{j\pm}^S, w_{j\pm}^P$ and $w_{j\pm}^Q$ causing the increase or decrease of the variables S_j, P_j and Q_j, respectively, by one unit. They are generated by decisions of firm F_j.

Firstly we choose *transition rates w_{j+}^S and w_{j-}^S for changes of the production* $S_j \Rightarrow (S_j + 1)$ and $S_j \Rightarrow (S_j - 1)$, respectively, by which the firm F_j adjusts its supply.

The simplest assumption is, that each firm F_j strives to improve its profit at the momentarily given price P_j.

In the stationary case the maximisation of the profit

$$G_j = P_j S_j - C_j(S_j), \tag{7.13}$$

where $C_j(S_j)$ are the costs per unit of time for the production of supply S_j, would lead to the wellknown first order condition

$$(P_j - C_j'(S_j)) = 0, \tag{7.14}$$

where $C_j'(S_j) > 0$ denotes the marginal costs, i.e. the costs for producing *one unit c_j more* per unit of time.

In the dynamic situation the firm will in general not be in its profit optimum so that the variable $(P_j - C_j'(S_j))$ can assume positive or negative values as well. However it is plausible to assume that the transition rates w_{j+}^S and w_{j-}^S are *functions* of $(P_j - C_j'(S_j))$ to be chosen in a manner so as to induce adjustment transitions of S_j which lead back to the optimum (7.14).

For increasingly *positive* values of the variable $(P_j - C_j'(S_j))$ there will exist an increasing propensity to *enhance* the production, whereas for negative values this propensity vanishes. On the other hand there will exist an increasing propensity to *diminish* the production for increasingly *negative* values of the variable $(P_j - C_j'(S_j))$, whereas this propensity vanishes for positive values.

The real production enhancement or diminution steps of the firm F_j induced by positive or negative values of $(P_j - C_j'(S_j))$ will usually take place in *percentages* of the existing production S_j. Since, on the other hand, we consider in our model only steps $S_j \Rightarrow S_j \pm 1$ of *one unit* at one moment, we are led to assume the rate of such a single *one-unit-step* to be not only proportional to $(P_j - C_j'(S_j))$ but also to S_j, that means proportional to

$$X_j = (P_j - C_j'(S_j)) \cdot S_j. \tag{7.15}$$

The simplest specification of rates $w_{j\pm}^S$ consistent with these considerations is

$$\begin{aligned} \tilde{w}_{j+}^S &= \tilde{w}_{j+}^S(X_j) = \tilde{\beta} \cdot X_j \cdot \vartheta(X_j) \geq 0; \\ \tilde{w}_{j-}^S &= \tilde{w}_{j-}^S(X_j) = \tilde{\beta} \cdot (-X_j) \cdot \vartheta(-X_j) \geq 0 \\ \text{hence} \quad &\tilde{w}_{j-}^S(-X_j) = \tilde{w}_{j+}^S(X_j), \end{aligned} \tag{7.16}$$

where $\tilde{\beta}$ is a production adjustment parameter and where

$$\begin{aligned} \vartheta(X) &= 1 \quad \text{for} \quad X \geq 0; \\ \vartheta(X) &= 0 \quad \text{for} \quad X < 0. \end{aligned} \tag{7.17}$$

Secondly, we choose *transition rates* w_{j+}^P and w_{j-}^P for *the adjustments of prices* $P_j \Rightarrow (P_j + 1)$ and $P_j \Rightarrow (P_j - 1)$, respectively, by the firm F_j and follow a similar argumentation: If a positive excess demand $(D_j - S_j)$ exists, this will lead to a corresponding propensity of the firm to raise its price P_j, whereas a positive excess production $(S_j - D_j)$ leads to a propensity to lower the price. The rate of this price raising or lowering by *one unit* will then *also* be proportional to the already existing price level, i.e. proportional to the *excess variable*

$$Z_j = (D_j - S_j)P_j \tag{7.18}$$

and we are led to the choice:

$$\tilde{w}_{j+}^P = \tilde{w}_{j+}^P(Z_j) = \tilde{\alpha} \cdot Z_j \cdot \vartheta(Z_j) \geq 0;$$
$$\tilde{w}_{j-}^P = \tilde{w}_{j-}^P(Z_j) = \tilde{\alpha} \cdot (-Z_j) \cdot \vartheta(-Z_j) \geq 0 \tag{7.19}$$
$$\text{hence} \quad \tilde{w}_{j-}^P(-Z_j) = \tilde{w}_{j+}^P(+Z_j)$$

Although the rates (7.16) and (7.19) are plausible and simple, we modify them because of the fact, that the *real value* of a variable x on which a transition rate $\tilde{w}(x)$ such as (7.16) or (7.19) depends, is perceived or known with some *uncertainty* only by the decision maker. Let for instance $p(\xi)d\xi$, with

$$p(\xi) = p(-\xi) > 0 \quad \text{and} \quad \int_{-\infty}^{+\infty} p(\xi)d\xi = 1 \tag{7.20}$$

be the probability of an agent to perceiving instead of the true value x the value $(x + \xi)$ in the interval $[\xi, \xi + d\xi]$. Accordingly, the transition rate $\tilde{w}(x)$ should be modified to become the weighted average over the perceived values of x. That means

$$\tilde{w}(x) \Rightarrow w(x) = \int_{-\infty}^{+\infty} p(\xi)\tilde{w}(x + \xi)d\xi. \tag{7.21}$$

Choosing a Gaussfunction with variance v^2 for the probability of an uncertainty ξ of perception:

$$p_v(\xi) = \frac{1}{v\sqrt{2\pi}}\exp\left[-\frac{\xi^2}{2v^2}\right], \tag{7.22}$$

one obtains by applying (7.21) instead of (7.16) and (7.19) the somewhat modified (that means smeared out by perception uncertainty) transition rates:

$$w_{j+}^S(X_j) = \tilde{\beta}\left\{X_j \cdot \frac{1}{2}\left[1 + \phi\left(\frac{X_j}{v}\right)\right] + \frac{v}{\sqrt{2\pi}}\exp\left[-\frac{X_j^2}{2v^2}\right]\right\}; \tag{7.23}$$
$$w_{j-}^S(-X_j) = w_{j+}^S(X_j)$$

and

$$w_{j+}^P(Z_j) = \tilde{\alpha}\left\{Z_j \cdot \frac{1}{2}\left[1 + \phi\left(\frac{Z_j}{v}\right)\right] + \frac{v}{\sqrt{2\pi}}\exp\left[-\frac{Z_j^2}{2v^2}\right]\right\}; \tag{7.24}$$
$$w_{j-}^P(-Z_j) = w_{j+}^P(Z_j)$$

where

$$\phi\left(\frac{X}{v}\right) = 2 \int_0^X p_v(\xi)d\xi = -\phi\left(-\frac{X}{v}\right).\tag{7.25}$$

It is remarkable and important for the quasimeanvalue equations, that the *differences* of the up and down rates are *not* affected by the averaging procedure. This means, with (7.16) and (7.23) there holds:

$$\tilde{w}_{j+}^S(X_j) - \tilde{w}_{j-}^S(X_j) = w_{j+}^S(X_j) - w_{j-}^S(X_j)$$
$$= \tilde{\beta}X_j \quad \text{for} \quad -\infty < X_j < +\infty \tag{7.26}$$

and with (7.19) and (7.24) there follows

$$\tilde{w}_{j+}^P(Z_j) - \tilde{w}_{j-}^P(Z_j) = w_{j+}^P(Z_j) - w_{j-}^P(Z_j)$$
$$= \tilde{\alpha}Z_j \quad \text{for} \quad -\infty < Z_j < +\infty. \tag{7.27}$$

Finally the transition rates w_{j+}^Q and w_{j-}^Q for adjusting the quality Q_j of the product c_j must be appropriately chosen. In contrast to the production- and price-adjustment processes there seems not to exist a single variable, such as X_j or Z_j, on which the up and down rates of quality could depend. We assume the quality enhancement and quality diminution rates

$$w_{j+}^Q = \tilde{\eta}D_j; \tag{7.28}$$
$$w_{j-}^Q = \tilde{\gamma}Q_j \tag{7.29}$$

to which the following interpretation can be given:

At first, the form (7.28) and (7.29) of the quality transition rates implies that the whole quality dynamics is, in effect, endogenously coupled to the variables introduced so far. Thus we assume implicitly in (7.28) that technological progress leading to *quality improvement steps* is possible by higher r&d expenditures and that this endeavour is proportional to demand. The *responsiveness parameter* $\tilde{\eta}$ describes the degree of the firms reaction to higher demand by improving further its product quality.

On the other hand, the form (7.29) has been chosen in view of the fact that there also exists a certain *quality decay* in the case of lack of demand, or more generally of quality adaptation if some demand exists. This decay- and adaptation-process is assumed to be proportional to the already reached level of quality and to be due to a certain complacency on the side of firms. The *quality adjustment parameter* $\tilde{\gamma}$ is a measure of the speed of this adaptation process.

In the formulas for $w_{j\pm}^S, w_{j\pm}^P, w_{j\pm}^Q$ we have assumed the *same* values $\tilde{\alpha}, \tilde{\beta}, \tilde{\eta}, \tilde{\gamma}$ of the global speed parameters of all firms. This means that we treat the firms as "strategically equivalent" in this respect.

7.2.2 The Dynamic Equations

The transition rates w_{j0}^C; w_{0j}^C; $w_{j\pm}^S$, $w_{j\pm}^P$; $w_{j\pm}^Q$ set up in Section 7.2.1 describe the frequency of elementary transitions between a given economic configuration $\mathbf{E} = \{\mathbf{n, S, P, Q}\}$ and neighbouring configurations $\mathbf{E}_{j0}^C = \{\mathbf{n}_{j0}, \mathbf{S, P, Q}\}$; $\mathbf{F}_{0j}^C - \{\mathbf{n}_{0j}, \mathbf{S, P, Q}\}$; $\mathbf{E}_{j\pm}^S = \{\mathbf{n}, \mathbf{S}_{j\pm}, \mathbf{P, Q}\}$; $\mathbf{E}_{j\pm}^P = \{\mathbf{n, S}, \mathbf{P}_{j\pm}, \mathbf{Q}\}$ and $\mathbf{E}_{j\pm}^Q = \{\mathbf{n, S, P}, \mathbf{Q}_{j\pm}\}$. Here we have introduced the notation:

$$
\begin{aligned}
\mathbf{n}_{j0} &= \{(n_0 - 1), \ldots, (n_j + 1), \ldots, n_L\}; \\
\mathbf{n}_{0j} &= \{(n_0 + 1), \ldots, (n_j - 1), \ldots, n_L\}; \\
\mathbf{S}_{j\pm} &= \{S_1, \ldots, (S_j \pm 1), \ldots, S_L\}; \\
\mathbf{P}_{j\pm} &= \{P_1, \ldots, (P_j \pm 1), \ldots, P_L\}; \\
\mathbf{Q}_{j\pm} &= \{Q_1, \ldots, (Q_j \pm 1), \ldots, Q_L\}.
\end{aligned}
\tag{7.30}
$$

According to the general procedure outlined in Chapter 3 it is now straight forward to set up the master equation and the quasimeanvalue-equations.

The Master Equation

The master equation is the equation of motion for the probability $P(\mathbf{E}; t)$ to find the economic configuration $\mathbf{E}$ at time t. It reads

$$
\begin{aligned}
\frac{dP(\mathbf{E}; t)}{dt} ={} & \sum_{j=1}^{L} w_{j0}^C(\mathbf{E}_{0j}^C) P(\mathbf{E}_{0j}^C; t) - \sum_{j=1}^{L} w_{j0}^C(\mathbf{E}) P(\mathbf{E}; t) \\
& + \sum_{j=1}^{L} w_{0j}^C(\mathbf{E}_{j0}^C) P(\mathbf{E}_{j0}^C; t) - \sum_{j=1}^{L} w_{0j}^C(\mathbf{E}) P(\mathbf{E}; t) \\
& + \sum_{j=1}^{L} w_{j+}^S(\mathbf{E}_{j-}^S) P(\mathbf{E}_{j-}^S; t) - \sum_{j=1}^{L} w_{j+}^S(\mathbf{E}) P(\mathbf{E}; t) \\
& + \sum_{j=1}^{L} w_{j-}^S(\mathbf{E}_{j+}^S) P(\mathbf{E}_{j+}^S; t) - \sum_{j=1}^{L} w_{j-}^S(\mathbf{E}) P(\mathbf{E}; t) \\
& + \sum_{j=1}^{L} w_{j+}^P(\mathbf{E}_{j-}^P) P(\mathbf{E}_{j-}^P; t) - \sum_{j=1}^{L} w_{j+}^P(\mathbf{E}) P(\mathbf{E}; t) \\
& + \sum_{j=1}^{L} w_{j-}^P(\mathbf{E}_{j+}^P) P(\mathbf{E}_{j+}^P; t) - \sum_{j=1}^{L} w_{j-}^P(\mathbf{E}) P(\mathbf{E}; t) \\
& + \sum_{j=1}^{L} w_{j+}^Q(\mathbf{E}_{j-}^Q) P(\mathbf{E}_{j-}^Q; t) - \sum_{j=1}^{L} w_{j+}^Q(\mathbf{E}) P(\mathbf{E}; t) \\
& + \sum_{j=1}^{L} w_{j-}^Q(\mathbf{E}_{j+}^Q) P(\mathbf{E}_{j+}^Q; t) - \sum_{j=1}^{L} w_{j-}^Q(\mathbf{E}) P(\mathbf{E}; t).
\end{aligned}
\tag{7.31}
$$

The right hand side of this equation contains eight lines. All of them contribute to changes with time of the probability $P(\mathbf{E}; t)$ of the configuration $\mathbf{E}$ by probability *inflows* from neighbouring configurations (positive terms) and *outflows* into neighbouring configurations (negative terms). The first two lines are generated by consumer movements from nonownership to ownership of one unit of the versions c_j of the commodity, and inversely from abandoning these goods. Lines three and four are due to supply adjustment steps; lines five and six stem from price adjustment steps, and lines seven and eight are generated by quality enhancement and diminution processes.

The Quasi-meanvalue Equations

The quasi-meanvalue equations for $\hat{n}_j, \hat{S}_j, \hat{P}_j, \hat{Q}_j$ which are closely related to the master equation (for their derivation see Chapter 3 and Chapter 12) describe the evolution with time of the *mean trajectory of a bundle of stochastic trajectories* at each system point. They read (omitting the hat over the variables)

$$\frac{dn_j(t)}{dt} = w_{j0}^C - w_{0j}^C = \tilde{\nu}\exp[\kappa Q_j - \sigma P_j]n_0 - \tilde{\rho}n_j; \tag{7.32}$$

$$\frac{dn_0(t)}{dt} = \sum_{j=1}^{L} w_{0j}^C - \sum_{j=1}^{L} w_{j0}^C = -\sum_{j=1}^{L} \frac{dn_j(t)}{dt}; \tag{7.33}$$

$$\frac{dS_j(t)}{dt} = w_{j+}^S(X_j) - w_{j-}^S(X_j) = \tilde{\beta}X_j = \tilde{\beta}(P_j - C_j'(S_j))S_j; \tag{7.34}$$

$$\frac{dP_j(t)}{dt} = w_{j+}^P(Z_j) - w_{j-}^P(Z_j) = \tilde{\alpha}Z_j = \tilde{\alpha}(D_j - S_j)P_j; \tag{7.35}$$

$$\frac{dQ_j(t)}{dt} = w_{j+}^Q - w_{j-}^Q = \tilde{\eta}D_j - \tilde{\gamma}Q_j. \tag{7.36}$$

The equation (7.33) is compatible with the conservation law (7.2) and can be eliminated.

Transition to Scaled Variables

It is now convenient to introduce in the quasi-meanvalue equations dimensionless scaled variables.

The relative shares of owners and nonowners are given by:

$$x_j = \frac{n_j}{N} \quad j = 1, 2, \ldots, L; \quad x_0 = \frac{n_0}{N} \tag{7.37}$$

and the conservation law (7.2) now reads

$$x_0 + \sum_{j=1}^{L} x_j = 1. \tag{7.38}$$

Furthermore we introduce the demand d_j and supply s_j per person in the time interval $\tilde{\nu}^{-1}$ by putting

$$D_j = \tilde{\nu}Nd_j; \quad S_j = \tilde{\nu}Ns_j. \tag{7.39}$$

The demand formula (7.10) is then transformed into:

$$d_j = \exp[u_j]x_0 = \exp[\kappa Q_j - \sigma P_j]x_0. \tag{7.40}$$

Finally we go over to the dimensionless time

$$\tau = \tilde{\nu}t \tag{7.41}$$

so that the interval 1 in τ corresponds to the interval $\tilde{\nu}^{-1}$ in t, and introduce the dimensionless frequencies:

$$\rho = \frac{\tilde{\rho}}{\tilde{\nu}}; \quad \beta = \frac{\tilde{\beta}}{\tilde{\nu}}; \quad \gamma = \frac{\tilde{\gamma}}{\tilde{\nu}}; \quad \alpha = \tilde{\alpha}N; \quad \eta = \tilde{\eta}N. \tag{7.42}$$

The scaled form of the quasi-meanvalue equations thereupon reads:

$$\frac{dx_j}{d\tau} = d_j - \rho x_j = \exp[\kappa Q_j - \sigma P_j]x_0 - \rho x_j \quad \text{for} \quad j = 1, 2, \ldots, L; \tag{7.43}$$

$$\frac{dx_0}{d\tau} = \rho \sum_{j=1}^{L} x_j - \sum_{j=1}^{L} d_j; \tag{7.44}$$

$$\frac{ds_j}{d\tau} = \beta s_j(P_j - C'(\tilde{\nu}Ns_j)); \tag{7.45}$$

$$\frac{dP_j}{d\tau} = \alpha(d_j - s_j)P_j; \tag{7.46}$$

$$\frac{dQ_j}{d\tau} = \eta d_j - \gamma Q_j. \tag{7.47}$$

The master equation (7.31) and the $(4L + 1)$ quasi-meanvalue equations, either in direct form (7.32)–(7.36) or in scaled form (7.43)–(7.47) constitute the mathematical form of the proposed general model.

7.3   The Case of Two Competing Firms

The general model presented in Section 7.2 is still too complex to obtain a survey of its solutions. Therefore we restrict it to the simplest case of two firms F_1 and F_2 and make some further simplifying assumptions which lead to the possibility of a partially analytic treatment. However, the most important instrument for deriving tractable reduced dynamic equations is the "slaving principle".

7.3.1 The "Slaving Principle" and the Transition to Equations for Order Parameters

The quasimeanvalue equations for two firms $j = 1, 2$ in unscaled form are special cases of equations (7.32), (7.34), (7.35) and (7.36) and have the general form

$$\frac{dA_j^{(K)}}{dt} = w_{j\uparrow}^{(K)}\{\mathbf{A}\} - w_{j\downarrow}^{(K)}\{\mathbf{A}\}; \quad j = 1, 2, \tag{7.48}$$

where:

$$A_j^{(1)} = n_j; \quad A_j^{(2)} = S_j; \quad A_j^{(3)} = P_j; \quad A_j^{(4)} = Q_j. \tag{7.49}$$

These eight equations are still complicated. But they can be considerably simplified, if the so-called "slaving principle" can be applied. (The slaving principle, introduced in full generality by H. Haken [30], is a central concept of Synergetics. We have treated it in some detail in Chapter 1.3.)

This slaving principle sets in, if in a dynamic system different time scales exist for the evolution of variables, in other words if slow variables $A^{(s)}$ and fast variables $A^{(f)}$ can be clearly distinguished. In this case the following process occurs: The fast variables quickly develop into their momentary equilibrium values, whereas the remaining slow variables do not move substantially in this short adaptation time of the fast variables. The momentary equilibrium values of the fast variables can thereupon be expressed by the values of the remaining slow variables. Illustratively spoken they are "slaved" (or entrained) by the slow variables.

After the elimination of the fast variables – sometimes also denoted as adiabatic elimination – there arises a *reduced approximate system of equations* of motion for the *slow variables* alone. Evidently the latter *dominate* the dynamics of the system, since the quickly adapted values of the fast variables can be re-expressed by the slow variables. The slow variables are therefore denoted as *orderparameters*.

The slaving principle can also be applied to the equations (7.48) under the condition that slow variables $A_j^{(s)}$ and fast variables $A_j^{(f)}$ can be distinguished. That means the relaxation constants and corresponding transition rates of fast variables must be large, and those of the slow variables must be small. The large right hand sides of (7.48) for the fast variables $A_j^{(f)}$ lead to a fast evolution of $A_j^{(f)}$ according to (7.48) so that they quickly reach their *momentary equilibrium values* $\hat{A}_j^{(f)}$ for which $dA_j^{(f)}/dt$ vanishes approximately. Hence, these momentary equilibrium values are defined by

$$0 = w_{j\uparrow}^{(f)}\{\hat{\mathbf{A}}^{(f)}, \mathbf{A}^{(s)}\} - w_{j\downarrow}^{(f)}\{\hat{\mathbf{A}}^{(f)}, \mathbf{A}^{(s)}\}, \tag{7.50}$$

where $j = 1, 2$ and (f) runs through all fast variables.

The equations (7.50) can now be used to *eliminate* the $\hat{\mathbf{A}}^{(f)}$, i.e. to express their "slaved" values $\hat{\mathbf{A}}^{(f)}$ by the momentary values of the slowly varying $\mathbf{A}^{(s)}$. Let us denote the result of this elimination procedure by

$$\hat{\mathbf{A}}^{(f)} = \hat{\mathbf{A}}^{(f)}\left(\mathbf{A}^{(s)}\right). \tag{7.51}$$

On re-inserting (7.51) into the equations (7.48) for the remaining slow variables one obtains

$$\frac{dA_j^{(s)}}{dt} = w_{j+}^{(s)}\left[\hat{\mathbf{A}}^{(f)}\left(\mathbf{A}^{(s)}\right), \mathbf{A}^{(s)}\right] - w_{j-}^{(s)}\left[\hat{\mathbf{A}}^{(f)}\left(\mathbf{A}^{(s)}\right), \mathbf{A}^{(s)}\right] \tag{7.52}$$

These are the approximate selfcontained equations for the slow motion of the "*orderparameters*" $A_j^{(s)}$.

We will now apply this elimination procedure of the fast adaptive variables in two steps in order to obtain the orderparameter equations for the slowest variables.

Adiabatic Elimination of Supply and Prices

The prices P_j and the supply s_j are now assumed to be *fast variables* quickly adapting to the momentary values of the other variables. This means we consider the relaxation constants β and α as large against $\rho, 1, \eta, \gamma$ in the scaled equations (7.43)–(7.47). The "slaved" values $\hat{P}_j$ and $\hat{s}_j$ then follow according to (7.50) from the equations

$$0 = \alpha(d_j - \hat{s}_j)\hat{P}_j; \tag{7.53}$$

$$0 = \beta\hat{s}_j \cdot (\hat{P}_j - C'(\tilde{\nu}N\hat{s}_j)), \tag{7.54}$$

where d_j is given by (7.40). From (7.53) and (7.54) follow

$$\hat{s}_j = d_j = \exp[\kappa Q_j - \sigma\hat{P}_j]x_0; \tag{7.55}$$

$$\hat{P}_j = C'(\tilde{\nu}N\hat{s}_j(Q_j, \hat{P}_j, x_0)). \tag{7.56}$$

For known costfunction $C(S_j)$ the equations. (7.55) and (7.56) can be solved for $\hat{s}_j$ and $\hat{P}_j$, so that

$$\hat{s}_j = \hat{s}_j(Q_j, x_0); \quad \hat{P}_j = \hat{P}_j(Q_j, x_0). \tag{7.57}$$

Henceforth we make the assumptions

$$\rho = 1; \tag{7.58}$$

$$\sigma = 0 \tag{7.59}$$

which do not change the principal model structure but simplify equation (7.57) and make analytical treatments possible. Equation (7.58) means that the global demand parameter $\tilde{\nu}$ coincides with the inverse mean lifetime $\tilde{\rho}$, and (7.59) means that we consider "rich" customers who are sensitive to quality but not to prices. This assumption is plausible for the high-tech commodities in which customers are so interested that they do not care about prices. In this case one obtains easily from (7.55) and (7.56) the adapted supply $\hat{s}_j$ and price $\hat{P}_j$ as *explicit functions* of x_0 and Q_j:

$$\hat{s}_j = \exp[\kappa Q_j]x_0 ; \quad \hat{P}_j = C'(\tilde{\nu}N\exp[\kappa Q_j]x_0) \tag{7.60}$$

and the remaining equations for x_j and Q_j assume the simple form:

$$\frac{dx_j}{d\tau} = \{e^{q_j}(1 - x_1 - x_2) - x_j\}; \quad j = 1,2; \tag{7.61}$$

$$\frac{dq_j}{d\tau} = \gamma\{\phi e^{q_j}(1 - x_1 - x_2) - q_j\}; \quad j = 1,2. \tag{7.62}$$

In these equations we have eliminated x_0 by use of (7.38) and introduced the abbreviation

$$q_j = \kappa Q_j. \tag{7.63}$$

Furthermore there appears in (7.62) the "*competitiveness parameter*"

$$\phi = \frac{\kappa\eta}{\gamma} \tag{7.64}$$

which will turn out to be of crucial importance for the global dynamical behaviour of the system. It should be noted that the numerical value of ϕ depends on consumers reactions (via κ) as well as on the reactions of firms (via η and γ).

Quality Variables as Order Parameters

The equations (7.61) and (7.62) describe the coupled quality-driven purchasing-behaviour of customers and the demand-driven development of quality by firms. If $\gamma = 0(1)$, i.e. if both processes occur on the same time-scale, no further simplifications in the solution of the four coupled equations (7.61) and (7.62) are possible. However, let us now treat the plausible case in which

$$\gamma \ll 1 \tag{7.65}$$

holds. In this case the evolution of the quality of the products c_1 and c_2 is much slower than the adaptive purchasing activity of the customers in selecting one of the commodities c_j.

Then one can once more apply the slaving principle which now amounts to the application of the adiabatic elimination procedure to the fast variables x_j. Their "slaved" values $\hat{x}_j$ are obtained from

$$\{e^{q_j}(1 - x_1 - x_2) - x_j\} \approx 0; \quad j = 1,2 \tag{7.66}$$

yielding

$$\hat{x}_1 = \frac{e^{q_1}}{1 + e^{q_1} + e^{q_2}}; \quad \hat{x}_2 = \frac{e^{q_2}}{1 + e^{q_1} + e^{q_2}}$$

$$\text{and} \quad \hat{x}_0 = (1 - \hat{x}_1 - \hat{x}_2) = \frac{1}{1 + e^{q_1} + e^{q_2}}. \tag{7.67}$$

Inserting these values into (7.62) one obtains equations for the qualities q_j alone which are now the slowly evolving orderparameters. These *orderparameter equations* read:

$$\frac{dq_j}{d\tau} = \gamma \left\{ \phi \frac{e^{q_j}}{1 + e^{q_1} + e^{q_2}} - q_j \right\}; \quad j = 1, 2. \tag{7.68}$$

After the substitution (where $q_j \geq 0; z_j \geq 1$)

$$z_j = e^{q_j}; \quad q_j = \ln(z_j) \tag{7.69}$$

the orderparameter equations assume the equivalent form

$$\frac{dz_j}{d\tau} = \gamma z_j \left\{ \phi \frac{z_j}{1 + z_1 + z_2} - \ln(z_j) \right\}; \quad j = 1, 2. \tag{7.70}$$

7.3.2 Analysis of Stationary Solutions and their Stability

Stationary Solutions

The stationary solutions $\bar{x}_j, \bar{q}_j, \bar{z}_j$ of (7.61) and (7.62) are obtained by putting the time derivative in these equations equal to zero, which leads to

$$0 = \bar{z}_j(1 - \bar{x}_1 - \bar{x}_2) - \bar{x}_j; \quad j = 1, 2; \tag{7.71}$$
$$0 = \phi \cdot \bar{z}_j(1 - \bar{x}_1 - \bar{x}_2) - \ln(\bar{z}_j); \quad j = 1, 2. \tag{7.72}$$

It can easily be seen from (7.71) that

$$\bar{x}_0 = (1 - \bar{x}_1 - \bar{x}_2) = r(\bar{z}_1, \bar{z}_2) \equiv \frac{1}{(1 + \bar{z}_1 + \bar{z}_2)} \tag{7.73}$$

and therefore

$$\bar{x}_1 = \bar{z}_1 r(\bar{z}_1, \bar{z}_2); \quad \bar{x}_2 = \bar{z}_2 r(\bar{z}_1, \bar{z}_2) \tag{7.74}$$

and

$$f(\bar{z}_j) \equiv \frac{\ln(\bar{z}_j)}{\bar{z}_j} = \phi \cdot r(\bar{z}_1, \bar{z}_2) \quad \text{for} \quad j = 1, 2. \tag{7.75}$$

The crucial equation is equation (7.75). It is to be solved in the domain

$$0 < \bar{q}_j < \infty \quad \text{or} \quad 1 < \bar{z}_j < \infty \qquad (7.76)$$

for all given values $0 < \phi < \infty$ of the competitivity parameter.

It can now easily be seen from the form of the functions $f(z)$ and $r(z, z)$, that for all positive values of ϕ a *symmetrical solution* of (7.75) exists:

$$\bar{z}_1 = \bar{z}_2 = z_0(\phi); \quad \bar{q}_1 = \bar{q}_2 \equiv \bar{q} = q_0(\phi) \qquad (7.77)$$

which obeys

$$\frac{\ln(z_0)}{z_0} = \phi \cdot r(z_0, z_0) \equiv \phi \frac{1}{1 + 2z_0} \qquad (7.78)$$

and which leads according to (7.74) to

$$\bar{x}_1 = \bar{x}_2 \equiv \bar{x} = z_0 \cdot r(z_0, z_0) = \frac{z_0}{1 + 2z_0}. \qquad (7.79)$$

This solution describes situations with equal market share $\bar{x}_1 = \bar{x}_2$ and equal product quality $\bar{Q}_1 = \bar{Q}_2$, which grows for growing ϕ, for both firms F_1 and F_2.

However, a close analysis of equation (7.75) shows (see [27] and [28]) that it possesses for

$$\phi > \phi_c = \frac{1 + 2e}{e} = 2.367879441 \ldots \qquad (7.80)$$

beyond the symmetrical solution also two *unsymmetrical solutions*:

$$\begin{aligned} &\bar{z}_1 = z_+(\phi); \quad \bar{z}_2 = z_-(\phi) \quad \text{or} \quad \bar{q}_1 = q_+(\phi); \quad \bar{q}_2 = q_-(\phi) \\ \text{and} \quad &\bar{z}_1 = z_-(\phi); \quad \bar{z}_2 = z_+(\phi) \quad \text{or} \quad \bar{q}_1 = q_-(\phi); \quad \bar{q}_2 = q_-(\phi) \end{aligned} \qquad (7.81)$$

with corresponding market shares

$$\begin{aligned} &\bar{x}_1 = z_+ \cdot r(z_+, z_-); \quad \bar{x}_2 = z_- \cdot r(z_+, z_-) \\ \text{and} \quad &\bar{x}_1 = z_- \cdot r(z_+, z_-); \quad \bar{x}_2 = z_+ \cdot r(z_+, z_-), \end{aligned} \qquad (7.82)$$

where $q_0(\phi), q_+(\phi)$ and $q_-(\phi)$ are depicted in Figure 7.1.

The following stability analysis will show that the symmetrical solution (7.77), becomes *unstable* for $\phi > \phi_c$, whereas the unsymmetrical solutions (7.81), are stable.

The remarkable fact of this *destabilisation of a symmetrical market* is that although the firms behave in a *strategically equivalent* manner (because they have the same trend parameters η, γ, and the customers have *no preference* for one of the firms since

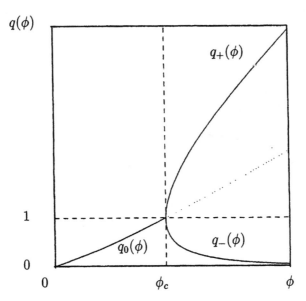

Figure 7.1 The quality parameter $q_0(\phi)$ for the symmetrical, and $q_+(\phi)$, $q_-(\phi)$ for the unsymmetrical solution of equation (7.75) as function of the competitiveness ϕ.

they have the same quality sensitivity κ for each product), nevertheless the *nonlinear interaction* between producers and consumers leads to a *symmetry breaking bifurcation process*, if the competitivity parameter ϕ (considered as a slowly varying composite trend parameter) passes a certain critical threshold value ϕ_c. The result of this destabilisation process is that the one firm becomes the *winner firm* and the other the *loser firm*. How the symmetry breaking of the firms market is engendered by *initial fluctuations* will now be analyzed.

Stability Analysis

In order to decide whether a stationary solution is stable or unstable we perform a conventional linear stability analysis. We apply it to the symmetrical market only. For the unsymmetrical states one could proceed on analogous lines. Starting from the symmetrical solution (7.77) with (7.79) we put

$$\begin{aligned} x_j(\tau) &= \bar{x} + \xi_j(\tau); \quad j = 1, 2; \\ q_j(\tau) &= \bar{q} + \chi_j(\tau); \quad j = 1, 2, \end{aligned} \tag{7.83}$$

where $\xi_j(\tau)$ and $\chi_j(\tau)$ are small deviations from the stationary state. It is convenient to introduce the symmetrical and antisymmetrical combinations of these deviations:

$$\begin{aligned} \xi_s(\tau) &= \xi_1(\tau) + \xi_2(\tau); \quad \xi_{as}(\tau) = \xi_1(\tau) - \xi_2(\tau); \\ \chi_s(\tau) &= \chi_1(\tau) + \chi_2(\tau); \quad \chi_{as}(\tau) = \chi_1(\tau) - \chi_2(\tau). \end{aligned} \tag{7.84}$$

The equations of motion (7.61), (7.62) yield, if linearized with respect to the deviations, two separate sets of equations:

$$\frac{d\xi_{as}}{d\tau} = (-1) \cdot \xi_{as} + \phi^{-1}\bar{q}\chi_{as};$$

$$\frac{d\chi_{as}}{d\tau} = 0 + \gamma(\bar{q}-1)\chi_{as} \tag{7.85}$$

and

$$\frac{d\xi_s}{d\tau} = -(2e^{\bar{q}}+1)\xi_s + \phi^{-1}\bar{q}\chi_s;$$

$$\frac{d\chi_s}{d\tau} = -2\gamma\phi e^{\bar{q}}\xi_s + \gamma(\bar{q}-1)\chi_s. \tag{7.86}$$

Evidently, symmetric and antisymmetric deviations do not couple to each other.
  The equations (7.85) and (7.86) can be solved by

$$\begin{pmatrix} \xi_s(\tau) \\ \chi_s(\tau) \end{pmatrix} = \begin{pmatrix} \xi_s \\ \chi_s \end{pmatrix} \exp(\lambda_s\tau); \quad \begin{pmatrix} \xi_{as}(\tau) \\ \chi_{as}(\tau) \end{pmatrix} = \begin{pmatrix} \xi_{as} \\ \chi_{as} \end{pmatrix} \exp(\lambda_{as}\tau), \tag{7.87}$$

where λ_s and λ_{as} must satisfy the respective secular equations:

$$\left\| \begin{array}{ccc} [-\lambda_{as}-1] & ; & \phi^{-1}\bar{q} \\ 0 & ; & [-\lambda_{as}+\gamma(\bar{q}-1)] \end{array} \right\| \overset{!}{=} 0 \tag{7.88}$$

and

$$\left\| \begin{array}{ccc} [-\lambda_s-(2e^{\bar{q}}+1)] & ; & \phi^{-1}\bar{q} \\ -2\gamma\phi e^{\bar{q}} & ; & [-\lambda_s+\gamma(\bar{q}-1)] \end{array} \right\| \overset{!}{=} 0 \tag{7.89}$$

with solutions

$$\lambda_{as}^{(1)} = (-1); \quad \lambda_{as}^{(2)} = \gamma(\bar{q}-1) \tag{7.90}$$

and

$$\lambda_s^{(1,2)} = -\frac{1}{2}\left[(2e^{\bar{q}}+1)-\gamma(\bar{q}-1)\right] \pm \sqrt{\frac{1}{4}[(2e^{\bar{q}}+1)+\gamma(\bar{q}-1)]^2 - 2\gamma\bar{q}e^{\bar{q}}}. \tag{7.91}$$

The amplitudes belonging to $\lambda_{as}^{(1)}$ and $\lambda_{as}^{(2)}$ are

$$\begin{pmatrix} \xi_{as}^{(1)} \\ 0 \end{pmatrix} \quad \text{and} \quad \begin{pmatrix} \xi_{as}^{(2)} \\ \chi_{as}^{(2)} = \phi\bar{q}^{-1}(1+\gamma(\bar{q}-1))\xi_{as}^{(2)} \end{pmatrix} \tag{7.92)}$$

We omit the not so interesting amplitudes belonging to $\lambda_s^{(1)}$ and $\lambda_s^{(2)}$.

Analyzing the eigenvalues we observe that for

$$\bar{q} < 1 \quad \text{belonging to} \quad \phi < \phi_c = \frac{(1+2e)}{e} \tag{7.93}$$

all four eigenvalues $\lambda_{as}^{(1)}, \lambda_{as}^{(2)}, \lambda_s^{(1)}, \lambda_s^{(2)}$ are negative or have negative real part. Therefore every deviation from the stationary state (7.87) relaxes to zero, which means that *the symmetrical stationary market state is stable for a competitiveness parameter ϕ below the threshold ϕ_c.*
On the other hand, for

$$\bar{q} > 1 \quad \text{belonging to} \quad \phi > \phi_c = \frac{(1+2e)}{e} \tag{7.94}$$

at least the eigenvalue $\lambda_{as}^{(2)}$ becomes positive, so that the corresponding deviation mode (7.87) is exponentially growing and leads to the destabilisation of the symmetrical market situation.

The form of $\begin{pmatrix} \xi_{as}^{(2)} \\ \chi_{as}^{(2)} \end{pmatrix}$ pertaining to the positive eigenvalue $\lambda_{as}^{(2)}$ is elucidatory: it consists of a quality deviation from $\bar{q}$ of opposite direction in firms F_1 and F_2 (e.g. $\xi_1 > 0, \xi_2 < 0$, so that $\xi_{as}^{(2)} > 0$) and a *simultaneous* customers share deviation from $\bar{x}$ (namely $\chi_1 > 0, \chi_2 < 0$, so that $\chi_{as}^{(2)} = \phi\bar{q}^{-1}(1 + \gamma(\bar{q} - 1))\xi_{as}^{(2)} > 0$)). Hence, if F_1 enhances quality a little bit above $\bar{q}$ and *simultaneously* wins a few customers x_1 above $\bar{x}$, whereas F_2 diminishes quality a little bit below $\bar{q}$ and *simultaneously* loses a few customers so that x_2 falls below $\bar{x}$, this fluctuation will become decisive and begin to grow, if $\phi > \phi_c$. This will be the case, if the customers quality sensitivity κ is high enough and the responsiveness η of the firms is also high enough. The further evolution of a small deviation from stationarity can only be studied by solving the exact nonlinear equations numerically.

7.3.3 Numerical Solutions of the Quasi-meanvalue Equations

We now go beyond the linear stability analysis and solve firstly the orderparameter equations (7.68), which are a good approximation if (7.65) holds, for values of the competitiveness ϕ below and above the threshold ϕ_c. In the Figures 7.2 and 7.3 we exhibit the fluxlines of the solution $\{q_1(\tau), q_2(\tau)\}$ of (7.68) in the q_1/q_2-space for the values $\phi = 0.8\phi_c$ and $\phi = 1.2\phi_c$.

Whereas for $\phi = 0.8\phi_c$ in Figure 7.2 all fluxlines converge to the unique equilibrium point $\{\bar{q}_1 = \bar{q}_2\}$, Figure 7.3 demonstrates that for $\phi = 1.2\phi_c$ two stable stationary points $\{\bar{q}_1 = q_+, \bar{q}_2 = q_-\}$ and $\{\bar{q}_1 = q_-, \bar{q}_2 = q_+\}$ exist. In this case all fluxlines converge in one of these stationary points, whereas the symmetrical stationary point $\{\bar{q}_1 = \bar{q}_2\}$ is now an unstable saddle point.

It is now possible to compare the solutions of the exact set (7.61) and (7.62) of coupled equations for x_j and q_j with the solutions of the approximate orderparameter equations (7.68) obtained for $\gamma \ll 1$ under application of the slaving principle.

In Figures 7.4 and 7.5 we compare the fluxlines $\{q_1, q_2\}$ of the orderparameter equations with the $\{q_1, q_2\}$-projection of the fluxlines of the exact equations (7.61) and (7.62) for $\gamma = 1$ and $\gamma = 2$, respectively. (The initial values of the consumer variables $\{x_1(0), x_2(0)\}$ in (7.61) and (7.62) are taken to be the slaved values $\{\hat{x}_1(0), \hat{x}_2(0)\}$. It can be seen, that for increasing values of γ the coincidence between the exact and the approximate fluxlines becomes worse but is still acceptable.

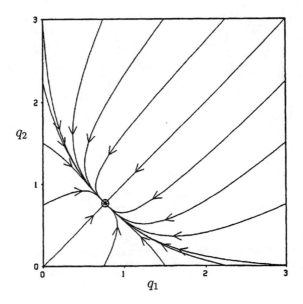

Figure 7.2 Fluxlines of the solution of the orderparameter equations (7.68) for competitiveness $\phi = 0.8\phi_c$.

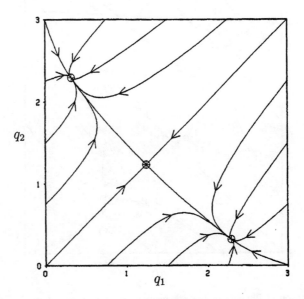

Figure 7.3 Fluxlines of the solution of the orderparameter equations (7.68) for competitiveness $\phi = 1.2\phi_c$.

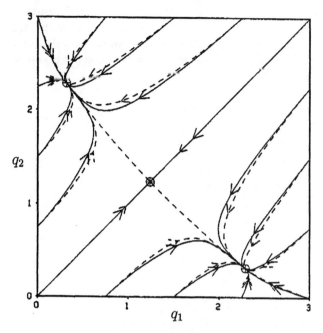

Figure 7.4 Comparison of fluxlines in $\{q_1, q_2\}$ space between solutions of exact equations (7.61) and (7.62) (straight lines) and of orderparameter equations (7.68) (dashed lines) $\phi = 1.2\phi_c$ and $\gamma = 1$.

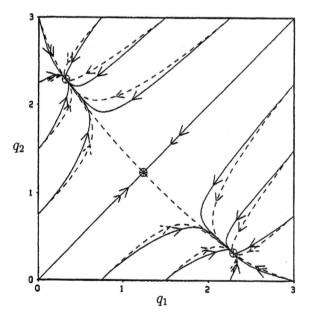

Figure 7.5 Comparison of fluxlines in $\{q_1, q_2\}$ space between solutions of exact equations (7.61) and (7.62) (straight lines) and of orderparameter equations (7.68) (dashed lines) $\phi = 1.2\phi_c$ and $\gamma = 2$.

7.4   Truncated Master Equations for the Two Firms Case

In Section 7.3 we have seen that the application of the slaving principle to the quasimeanvalue equations leads to considerable simplifications. We will now see that the application of the same principle also leads to simplified *"truncated" forms of the master equation* for two firms.

7.4.1   Derivation of Reduced and Decoupled Master Equations

As in Section 7.3.1 we assume that the supply and price variables S_j and P_j have already assumed their "slaved" values $\hat{S}_j(\mathbf{n}, \mathbf{Q})$ and $\hat{P}_j(\mathbf{n}, \mathbf{Q})$ by adapting to each given set $\{\mathbf{n}, \mathbf{Q}\} = \{n_1, n_2; Q_1, Q_2\}$ of the consumer and quality variables. This is however equivalent to saying that the probability fluxes

$$
\sum_{j=1}^{2} w_{j+}^{S}(\mathbf{E}_{j-}^{S}) P(\mathbf{E}_{j-}^{S}; t) - \sum_{j=1}^{2} w_{j+}^{S}(\mathbf{E}) P(\mathbf{E}; t)
$$
$$
+ \sum_{j=1}^{2} w_{j-}^{S}(\mathbf{E}_{j+}^{S}) P(\mathbf{E}_{j+}^{S}; t) - \sum_{j=1}^{2} w_{j-}^{S}(\mathbf{E}) P(\mathbf{E}; t)
$$
$$
+ \sum_{j=1}^{2} w_{j+}^{P}(\mathbf{E}_{j-}^{P}) P(\mathbf{E}_{j-}^{P}; t) - \sum_{j=1}^{2} w_{j+}^{P}(\mathbf{E}) P(\mathbf{E}; t) \tag{7.95}
$$
$$
+ \sum_{j=1}^{2} w_{j-}^{P}(\mathbf{E}_{j+}^{P}) P(\mathbf{E}_{j+}^{P}; t) - \sum_{j=1}^{2} w_{j-}^{P}(\mathbf{E}) P(\mathbf{E}; t)
$$

on the right hand side of the full master equation *cancel mutually* if the values $\hat{S}_j(\mathbf{n}, \mathbf{Q})$ and $\hat{P}_j(\mathbf{n}, \mathbf{Q})$ are inserted in $\mathbf{E} = \{\mathbf{n}, \mathbf{S}, \mathbf{P}, \mathbf{Q}\}$ so that they no more contribute to the change with time of the probability distribution $P(\mathbf{n}, \mathbf{S}, \mathbf{P}, \mathbf{Q}; t)$.

After having everywhere $\mathbf{S}$ and $\mathbf{P}$ expressed by their slaved values $\hat{\mathbf{S}}(\mathbf{n}, \mathbf{Q})$ and $\hat{\mathbf{P}}(\mathbf{n}, \mathbf{Q})$, there arises instead of (7.31) a reduced or "truncated" master equation for the probability distribution $P(\mathbf{n}, \mathbf{Q}; t) \equiv P(n_1, n_2, Q_1, Q_2; t)$ over the relevant variables $\{\mathbf{n}, \mathbf{Q}\}$ only:

$$
\frac{dP(n_1, n_2, Q_1, Q_2; t)}{dt} = \sum_{j=1}^{2} w_{j0}^{C}(\mathbf{n}_{0j}, \mathbf{Q}) P(\mathbf{n}_{0j}, \mathbf{Q}; t) - \sum_{j=1}^{2} w_{j0}^{C}(\mathbf{n}, \mathbf{Q}) P(\mathbf{n}, \mathbf{Q}; t)
$$
$$
+ \sum_{j=1}^{2} w_{0j}^{C}(\mathbf{n}_{j0}, \mathbf{Q}) P(\mathbf{n}_{j0}, \mathbf{Q}; t) - \sum_{j=1}^{2} w_{0j}^{C}(\mathbf{n}, \mathbf{Q}) P(\mathbf{n}, \mathbf{Q}; t)
$$
$$
+ \sum_{j=1}^{2} w_{j+}^{Q}(\mathbf{n}, \mathbf{Q}_{j-}) P(\mathbf{n}, \mathbf{Q}_{j-}; t) - \sum_{j=1}^{2} w_{j+}^{Q}(\mathbf{n}, \mathbf{Q}) P(\mathbf{n}, \mathbf{Q}; t)
$$
$$
+ \sum_{j=1}^{2} w_{j-}^{Q}(\mathbf{n}, \mathbf{Q}_{j+}) P(\mathbf{n}, \mathbf{Q}_{j+}; t) - \sum_{j=1}^{2} w_{j-}^{Q}(\mathbf{n}, \mathbf{Q}) P(\mathbf{n}, \mathbf{Q}; t), \tag{7.96}
$$

where the transition rates follow from (7.5), (7.9), (7.28) and (7.29), making use of (7.42) and of (7.58), (7.59).

$$w_{j0}^C(\mathbf{n}, \mathbf{Q}) = \tilde{\nu} \exp[\kappa Q_j](N - n_1 - n_2);$$
$$w_{0j}^C(\mathbf{n}, \mathbf{Q}) = \tilde{\nu} n_j \qquad (7.97)$$

and

$$w_{j+}^Q(\mathbf{n}, \mathbf{Q}) = \tilde{\eta} w_{j0}^C(\mathbf{n}, \mathbf{Q}) \cdot \vartheta(Q_M - 1 - Q_j)$$
$$= \tilde{\nu} \frac{\gamma}{\kappa} \phi \exp[\kappa Q_j] \frac{(N - n_1 - n_2)}{N} \cdot \vartheta(Q_M - 1 - Q_j); \qquad (7.98)$$
$$w_{j-}^Q(\mathbf{n}, \mathbf{Q}) = \tilde{\nu} \cdot \frac{\gamma}{\kappa} \cdot (\kappa Q_j) \cdot \vartheta(Q_M - Q_j).$$

In (7.98) we have multiplied with a ϑ-function (for its definition see (7.17)) which prevents transitions from an assumed maximal quality Q_M into higher values or from higher values. Hence the transition rates (7.97) and (7.98) restrict the values of variables for which $P(\mathbf{n}, \mathbf{Q}; t)$ can be positive to the finite domain

$$n_1 \geq 0; \quad n_2 \geq 0; \quad (N - n_1 - n_2) \geq 0; \quad 0 \leq Q_1 \leq Q_M; \quad 0 \leq Q_2 \leq Q_M. \qquad (7.99)$$

The master equation (7.96) for a probability distribution over four variables is still complicated. However, under the conditions treated in Section 7.3 leading to the orderparameter equations (7.68) for the quality variables, the master equation (7.96) can be *further simplified* and be split into *two separate and decoupled master equations*.

The relevant condition for setting up orderparameter equations for $\{q_1(\tau), q_2(\tau)\}$ was that the variables $\{x_1, x_2\}$, and correspondingly $\{n_1, n_2\}$ are fast variables quickly assuming their slaved values (see (7.67)):

$$\hat{n}_1(\mathbf{Q}) = N\hat{x}_1(\mathbf{Q}); \quad \hat{n}_2(\mathbf{Q}) = N\hat{x}_2(\mathbf{Q}). \qquad (7.100)$$

Under this condition it is justifiable to substitute the – anyway small – transition rates (7.98) by the *approximate rates*

$$\hat{w}_{j+}^Q(\mathbf{Q}) = \tilde{\eta} w_{j0}^C(\hat{\mathbf{n}}(\mathbf{Q}), \mathbf{Q}) \cdot \vartheta(Q_M - 1 - Q_j);$$
$$\hat{w}_{j-}^Q(\mathbf{Q}) = \tilde{\gamma} Q_j \cdot \vartheta(Q_M - Q_j) \qquad (7.101)$$

which only depend on the variables $\mathbf{Q} = \{Q_1, Q_2\}$.

With the transition rates (7.97) and (7.101) instead of (7.97) and (7.98), the master equation (7.96) can be solved in the form:

$$P(\mathbf{n}, \mathbf{Q}; t) = p(\mathbf{n} \,|\, \mathbf{Q}; t) P(\mathbf{Q}; t) \qquad (7.102)$$

with

$$\sum_{\mathbf{n}} p(\mathbf{n}\,|\,\mathbf{Q};t) = 1\,; \quad \sum_{\mathbf{Q}} P(\mathbf{Q};t) = 1$$

$$\text{and} \quad \sum_{\mathbf{n},\mathbf{Q}} P(\mathbf{n},\mathbf{Q};t) = 1,$$

(7.103)

where the two probability distributions $p(\mathbf{n}\,|\,\mathbf{Q};t)$ and $P(\mathbf{Q};t)$ satisfy two *separate* and *decoupled master equations*, namely

$$
\frac{dp(\mathbf{n}\,|\,\mathbf{Q};t)}{dt} = \sum_{j=1}^{2} w_{j0}^{C}(\mathbf{n}_{0j},\mathbf{Q})p(\mathbf{n}_{0j}\,|\,\mathbf{Q};t) - \sum_{j=1}^{2} w_{j0}^{C}(\mathbf{n},\mathbf{Q})p(\mathbf{n}\,|\,\mathbf{Q};t)
$$

$$
+ \sum_{j=1}^{2} w_{0j}^{C}(\mathbf{n}_{j0},\mathbf{Q})p(\mathbf{n}_{j0}\,|\,\mathbf{Q};t) - \sum_{j=1}^{2} w_{0j}^{C}(\mathbf{n},\mathbf{Q})p(\mathbf{n}\,|\,\mathbf{Q};t)
$$

(7.104)

and

$$
\frac{dp(\mathbf{Q};t)}{dt} = \sum_{j=1}^{2} \hat{w}_{j+}^{Q}(\mathbf{Q}_{j-})P(\mathbf{Q}_{j-};t) - \sum_{j=1}^{2} \hat{w}_{j+}^{Q}(\mathbf{Q})P(\mathbf{Q})
$$

$$
+ \sum_{j=1}^{2} \hat{w}_{j-}^{Q}(\mathbf{Q}_{j+})P(\mathbf{Q}_{j+};t) - \sum_{j=1}^{2} \hat{w}_{j-}^{Q}(\mathbf{Q})P(\mathbf{Q};t).
$$

(7.105)

It can easily be checked, that $P(\mathbf{n},\mathbf{Q};t)$ of the form (7.102) satisfies the full master equation (7.96) with rates (7.97) and (7.101), if $p(\mathbf{n}\,|\,\mathbf{Q};t)$ and $P(\mathbf{Q};t)$ fulfil (7.104) and (7.105), respectively.

The form (7.102) of the probability distribution can easily be interpreted: The probability $P(\mathbf{n},\mathbf{Q};t)$ consists of the *quickly evolving* conditional probability $p(\mathbf{n}\,|\,\mathbf{Q};t)$ under *given values* of $\mathbf{Q}$ times the *slowly evolving* probability $P(\mathbf{Q};t)$ of the variable $\mathbf{Q}$.

The approximation (7.101) of the (slow) transition rates $w_{j+}^{Q}(\mathbf{n},\mathbf{Q}) \Rightarrow \hat{w}_{j+}^{Q}(\hat{\mathbf{n}}(\mathbf{Q}),\mathbf{Q})$ can retrospectively be well justified by the fact that the conditional meanvalues

$$\bar{n}_j(\mathbf{Q};t) = \sum_{\mathbf{n}} n_j p(\mathbf{n}\,|\,\mathbf{Q};t)$$

(7.106)

quickly approach – because of the fast transition rates in master equation (7.104) – their $\mathbf{Q}$-adapted values

$$\bar{n}_j(\mathbf{Q}) = \sum_{\mathbf{n}} n_j p_{st}(\mathbf{n}\,|\,\mathbf{Q}),$$

(7.107)

where $p_{st}(\mathbf{n}|\mathbf{Q})$ is the stationary solution of (7.104) for parametrically given values of $\mathbf{Q}$.

The latter stationary solution $p_{st}(\mathbf{n}|\mathbf{Q})$ can even be explicitly constructed according to the methods derived in Chapter 10.5 because the transition rates (7.97) fulfil *detailed balance*. One obtains

$$p_{st}(n_1, n_2 \,|\, Q_1 Q_2) = \prod_{\mu=0}^{n_2-1} \frac{w_{20}^C(n_1, \mu; \mathbf{Q})}{w_{02}^C(n_1, \mu+1; \mathbf{Q})} \prod_{\nu=0}^{n_1-1} \frac{w_{10}^C(\nu, 0; \mathbf{Q})}{w_{01}^C(\nu+1, 0; \mathbf{Q})} p_{st}(0, 0 \,|\, Q_1 Q_2)$$

(7.108)

or in explicit form

$$p_{st}(n_1 n_2 \,|\, Q_1 Q_2) = \frac{N!}{n_0! n_1! n_2!} \exp[\kappa(n_1 Q_1 + n_2 Q_2)] p_{st}(0, 0 \,|\, Q_1 Q_2),$$

(7.109)

where $p_{st}(0, 0 \,|\, Q_1 Q_2)$ must be determined making use of the normalization condition (7.103).

One easily finds that the point of maximal probability $p_{st}(n_1 n_2 \,|\, Q_1 Q_2)$ in $\{n_1, n_2\}$ space, which practically agrees with the *meanvalues* $\bar{n}_j(\mathbf{Q})$, depends on $\mathbf{Q}$ and lies at

$$\bar{n}_1(\mathbf{Q}) = \frac{N e^{\kappa Q_1}}{1 + e^{\kappa Q_1} + e^{\kappa Q_2}} \; ; \quad \bar{n}_2(\mathbf{Q}) = \frac{N e^{\kappa Q_2}}{1 + e^{\kappa Q_1} + e^{\kappa Q_2}}.$$

(7.110)

These values coincide with the slaved values $\hat{n}_1(\mathbf{Q})$ and $\hat{n}_2(\mathbf{Q})$ obtained from the quasimeanvalue equations (see (7.67)).

The master equation (7.105) thereupon describes the slow evolution of the probability distribution $P(\mathbf{Q}; t)$ of the orderparameters $\{Q_1, Q_2\}$ into the stationary distribution $P_{st}(\mathbf{Q})$. The full stationary solution is then given by

$$P_{st}(\mathbf{n}, \mathbf{Q}) = p_{st}(\mathbf{n} \,|\, \mathbf{Q}) P_{st}(\mathbf{Q})$$

(7.111)

from which there follow reduced stationary probability distributions for $\mathbf{n}$ and $\mathbf{Q}$ alone:

$$\sum_{\mathbf{n}} P_{st}(\mathbf{n}, \mathbf{Q}) = \sum_{\mathbf{n}} p_{st}(\mathbf{n} \,|\, \mathbf{Q}) P_{st}(\mathbf{Q}) = P_{st}(\mathbf{Q});$$

$$\sum_{\mathbf{Q}} P_{st}(\mathbf{n}, \mathbf{Q}) = \sum_{\mathbf{Q}} p_{st}(\mathbf{n} \,|\, \mathbf{Q}) P_{st}(\mathbf{Q}) \equiv \Pi_{st}(\mathbf{n}).$$

(7.112)

7.4.2 Numerical Evaluation of Stationary Distributions

The Figures 7.6 and 7.7 demonstrate the reduced stationary probability distributions $P_{st}(Q_1, Q_2)$ and $\Pi_{st}(n_1, n_2)$ for two characteristic values of competitiveness ϕ, namely for $\phi = 0.8 \phi_C$ and $\phi = 1.2 \phi_C$. For illustrative purposes all distributions are normalized to the same height of their maxima. Near the probability distributions their contour lines are also shown, which clearly exhibit a unimodal form for $\phi < \phi_C$ and a bimodal form for $\phi > \phi_C$.

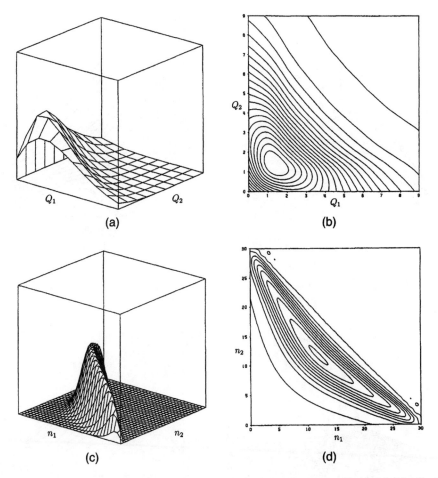

Figure 7.6 (a) The stationary probability distribution $P_{st}(Q_1, Q_2)$; (b) Contour lines of the distribution $P_{st}(Q_1, Q_2)$; (c) The stationary probability distribution $\Pi_{st}(n_1, n_2)$; (d) Contour lines of the distribution $\Pi_{st}(n_1, n_2)$. Parameters: $Q_M = 9$, $\kappa = 1/3$; $N = 30$, and competitiveness $\phi = 0.8\phi_C$.

It is assumed that the qualities Q_j can take ten integer values between $Q_j = 0$ and $Q_j = Q_M = 9$ only. The value of the quality sensitivity has been chosen to be $\kappa = 1/3$. Hence the quality variable $q_j = \kappa Q_j$ varies in the interval $0 \le q_j \le 3$.

The critical values of Q_j and q_j, where the quality bifurcation between firm 1 and firm 2 takes place, are $Q_C = 3$ and $q_C = 1$. They belong to $\phi = \phi_C$.

Again for illustrative purposes a small total number $N = 30$ of customers has been chosen in order to show their fluctuations in the stationary state. The number N can be interpreted as the total number of a representative subgroup of customers.

Outlook

We have only treated the simplest version of a simple model in which never-theless characteristic phenomena of nonlinear nonequilibrium dynamics appeared.

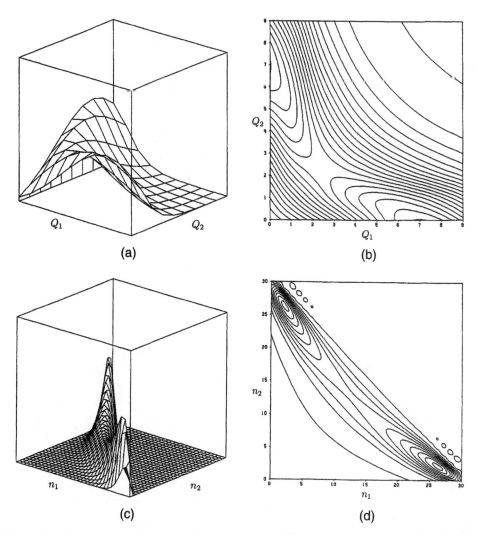

Figure 7.7 (a) The stationary probability distribution $P_{st}(Q_1, Q_2)$; (b) Contour lines of the distribution $P_{st}(Q_1, Q_2)$; (c) The stationary probability distribution $\Pi_{st}(n_1, n_2)$; (d) Contour lines of the distribution $\Pi_{st}(n_1, n_2)$. Parameters: $Q_M = 9$, $\kappa = 1/3$; $N = 30$, and competitiveness $\phi = 1.2\phi_C$.

Generalisations lying still within the scope of the model are feasible. For instance one could *give up the "strategic equivalence"* of the two firms by choosing different trendparameters η_j, γ_j for them. Of course, the *interaction of more than two firms* would lead to further complications. However, the most important possibility of extending the model would lie in *giving up the time-independence of all trendparameters* of the model, in particular of the firms strategy parameters η, γ and of consumers' quality sensitivities. It can be expected that the introduction of such a *trendparameter dynamics* would considerably extend the manifold of possible dynamic modes even in this easily surveyable model.

8. Dynamics of Conventional and Fashion Demand

In trying to identify processes with a dynamics beyond the neo-classical framework we have treated in Chapter 7 *innovation processes* leading to a specific interaction between firms and consumers in which the quality of the innovative product played a central role.

A further class of dynamic processes which may lead to a destabilisation of equilibrium is generated by cooperative and/or antagonistic interactions between agents belonging to the same or to different economic groups.

One example of this type was set up in an article of G. Mensch, G. Haag and the author [9] wherein a *Schumpetarian interaction* including imitation behaviour within two groups of entrepreneurs with innovative and rationalizing investment-inclination, respectively, was treated. *Supply-side induced business cycles* were the consequence of the dynamics engendered by this interaction.

In the following model we will treat another example of this kind, which also includes imitation- and marking off-behaviour within and between groups of economic agents. However, in this case the groups belong to the *demand-side*.

8.1 Lines of Model Design

We have selected the dynamics of fashion demand (extending the case of conventional demand), because fashion is a driving force in the economy as well as in the total society.

Therefore this phenomenon has been investigated in various social sciences, particularly in psychology [31], [32], sociology [33], [34], [35] and more recently also in economics [36], [37], [38], [39], although, as Adams and McCormick put it, "mainstream economics has no theory of fashion changes" [37]. A recent interesting work about fashion demand which includes the psychological interactions between consumers and follows the modelling concepts of Sociodynamics is that of P. Weise [40].

The present model [29] is designed to capture two psychological trends which seem to play the main role in fashion demand: The one is the *snob-trend* consisting in the wish of a priviledged group of "prominent" people to maintain their prestige, to boast of something, to show up against others. The other is the *imitation-trend* of a group of not so prominent people to gain prestige by imitating and conforming to the prestigious group.

If these trends find their expression in the demand for fashion goods they turn out to be antagonistic: The members of the snob-group want to buy fashion-goods, which *differ* from the goods bought by people not belonging to the "elitist" group. Instead, the members of the imitation-group want to buy fashion-goods which are *equal* or at least *similar* to those bought by the members of the snob-group. Evidently both trends are not reconcilable: If the intention of the one group is satisfied, the intention of the other is frustrated.

Whereas the utility functions for *conventional commodities* are only measures of their *plain usefulness*, the utility functions for *fashion goods* must include these psychological trends of the corresponding group and measure their prestige-value beyond pure usefulness.

Since the snob- or imitation-effect can formally be "switched on or off" in the utility functions, the model includes cases of fashion goods *and* conventional goods *as well*. This fact will allow us to compare conventional (equilibrium) demand theory with the new dynamics arising from "fashion psychology".

Along with this special choice of utility functions the model is designed according to the procedure outlined in Chapter 3. It is a *partial model* only for the demand side taking the supply of the desired commodities at fixed prices for granted. After introduction of the variables – i.e. amounts of commodities in the households of different consumer populations – and the corresponding population-specific utility functions the latter enter the transition rates between neighboring "demand configurations". Thereupon the probabilistic and deterministic evolution equations can be set up and analyzed.

8.2   The General Model

8.2.1   Variables, Dynamic Utilities and Transition Rates

Let us assume a market of L different goods $i = 1, 2, \ldots, L$ including *conventional goods* and *fancy goods*. All further goods which are not explicitly enumerated are gathered up in one *composite good* $i = (L + 1)$. For these $(L + 1)$ goods fixed prices $p_i, i = 1, \ldots, (L + 1)$, per unit are assumed so that the consumers are price takers.

It will be essential for our model to divide the total consumer population $\mathcal{P}$ into several, say P, consumer subpopulations $\mathcal{P}^{(\mu)}$, with $\mu = 1, \ldots, P$. Each subpopulation $\mathcal{P}^{(\mu)}$ is considered as a homogeneous group consisting of households exhibiting the same demand behaviour concerning all general parameters such as available budget, preferences for goods and consumer psychology within this group and in interaction with the purchase behaviour of other groups.

The Variables

Let $\mathcal{P}^{(\mu)}$ consist of $N^{(\mu)}$ households so that the whole consumer population $\mathcal{P}$ comprises

$$N = \sum_{\mu=1}^{P} N^{(\mu)} \tag{8.1}$$

households. After choosing an appropriate time period and appropriate units of goods, we introduce the integer $X_i^{(\mu)}$ as the number of units of good i consumed per period of time by subpopulation $\mathcal{P}^{(\mu)}$.

The multiple of positive integers

$$\mathbf{X} = \left\{ X_1^{(1)}, \ldots, X_i^{(\mu)}, \ldots, X_L^{(P)} \right\} \tag{8.2}$$

is denoted as the *demand configuration*. For each consumer population $\mathcal{P}^{(\mu)}$ this multiple is a function of time. The elementary changes of the demand configuration

$$\mathbf{X} \Rightarrow \mathbf{X}_{i\pm}^{(\mu)} = \left\{ X_1^{(1)}, \ldots, (X_i^{(\mu)} \pm 1), \ldots, X_L^{(P)} \right\} \tag{8.3}$$

are always effected by steps of *one* of the $N^{(\mu)}$ members of $\mathcal{P}^{(\mu)}$ who buys one unit of good i more or less than before in the period of time.

For later use we also introduce the average number of units of good i consumed in *one household* of $\mathcal{P}^{(\mu)}$ per period of time. It is given by

$$x_i^{(\mu)} = \frac{X_i^{(\mu)}}{N^{(\mu)}} \tag{8.4}$$

so that the *scaled demand configuration* reads

$$\mathbf{x} = \left\{ x_1^{(1)}, \ldots, x_i^{(\mu)}, \ldots, x_L^{(P)} \right\}. \tag{8.5}$$

To the transitions (8.3) now correspond the transitions

$$\mathbf{x} \Rightarrow x_{i\pm}^{(\mu)} = \left\{ x_1^{(1)}, \ldots, \left(x_i^{(\mu)} \pm \Delta x_i^{(\mu)} \right), \ldots, x_L^{(P)} \right\} \tag{8.6}$$

with

$$\Delta x_i^{(\mu)} = \frac{1}{N^{(\mu)}} \tag{8.7}$$

of the scaled demand configuration.

The Utility Functions

We have now to choose *utility functions* $U^{(\mu)}(\mathbf{X})$ attributed to a representative member of the consumer subpopulation $\mathcal{P}^{(\mu)}$ and being a measure of the material and psychological satisfaction assigned to the configuration $\mathbf{X}$ by this member. The only dynamic effect of these utility functions will be, that their differences show up, according to the general formulas (3.27), in the transition rates for a transition $\mathbf{X} \Rightarrow \mathbf{X}_{i\pm}^{(\mu)}$, which is effected by this member of $\mathcal{P}^{(\mu)}$.

We now make the (very plausible) assumption, that the utility difference $[U^{(\mu)}(\mathbf{X}_{i\pm}^{(\mu)}) - U(\mathbf{X})]$ for the member of $\mathcal{P}^{(\mu)}$ executing the step $\mathbf{X} \Rightarrow \mathbf{X}_{i\pm}^{(\mu)}$ only depends on the *consumption per household* in the group $\mathcal{P}^{(\mu)}$ and perhaps other groups $\mathcal{P}^{(\nu)}, \ldots$, but *not on the magnitudes $N^{(\mu)}, N^{(\nu)}, \ldots$* of these groups.

This assumption is fulfilled, if $U^{(\mu)}(\mathbf{X})$ has the form

$$U^{(\mu)}(\mathbf{X}) = N^{(\mu)} u^{(\mu)}(\mathbf{x}) \tag{8.8}$$

because then there holds:

$$\left[U^{(\mu)}\left(\mathbf{X}_{i\pm}^{(\mu)}\right) - U^{(\mu)}(\mathbf{X}) \right] = N^{(\mu)} \left[u^{(\mu)}\left(\mathbf{x}_{i\pm}^{(\mu)}\right) - u^{(\mu)}(\mathbf{x}) \right]$$

$$\approx \pm N^{(\mu)} \frac{\partial u^{(\mu)}(\mathbf{x})}{\partial x_i^{(\mu)}} \Delta x_i^{(\mu)} = \pm \frac{\partial u^{(\mu)}(\mathbf{x})}{\partial x_i^{(\mu)}}. \tag{8.9}$$

Let us now consider in detail the structure of the utility functions $u^{(\mu)}(\mathbf{x})$ of members of $\mathcal{P}^{(\mu)}$.

At first there exists an *independent plain usefulness* of each good $i = 1, \ldots, (L+1)$. This corresponds to a conventional term $u_0^{(\mu)}(\mathbf{x})$ (as part of $u^{(\mu)}(\mathbf{x})$) composed of additive contributions of the utilities of the quantities $x_i^{(\mu)}$ of goods i.

$$u_0^{(\mu)}(\mathbf{x}) = \sum_{i=1}^{L+1} u_{0i}^{(\mu)}\left(x_i^{(\mu)}\right). \tag{8.10}$$

To be concrete we choose a logarithmic form for the $u_{0i}^{(\mu)}\left(x_i^{(\mu)}\right)$:

$$u_{0i}^{(\mu)}\left(x_i^{(\mu)}\right) = a_i^{(\mu)} \ln\left(x_i^{(\mu)}\right). \tag{8.11}$$

The $a_i^{(\mu)} > 0$ characterize the preferences for good i and the logarithmic dependence on $x_i^{(\mu)}$ takes into account the decrease of the marginal utility of each good i.

Although so far all $x_i^{(\mu)}$ can vary in the interval $0 < x_i^{(\mu)} < \infty$, a *trade off* between the goods is already implied in the form (8.10) if the budget constraint for members of $\mathcal{P}^{(\mu)}$

$$\tilde{b}^{(\mu)} = \sum_{i=1}^{L+1} \tilde{p}_i x_i^{(\mu)} \tag{8.12}$$

is taken into account, where $\tilde{p}_i$ is the price for one unit of good i. Solving (8.12) for the composite good x_{L+1} (which includes saving and spending for all other goods except for $i = 1, 2, \ldots, L$) one obtains

$$x_{L+1}^{(\mu)} = \left(b^{(\mu)} - \sum_{i=1}^{L} p_i x_i^{(\mu)} \right) \tag{8.13}$$

with rescaled budget and prices:

$$b^{(\mu)} = \tilde{b}^{(\mu)}/p_{L+1}; \quad p_i = \tilde{p}_i/p_{L+1}. \tag{8.14}$$

Inserting (8.11) and (8.13) in (8.10) one obtains the *conventional traded off utility* term:

$$u_0^{(\mu)}(\mathbf{x}) = \sum_{i=1}^{L} a_i^{(\mu)} \ln\left(x_i^{(\mu)}\right) + a_{L+1}^{(\mu)} \ln\left(b^{(\mu)} - \sum_{i=1}^{L} p_i x_i^{(\mu)}\right). \qquad (8.15)$$

The domain of variation of all $x_i^{(\mu)}$ must now be finite and is confined by the evident condition

$$x_i^{(\mu)} > 0 \quad i = 1, 2, \ldots, L;$$
$$\sum_{i=1}^{L} p_i x_i^{(\mu)} < b^{(\mu)}. \qquad (8.16)$$

Transitions beyond the boundary of domain (8.16) will not take place, because transition rates of the form (8.21) will vanish if one of the terms of $u_0^{(\mu)}(\mathbf{x})$ approaches $(-\infty)$.

Next we consider terms in $u^{(\mu)}(\mathbf{x})$ which take into account that the satisfaction obtained from different goods i and j consumed by members of the *same group* $\mathcal{P}^{(\mu)}$ may be *correlated*. The simplest possible form of an *intra-group interaction utility* between goods i and j within the same group $\mathcal{P}^{(\mu)}$ is given by a term:

$$u_{ij}^{\mu\mu} = \kappa_{ij}^{(\mu\mu)}\left(x_i^{(\mu)} - x_j^{(\mu)}\right)^2, \qquad (8.17)$$

where $\kappa_{ij}^{(\mu\mu)} > 0$ is a positive trend parameter.

If the goods i and j are *substitutable fancy goods*, the following interpretation can be given to the term (8.17): It describes the utility effect of an *intra-group conformation trend*. This term is only large and leads to a *high utility* for each member of $\mathcal{P}^{(\mu)}$ if this member prefers (together with all other members of $\mathcal{P}^{(\mu)}$) either good i to good j, or alternatively good j to good i, because only then $(x_i^{(\mu)} - x_j^{(\mu)})^2$ assumes a large value. Since $\kappa_{ij}^{(\mu\mu)}$ measures the strength of this intra-group conformation trend we denote it as the *internal conformity parameter*. The high interaction utility (8.17) is then due to the psychological satisfaction by conformation (or due to the psychological relief by complying with the social pressure exerted by members of the host group).

Finally we consider a term in $u^{(\mu)}(\mathbf{x})$ describing an interaction utility for members of $\mathcal{P}^{(\mu)}$ which depends on the consumption of two fancy goods i and j in the *host group* $\mathcal{P}^{(\mu)}$ and in *other groups*, say $\mathcal{P}^{(\rho)}$. The simplest possible form of such an *intergroup interaction utility* term reads:

$$u_{ij}^{\mu\rho} = \kappa_{ij}^{\mu\rho}\left(x_i^{(\mu)} - x_j^{(\mu)}\right) \cdot \left(x_i^{(\rho)} - x_j^{(\rho)}\right), \qquad (8.18)$$

where $\kappa_{ij}^{\mu\rho}$ is an *intergroup interaction parameter*.

The appearance of a term of type (8.18) is again typical for substitutable fancy goods. However, two characteristic cases can now appear:

- *The case $\kappa_{ij}^{\mu\rho} > 0$*: Here the intergroup interaction utility of the group $\mathcal{P}^{(\mu)}$ becomes positive, if the members of $\mathcal{P}^{(\mu)}$ prefer *the same* fancy good as those of group $\mathcal{P}^{(\rho)}$, i.e. if $(x_i^{(\mu)} - x_j^{(\mu)})$ and $(x_i^{(\rho)} - x_j^{(\rho)})$ have *the same* sign. Evidently, in this case the fashion psychology of $\mathcal{P}^{(\mu)}$ is *imitative*, because the members of $\mathcal{P}^{(\mu)}$ feel higher utility, i.e. satisfaction, if they *imitate* the preferences of the members of $\mathcal{P}^{(\rho)}$ for one of the fashion goods. Therefore we denote $\kappa_{ij}^{\mu\rho} > 0$ as *intergroup imitation parameter*.

- *The case $\kappa_{ij}^{\mu\rho} < 0$*: Here the intergroup interaction utility of $\mathcal{P}^{(\mu)}$ becomes positive, if the members of group $\mathcal{P}^{(\mu)}$ prefer a *different* fancy good than those of group $\mathcal{P}^{(\rho)}$, i.e. if $(x_i^{(\mu)} - x_j^{(\mu)})$ and $(x_i^{(\rho)} - x_j^{(\rho)})$ have *different* signs. Evidently, in this case the fashion psychology of $\mathcal{P}^{(\mu)}$ is *exclusivist, elitist and snobbish*, because the members of $\mathcal{P}^{(\mu)}$ derive satisfaction from being unique and *different* from the other group $\mathcal{P}^{(\rho)}$. Therefore $\kappa_{ij}^{\mu\rho} < 0$ may be denoted as *the intergroup demarcation parameter*.

In the general case the utility of the whole consumption basket x comprises for a representative member of $\mathcal{P}^{(\mu)}$ the terms

$$u^{(\mu)}(\mathbf{x}) = u_0^{(\mu)}\left(\mathbf{x}^{(\mu)}\right) + \sum_{\rho}\sum_{i,j\neq i} u_{i,j}^{\mu\rho}\left(\mathbf{x}^{(\mu)}, \mathbf{x}^{(\rho)}\right)$$

$$= \sum_{i=1}^{L} a_i^{(\mu)} \ln\left(x_i^{(\mu)}\right) + a_{L+1}^{(\mu)} \ln\left(b^{(\mu)} - \sum_{i=1}^{L} p_i x_i^{(\mu)}\right)$$

$$+ \sum_{\rho}\sum_{i,j\neq i} \kappa_{ij}^{\mu\rho}\left(x_i^{(\mu)} - x_j^{(\mu)}\right)\cdot\left(x_i^{(\rho)} - x_j^{(\rho)}\right). \tag{8.19}$$

The coefficients $a_i^{(\mu)}$ and $\kappa_{ij}^{\mu\rho}$ have to be chosen according to the nature of the goods (conventional or fancy) and the psychology of the group $\mathcal{P}^{(\mu)}$ (imitative or snobbish). We remark that the interaction between the members of the groups $\mathcal{P}^{(\mu)}, \mathcal{P}^{(\rho)}, \ldots$ is an *indirect* one and not a *pairwise* one: They only interact via their knowledge of the average group-specific demands $\mathbf{x}^{(\mu)}, \mathbf{x}^{(\rho)}, \ldots$ within their own and the other group.

The Transition Rates

The transition rates for the elementary changes of the demand configuration (8.3), or in scaled variables (8.6), can now be set up in straight forward manner. Since the transition (8.3) or (8.6) can be caused statistically independently by each of the $N^{(\mu)}$ members of the consumer group $\mathcal{P}^{(\mu)}$, the transition rates have the form

$$\begin{aligned} W_{i\uparrow}^{(\mu)} &= N^{(\mu)} w_{i\uparrow}^{(\mu)}(\mathbf{X}) \quad \text{for} \quad \mathbf{X} \Rightarrow \mathbf{X}_{i+}^{(\mu)}; \\ W_{i\downarrow}^{(\mu)} &= N^{(\mu)} w_{i\downarrow}^{(\mu)}(\mathbf{X}) \quad \text{for} \quad \mathbf{X} \Rightarrow \mathbf{X}_{i-}^{(\mu)}, \end{aligned} \tag{8.20}$$

where $w_{i\uparrow}^{(\mu)}$ and $w_{i\downarrow}^{(\mu)}$ are the individual transition rates for consuming one unit more or less of good i per unit of time. Their general form was derived in Chapter 3. Applying this form to the present case and taking into account equation (8.8) one obtains:

$$w_{i\uparrow}^{(\mu)}\mathbf{X} = \nu^{(\mu)}\exp\left\{U^{(\mu)}\left(\mathbf{X}_{i+}^{(\mu)}\right) - U^{(\mu)}(\mathbf{X})\right\} \approx \nu^{(\mu)}\exp\left\{\frac{\partial u^{(\mu)}(\mathbf{x})}{\partial x_i^{(\mu)}}\right\};$$

$$w_{i\downarrow}^{(\mu)}\mathbf{X} = \nu^{(\mu)}\exp\left\{U^{(\mu)}\left(\mathbf{X}_{i-}^{(\mu)}\right) - U^{(\mu)}(\mathbf{X})\right\} \approx \nu^{(\mu)}\exp\left\{-\frac{\partial u^{(\mu)}(\mathbf{x})}{\partial x_i^{(\mu)}}\right\}. \tag{8.21}$$

Due to the assumption (8.8) the individual rates only depend on the scaled variables $\mathbf{x}$ and not on the size $\sim N^{(\mu)}$ of the group $P^{(\mu)}$. The parameter $\nu^{(\mu)}$ describes a global flexibility within the group $\mathcal{P}^{(\mu)}$. We assume that $\nu^{(\mu)}$ is independent of $\mathbf{X}$.

8.2.2 Dynamic Equations

According to the general procedure of Chapter 3 we can now immediately write down the dynamic equations on the probabilistic and deterministic level of description

The Master Equation

By $P(\mathbf{X};t)$ we mean the probability of finding the demand configuration $\mathbf{X}$ at time t. The probability distribution function $P(\mathbf{X};t)$ fulfils the normalisation condition

$$\sum_{\mathbf{X}} P(\mathbf{X};t) = 1, \tag{8.22}$$

where the sum extends over all allowed configurations and evolves with time according to the *master equation* (see (3.35)), which reads, if applied to the present model:

$$\frac{dP(\mathbf{X};t)}{dt} = \sum_{i,\mu}\left\{W_{\uparrow i}^{(\mu)}\left(\mathbf{X}_{i-}^{(\mu)}\right)P\left(\mathbf{X}_{i-}^{(\mu)};t\right) + W_{\downarrow i}^{(\mu)}\left(\mathbf{X}_{i+}^{(\mu)}\right)P\left(\mathbf{X}_{i+}^{(\mu)};t\right)\right\}$$

$$- \sum_{i,\mu}\left\{W_{\uparrow i}^{(\mu)}(\mathbf{X})P(\mathbf{X};t) + W_{\downarrow i}^{(\mu)}(\mathbf{X})P(\mathbf{X};t)\right\}. \tag{8.23}$$

As always, the change with time of the probability $P(\mathbf{X};t)$ of the given configuration $\mathbf{X}$ comes about by two counteractive terms on the r.h.s. of equation (8.23), namely the probability flow *into* configuration $\mathbf{X}$ from the neighboring configurations $\mathbf{X}_{i-}^{(\mu)}$ and $\mathbf{X}_{i+}^{(\mu)}$ (first line of r.h.s.), and the probability flow *out of* configuration $\mathbf{X}$ into the neighboring configurations $\mathbf{X}_{i-}^{(\mu)}$ and $\mathbf{X}_{i+}^{(\mu)}$ (second line of r.h.s.).

Quasi-meanvalue Equations

In Chapters 10 and 12 we demonstrate, how in the context of the master equation formalism deterministic equations of motion for quasi-meanvalues $\hat{\mathbf{X}}$ can be derived.

As derived in Chapter 12, the quasi-meanvalue equations describe the mean path of a bundle of stochastic trajectories at each point $\mathbf{X}$ in configuration space. For the present model they read:

$$\frac{d\hat{X}_i^{(\mu)}}{dt} = W_{i\uparrow}^{(\mu)}(\hat{\mathbf{X}}) - W_{i\downarrow}^{(\mu)}(\hat{\mathbf{X}}) \tag{8.24}$$

or, going over to scaled variables (8.4) and taking into account the form (8.20) of the transition rates,

$$\frac{d\hat{x}_i^{(\mu)}}{dt} = w_{i\uparrow}^{(\mu)}(\hat{\mathbf{x}}) - w_{i\downarrow}^{(\mu)}(\hat{\mathbf{x}}) \tag{8.25}$$

in which the magnitudes $N^{(\mu)}, \ldots$ of the groups $\mathcal{P}^{(\mu)}$ do not appear due to assumption (8.8).

Inserting the explicit transition rates (8.21) one obtains the quasi-meanvalue-equations in the form

$$\frac{d\hat{x}_i^{(\mu)}}{dt} = 2\nu^{(\mu)} \sinh\left\{\frac{\partial u^{(\mu)}(\hat{\mathbf{x}})}{\partial \hat{x}_i^{(\mu)}}\right\} \quad \begin{matrix} i = 1, 2, \ldots, L; \\ \mu = 1, 2, \ldots, P. \end{matrix} \tag{8.26}$$

These equations are a set of $L \cdot P$ autonomous nonlinear differential equations for the quasi-meanvalues $\hat{x}_i^{(\mu)}$ of the scaled consumption variables $x_i^{(\mu)}$. Together with the master equation (8.23) the equations (8.26) provide the basis for the analysis of the model in the following Sections.

8.2.3 Stationary Solutions and Stability Analysis

Stationary Quasi-meanvalues

We begin with the analysis of the stationary solutions $\hat{\hat{x}}_i^{(\mu)}$ of the quasi-meanvalue equations (8.26) which satisfy (8.26) after putting all time derivatives $d\hat{x}_i^{(\mu)}/dt$ equal to zero. There follow the conditions for the stationary $\hat{\hat{x}}_i^{(\mu)}$:

$$\left(\frac{\partial u^{(\mu)}(\mathbf{x})}{\partial x_i^{(\mu)}}\right)_{\hat{\hat{\mathbf{x}}}} = 0; \quad \begin{matrix} i = 1, 2, \ldots, L \\ \mu = 1, 2, \ldots, P \end{matrix} \tag{8.27}$$

since the hyperbolic sinus only vanishes if its argument is zero.

The conditions (8.27) coincide with those determining the simultaneous extremum for all $u^{(\mu)}(\mathbf{x})$ if the composite good $(L + 1)$ is included in $\mathbf{x}$ and if, on the other hand, the budget constraint (8.12) is taken into account by the Lagrange multiplier method. In so far the search for stationary states of the dynamic equations and the search leading to extremal values of the utilities are equivalent.

This means that the dynamic equations include *stationary states* which fully correspond to those states found by *utility maximisation* in the conventional equilibrium theory.

This holds also concerning the *second order conditions* for a true maximum of the utility functions. Indeed, the conditions derived below for a *stable stationary state* fully correspond to the second order conditions for a true maximum of the utility functions.

On the other hand the dynamic equations do of course comprise much more general cases than stable stationarity. These will be discussed in detail in the next Section.

Stability of Stationary Quasi-meanvalues

The *stability* of the stationary solutions satisfying equations (8.27) can now be examined by means of a *linear stability analysis*. Expanding the components $\hat{x}_i^{(\mu)}(t)$ of the quasi-meanvalue near a stationary point $\hat{\bar{x}}$

$$\hat{x}_i^{(\mu)}(t) = \hat{\bar{x}}_i^{(\mu)} + \xi_i^{(\mu)}(t) \tag{8.28}$$

and linearizing the equations (8.26) with respect to $\xi_i^{(\mu)}(t)$, one easily obtains a set of linear equations

$$\frac{d\xi_i^{(\mu)}(t)}{dt} = \sum_{\rho,j}^{P,L} D_{ij}^{\mu\rho} \xi_j^{(\rho)}(t) \qquad \begin{matrix} \mu = 1, 2, \ldots, P \\ i = 1, 2, \ldots, L \end{matrix} \tag{8.29}$$

with coefficients

$$D_{ij}^{\mu\rho} = 2\nu^{(\mu)} \left(\frac{\partial^2 u^{(\mu)}(\mathbf{x})}{\partial x_i^{(\mu)} \partial x_j^{(\rho)}} \right)_{\hat{\bar{x}}} \tag{8.30}$$

for the small deviations $\xi_i^{(\mu)}$ from the stationary state. Solving equation (8.29) by

$$\xi_i^{(\mu)}(t) = \xi_{i0}^{(\mu)} \exp(\lambda t) \tag{8.31}$$

one obtains by inserting (8.31) into (8.29) a set of $P \cdot L$ homogeneous linear equations for the amplitudes $\xi_{i0}^{(\mu)}$, which has nontrivial solutions only, if the determinant of the $P \cdot L$-dimensional coefficient matrix vanishes. This leads to the condition

$$\left\| D_{ij}^{\mu\rho} - \delta_{\mu\rho}\delta_{ij}\lambda \right\| \overset{!}{=} 0 \tag{8.32}$$

for the possible values of λ, which are denoted as *eigenvalues*.

The *stability* of the stationary state $\hat{\bar{x}}$ is only warranted if *all eigenvalues λ have a negative real part*, such as leading to an exponential decay with time of any deviation (8.31). In Section 8.3 we will see that this needs not always be fulfilled and that – depending on the trendparameters $\kappa_{ij}^{\mu\rho}$ – a stationary state may become unstable.

However, let us here consider a case for which the equations (8.29) can be further evaluated, and for which, after explicit choice of the utility functions $u^{(\mu)}(\mathbf{x}^{(\mu)})$, the unique stationary state can be explicitly found and proves to be stable.

If the consumer groups $\mathcal{P}^{(\mu)}$ *do not interact*, i.e. if their respective utility functions $u^{(\mu)}(\mathbf{x})$ only depend on the demand configuration $\mathbf{x}^{(\mu)}$ of their own group and *not* on the demand configurations $\mathbf{x}^{(\nu)}, \mathbf{x}^{(\rho)}, \ldots$ of other groups $\mathcal{P}^{(\nu)}, \mathcal{P}^{(\rho)}, \ldots$, then there exists a global utility function

$$U(\mathbf{X}) = \sum_{\mu=1}^{P} U^{(\mu)}\left(\mathbf{X}^{(\mu)}\right) = \sum_{\mu=1}^{P} N^{(\mu)} u^{(\mu)}\left(\mathbf{x}^{(\mu)}\right) \tag{8.33}$$

for which holds:

$$U\left(\mathbf{X}_{i\pm}^{(\mu)}\right) - U(\mathbf{X}) = U^{(\mu)}\left(\mathbf{X}_{i\pm}^{(\mu)}\right) - U^{(\mu)}\left(\mathbf{X}^{(\mu)}\right). \tag{8.34}$$

Furthermore, the coefficients (8.30) assume the form

$$D_{ij}^{\mu\rho} = \delta_{\mu\rho} D_{ij}^{\mu\mu}$$

$$\text{with} \quad D_{ij}^{\mu\mu} = D_{ji}^{\mu\mu} = 2\nu^{(\mu)} \cdot \left(\frac{\partial^2 u^{(\mu)}\left(\mathbf{x}^{(\mu)}\right)}{\partial x_i^{(\mu)} \partial x_j^{(\mu)}}\right)_{\hat{\mathbf{x}}^{(\mu)}}. \tag{8.35}$$

The $P \cdot L$ *coupled* linear equations (8.29) then split into P *independent sets of equations*

$$\frac{d\xi_i^{(\mu)}}{dt} = \sum_{j=1}^{L} D_{ij}^{\mu\mu} \xi_j^{(\mu)}(t) \qquad \begin{array}{l} i = 1, 2, \ldots, L \\ \mu = 1, 2, \ldots, P \end{array} \tag{8.36}$$

which are of course more easily tractable.

As a concrete case let us assume that $u^{(\mu)}(\mathbf{x})$ only consists of the conventional term $u_0^{(\mu)}(\mathbf{x}^{(\mu)})$ given by (8.15) without inter-group interaction terms. The global utility function $U(\mathbf{X})$ then reads

$$U(\mathbf{X}) = \sum_{\mu=1}^{P} N^{(\mu)} u_0^{(\mu)}\left(\mathbf{x}^{(\mu)}\right)$$

$$= \sum_{\mu=1}^{P} N^{(\mu)} \left\{ \sum_{i=1}^{L} a_i^{(\mu)} \ln\left(x_i^{(\mu)}\right) + a_{L+1}^{(\mu)} \ln\left(b^{(\mu)} - \sum_{j=1}^{L} p_j x_j^{(\mu)}\right) \right\}. \tag{8.37}$$

The stationary states of the quasi-meanvalue equations follow from (8.27) with $u^{(\mu)}(\mathbf{x}) \Rightarrow u_0^{(\mu)}(\mathbf{x}^{(\mu)})$. Here there exists one *unique solution* of (8.27) only. It reads

$$\hat{\bar{x}}_j^{(\mu)} = \frac{b^{(\mu)}}{p_j} \frac{a_j^{(\mu)}}{\sum_{i=1}^{L+1} a_i^{(\mu)}}. \tag{8.38}$$

Furthermore it can easily be shown that the matrix

$$\left(\frac{\partial^2 u_0^{(\mu)}}{\partial x_i^{(\mu)} \partial x_j^{(\mu)}}\right)_{\hat{\hat{\mathbf{x}}}} = -\frac{\left(\sum_{l=1}^{L+1} a_l^{(\mu)}\right)^2}{b^{(\mu)2}} \left[\delta_{ij}\left(\frac{p_i}{\sqrt{a_i^{(\mu)}}}\right)^2 + \frac{p_i}{\sqrt{a_{L+1}^{(\mu)}}} \cdot \frac{p_j}{\sqrt{a_{L+1}^{(\mu)}}}\right] \qquad (8.39)$$

is *negatively definite*. Hence all eigenvalues of the solutions of (8.36) are negative, which means that the stationary solution (8.38) is stable. Simultaneously it follows that $u_0^{(\mu)}(\mathbf{x}^{(\mu)})$ has a *true maximum* at $\mathbf{x}^{(\mu)} = \hat{\hat{\mathbf{x}}}^{(\mu)}$.

Stationary Solution of the Master Equation

It is remarkable that the existence of a global utility function for which the condition (8.34) holds, does already lead to the construction of the stationary solution of the master equation (8.23). The stationary solution $P_{st}(\mathbf{X})$ does not depend on time and therefore has to satisfy, according to (8.23):

$$\sum_{i,\mu} W_{\uparrow i}^{(\mu)}\left(\mathbf{X}_{i-}^{(\mu)}\right) P_{st}\left(\mathbf{X}_{i-}^{(\mu)}\right) + \sum_{i,\mu} W_{\downarrow i}^{(\mu)}\left(\mathbf{X}_{i+}^{(\mu)}\right) P_{st}\left(\mathbf{X}_{i+}^{(\mu)}\right)$$
$$= \sum_{i,\mu} W_{\uparrow i}^{(\mu)}(\mathbf{X}) P_{st}(\mathbf{X}) + \sum_{i,\mu} W_{\downarrow i}^{(\mu)}(\mathbf{X}) P_{st}(\mathbf{X}). \qquad (8.40)$$

The stationary equation (8.40) is automatically fulfilled, if it happens that for $P_{st}(\mathbf{X})$ the *condition of detailed balance* holds:

$$W_{\uparrow i}^{(\mu)}\left(\mathbf{X}_{i-}^{(\mu)}\right) P_{st}\left(\mathbf{X}_{i-}^{(\mu)}\right) = W_{\downarrow i}^{(\mu)}(\mathbf{X}) P_{st}(\mathbf{X});$$
$$W_{\downarrow i}^{(\mu)}\left(\mathbf{X}_{i+}^{(\mu)}\right) P_{st}\left(\mathbf{X}_{i+}^{(\mu)}\right) = W_{\uparrow i}^{(\mu)}(\mathbf{X}) P_{st}(\mathbf{X}) \qquad (8.41)$$

which means that the probability flows between $\mathbf{X}$ and each of the neighboring configurations $\mathbf{X}_{i-}^{(\mu)}$ and $\mathbf{X}_{i+}^{(\mu)}$ *cancel individually*, so that the corresponding i, μ-terms in (8.40) cancel pairwise.

It can now easily be seen that in the case of the existence of a global utility $U(\mathbf{X})$, which fulfils (8.34), the transition rates (8.20) assume the form:

$$W_{\uparrow i}^{(\mu)}(\mathbf{X}) = \nu^{(\mu)} N^{(\mu)} \exp\left[U\left(\mathbf{X}_{i+}^{(\mu)}\right) - U(\mathbf{X})\right]$$
$$W_{\downarrow i}^{(\mu)}(\mathbf{X}) = \nu^{(\mu)} N^{(\mu)} \exp\left[U\left(\mathbf{X}_{i-}^{(\mu)}\right) - U(\mathbf{X})\right] \qquad (8.42)$$

and that the following form of $P_{st}(\mathbf{X})$

$$P_{st}(\mathbf{X}) = C \cdot \exp[2U(\mathbf{X})] \qquad (8.43)$$

satisfies detailed balance (8.41) and is therefore a solution of the stationary master equation (8.40). In Chapter 10 it is shown that (under conditions which are satisfied here) there exists *one unique* stationary solution only; hence (8.43) must be this solution.

Inserting the explicit form (8.37) of $2U(\mathbf{X})$ one observes that – as a consequence of the presumed independence of the consumer groups $\mathcal{P}^{(\mu)}$ in their demand behaviour – the stationary probability distribution (8.43) factorizes

$$P_{st}(\mathbf{X}) = C \prod_{\mu=1}^{P} P_{st}^{(\mu)}\left(\mathbf{X}^{(\mu)}\right) \tag{8.44}$$

and that the distribution for the group $\mathcal{P}^{(\mu)}$ takes the explicit form

$$P_{st}^{(\mu)}\left(\mathbf{X}^{(\mu)}\right) = \left\{ \left[b^{(\mu)} - \sum_{j=1}^{L} p_j x_j^{(\mu)} \right]^{a_{L+1}^{(\mu)}} \cdot \prod_{i=1}^{L} \left[x_i^{(\mu)} \right]^{a_i^{(\mu)}} \right\}^{2N^{(\mu)}}. \tag{8.45}$$

The maximum of this unimodal probability distribution coincides with the stable stationary state (8.38) of the quasimeanvalue equations. The width of this probability peak describes the natural fluctuations around the stationary state due to the stochastic purchasing behaviour of the consumers.

8.3 Demand Dynamics for Two Consumer Groups

Let us now specialize the general model to the case of two consumer groups $\mathcal{P}^{(\alpha)}$ and $\mathcal{P}^{(\beta)}$ exhibiting *intra-group* and *inter-group* interaction concerning their purchasing behaviour. This interaction will lead to essential differences of the demand dynamics as compared to groups without this kind of interaction.

For reasons of simplicity we consider two goods $i = 1, 2$ only, which have the quality of *fancy goods*, while all other goods are included in the composite good.

Further simplifications are introduced in order to let the groups $\mathcal{P}^{(\alpha)}$ and $\mathcal{P}^{(\beta)}$ and the goods $i = 1, 2$ be as similar as possible so that the effects of intra-group and inter-group interaction can be studied in *pure form*. In this sense we assume that the groups have the same size and the same reaction speed. The available budget of the members of both groups should also be the same. Apart from their fancy character the two goods $i = 1, 2$ should be fully substitutable, i.e. they should have the same price per unit and the same "natural" utility in both groups. Thus let us think of the legendary "red dresses and blue dresses".

These specifications lead to the following choice of model coefficients:

$$
\begin{aligned}
N^{(\alpha)} &= N^{(\beta)} = N \\
\nu^{(\alpha)} &= \nu^{(\beta)} = \nu; \quad 2\nu t = \tau \\
b^{(\alpha)} &= b^{(\beta)} = b \\
p_1 &= p_2 = p \\
a_1^{(\alpha)} &= a_2^{(\alpha)} = a_1^{(\beta)} = a_2^{(\beta)} = a \\
a_{L+1}^{(\alpha)} &= a_{L+1}^{(\beta)} = c \\
\kappa_{12}^{\mu\rho} &= \kappa_{21}^{\mu\rho} = \kappa^{\mu\rho}.
\end{aligned}
\tag{8.46}
$$

Correspondingly, the utility functions (8.19) now assume the form:

$$u^{(\alpha)}\left(x_1^{(\alpha)}, x_2^{(\alpha)}; x_1^{(\beta)}, x_2^{(\beta)}\right) = a \ln\left(x_1^{(\alpha)} \cdot x_2^{(\alpha)}\right) + c \ln\left(b - p\left(x_1^{(\alpha)} + x_2^{(\alpha)}\right)\right)$$

$$+ \kappa^{\alpha\alpha}\left(x_1^{(\alpha)} - x_2^{(\alpha)}\right)^2 + \kappa^{\alpha\beta}\left(x_1^{(\alpha)} - x_2^{(\alpha)}\right) \cdot \left(x_1^{(\beta)} - x_2^{(\beta)}\right)$$

(8.47a)

and

$$u^{(\beta)}\left(x_1^{(\beta)}, x_2^{(\beta)}; x_1^{(\alpha)}, x_2^{(\alpha)}\right) = a \ln\left(x_1^{(\beta)} \cdot x_2^{(\beta)}\right) + c \ln\left(b - p\left(x_1^{(\beta)} + x_2^{(\beta)}\right)\right)$$

$$+ \kappa^{\beta\beta}\left(x_1^{(\beta)} - x_2^{(\beta)}\right)^2 + \kappa^{\beta\alpha}\left(x_1^{(\beta)} - x_2^{(\beta)}\right) \cdot \left(x_1^{(\alpha)} - x_2^{(\alpha)}\right).$$

(8.47b)

From (8.47) there follow in straight forward manner the equations of type (8.27) for the stationary quasimeanvalues $\hat{\bar{x}}_i^{(\alpha)}$ and $\hat{\bar{x}}_i^{(\beta)}$ (For simplicity we henceforth use the notation $\bar{x}_i^{(\alpha)}$ and $\bar{x}_i^{(\beta)}$ instead of $\hat{\bar{x}}_i^{(\alpha)}$ and $\hat{\bar{x}}_i^{(\beta)}$):

$$\frac{a}{\bar{x}_1^{(\alpha)}} - \frac{cp}{\left[b - p\left(\bar{x}_1^{(\alpha)} + \bar{x}_2^{(\alpha)}\right)\right]} + 2\kappa^{\alpha\alpha}\left(\bar{x}_1^{(\alpha)} - \bar{x}_2^{(\alpha)}\right) + \kappa^{\alpha\beta}\left(\bar{x}_1^{(\beta)} - \bar{x}_2^{(\beta)}\right) \overset{!}{=} 0; \quad (8.48a)$$

$$\frac{a}{\bar{x}_2^{(\alpha)}} - \frac{cp}{\left[b - p\left(\bar{x}_1^{(\alpha)} + \bar{x}_2^{(\alpha)}\right)\right]} - 2\kappa^{\alpha\alpha}\left(\bar{x}_1^{(\alpha)} - \bar{x}_2^{(\alpha)}\right) - \kappa^{\alpha\beta}\left(\bar{x}_1^{(\beta)} - \bar{x}_2^{(\beta)}\right) \overset{!}{=} 0; \quad (8.48b)$$

$$\frac{a}{\bar{x}_1^{(\beta)}} - \frac{cp}{\left[b - p\left(\bar{x}_1^{(\beta)} + \bar{x}_2^{(\beta)}\right)\right]} + 2\kappa^{\beta\beta}\left(\bar{x}_1^{(\beta)} - \bar{x}_2^{(\beta)}\right) + \kappa^{\beta\alpha}\left(\bar{x}_1^{(\alpha)} - \bar{x}_2^{(\alpha)}\right) \overset{!}{=} 0; \quad (8.48c)$$

$$\frac{a}{\bar{x}_2^{(\beta)}} - \frac{cp}{\left[b - p\left(\bar{x}_1^{(\beta)} + \bar{x}_2^{(\beta)}\right)\right]} - 2\kappa^{\beta\beta}\left(\bar{x}_1^{(\beta)} - \bar{x}_2^{(\beta)}\right) - \kappa^{\beta\alpha}\left(\bar{x}_1^{(\alpha)} - \bar{x}_2^{(\alpha)}\right) \overset{!}{=} 0. \quad (8.48d)$$

In the following subsections we will consider in detail – analytically and numerically – special cases of the interaction within and between the groups making use of the utility functions (8.47) and the equations for stationary states (8.48).

8.3.1 Independent Groups with Intra-Group Interaction Only

In this Section we "switch off" the inter-group interaction parameters by putting

$$\kappa^{\alpha\beta} = \kappa^{\beta\alpha} = 0 \qquad (8.49)$$

and assume that the internal conformity parameters of both groups are equal:

$$\kappa^{\alpha\alpha} = \kappa^{\beta\beta} = \kappa. \qquad (8.50)$$

This means that $u^{(\alpha)}$ only depends on $\{x_1^{(\alpha)}, x_2^{(\alpha)}\}$ and $u^{(\beta)}$ only on $\{x_1^{(\beta)}, x_2^{(\beta)}\}$. As a consequence, the quasimeanvalue equations now read

$$\frac{d\hat{x}_i^{(\mu)}}{d\tau} = \sinh\left[\frac{\partial u^{(\mu)}(\hat{\mathbf{x}}^{(\mu)})}{\partial \hat{x}_i^{(\mu)}}\right] \quad \begin{array}{l} \mu = \alpha, \beta \\ i = 1, 2 \end{array} \tag{8.51}$$

and the *stationary equations* (8.48a,b) for group $\mathcal{P}^{(\alpha)}$ and (8.48c,d) for group $\mathcal{P}^{(\beta)}$ are now decoupled and belong to two in all respects equivalent non-interacting groups $\mathcal{P}^{(\alpha)}$ and $\mathcal{P}^{(\beta)}$ with internal conformity.

After introducing for $\mathcal{P}^{(\alpha)}$ the symmetrical and antisymmetrical variables:

$$x^{(\alpha)} = \bar{x}_1^{(\alpha)} + \bar{x}_2^{(\alpha)} \quad \text{and} \quad y^{(\alpha)} = \bar{x}_1^{(\alpha)} - \bar{x}_2^{(\alpha)},$$
$$\text{hence} \quad \bar{x}_1^{(\alpha)} = \frac{1}{2}\left(x^{(\alpha)} + y^{(\alpha)}\right) \quad \text{and} \quad \bar{x}_2^{(\alpha)} = \frac{1}{2}\left(x^{(\alpha)} - y^{(\alpha)}\right) \tag{8.52}$$

one obtains from (8.48a) and (8.48b):

$$y^{(\alpha)} \cdot \left[\left(x^{(\alpha)2} - y^{(\alpha)2}\right) - \frac{a}{\kappa}\right] = 0 \tag{8.53}$$

and

$$2a\left(b - px^{(\alpha)}\right)x^{(\alpha)} - cp\left[x^{(\alpha)2} - y^{(\alpha)2}\right] = 0. \tag{8.54}$$

The analogous holds for $\mathcal{P}^{(\beta)}$.

The equations (8.53) and (8.54) have two solutions, namely a *symmetrical* one with $\bar{x}_1^{(\alpha)} = \bar{x}_2^{(\alpha)}$ or $y^{(\alpha)} = 0$ and an *unsymmetrical* one with $\bar{x}_1^{(\alpha)} \neq \bar{x}_2^{(\alpha)}$, or $y^{(\alpha)} \neq 0$. The symmetrical solution reads:

$$y_s = 0; \quad x_s = \frac{2ab}{(2a + c)p} \tag{8.55}$$

and the unsymmetrical one is given by

$$x_u = \frac{b}{2p} + \sqrt{\left(\frac{b}{2p}\right)^2 - \frac{c}{2\kappa}}; \tag{8.56}$$

$$y_{u\pm} = \pm\sqrt{x_u^2 - \frac{a}{\kappa}}.$$

The same solutions (8.55) and (8.56) hold for group $\mathcal{P}^{(\beta)}$.

Since only *real* solutions x_u and y_u are admissible, the unsymmetrical solution (8.56) only exists, if the internal conformity parameter κ fulfils the two conditions:

$$\frac{c}{2\kappa} < \left(\frac{b}{2p}\right)^2 \quad \text{and} \quad \frac{a}{\kappa} < x_u^2. \tag{8.57}$$

The conditions (8.57) can both be satisfied if κ is sufficiently large. Otherwise only the symmetrical solution exist.

If (8.57) is fulfilled, then there exist – beyond the symmetrical one – four unsymmetrical stationary solutions for both groups $\mathcal{P}^{(\alpha)}$ and $\mathcal{P}^{(\beta)}$ together, namely

$$
\begin{aligned}
x^{(\alpha)} = x^{(\beta)} = x_u \quad & y^{(\alpha)} = y_{u+} \quad y^{(\beta)} = y_{u+}; \\
x^{(\alpha)} = x^{(\beta)} = x_u \quad & y^{(\alpha)} = y_{u+} \quad y^{(\beta)} = y_{u-}; \\
x^{(\alpha)} = x^{(\beta)} = x_u \quad & y^{(\alpha)} = y_{u-} \quad y^{(\beta)} = y_{u+}; \\
x^{(\alpha)} = x^{(\beta)} = x_u \quad & y^{(\alpha)} = y_{u-} \quad y^{(\beta)} = y_{u-}.
\end{aligned}
\tag{8.58}
$$

It is also possible to construct the stationary solution $P_{st}(x_1^{(\alpha)}, x_2^{(\alpha)}, x_1^{(\beta)}, x_2^{(\beta)})$ of the master equation because for utility functions (8.47) there exists a global utility function $U(\mathbf{X})$ which satisfies the condition (8.34). It reads

$$
U(\mathbf{X}) = N\left[u^{(\alpha)}\left(x_1^{(\alpha)}, x_2^{(\alpha)} \right) + u^{(\beta)}\left(x_1^{(\beta)}, x_2^{(\beta)} \right) \right]
\tag{8.59}
$$

with

$$
u^{(\mu)}\left(x_1^{(\mu)}, x_2^{(\mu)} \right) = a \ln\left(x_1^{(\mu)}, x_2^{(\mu)} \right) + c \ln\left(b - p \cdot \left(x_1^{(\mu)} + x_2^{(\mu)} \right) \right) + \kappa\left(x_1^{(\mu)} - x_2^{(\mu)} \right)^2.
\tag{8.60}
$$

Therefore $P_{st}(\mathbf{x}^{(\alpha)}, \mathbf{x}^{(\beta)})$ has, according to (8.43), the form:

$$
P_{st}\left(\mathbf{x}^{(\alpha)}, \mathbf{x}^{(\beta)} \right) = P_{st}^{(\alpha)}\left(\mathbf{x}^{(\alpha)} \right) \cdot P_{st}^{(\beta)}\left(\mathbf{x}^{(\beta)} \right)
\tag{8.61}
$$

with

$$
P_{st}^{(\mu)}\left(\mathbf{x}^{(\mu)} \right) = c\left[x_1^{(\mu)} \cdot x_2^{(\mu)} \right]^{2Na} \cdot \left[b - p \cdot \left(x_1^{(\mu)} + x_2^{(\mu)} \right) \right]^{2Nc} \exp\left[2N\kappa\left(x_1^{(\mu)} - x_2^{(\mu)} \right)^2 \right].
\tag{8.62}
$$

We now illustrate the case of intra-group conformity interaction by numerical solutions of the quasimeanvalue equations (8.51) and the stationary master equation. The representation of the dynamics of the four variables $\{\hat{x}_1^{(\alpha)}(\tau), \hat{x}_2^{(\alpha)}(\tau), \hat{x}_1^{(\beta)}(\tau), \hat{x}_2^{(\beta)}(\tau)\}$ is facilitated by the fact that the sum variables $x^{(\alpha)}(\tau), x^{(\beta)}(\tau)$ exhibit a "harmless" behaviour by always tending to some equilibrium value, whereas the difference variables $y^{(\alpha)}(\tau), y^{(\beta)}(\tau)$ exhibit a more "dramatic" dynamics depending on the choice of the internal conformity parameter κ. Therefore we will only represent the *projection* of the fluxlines in the four-dimensional space into the *two-dimensional plane* of the difference variables $y^{(\alpha)}$ and $y^{(\beta)}$.

Correspondingly we only represent the reduced stationary probability distribution:

$$
P_{st}\left[y^{(\alpha)}, y^{(\beta)} \right] = \sum_{x^{(\alpha)}, x^{(\beta)}} P_{st}\left[x^{(\alpha)}, y^{(\alpha)}; x^{(\beta)}, y^{(\beta)} \right],
\tag{8.63}
$$

where the sum in (8.63) must be extended over all admissible values of the sum variables $x^{(\alpha)}$ and $x^{(\beta)}$ for given difference variables $y^{(\alpha)}$ and $y^{(\beta)}$.

Beginning with the *fluxlines* we exhibit them in the $y^{(\alpha)}/y^{(\beta)}$-space in Figure 8.1 for the case $\kappa = 0$, i.e. for vanishing internal conformity, and in Figure 8.2 for the case $\kappa = 0.2$, i.e. for a large internal conformity parameter, which fulfils the conditions (8.57), after choice of the parameters $b = 10$; $p = 1$, $a = 1$, $c = 1$.

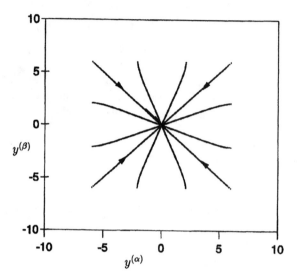

Figure 8.1 Demand fluxlines in $y^{(\alpha)}/y^{(\beta)}$-space for vanishing internal conformity parameter $\kappa = 0$. They converge to the stable stationary point $(y^{(\alpha)}, y^{(\beta)}) = (0,0)$. Parameters: $b = 10$; $p = 1, a = 1, c = 1$.

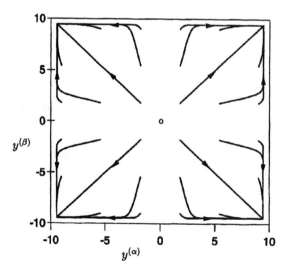

Figure 8.2 Demand fluxlines in $y^{(\alpha)}/y^{(\beta)}$-space for large internal conformity parameter $\kappa = 0.2$. They approach one of the stable stationary points $(y^{(\alpha)}, y^{(\beta)}) = (y_{u+}, y_{u+}); (y_{u-}, y_{u+}); (y_{u-}, y_{u-}); (y_{u+}, y_{u-})$. Parameters: $b = 10$; $p = 1, a = 1, c = 1$.

As expected, the fluxlines merge in Figure 8.1 in the stationary state $y^{(\alpha)} = y^{(\beta)} = 0$ which is the only stable stationary state for $\kappa = 0$, whereas the fluxlines approach in Figure 8.2 one of the four stable stationary states (8.58) present in the case of the large internal conformity parameter $\kappa = 0.2$. In the latter case one of the goods 1 or 2 strongly prevails over the other good in each group due to the strong conformation trend.

Next we represent the reduced stationary probability distributions $P_{st}(y^{(\alpha)}, y^{(\beta)})$ in Figure 8.3 for vanishing internal conformity parameter $\kappa = 0$ and in Figure 8.4 for a relatively large value $\kappa = 0.07$, and for parameters $a = 1; c = 1; b = 10;$ and $p = 1$. The rather small values $N = 20$ and $N = 10$ have been chosen for illustrative purposes yielding distributions that are not too steep. (Large N lead to sharply peaked, small N to broad distributions.)

As expected, for $\kappa = 0$ the distribution $P_{st}(y^{(\alpha)}, y^{(\beta)})$ is unimodal with one probability peak at $(y^{(\alpha)}, y^{(\beta)}) = (0, 0)$, the stable stationary state, whereas for $\kappa = 0.07$ the distribution exhibits *four peaks of equal height*, because of the symmetry between goods $i = 1, 2$, with maxima at the stationary points $(y^{(\alpha)}, y^{(\beta)}) = (y_{u+}, y_{u+})$; (y_{u-}, y_{u+}); (y_{u-}, y_{u-}); and (y_{u+}, y_{u-}). The width of the peaks is due to the probabilistic fluctuations of the purchasing behaviour among the members of $\mathcal{P}^{(\alpha)}$ and $\mathcal{P}^{(\beta)}$.

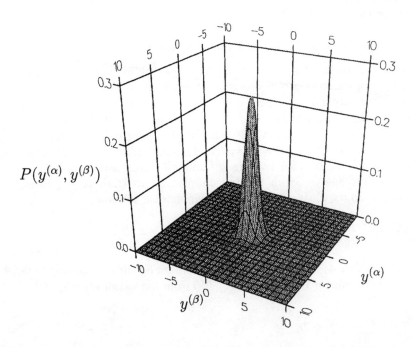

Figure 8.3 Reduced probability distribution $P_{st}(y^{(\alpha)}, y^{(\beta)})$ for vanishing internal conformity parameter $\kappa = 0$ and parameters $b = 10; a = 1; c = 1; p = 1; N = 20$. The distribution is unimodal with maximum at the stable stationary point $(y^{(\alpha)}, y^{(\beta)}) = (0, 0)$.

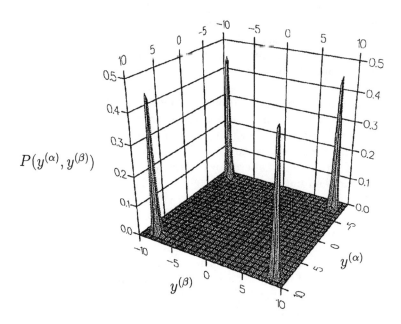

Figure 8.4 Reduced probability distribution $P_{st}(y^{(\alpha)}, y^{(\beta)})$ for large internal conformity parameter $\kappa = 0.07$ and parameters $b = 10; a = 1; c = 1; p = 1; N = 10$. The distribution is multimodal with maxima at the stable stationary points $(y^{(\alpha)}, y^{(\beta)}) = (y_{u+}, y_{u+}), (y_{u-}, y_{u+}), (y_{u-}, y_{u-})$ and (y_{u+}, y_{u-}).

8.3.2 Groups with Intra- and Inter-Group Interaction

Let us now consider the case where *both types* of interaction, the intra-group *conformity* and the inter-group *imitation* or *marking off* behaviour, are taken into account. The interplay of all these interactions performs – as already discussed – a prominent role in purchasing fancy goods. Since now not only the *internal conformity parameter* $\kappa = \kappa^{\alpha\alpha} = \kappa^{\beta\beta}$ (see (8.50)), but also the *intergroup interaction parameters* $\kappa^{\alpha\beta}$ and $\kappa^{\beta\alpha}$ relevantly influence the system dynamics, we must expect more complex situations than in Section 8.3.1 where $\kappa^{\alpha\beta}$ and $\kappa^{\beta\alpha}$ were "switched off".

We begin the analysis with the full coupled set of stationary quasimeanvalue equations (8.48a,b,c,d). It still has a fully symmetrical solution:

$$\bar{x}_1^{(\alpha)} = \bar{x}_2^{(\alpha)} = \bar{x}_1^{(\beta)} = \bar{x}_2^{(\beta)} \equiv \bar{x} = \frac{ab}{(2a+c)p}. \tag{8.64}$$

The *linear stability analysis* of this stationary solution yields, according to (8.29), the following equations for the deviations $\xi_i^{(\mu)}(\tau)$ from the stationary state $\bar{x}_i^{(\mu)}$:

$$\frac{d\xi_1^{(\alpha)}}{d\tau} = [-(r+q) + 2\kappa^{\alpha\alpha}]\xi_1^{(\alpha)} - (q + 2\kappa^{\alpha\alpha})\xi_2^{(\alpha)} + \kappa^{\alpha\beta}\xi_1^{(\beta)} - \kappa^{\alpha\beta}\xi_2^{(\beta)}; \tag{8.65a}$$

$$\frac{d\xi_2^{(\alpha)}}{d\tau} = -(q + 2\kappa^{\alpha\alpha})\xi_1^{(\alpha)} + [-(r+q) + 2\kappa^{\alpha\alpha}]\xi_2^{(\alpha)} - \kappa^{\alpha\beta}\xi_1^{(\beta)} + \kappa^{\alpha\beta}\xi_2^{(\beta)}; \tag{8.65b}$$

$$\frac{d\xi_1^{(\beta)}}{d\tau} = \kappa^{\beta\alpha}\xi_1^{(\alpha)} - \kappa^{\beta\alpha}\xi_2^{(\alpha)} + [-(r+q) + 2\kappa^{\beta\beta}]\xi_1^{(\beta)} - (q + 2\kappa^{\beta\beta})\xi_2^{(\beta)}; \qquad (8.65c)$$

$$\frac{d\xi_2^{(\beta)}}{d\tau} = -\kappa^{\beta\alpha}\xi_1^{(\alpha)} + \kappa^{\beta\alpha}\xi_2^{(\alpha)} - (q + 2\kappa^{\beta\beta})\xi_1^{(\beta)} + [-(r+q) + 2\kappa^{\beta\beta}]\xi_2^{(\beta)}. \qquad (8.65d)$$

Here we have made use of the abbreviations

$$r = \frac{a}{\bar{x}^2} > 0 \qquad q = \frac{cp}{(b - 2p\bar{x})^2} > 0. \qquad (8.66)$$

After introducing the sum and difference variables

$$
\begin{aligned}
\sigma^{(\alpha)} &= \xi_1^{(\alpha)} + \xi_2^{(\alpha)} \quad \sigma^{(\beta)} = \xi_1^{(\beta)} + \xi_2^{(\beta)}; \\
\delta^{(\alpha)} &= \xi_1^{(\alpha)} - \xi_2^{(\alpha)} \quad \delta^{(\beta)} = \xi_1^{(\beta)} - \xi_2^{(\beta)}
\end{aligned}
\qquad (8.67)
$$

we obtain from (8.65) two de-coupled systems of linear differential equations:

$$
\begin{aligned}
\frac{d\sigma^{(\alpha)}}{d\tau} &= -(2q + r)\sigma^{(\alpha)}; \\
\frac{d\sigma^{(\beta)}}{d\tau} &= -(2q + r)\sigma^{(\beta)}
\end{aligned}
\qquad (8.68)
$$

and

$$
\begin{aligned}
\frac{d\delta^{(\alpha)}}{d\tau} &= [4\kappa^{\alpha\alpha} - r]\delta^{(\alpha)} + 2\kappa^{\alpha\beta}\delta^{(\beta)}; \\
\frac{d\delta^{(\beta)}}{d\tau} &= 2\kappa^{\beta\alpha}\delta^{(\alpha)} + [4\kappa^{\beta\beta} - r]\delta^{(\beta)}.
\end{aligned}
\qquad (8.69)
$$

Whereas the equations (8.68) lead to a simple relaxation behaviour of $\sigma^{(\mu)}(\tau)$, which need not be further considered, the solution of (8.69):

$$\delta^{(\alpha)}(\tau) = \delta_0^{(\alpha)}\exp(\lambda t); \quad \delta^{(\beta)}(\tau) = \delta_0^{(\beta)}\exp(\lambda t) \qquad (8.70)$$

leads to the eigenvalue equation

$$
\left\|
\begin{array}{cc}
[4\kappa^{\alpha\alpha} - r - \lambda] & ; \quad 2\kappa^{\alpha\beta} \\
2\kappa^{\beta\alpha} & ; \quad [4\kappa^{\beta\beta} - r - \lambda]
\end{array}
\right\|
\qquad (8.71)
$$

with the solutions

$$\lambda_\pm = \left[2\left(\kappa^{\alpha\alpha} + \kappa^{\beta\beta}\right) - r\right] \pm 2\sqrt{(\kappa^{\alpha\alpha} - \kappa^{\beta\beta})^2 + \kappa^{\alpha\beta}\kappa^{\beta\alpha}} \qquad (8.72)$$

which will now be evaluated.

In the further discussion we assume, as in Section 8.3.1, equal internal conformity parameters $\kappa^{\alpha\alpha} = \kappa^{\beta\beta} = \kappa$ (see equation (8.50)), so that the *eigenvalues* assume the form

$$\lambda_\pm = [4\kappa \quad r] \pm 2\sqrt{\kappa^{\alpha\beta}\kappa^{\beta\alpha}}. \tag{8.73}$$

Evidently the answer to the question whether the eigenvalues $\lambda_\pm$ are *real* or *conjugate complex* depends on whether $\kappa^{\alpha\beta}$ and $\kappa^{\beta\alpha}$ have *equal* or *opposite* sign.

In the case 1 of *equal sign* of $\kappa^{\alpha\beta}$ and $\kappa^{\beta\alpha}$ either *both* groups $\mathcal{P}^{(\alpha)}$ and $\mathcal{P}^{(\beta)}$ have a *tendency to imitate* the other group (if $\kappa^{\alpha\beta}$ and $\kappa^{\beta\alpha}$ are positive) or both groups $\mathcal{P}^{(\alpha)}$ and $\mathcal{P}^{(\beta)}$ have a *tendency to differ* from the other group (if $\kappa^{\alpha\beta}$ and $\kappa^{\beta\alpha}$ are negative). That means in case 1 for which the *eigenvalues are real*, both groups are either *imitator* groups or *snob groups*.

In the case 2 of *opposite sign* of $\kappa^{\alpha\beta}$ and $\kappa^{\beta\alpha}$ one of the groups (say $\mathcal{P}^{(\beta)}$, if $\kappa^{\beta\alpha}$ is positive) is an *imitator group*, because of its tendency to buy the *same good* as the other group, whereas the other group (say $\mathcal{P}^{(\alpha)}$, if $\kappa^{\alpha\beta}$ is negative) is a *snob group*, because of its trend to buy *different goods* than those bought by the other group. That means in case 2 for which the eigenvalues are *conjugate complex*, one of the group is a *snob group* and the other group is an *imitator group*.

Let us now further analyze the cases 1 and 2.

Case 1: Real Eigenvalues $\lambda_\pm$

Case (1a)   Both eigenvalues λ_+ and λ_- are negative
This sub-case is realized, if, according to (8.73), the following inequalities hold:

$$\left(4\kappa + 2\sqrt{\kappa^{\alpha\beta}\kappa^{\beta\alpha}}\right) < r; $$
$$\left(4\kappa - 2\sqrt{\kappa^{\alpha\beta}\kappa^{\beta\alpha}}\right) < r. \tag{8.74}$$

The condition (8.74) is satisfied if both the internal conformity parameter κ and the intergroup interaction parameters $\kappa^{\alpha\beta}, \kappa^{\beta\alpha}$ are small. Then the symmetrical state (8.64) remains stable and all fluxlines converge to this stable stationary state. That means the fluxlines still behave in qualitatively similar fashion to those in Figure 8.1.

Case (1b)   Eigenvalue λ_+ positive and λ_- negative
This sub-case is realized if the following inequalities hold:

$$\left(4\kappa + 2\sqrt{\kappa^{\alpha\beta}\kappa^{\beta\alpha}}\right) > r; $$
$$\left(4\kappa - 2\sqrt{\kappa^{\alpha\beta}\kappa^{\beta\alpha}}\right) < r. \tag{8.75}$$

The condition (8.75) can only be satisfied if the magnitude of the intergroup interaction parameters dominates that of the internal conformity parameter. Since now one eigenvalue is positive, the symmetrical state (8.64) becomes an unstable saddle point.

The global evolution of the fluxlines depends on whether both groups $\mathcal{P}^{(\alpha)}$ and $\mathcal{P}^{(\beta)}$ are *imitator groups* or *snob groups*.

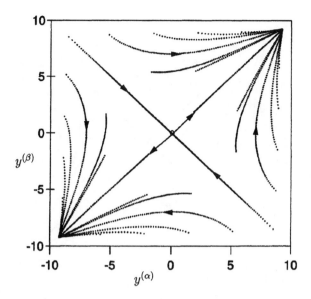

Figure 8.5   Demand fluxlines in $y^{(\alpha)}/y^{(\beta)}$-space for small internal conformity parameter $\kappa = 0.04$ and large intergroup imitation parameters $\kappa^{\alpha\beta} = \kappa^{\beta\alpha} = 0.2$. They converge to stationary points where $\mathcal{P}^{(\alpha)}$ and $\mathcal{P}^{(\beta)}$ prefer the same fancy good. Further parameters: $b = 10$; $p = 1$; $a = 1$; $c = 1$.

In the case of *imitator groups* with $\kappa^{\alpha\beta} > 0$ and $\kappa^{\beta\alpha} > 0$ the fluxlines approach stable stationary states in the first or third quadrant in the $y^{(\alpha)}/y^{(\beta)}$-space. These stationary states describe situations in which both groups $\mathcal{P}^{(\alpha)}$ and $\mathcal{P}^{(\beta)}$ prefer the *same fancy good* (namely good 1 in the first quadrant, or good 2 in the third quadrant). Figure 8.5 illustrates this case for a *small internal conformity parameter* $\kappa = 0.04$ and for *large intergroup imitation parameters* $\kappa^{\alpha\beta} = \kappa^{\beta\alpha} = 0.2$.

In the case of *snob groups* with $\kappa^{\alpha\beta} < 0$ and $\kappa^{\beta\alpha} < 0$ the fluxlines approach stable stationary states in the second or fourth quadrant in the $y^{(\alpha)}/y^{(\beta)}$-space. These stationary states describe situations in which groups $\mathcal{P}^{(\alpha)}$ and $\mathcal{P}^{(\beta)}$ prefer *different fancy goods* (namely $\mathcal{P}^{(\alpha)}$ good 2 and $\mathcal{P}^{(\beta)}$ good 1 in the second quadrant, or alternatively $\mathcal{P}^{(\alpha)}$ good 1 and $\mathcal{P}^{(\beta)}$ good 2 in the fourth quadrant). Figure 8.6 illustrates this case for a *small internal conformity parameter* $\kappa = 0.04$ and for *large intergroup marking off parameters* $\kappa^{\alpha\beta} = \kappa^{\beta\alpha} = -0.2$.

Case (1c)   Eigenvalue λ_+ positive and λ_- positive
This sub-case is realized if the following inequalities hold:

$$\left(4\kappa + 2\sqrt{\kappa^{\alpha\beta}\kappa^{\beta\alpha}}\right) > r;$$
$$\left(4\kappa - 2\sqrt{\kappa^{\alpha\beta}\kappa^{\beta\alpha}}\right) > r. \tag{8.76}$$

The condition (8.76) can only be satisfied, if the magnitude of the internal conformity parameter κ dominates the values of the intergroup interaction parameters. Since both eigenvalues are positive, the symmetrical state (8.64) is unstable. The

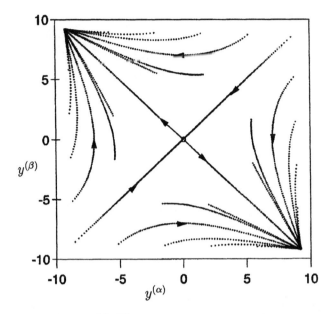

Figure 8.6 Demand fluxlines in $y^{(\alpha)}/y^{(\beta)}$-space for small internal conformity parameter $\kappa = 0.04$ and large intergroup marking off parameters $\kappa^{\alpha\beta} = \kappa^{\beta\alpha} = -0.2$. They converge to stationary points where $\mathcal{P}^{(\alpha)}$ and $\mathcal{P}^{(\beta)}$ prefer different fancy goods. Further parameters: $b = 10$; $p = 1$; $a = 1$; $c = 1$.

fluxlines now behave in qualitatively similar fashion to those in Figure 8.2 where they approach one of four stationary states.

The inequalities (8.74), (8.75) and (8.76) belonging to the sub-cases (1a), (1b) and (1c), respectively, are graphically exhibited in Figure 8.7.

Case 2: Conjugate Complex Eigenvalues λ_+ and λ_-

As already mentioned the intergroup interaction parameters $\kappa^{\alpha\beta}$ and $\kappa^{\beta\alpha}$ must now have opposite sign, so that one group, say $\mathcal{P}^{(\beta)}$, is a snob group with $\kappa^{\beta\alpha} < 0$, and the other group $\mathcal{P}^{(\alpha)}$ is an imitator group with $\kappa^{\alpha\beta} > 0$. We may again distinguish between *three sub-cases*.

Case (2a)   The eigenvalues λ_+ and λ_- have a negative real part
According to (8.73) this sub-case amounts to the condition

$$(4\kappa - r) < 0 \tag{8.77}$$

so that the internal conformity parameter κ must be small. Then the symmetrical state (8.64) is a stable focus and all fluxlines spiral into this stationary state. Figure 8.8 illustrates this case for a vanishing internal conformity parameter $\kappa = 0$ and antisymmetrical intergroup interaction parameters $\kappa^{\alpha\beta} = -\kappa^{\beta\alpha} = 0.8$.

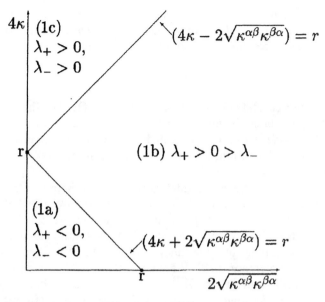

Figure 8.7 Domains of the parameters 4κ and $2\sqrt{\kappa^{\alpha\beta}\kappa^{\beta\alpha}}$ for the sub-cases (1a), (1b) and (1c) of real eigenvalues λ_+ and λ_-.

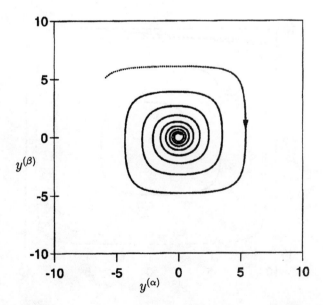

Figure 8.8 Demand fluxlines in $y^{(\alpha)}/y^{(\beta)}$-space for vanishing internal conformity parameter $\kappa = 0$ and strong antisymmetrical intergroup interaction parameters $\kappa^{\alpha\beta} = -\kappa^{\beta\alpha} = 0.8$. The fluxlines approach the stable focus P_0. Further parameters: $b = 10; p = 1; a = 1; c = 1$.

Case (2b)   The eigenvalues λ_+ and λ_- have a positive real part and the intergroup interaction parameters $\kappa^{\alpha\beta}$ and $\kappa^{\beta\alpha}$ dominate over the internal conformity parameter κ
According to (8.73) there must now hold the condition

$$(4\kappa - r) > 0 \tag{8.78}$$

so that the symmetrical state (8.64) is an *unstable focus*. On the other hand there exist no other stationary states. Numerical analysis shows that in this case the fluxlines merge into a *limit cycle*. This is demonstrated in Figure 8.9 for an internal conformity parameter $\kappa = 0.08$ which fulfils (8.78) and strong antisymmetrical intergroup interaction parameters $\kappa^{\alpha\beta} = -\kappa^{\beta\alpha} = 0.8$.

This case and its psycho-social interpretation is perhaps the most interesting scenario covered by the model. We assume as in Figure 8.9 that $\kappa^{\alpha\beta} > 0$ and $\kappa^{\beta\alpha} < 0$. Hence $\mathcal{P}^{(\alpha)}$ is an *imitator group* and $\mathcal{P}^{(\beta)}$ a *snob group*.

Let us start with a situation in the first quadrant of Figure 8.9 where both groups $\mathcal{P}^{(\alpha)}$ and $\mathcal{P}^{(\beta)}$ prevailingly buy the fancy good 1. Thus the members of $\mathcal{P}^{(\alpha)}$ who *imitate* the buying preferences of $\mathcal{P}^{(\beta)}$ are content with the situation.

Not so the members of group $\mathcal{P}^{(\beta)}$ who *dislike to be imitated* by group $\mathcal{P}^{(\alpha)}$. Therefore they *evade the situation* by buying a *different good*. (In our simple model the only available fancy good different from good 1 is good 2.) Since group $\mathcal{P}^{(\beta)}$ has, according to (8.78), a relatively high internal conformity parameter, they like to act *together*, so that now a preference for good 2 prevails in $\mathcal{P}^{(\beta)}$. This dynamics has led the fluxline into quadrant four.

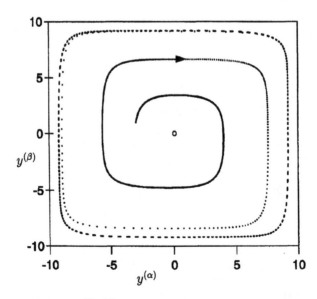

Figure 8.9 Demand fluxlines in $y^{(\alpha)}/y^{(\beta)}$-space for a moderate internal conformity parameter $\kappa = 0.08$ and strong antisymmetrical intergroup interaction parameters $\kappa^{\alpha\beta} = -\kappa^{\beta\alpha} = 0.8$. The fluxlines starting from the unstable P_0 approach a limit cycle. Further parameters: $b = 10; p = 1; a = 1; c = 1$.

However, the new situation is not appreciated by the members of group $\mathcal{P}^{(\alpha)}$ who now prevailingly own a different fancy good to that of the snobs of $\mathcal{P}^{(\beta)}$. Following their nature as imitators they begin to buy good 2, too, because it is more prestigious to have what group $\mathcal{P}^{(\beta)}$ has. Sooner or later the majority of $\mathcal{P}^{(\alpha)}$ conforms in possessing good 2, and the fluxlines have reached quadrant three.

This egalitarian situation is however disappointing to members of $\mathcal{P}^{(\beta)}$ who want to differentiate themselves from group $\mathcal{P}^{(\alpha)}$ and once more evade by buying conformingly a different fancy good (namely good 1). Thus the fluxline has reached quadrant 2.

It will return to quadrant 1 if thereupon the imitators of group $\mathcal{P}^{(\alpha)}$ once more imitate the snobs of $\mathcal{P}^{(\beta)}$ by buying preferentially good 1 which has won new prestige by being now preferred by the snobs.

Evidently this cyclical dynamics will repeat as long and often as the trend parameters κ, $\kappa^{\alpha\beta}$ and $\kappa^{\beta\alpha}$ remain the same.

Case (2c)   The eigenvalues λ_+ and λ_- have positive real part and the internal conformity parameter κ dominates the intergroup interaction parameters $\kappa^{\alpha\beta}$ and $\kappa^{\beta\alpha}$
The condition (8.78) still holds and the symmetrical state (8.64) remains an unstable focus. However, since the intergroup interaction parameters which were the reason for the restless dynamics of case (2b) are now *too weak to maintain this dynamics*, the limit cycle breaks up and the fluxlines end in one of four stable stationary states which have now come into existence as solutions of equations (8.48). This situation is illustrated by Figure 8.10 for which a strong internal conformity parameter $\kappa = 0.08$ and weak antisymmetrical intergroup interaction parameters $\kappa^{\alpha\beta} = -\kappa^{\beta\alpha} = 0.04$

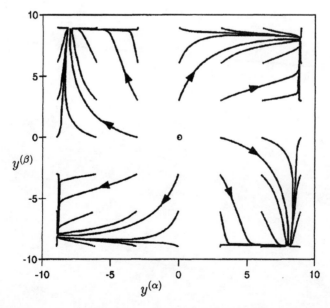

Figure 8.10   Demand fluxlines in $y^{(\alpha)}/y^{(\beta)}$-space for a moderate internal conformity parameter $\kappa = 0.08$ and weak antisymmetrical intergroup interaction parameters $\kappa^{\alpha\beta} = -\kappa^{\beta\alpha} = 0.4$. The fluxlines starting from the unstable P_0 approach one of the four stable stationary states. Further parameters: $b = 10$; $p = 1$; $a = 1$; $c = 1$.

have been chosen. Although the dynamics is different from that of case (1c) there appear four stationary states similar to those of Figure 8.2.

Outlook

The evaluation of the model in the simplest nontrivial cases in Sections 8.3.1 and 8.3.2 has already shown a manifold of scenarios for demand dynamics of fancy goods. It is to be expected that in more general cases with more than two fancy goods and more than two partially conforming and partially antagonistic consumer groups chaotic dynamics (i.e. strange attractors of the dynamic equations) could appear. Another natural step which would increase the complexity of the model would be its extension towards an adequate supply side dynamics which should include adaptation to, and even anticipation of, the consumer dynamics by the producers of fancy goods.

II.4 Application to Regional Science

Introductory Remarks

Urbanisation – meaning the *formation of new metropolitan areas* – is one of the mega-trends of the modern world and belongs to the most dramatic social evolutions of recent times. It is one of the central problems of Regional Science. Consequently we are going to treat some aspects of this problem with the method of Sociodynamics in the model outlined below.

Whereas in 1860 there existed 5 conurbations only of over one million inhabitants (Berlin, London, Paris, Beijing and Vienna) there appeared 109 such metropoles in 1960 and already 191 in 1975 (see [1], [2]); nowadays (1998) there exist more than 300 of them and their number is still growing. The cause for this steep increase of the number of inhabitants in metropoles is not primarily the general increase of the total average population but a *population rush* from hinterland to city generating a *migratory phase-transition*. This process will be treated in Section 9.4.1 of the following model. (For more details see also [3].)

Urban agglomerations, whether growing suddenly or smoothly, establish the *most complex systems* created so far by mankind.

The reason for this complexity is the existence of many *material* and *abstract organisational structures* which are *strongly intertwined* and *interdependent*. These substructures may be either ordered *"vertically"* – such as in the sequence person-family-group-community – and may then have a *bottom-up* and *top-down* interaction, or *"horizontally"* – e.g. in overlapping organisations such as firms, companies, corporations, associations, parties, churches – having a mutual groupwise or institutional interaction. We mention obvious examples: The distribution of firms, residential areas, universities, theaters and churches over the city interacts with the material, intellectual, political and religious life of the city's inhabitants.

The size of these substructures evidently ranges from small to large ones, and their evolution speed from fast to slow. One observes that *small* structures exhibit *flexibility* and a *fast* dynamics whereas *large* structures exhibit *inertia* and a *slow* dynamics.

Obviously the *city* can be considered as the *container* of these vertically and horizontally intertwined and interacting organized substructures.

261

In view of this complexity which cannot be fully captured in *one* model it is inevitable to find a *window of perception* which restricts the scope and space-time-scale of events to be taken into account within the frame of a partial model (see [4] and [5]).

However, the choice of the pertaining window of perception should be consistent in so far as it allows of a clear distinction between the endogenous strongly interacting variables whose dynamics is explicitly considered, and the exogenous trend-parameters which influence this dynamics from outside.

Once more, the *slaving- or entrainment-principle* yields some guideline for this choice if it is appropriately adapted and applied to the case of urban structures and their dynamics, in particular to the *visible material city structures*.

We have already mentioned that *small structures*, e.g. on the local level of individual buildings being erected or torn down, exhibit a *fast change* whereas *large structures*, e.g. the central area, the suburbs and street networks of a city exhibit a *slow change*. The relation between the fast development of local structures and the slow one of whole city areas is now explained by the slaving principle:

On the one side the fast development of local structures is driven and guided by the quasi-constant area structure into which it is embedded. That means the surrounding area serves as the (only slowly changing) environment and boundary condition under which each local structure evolves.

On the other side, the (slowly changing) area structure is of course nothing but the global resultant of the many local structures (i.e. houses, street-sections) of which an urban settlement is composed. However, similar to the longevity of the body of an animal whose organs are regenerating on a shorter time-scale than the life time of the whole body, the time of persistence of a whole urban area is much higher than the decay- and regeneration time of its local substructures.

This relation between the local and global level of urban structures will help us in finding a window of perception for a model of urban dynamics interacting with population evolution, which will be set up in the following chapter (see also [6]).

It should be mentioned that in the last two decades intense quantitative research about urban structures and urban dynamics has been implemented by several research groups who developed and applied different complementary model approaches in order to capture aspects of the complex urban system. We can only give an incomplete account of these comprehensive achievements by referring to the work of P. Allen and M. Sanglier [7], [8], [9], of R. White and G. Engelen [10], [11], [12], [13], and of D. Pumain, L. Sanders and T. Saint-Julien [14], [15], [16], [17]. The Sociodynamics group made the contributions [18], [19], [20], [21], [22], [23], [24], and [6], and the close cooperation of this group with the groups of D. Pumain and Y. Popkov has led to models integrating migration, urban dynamics, and settlement formation [25], [26], [27].

9. Urban Evolution and Population Pressure

9.1 Lines of Model Design

The model restricts its set of dynamic variables to *visible material structures* of the city (the city-configuration) and to the *distribution of the population* between the city and the hinterland (the population-configuration). Hence the economic and cultural background of the city is *only indirectly shown up* by the parameters and processes determining the dynamics of the configurations.

The relevant "*window of perception*" is chosen by considering a system of sites tessellating the city area on which different kinds of buildings (dwellings, factories, schools, stores, service-stations...) can be erected. These erection- or tearing-down-processes constitute the *relatively fast local dynamics* which are embedded into and guided by its *slowly changing urban environment*.

On the population side the most interesting process will be the migration between hinterland and city which is coupled to the evolution of the city-configuration. Therefore the model describes an *integrated dynamics of city- and population-evolution*.

The *type of the dynamics* must now be discussed:

It may be the ideal of city-planners to make and to realize far-reaching plans for the evolution of a city and to leave no space for uncoordinated random growth. If their plans would fully come true, city-evolution models would make no sense, because the plan would then uniquely determine the future evolution.

However, this ideal is normally thwarted for the following reasons:

(a) In the *short run* many competing and controversial interests of individuals and pressure groups (such as influential citizens, communal politicians, firms, environment protectors etc.) influence the planning process and make the eventual result partially unpredictable.

(b) Unforeseen events such as an unplanned population rush into the city or catastrophies may thwart the planning measures.

(c) In the medium run the ideals of planners, as well as the styles and ideologies of architects change after at most a few decades, together with the "Zeitgeist",

263

i.e. the spirit of the age. Since the life-time of urban structures is longer than zeitgeist-periods, sufficiently old cities will in general exhibit a mixture of styles and functions of the buildings.

For all these reasons a design for modelling urban dynamics is required which contains *both components*:

(a) planning trends and intentions which determine to a more or less high degree, and for a given era, the general direction of the step by step evolution of the city.

(b) an element of chance and randomness taking into account the not eliminable probabilistic character of communal decision making.

The modelling procedure of Sociodynamics takes into consideration both aspects: *Probabilistic transition rates* which determine the mean trend as well as the stochastic realisation of the step by step evolution of the city are the central element of model design. Evidently these rates should depend on the – sometimes conformist, sometimes controversial – *utility considerations* of the influential groups participating in the communal decision making. Here the concept "utility" must not be interpreted in too narrow a manner! It comprises the valuation of aesthetic, social, economic and environmental points of view as well as of material interests. The choice of the *utility functions*, which valuate the city configuration and determine the form of the transition rates is therefore of crucial importance.

   With given transition rates the *coupled equations for city- and population-evolution* can be set up. They comprise, according to the general modelling procedure of Sociodynamics, the *master equation* for the probability distribution over city- and population-configurations, and the *quasimeanvalue equations* for all variables of these configurations. Since both configurations consist of many variables we will restrict further analysis to the quasimeanvalue-equations.

9.2   The General Integrated Model for Urban and Population Evolution

9.2.1   The Variables of the City- and Population-Configuration

We make use of two kinds of variables describing the integrated system of the city and the population:

(a) *material variables* characterizing the city configuration, and

(b) *personal variables* characterizing the population configuration, i.e. the distribution of the population over the city and the hinterland.

Material Variables

Firstly, we introduce the material variables. Let the whole landscape under consideration be tessellated into a lattice of plots. Each plot is chosen *small enough* to be a homogenous piece of land, but *large enough* to erect, after being opened up, a considerable number ($\gg 1$) of even different kinds of buildings upon it. The plots are enumerated by $i(i_1, i_2)$, $j(j_1, j_2), \ldots$, where (i_1, i_2), $(j_1, j_2), \ldots$ are integer lattice coordinates. The whole landscape is, at a given time, separated into the area c of the city and the area h of the hinterland, so that each plot belongs to one of these areas. In the course of time the city can expand or shrink, so that the areas c and h can change with time. The demarcation between both areas is defined below.

At a given time the city planners open up a certain *capacity C_i at plot i* providing the possibility of building different kinds of structures or traffic infrastructure on that plot. Since all kinds of buildings will be subdivided into construction units, the capacity C_i is an integer, too, denoting the maximal number of construction units erectable on plot i. If C_i exceeds a certain threshold, say C_{thr}, the plot i belongs by definition to the city area c, otherwise the plot i belongs to the hinterland area h. Since the opened up capacities will slowly change with time, the city- and hinterland areas will slowly shift, too.

On each plot different kinds of *buildings* (such as lodgings, factories, schools, shops, supermarkets, service stations) and *traffic infrastructure elements* (such as street segments, tram- or subway-line segments or stations) may be erected or constructed. We denote the different *kinds* of erected or constructed buildings or structures by $K, L, \ldots$, and the integer $m_i^{(K)}$ denotes the number of construction units of kind K erected on plot i. (For instance, if "L" means "lodgings", the integer $m_i^{(L)}$ denotes the number of apartments = lodging construction units erected on plot i.)

The total set of all variables $m_i^{(K)}$ and of the capacities C_i, namely

$$\mathbf{m} = \{\ldots; \ldots, m_i^{(K)}, \ldots, m_i^{(L)}, \ldots, C_i; \ldots, m_j^{(K)}, \ldots, m_j^{(L)}, \ldots, C_j; \ldots\} = \{\mathbf{m}_i; \mathbf{m}_j; \ldots\}$$

(9.1)

is denoted as the *city configuration*. It provides an occupation number representation of the developmental state of the city (if $i \in c$) and of the hinterland (if $j \in h$), because it comprises the numbers of erected building- and construction-units of all kinds and the opened up capacities on all plots $i \in c$ and $j \in h$.

Since C_i is the (momentary) maximal capacity on plot i, the relation

$$\sum_K m_i^{(K)} \le C_i$$

(9.2)

must always be satisfied. For later use we introduce the aggregated quantities of the *total capacity* of the city and the hinterland, respectively:

$$C_c = \sum_{i \in c} C_i; \quad C_h = \sum_{i \in h} C_i.$$

(9.3)

Personal Variables

Secondly, we introduce personal variables in order to describe the distribution of the population over the city and the hinterland. In general one may distinguish sub-populations $\mathcal{P}^{(\alpha)}, \mathcal{P}^{(\beta)}$ differentiated by profession, age, sex, etc. Let $N_i^{(\alpha)}$ be the number of members of subpopulation $\mathcal{P}^{(\alpha)}$ living on plot i. Then we denote as *population configuration* the set of all variables $N_i^{(\alpha)}$:

$$\mathbf{N} = \{\ldots; \ldots, N_i^{(\alpha)}, \ldots; \ldots; \ldots, N_j^{(\beta)}, \ldots, ; \quad \} - \{\ldots; \mathbf{N}_i; \ldots; \mathbf{N}_j; \ldots\} \qquad (9.4)$$

This population configuration gives a rather detailed picture of the distribution of the members of different subpopulations over the sites $i \in c$ of the city and $j \in h$ of the hinterland.

It is now easy to introduce *aggregated personal variables*, in particular

$$N_c^{(\alpha)} = \sum_{i \in c} N_i^{(\alpha)} = \text{number of members of } \mathcal{P}^{(\alpha)} \text{ in the city;}$$

$$N_h^{(\alpha)} = \sum_{i \in h} N_i^{(\alpha)} = \text{number of members of } \mathcal{P}^{(\alpha)} \text{ in the hinterland;}$$

$$N_c = \sum_{\alpha} N_c^{(\alpha)} = \text{number of city inhabitants;} \qquad (9.5)$$

$$N_h = \sum_{\alpha} N_h^{(\alpha)} = \text{number of hinterland inhabitants;}$$

$$P = N_c + N_h = \text{total number of population.}$$

The *total configuration of macrovariables* is then given by

$$\mathbf{V} = \{\ldots; \mathbf{m}_i, \mathbf{N}_i; \ldots; \mathbf{m}_j, \mathbf{N}_j; \ldots\} = \{\mathbf{m}, \mathbf{N}\}. \qquad (9.6)$$

9.2.2   Utility-Driven Transition Rates

Elementary Evolution Steps

Let us first consider the elementary steps of the city- and population-evolution.

$$\mathbf{m} = \left\{\ldots, m_i^{(K)}, \ldots\right\} \Rightarrow \mathbf{m}_{i\pm}^{(K)} = \left\{\ldots, (m_i^{(K)} \pm 1), \ldots\right\}; \qquad (9.7)$$

$$\mathbf{N} = \left\{\ldots, N_i^{(\alpha)}, \ldots\right\} \Rightarrow \mathbf{N}_{i\pm}^{(\alpha)} = \left\{\ldots, (N_i^{(\alpha)} \pm 1), \ldots\right\}; \qquad (9.8)$$

$$\mathbf{N} = \left\{\ldots, N_j^{(\alpha)}, \ldots, N_i^{(\alpha)}, \ldots\right\} \Rightarrow \mathbf{N}_{ji}^{(\alpha)} = \left\{\ldots, (N_j^{(\alpha)} + 1), \ldots, (N_i^{(\alpha)} - 1), \ldots\right\}. \qquad (9.9)$$

The step $\mathbf{m} \Rightarrow \mathbf{m}_{i+}^{(K)}$ means, that one unit of kind K has been *erected* at plot i, and $\mathbf{m} \Rightarrow \mathbf{m}_{i-}^{(K)}$ means, that one unit of kind K has been *torn down* at plot i, whereas all other plots remain unchanged. The steps $\mathbf{N} \Rightarrow \mathbf{N}_{i\pm}^{(\alpha)}$ correspond to the *birth* or *death*, respectively, of one member of subpopulation $\mathcal{P}^{(\alpha)}$ at plot i, and the step $\mathbf{N} \Rightarrow \mathbf{N}_{ji}^{(\alpha)}$ corresponds to the *migration* of one member of subpopulation $\mathcal{P}^{(\alpha)}$ from plot i to plot j.

The Transition Rates

The steps (9.7), (9.8) and (9.9) are put into effect by probabilistic transition rates. Their general form was introduced in Chapter 3 and can immediately be applied to the present model.

For the case of transitions (9.7) within the *city-configuration* the rates read

$$w_i^K\left(\mathbf{m}_{i+}^{(K)}, \mathbf{m}; \mathbf{N}\right) \equiv w_{i\uparrow}^K(\mathbf{m}; \mathbf{N}) = \mu_i^K \exp[\Delta_{i+}^K(\mathbf{m}; \mathbf{N})];$$

$$w_i^K\left(\mathbf{m}_{i-}^{(K)}, \mathbf{m}; \mathbf{N}\right) \equiv w_{i\downarrow}^K(\mathbf{m}; \mathbf{N}) = \mu_i^K \exp[\Delta_{i-}^K(\mathbf{m}; \mathbf{N})],$$

(9.10)

where

$$\Delta_{i+}^K(\mathbf{m}; \mathbf{N}) = u\left(\mathbf{m}_{i+}^{(K)}, \mathbf{N}\right) - u(\mathbf{m}; \mathbf{N});$$

$$\Delta_{i-}^K(\mathbf{m}; \mathbf{N}) = u\left(\mathbf{m}_{i-}^{(K)}, \mathbf{N}\right) - u(\mathbf{m}; \mathbf{N}).$$

(9.11)

The factors μ_i^K are *mobilities*, i.e. measures for the general speed with which the corresponding transition takes place. They will in general depend on the plot i and the kind K of buildings, but not on the whole configuration $\{\mathbf{m}; \mathbf{N}\}$.

The $u(\mathbf{m}, \mathbf{N})$ are to be interpreted as measures of the "*utility*", or better "*appropriateness*" of the whole city- and population-configuration $\{\mathbf{m}, \mathbf{N}\}$, estimated and attributed to $\{\mathbf{m}, \mathbf{N}\}$ by all groups responsible for city development decisions. (If these influential groups $\mathcal{G}^{(\delta)}$, e.g. municipal authorities, city planners, architects, civil engineers, do *not* agree in their estimation of a given configuration $\{\mathbf{m}, \mathbf{N}\}$ and come to different utility functions $u^{(\delta)}(\mathbf{m}, \mathbf{N})$, one must take a weighted mean of these $u^{(\delta)}$ according to the relative influence of the groups $\mathcal{G}^{(\delta)}$.) The transition rates (9.10) thereupon depend on the *differences* of the configuration-utility *after* and *before* the step carried out at plot i concerning kind K of buildings. These utility-differences evidently play the role of "*driving forces*". If the utility *after the step* is higher (lower) than that *before the step*, the transition rate is enhanced (diminished).

The transition rates putting into effect the transitions (9.8) and (9.9) within the *population configuration* read, according to Chapter 3:

$$w_{i+}^\alpha(\mathbf{m}; \mathbf{N}_{i+}^{(\alpha)}, \mathbf{N}) \equiv w_{i\uparrow}^\alpha(\mathbf{m}; \mathbf{N}) = \beta_i^\alpha N_i^{(\alpha)};$$
(9.12a)

$$w_{i-}^\alpha(\mathbf{m}; \mathbf{N}_{i-}^{(\alpha)}, \mathbf{N}) \equiv w_{i\downarrow}^\alpha(\mathbf{m}; \mathbf{N}) = \delta_i^\alpha N_i^{(\alpha)}$$
(9.12b)

and

$$w_{ji}^\alpha(\mathbf{m}; \mathbf{N}_{ji}^{(\alpha)}, \mathbf{N}) \equiv w_{ji}^\alpha(\mathbf{m}; \mathbf{N}) = N_i^{(\alpha)} p_{ji}^\alpha[\mathbf{m}; \mathbf{N}],$$
(9.13)

where

$$p_{ji}^\alpha[\mathbf{m}; \mathbf{N}] = \nu_{ji}^\alpha[\mathbf{m}; \mathbf{N}] \exp[\Delta_{ji}^\alpha(\mathbf{m}; \mathbf{N})]$$
(9.14)

with

$$\Delta_{ji}^\alpha(\mathbf{m}; \mathbf{N}) = u_j^\alpha(\mathbf{m}; \mathbf{N}_{ji}^{(\alpha)}) - u_i^\alpha(\mathbf{m}; \mathbf{N}).$$
(9.15)

The rates (9.12a) and (9.12b) are birth- and death rates, respectively, within subpopulation $\mathcal{P}^{(\alpha)}$ at plot i. The rate (9.13) comes about by the migration of anyone of the $N_i^{(\alpha)}$ members of $\mathcal{P}^{(\alpha)}$ living on plot i to plot j, thus effecting the transition $\mathbf{N} \Rightarrow \mathbf{N}_{ji}^{(\alpha)}$. The $p_{ji}^{\alpha}[\mathbf{m}; \mathbf{N}]$ of (9.14) are *individual transition rates*. They depend on a *mobility* of members of $\mathcal{P}^{(\alpha)}$ between plots i and j, which is symmetrical: $\nu_{ji}^{\alpha} = \nu_{ij}^{\alpha}$, and the *difference* (9.15) of the utility *after* and *before* the migration from plot i to plot j of a member of $\mathcal{P}^{(\alpha)}$. The utility differences (9.15) again play the role of *driving forces* in the transition rates (9.13): If the utility for a member of $\mathcal{P}^{(\alpha)}$ is higher (lower) *after* the migration step from plot i to plot j than *before*, the transition rate is enhanced (diminished).

9.2.3 Evolution Equations

After having determined the general form of the transition rates for all elementary steps the evolution equations on the probabilistic and deterministic levels of description can be set up in straight-forward manner.

Master Equation

The central evolution equation on the probabilistic level is the master equation. It describes how the probability distribution $P(\mathbf{m}; \mathbf{N}; t)$ changes with time. The definition of the latter reads:

$$P(\mathbf{m}; \mathbf{N}; t) = \text{probability that the configuration} \{\mathbf{m}; \mathbf{N}\} \text{ is realized at time } t. \quad (9.16)$$

Because anyone out of the alternative configurations $\{\mathbf{m}; \mathbf{N}\}$ must *always be realized*, the distribution function (9.16) must satisfy the normalization condition

$$\sum_{\mathbf{m}, \mathbf{N}} P(\mathbf{m}; \mathbf{N}; t) = 1. \quad (9.17)$$

The master equation has the form:

$$
\frac{dP(\mathbf{m}; \mathbf{N}; t)}{dt} = \sum_K \sum_j \left[w_{j\uparrow}^K \left(\mathbf{m}_{j-}^{(K)}; \mathbf{N} \right) \cdot P\left(\mathbf{m}_{j-}^{(K)}; \mathbf{N}; t \right) - w_{j\uparrow}^K(\mathbf{m}; \mathbf{N}) \cdot P(\mathbf{m}; \mathbf{N}; t) \right]
$$
$$
+ \sum_K \sum_j \left[w_{j\downarrow}^K \left(\mathbf{m}_{j+}^{(K)}; \mathbf{N} \right) \cdot P\left(\mathbf{m}_{j+}^{(K)}; \mathbf{N}; t \right) - w_{j\downarrow}^K(\mathbf{m}; \mathbf{N}) \cdot P(\mathbf{m}; \mathbf{N}; t) \right]
$$
$$
+ \sum_\alpha \sum_{i,j(i \neq j)} \left[w_{ji}^\alpha \left(\mathbf{m}; \mathbf{N}_{ij}^{(\alpha)} \right) \cdot P\left(\mathbf{m}; \mathbf{N}_{ij}^{(\alpha)}; t \right) - w_{ji}^\alpha(\mathbf{m}; \mathbf{N}) \cdot P(\mathbf{m}; \mathbf{N}; t) \right]
$$
$$
+ \sum_\alpha \sum_i \left[w_{i\uparrow}^\alpha \left(\mathbf{m}; \mathbf{N}_{i-}^{(\alpha)} \right) \cdot P\left(\mathbf{m}; \mathbf{N}_{i-}^{(\alpha)}; t \right) - w_{i\uparrow}^\alpha(\mathbf{m}; \mathbf{N}) \cdot P(\mathbf{m}; \mathbf{N}; t) \right]
$$
$$
+ \sum_\alpha \sum_i \left[w_{i\downarrow}^\alpha \left(\mathbf{m}; \mathbf{N}_{i+}^{(\alpha)} \right) \cdot P\left(\mathbf{m}; \mathbf{N}_{i+}^{(\alpha)}; t \right) - w_{i\downarrow}^\alpha(\mathbf{m}; \mathbf{N}) \cdot P(\mathbf{m}; \mathbf{N}; t) \right]. \quad (9.18)
$$

The first line on the r.h.s. contains the probability flows into and out of configuration $\{\mathbf{m}, \mathbf{N}\}$ induced by *erection processes* of all kinds K on all sites j. The second line contains the corresponding flows induced by *tearing down processes*. The third line contains the flows into and out of configuration $\{m, N\}$ induced by *migration processes* of members of all subpopulations $\mathcal{P}^{(\alpha)}$ from all plots i to all plots $j(\neq i)$. The forth and fifth lines contain the corresponding probability flows induced by *birth- and death-processes*, respectively.

Quasi-meanvalue Equations

The true probabilistic evolution of a *single configuration* $\{m, N\}$ (out of the ensemble of configurations where probabilistic evolution is described by the master equation) is a *stochastic hopping process* from $\{m, N\}$ to neighbouring configurations $\{m', N'\}$. In the course of time this process produces a *stochastic trajectory* (see Chapter 12).

The probability of making one step of this process from $\{m, N\}$ in the small time interval δt is given by $w(m', N'; m, N)\delta t$, where $w(m', N'; m, N)$ is the transition rate from (m, N) to the corresponding neighbour configuration (m', N'). However, for most purposes it is sufficient to consider the path of the *mean evolution* from any $\{m, N\}$ through the configuration space. This path traversed with time is described by evolution equations for *quasi-meanvalues*. For the quasi-meanvalues $\hat{m}_j^{(K)}$ and $\hat{N}_j^{(\alpha)}$ of the variables of our model they read (see Chapter 12):

$$\frac{d\hat{m}_j^{(K)}}{dt} = w_{j\uparrow}^K(\hat{m}, \hat{N}) - w_{j\downarrow}^K(\hat{m}, \hat{N}); \tag{9.19}$$

$$\frac{d\hat{N}_j^{(\alpha)}}{dt} = \sum_i w_{ji}^\alpha(\hat{m}, \hat{N}) - \sum_i w_{ij}^\alpha(\hat{m}, \hat{N}) + w_{j\uparrow}^\alpha(\hat{m}, \hat{N}) - w_{j\downarrow}^\alpha(\hat{m}, \hat{N}). \tag{9.20}$$

Finally we have to make a plausible assumption about the capacities opened up on the plots i, in particular in the city area c, by city planners. We assume that the capacities C_i of the individual plots i contribute to the global capacity C_c of the city in the following manner:

$$C_i = f(i) \cdot C_c \quad \text{with} \quad \sum_{i \in c} f(i) = 1, \tag{9.21}$$

where $f(i)$ is a *capacity distribution function*. With respect to $f(i)$ we assume that there exist "cognitive maps" [28] in the mind of city planners leading to certain amazingly stable visions about the shape of the distribution of capacities over a city area. Explicit assumptions of the form of $f(i)$ will be discussed in Section 9.3. For the *global capacities* C_c and C_h of the city and the hinterland, respectively, we make the simplest possible assumption that they are functions of the respective global populations:

$$C_c = C_c(N_c); \quad C_h = C_h(N_h). \tag{9.22}$$

The master equation (9.18) and the quasi-meanvalue equations (9.19) and (9.20) together with assumptions (9.21) and (9.22) constitute the general form of the evolution equations for the coupled development of the city-configuration and the population-configuration.

However, the general model in this form is not yet fully explicit. Rather it provides a *modelling frame* for fully implemented models generated by explicit choice of the plot system, the variables, the utility functions and the capacities. In the next section we implement a simple explicit version of the model.

9.3   A Concrete Implementation of the Model

9.3.1   The Tessellated City; Hinterland- and City-Population

Tessellation and Distance

Firstly, in the implementation of the model, we choose a tessellation of the city-area into a square-lattice of plots $i(i_1, i_2); j(j_1, j_2), \ldots$ with integer cartesian coordinates $(i_1, i_2), (j_1, j_2), \ldots$ and a square network of streets in between.

The *distance* between plots will play an important role in the selforganizing formation of the city-structure. The most natural choice of distance in the case of a square-lattice is the so-called *Manhattan-distance*:

$$d(i, j) = |i_1 - j_1| + |i_2 - j_2|. \tag{9.23}$$

Buildings and Infrastructure

Since we are mainly interested in the distribution of places of *residence* and *work*, we restrict the material configuration, namely the different kinds of buildings and infrastructure to "*lodgings*" and "*factories*", i.e. to

$$\begin{aligned} m_i^{(1)} &= x_i = \text{number of lodging units on plot } i; \\ m_i^{(2)} &= y_i = \text{number of factory units on plot } i. \end{aligned} \tag{9.24}$$

The city configuration, which also includes the capacities $C = \{\ldots, C_i, \ldots\}$ on all plots $i \in c$, then reads:

$$\mathbf{m} = \{\ldots; x_i, y_i, C_i; \ldots\} = \{\mathbf{x}, \mathbf{y}, \mathbf{C}\}. \tag{9.25}$$

This implies that we do not explicitly treat the traffic infrastructure as a system with independent variables but simply consider it as adapting to the momentary distribution of buildings.

City- and Hinterland-Population

The general model of Section 9.2 provides in principle a rather detailed description of the population because it is subdivided into subpopulations $\mathcal{P}^{(\beta)}$ whose members are distributed over the plots i. However, in the present simple version of the model we assume a *homogeneous population* (omitting the index (β)) and are only interested in the question, which part of the population lives in the *city* and which in the *hinterland*. That means we only make use of the following global population variables (see also (9.5)).

$$N_c = n_c P = \text{ population of the city;} \tag{9.26a}$$

$$N_h = n_h P = \text{ population of the hinterland;} \tag{9.26b}$$

$$P = N_c + N_h = pP_0 \equiv pP(t = 0) = \text{ total population;} \tag{9.26c}$$

$$n_c + n_h = 1. \tag{9.26d}$$

Furthermore we introduce for later use the convenient variables:

$$N = N_c - N_h = n \cdot P; \quad n = n_c - n_h; \tag{9.27a}$$

$$N_c = \frac{1}{2}(P + N); \quad N_h = \frac{1}{2}(P - N); \tag{9.27b}$$

$$n_c = \frac{1}{2}(1 + n); \quad n_h = \frac{1}{2}(1 - n); \tag{9.27c}$$

$$-P \le N \le +P; \quad -1 \le n \le +1. \tag{9.27d}$$

The population configuration now takes the simple form:

$$\mathbf{N} = \{N_c, N_h\}. \tag{9.28}$$

9.3.2 Choice of Utility Functions

In order to have a fully explicit model we must now make explicit assumptions about

(a) the *utility of a city configuration* in the view of the municipal authorities comprising all decision makers for the development of the city

(b) the *personal utilities* of members of the city- and hinterland-population with respect to possible migration between both areas.

The Utility of City Configurations

We assume that the utility of a city configuration consists of two main terms:

$$u(\mathbf{x}, \mathbf{y}, \mathbf{C}) = u_L(\mathbf{x}, \mathbf{y}, \mathbf{C}) + u_I(\mathbf{x}, \mathbf{y}). \tag{9.29}$$

Here, $u_L(\mathbf{x}, \mathbf{y}, \mathbf{C})$ is a sum of *local utilities* $u_j(x_j, y_j, C_j)$ describing the measure of usefulness to erect x_j lodging units and y_j factory units and to leave z_j units of empty disposable space on plot j, where the local capacity is given by

$$C_j = x_j + y_j + z_j. \tag{9.30}$$

Evidently, $u_L(\mathbf{x}, \mathbf{y}, \mathbf{C})$ takes the form

$$u_L(\mathbf{x}, \mathbf{y}, \mathbf{C}) = \sum_{j \in c} u_j(x_j, y_j, C_j), \tag{9.31}$$

where the following form of the local utilities is sufficiently flexible and general:

$$
\begin{aligned}
u_j(x_j, y_j, C_j) &= p_j^x \ln(x_j + 1) + p_j^y \ln(y_j + 1) + p_j^z \ln(z_j + 1) + g_j^x x_j + g_j^y y_j \\
&= [p_j^x \ln(x_j + 1) + g_j^x x_j] + [p_j^y \ln(y_j + 1) + g_j^y y_j] \\
&\quad + p_j^z \ln(C_j + 1 - x_j - y_j).
\end{aligned}
\tag{9.32}
$$

In the last line of the r.h.s. of (9.32) the local capacity (9.30) has been used to eliminate the empty space z_j.

The logarithmic terms in (9.32) take into account that the marginal utility of one kind of building units on plot j slowly decreases with the growing number of units. Furthermore, the logarithmic terms prohibit x_j or y_j or z_j assuming the forbidden negative values (-1). For these values the logarithmic terms approach $(-\infty)$ with the consequence that the transition rates to such states vanish "automatically" because of their form (9.10). In the same way the last term on the r.h.s. of (9.32) prohibits transitions to states in which $(x_j + y_j)$ exceeds the capacity C_j. The coefficients p_j^x together with g_j^x, and p_j^y together with g_j^y, describe the "natural" preferences of plot j to erect on it buildings of kind x or y, respectively.

Against this, the *interaction utility* $u_I(\mathbf{x}, \mathbf{y})$ takes into account, that the utility of certain kinds of buildings on a plot i is not independent of the existence of the same kind or complementary kinds of buildings on neighbouring or distant plots j.

This positive or negative influence of the *relative position and distance* of the various kinds of buildings on the utility of the whole configuration is assumed to have the following *simplest possible form*:

$$
u_I(\mathbf{x}, \mathbf{y}) = \sum_{i,j \in c} a_{ij}^{xx} x_i x_j + \sum_{i,j \in c} a_{ij}^{xy} x_i y_j + \sum_{i,j \in c} a_{ij}^{yy} y_i y_j.
\tag{9.33}
$$

The signs and magnitudes of the coefficients in the interaction utility (9.33) determine the interaction effect. If one choses for instance $a_{ii}^{xy} \ll 0$ this means that it is *strongly disfavoured* and detrimental to build lodgings *and* factories on the *same* plot i. If, on the other hand, a_{ij}^{xy} is chosen as a *positive* coefficient for $d(i, j) \approx d_0$ this means that lodgings on plot i and factories on plot j at a distance $d(i, j) \approx d_0$ lead to a positive utility contribution. This is a plausible choice, since workers living in the lodgings need working places in factories in a neighbourhood of a reasonable distance d_0. The choice of positive coefficients a_{ij}^{xx} and a_{ij}^{yy} for $d(i, j) \approx d_1 \ll d_0$ is also plausible since it means, that it is useful to have further lodgings in the neighbourhood of lodgings, and further factories in the near neighbourhood of factories.

The interaction term in the configurational utility will turn out to be decisive for an urban dynamics leading to the selforganisation of a city structured into *residential* and *industrial* parts. The transition rates in the evolution equations lead to the successive generation of configurations for which the configurational utility approaches one of its relative optima.

The Personal Utilities

In the coarse-grained description chosen in this model for the population distribution the migrants only see the "city as such" and the "hinterland as such", i.e. they *do not differentiate* between *different* plots in the city or hinterland. Therefore, the personal utilities providing the driving forces for the migration can only depend on *global variables* characterizing the actual or foreseeable state of the city or hinterland.

We propose that the *global capacity* of the city and of the hinterland – rather than the already realized set of buildings – is the adequate measure for the utility of the city and the hinterland, respectively, in the view of potential migrants. Hence we propose the utilities:

$$v_c = S \cdot C_c; \quad v_h = S \cdot C_h, \tag{9.34}$$

where S is a sensibility factor and where C_c and C_h are the global capacities of city and hinterland, respectively (see (9.3)).

The utilities (9.34) will, at least in first approximation, *not* depend on the absolute size of the city-hinterland-system. Therefore we assume that the value of S scales as follows:

$$S = sP_0^{-1} \tag{9.35}$$

(where P_0 is the total population P at time $t = 0$), so that e.g. a doubling of all extensive quantities $C_h, C_c, N_h, N_c, P_0, \ldots$ leaves v_h and v_c invariant.

9.3.3 Choice of Capacity Distribution Functions

The only remaining functions to be concretely chosen are the global capacities C_c and C_h according to (9.22) and the – in general time-dependent – capacity distribution functions $f(i, t)$ according to (9.21).

The simplest proposal for the global capacities (which are determined by city-planners) is that they depend on the momentary population in the respective area as follows

$$\begin{aligned} C_c(t) &= C_{c0} + \kappa_c N_c(t); \\ C_h(t) &= C_{h0} + \kappa_h N_h(t) \end{aligned} \tag{9.36}$$

which means that they consist of a time-independent term representing a fundamental capacity provided for public buildings, and a time-dependent term proportional to the respective population. Here, the parameters κ_c and κ_h mean the number of capacity units being provided per inhabitant in the city and the hinterland, respectively.

Among the possibilities of choosing, according to the cognitive map [28] of city planners, capacity distribution functions $f(i, t)$ within the city (see (9.21)):

$$C_j(t) = f(j, t) \cdot C_c(t) \tag{9.37}$$

we only discuss here the *Gauss-distribution*. (A second plausible choice of $f(i, t)$ derived from the *Pareto rank-size-distribution* of city-clusters is explicitly discussed in [29].)

We start from the observation that normally in a city there exists a "central site" or a "central cluster of buildings" to which the highest capacity belongs. Around this central site further sites or plots of decreasing capacity are arranged, which end at plots of lowest capacity $C_j = C_{thr}$ at the boundary of the city. We assume that this capacity decrease depends on the distance $d(j, j_0)$ of a given plot j from the central site j_0, and has the form of a Gauss-function:

$$f(j, t) = f(j_0, t) \exp\left[-\frac{d^2(j, j_0)}{\sigma^2(t)}\right], \tag{9.38}$$

where the central site has the coordinates $j_0 = (0, 0)$ and $d(j, j_0)$ is the Manhattan-distance (9.23), and where $\sigma^2(t)$ is the variance of the Gauss-distribution. If the capacity on plots $j = b$ at the boundary of the city with distance $d(b, j_0) \equiv d_b$ is much smaller than that of the central site, i.e. if

$$f(b, t) = f(j_0, t) \exp\left[-\frac{d_b^2}{\sigma^2(t)}\right] \ll f(j_0, t) \tag{9.39}$$

the normalisation condition (9.21) leads to

$$\sum_{i \in c} f(i, t) \approx \sum_i^\infty f(i, t)$$

$$\approx f(j_0, t) \int_{-\infty}^{+\infty} \int_{-\infty}^{+\infty} \exp\left[-\frac{(|i_1| + |i_2|)^2}{\sigma^2(t)}\right] di_1 di_2 \tag{9.40}$$

$$= 2f(j_0, t) \cdot \sigma^2(t) \overset{!}{=} 1.$$

The result (9.40) can be inserted in (9.38) to yield the final form of the capacity distribution function:

$$f(j, t) = \frac{1}{2\sigma^2(t)} \exp\left[-\frac{d^2(j, j_0)}{\sigma^2(t)}\right]. \tag{9.41}$$

This function still depends on the width $\sigma(t)$ which has been left open so far. However under two extreme conditions of city-growth it can be determined completely.

The Case A of Fixed Capacity of Central Site

This case describes a city for which the central site $j = (0, 0)$ maintains a *stationary capacity* C_{cs} – which is normally fully exhausted by central buildings – whereas its boundary can freely expand. By definition the plots at the boundary of the city are those which have reached – due to the development of the city – a *threshold capacity* C_{thr}. The relation between C_{cs} and C_{thr} with the Gauss-distribution and the global city-capacity $C_c(t)$ follows from their definition and from equations (9.37) and (9.41):

$$C_{cs} \equiv C(j = j_0) = \frac{1}{2\sigma^2(t)} C_c(t); \tag{9.42}$$

$$C_{thr} \equiv C(j = b(t)) = \frac{1}{2\sigma^2(t)} \exp\left[-\frac{d_b^2(t)}{\sigma^2(t)}\right] C_c(t). \tag{9.43}$$

Solving (9.42) and (9.43) for the two quantities $\sigma^2(t)$ and $d_b(t)$ to be determined, one obtains:

$$\sigma^2(t) = \frac{C_c(t)}{2C_{cs}} \tag{9.44}$$

and

$$d_b^2(t) = \frac{C_c(t)}{2C_{cs}} \cdot \ln\left[\frac{C_{cs}}{C_{thr}}\right]. \tag{9.45}$$

This means that the width $\sigma(t)$ of the Gauss-distribution and the distance $d_b(t)$ of the boundary from the central site grow proportionally to the square root of the global capacity $C_c(t)$. Inserting (9.44) into (9.41) and (9.37), the capacity $C_j(t)$ at plot j takes the explicit form

$$C_j(t) = C_{cs} \exp\left[-\frac{2C_{cs}}{C_c(t)} d^2(j,j_0)\right]. \tag{9.46}$$

Many cities in countries with sufficient space for spreading out are examples for case A.

The Case B of Fixed Boundary

This case describes a city confined to an area with a boundary fixed by the environmental landscape (e.g. mountains or ocean). Then the only possibility of allowing of an increasing global capacity $C_c(t)$ is to increase the capacities of all city-plots including the central one (for instance by allowing of skyscrapers).

Having now a constant distance d_b of the boundary from the central site and still a constant threshold capacity C_{thr}, the time-dependence of the capacity $C_{cs}(t)$ of the central site must now be calculated. It follows from the assumption of a Gauss-distribution of the capacities and the conditions of case B:

$$C_{cs}(t) \equiv C(j=j_0) = \frac{1}{2\sigma^2(t)} C_c(t) \tag{9.47}$$

and

$$C(j=b) = C_{thr} = \frac{1}{2\sigma^2(t)} \exp\left[-\frac{d_b^2}{\sigma^2(t)}\right] C_c(t) \tag{9.48a}$$

or

$$\ln(\sigma^2(t)) + \frac{d_b^2}{\sigma^2(t)} = \ln\left[\frac{C_c(t)}{2C_{thr}}\right]. \tag{9.48b}$$

Equation (9.48) has two solutions for the variance $\sigma^2(t)$, of which only that with $\sigma^2(t) \ll d_b^2$ is allowed, since only then the capacities outside the boundary of the city can be neglected. By inserting the result in equation (9.47) there follows the time-dependent capacity $C_{cs}(t)$ of the central site.

In contrast to case A it follows from (9.48) that the width $\sigma(t)$ of the Gauss-distribution (9.41) is now shrinking for growing $C_c(t)$ and that the capacity $C_{cs}(t)$ of the central site even grows overproportionally with $C_c(t)$. The city of New York may approximately conform to this case B.

9.3.4 The Quasi-meanvalue Equations of the Concrete Model

After the choice of concrete utility functions (9.29), with (9.31), (9.32), (9.33) and (9.34) and concrete forms (9.37) of capacity functions, with (9.36), (9.41), we are now able to write down fully explicit evolution equations for the concrete model. Even this version of the model still contains many variables. Therefore we restrict the further consideration to the quasi-meanvalue equations only. They consist of three parts: (a) the evolution equations for the city configuration, (b) the evolution equations for the population configuration, and (c) the form of the time-dependent capacity functions for the city and the hinterland.

(a) Equations for the City Configuration

The variables are the quasi-meanvalues $\hat{x}_j$, $\hat{y}_j$ of lodging and factory units on plots $j(j_1, j_2)$. Their equations read

$$\frac{d\hat{x}_j}{dt} = w_{j\uparrow}^x(\hat{\mathbf{x}}, \hat{\mathbf{y}}; \mathbf{C}) - w_{j\downarrow}^x(\hat{\mathbf{x}}, \hat{\mathbf{y}}; \mathbf{C})$$
$$= \mu_j^x \exp[\Delta_{j+}^x(\hat{\mathbf{x}}, \hat{\mathbf{y}}; \mathbf{C})] - \mu_j^x \exp[\Delta_{j-}^x(\hat{\mathbf{x}}, \hat{\mathbf{y}}; \mathbf{C})] \qquad (9.49)$$

and

$$\frac{d\hat{y}_j}{dt} = w_{j\uparrow}^y(\hat{\mathbf{x}}, \hat{\mathbf{y}}; \mathbf{C}) - w_{j\downarrow}^y(\hat{\mathbf{x}}, \hat{\mathbf{y}}; \mathbf{C})$$
$$= \mu_j^y \exp[\Delta_{j+}^y(\hat{\mathbf{x}}, \hat{\mathbf{y}}; \mathbf{C})] - \mu_j^y \exp[\Delta_{j-}^y(\hat{\mathbf{x}}, \hat{\mathbf{y}}; \mathbf{C})] \qquad (9.50)$$

with the utility differences

$$\Delta_{j+}^x(\hat{\mathbf{x}}, \hat{\mathbf{y}}; \mathbf{C}) = u(\hat{\mathbf{x}}_{j+}, \hat{\mathbf{y}}; \mathbf{C}) - u(\hat{\mathbf{x}}, \hat{\mathbf{y}}; \mathbf{C})$$
$$= \left[p_j^x \ln \frac{\hat{x}_j + 2}{\hat{x}_j + 1} + g_j^x + a_{jj}^{xx} \right] + p_j^z \ln \frac{C_j - \hat{x}_j - \hat{y}_j}{C_j + 1 - \hat{x}_j - \hat{y}_j}$$
$$+ \sum_i a_{ji}^{xy} \hat{y}_i + \sum_i \left(a_{ji}^{xx} + a_{ij}^{xx} \right) \hat{x}_i \qquad (9.51a)$$

and

$$\Delta_{j-}^x(\hat{\mathbf{x}}, \hat{\mathbf{y}}; \mathbf{C}) = u(\hat{\mathbf{x}}_{j-}, \hat{\mathbf{y}}; \mathbf{C}) - u(\hat{\mathbf{x}}, \hat{\mathbf{y}}; \mathbf{C})$$
$$= \left[p_j^x \ln \frac{\hat{x}_j}{\hat{x}_j + 1} - g_j^x + a_{jj}^{xx} \right] + p_j^z \ln \frac{C_j + 2 - \hat{x}_j - \hat{y}_j}{C_j + 1 - \hat{x}_j - \hat{y}_j}$$
$$- \sum_i a_{ji}^{xy} \hat{y}_i - \sum_i \left(a_{ji}^{xx} + a_{ij}^{xx} \right) \hat{x}_i \qquad (9.51b)$$

and analogously:

$$\Delta^y_{j+}(\hat{\mathbf{x}}, \hat{\mathbf{y}}; \mathbf{C}) = u(\hat{\mathbf{x}}, \hat{\mathbf{y}}_{j+}; \mathbf{C}) - u(\hat{\mathbf{x}}, \hat{\mathbf{y}}; \mathbf{C})$$
$$= \left[p^y_j \ln \frac{\hat{y}_j + 2}{\hat{y}_j + 1} + g^y_j + a^{yy}_{jj} \right] + p^z_j \ln \frac{C_j - \hat{x}_j - \hat{y}_j}{C_j + 1 - \hat{x}_j - \hat{y}_j}$$
$$+ \sum_i a^{xy}_{ji} \hat{x}_i + \sum_i \left(a^{yy}_{ji} + a^{yy}_{ij} \right) \hat{y}_i \qquad (9.52\text{a})$$

and

$$\Delta^y_{j-}(\hat{\mathbf{x}}, \hat{\mathbf{y}}; \mathbf{C}) = u(\hat{\mathbf{x}}, \hat{\mathbf{y}}_{j-}; \mathbf{C}) - u(\hat{\mathbf{x}}, \hat{\mathbf{y}}; \mathbf{C})$$
$$= \left[p^y_j \ln \frac{\hat{y}_j}{\hat{y}_j + 1} - g^y_j + a^{yy}_{jj} \right] + p^z_j \ln \frac{C_j + 2 - \hat{x}_j - \hat{y}_j}{C_j + 1 - \hat{x}_j - \hat{y}_j}$$
$$- \sum_i a^{xy}_{ji} \hat{x}_i - \sum_i \left(a^{yy}_{ji} + a^{yy}_{ij} \right) \hat{y}_i. \qquad (9.52\text{b})$$

(b) Equations for the Population Configuration

The variables are the quasi-meanvalues $\hat{N}_c$, $\hat{N}_h$ of the population numbers of the city and the hinterland. Their equations read:

$$\frac{d\hat{N}_c}{dt} = w_{ch}(\hat{\mathbf{N}}) - w_{hc}(\hat{\mathbf{N}}) + w_{c\uparrow}(\hat{\mathbf{N}}) - w_{c\downarrow}(\hat{\mathbf{N}})$$
$$= p_{ch}(\hat{\mathbf{N}}) \cdot \hat{N}_h - p_{hc}(\hat{\mathbf{N}}) \cdot \hat{N}_c + \gamma_c \cdot \hat{N}_c \qquad (9.53)$$

and

$$\frac{d\hat{N}_h}{dt} = w_{hc}(\hat{\mathbf{N}}) - w_{ch}(\hat{\mathbf{N}}) + w_{h\uparrow}(\hat{\mathbf{N}}) - w_{h\downarrow}(\hat{\mathbf{N}})$$
$$= p_{hc}(\hat{\mathbf{N}}) \cdot \hat{N}_c - p_{ch}(\hat{\mathbf{N}}) \cdot \hat{N}_h + \gamma_h \cdot \hat{N}_h \qquad (9.54)$$

with the individual migration rates

$$p_{ch} = \nu \exp[v_c - v_h]; \quad p_{hc} = \nu \exp[v_h - v_c], \qquad (9.55)$$

where the utilities v_c and v_h of the city and the hinterland, respectively, are given by (9.34). The factor ν is the global mobility of the migrants between c and h and

$$\gamma_c = (\beta_c - \delta_c); \quad \gamma_h = (\beta_h - \delta_h) \qquad (9.56)$$

are the net birth rates (i.e. birth rates minus death rates) in the city and the hinterland, respectively.

(c) The Capacity Functions

The capacity functions provide the link between the equations (9.49), (9.50) of the city configuration and the equations (9.53), (9.54) of the population configuration, because they appear in both sets of equations. We repeat their form here:

$$C_c(t) = C_{c0} + \kappa_c N_c(t);$$
$$C_h(t) = C_{h0} + \kappa_h N_h(t) \tag{9.57}$$

and for plots j within the city:

$$C_j(t) = f(j, t) C_c(t)$$
$$= \frac{1}{2\sigma^2(t)} \cdot \exp\left[-\frac{d^2(j, j_0)}{\sigma^2(t)}\right] \cdot C_c(t). \tag{9.58}$$

9.4 Solutions of the Concrete Model

Looking at the structure of the total set of the equations (9.49)–(9.58) for the dynamics of the integrated city-plus-population system one observes that the equations (9.53) and (9.54) after inserting (9.34), (9.55), (9.56) and (9.57) form a system of two autonomous, nonlinear differential equations for $N_c(t)$ and $N_h(t)$. Therefore we can *separate off* these equations for the population sector and treat them first.

9.4.1 The Population Sector

We now make use of all quantities introduced in equations (9.26) and (9.27). All variables $\hat{N}_c, \hat{N}_h, \hat{N}; \hat{n}_c, \hat{n}_h, \hat{n}; \hat{P}, \hat{p}$ are functions of time. (The hat ^ reminds us of their quasimeanvalue nature.)

It turns out that the equations (9.53) and (9.54) can be further simplified if the *net birth rates* in the city and the hinterland *coincide*. Therefore we will firstly analyze this case.

Equal Net Birth Rates in City and Hinterland

In this case we presume

$$\gamma_c = \gamma_h = \gamma. \tag{9.59}$$

Taking the sum of equations (9.53) and (9.54) one obtains under condition (9.59)

$$\frac{d\hat{P}(t)}{dt} = \gamma(\hat{P})\hat{P}(t) \quad \text{or} \quad \frac{d\hat{p}}{dt} = \gamma(\hat{P})\hat{p}(t) \tag{9.60}$$

so that the evolution of the *total population* $\hat{P}(t)$ is *decoupled from the migration process* between city and hinterland. This holds, even if the global net birth rate $\gamma(\hat{P})$ still depends on the size of the population $\hat{P}$. We solve (9.60) explicitly for two choices of $\gamma(\hat{P})$:

$$\gamma(\hat{P}) = \gamma_0 = \text{const}; \tag{9.61a}$$

$$\gamma(\hat{P}) = \gamma_0 \left(1 - \frac{\hat{P}}{P_S}\right), \tag{9.61b}$$

where (9.61a) describes the case of an unrestricted growth and (9.61b) the case of a saturating growth of the total population. It is easy to solve (9.60) for both cases (9.61a) or (9.61b), respectively, with the results:

$$\hat{P}(t) = \hat{p}(t)P_0 = \exp(\gamma_0 t)P_0 \tag{9.62a}$$

or

$$\hat{P}(t) = \hat{p}(t)P_0 = \frac{P_S \exp(\gamma_0 t)P_0}{\{P_S + P_0[\exp(\gamma_0 t) - 1]\}}. \tag{9.62b}$$

Here, P_0 is the total population at time $t = 0$, and P_S is the saturation level of the total population reached at $t = \infty$ in case (9.62b).

Inserting (9.62a) or (9.62b) in the equations (9.53) and (9.54) and making use of (9.60) and (9.55) one now obtains equations for the migratory process alone, namely:

$$\frac{d\hat{n}_c(t)}{dt} = -p_{hc}\hat{n}_c + p_{ch}\hat{n}_h$$
$$= \nu\{-\exp[v_h - v_c] \cdot \hat{n}_c + \exp[v_c - v_h] \cdot \hat{n}_h\}; \tag{9.63}$$

$$\frac{d\hat{n}_h(t)}{dt} = +p_{hc}\hat{n}_c - p_{ch}\hat{n}_h$$
$$= \nu\{+\exp[v_h - v_c] \cdot \hat{n}_c - \exp[v_c - v_h] \cdot \hat{n}_h\}. \tag{9.64}$$

Both equations are not independent, because there holds (9.26d). Therefore the only relevant dynamic equation concerns the *difference of the population shares in city and hinterland*, namely $\hat{n} = \hat{n}_c - \hat{n}_h$. It reads:

$$\frac{d\hat{n}(t)}{dt} = (p_{ch} - p_{hc}) - (p_{hc} + p_{ch}) \cdot \hat{n}$$
$$= 2\nu\{\sinh(v_c - v_h) - \cosh(v_c - v_h) \cdot \hat{n}\}. \tag{9.65}$$

The equations (9.63), (9.64) and (9.65) become fully explicit, if the utility functions v_c and v_h are expressed by the capacities C_c and C_h (see (9.34)) and if the dependence of the capacities on the populations is inserted (see (9.36)). One obtains:

$$v_c = S \cdot C_c = s \cdot P_0^{-1}C_c = s \cdot [c_{c0} + \kappa_c p(t)\hat{n}_c]; \tag{9.66}$$
$$v_h = S \cdot C_h = s \cdot P_0^{-1}C_h = s \cdot [c_{h0} + \kappa_h p(t)\hat{n}_h] \tag{9.67}$$

with

$$C_{c0} = c_{c0} \cdot P_0; \quad C_{h0} = c_{h0} \cdot P_0 \tag{9.68}$$

and for the individual transition rates there follows:

$$p_{ch} = \nu \cdot \exp[v_c - v_h] = \nu \exp[a(t) + b(t) \cdot \hat{n}], \tag{9.69}$$
$$p_{hc} = \nu \cdot \exp[v_h - v_c] = \nu \exp[-a(t) - b(t) \cdot \hat{n}] \tag{9.70}$$

with the coefficients

$$a(t) = s\left[(c_{c0} - c_{h0}) + \frac{1}{2}(\kappa_c - \kappa_h)p(t)\right] \tag{9.71}$$

$$\text{and}\quad b(t) = \frac{1}{2}s(\kappa_c + \kappa_h)p(t). \tag{9.72}$$

The time-dependence of these coefficients stems from the growth factor $p(t)$ of the total population which must be taken from (9.62a) or (9.62b).

Insertion of (9.69) and (9.70) in (9.63) and (9.64), and in particular in (9.65) yields the final nonlinear evolution equations for $\hat{n}_c, \hat{n}_h$, and in particular for $\hat{n}$.

For the further discussion of equation (9.65) it is now very convenient and simultaneously illustrative to introduce an *evolution potential* $V(\hat{n}; t)$ by writing (9.65) in the form

$$\frac{d\hat{n}}{dt} = \nu\left\{e^{(a(t)+b(t)\hat{n})} \cdot (1 - \hat{n}) - e^{-(a(t)+b(t)\hat{n})} \cdot (1 + \hat{n})\right\}$$

$$\overset{!}{=} -\frac{\partial V(\hat{n}; t)}{\partial \hat{n}}. \tag{9.73}$$

The evolution potential, which is slowly time dependent due to the growth factor $p(t)$, can easily be found and reads:

$$V(\hat{n}; t) = V[\hat{n}; a, b] = \nu\left\{e^{(a(t)+b(t)\hat{n})}\left[\frac{b(t)\hat{n} - 1}{b^2(t)} - \frac{1}{b(t)}\right]\right.$$

$$\left. - e^{-(a(t)+b(t)\hat{n})}\left[\frac{b(t)\hat{n} + 1}{b^2(t)} + \frac{1}{b(t)}\right]\right\}. \tag{9.74}$$

Before proceeding with the analysis of the potential a remark should be made as to why it is useful and illustrative to write the evolution equation for $\hat{n}$ in the form (9.73) making use of a potential $V(\hat{n}, t)$. This comes from physics: The one-dimensional motion of a particle with mass m and coordinate $x(t)$ under the influence of a "conservative" force $f_1(x)$ which can be written in the form $f_1(x) = -\partial \tilde{V}(x)/\partial x$, and of a frictional force $f_2 = -gdx/dt$ obeys the Newtonian equation of motion: $m\frac{d^2x}{dt^2} = f_1(x) + f_2$, or $m\frac{d^2x}{dt^2} + g\frac{dx}{dt} = -\frac{\partial \tilde{V}(x)}{\partial x}$. In the case of a light particle with a very small mass m and a large frictional constant g this equation reads approximately $dx/dt = -\partial V/\partial x$, with $V = g^{-1}\tilde{V}$, and describes the motion of a light particle under the conservative force $f_1(x)$ in a viscous fluid – like syrup. After re-interpretation $x \Rightarrow \hat{n}$ and $V(x) \Rightarrow V(\hat{n}, t)$ the equation (9.73) has exactly the form of the approximate Newtonian equation of motion.

Let us now discuss the consequences of writing the evolution equation in the form (9.73): We denote the extrema $\hat{\hat{n}}(t)$ of $V(\hat{n}, t)$, i.e. its minima and maxima as *quasi-stationary states*. They are defined by

$$\left.\frac{\partial V(\hat{n}, t)}{\partial \hat{n}}\right|_{\hat{n}=\hat{\hat{n}}(t)} \overset{!}{=} 0. \tag{9.75}$$

After rearranging the r.h.s. of (9.73) it follows that (9.75) is equivalent to the equation

$$\ln\left(\frac{1+\hat{\bar{n}}(t)}{1-\hat{\bar{n}}(t)}\right) = 2(a(t)+b(t)\hat{\bar{n}}(t)). \qquad (9.76)$$

If the coefficients a and b were constant with time – which could only be so for constant growth factor $p(t) \Rightarrow p_0$ – the $\hat{\bar{n}}(t)$ would also become constant with time, i.e. $\hat{\bar{n}}(t) \Rightarrow \hat{\bar{n}}$, and would be *exact stationary solutions* of the evolution equation (9.73).

However, for a time-dependent potential, i.e. for time-dependent coefficients $a(t)$ and $b(t)$, the equation (9.73) does not possess stationary solutions at all.

Nevertheless there exist for slowly varying $a(t)$ and $b(t)$ slowly varying solutions of (9.73) which always remain *in the vicinity of the momentary minimum* of the slowly varying potential. These "almost equilibrium"-solutions of (9.73) are approximated by the quasistationary states $\hat{\bar{n}}(t)$.

It is therefore instructive to analyze these extrema of the potential and their slow evolution with time, before discussing the full dynamics of $\hat{n}(t)$ according to (9.73). The equation (9.76) will now be discussed in terms of a graphical representation of its l.h.s. and r.h.s. in Figure 9.1.

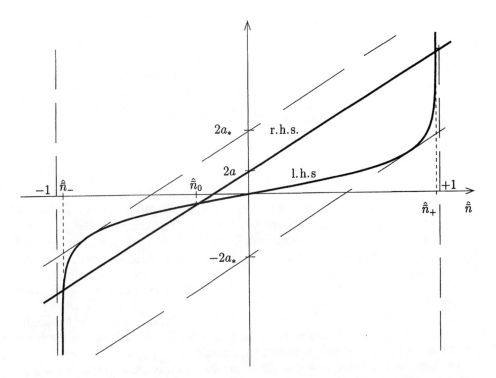

Figure 9.1 Graphical representation of the l.h.s. and r.h.s. of equation (9.76) for $a > 0$ and $b > 1$. In the depicted case there exist three solutions of (9.76) corresponding to two minima at $\hat{\bar{n}}_+$ and $\hat{\bar{n}}_-$ and one maximum at $\hat{\bar{n}}_0$ of the potential $V(\hat{n}; t) = V[\hat{n}; a, b]$.

The Figure (9.1) represents a case for which the slope $2b$ of the straight line $(2a + 2b\hat{n})$ exceeds 2 and where $-2a_* < 2a < 2a_*$. Then there exist three quasi-stationary states $\hat{\hat{n}}_-, \hat{\hat{n}}_0$ and $\hat{\hat{n}}_+$.

In general there can exist one, two or three quasistationary states. The corresponding conditions for the parameters b and a read:

(1) $b < 1$; a arbitrary:
     there exists *one* quasistationary point

(2) $b \geq 1$; $|a| > a_*(b)$
     there exists *one* quasistationary point

(3) $b \geq 1$; $|a| = a_*(b)$
     there exist *two* quasistationary points

(4) $b \geq 1$; $|a| < a_*(b)$
     there exist *three* quasistationary points

The parameter

$$a_*(b) = \frac{1}{2}\ln\left(\frac{1 - \sqrt{1 - 1/b}}{1 + \sqrt{1 - 1/b}}\right) + b\sqrt{1 - \frac{1}{b}} > 0 \tag{9.77}$$

determines the marginal value of $|a|$ for the transition from one to three quasistationary points.

Let us now discuss two characteristic scenarios for the slowly timedependent coefficients $a(t)$ and $b(t)$ in terms of the capacity parameters c_{c0}, c_{h0}, κ_c and κ_h. In addition, both coefficients depend on the growth parameter $p(t)$ and according to (9.61) and (9.72) there holds between them the relation:

$$a(t) = s(c_{c0} - c_{h0}) + \frac{(\kappa_c - \kappa_h)}{(\kappa_c + \kappa_h)}b(t). \tag{9.78}$$

In the first scenario we assume a *"constructive competition" between city and hinterland*. This means, both areas react positively to a growing population by providing capacity for them. This means that κ_c and κ_h, where perhaps $\kappa_c \gtrsim \kappa_h > 0$, are both positive and have the same order of magnitude. Also the basic capacities $C_{0c} = c_{0c}P_0$ and $C_{0h} = c_{0h}P_0$ are assumed to have the same order of magnitude. This means, that for $t = 0$, where $p(0) = 1$, the condition (4) can be fulfilled. Hence, two stable quasistationary states $\hat{\hat{n}}_- < 0$ and $\hat{\hat{n}}_+ > 0$ exist.

If $\hat{\hat{n}}_- < 0$ is realized, the majority of the total population lives in the hinterland, and if $\hat{\hat{n}}_+ > 0$ is realized, the majority lives in the city. It depends on the initial conditions, *which* of the two possibilities is realized.

The important question now arises, whether this situation persists for $t > 0$ and for growing population factor $p(t)$. The answer is *positive* for the following reasons: According to (9.72), $b(t)$ will grow with time, for growing $p(t)$, and therefore fulfil $b(t) \geq 1$ for all times $t > 0$, if $b(0) \geq 1$ was satisfied. Furthermore, whereas $a_*(b)$

grows with time essentially like $b(t)$ according to (9.77), the growth of $a(t)$ is given by (9.78) and is slower than that of $b(t)$ because of $(\kappa_c - \kappa_h)/(\kappa_c + \kappa_h) < 1$. Therefore the condition $|a(t)| < a_*(b(t))$ remains valid for all times $t > 0$, too. The result is, that *under conditions of constructive competition* between city and hinterland a stable situation of population distribution between c and h is *permanent*, even if the total population grows.

In the second, more dramatic scenario we assume a *worsening balance between city and hinterland.*

Such a situation is realized if C_{0h} and C_{0c} still have the same order of magnitude and if the condition (4) is still fulfilled at time $t = 0$, so that $\hat{n}_-$ and $\hat{n}_+$ exist and $\hat{n}_-$ can be realized at this initial time, i.e. the majority of the population can initially live in stable manner in the hinterland. However we now assume that $|\kappa_c| > |\kappa_h|$, but $\kappa_c > 0$ and $\kappa_h < 0$. The latter assumption means that growing hinterland population N_h leads to a *diminution* of the hinterland capacity $C_h(t)$.

Unfortunately, this case can be realistic and occurs for instance if the cattle of the growing hinterland population is over-grazing the pasture-ground so that the capacity $C_h(t)$ for living there is shrinking!

Let us discuss the consequences! Whereas $b(t)$ is still growing proportional to $p(t)$, so that $b(t) \geq 1$ is fulfilled for all times $t > 0$, if $b(0) \geq 1$, the situation changes concerning the second condition of (4): We have assumed that $|a| < a_*(b)$ for $t = 0$. However, because of $(\kappa_c - \kappa_h)/(\kappa_c + \kappa_h) > 1$ the coefficient $|a(t)|$ grows *faster than* $a_*(b(t))$. This means, there exists a time t^* for which $|a(t^*)| = a_*(b(t^*))$ is satisfied, and for $t > t^*$ there obtains $|a(t)| > a_*(b(t))$. At the critical time $t = t^*$ the stable quasi-stationary state $\hat{n}_-$ *disappears* and for $t > t^*$ the case (2) with only one (stable) quasistationary state is realized. The Figure 9.1 tells us that after the corresponding shift of the straight line the state $\hat{n}_+$ will be the only surviving quasistationary state. Correspondingly, the potential $V(\hat{n}; t) = V[\hat{n}; a(t), b(t)]$ will have changed its form from a "two minima and one maximum shape" to a "one-minimum shape".

One may guess that the disappearance of the quasistationary state $\hat{n}_-$ wherein the population majority lives in the hinterland leads to a dramatic *population rush from hinterland to city*, that means to a *migratory phase transition*. This is indeed true, but can only be proved by solving the fully dynamic equation (9.73).

We demonstrate this sudden population rush in two cases and with two different ways of presentation. Both cases are scenarios with a worsening balance between city and hinterland.

First Case

In the first case we assume an exponential growth of the total population according to (9.62a). Furthermore we assume the parameters:

$$s = 1; \quad \nu = 1; \quad (c_{c0} - c_{h0}) = -3.5; \quad \kappa_c = 6; \quad \kappa_h = -2$$

$$\text{and} \quad \gamma_0 = 0.001; \quad \text{there follows:} \quad t^* = 12.64. \tag{9.79}$$

The solution of (9.73) leads to $\hat{n}(t)$ (see Figure 9.2a) and from

$$\hat{N}_c(t) = \frac{1 + \hat{n}(t)}{2} P(t); \quad \hat{N}_h(t) = \frac{1 - \hat{n}(t)}{2} P(t) \tag{9.80}$$

one obtains $\hat{N}_c(t)$ and $\hat{N}_h(t)$ (see Figures 9.2(b) and 9.2(c)).

The evolution of $\hat{n}(t)$ is particularly interesting. The population at first practically remains in the quasistationary state: $\hat{n}(t) \approx \hat{\hat{n}}_-$. Even for $t \gtrsim t^*$, that means after disappearance of $\hat{\hat{n}}_-$, the evolution of $\hat{n}(t)$ is still remarkably slow, and only after $t \approx 21$ a sudden transition of $\hat{n}(t)$ to the surviving quasistationary state $\hat{\hat{n}}_+$ sets in (see Figure 9.2(a). The Figures 9.2(b) and 9.2(c) confirm this picture and show that after the migratory phase-transition practically the whole population is now settling in the city whereas there remains a depleted hinterland.

Second Case

In the second case we assume a logistic growth of the total population reaching a saturation level according to (9.62b). Furthermore we assume the parameters:

$$s = 1; \quad \nu = 1; \quad (c_{c0} - c_{h0}) = -4.5; \quad \kappa_c = 6; \quad \kappa_h = -2; \quad \gamma_0 = 0.001;$$
$$P_0 = 1; \quad P_S = 5; \quad \text{there follows } t^* = 458.93; \tag{9.81}$$
$$\hat{\hat{n}}_-(0) = -0.985840; \quad \hat{\hat{n}}_+ = 0.801759.$$

Here we make use of the evolution potential $V(\hat{n}; t)$ (see equation (9.74)) which gives an even more illustrative picture of what happens at a migratory phase transition for a worsening balance between city and hinterland.

The Figure 9.3(a) represents the evolution potential which slowly changes its shape with growing time. For small times it possesses two minima corresponding to the two stable quasistationary states $\hat{\hat{n}}_-$ and $\hat{\hat{n}}_+$. For growing time the one minimum at $\hat{\hat{n}}_-$ becomes more and more shallow whereas the other one at $\hat{\hat{n}}_+$ more and more deepens. At $t = t^* = 458.93$ the shallow minimum vanishes completely and for $t > t^*$ the potential possesses one minimum at $\hat{\hat{n}}_+$ only.

The Figure 9.3(b) shows the same potential together with the evolution of $\hat{n}(t)$ according to equation (9.73) which is represented by a "system-ball" which first stays in the shallow minimum until it suddenly "rolls down" into the deep minimum at $\hat{n} = \hat{\hat{n}}_+$.

Different Net Birth Rates in City and Hinterland

Now we allow of different net birth rates in the area of the city and the hinterland; that means we no longer presume (9.59). In this case the evolution of the total population $P(t)$ *cannot be separated* from the migration between c and h and it is also *impossible* to introduce an evolution potential.

(a)

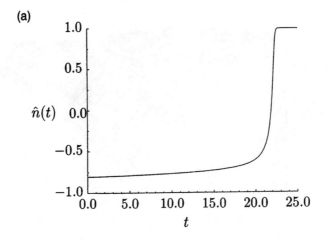

(b)

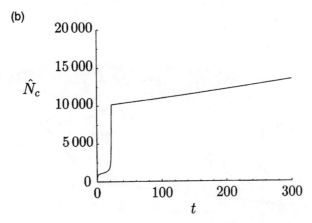

(c)

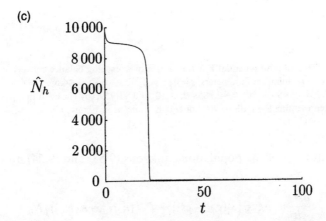

Figure 9.2   (a) Evolution of $\hat{n}(t)$ at worsening balance between c and h for exponential growth of the total population. Parameters: $s = 1; \nu = 1; c_{c0} - c_{h0} = -3.5; \kappa_c = 6; \kappa_h = -2; \gamma_0 = 0.001; t^* = 12.64$; (b) Evolution of $\hat{N}_c(t)$ under conditions as in Figure 9.2(a); (c) Evolution of $\hat{N}_h(t)$ under conditions as in Figure 9.2(a).

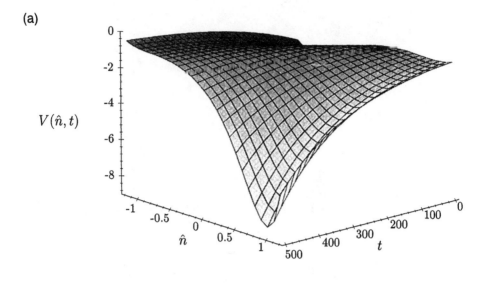

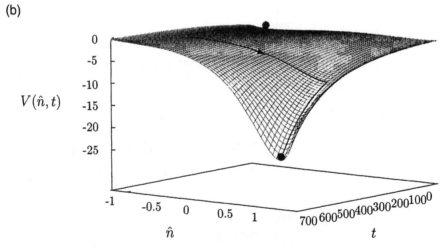

Figure 9.3 (a) The evolution potential $V(\hat{n}, t)$ in a case of worsening balance between c and h for logistic growth of the total population. Parameters: $s = 1$; $\nu = 1$; $(c_{c0} - c_{h0}) = -4.5$; $\kappa_c = 6$; $\kappa_h = -2$; $\gamma_0 = 0.001$; $P_0 = 1$; $P_S = 5$. $t^* = 458.93$; $\hat{n}_-(0) = -0.985840$; $\hat{n}_+(0) = 0.801759$; (b) The evolution potential $V(\hat{n}, t)$ with "system ball" representing the path of $\hat{n}(t)$ under conditions as in Figure 9.3(a).

The explicit form of the population equations (9.53) and (9.54) now reads

$$
\begin{aligned}
\frac{d\hat{N}_c}{dt} = {} & \nu \exp\left\{s[(c_{c0} - c_{h0}) + P_0^{-1}(\kappa_c\hat{N}_c - \kappa_h\hat{N}_h)]\right\}\hat{N}_h \\
& - \nu \exp\left\{-s[(c_{c0} - c_{h0}) + P_0^{-1}(\kappa_c\hat{N}_c - \kappa_h\hat{N}_h)]\right\}\hat{N}_c \\
& + \gamma_c\hat{N}_c
\end{aligned}
\tag{9.82}
$$

and

$$\frac{d\hat{N}_h}{dt} = -\nu \exp\left\{s[(c_{c0} - c_{h0}) + P_0^{-1}(\kappa_c \hat{N}_c - \kappa_h \hat{N}_h)]\right\}\hat{N}_h$$
$$+ \nu \exp\left\{-s[(c_{c0} - c_{h0}) + P_0^{-1}(\kappa_c \hat{N}_c - \kappa_h \hat{N}_h)]\right\}\hat{N}_c$$
$$+ \gamma_h \hat{N}_c \qquad (9.83)$$

We remark that the equations (9.82) and (9.83) are invariant against a rescaling of $\hat{N}_c(t)$, $\hat{N}_h(t)$ and $P_0 = (\hat{N}_c(0) + \hat{N}_h(0))$ with the *same factor*. Therefore it is convenient for numerical treatment to use small numbers for $\hat{N}_c(0)$ and $\hat{N}_h(0)$ and to rescale $\hat{N}_c(t)$, $\hat{N}_h(t)$ and P_0 afterwards.

We are interested in the question whether for different birth rates there might exist realistic cases in which the total population evolution reaches a *stationary state*. Such cases do indeed exist and one characteristic case will now be discussed.

In this case the *hinterland* has an initially high population, a *positive* constant net birth rate γ_h and a good fundamental capacity outfit c_{h0}, but a trend of *diminishing capacity* with growing population (i.e. a negative κ_h).

On the other hand, the *city* has an initially lower population, a smaller fundamental capacity outfit c_{c0}, but manifests a trend of extending its capacity with growing population (i.e. a positive κ_c); however it has a *negative net birth rate* γ_c. The parameters calibrating this case are chosen as follows:

$$\hat{N}_h(0) = 1.0; \quad \gamma_h = 1.0; \quad \kappa_h = -1.1;$$
$$\hat{N}_c(0) = 0.1; \quad \gamma_c = -0.5; \quad \kappa_c = +3.3; \qquad (9.84)$$
$$(c_{c0} - c_{h0}) = -1.$$

The result of these scenario assumptions can be seen in Figure 9.4(a),(b),(c).

The Figure 9.4(a) depicts the evolution of $\hat{N}_h$ versus $\hat{N}_c$ and shows that after an initial strong decrease of $\hat{N}_h$ and strong increase of $\hat{N}_c$ eventually a stationary equilibrium between $\hat{N}_h$ and $\hat{N}_c$ is levelling in at the stable fixpoint $\hat{N}_c = 0.4838$ and $\hat{N}_h = 0.2419$. The Figures 9.4(b) and (c) show separately the evolution with time of $\hat{N}_c(t)$ and $\hat{N}_h(t)$.

However, behind the seemingly harmless final end-state of $\hat{N}_c$ and $\hat{N}_h$ at $\hat{N}_c$ and $\hat{N}_h$ a permanent population dynamics is hidden: In the hinterland more people are born than die, and in the city the inverse is true; i.e. the hinterland is a population source and the city a population sink. On the other hand, the capacity of the hinterland is worsening, and that of the city is enhanced with increasing population. Therefore the reproductively prolific families of the hinterland have no other choice than to migrate into the city and there to compensate the lack of aftergrowth.

9.4.2 The City Sector

The evolution of the city configuration is of course a much more complicated process with many variables involved than the global migration process of the population

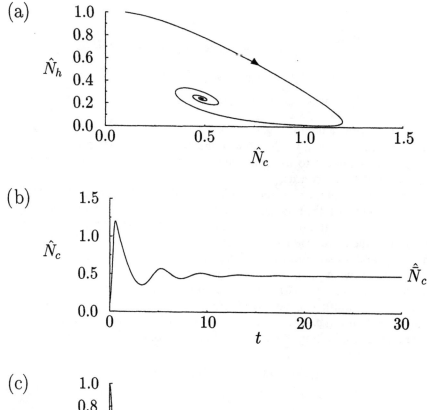

Figure 9.4 (a) Phasespace representation of the evolution of hinterland- versus city-population; (b) evolution with time of $\hat{N}_c(t)$; (c) evolution with time of $\hat{N}_h(t)$. Parameters: $\hat{N}_c(0) = 0.1$; $\hat{N}_h(0) = 1.0$; $(c_{c0} - c_{h0}) = -1$; $\kappa_c = 3.3$; $\kappa_h = -1.1$; $\gamma_c = -0.5, \gamma_h = 1.0$.

between hinterland and city. Therefore some general remarks are due before we go into the details of the numerical simulations of the set of equations (9.49) and (9.50).

Whereas the equations (9.53) and (9.54) of the population sector turned out to be *selfcontained*, this is not the case with the equations for the city sector! The capacities which depend on the population dynamics enter the equations (9.49) and (9.50) and therefore influence the evolution of the city.

We will restrict ourselves to cases where the population numbers N_h and N_c approach stationary states. Since the capacities $C_c(t)$ and $C_j(t)$ then also approach stationary values and simultaneously provide a limit for the number of building units x_j and y_j on each plot j it can be assumed that the city configuration, having started from some initial configuration, will also eventually reach a *stationary state*. The numerical simulations confirm this expectation!

The nonlinear equations (9.49) and (9.50) describing the city evolution in the multidimensional $\{x, y\}$-space will however in general possess *not only one but several attractors*, which will turn out to be fixed points, i.e. stable stationary states. Then the evolution of the city will exhibit the *fundamental phenomenon of path dependence*: This means that in the case of several attractors it will depend on the initial conditions as to *which one* of the attractors will eventually be approached. We will *demonstrate by example* that this path dependence exists for our model.

The model allows of a city with *fixed* boundary, or alternatively of a city with *expanding* boundary. In the simulations it has turned out that the latter case does not lead to principally new insights. Therefore we restrict ourselves to simulations of a *model-city with fixed boundaries*.

Even then, the model design is flexible enough to proceed from simple to more realistic scenarios by "switching on" complications of the city structure.

In the presentation of the "simple" and "realistic" scenarios we follow Stefan Stöckle [3], who has thoroughly investigated and extended (by introducing a special decision process for laying out parks) the model and worked out the following numerical simulations.

Thus we will start with a "*simple city*" possessing only lodgings and factories erected on a homogeneous area and proceed with a "*realistic city*" by including into the scenario at least a few realistic aspects such as the laying out of parks and the existence of preferred districts and of a river flowing through the city.

The "Simple" City

Scenario 1

In this scenario the city area (with fixed boundary) consists of a square lattice of 15×15 plots j, with coordinates $j(p, q)$. Only lodgings or factories can be erected on these plots and all plots have the same local utility.

The following parameter calibrations are made:

Initial Conditions

We assume the simplest possible initial condition

$$x_i(t = 0) = 0; \quad y_i(t = 0) = 0 \quad \text{for all plots } i \qquad (9.85)$$

that means we begin with an *empty city area*.

Population Sector

$$\hat{N}_c(0) = 200; \quad \hat{N}_h(0) = 500; \quad \gamma_c = -2.0; \quad \gamma_h = 3.1; \quad \nu = 1; \quad s = 1. \qquad (9.86)$$

Capacities

$$C_{c0} = 700; \quad C_{h0} = 400; \quad \kappa_c = 5; \quad \kappa_h = -2;$$
$$\sigma = 8 \text{ (width of Gauss-distribution)} \tag{9.87}$$

Transition Rates of City Configuration

$$\mu_j^x = 2; \quad \mu_j^y = 1 \text{ (erecting and tearing down mobilities)}$$
$$p_j^x = p_j^y = p_j^z = 1 \text{ (coefficients of local utilities)}$$
$$a^{xx}(0) = 0.01; \quad a^{xy}(0) = a^{yx}(0) = -0.015; \quad a^{yy}(0) = 0.01;$$
$$a^{xx}(1) = 0.004; \quad a^{xy}(1) = a^{yx}(1) = -0.005; \quad a^{yy}(1) = 0.0015;$$
$$a^{xx}(2) = -0.002; \quad a^{xy}(2) = a^{yx}(2) = 0.007; \quad a^{yy}(2) = -0.002; \tag{9.88}$$
$$a^{xx}(3) = -0.01; \quad a^{xy}(3) = a^{yx}(3) = 0.02; \quad a^{yy}(3) = -0.01;$$
$$a^{xx}(4) = 0.0005; \quad a^{xy}(4) = a^{yx}(4) = 0.003; \quad a^{yy}(4) = 0.0005;$$
$$a^{xx}(5) = 0.005; \quad a^{xy}(5) = a^{yx}(5) = -0.01; \quad a^{yy}(5) = 0.005.$$

(coefficients of interaction utilities)

The coefficients $a_{ij}^{\rho\sigma}$ are assumed to depend on the distance $d(i, j)$ between plot i and plot j only. Therefore we have used the notation $a_{ij}^{\rho\sigma} \Rightarrow a^{\rho\sigma}(d(i, j))$.

The results of the first scenario are depicted in Figures 9.5(a),(b),(c).

Figure 9.5(a) shows the (Gaussian) capacity distribution (9.58) over the plots of the city, where the Manhattan distance (9.23) between plots has been used.

Figure 9.5(b) shows the stationary distribution of lodgings, and Figure 9.5(c) the stationary distribution of factories having developed after a sufficiently long evolution time.

The distance-dependence of the coefficients of the interaction utilities has led to a *"selforganized" city structure, with separated lodging-districts and factory-districts.* The arrangement of the districts is symmetrical. This could have been predicted since the capacity and the interaction coefficients are only functions of Manhattan distances and the homogeneous initial condition (9.85) does not break the symmetry.

We remark that the model results react sensitively to changes of the distance dependence of the interaction coefficients: Modified changes may lead to a different arrangement of lodging- and factory-districts (see [3]).

Scenario 2

In this second scenario we wish to answer the question as to whether there already exists in the case of a "simple city" an *evolutionary path dependence*, i.e. whether the evolution can end in a different final stationary state (a different attractor), if one starts from a different initial state. We will demonstrate that the answer is positive!

All parameters of the second scenario are the same, namely chosen according to (9.86), (9.87) and (9.88), as in the first scenario. However we start from a different initial distribution of lodgings and factories over the plots (see Figure 9.6(a) and Figure 9.7(a), respectively).

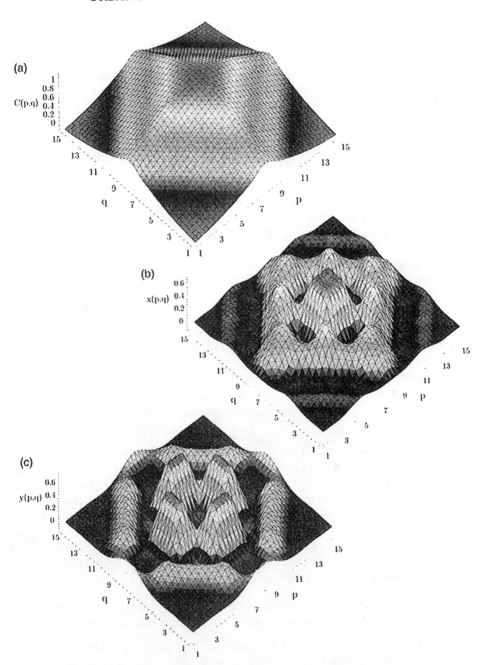

Figure 9.5 (a) Gaussian capacity distribution over the plots of the city assuming its dependence on the Manhattan distance from the central site according to (9.58); (b) Stationary distribution of *lodgings* eventually reached after starting from the initial condition (9.85) of an "empty city", and with parameters chosen according to (9.86), (9.87) and (9.88); (c) Stationary distribution of *factories* eventually reached after starting from the initial condition (9.85) of an "empty city", and with parameters chosen according to (9.86), (9.87) and (9.88).

The further evolution of the city configuration after 10000 and 50000 time steps is depicted for lodgings and factories in Figures 9.6(b),(c) and Figures 9.7(b),(c), respectively. Evidently the final state eventually reached in Figure 9.6(c) and Figure 9.7(c) concerning the lodging- and factory-distribution is *completely different* from that of the first scenario, presented in Figure 9.5(b) and 9.5(c). This proves the *appearance of path dependence in our model.*

The "Realistic" City

Scenario 3

In the following third scenario we try to imitate, still within the framework of the model, the evolution of a city under somewhat more realistic circumstances. We do this by taking into account two additional facts:

(a) The *geographical situation* within the city area is usually not so homogeneous as presumed in the "simple city scenarios" discussed above. For instance, a river may flow through the city, and there may exist a natural preference for some districts to erect certain kinds of buildings just there and not elsewhere.

   Such *exogenous causes* will of course destroy the equivalence among plots. They can however relatively easily be included in the model as *given facts*: Where a river flows or a steep hill prohibits the construction of buildings, the local capacity C_i must be made equivalent to zero. On the other hand, preferences for certain advantageous plots or districts to erect buildings there can be taken into account in the local utility terms (i.e. by the terms $g_j^x x_j$ and $g_j^y y_j$ in (9.32)).

(b) *Green parks* will usually disaggregate the otherwise too compact formations of buildings in a city and will serve for the recreation of its inhabitants. The laying out of parks is a *planned event* depending on decisions of the municipal authorities. Therefore the process of creating parks should be *endogenized* in the model in an appropriate way. This can be done by the following computerized decision and laying out algorithms added to the hitherto existing model:

   (1) Parks are created in residential districts with many lodgings. Therefore the first step consists in checking, on which site i_0 the number of lodgings x_{i0} exceeds a threshold value x_{thr} during the evolution.

   (2) The park should thereupon be created on that plot i in the neighbourhood of i_0 with the minimal number $(x_i + y_i)$ of building units on it.

   (3) After selecting this plot i the buildings on it are torn down and instead a park or recreation area r_i is layed out there.

   (4) Afterwards once and for all no buildings or further parks can be erected on plots with a park. Therefore the capacity is put equal to zero there.

   (5) The total number of parks generated in this manner is to be restricted appropriately in the city.

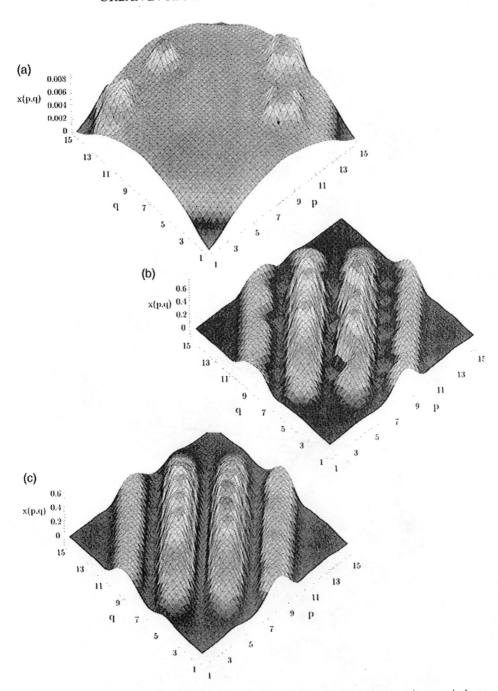

Figure 9.6 Evolution of the distribution of *lodgings* with model parameters chosen as in scenario 1, see Figure 9.5. (a) Initial distribution; (b) distribution after 10000 time steps; (c) distribution eventually reached after 50000 time steps.

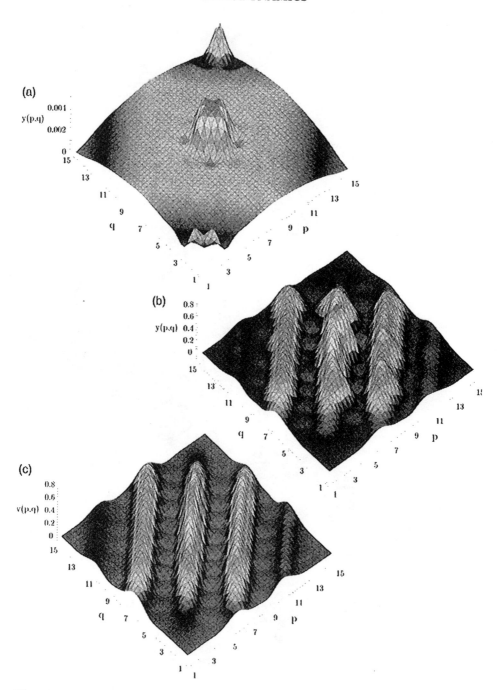

Figure 9.7 Evolution of the distribution of *factories* with model parameters chosen as in scenario 1, see Figure 9.5. (a) Initial distribution; (b) distribution after 10000 time steps; (c) distribution eventually reached after 50000 time steps.

Scenario 3 now assumes the same lattice of plots as in scenario 1 and 2; however there exists a "river" (hatched plots in Figures 9.8(a),(b) with capacity zero) in the city area and districts with positive or negative preferences for lodgings or for factories.

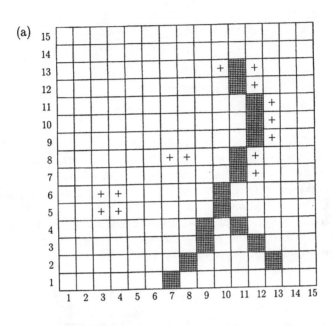

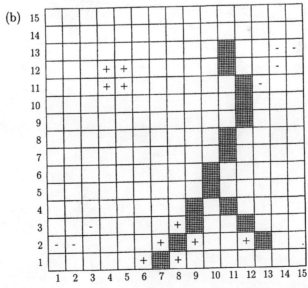

Figure 9.8 City area with lattice of plots, and a "river" (hatched plots with capacity zero). (a) shows the preferred districts for lodgings; (b) shows the preferred and rejected districts for factories.

The initial condition of scenario 3, namely "no lodgings, no factories, no parks" coincide with those of scenario 1, and also all parameters agree with those of scenario 1. The laying out of parks is now admitted, however their total number is restricted to 10. Therefore the parameter choice (9.88) must be complemented by additional interaction coefficients between lodgings and parks as well as factories and parks. They are chosen as follows:

$$
\begin{aligned}
a^{xr}(1) &= a^{rx}(1) = 0.05; & a^{yr}(1) &= a^{ry}(1) = -0.03; \\
a^{xr}(2) &= a^{rx}(2) = 0.01; & a^{yr}(2) &= a^{ry}(2) = -0.003; \\
a^{xr}(3) &= a^{rx}(3) = 0.006; & a^{yr}(3) &= a^{ry}(3) = 0.01; \\
a^{xr}(4) &= a^{rx}(4) = 0.005; & a^{yr}(4) &= a^{ry}(4) = -0.02; \\
a^{xr}(5) &= a^{rx}(5) = -0.005; & a^{yr}(5) &= a^{ry}(5) = 0.01.
\end{aligned}
\tag{9.89}
$$

The results of the simulation of scenario 3 which includes the algorithm for generating parks are presented in Figures 9.9, 9.10 and 9.11(a),(b), 9.12(a),(b).

Figure 9.9 shows the positions of the 10 parks. A comparison with Figure 9.11 confirms that they are situated in between the residential districts in accordance with the principles of their creation-algorithm.

Figure 9.10 exhibits the capacity distribution. Although still recognizable, the original Gaussian distribution is now strongly distorted, because the capacity is zero on the river and on plots occupied by a park.

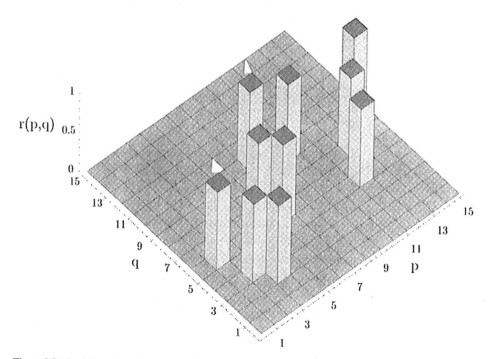

Figure 9.9 Position of parks endogenously generated by a decision algorithm in scenario 3.

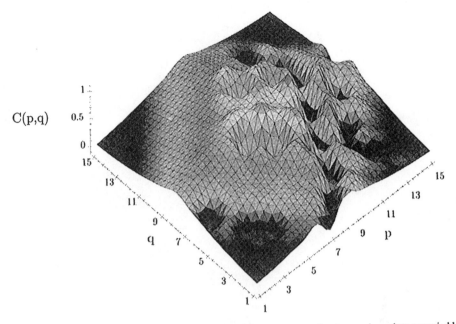

Figure 9.10 Capacity distribution of scenario 3. The capacity is zero on the river and on plots occupied by a park.

(a)

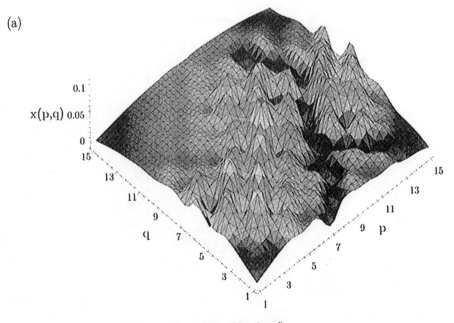

Figure 9.11 (Continued)

(b)

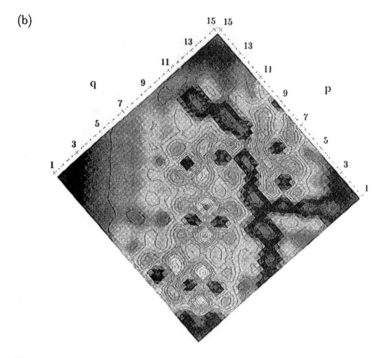

Figure 9.11 Stationary distribution of lodgings having evolved under the conditions of scenario 3. (a) Perspective representation of the density of lodgings; (b) Topographic representation of the density of lodgings.

(a)

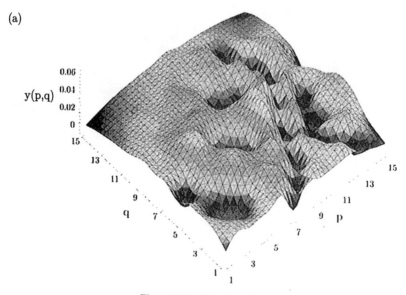

Figure 9.12 (Continued)

(b)

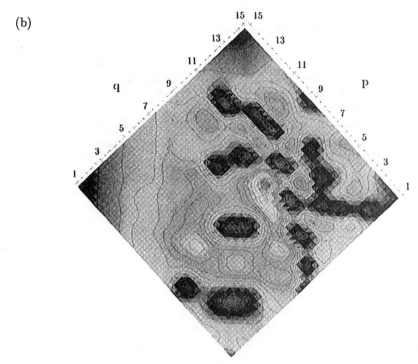

Figure 9.12 Stationary distribution of factories having evolved under the conditions of scenario 3. (a) Perspective representation of the density of factories; (b) Topographic representation of the density of factories.

The main results of the simulation are represented in Figures 9.11 and 9.12 which show the stationary distributions of lodgings and factories, respectively, which have now developed. Many "forces" have contributed to their form: Not only the distance-dependent interactions within and between lodgings, factories and parks, but also the capacity distribution and the existence of a river and of preferred districts for the erection of either lodgings or factories.

Concluding Remarks

The three scenarios, in particular the third one, have demonstrated that relatively complex city configurations can be generated on the basis of the model equations after appropriate calibration of the parameters. In order to simulate an existing real city structure there must of course be chosen an appropriately adapted grid of plots and all parameters must be calibrated accordingly.

It could be objected that such a model does not yield more than a plain imitation of a real city which exists anyway.

This objection would however *underestimate the predictive capacity of models* such as that presented above for the following reason: We have seen that all parameters appearing in the model have a *concrete and interpretable meaning* and that the relatively complex results *react sensitively to changes of parameters*. Also the effect of *path dependence*, i.e. the dependence of the final state on initial conditions was demonstrated.

Therefore one can *trace back* the simulation results to special choices of parameters and initial conditions in an ensemble of intelligently selected scenarios. This makes possible the *analysis and interpretation of chains of causation in the complex evolution of a city*.

On the other hand, such an analysis is much more difficult if not impossible if only a few really existing cities are at our disposal for analysis, because in all real cases the existing state is generated by *many superimposed causes* which cannot be disentangled, because their influence cannot be systematically varied or even switched on and off as in the case of scenario simulations on the basis of a quantitative model!

Part III
Mathematical Methods

Remarks about the Choice of an Appropriate Mathematical Formalism for Modelling Social Dynamics

In part I of this book some principles have been established for a broad approach towards a quantitative modelling of dynamic processes in human society. Some arguments which are relevant for the choice of appropriate mathematical methods are repeated here:

(1) In all social sciences we have the *micro-level* of decisions and actions of individuals and the *macro-level* of appropriately defined macro-variables which evolve rather smoothly and dominate the social process. The latter are also denoted as *order parameters*.

   Often we must interpolate between micro- and macro-level several *meso-levels*, for instance groups, institutions and other structures which behave as entities and units of their own and exhibit a characteristic shape ("Gestalt").

(2) Between all levels there exists interaction. This interaction takes place "*bottom up*" from the lower (micro-)levels to the higher (macro-)levels as well as inversely "*top down*" from the higher to the lower levels.

   Both kinds of interaction together establish a *form of causal interdependence* which differs from the unidirectional relation between causes and effects. The mathematical formalism must embrace this more complex causality from the very beginning!

(3) On the micro-level of decisions and actions of individuals there are *not (yet) available any micro-equations of motion*! (Such equations, if they could be found, would have to include the brain-dynamics of individuals in terms of appropriate brain variables capable of describing cognitions, decisions and actions as dependent upon internal motivations and external conditions. Such equations would however introduce the immense complexity of brain processes into sociodynamics, whereas we need only the *outcomes of these processes*, namely the individual decisions and actions influencing the social process.)

303

Our conclusion is therefore, that formalisms which would include brain micro-equations in order to obtain social macrodynamics are not the appropriate starting point for a sufficiently concise formulation of sociodynamics.

Instead, the elementary concepts at the bottom of the microlevel should contain *probabilistic* and *deterministic* ingredients as well in order to describe the socially relevant decisions and actions of individuals *resulting* from their rational and emotional dealing with their *internal disposition* and *external condition.*

On the one side the *probabilistic nature* of these elementary concepts is necessary because the decisions and actions of individuals always contain a random element of "free will", "free choice" and "chance" which cannot be included within a fully deterministic description.

On the other side, decisions and actions are always guided, directed and channelled and therefore *partially predetermined* by internal dispositions characterized by trendparameters and by external conditions characterized by the macrovariables of the society.

In Chapter 3 we have introduced *probabilistic transition rates* which describe the changes of attitudes and actions of individuals in dependence on trendparameters and macrovariables.

These transition rates seem to meet all the requirements of elementary concepts for sociodynamics: They contain by definition probabilistic and deterministic ingredients as required in 3. Simultaneously they provide the connection between the micro- and macro-level of the society as required in 2: Describing individual activities in dependence on the macrovariables of the society, the transition rates imply the *top-down interaction*. On the other hand, the aggregated cooperative effect of the individual changes of attitudes or actions induced by the transition rates leads to a change of the macrovariables, hence of the macrostate of the society; thus it provides the *bottom-up interaction* from micro- to macro-level.

We therefore require a *mathematical formalism which makes use of these transition rates* in order to describe the global probabilistic evolution of the society or its sectors on the macrolevel. Simultaneously this formalism will then imply the mutual relation between macro- and micro-level!

This *universal mathematical formalism for stochastic dynamic systems* does indeed exist and has been developed by several great mathematicians. In the center of this formalism there stands the *master equation* describing the evolution with time of the probability distribution over the variables of stochastically moving members of an ensemble of systems.

Due to its great generality this formalism can be applied to systems of very different nature. In the natural sciences, in particular in Statistical Physics, widespread applications of the master equation formalism in thousands of articles has existed for many decades, whereas in the social sciences the comprehensive use of this formalism is of more recent date. It was the intention of the author together with his research group, and it is the intention of this book to demonstrate the universal capacity of this formalism for a broad spectrum of applications in the social sciences.

In the following chapters we shall give an introduction into the master equation formalism which should be readable without too specialized a mathematical knowledge. Completeness of methods is not the purpose of these chapters. Instead it is intended to give a coherent insight into the properties of the master equation and the equations derived from it. Our intention is to focus on those problems which are relevant for the purpose of modelling social systems with this formalism.

Although the Chapters 10, 11, and 12 are practically selfcontained we give some references to related literature about the mathematical methods and their applications for the interested reader. One part of this literature treats the mathematics of probabilistically or stochastically evolving systems [1], [2], [3], [4], [5], [6], [7], [8], whereas the other part treats nonlinear dynamic systems including those exhibiting deterministic chaos: [9], [10], [11], [12], [13] and [14].

10. The Master Equation

This chapter contains a selfcontained description of the main general properties of the master equation and its solutions. It comprises in Section 10.1 the derivation of the master equation and in Section 10.2 the formulation of the master equation in configuration space which is of particular value for sociodynamics because it allows us to describe configuration-dependent migratory processes within a population consisting of different kinds of subpopulations.

The next sections are devoted to the properties of solutions of the master equation. In Section 10.3 the famous Boltzmannian *H*-theorem is derived which shows that – under certain weak conditions for the transition rates – all time-dependent solutions merge into the same unique stationary solution. In Section 10.4 an exact time-dependent solution of a special master equation in configuration space is derived and discussed as an example. In Section 10.5 the condition of detailed balance is introduced which sometimes may be satisfied for the transition rates. If detailed balance holds it is easy to construct the stationary solution of the master equation.

10.1 The Derivation of the Master Equation

We begin with a comparison between the deterministic and the probabilistic description of evolving systems:

Deterministically versus Probabilistically Evolving Systems

Consider a system which can pass through different states in the course of time. For simplicity we assume that the states of the system are discrete (noncontinuous), so that the index i characterizing each state is a discrete number or a set $i = \{i_1, i_2, \ldots, i_n\}$ of discrete numbers. Let us further assume that at an initial time t_0 the system is in state $i_0 = i(t_0)$. Two possible descriptions of its evolution with time are then feasible:

(a)   The information about the dynamics of the system can be *complete*. In this case the description is *fully deterministic* and leads to the unique determination of the states $i(t)$ at later times.

Any computer can be taken as an example for such a deterministic system with a finite – though very large – number of states i. Beginning with an initial state i_0 set by the program, the central processor, the memory units and the peripheral devices of the computer traverse a sequence of states $i_1, i_2, \ldots i_N$ which are fully predetermined by the program. The unique unambiguous result of the calculation represents the final state of the system.

(b) Alternatively, the information about the dynamics of the systems under consideration can be *incomplete*. In this case the description of the evolution with time can only be a *probabilistic* one. That means, an exact prediction of the state $i(t)$ reached by an individual system is not possible. Instead, the members of an *ensemble of systems* of identical structure – each of them prepared in the same initial state $i(t_0)$ – will develop into in general *different* states $i(t)$ at time t. The best information available in this situation is the *probability* (measured approximately by the relative frequency within the ensemble) that a system reaches the state i at time t, given that it was prepared in state i_0 at time t_0. This special probability $P(i, t \,|\, i_0 t_0)$ is denoted as "conditional probability". The master equation will turn out to be the tool for determining this quantity.

Comparing the deterministic with the probabilistic evolution we must state that the latter is the more general form of dynamics, since the case of incomplete knowledge about the system comprises complete knowledge as a limit case whereas the converse is not true. The limit case of (almost) complete knowledge of the dynamics is revealed by the shape of the probability distribution $P(i; t)$ itself: In this case the master equation leads to the evolution of a distribution having one and only one outstanding mode sharply peaked around the most likely state $i_{max}(t)$. This means that the systems of the ensemble assume the state $i = i_{max}(t)$ with overwhelming probability ($\widehat{=}$ relative frequency) at time t, whereas all other states $i \neq i_{max}(t)$ are highly improbable at the same time. Evidently this case describes an almost deterministic evolution of the systems along the path $i(t) \approx i_{max}(t)$.

Some General Concepts of Probability Theory

Before deriving the master equation it is useful to introduce some fundamental concepts of probability theory that especially apply to *dynamic systems* exhibiting stochastic evolution.

As before, it is assumed that the system can be in one of a number of mutually exclusive states which are characterized by an index i consisting of one discrete number or a multiple of discrete numbers. In the course of time transitions between different states of a system can take place. Since in general one does not know with certainty in which state an individual system is, the (by definition positive semidefinite) probability distribution function

$$P(i; t) \geq 0 \qquad\qquad (10.1)$$

is introduced. By definition $P(i; t)$ is the probability of finding the system in state i at time t. This probability has the following *statistical interpretation*: In an ensemble of a very large number of systems of the same structure and the same set of possible states $i, j, \ldots$ one would find systems in state i at time t with the *relative frequency* $P(i; t)$. (Strictly speaking, this holds only in the limit of an ensemble with an *infinite* number of systems.)

Since each system is with certainty in exactly one of the states i at any time t, the probability distribution function has to satisfy the condition

$$\sum_{\{i\}} P(i; t) = 1. \tag{10.2}$$

Furthermore, we now introduce the most important quantity for the time evolution of the system, the *conditional probability*

$$P(i_2, t_2 \mid i_1, t_1; \text{p.h.}). \tag{10.3}$$

By definition, this is the probability of finding the system in the state i_2 at time t_2, *given* that it was with *certainty* in the state i_1 at time t_1. The conditional probability is fundamental for the dynamics of the systems of the ensemble, since it describes how the probability spreads out in the time interval $(t_2 - t_1)$, given that it was concentrated on the state i_1 at time t_1.

The letters "p.h." in (10.3) indicate that the conditional probability may also depend on the *previous history* of the system, that means on states traversed *before* arriving at state i_1 at time t_1.

Fortunately, for many dynamic systems the so called *Markov assumption* holds. The Markov assumption postulates that the evolution within time of the conditional probability $P(i_2, t_2 \mid i_1, t_1)$ *only depends* on the initial state i_1 at time t_1 and the state i_2 at t_2, but *not* on states of the system *prior* to t_1. In other words: After arriving at state i_1 at time t_1 the system has "*lost its memory*" so that states before t_1 *do not matter* in the process of the further probabilistic evolution. (We remark that non-Markovian processes for which $P(i_2, t_2 \mid i_1, t_1, \text{p.h.})$ depends on the previous history may often be transformed into Markovian processes by extending the space of states $i, j, \ldots$ into a more comprehensive set of states $I, J, \ldots$: If the state I at time t also comprises the *memory* about the history of the system before time t, the non-Markovian conditional probability $P(i_2, t_2 \mid i_1, t_1, \text{p.h.})$ may be transformed into a Markovian conditional probability $P(I_2, t_2 \mid I_1, t_1)$ in the extended state space.)

Since the space of states i characterizing the systems at one time t can in most cases be chosen in a manner guaranteing that the Markov assumption holds we shall presume its validity from now on and cancel the "p.h." in (10.3).

Let us now draw some conclusions about the properties of the conditional probability. As a consequence of its definition the following equations must be satisfied:

$$P(i_2, t_1 \mid i_1, t_1) = \delta_{i_2 i_1}, \tag{10.4}$$

where $\delta_{i_2 i_1}$ is the Kronecker symbol defined by

$$\begin{aligned} \delta_{i_2 i_1} &= 1 \quad \text{for} \quad i_2 = i_1; \\ \delta_{i_2 i_1} &= 0 \quad \text{for} \quad i_2 \neq i_1 \end{aligned} \tag{10.5}$$

and

$$\sum_{\{i_2\}} P(i_2, t_2 \,|\, i_1, t_1) = 1. \tag{10.6}$$

Equation (10.4) follows because at time $t_2 = t_1$ an evolution has not yet taken place and the probability must still be fully concentrated at the state i_1. Equation (10.6) holds since each system at any time t_2 will have to be *with certainty* in one of the states $\{i_2\}$.

From equations (10.4) and (10.6) it becomes clear that the conditional probability is nothing but a special probability distribution $P_{i_1 t_1}(i_2; t_2)$, namely that one, which evolves from the initial distribution $P(i; t_1) = \delta_{i i_1}$.

A further important concept is the *joint probability*

$$P(i_n t_n, i_{n-1} t_{n-1}, \dots, i_2 t_2, i_1 t_1). \tag{10.7}$$

By definition the n-fold joint probability (10.7) is the probability of finding the system in state i_1 at t_1, i_2 at $t_2 \dots$ and jointly in state i_{n-1} at t_{n-1} as well as in state i_n at t_n.

From this definition it follows that the lower joint probabilities can be obtained from the higher ones by the following *reduction formula*:

$$P(i_3 t_3, i_1 t_1) = \sum_{\{i_2\}} P(i_3 t_3, i_2 t_2, i_1 t_1) \tag{10.8}$$

or, in the general case, by

$$P(i_n t_n, \dots, i_{k+1} t_{k+1}, i_{k-1} t_{k-1}, \dots, i_1 t_1) = \sum_{\{i_k\}} P(i_n t_n, \dots, i_{k+1} t_{k+1}, i_k t_k, i_{k-1} t_{k-1}, \dots, i_1 t_1).$$
$$\tag{10.9}$$

Clearly, the summation of $P(i_3 t_3, i_2 t_2, i_1 t_1)$ in (10.8) over all possible states $\{i_2\}$ at time t_2 leads to the probability of being in state i_1 at t_1 and jointly in state i_3 at t_3 *irrespective* of the state at time t_2. That means it leads to $P(i_3 t_3, i_1 t_1)$.

Under the Markov assumption all joint probabilities can now be expressed by the simple probability (10.1) and by the conditional probability (10.3). For the two-fold joint probability this can be seen as follows:

For a system, the event of being in state i_1 at time t_1 and the event of reaching state i_2 at time t_2 after starting from i_1 at t_1 are independently occurring (if they occur at all). The first event has probability $P(i_1; t_1)$ and the second event the probability $P(i_2, t_2 \,|\, i_1, t_1)$. The probability that both independent events occur is the product of the occurrence probability of the single events, i.e. $P(i_2, t_2 \,|\, i_1, t_1) \cdot P(i_1; t_1)$. On the other hand, the joint probability $P(i_2 t_2, i_1 t_1)$ is synonymous with the probability for the occurrence of both events, namely that the system is in i_2 at t_2 and in i_1 at t_1.

Therefore we obtain the formula

$$P(i_2 t_2, i_1 t_1) = P(i_2, t_2 \,|\, i_1, t_1) P(i_1; t_1). \tag{10.10}$$

The argumentation can easily be generalized and then leads to the *composition formula* for the *n*-fold joint probability in terms of conditional probabilities and $P(i_1, t_1)$

$$P(i_n t_n, i_{n-1} t_{n-1}, \ldots, i_2 t_2, i_1 t_1) = P(i_n, t_n \,|\, i_{n-1}, t_{n-1}) \ldots P(i_2, t_2 \,|\, i_1, t_1) P(i_1; t_1). \tag{10.11}$$

Combining now the *reduction formulas* of the type (10.8), (10.9) with the *composition formulas* of the type (10.10), (10.11), we obtain further important equations, namely the formula for the *propagation of probabilities* and the famous *Chapman-Kolmogorov equation*.

From equation (10.10) we obtain by taking the sum over i_1 and making use of the reduction formula:

$$\begin{aligned}
P(i_2; t_2) &= \sum_{\{i_1\}} P(i_2 t_2, i_1 t_1) \\
&= \sum_{\{i_1\}} P(i_2, t_2 \,|\, i_1, t_1) P(i_1; t_1).
\end{aligned} \tag{10.12}$$

Equation (10.12) shows how the probability distribution $P(i; t)$ is propagated from t_1 to t_2 by means of the conditional probability $P(i_2, t_2 \,|\, i_1, t_1)$. Therefore, the latter is also referred to as *the propagator*.

Furthermore, inserting in the reduction formula (10.8) on both sides of the composition formula (10.11), one obtains:

$$P(i_3, t_3 \,|\, i_1, t_1) P(i_1; t_1) = \sum_{\{i_2\}} P(i_3, t_3 \,|\, i_2, t_2) P(i_2, t_2 \,|\, i_1, t_1) P(i_1; t_1) \tag{10.13}$$

Since equation (10.13) holds for *arbitrary* initial distributions $P(i_1; t_1)$, one concludes that also

$$P(i_3, t_3 \,|\, i_1, t_1) = \sum_{\{i_2\}} P(i_3, t_3 \,|\, i_2, t_2) P(i_2, t_2 \,|\, i_1, t_1) \tag{10.14}$$

must hold. Equation (10.14) is the *Chapman-Kolmogorov equation*. It shows how the propagator from t_1 to t_3 can be decomposed into propagators from t_1 to t_2 and from t_2 to t_3.

The Master Equation

The master equation is now easily derived from the propagation equation (10.12). Whereas the latter equation describes how the distribution $P(i_1; t_1)$ evolves into the distribution $P(i_2; t_2)$ within the *finite* time interval $(t_2 - t_1)$ – under the proviso that the form of the propagator is already known – the master equation is nothing but *a differential equation version* of the propagation equation (10.12). This form is however more appropriate for further treatment. It follows from considering equation (10.12) for times $t_1 = t$ $t_2 = t + \tau$, where $\tau = (t_2 - t_1)$ is an *infinitesimally short* time interval.

The short time evolution equation (10.12) then reads:

$$P(i_2; t + \tau) = \sum_{\{i_1\}} P(i_2, t + \tau \mid i_1, t) P(i_1; t). \tag{10.15}$$

The short-time propagator in (10.15) is now expanded in a Taylor series around t with respect to the variable $t_2 = t + \tau$, yielding

$$P(i_2, t + \tau \mid i_1, t) = P(i_2, t \mid i_1, t) + \tau \frac{\partial P(i_2, t_2 \mid i_1, t)}{\partial t_2}\bigg|_{t_2=t} + 0(\tau^2). \tag{10.16}$$

Making use of (10.4) and (10.6) one obtains

$$P(i_2, t \mid i_1, t) = \delta_{i_2 i_1} \tag{10.17}$$

and

$$\sum_{\{i_2\}} \frac{\partial P(i_2, t_2 \mid i_1, t)}{\partial t_2}\bigg|_{t_2=t} = 0, \tag{10.18}$$

where the sum extends over *all* states i_2 of the system. Introducing now the *probability transition rate*

$$w_t(i_2 \mid i_1) \equiv \frac{\partial P(i_2, t_2 \mid i_1, t)}{\partial t_2}\bigg|_{t_2=t} \tag{10.19}$$

and taking into account (10.17) and (10.18), we may now reformulate (10.16) as follows:

$$P(i_2, t + \tau \mid i_1, t) = \tau w_t(i_2 \mid i_1) + 0(\tau^2) \quad \text{for} \quad i_2 \neq i_1 \tag{10.20}$$

and

$$P(i_2, t + \tau \mid i_1, t) = 1 - \sum_{i \neq i_1} \tau w_t(i \mid i_1) + 0(\tau^2) \quad \text{for} \quad i_2 = i_1. \tag{10.21}$$

The interpretation of equations (10.20), (10.21) is straight forward: Given that the system was in state i_1 at time t, the probability (10.20) that it reaches a state $i_2(\neq i_1)$ in the infinitesimally small time interval τ is proportional to that interval τ and to the transition rate from i_1 to i_2 at time t. On the other hand, the probability (10.21) of remaining in the same state i_1 during the infinitesimally small time interval τ is equal to 1 minus the probability transferred to all other states $\mathbf{i} \neq \mathbf{i}_1$ within that time interval τ.

The *master equation* is now established by inserting (10.20), (10.21) into (10.15). Dividing equation (10.15) through τ and going over to the limit $\tau \to 0$ it follows after trivial rearrangements of terms:

$$\lim_{\tau \to 0} \frac{P(\mathbf{i}_2; t + \tau) - P(\mathbf{i}_2; t)}{\tau} \equiv \frac{dP(\mathbf{i}_2; t)}{dt}$$
$$= \sum_{\mathbf{i}_1} w_t(\mathbf{i}_2 \mid \mathbf{i}_1) P(\mathbf{i}_1; t) - \sum_{\mathbf{i}_1} w_t(\mathbf{i}_1 \mid \mathbf{i}_2) P(\mathbf{i}_2; t), \tag{10.22}$$

where the sums extend over all $\mathbf{i}_1 \neq \mathbf{i}_2$. (Formally one may extend the sums over all $\mathbf{i}_1$ including $\mathbf{i}_1 = \mathbf{i}_2$ with arbitrary $w_t(\mathbf{i}_2 \mid \mathbf{i}_2)$, since the additional terms cancel in (10.22).)

Since the master equation (10.22) is valid for any probability distribution $P(\mathbf{i}; t)$ it holds in particular for the conditional probability, i.e. the propagator $P(\mathbf{i}, t \mid \mathbf{i}_0, t_0)$.

We shall now give a plausible interpretation to the master equation: At first we note that evidently the term $\tau \cdot w_t(\mathbf{i}_2 \mid \mathbf{i}_1) P(\mathbf{i}_1; t)$ is the probability transferred from state $\mathbf{i}_1$ to state $\mathbf{i}_2$ in the time interval τ. Since this probability amount is by definition positive, the *transition rate $w_t(\mathbf{i}_2 \mid \mathbf{i}_1)$ must also be a positive (semi-)definite quantity.* The term $w_t(\mathbf{i}_2 \mid \mathbf{i}_1) P(\mathbf{i}_1; t)$ can now be denoted as the *probability flow* (per unit of time) from state $\mathbf{i}_1$ to state $\mathbf{i}_2$. Then the master equation turns out to be a *rate equation for probabilities*: The change per unit of time of the probability of a state $\mathbf{i}_2$, that is the l.h.s. of (10.22), is the consequence of two counteractive terms: The first term on the r.h.s. of (10.22) describes the probability flow from all other states $\mathbf{i}_1$ *into* state $\mathbf{i}_2$. The second term on the r.h.s. of (10.22) describes the probability flow *from* the state $\mathbf{i}_2$ into all other states $\mathbf{i}_1$. Both terms have opposite sign and their net effect determines the increase or decrease per unit of time of the probability $P(\mathbf{i}_2, t)$.

The master equation gives the most detailed knowledge available about the evolution of an ensemble of stochastic systems. Evidently the (probabilistic) transition rates $w_t(\mathbf{i}_2 \mid \mathbf{i}_1)$ are the decisive quantities determining that probabilistic evolution.

10.2 The Master Equation for the Configuration Space (Migratory and Birth/Death-Processes within Population Configurations)

In Section 10.1 the space of discrete states $\mathbf{i}$ was left in full generality and for many general considerations we remain in this unspecified space of states. For the purposes of sociodynamics, however, we frequently need more specialized states which characterize systems composed of different kinds (or sorts) of populations. The space of these states will then be denoted as *the configuration space*.

We consider systems (e.g. "societies") consisting of a total population whose individuals can be subdivided into different "kinds" or "sorts" or "species". (Here we need not specify the nature of the "kinds" or "sorts"; this is done in detail in parts I and II of the book.) We use the index i, where $i = 1, 2, \ldots, L$, to distinguish the L different kinds of individuals.

Be now n_i the number of individuals of kind i. Then the *population configurations* (p.c.)

$$\mathbf{n} = \{n_1, \ldots, n_i, \ldots, n_L\} \tag{10.23}$$

consisting of a multiple of positive integers $n_i \geq 0$ are the possible states of the systems under consideration. These states are elements of the configuration space.

Let us now introduce three types of neighboring configurations to the configuration (10.23):

$$\mathbf{n}_{ji} = \{n_1, \ldots, (n_j + 1), \ldots, (n_i - 1), \ldots, n_L\}; \tag{10.24}$$

$$\mathbf{n}_{i+} = \{n_1, \ldots, (n_i + 1), \ldots, n_L\}; \tag{10.25}$$

$$\mathbf{n}_{i-} = \{n_1, \ldots, (n_i - 1), \ldots, n_L\}. \tag{10.26}$$

Evidently, $\mathbf{n}_{ji}$ arises from $\mathbf{n}$ if one individual of kind i "mutates" or "migrates" from kind i to kind j. Similarly, $\mathbf{n}_{i+}$ arises from $\mathbf{n}$ if one individual of kind i is "born", and $\mathbf{n}_{i-}$ arises from $\mathbf{n}$ if one individual of kind i "dies".

In order to describe the elementary dynamic steps belonging to these transitions we introduce the corresponding transition rates, namely the migratory transition rate from i to j

$$w_{t;ji}(\mathbf{n}_{ji} \mid \mathbf{n}) \equiv w_{ji}(\mathbf{n}; t) \tag{10.27}$$

the birth rate of kind i

$$w_{t;i+}(\mathbf{n}_{i+} \mid \mathbf{n}) \equiv w_{i+}(\mathbf{n}; t) \tag{10.28}$$

and the death rate of kind i

$$w_{t;i-}(\mathbf{n}_{i-} \mid \mathbf{n}) \equiv w_{i-}(\mathbf{n}; t). \tag{10.29}$$

It should be clear that the words "migration", "birth" and "death" are used here in a generalized sense and have not necessarily to do with spatial migration or birth/death at some location.

If each of the n_i individuals of kind i has the same independent *individual transition rate* $p_{ji}(\mathbf{n}; t)$ from i to j (i.e. the probability per unit of time to go over from i to j), then the *configuration transition rate* (10.27) can be written in the form

$$w_{ji}(\mathbf{n}; t) = p_{ji}(\mathbf{n}; t) \cdot n_i \tag{10.30}$$

since each of the n_i individuals of kind i can independently produce the transition from $\mathbf{n}$ to $\mathbf{n}_{ji}$. The form of the individual transition rate must not be further specified here. For sociodynamic processes, however, $p_{ji}(\mathbf{n}; t)$ assumes a characteristic form which is discussed in detail in Chapter 3. Similarly, the configurational birth- and death-rates of kind i can be put proportional to n_i:

$$w_{i+}(\mathbf{n}; t) = \beta_i(\mathbf{n}; t) \cdot n_i ; \tag{10.31}$$

$$w_{i-}(\mathbf{n}; t) = \mu_i(\mathbf{n}; t) \cdot n_i , \tag{10.32}$$

where $\beta_i(\mathbf{n}; t)$ and $\mu_i(\mathbf{n}; t)$ are the birth- and death-rates of one individual of kind i, respectively.

Furthermore we assume that no other elementary transition rates exist, that means we assume

$$w_t(\mathbf{n}' \mid \mathbf{n}) = 0 \quad \text{for} \quad \mathbf{n}' \neq \mathbf{n}_{ji}, \mathbf{n}_{i+}, \mathbf{n}_{i-} \quad \text{with} \quad j, i = 1, 2, \ldots, L. \tag{10.33}$$

The probabilistic evolution of the configurations $\mathbf{n}$ is now governed by the probability distribution

$$P(\mathbf{n}; t) = \text{probability of finding configuration } \mathbf{n} \text{ at time } t \geq 0 \tag{10.34}$$

to which all concepts developed in Section (10.1) apply: It is normalized by

$$\sum_{\mathbf{n}}^{p.c.} P(\mathbf{n}; t) = 1, \tag{10.35}$$

where the sum extends over all possible population configurations p.c. Furthermore, there exists the conditional probability

$$P(\mathbf{n}, t_2 \mid \mathbf{n}', t_1) \tag{10.36}$$

of finding the configuration $\mathbf{n}$ at time t_2, given that the system was in the configuration $\mathbf{n}'$ at time t_1.

The fundamental propagation equation which corresponds to equation (10.12) now reads

$$P(\mathbf{n}; t_2) = \sum_{\mathbf{n}'}^{p.c.} P(\mathbf{n}, t_2 \mid \mathbf{n}', t_1) P(\mathbf{n}'; t_1). \tag{10.37}$$

From equation (10.37) the *configurational master equation* for stochastic systems with generalized migration-birth- and death-processes can be derived in the same manner as in Section 10.1. It reads:

$$
\begin{aligned}
\frac{dP(\mathbf{n}; t)}{dt} = {} & \sum_{i,j(i \neq j)}^{L} w_{ij}(\mathbf{n}_{ji}; t) P(\mathbf{n}_{ji}; t) - \sum_{i,j(i \neq j)}^{L} w_{ji}(\mathbf{n}; t) P(\mathbf{n}; t) \\
& + \sum_{i=1}^{L} w_{i+}(\mathbf{n}_{i-}; t) P(\mathbf{n}_{i-}; t) - \sum_{i=1}^{L} w_{i+}(\mathbf{n}; t) P(\mathbf{n}; t) \\
& + \sum_{i=1}^{L} w_{i-}(\mathbf{n}_{i+}; t) P(\mathbf{n}_{i+}; t) - \sum_{i=1}^{L} w_{i-}(\mathbf{n}; t) P(\mathbf{n}; t).
\end{aligned} \tag{10.38}
$$

The first, second and third line on the r.h.s. of the master equation (10.38) contain the net probability flows due to migration-, birth- and death-processes, respectively, which lead to corresponding changes of the probability of configuration **n**.

10.3 General Properties of the Solutions of the Master Equation

We now return to the master equation in the general state space (with system states denoted by $\mathbf{i}, \mathbf{j}, \mathbf{k}, \ldots$) in order to discuss some general properties of its solutions. Beforehand we make some assumptions about the transition rates $w_t(\mathbf{j}|\mathbf{i})$, which are in most cases fulfilled.

(1) *Time-independence*
     We presume

$$w_t(\mathbf{j}|\mathbf{i}) = w(\mathbf{j}|\mathbf{i}) \tag{10.39}$$

  that means, the transition rates depend on the initial state $\mathbf{i}$ and the destination state $\mathbf{j}$, but not on the time t when the transition occurs.

(2) *Connectiveness* We presume that each state $\mathbf{j}_0$ is connected with each other state $\mathbf{i}_0$ by at least one chain of nonvanishing transition rates leading from $\mathbf{i}_0$ to $\mathbf{j}_0$. This means that for each pair of states $(\mathbf{i}_0, \mathbf{j}_0)$ there exists at least one chain of system states $\mathbf{i}_0, \mathbf{i}_1, \mathbf{i}_2, \ldots \mathbf{i}_{n-1}, \mathbf{i}_n \equiv \mathbf{j}_0$ so that

$$w(\mathbf{j}_0|\mathbf{i}_{n-1}) \cdot w(\mathbf{i}_{n-1}|\mathbf{i}_{n-2}) \ldots \cdot w(\mathbf{i}_1|\mathbf{i}_0) > 0. \tag{10.40}$$

Now we prove the following properties of the distribution function $P(\mathbf{j}; t)$:

Normalisation of $P(\mathbf{j}; t)$

At first we show that the probability normalisation condition (10.2) is compatible with the master equation (10.22):

$$\frac{dP(\mathbf{j}; t)}{dt} = \sum_i w(\mathbf{j}|\mathbf{i}) P(\mathbf{i}; t) - \sum_i w(\mathbf{i}|\mathbf{j}) P(\mathbf{j}; t).$$

This follows from taking the sum over $\mathbf{j}$ in (10.22):

$$\frac{d}{dt} \sum_{\mathbf{j}} P(\mathbf{j}; t) = \sum_{\mathbf{j}, \mathbf{i}} w(\mathbf{j}|\mathbf{i}) P(\mathbf{i}; t) - \sum_{\mathbf{j}, \mathbf{i}} w(\mathbf{i}|\mathbf{j}) P(\mathbf{j}; t) \equiv 0. \tag{10.41}$$

Existence of a Stationary Solution $P_{st}(\mathbf{i})$

Furthermore we prove that there exists at least one solution $P_{st}(\mathbf{i})$ of the stationary master equation.

For $P_{st}(\mathbf{i})$ there vanishes the time derivative. For all states enumerated by $\mathbf{j} = 1, 2, \ldots, c$, where c is the number of states, there must therefore hold

$$0 = \sum_{\mathbf{i}=1}^{c} [w(\mathbf{j}|\mathbf{i})P_{st}(\mathbf{i}) - w(\mathbf{i}|\mathbf{j})P_{st}(\mathbf{j})]$$

$$\equiv \sum_{\mathbf{i}=1}^{c} L(\mathbf{j}|\mathbf{i})P_{st}(\mathbf{i}) \quad \text{for} \quad \mathbf{j} = 1, 2, \ldots, c$$

(10.42)

with coefficients

$$L(\mathbf{j}|\mathbf{i}) = w(\mathbf{j}|\mathbf{i}) - \delta_{\mathbf{ji}} \sum_{\mathbf{k}} w(\mathbf{k}|\mathbf{i}).$$

(10.43)

This is a system of c linear homogeneous equations for $P_{st}(\mathbf{i})$. It has a nontrivial solution $P_{st}(\mathbf{i}) \not\equiv 0$ if and only if the determinant of the coefficients vanishes, that means if

$$||L(\mathbf{j}|\mathbf{i})|| = 0$$

(10.44)

holds. The vanishing of the determinant of $L(\mathbf{j}|\mathbf{i})$ now follows from the fact, that the equations (10.42) are not linearly independent. Indeed, taking the sum over $\mathbf{j}$ there follows:

$$\sum_{\mathbf{j},\mathbf{i}} L(\mathbf{j}|\mathbf{i})P_{st}(\mathbf{i}) = 0$$

$$\text{and also} \quad \sum_{\mathbf{j}} L(\mathbf{j}|\mathbf{i}) = 0$$

(10.44)

so that (10.44) is satisfied, with the consequence that at least one nontrivial solution $P_{st}(\mathbf{i}) \not\equiv 0$ exists. This solution is only determined up to an open common factor which is finally found out making use of the normalisation condition

$$\sum_{\mathbf{i}=1}^{c} P_{st}(\mathbf{i}) = 1.$$

(10.45)

Positive Semi-Definiteness of $P(\mathbf{j}; t)$ and Positive Definiteness of $P_{st}(\mathbf{j})$

At first we prove the statement:
If the initial distribution $P(\mathbf{j}; 0)$ is positive semi-definite, i.e. if

$$P(\mathbf{j}; 0) \geq 0$$

(10.47)

is fulfilled, then

$$P(\mathbf{j}; t_0) \geq 0$$

(10.48)

holds for all times $t_0 > 0$, if $P(\mathbf{j}; t)$ obeys the master equation (10.25).

Proof Presume that at t_0 a state j_0 reaches the probability zero whereas the other states $i \neq j_0$ still have positive semidefinite probabilities:

$$P(j_0; t_0) = 0; \quad P(i; t_0) \geq 0 \quad \text{for} \quad i \neq j_0. \tag{10.49}$$

Then

$$\left. \frac{dP(j_0; t)}{dt} \right|_{t=t_0} = \left(\sum_i \underbrace{w(j_0 \mid i)}_{\geq 0} \underbrace{P(i; t_0)}_{\geq 0} - \sum_i \underbrace{w(i \mid j_0)}_{\geq 0} \underbrace{P(j_0; t_0)}_{0} \right) \geq 0. \tag{10.50}$$

According to equation (10.50) the time derivative of $P(j_0; t)$ is positive or zero at $t = t_0$. Therefore, $P(j_0; t_0 + \tau)$ cannot become negative!

This conclusion proves true for all states j_0 at all times t_0 for which the presumption (10.49) holds. Therefore we conclude that

$$P(j; t) \geq 0 \tag{10.51}$$

holds for all times, if the initial condition (10.47) is fulfilled.

In a following theorem we shall prove that $P(j; t)$ approaches the (unambiguous) stationary solution $P_{st}(j)$ for $t \to \infty$; therefore it follows from (10.51), that also

$$P_{st}(j) \geq 0 \tag{10.52}$$

must hold. It can now even be shown, that $P_{st}(j)$ is *strictly positive*, i.e. that

$$P_{st}(j) > 0 \quad \text{for all states } j \tag{10.53}$$

is fulfilled.

Proof We show that the *contrary* assumption, namely that there exist states j_0 for which

$$P_{st}(j_0) = 0 \tag{10.54}$$

holds, leads to a *contradiction*. Indeed, it would follow from (10.54) and the stationary master equation (10.42) taken for $j = j_0$, that also

$$\sum_i^c \underbrace{w(j_0 \mid i)}_{\geq 0} \underbrace{P_{st}(i)}_{\geq 0} = 0 \tag{10.55}$$

must hold. Since all terms in the sum (10.55) are positive semidefinite, each term $w(j_0 \mid i)P_{st}(i)$, for all states $i \neq j_0$, must then vanish individually; furthermore, there exists a chain of states $i_0, i_1, i_2, \ldots, i_{n-1}, i_n \equiv j_0$ from an arbitrary state i_0 to state j_0, with positive transition rates $w(j_0 \mid i_{n-1}) > 0, w(i_{n-1} \mid i_{n-2}) > 0, \ldots, w(i_1 \mid i_0) > 0$ according to the presumption of connectiveness. Therefore, one must conclude successively, that at least the stationary probabilities along this chain must vanish, i.e.

$$P_{st}(\mathbf{i}_{n-1}) = P_{st}(\mathbf{i}_{n-2}) = \cdots = P_{st}(\mathbf{i}_0) = 0. \tag{10.56}$$

Because $\mathbf{i}_0$ is an *arbitrary state*, there follows from the presumption (10.54) for *one* state $\mathbf{j}_0$, that

$$P_{st}(\mathbf{i}_0) = 0 \tag{10.57}$$

must hold for *every state* $\mathbf{i}_0$, i.e. that the stationary solution would have to vanish completely. This, however, contradicts the normalisation condition (10.46) so that the assumption (10.54) must be rejected, which means that (10.53) has been proven.

Convergence of all $P(\mathbf{j};t)$ to the same Stationary Solution $P_{st}(\mathbf{j})$

Finally we prove the following theorem which provides an insight into the behavior of all time-dependent solutions of the master equation (10.25).

Theorem   Any time-dependent solution $P(\mathbf{i};t)$ of the master equation approaches for $t \to \infty$ one and the same stationary solution $P_{st}(\mathbf{i})$ of the master equation, if the conditions 1) and 2) for the transition rates are fulfilled. The proof proceeds along the lines of the famous H-theorem of Ludwig Boltzmann for his gas-kinetic equation. It can mutatis mutandis also be applied to the master equation.

The core of the proof consists in the construction of a functional $H(t) = F\{\mathbf{P}(t); \mathbf{P}_{st}\}$ which depends on both, the whole time-dependent and the whole stationary distribution function, and satisfies the following conditions:

(1) $H(t) \geq 0$, and $H = 0$ if and only if $\mathbf{P}(t) = \mathbf{P}_{st}$;

(2) $\dfrac{dH(t)}{dt} \leq 0$, if $\mathbf{P}(t)$ and $\mathbf{P}_{st}$ satisfy the master equation;

(3) $\dfrac{dH}{dt} = 0$, if and only if $\mathbf{P}(t) = \mathbf{P}_{st}$.

If such a functional $H(t)$ has been found, the proof of the theorem has already been accomplished, which can be seen as follows:

Because of (1) and (2) the positive semidefinite $H(t)$ decreases monotonously. However, since $H(t)$ cannot become negative, its time-derivative must asymptotically approach zero. According to (3) this takes place then and only then, if the time-dependent solution $\mathbf{P}(t)$ has approached $\mathbf{P}_{st}$, that means if $P(\mathbf{i};t)$ has approached $P_{st}(\mathbf{i})$ for every state $\mathbf{i}$. According to 1), $H(t)$ then has reached zero, its lowest possible value.

Following Boltzmann we now choose the appropriate form of $H(t)$ and prove the properties (1), (2) and (3). For the first we can even admit time-dependent transition rates $w_t(\mathbf{j}|\mathbf{i})$ and a time-dependent solution $\mathbf{P}_1(t)$ instead of $\mathbf{P}_{st}$ and go over to time-independent $w(\mathbf{j}|\mathbf{i})$ and $\mathbf{P}_1(t) \Rightarrow \mathbf{P}_{st}$ only at the end of the proof. Our choice is:

$$H(t) = \sum_{\mathbf{j}} P(\mathbf{j};t) \ln\left(\frac{P(\mathbf{j};t)}{P_1(\mathbf{j};t)}\right), \tag{10.58}$$

where $P(\mathbf{j}; t)$ and $P_1(\mathbf{j}; t)$, with

$$
\begin{aligned}
0 &< P(\mathbf{j}; t) < 1; \\
0 &< P_1(\mathbf{j}; t) < 1
\end{aligned}
\tag{10.59}
$$

and

$$
\sum_{\mathbf{j}} P(\mathbf{j}; t) = \sum_{\mathbf{j}} P_1(\mathbf{j}; t) = 1
\tag{10.60}
$$

are two correctly normalized solutions of the master equation (10.22).

Proof of (1)   At first it can immediately be seen that

$$
H(t) = 0 \quad \text{for} \quad P(\mathbf{j}; t) = P_1(\mathbf{j}; t)
\tag{10.61}
$$

because of the form (10.58) of H and since $\ln(1) = 0$. Secondly we write $H(t)$ in the form

$$
\begin{aligned}
H(t) &= \sum_{\mathbf{j}} \left\{ P(\mathbf{j}; t) \ln\left(\frac{P(\mathbf{j}; t)}{P_1(\mathbf{j}; t)}\right) - P(\mathbf{j}; t) + P_1(\mathbf{j}; t) \right\} \\
&= \sum_{\mathbf{j}} P_1(\mathbf{j}; t) \{ R(\mathbf{j}; t) \ln(R(\mathbf{j}; t)) - R(\mathbf{j}; t) + 1 \}
\end{aligned}
\tag{10.62}
$$

with

$$
R(\mathbf{j}; t) = \frac{P(\mathbf{j}; t)}{P_1(\mathbf{j}; t)} > 0.
\tag{10.63}
$$

In (10.62) we have made use of (10.60). Now we observe that the terms under the sum in (10.62) are always positive or zero. This follows because of (10.59) and

$$
\{ R \ln R - R + 1 \} = \int_1^R \ln(x)\, dx \geq 0
\tag{10.64}
$$
$$
\text{for} \quad R > 0.
$$

This proves the property $H(t) \geq 0$.

Proof of (2)   The proof of property 2 is accomplished after some tricky rearrangements of terms. At first the straight-forward calculation of the time derivative of $H(t)$ leads to

$$
\begin{aligned}
\frac{dH(t)}{dt} &= \sum_{\mathbf{j}} \left\{ \dot{P}(\mathbf{j}; t) \ln\left(\frac{P(\mathbf{j}; t)}{P_1(\mathbf{j}; t)}\right) + P(\mathbf{j}; t) \cdot \frac{P_1(\mathbf{j}; t)}{P(\mathbf{j}; t)} \cdot \frac{[\dot{P}(\mathbf{j}; t)P_1(\mathbf{j}; t) - \dot{P}_1(\mathbf{j}; t)P(\mathbf{j}; t)]}{P_1^2(\mathbf{j}; t)} \right\} \\
&= \sum_{\mathbf{j}} \left\{ \dot{P}(\mathbf{j}; t) \left[\ln\left(\frac{P(\mathbf{j}; t)}{P_1(\mathbf{j}; t)}\right) + 1 \right] - \dot{P}_1(\mathbf{j}; t) \cdot \left(\frac{P(\mathbf{j}; t)}{P_1(\mathbf{j}; t)}\right) \right\},
\end{aligned}
\tag{10.65}
$$

where we have used the abbreviation

$$\frac{dP(\mathbf{j}; t)}{dt} \equiv \dot{P}(\mathbf{j}; t).$$

(10.66)

Now we insert the master equation for $\dot{P}(\mathbf{j}; t)$ and $\dot{P}_1(\mathbf{j}; t)$ into (10.64). There follows

$$\frac{dH(t)}{dt} = \sum_{\mathbf{j}} \sum_{\mathbf{i}} [w_t(\mathbf{j}|\mathbf{i})P(\mathbf{i}; t) - w_t(\mathbf{i}|\mathbf{j})P(\mathbf{j}; t)] \ln\left(\frac{P(\mathbf{j}; t)}{P_1(\mathbf{j}; t)}\right) \quad \text{(I)}$$

$$+ \sum_{\mathbf{j}} \sum_{\mathbf{i}} [w_t(\mathbf{j}|\mathbf{i})P(\mathbf{i}; t) - w_t(\mathbf{i}|\mathbf{j})P(\mathbf{j}; t)] \quad \text{(II)}$$

$$- \sum_{\mathbf{j}} \sum_{\mathbf{i}} [w_t(\mathbf{j}|\mathbf{i})P_1(\mathbf{i}; t) - w_t(\mathbf{i}|\mathbf{j})P_1(\mathbf{j}; t)]\left(\frac{P(\mathbf{j}; t)}{P_1(\mathbf{j}; t)}\right) \quad \text{(III)} \qquad \text{(10.67)}$$

It can be seen immediately, that the term (II) vanishes. In a next step we take the expression (10.67) twice:

$$2\frac{dH(t)}{dt} = \text{I} + \text{I}' + \text{III} + \text{III}',$$

(10.68)

where however I′ arises from I, and III′ from III – without changing their value – by interchanging the summation indices **i** and **j**. In this way one obtains:

$$\text{I} + \text{I}' = \sum_{\mathbf{j}, \mathbf{i}} [w_t(\mathbf{j}|\mathbf{i})P(\mathbf{i}; t) - w_t(\mathbf{i}|\mathbf{j})P(\mathbf{j}; t)] \cdot \left[\ln\left(\frac{P(\mathbf{j}; t)}{P_1(\mathbf{j}; t)}\right) - \ln\left(\frac{P(\mathbf{i}; t)}{P_1(\mathbf{i}; t)}\right)\right]$$

$$= \sum_{\mathbf{j}, \mathbf{i}} [w_t(\mathbf{j}|\mathbf{i})P(\mathbf{i}; t) - w_t(\mathbf{i}|\mathbf{j})P(\mathbf{j}; t)] \ln X(\mathbf{j}, \mathbf{i}; t)$$

$$= 2 \sum_{\mathbf{j}, \mathbf{i}} w_t(\mathbf{j}|\mathbf{i})P(\mathbf{i}; t) \ln X(\mathbf{j}, \mathbf{i}; t)$$

(10.69)

with the abbreviation

$$X(\mathbf{j}, \mathbf{i}; t) = \frac{P(\mathbf{j}; t)}{P_1(\mathbf{j}; t)} \cdot \frac{P_1(\mathbf{i}; t)}{P(\mathbf{i}; t)} = X^{-1}(\mathbf{i}, \mathbf{j}; t).$$

(10.70)

Similarly there follows after rearrangements of the fractions and interchange of indices

$$\text{III} + \text{III}' = \sum_{\mathbf{j}, \mathbf{i}} [w_t(\mathbf{i}|\mathbf{j})P_1(\mathbf{j}; t) - w_t(\mathbf{j}|\mathbf{i})P_1(\mathbf{i}; t)] \cdot \left[\frac{P(\mathbf{j}; t)}{P_1(\mathbf{j}; t)} - \frac{P(\mathbf{i}; t)}{P_1(\mathbf{i}; t)}\right]$$

$$= \sum_{\mathbf{j}, \mathbf{i}} \left\{ w_t(\mathbf{i}|\mathbf{j})P(\mathbf{j}; t) - w_t(\mathbf{i}|\mathbf{j})P_1(\mathbf{j}; t)\frac{P(\mathbf{i}; t)}{P_1(\mathbf{i}; t)} \cdot \frac{P(\mathbf{j}; t)}{P(\mathbf{j}; t)} \right.$$

$$\left. - w_t(\mathbf{j}|\mathbf{i})P_1(\mathbf{i}; t)\frac{P(\mathbf{j}; t)}{P_1(\mathbf{j}; t)} \cdot \frac{P(\mathbf{i}; t)}{P(\mathbf{i}; t)} + w_t(\mathbf{j}|\mathbf{i})P(\mathbf{i}; t) \right\}$$

$$= 2 \sum_{\mathbf{j}, \mathbf{i}} w_t(\mathbf{j}|\mathbf{i})P(\mathbf{i}; t) \cdot [1 - X(\mathbf{j}, \mathbf{i}; t)].$$

(10.71)

On inserting (10.69) and (10.71) in (10.68) there follows the final form of the derivative of $H(t)$:

$$\frac{dH(t)}{dt} = \sum_{i,j} w_t(\mathbf{j}\,|\,\mathbf{i}) P(\mathbf{i};t)\{\ln X(\mathbf{j},\mathbf{i};t) - X(\mathbf{j},\mathbf{i};t) \mid 1\}. \qquad (10.72)$$

It can now easily be checked that

$$\begin{aligned} \{\ln(X) - X + 1\} &\le 0 \quad \text{for} \quad X > 0; \\ \{\ln(X) - X + 1\} &= 0 \quad \text{only for} \quad X = 1. \end{aligned} \qquad (10.73)$$

Since $w_t(\mathbf{j}\,|\,\mathbf{i}) P(\mathbf{i};t) > 0$, there follows from (10.72) with (10.73), that the derivative of $H(t)$ is always negative semidefinite, i.e. that property (2) holds.

Proof of (3)   If $X(\mathbf{j},\mathbf{i};t) = 1$ for all pairs $\mathbf{j},\mathbf{i}$ of states, $P_1(\mathbf{j};t)$ must be proportional to $P(\mathbf{j};t)$ for all j. Because of the normalisation (10.60) both distributions must then even be identical. Due to (10.73) and (10.72) the time derivative of $H(t)$ vanishes in the case, when $P(\mathbf{j};t)$ coincides with $P_1(\mathbf{j};t)$. But also the inverse statement is true under the condition of connectiveness of the $w_t(\mathbf{j}\,|\,\mathbf{i})$ and with $P(\mathbf{i};t) > 0$:

If $dH/dt = 0$ and if for chains of states $\mathbf{i}_0, \mathbf{i}_1, \ldots, \mathbf{i}_{n-1}, \mathbf{i}_n = \mathbf{j}_0$ with arbitrary $\mathbf{i}_0$ and $\mathbf{j}_0$ one has positive flows $w_t(\mathbf{i}_1\,|\,\mathbf{i}_0) P(\mathbf{i}_0;t) > 0, \ldots, w_t(\mathbf{j}_0\,|\,\mathbf{i}_{n-1}) P(\mathbf{i}_{n-1};t) > 0$, then (10.72) can only be fulfilled for

$$X(\mathbf{i}_1,\mathbf{i}_0;t) = X(\mathbf{i}_2,\mathbf{i}_1;t) = \cdots = X(\mathbf{j}_0,\mathbf{i}_{n-1};t) = 1 \qquad (10.74)$$

that means for

$$\frac{P(\mathbf{i}_0;t)}{P_1(\mathbf{i}_0;t)} = \frac{P(\mathbf{i}_1;t)}{P_1(\mathbf{i}_1;t)} = \cdots = \frac{P(\mathbf{j}_0;t)}{P_1(\mathbf{j}_0;t)} \qquad (10.75)$$

with arbitrary $\mathbf{i}_0$ and $\mathbf{j}_0$. This means, the distributions $\mathbf{P}(t)$ and $\mathbf{P}_1(t)$ must be proportional. Because of their normalisation they must even be equal.

Summarizing we conclude, that due to the properties (1), (2) and (3) of the functional $H(t)$ any two solutions $P(\mathbf{j};t)$ and $P_1(\mathbf{j};t)$ of the master equation must approach each other in the course of time. For $t \to \infty$ they coincide and $H(t)$ reaches its minimal value $H(\infty) = 0$. This statement holds even for time-dependent transition rates $w_t(\mathbf{j}\,|\,\mathbf{i})$ which only fulfil the condition of connectiveness. If the transition rates are in addition time-independent, then there exists (at least) one stationary solution $P_{st}(\mathbf{j})$ of the master equation and one can identify $P_1(\mathbf{j};t)$ with $P_{st}(\mathbf{j})$. Then all time-dependent solutions must approach $P_{st}(\mathbf{j})$ and this solution must even be the unique one, because all time-dependent solutions approach each other and therefore one and the same stationary solution.

10.4 An Exact Time-Dependent Solution of a Special Configurational Master Equation

The general form of a solution of the time-dependent configurational master equation (10.38) is complicated and is normally only obtained numerically. In a special case, however, a fully analytical solution of (10.38) is available. Furthermore, in this case the relation between the probability distribution and its meanvalue becomes very transparent. In this special case the transition rates in equation (10.38) have the special form

$$w_{ji}(\mathbf{n}; t) = p_{ji}(t)n_i \tag{10.76}$$

and

$$w_{i+}(\mathbf{n}; t) = \beta_i n_i; \tag{10.77}$$

$$w_{i-}(\mathbf{n}; t) = \mu_i n_i. \tag{10.78}$$

In contrast to (10.30), (10.31) and (10.32) the individual rates $p_{ji}(t)$, β_i and μ_i do not depend on $\mathbf{n}$ here, so that w_{ji}, w_{i+}, w_{i-} are linear in n_i. The individual migration rate from i to j, however, may still depend on time and can be decomposed in the form

$$p_{ji}(t) = \mu_{ji}(t) \exp[u_j(t) - u_i(t)], \tag{10.79}$$

where

$$\mu_{ji}(t) = \mu_{ij}(t) = [p_{ji}(t)p_{ij}(t)]^{\frac{1}{2}} \tag{10.80}$$

is a symmetrical mobility factor, and

$$[u_j(t) - u_i(t)] = \frac{1}{2} \ln \left[\frac{p_{ji}(t)}{p_{ij}(t)} \right] \tag{10.81}$$

can be interpreted as the difference between the attractiveness ("utility") of state j and i.

Let us begin with the purely migratory case by putting $\beta_i = \mu_i = 0$ for the first. We try the following form of the probability distribution:

$$P(\mathbf{n}; t) = \frac{\pi(\mathbf{n}; t)}{n_1! n_2! \dots n_L!} \tag{10.82}$$

from which there follows immediately

$$P(\mathbf{n}_{ji}; t) = \frac{\pi(\mathbf{n}_{ji}; t)}{n_1! n_2! \dots n_L!} \cdot \frac{n_i}{(n_j + 1)}. \tag{10.83}$$

On inserting (10.83) into the configurational master equation (10.38) and making use of (10.76), one obtains the equation of motion for $\pi(\mathbf{n}; t)$:

$$\frac{d\pi(\mathbf{n}; t)}{dt} = \sum_{i,j=1}^{L} \{n_i p_{ij}(t)\pi(\mathbf{n}_{ji}; t) - n_i p_{ij}(t)\pi(\mathbf{n}; t)\} \tag{10.84}$$

which, as we shall see, can be solved by the form

$$\pi(\mathbf{n}; t) = \prod_{l=1}^{L} [\nu_l(t)]^{n_l} \cdot e^{-\nu_l(t)}. \tag{10.85}$$

if $\nu_l(t)$ is determined appropriately.

Before doing this we show that the form (10.85) of $\pi(\mathbf{n}; t)$ leads to an easily interpretable form of the probability distribution: Inserting (10.85) into (10.82) one obtains

$$P(\mathbf{n}; t) = \prod_{l=1}^{L} \frac{[\nu_l(t)]^{n_l}}{n_l!} e^{-\nu_l(t)}. \tag{10.86}$$

This is nothing but a *L-dimensional Poisson probability distribution*! This distribution is already correctly normalized, because of

$$\sum_{\mathbf{n}} P(\mathbf{n}; t) = \prod_{l=1}^{L} \left(\sum_{n_l=0}^{\infty} \frac{[\nu_l(t)]^{n_l}}{n_l!} e^{-\nu_l(t)} \right) = \prod_{l=1}^{L} 1_{(l)} = 1. \tag{10.87}$$

Furthermore, it can easily be seen that in the multi-Poisson-distribution (10.86) the $\nu_i(t)$ have the meaning of mean values $\bar{n}_i(t)$. Indeed there follows:

$$\bar{n}_i(t) = \sum_{\mathbf{n}} n_i P(\mathbf{n}; t) = \sum_{\mathbf{n}} n_i \prod_{l=1}^{L} \frac{[\nu_l(t)]^{n_l}}{n_l!} e^{-\nu_l(t)}$$

$$= \sum_{\mathbf{n}} \left[\frac{\partial P(\mathbf{n}; t)}{\partial \nu_i(t)} + P(\mathbf{n}; t) \right] \nu_i(t) = \nu_i(t). \tag{10.88}$$

In the last line of (10.88) we have made use of the normalization (10.87) and of its consequence

$$\frac{\partial}{\partial \nu_i(t)} \sum_{\mathbf{n}} P(\mathbf{n}; t) = 0. \tag{10.89}$$

It must now be checked under which conditions for $\nu_l(t)$ the form (10.85) solves equation (10.84) and, as a consequence, the master equation (10.38) for the probability distribution (10.82).

At first we note that according to (10.85) the relations

$$\frac{d\pi(\mathbf{n}; t)}{dt} \equiv \dot{\pi}(\mathbf{n}; t) = \sum_{i=1}^{L} \left(n_i \frac{\dot{\nu}_i}{\nu_i} - \dot{\nu}_i \right) \pi(\mathbf{n}; t) \tag{10.90}$$

and

$$\pi(\mathbf{n}_{ji}; t) = \frac{\nu_j}{\nu_i} \pi(\mathbf{n}; t) \tag{10.91}$$

are satisfied. Making use of them in the equation (10.84) which is to be fulfilled, we obtain:

$$\sum_{i=1}^{L} \left(n_i \frac{\dot{\nu}_i}{\nu_i} - \dot{\nu}_i \right) \pi(\mathbf{n}; t) = \sum_{i=1}^{L} n_i \pi(\mathbf{n}; t) \cdot \sum_{j=1}^{L} \left[p_{ij}(t) \frac{\nu_j}{\nu_i} - p_{ji}(t) \right]. \tag{10.92}$$

This relation can only hold if the coefficients of $n_i \pi(\mathbf{n}; t)$ and of $\pi(\mathbf{n}; t)$ under the sum $\sum_{i=1}^{L}$ coincide on both sides of (10.92). This leads to the final conditions for the $\nu_i(t)$:

$$\dot{\nu}_i(t) = \sum_{j=1}^{L} [p_{ij}(t)\nu_j(t) - p_{ji}(t)\nu_i(t)] \tag{10.93}$$

and to

$$\sum_{i=1}^{L} \dot{\nu}_i(t) = 0. \tag{10.94}$$

where (10.94) turns out to be a consequence of (10.93). In Chapter 11 we shall prove that equations (10.93) are – in the case of the presently chosen transition rates – the *exact equations of motion for the meanvalues* $\bar{n}_i(t) = \nu_i(t)$.

If the transition rates p_{ji} and the corresponding mobilities μ_{ji} and utilities u_j, u_i are time-independent, the meanvalue equations (10.93), which now read

$$\dot{\nu}_i(t) = \sum_{j=1}^{L} \mu_{ij} \left[e^{(u_i - u_j)} \nu_j(t) - e^{(u_j - u_i)} \nu_i(t) \right] \tag{10.95}$$

have a *unique stationary solution*, which can easily be verified:

$$\nu_i^{st} = \bar{n}_i^{st} = \frac{N \exp[2u_i]}{\sum_{j=1}^{L} \exp[2u_j]}, \tag{10.96}$$

where

$$N = \sum_{i=1}^{L} \nu_i(t) = \sum_{i=1}^{L} \nu_i^{st} \tag{10.97}$$

is the total mean number of all individuals which remains constant during the migratory motion.

Correspondingly, the solution (10.86) evolves in this case into the stationary probability distribution

$$P_{st}(\mathbf{n}) = \frac{C}{n_1! n_2! \ldots n_L!} \exp \left\{ 2 \sum_{l=1}^{L} u_l n_l \right\}, \tag{10.98}$$

where C is a normalisation factor determined by (10.87).

Finally we prove that a moving multi-dimensional Poisson-distribution is also an *approximate solution* for the full master equation which now includes not only migratory but also birth–death-processes with rates (10.77), (10.78).

The approximation consists in making the substitution

$$w_{i+}(\mathbf{n}) = \beta_i n_i \Rightarrow \beta_i \bar{n}_i \qquad (10.99)$$

in the birth rate, which is certainly justified for large meanvalues $\bar{n}_i \gg 1$, where the relative deviations of the realized value n_i from $\bar{n}_i$ are small in the Poisson-distribution.

Inserting the form (10.82) into the full master equation (10.38), with transition rates (10.76), (10.77) and (10.78) and approximation (10.99) one now obtains instead of (10.84) the following equation for $\pi(\mathbf{n}; t)$:

$$\frac{d\pi(\mathbf{n}; t)}{dt} = \sum_{i,j} \left\{ n_i p_{ij}(t)\pi(\mathbf{n}_{ji}; t) - n_i p_{ji}(t)\pi(\mathbf{n}; t) \right\}$$

$$+ \sum_i \left\{ \beta_i(\bar{n}_i - 1)n_i \pi(\mathbf{n}_{i-}; t) - \beta_i \bar{n}_i \pi(\mathbf{n}; t) \right\}$$

$$+ \sum_i \left\{ \mu_i \pi(\mathbf{n}_{i+}; t) - \mu_i n_i \pi(\mathbf{n}; t) \right\}. \qquad (10.100)$$

Making use of (10.90), (10.91) and

$$\pi(\mathbf{n}_{i-}; t) = \frac{1}{\nu_i}\pi(\mathbf{n}; t); \quad \pi(\mathbf{n}_{i+}; t) = \nu_i \pi(\mathbf{n}; t) \qquad (10.101)$$

on both sides of (10.100) there follows now

$$\sum_{i=1}^{L} \left(n_i \frac{\dot{\nu}_i}{\nu_i} - \dot{\nu}_i \right) \pi(\mathbf{n}; t) = \sum_{i=1}^{L} n_i \pi(\mathbf{n}; t) \sum_{j=1}^{L} \left[p_{ij}(t)\frac{\nu_j}{\nu_i} - p_{ji}(t) \right]$$

$$+ \sum_{i=1}^{L} \left\{ \beta_i(\bar{n}_i - 1) \cdot n_i \cdot \pi(\mathbf{n}; t) \cdot \frac{1}{\nu_i} - \beta_i \cdot \bar{n}_i \pi(\mathbf{n}; t) \right\}$$

$$+ \sum_{i=1}^{L} \left\{ \mu_i \pi(\mathbf{n}; t) \cdot \nu_i - \mu_i n_i \pi(\mathbf{n}; t) \right\}. \qquad (10.102)$$

Identifying, as before, $\bar{n}_i$ with ν_i and putting $(\bar{n}_i - 1) \approx \bar{n}_i$, we may again compare the coefficients of $n_i \pi(\mathbf{n}; t)$ and $\pi(\mathbf{n}; t)$ in (10.102), in order to obtain conditions to be fulfilled by $\nu_i(t)$. The comparison now yields:

$$\dot{\nu}_i = \sum_{j=1}^{L} \left[p_{ij}(t)\nu_j(t) - p_{ji}(t)\nu_i(t) \right] + (\beta_i - \mu_i)\nu_i(t) \quad \text{for} \quad i = 1, 2, \ldots, L \qquad (10.103)$$

and

$$\sum_{i=1}^{L} \dot{\nu}_i = \sum_{i=1}^{L} (\beta_i - \mu_i)\nu_i(t), \tag{10.104}$$

where again equation (10.104) is a consequence of equation (10.103).

The equations (10.103) turn out to be the equations of motion for the meanvalues $\nu_i(t) = \bar{n}_i(t)$ in the case of simultaneous migratory and birth–death processes for the subpopulations of kinds i, where $i = 1, 2, \ldots, L$.

Of course, in the presence of birth-death processes, $N = \sum_{i=1}^{L} \bar{n}_i(t)$ is no longer a constant of motion. Instead, N may go to infinity, if the birth rates prevail, or to zero, if the death rates prevail. (The master equation has only one *exact stationary solution* in the presence of birth–death-processes, namely the state of completely extinct subpopulations.)

We summarize the main result of Section 10.4:

If we assume special transition rates (10.76), (10.77), (10.78), in which the individual rates do not depend on the configuration $\mathbf{n}$, the master equation (10.38) has a solution, which is exact in the case of pure migration and a very good approximation in the case of migration and birth–death-processes. This solution has the form of a multi-Poisson distribution (10.86) with time-dependent meanvalues obeying the equations of motion (10.93) or (10.103) for cases of pure migration or cases of migration plus birth–death-processes, respectively. In the case of pure migration and time-independent utilities u_i the meanvalue equations possess a unique stationary solution (10.96) and the probability distribution approaches the corresponding stationary solution (10.98). The form of this solution demonstrates the relation between the probability distribution and its meanvalues in a simple case. Whereas the probability distribution includes the probability of deviations of the variables n_i from their meanvalues $\bar{n}_i(t) = \nu_i(t)$ due to the stochastic transition behavior of the individuals, the meanvalues follow the peak of the – in our example unimodal – probability distribution function.

10.5 Detailed Balance and the Construction of the Solution of the Stationary Master Equation

We now return to the discussion of the stationary master equation which we repeat here for convenience:

$$\sum_{i=1}^{c} w(\mathbf{j}|\mathbf{i})P_{st}(\mathbf{i}) = \sum_{i=1}^{c} w(\mathbf{i}|\mathbf{j})P_{st}(\mathbf{j}) \quad \text{for} \quad \mathbf{j} = 1, 2, \ldots, c. \tag{10.105}$$

We have seen in Section 10.3, that the unique stationary solution $P_{st}(\mathbf{i})$, normalized to

$$\sum_{i=1}^{c} P_{st}(\mathbf{i}) = 1 \tag{10.106}$$

always exists under certain weak conditions for the transition rates. Its meaning is clear from equation (10.105), which says that in the stationary case the probability flow from all states $\mathbf{i}$ *towards* the reference state $\mathbf{j}$ (i.e. the l.h.s.) has to be equal to the probability flow *out of* the reference state $\mathbf{j}$ into all states $\mathbf{i}$ (i.e. the r.h.s.).

Although the nontrivial solution of the system of c linear equations for the $P_{st}(\mathbf{j})$ can always be found in principle, since the determinant of coefficients vanishes (see (10.44)), the solution has a very cumbersome form in the general case. This solution may be represented in graph-theoretical terms. In special cases, however, the transition rates $w(\mathbf{j}|\mathbf{i})$ fulfil the condition of *Detailed Balance*

$$w(\mathbf{j}|\mathbf{i})P_{st}(\mathbf{i}) = w(\mathbf{i}|\mathbf{j})P_{st}(\mathbf{j}) \quad \text{for all} \quad \mathbf{i} \text{ and } \mathbf{j}. \tag{10.107}$$

Its meaning can easily be found by comparing (10.105) with (10.107): Whereas (10.105) states that the *total* probability flow into state $\mathbf{j}$ is equal to the *total* probability flow out of state $\mathbf{j}$, equation (10.107) is a more detailed requirement, stating that the probability flow from an individual state $\mathbf{i}$ to another individual state $\mathbf{j}$ is equal to the back-flow from the state $\mathbf{j}$ to the state $\mathbf{i}$.

If the condition (10.107) of detailed balance is fulfilled, then it is easy to construct the explicit form of the stationary solution $P_{st}(\mathbf{i})$ for all states $\mathbf{i}$.

For this aim we may take any chain C of states $\mathbf{i}_0, \mathbf{i}_1, \ldots, \mathbf{i}_{n-1}, \mathbf{i}_n$ from a reference state $\mathbf{i}_0$ to an *arbitrary state* $\mathbf{i}_n$ for which the forward and backward transition rates between two neighboring chain-states are nonvanishing, i.e. all $w(\mathbf{i}_1|\mathbf{i}_0)$, $w(\mathbf{i}_0|\mathbf{i}_1)$; $w(\mathbf{i}_2|\mathbf{i}_1)$, $w(\mathbf{i}_1|\mathbf{i}_2)$; $\ldots$; $w(\mathbf{i}_n|\mathbf{i}_{n-1})$, $w(\mathbf{i}_{n-1}|\mathbf{i}_n)$ are strictly positive definite. Then the repeated application of (10.107) along the chain C yields

$$P_{st}(\mathbf{i}_n) = {}^{(C)}\prod_{\nu=0}^{n-1} \frac{w(\mathbf{i}_{\nu+1}|\mathbf{i}_\nu)}{w(\mathbf{i}_\nu|\mathbf{i}_{\nu+1})} P_{st}(\mathbf{i}_0). \tag{10.108}$$

Thus we obtain $P_{st}(\mathbf{i}_n)$ for the arbitrary state $\mathbf{i}_n$ from $P_{st}(\mathbf{i}_0)$. Note that (10.108) must hold for *any chain* from $\mathbf{i}_0$ to $\mathbf{i}_n$ with nonvanishing forward and backward transition rates between neighboring chain-states. The value of $P_{st}(\mathbf{i}_0)$ can finally be determined by inserting (10.108) into the normalisation condition (10.106).

Now the problem arises of checking for a given master equation with given transition rates, whether detailed balance is fulfilled or not. The formulation of detailed balance by formula (10.107) is not immediately appropriate for this test, because it implies the stationary solution which is not known beforehand and can only be written in the form (10.108), *if* detailed balance holds!

Therefore we must first derive conditions for the transition rates which are *equivalent* to (10.107) but which *do not* contain the unknown stationary solution. In other words: we must *eliminate* the stationary state in the condition of detailed balance.

At first a *set of necessary relations* for the transition rates, which do not contain the unknown $\mathbf{P}_{st}$, can be derived from detailed balance in the form (10.107): The consequence of (10.107) was formula (10.108) for any chain C with nonvanishing transition rates between its links and for arbitrary end states $\mathbf{i}_n$. Let now C be a *closed loop*

$\mathcal{L}$ for which the end state $\mathbf{i}_n$ coincides with the initial reference state $\mathbf{i}_0$. In this case there follows:

$$P_{st}(\mathbf{i}_0) = {}^{(\mathcal{L})}\prod_{\nu=0}^{n-1} \frac{w(\mathbf{i}_{\nu+1}\,|\,\mathbf{i}_\nu)}{w(\mathbf{i}_\nu\,|\,\mathbf{i}_{\nu+1})} P_{st}(\mathbf{i}_0) \qquad (10.109)$$

or

$${}^{(\mathcal{L})}\prod_{\nu=0}^{n-1} \frac{w(\mathbf{i}_{\nu+1}\,|\,\mathbf{i}_\nu)}{w(\mathbf{i}_\nu\,|\,\mathbf{i}_{\nu+1})} = 1 \quad \text{for every closed loop } \mathcal{L}(\mathbf{i}_0,\mathbf{i}_1,\dots,\mathbf{i}_n = \mathbf{i}_0)$$

$$\text{with nonvanishing quotients} \quad \frac{w(\mathbf{i}_{\nu+1}\,|\,\mathbf{i}_\nu)}{w(\mathbf{i}_\nu\,|\,\mathbf{i}_{\nu+1})} \qquad (10.110)$$

as a *necessary* consequence of detailed balance (10.107). Evidently, the conditions (10.110) do not contain the unknown $\mathbf{P}_{st}$.

We shall now prove that (10.110) is not only a necessary but also a *sufficient* set of relations for detailed balance. That means, equations (10.110) are equivalent to the original formulation (10.107) of detailed balance. For this aim we presume that (10.110) holds and show, that the construction of $P_{st}(\mathbf{i}_n)$ via formula (10.108) is under this presumption *independent* of the chosen chain $\mathcal{C}$, and therefore *consistent* and *unique*.

In order to show this let us choose another chain $\mathcal{C}'\{\mathbf{j}_0 = \mathbf{i}_0, \mathbf{j}_1, \mathbf{j}_2, \dots, \mathbf{j}_{n'} = \mathbf{i}_n\}$ with the same initial state $\mathbf{j}_0 \cong \mathbf{i}_0$ and the same final state $\mathbf{j}_{n'} \cong \mathbf{i}_n$. We then have to prove that the formula

$$P_{st}(\mathbf{j}_{n'}) = {}^{(\mathcal{C}')}\prod_{\nu=0}^{n'-1} \frac{w(\mathbf{j}_{\nu+1}\,|\,\mathbf{j}_\nu)}{w(\mathbf{j}_\nu\,|\,\mathbf{j}_{\nu+1})} P_{st}(\mathbf{j}_0) \qquad (10.111)$$

using chain $\mathcal{C}'$ instead of $\mathcal{C}$, leads to the same $P_{st}(\mathbf{j}_{n'}) = P_{st}(\mathbf{i}_n)$ as formula (10.108). This leads to the requirement:

$${}^{(\mathcal{C})}\prod_{\nu=0}^{n-1} \frac{w(\mathbf{i}_{\nu+1}\,|\,\mathbf{i}_\nu)}{w(\mathbf{i}_\nu\,|\,\mathbf{i}_{\nu+1})} = {}^{(\mathcal{C}')}\prod_{\nu=0}^{n'-1} \frac{w(\mathbf{j}_{\nu+1}\,|\,\mathbf{j}_\nu)}{w(\mathbf{j}_\nu\,|\,\mathbf{j}_{\nu+1})} \qquad (10.112)$$

which is however equivalent to the formula

$${}^{(\mathcal{L})}\prod_{\nu=0}^{n+n'-1} \frac{w(\mathbf{i}_{\nu+1}\,|\,\mathbf{i}_\nu)}{w(\mathbf{i}_\nu\,|\,\mathbf{i}_{\nu+1})} = 1 \qquad (10.113)$$

for the closed loop

$$\mathcal{L}\{\mathbf{i}_0,\mathbf{i}_1,\dots,\mathbf{i}_n = \mathbf{j}_{n'}, \mathbf{i}_{n+1} \cong \mathbf{j}_{n'-1}, \dots, \mathbf{i}_{n+n'-1} \cong \mathbf{j}_1, \mathbf{i}_{n+n'} \cong \mathbf{j}_0 \cong \mathbf{i}_0\}.$$

Since (10.113) is fulfilled because of the presumption (10.110), our statement holds true.

To complete the proof of equivalence of the formulations (10.110) and (10.107) of detailed balance, we show that (10.107) follows from (10.108), which has now been proven to be a consistent and unique construction formula for $\mathbf{P}_{st}$ under the presumption (10.110). For this aim let us include the states $\mathbf{i}$ and $\mathbf{j}$ as the last but one $(\mathbf{i} \hat{=} \mathbf{i}_{n-1})$ and last $(\mathbf{j} \hat{=} \mathbf{i}_n)$ state in a chain $C\{\mathbf{i}_0, \mathbf{i}_1, \dots, \mathbf{i}_{n-1}, \mathbf{i}_n\}$. The application of construction formula (10.108) then yields

$$
\begin{aligned}
P_{st}(\mathbf{j}) &= {}^{(C)}\prod_{\nu=0}^{n-1} \frac{w(\mathbf{i}_{\nu+1} \mid \mathbf{i}_\nu)}{w(\mathbf{i}_\nu \mid \mathbf{i}_{\nu+1})} P_{st}(\mathbf{i}_0) \\
&= \frac{w(\mathbf{j} \mid \mathbf{i})}{w(\mathbf{i} \mid \mathbf{j})} {}^{(C)}\prod_{\nu=0}^{n-2} \frac{w(\mathbf{i}_{\nu+1} \mid \mathbf{i}_\nu)}{w(\mathbf{i}_\nu \mid \mathbf{i}_{\nu+1})} P_{st}(\mathbf{i}_0) \\
&= \frac{w(\mathbf{j} \mid \mathbf{i})}{w(\mathbf{i} \mid \mathbf{j})} P_{st}(\mathbf{i}).
\end{aligned}
\tag{10.114}
$$

Formula (10.114) finishes the proof of the equivalence of the two formulations (10.107) and (10.110) of the condition of detailed balance.

Example: Application to the Configurational Master Equation

We now apply the construction method of stationary solutions for cases where detailed balance is fulfilled to the configurational master equation (10.38) for purely migratory processes without birth- and death-processes. Since migration of individuals between kinds of states $i, j, k \dots$ does not change the total number of population

$$
N = \sum_{i=1}^{L} n_i
\tag{10.115}
$$

it is compatible with the migratory master equation to put $N = \text{const.}$ during the evolution of the system and of course also for the stationary solution. This implies that the total number of accessible states $\mathbf{n} = \{n_1, \dots, n_i, \dots, n_L\}$ with integers $n_i \geq 0$ is finite, and the master equation must possess a stationary solution.

We now choose the rather general form

$$
\begin{aligned}
w_{ji}(\mathbf{n}_{ji} \mid \mathbf{n}) &= p_{ji}(\mathbf{n}) \cdot n_i = \mu_{ji} \exp[u_j(\mathbf{n}_{ji}) - u_i(\mathbf{n})] \cdot n_i \\
&\quad \text{with} \quad \mu_{ji} = \mu_{ij}
\end{aligned}
\tag{10.116}
$$

for the nonvanishing transition rates from $\mathbf{n}$ to $\mathbf{n}_{ji}$. They differ from (10.76) and (10.79) in one important respect: The utility functions u_i, u_j in general now depend on the initial configuration $\mathbf{n}$ or the final configuration $\mathbf{n}_{ji}$, respectively.

This generalisation leads to transition rates which are *nonlinear functions of the configuration variables*, and this fact changes the dynamics of the system fundamentally. (In particular, the multi-Poissonian distribution of Section 10.4 is no longer a solution of the master equation.)

In cases where the utility functions u_i, u_j depend on *all* numbers $\{n_1, n_2, \dots, n_i, \dots, n_j, \dots, n_L\}$ it can also be shown, that detailed balance is in general not fulfilled. (Such cases are even of high sociodynamic interest and are e.g. treated in Chapter 4.) Therefore we reduce somewhat the generality of (10.116) and assume the form

$$w_{ji}(\mathbf{n}_{ji}\,|\,\mathbf{n}) = \mu_{ji}\exp[u_j(n_j+1) - u_i(n_i)]\cdot n_i$$
$$\text{with}\quad \mu_{ji} = \mu_{ij}, \tag{10.117}$$

where the utility u_i of kind i only depends on the number n_i of individuals belonging to this kind. The corresponding holds for u_j (Note that n_i is the number of kind i *before* migration and $(n_j + 1)$ is the number of kind j *after* migration of one individual from i to j).

For transition rates of the form (10.117) it can now be proved, that *the condition of detailed balance is satisfied*!

The proof is simple in principle but somewhat cumbersome because (10.110) must be proved for *all closed loops* of configuration states with nonvanishing quotients of transition rates between adjacent states. Such adjacent states are e.g. $\mathbf{n}$ and $\mathbf{n}_{ji}$ with

$$\frac{w_{ji}(\mathbf{n}_{ji}\,|\,\mathbf{n})}{w_{ij}(\mathbf{n}\,|\,\mathbf{n}_{ji})} = \frac{\mu_{ji}\exp[u_j(n_j+1) - u_i(n_i)]\cdot n_i}{\mu_{ij}\exp[u_i(n_i) - u_j(n_j+1)]\cdot(n_j+1)}$$
$$= \left[\frac{\exp[2u_j(n_j+1)]}{(n_j+1)}\right]\cdot\left[\frac{\exp[2u_i(n_i)]}{n_i}\right]^{-1}. \tag{10.118}$$

A general closed loop starts from a configuration $\mathbf{n} = \{n_1, n_2, \ldots, n_L\}$. Intermediate configuration states $\mathbf{n} + \mathbf{k}$ of the loop are reached by several sequential migration steps of individuals from any index i to any other index j, where each step contributes a quotient of form (10.118). Each intermediate configuration must have the form

$$\mathbf{n} + \mathbf{k} = \{n_1 + k_1, n_2 + k_2, \ldots, n_l + k_L\}\quad\text{where}\quad n_i + k_i \geq 0,\ \text{with}\ k_i = 0, \pm 1, \pm 2, \ldots$$

$$\text{and where}\quad \sum_{i=1}^{L} k_i = 0 \tag{10.119}$$

Because the loop is closed, the end configuration coincides with the initial configuration $\mathbf{n} = \{n_1, n_2, \ldots, n_L\}$, i.e. with $\mathbf{k} = \{0, 0, \ldots, 0\}$.

We have to prove that the product of quotients of the form (10.118) belonging to the steps leading from state to state of the loop has the value 1. Indeed, we will now show that all factors belonging to the product of quotients of a closed loop do cancel mutually, so that the result is immediately evident.

We show this by presenting the steps and the intermediate states of a loop in *graphic form*. Discussing an arbitrarily chosen closed loop and its graphic representation we then can see that the cancelling of all terms in the product of quotients belonging to this loop takes place *with necessity* and is a *general result* for all loops.

The configuration states (10.119) can be depicted in a *two-dimensional square-lattice* with points having the coordinates $(x, y) = (i, k)$ with $i = 1, 2, \ldots, L$ and $k_i = 0, \pm 1, \pm 2, \pm 3, \ldots$. The general configuration $\mathbf{n} + \mathbf{k}$ is represented by the set of points $\{1, k_1; 2, k_2; \ldots; L, k_L\}$ with $\sum_{i=1}^{L} k_i = 0$. The configuration $\mathbf{n}$ corresponds to $\{1, 0; 2, 0; \ldots; L, 0\}$ and the transition from state $\mathbf{n} + \mathbf{k}$ to an adjacent state by migration of an individual from kind i to kind j corresponds to

$$\{1, k_1; \ldots; i, k_i; \ldots; j, k_j; \ldots; L, k_L\} \Rightarrow \{1, k_1; \ldots; i, k_i - 1; \ldots; j, k_j + 1; \ldots; L, k_L\}.$$

This transition step can be represented by two arrows, an upward arrow from point (j, k_j) to $(j, k_j + 1)$ and a downward arrow from point (i, k_i) to $(i, k_i - 1)$.

Furthermore we stipulate that to the *upward arrow* there belongs the factor

$$\uparrow \; \cong \left[\frac{\exp[2u_j(n_j + k_j + 1)]}{(n_j + k_j + 1)}\right] \tag{10.120}$$

and to the *downward arrow* the factor

$$\downarrow \; \cong \left[\frac{\exp[2u_i(n_i + k_i)]}{(n_i + k_i)}\right]^{-1} \tag{10.121}$$

and to the transition step there belongs the product of the two factors (10.120) and (10.121), which amounts to a quotient of type (10.118).

As an example we choose a closed loop in a configuration space with $L = 7$ kinds $i = 1, 2, \ldots, 7$ which starts from an initial configuration state

$$\mathbf{0} = \{n_1, n_2, \ldots, n_7\} \cong \{1, 0; 2, 0; 3, 0; 4, 0; 5, 0; 6, 0; 7, 0\}$$

and reaches eight intermediate states I, II, ..., VIII by eight steps (1), (2), ..., (8). The last state VIII coincides with the initial state $\mathbf{0}$. In a step we only note those k-values which have changed, for instance $(k_i = 3, k_j = -2) \Rightarrow (k_i = 2, k_j = -1)$. The formal notation of the chosen closed loop reads:

Initial State $\mathbf{0} = \{1, 0; 2, 0; 3, 0; 4, 0; 5, 0; 6, 0; 7, 0\}$
Transition step (1) $\cong (k_2 = 0, k_4 = 0) \rightarrow (k_2 = -1, k_4 = +1)$
Reached state I $= \{1, 0; 2, -1; 3, 0; 4, +1; 5, 0; 6, 0; 7, 0\}$
Transition step (2) $\cong (k_3 = 0, k_4 = 1) \rightarrow (k_3 = -1, k_4 = +2)$
Reached state II $= \{1, 0; 2, -1; 3, -1; 4, +2; 5, 0; 6, 0; 7, 0\}$
Transition step (3) $\cong (k_6 = 0, k_2 = -1) \rightarrow (k_6 = -1, k_2 = 0)$
Reached state III $= \{1, 0; 2, 0; 3, -1; 4, +2; 5, 0; 6, -1; 7, 0\}$
Transition step (4) $\cong (k_6 = -1, k_5 = 0) \rightarrow (k_6 = -2, k_5 = 1)$
Reached state IV $= \{1, 0; 2, 0; 3, -1; 4, +2; 5, +1; 6, -2; 7, 0\}$ (10.122)
Transition step (5) $\cong (k_5 = +1; k_4 = +2) \rightarrow (k_5 = 0; k_4 = 3)$
Reached state V $= \{1, 0; 2, 0; 3, -1; 4, +3; 5, 0; 6, -2; 7, 0\}$
Transition step (6) $\cong (k_4 = 3, k_6 = -2) \rightarrow (k_4 = 2; k_6 = -1)$
Reached state VI $= \{1, 0; 2, 0; 3, -1; 4, +2; 5, 0; 6, -1; 7, 0\}$
Transition step (7) $\cong (k_4 = 2, k_3 = -1) \rightarrow (k_4 = 1; k_3 = 0)$
Reached state VII $= \{1, 0; 2, 0; 3, 0; 4, +1; 5, 0; 6, -1; 7, 0\}$
Transition step (8) $\cong (k_4 = 1, k_6 = -1) \rightarrow (k_4 = 0, k_6 = 0)$
Reached state VIII $= \mathbf{0} = \{1, 0; 2, 0; 3, 0; 4, 0; 5, 0; 6, 0; 7, 0\}$.

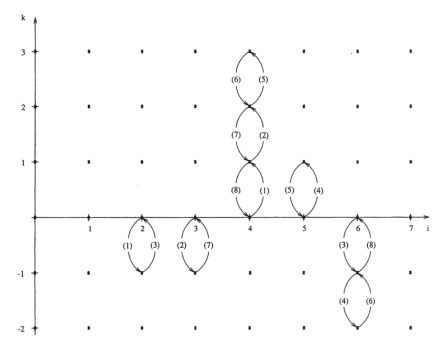

Figure 10.1 Graphical representation of the closed loop (10.122) consisting of 8 states and 8 transition steps between states. To each transition there belongs an upward and a downward arrow. To each upward arrow from k_i to $(k_i + 1)$ there must belong a downward arrow from $(k_i + 1)$ to k_i, because the loop is closed.

In Figure (10.1) we give the graphical representation of the loop (10.122) in terms of the arrow pairs belonging to each of the eight transitions in the lattice space.

In the figure there belongs to each of the 8 transition steps an upward and a downward arrow. Eventually to each upward arrow from k_i to $(k_i + 1)$ there *must belong* a downward arrow from $(k_i + 1)$ to k_i, because the loop is closed and the final state after all transition steps must coincide with the initial state $\{1, 0; 2, 0; 3, 0; 4, 0; 5, 0; 6, 0; 7, 0\}$.

To the whole loop we now assign the *product of all factors* (10.120), (10.121) *belonging to all upward and downward arrows*. This corresponds to the product of all quotients of type (10.118) belonging to the transitions. On the other hand we see that the factors (10.120), (10.121) belonging to an upward arrow from k_i to $(k_i + 1)$ and the corresponding downward arrow from $(k_i + 1)$ to k_i, respectively, cancel mutually. Therefore the whole product assigned to the closed loop has the value 1.

Evidently this holds for *every* closed loop whatsoever transition steps it may contain, because it must, in order to be closed, always contain pairs of upward and downward arrows between k_i and $(k_i + 1)$, the factors of which cancel mutually. Therefore condition (10.110) is satisfied for every closed loop.

This ends our proof that detailed balance holds for migratory master equations with transition rates (10.117).

Construction of the Stationary Solution $P_{st}(n_1, \ldots, n_L)$

We are now able to construct explicitly the stationary solution of the migratory master equation with transition rates (10.117) by applying the construction formula (10.108). Starting from an arbitrary initial state we must reach the general state $\{n_1, n_2, \ldots, n_L\}$ by a chain of intermediate states so that the transition rates between adjacent links of the chain are nonvanishing.

Starting from the initial state $\{N, 0, 0, \ldots, 0\}$ we choose the following "standard chain" to the general state $\mathbf{n} = \{n_1, n_2, \ldots, n_L\}$:

$$
\begin{aligned}
\mathcal{C} = \{ &(N, 0, \ldots, 0) \to (N-1, 1, 0, \ldots, 0) \ldots \to (N - n_2, n_2, 0, \ldots, 0) \\
&\to (N - n_2 - 1, n_2, 1, 0, \ldots, 0) \ldots \to (N - n_2 - n_3, n_2, n_3, 0, \ldots, 0) \\
&\to (N - n_2 - n_3 - 1, n_2, n_3, 1, 0, \ldots, 0) \ldots \to (n_1, n_2, n_3, \ldots, n_L) \}.
\end{aligned}
\tag{10.123}
$$

According to (10.108) and with the simplified notation of transition rates (10.117)

$$
\begin{aligned}
w_{ji}(\mathbf{n}_{ji} \,|\, \mathbf{n}) &\Rightarrow w_{ji}(n_j + 1, n_i - 1 \,|\, n_j, n_i) \\
&= \mu_{ji} \cdot n_i \cdot \exp[u_j(n_j + 1) - u_i(n_i)]
\end{aligned}
\tag{10.124}
$$

the first n_2 steps of the chain lead to

$$
P_{st}(N - n_2, n_2, 0, \ldots, 0) = \prod_{\nu=0}^{n_2-1} \frac{w_{21}(\nu + 1, N - \nu - 1 \,|\, \nu, N - \nu)}{w_{12}(N - \nu, \nu \,|\, N - \nu - 1, \nu + 1)} P_{st}(N, 0, \ldots, 0)
\tag{10.125}
$$

or explicitly, after inserting (10.124) in (10.125),

$$
P_{st}(N - n_2, n_2, 0, \ldots, 0) = \frac{N(N-1) \ldots (N - n_2 + 1)}{n_2!} \exp \left\{ 2 \sum_{\nu=1}^{n_2} u_2(\nu) \right.
$$
$$
\left. -2 \sum_{\nu=N-n_2+1}^{N} u_1(\nu) \right\} P_{st}(N, 0, \ldots, 0).
\tag{10.126}
$$

Continuing the construction procedure of $P_{st}(\ldots)$ along the chain (10.123) we finally obtain

$$
P_{st}(n_1, n_2, \ldots, n_L) = \frac{Z^{-1} \delta\left(\sum_{i=1}^{L} n_i - N \right)}{n_1! n_2! \ldots n_L!} \exp \left\{ 2 \sum_{i=1}^{L} U_i(n_i) \right\}.
\tag{10.127}
$$

Here we have introduced "*utility potentials*"

$$
U_i(n_i) = \sum_{\nu=1}^{n_i} u_i(\nu) \quad \text{for} \quad n_i \geq 1;
$$
$$
U_i(0) = 0.
\tag{10.128}
$$

Furthermore we have explicitly taken into account, that only configurations
$\mathbf{n} = \{n_1, n_2, \ldots, n_L\}$ with

$$\sum_{i=1}^{L} n_i = N \tag{10.129}$$

have a nonvanishing probability by introducing the Kronecker factor

$$\delta\left(\sum_{i=1}^{L} n_i - N\right) = \begin{cases} 1 & \text{for } \sum_{i=1}^{L} n_i = N \\ 0 & \text{for } \sum_{i=1}^{L} n_i \neq N \end{cases} \tag{10.130}$$

Finally we have put the probability of the initial state equal to

$$P_{st}(N, 0, \ldots, 0) = \frac{\exp\{2U_1(N)\}}{N!} \cdot \frac{1}{Z}, \tag{10.131}$$

where the factor Z now follows from the normalisation condition

$$\sum_{\mathbf{n}} P_{st}(n_1, n_2, \ldots, n_L) = 1 \tag{10.132}$$

and is given by

$$Z = \sum_{\mathbf{n}} \frac{\delta\left(\sum_{i=1}^{L} n_i - N\right) \exp\left\{2 \sum_{i=1}^{L} U_i(n_i)\right\}}{n_1! n_2! \ldots n_L!}. \tag{10.133}$$

The sum extends over all configurations $\mathbf{n}(n_1, \ldots, n_L)$.

If the utility functions $u_i(n_i)$ are explicitly known, the formula (10.127) may be
further evaluated. A plausible form of $u_i(n_i)$ which has been substantiated in empirical applications to interregional migration of populations is the following:

$$u_i(n_i) = \delta_i + \kappa_i n_i - \sigma_i n_i^2. \tag{10.134}$$

(Identifying the "species i" with the "population living in region i" one may interpret the three terms of the regional utility (10.134) as a natural preference term, an
agglomeration term and a saturation term, respectively.)

In this case we obtain for the utility potentials:

$$U_i(n_i) = \delta_i \sum_{\nu=1}^{n_i} 1 + \kappa_i \sum_{\nu=1}^{n_i} \nu - \sigma_i \sum_{\nu=1}^{n_i} \nu^2$$

$$= \delta_i n_i + \kappa_i \frac{n_i(n_i+1)}{2} - \sigma_i \frac{n_i(n_i+1)(2n_i+1)}{6} \tag{10.135}$$

which must be inserted into (10.127) to obtain the fully explicit stationary solution.

In the *special case* where the utility functions *do not* depend on n_i, i.e. for $\kappa_i = 0$ and $\sigma_i = 0$, the stationary solution (10.127) coincides with the stationary distribution (10.98), found as final state of the moving multi-Poissonian solution of Section 10.4, apart from the factor $\delta(\sum_{i=1}^{L} n_i - N)$, which restricts this solution to the "sheet" of fixed N.

In most practical applications one has to deal with large numbers $n_i \gg 1$, with $i = 1, 2, \ldots, L$. In these cases one can use Stirling's formula for the factorials

$$n! \cong n^n e^{-n} \tag{10.136}$$

and approximate the utility potentials by

$$U_i(n) \approx \int_0^n u_i(\nu) d\nu. \tag{10.137}$$

The approximate form of $P_{st}(\mathbf{n})$ then reads:

$$P_{st}(\mathbf{n}) = Z^{-1} \delta \left(\sum_{i=1}^{L} n_i - N \right) \exp \left\{ \sum_{i=1}^{L} \Phi(n_i) \right\} \tag{10.138}$$

with

$$\Phi_i(n_i) = 2U_i(n_i) - (n_i \ln(n_i) - n_i). \tag{10.139}$$

Since we are most interested in those configurations $\hat{\mathbf{n}} = \{\hat{n}_1, \hat{n}_2, \ldots, \hat{n}_L\}$ which have a maximal probability we determine now the extremum of the exponent in (10.138) under the constraint (10.129). This leads to the condition

$$\delta \left\{ \sum_{i=1}^{L} \Phi_i(n_i) - \lambda \left(\sum_{i=1}^{L} n_i - N \right) \right\} = \sum_{i=1}^{L} \delta n_i \left[2 \frac{\partial U_i(n_i)}{\partial n_i} - \ln(n_i) - \lambda \right] \overset{!}{=} 0 \tag{10.140}$$

with the Lagrangian parameter λ. Solving for n_i and making use of (10.137) leads to L equations determining the extremal configurations $\{\hat{n}_1, \hat{n}_2, \ldots, \hat{n}_L\}$:

$$\hat{n}_i = e^{-\lambda} \exp[2u_i(\hat{n}_i)] = \frac{N \exp[2u_i(\hat{n}_i)]}{\sum_{j=1}^{L} \exp[2u_i(\hat{n}_i)]} \tag{10.141}$$

$$\text{for } i = 1, 2, \ldots, L,$$

where the Lagrangian parameter λ has been chosen so that the constraint (10.129) is fulfilled.

If the u_i are *independent* of n_i, equation (10.141) immediately leads to the uniquely determined configuration $\{\hat{n}_1, \hat{n}_2, \ldots, \hat{n}_L\}$ where the unimodal probability distribution has its maximum. It is interesting to note that in this case the equation (10.141) for the configuration with maximal probability coincides with equation (10.96) for the *unique stationary solution* of the meanvalue equations (10.95).

However, the situation is *completely different* if the $u_i(n_i)$ depend on n_i, for instance by formula (10.134). Then equation (10.141) still holds, but represents now a *set of transcendental equations* for the determination of $\{\hat{n}_1, \hat{n}_2, \ldots, \hat{n}_L\}$. Depending on the parameters in the functions $u_i(n_i)$ (like $\delta_i, \kappa_i, \sigma_i$ in (10.134)), equation (10.141) may then have one, or also *more than one* solutions. In the latter case these solutions belong to the extrema (maxima, minima, saddle-points) of a *multimodal* probability distribution function given by (10.127) or approximately by (10.138).

Furthermore, the relation between the true meanvalue $\bar{\mathbf{n}}(t) = \{\bar{n}_1(t), \ldots, \bar{n}_L(t)\}$ and a multimodal probability distribution becomes more complex! The true meanvalue – in contrast to the quasi-meanvalues introduced in Chapter 12 – is always *uniquely defined*, because $P(\mathbf{n}; t)$ is a uniquely defined function. If $P(\mathbf{n}; t)$ approaches the stationary distribution $P_{st}(\mathbf{n})$, the true meanvalue will approach the uniquely defined stationary meanvalue $\bar{\mathbf{n}}^{st} = \{\bar{n}_1^{st}, \ldots, \bar{n}_L^{st}\}$, too, whatsoever form the exact meanvalue equations may have. It is intuitively clear that this *true meanvalue* will in the case of a multimodal probability distribution *not coincide* with one of its maxima but instead lie somehow *between these maxima*. The relation between the probability distribution, true meanvalues and quasi-meanvalues will be further elucidated in Chapters 11 and 12.

11. Evolution Equations for Meanvalues and Variances in Configuration Space

The solution of the master equation, i.e. the probability distribution $P(\mathbf{n}; t)$ depicts the whole process of the stochastic evolution of an ensemble of configurations $\mathbf{n} = \{n_1, n_2, \ldots, n_L\}$. However, in the case of social systems only one or a few samples of the ensemble described by $P(\mathbf{n}; t)$ are available empirically. The distribution function $P(\mathbf{n}; t)$ therefore contains – apart from principal insights – too much information about too many nonrealized systems. For most considerations it is sufficient to focus one's attention to the mean behaviour and the possible mean deviations from it among the systems under consideration. This holds in particular if the probability distribution can be expected to be unimodular and sharply peaked.

It is well known that the appropriate measures for the mean behavior and mean deviations from meanvalues of an ensemble of stochastic variables $\{n_1, \ldots, n_L\}$ are the *meanvalues*

$$\bar{n}_k(t) = \sum_{\mathbf{n}}^{PC} n_k P(\mathbf{n}; t) \tag{11.1}$$

and the *variance matrix* consisting of elements $v_{kl}(t)$ which are meanvalues of bilinear deviations of the variables from their meanvalues, i.e.

$$\begin{aligned}\bar{v}_{kl}(t) &= \overline{(n_k - \bar{n}_k(t)) \cdot (n_l - \bar{n}_l(t))} \\ &= \overline{n_k \cdot n_l} - \bar{n}_k \cdot \bar{n}_l.\end{aligned} \tag{11.2}$$

In terms of the deviation variables from the meanvalues

$$\Delta n_k(t) = (n_k - \bar{n}_k(t)) \tag{11.3}$$

the elements of the variance matrix read explicitly

$$\bar{v}_{kl}(t) = \sum_{\mathbf{n}}^{\{P.C.\}} \Delta n_k(t) \Delta n_l(t) P(\mathbf{n}; t). \tag{11.4}$$

339

The sums in (11.1) and (11.4) extend over all admissible population configurations *P.C.*, that means over all $\mathbf{n} = \{n_1, n_2, \ldots, n_L\}$ with $n_i \geq 0$.

In the following sections we will firstly introduce in 11.1 translation operators, a formal device which makes the derivation of dynamic equations for meanvalues and variances more transparent. This derivation of exact and approximate meanvalue- and variance equations from the master equation follows in Section 11.2. In Section 11.3 the limit of validity of the approximate equations is discussed in the case of nonlinear transition rates for which $P(\mathbf{n}; t)$ may evolve into a multimodal distribution. In Section 11.4 a simple exactly solvable example of meanvalue- and variance equations illustrates their meaning.

11.1   Translation Operators

Firstly we introduce in addition to the *true population configuration P.C.*: $\mathbf{n} = \{n_1, n_2, \ldots, n_L\}$ with positive semidefinite integers $n_i \geq 0$ the *general configurations G.C.*

$$\mathbf{n} = \{n_1, n_2, \ldots, n_L\} \quad n_i \gtrless 0, \tag{11.5}$$

where each n_i can be zero or a positive or a negative integer. *Virtual configurations V.C.* are those $\mathbf{n} = \{n_1, n_2, \ldots, n_L\}$ for which at least one of the n_i is negative. The space of general configurations $\{G.C.\}$ comprises all true and all virtual configurations, i.e. $\{G.C.\} = \{P.C.\} \oplus \{V.C.\}$.

All functions $F(\mathbf{n})$ like $P(\mathbf{n}; t)$, $w_{ij}(\mathbf{n}; t)$ etc. introduced so far are only defined on the space $\{P.C.\}$ of true population configurations. We may however extend their domain of definition to the space of general configurations $\{G.C.\}$ by putting

$$F(\mathbf{n}) = \begin{cases} F(\mathbf{n}) & \text{for} \quad \mathbf{n} \in \{P.C.\} \\ 0 & \text{for} \quad \mathbf{n} \in \{V.C.\} \end{cases} \tag{11.6}$$

The *translation operators* are now defined to act on functions in $\{G.C.\}$ as follows:

$$\begin{aligned} T_i F(n_1, \ldots, n_i, \ldots, n_L) &= F(n_1, \ldots, (n_i + 1), \ldots, n_L); \\ T_i^{-1} F(n_1, \ldots, n_i, \ldots, n_L) &= F(n_1, \ldots, (n_i - 1), \ldots, n_L). \end{aligned} \tag{11.7}$$

The definition (11.7) implies according to the notations (10.24), (10.25) and (10.26)

$$T_i^{\pm 1} F(\mathbf{n}) = F(\mathbf{n}_{i\pm}); \quad T_j^{+1} T_i^{-1} F(\mathbf{n}) = F(\mathbf{n}_{ji}) \tag{11.8}$$

and in particular the *commutation relations*

$$\begin{aligned} {[T_i, n_k]} &\equiv [T_i n_k - n_k T_i] = \delta_{ik} \cdot T_i \\ {[T_i^{-1}, n_k]} &\equiv [T_i^{-1} n_k - n_k T_i^{-1}] = -\delta_{ik} \cdot T_i^{-1} \end{aligned} \tag{11.9}$$

where δ_{ik} is the Kronecker symbol

$$
\begin{aligned}
\delta_{ik} &= 1 \quad \text{for} \quad i = k; \\
\delta_{ik} &= 0 \quad \text{for} \quad i \neq k.
\end{aligned}
\tag{11.10}
$$

Repeated application of (11.9) yields for instance

$$
n_k T_i^{\pm 1} F(\mathbf{n}) = T_i^{\pm 1} (n_k \mp \delta_{ik}) F(\mathbf{n}) \tag{a}
$$

$$
n_k T_j^{+1} T_i^{-1} F(\mathbf{n}) = T_j^{+1} T_i^{-1} (n_k - \delta_{jk} + \delta_{ik}) F(\mathbf{n}) \tag{b} \quad (11.11)
$$

$$
\Delta n_k \Delta n_l T_j^{+1} T_i^{-1} F(\mathbf{n}) = T_j^{+1} T_i^{-1} (\Delta n_k + \delta_{ik} - \delta_{jk})(\Delta n_l + \delta_{il} - \delta_{jl}) F(\mathbf{n}) \tag{c}
$$

Furthermore, it is evident that the relations hold

$$
\sum_{\mathbf{n}}^{\{G.C.\}} T_i^{\pm 1} F(\mathbf{n}) = \sum_{\mathbf{n}}^{\{G.C.\}} T_j^{+1} T_i^{-1} F(\mathbf{n}) = \sum_{\mathbf{n}}^{\{G.C.\}} F(\mathbf{n}) \tag{11.12}
$$

since the summation over all $\mathbf{n} \in \{G.C.\}$ extends over all $-\infty < n_i < +\infty$, $i = 1, 2, \ldots, L$, so that the translation of the variables in $F(\mathbf{n})$ does not matter.

The configurational master equation (10.38) may now be written in an equivalent compact form, making use of the translation operators:

$$
\begin{aligned}
\frac{dP(\mathbf{n}; t)}{dt} &= \sum_{i,j} (T_j^{+1} T_i^{-1} - 1) w_{ij}(\mathbf{n}; t) P(\mathbf{n}; t) \\
&\quad + \sum_i (T_i^{-1} - 1) w_{i+}(\mathbf{n}; t) P(\mathbf{n}; t) \\
&\quad + \sum_i (T_i^{+1} - 1) w_{i-}(\mathbf{n}; t) P(\mathbf{n}; t).
\end{aligned}
\tag{11.13}
$$

The conservation of the normalisation of $P(\mathbf{n}; t)$ follows now easily. (Note, that because of (11.6), sums over $\{P.C.\}$ can now be extended over $\{G.C.\}$.) Indeed, taking into account (11.12), one obtains from (11.13)

$$
\frac{d}{dt} \sum_{\mathbf{n}}^{\{G.C.\}} P(\mathbf{n}; t) = 0. \tag{11.14}
$$

11.2 Derivation of Dynamic Equations for Meanvalues and Variances

The equations of motion for the meanvalues (11.1) now follow by multiplying the master equation (11.13) by n_k and taking the sum over all configurations $\mathbf{n} \in \{G.C.\}$.

Furthermore the relations (11.11a) and (11.11b) and (11.12) are taken into account. One obtains sequentially:

$$\frac{d\bar{n}_k(t)}{dt} = \sum_{\mathbf{n}}^{\{G.C.\}} n_k \frac{dP(\mathbf{n}; t)}{dt}$$

$$= \sum_{i,j}^{L} \sum_{\mathbf{n}}^{\{G.C.\}} n_k (T_j^{+1} T_i^{-1} - 1) w_{ij}(\mathbf{n}; t) P(\mathbf{n}; t)$$

$$+ \sum_{i=1}^{L} \sum_{\mathbf{n}}^{\{G.C.\}} n_k (T_i^{-1} - 1) w_{i+}(\mathbf{n}; t) P(\mathbf{n}; t)$$

$$+ \sum_{i=1}^{L} \sum_{\mathbf{n}}^{\{G.C.\}} n_k (T_i^{+1} - 1) w_{i-}(\mathbf{n}; t) P(\mathbf{n}; t)$$

$$= \sum_{i,j}^{L} \sum_{\mathbf{n}}^{\{G.C.\}} T_j^{+1} T_i^{-1} (\delta_{ik} - \delta_{jk}) w_{ij}(\mathbf{n}; t) P(\mathbf{n}; t)$$

$$+ \sum_{i=1}^{L} \sum_{\mathbf{n}}^{\{G.C.\}} T_i^{-1} \delta_{ik} w_{i+}(\mathbf{n}; t) P(\mathbf{n}; t)$$

$$- \sum_{i=1}^{L} \sum_{\mathbf{n}}^{\{G.C.\}} T_i^{+1} \delta_{ik} w_{i-}(\mathbf{n}; t) P(\mathbf{n}; t)$$

$$= \sum_{j=1}^{L} \sum_{\mathbf{n}}^{\{G.C.\}} w_{kj}(\mathbf{n}; t) P(\mathbf{n}; t) - \sum_{i=1}^{L} \sum_{\mathbf{n}}^{\{G.C.\}} w_{ik}(\mathbf{n}; t) P(\mathbf{n}; t)$$

$$+ \sum_{\mathbf{n}}^{\{G.C.\}} w_{k+}(\mathbf{n}; t) P(\mathbf{n}; t)$$

$$- \sum_{\mathbf{n}}^{\{G.C.\}} w_{k-}(\mathbf{n}; t) P(\mathbf{n}; t). \tag{11.15}$$

The last line on the r.h.s. of (11.15) contains meanvalues over transition rates only. The *exact meanvalue equations* therefore can be written in the compact form:

$$\frac{d\bar{n}_k(t)}{dt} = \sum_{j=1}^{L} \overline{w_{kj}(\mathbf{n}; t)} - \sum_{i=1}^{L} \overline{w_{ik}(\mathbf{n}; t)} + \overline{w_{k+}(\mathbf{n}; t)} - \overline{w_{k-}(\mathbf{n}; t)} \tag{11.16}$$

$$\text{for} \quad k = 1, 2, \ldots, L.$$

The intuitive interpretation of these equations is clear: The change of the mean-value $\bar{n}_k(t)$ with time is due to the mean flow of population members *from all other states j* to state $k(\neq j)$ minus the mean flow of population members from state k *into all other states i($\neq k$)*, plus the mean birth rate minus the mean death rate of the population in state k.

Proceeding analogously the equations of motion for the variances (11.4) can also be derived. At first we state that

$$\frac{d\bar{v}_{kl}(t)}{dt} = \sum_{\mathbf{n}}^{\{G.C.\}} \Delta n_k(t) \Delta n_l(t) \frac{dP(\mathbf{n};t)}{dt}$$

$$- \frac{d\bar{n}_k}{dt} \sum_{\mathbf{n}}^{\{G.C.\}} \Delta n_l(t) P(\mathbf{n};t) - \frac{d\bar{n}_l}{dt} \sum_{\mathbf{n}}^{\{G.C.\}} \Delta n_k(t) P(\mathbf{n};t)$$

$$= \sum_{\mathbf{n}}^{\{G.C.\}} \Delta n_k(t) \Delta n_l(t) \frac{dP(\mathbf{n};t)}{dt}, \qquad (11.17)$$

where we have taken into account that

$$\overline{\Delta n_l(t)} = \overline{\Delta n_k(t)} \equiv 0. \qquad (11.18)$$

After inserting the master equation (11.13) on the r.h.s. of (11.17) and making use of (11.11) and (11.12) there follows:

$$\frac{d\bar{v}_{kl}(t)}{dt} = \sum_{i,j} \sum_{\mathbf{n}}^{\{G.C.\}} \Delta n_k(t) \Delta n_l(t) (T_j^{+1} T_i^{-1} - 1) w_{ij}(\mathbf{n};t) P(\mathbf{n};t)$$

$$+ \sum_{i} \sum_{\mathbf{n}}^{\{G.C.\}} \Delta n_k(t) \Delta n_l(t) (T_i^{-1} - 1) w_{i+}(\mathbf{n};t) P(\mathbf{n};t)$$

$$+ \sum_{i} \sum_{\mathbf{n}}^{\{G.C.\}} \Delta n_k(t) \Delta n_l(t) (T_i^{+1} - 1) w_{i-}(\mathbf{n};t) P(\mathbf{n};t)$$

$$= \sum_{i,j} \sum_{\mathbf{n}}^{\{G.C.\}} \left[(\delta_{ik} - \delta_{jk}) \Delta n_l(t) + (\delta_{il} - \delta_{jl}) \Delta n_k(t) + (\delta_{ik} - \delta_{jk})(\delta_{il} - \delta_{jl}) \right]$$
$$w_{ij}(\mathbf{n};t) P(\mathbf{n};t)$$

$$+ \sum_{i} \sum_{\mathbf{n}}^{\{G.C.\}} [\delta_{ik} \Delta n_l + \delta_{il} \Delta n_k + \delta_{ik} \delta_{il}] w_{i+}(\mathbf{n};t) P(\mathbf{n};t)$$

$$- \sum_{i} \sum_{\mathbf{n}}^{\{G.C.\}} [\delta_{ik} \Delta n_l + \delta_{il} \Delta n_k - \delta_{ik} \delta_{il}] w_{i-}(\mathbf{n};t) P(\mathbf{n};t)$$

$$= \left\{ \sum_{j} \overline{\Delta n_l(t) w_{kj}(\mathbf{n};t)} - \sum_{i} \overline{\Delta n_l(t) w_{ik}(\mathbf{n};t)} \right.$$

$$+ \sum_{j} \overline{\Delta n_k(t) w_{lj}(\mathbf{n};t)} - \sum_{i} \overline{\Delta n_k(t) w_{il}(\mathbf{n};t)}$$

$$\left. + \sum_{j} \delta_{kl} \overline{w_{kj}(\mathbf{n};t)} + \sum_{i} \delta_{kl} \overline{w_{ik}(\mathbf{n};t)} - \overline{w_{lk}(\mathbf{n};t)} - \overline{w_{kl}(\mathbf{n};t)} \right\}$$

$$+ \left\{ \overline{\Delta n_l w_{k+}(\mathbf{n};t)} + \overline{\Delta n_k w_{l+}(\mathbf{n};t)} + \delta_{kl} \overline{w_{k+}(\mathbf{n};t)} \right\}$$

$$- \left\{ \overline{\Delta n_l w_{k-}(\mathbf{n};t)} + \overline{\Delta n_k w_{l-}(\mathbf{n};t)} - \delta_{kl} \overline{w_{k-}(\mathbf{n};t)} \right\}. \qquad (11.19)$$

Introducing some abbreviations for the net migration rate into state k,

$$w_k^{NM}(\mathbf{n}; t) = \sum_j w_{kj}(\mathbf{n}; t) - \sum_i w_{ik}(\mathbf{n}; t), \qquad (11.20)$$

the sum of migration rates into and from state k,

$$w_k^{SM}(\mathbf{n}; t) = \sum_j w_{kj}(\mathbf{n}; t) + \sum_i w_{ik}(\mathbf{n}; t) \qquad (11.21)$$

and for the sum of rates between l and k:

$$w_{lk}^{SM}(\mathbf{n}; t) = w_{lk}(\mathbf{n}; t) + w_{kl}(\mathbf{n}; t), \qquad (11.22)$$

where we may put $w_{kk}(\mathbf{n}; t) \equiv 0$ in all formulas, as well as for the net birth/death rate of state k

$$w_k^{NBD}(\mathbf{n}; t) = w_{k+}(\mathbf{n}; t) - w_{k-}(\mathbf{n}; t) \qquad (11.23)$$

and the sum of birth/death rates of state k

$$w_k^{SBD}(\mathbf{n}; t) = w_{k+}(\mathbf{n}; t) + w_{k-}(\mathbf{n}; t), \qquad (11.24)$$

the final form of the *exact equations of motion* for the variances reads:

$$\frac{d\bar{v}_{kl}(t)}{dt} = \left\{ \overline{\Delta n_k w_l^{NM}(\mathbf{n}; t)} + \overline{\Delta n_l w_k^{NM}(\mathbf{n}; t)} + \delta_{kl}\overline{w_k^{SM}(\mathbf{n}; t)} - \overline{w_{kl}^{SM}(\mathbf{n}; t)} \right\}$$
$$+ \left\{ \overline{\Delta n_k w_l^{NBD}(\mathbf{n}; t)} + \overline{\Delta n_l w_k^{NBD}(\mathbf{n}; t)} + \delta_{kl}\overline{w_k^{SBD}(\mathbf{n}; t)} \right\}. \qquad (11.25)$$

The first bracket { } stems from migration processes and the second bracket { } from birth–death-processes.

Approximate meanvalue- and variance-equations

The sets of meanvalue equations (11.16) and variance equations (11.25) are *exact*, but have a decisive *disadvantage:* They are in general *not* closed, i.e. selfcontained equations for the variables under consideration!

Only in the case when the transition rates $w_{ji}(\mathbf{n}; t)$, $w_{j+}(\mathbf{n}; t)$ and $w_{j-}(\mathbf{n}; t)$ are *linear functions* of $\mathbf{n}$, the right hand sides of (11.16) and (11.25) are linear expressions in $\{\bar{n}_1, \ldots, \bar{n}_L\}$ and $\{\bar{v}_{pq}(t)\}$, so that these exact equations become selfcontained and can in simple cases even be solved exactly (see Section 13.4).

In all other cases, i.e. when the transition rates are *nonlinear functions* of the configuration variables $\{n_1, n_2, \ldots, n_L\}$, the right hand sides of (11.16) and (11.25) contain the meanvalues of higher powers of the variables $\{n_1, n_2, \ldots, n_L\}$. The equations of motion for these higher meanvalues contain meanvalues of still higher powers, and so on, so that this system of equations is not closed, at least not exactly.

The equations (11.16) and (11.25) may however be transformed into *approximate* but *closed* equations by expanding all transition rates $w(\mathbf{n}; t)$ and expressions composed of them in a Taylor series up to second order around the meanvalues $\bar{n}(t) = \{\bar{n}_1(t), \ldots \bar{n}_L(t)\}$, neglecting higher expansion terms. This means, all $w(\mathbf{n}; t)$ are substituted by

$$w(\mathbf{n}; t) = w(\bar{\mathbf{n}}(t); t) + \sum_p w_{|p}(\bar{\mathbf{n}}(t); t)\Delta n_p(t)$$

$$+ \frac{1}{2}\sum_{p,q} w_{|p|q}(\bar{\mathbf{n}}(t); t)\Delta n_p(t)\Delta n_q(t) + \cdots, \tag{11.26}$$

where we use the notation

$$w_{|p}(\mathbf{n}; t) = \frac{\partial w(\mathbf{n}; t)}{\partial n_p}. \tag{11.27}$$

The neglection of the higher terms anticipates that they play no role in the formation of the meanvalues on the r.h.s. of (11.16) and (11.25). This is however only fulfilled as long as the probability distribution $P(\mathbf{n}; t)$ remains unimodal and sufficiently sharply peaked during its temporal evolution. This question is further discussed in Section 11.3.

By inserting (11.26) in the r.h.s. of (11.16) and (11.25), regarding (11.18), and going to second order terms in $\Delta n_i(t)$ only, one obtains now the approximate meanvalue equation

$$\frac{d\bar{n}_k(t)}{dt} = \left\{\sum_{j=1}^{L}\left(w_{kj}(\bar{\mathbf{n}}(t); t) - w_{jk}(\bar{\mathbf{n}}(t); t)\right) + w_{k+}(\bar{\mathbf{n}}(t); t) - w_{k-}(\bar{\mathbf{n}}(t); t)\right\}$$

$$+ \frac{1}{2}\left\{\sum_{j,p,q}\left(w_{kj|p|q}(\bar{\mathbf{n}}(t); t) - w_{jk|p|q}(\bar{\mathbf{n}}(t); t)\right)\bar{v}_{pq}(t)\right.$$

$$\left. + \sum_{p,q}\left(w_{k+|p|q}(\bar{\mathbf{n}}(t); t) - w_{k-|p|q}(\bar{\mathbf{n}}(t); t)\right)\bar{v}_{pq}(t)\right\} \tag{11.28}$$

and the approximate variance equation:

$$\frac{d\bar{v}_{kl}(t)}{dt} = \left\{\sum_p w_{l|p}^{NM}(\bar{\mathbf{n}}(t); t)\bar{v}_{kp}(t) + \sum_p w_{k|p}^{NM}(\bar{\mathbf{n}}(t); t)\bar{v}_{lp}(t)\right.$$

$$+ \delta_{kl}\left[w_k^{SM}(\bar{\mathbf{n}}(t); t) + \frac{1}{2}\sum_{p,q} w_{k|p|q}^{SM}(\bar{\mathbf{n}}(t); t)\bar{v}_{pq}(t)\right]$$

$$\left. - \left[w_{kl}^{S}(\bar{\mathbf{n}}(t); t) + \frac{1}{2}\sum_{p,q} w_{kl|p|q}^{S}(\bar{\mathbf{n}}(t); t)\bar{v}_{pq}(t)\right]\right\}$$

$$+ \left\{\sum_p w_{l|p}^{NBD}(\bar{\mathbf{n}}(t); t)\bar{v}_{kp}(t) + \sum_p w_{k|p}^{NBD}(\bar{\mathbf{n}}(t); t)\bar{v}_{lp}(t)\right.$$

$$\left. + \delta_{kl}\left[w_k^{SBD}(\bar{\mathbf{n}}(t); t) + \frac{1}{2}\sum_{p,q} w_{k|p|q}^{SBD}(\bar{\mathbf{n}}(t); t)\bar{v}_{pq}(t)\right]\right\}, \tag{11.29}$$

where the first bracket { } on the r.h.s. refers to migratory processes, and the second bracket { } to birth–death-processes. In spite of their apparently complicated form equations (11.28) and (11.29) are selfcontained coupled differential equations for the variables $\{\bar{n}_1(t), \ldots, \bar{n}_L(t)\}$ and $\bar{v}_{kl}(t)$. If the transition rates do not explicitly depend on time (which means $w_{kj}(\bar{\mathbf{n}}(t); t) \Rightarrow w_{kj}(\bar{\mathbf{n}}(t)))$, the equations are even autonomous.

11.3   Limits of Validity of Closed Meanvalue and Variance Equations

Evidently the answer to the question whether the approximate equations (11.28) and (11.29) are valid and applicable or not depends on the order of magnitude of the neglected terms and the terms taken into account in the Taylor expansion (11.26) and their corresponding meanvalues.

At first we show how the *orders of magnitude of the transition rates* $w(\bar{\mathbf{n}}(t); t)$ and their derivatives and of the meanvalues $\bar{n}_i$ depend on the *system size*. For the system of configurations $\mathbf{n} = \{n_1, n_2, \ldots, n_L\}$ there exists an appropriate measure of system size, namely the total number of members of the population

$$N = \sum_{i=1}^{L} n_i \gg 1 \tag{11.30}$$

which is even a conserved quantity in the case of purely migratory processes. Introducing the size-independent scaled variables x_i by

$$n_i = N x_i \quad 0 \le x_i \le 1, \tag{11.31}$$

it is evident, that

$$O(x_i) = O(1); \quad O(n_i) = O(N), \tag{11.32}$$

where $O(a)$ means "order of magnitude of a". The transition rates, in particular the migratory transition rates, have the form (see (12.29)):

$$w_{ji}(\mathbf{n}; t) = p_{ji}(\mathbf{n}; t) \cdot n_i, \tag{11.33}$$

where n_i is the number of population members of kind i and p_{ji} is an individual transition rate from i to j, which should be practically *independent of the system size*, for instance by depending on $\mathbf{x} = \{x_1, \ldots, x_L\}$ only. Therefore we conclude

$$O(w_{ji}(\mathbf{n}; t)) = O(N), \tag{11.34}$$

The same holds for the birth/death rates (10.31) and (10.32). Because of

$$\frac{\partial F(\mathbf{n})}{\partial n_k} = \frac{\partial F}{\partial x_k} \cdot \frac{\partial x_k}{\partial n_k} = \frac{\partial F}{\partial x_k} \cdot N^{-1}$$

$$\text{and} \quad O\left(\frac{\partial F(\mathbf{n})}{\partial n_k}\right) = O\left(\frac{\partial F}{\partial x_k}\right) \cdot O(N^{-1}) = O(F)O(N^{-1}) \tag{11.35}$$

there follows, that the orders of magnitude of *derivatives* of $w_{ji}(\mathbf{n}; t)$ are:

$$(w_{ji|p}) = O(1); \quad O(w_{ji|p|q}) = O(N^{-1});$$
$$O(w_{ji|p|q|r}) = O(N^{-2}); \quad O(w_{ji|p|q|r|s}) = O(N^{-3}) \quad \text{and so on.}$$

$$(11.36)$$

Secondly we must consider the *order of magnitude of the variances* $\bar{v}_{pq}(t)$ and of higher order expressions like

$$\bar{v}_{pqr}(t) = \overline{(n_p - \bar{n}_p(t))(n_q - \bar{n}_q(t))(n_r - \bar{n}_r(t))};$$
$$\bar{v}_{pqrs}(t) = \overline{(n_p - \bar{n}_p(t))(n_q - \bar{n}_q(t))(n_r - \bar{n}_r(t))(n_s - \bar{n}_s(t))}$$

$$(11.37)$$

which have been neglected in the Taylor expansion (11.26). Their orders of magnitude evidently depend on the form of the probability distribution $P(\mathbf{n}; t)$.

If this distribution is *unimodal* and if $P(\mathbf{n}; t)$ possesses a small width $\sigma \ll N$ so that for the largest variance-expressions, namely the positive definite quantities $\bar{v}_{pp}; \bar{v}_{ppqq}$ there holds:

$$\bar{v}_{pp} \leq \sigma^2 \ll N^2 \quad \text{for all } p$$
$$\bar{v}_{ppqq} \leq \sigma^4 \lll N^4 \quad \text{for all } p \text{ and } q$$

$$(11.38)$$

(and accordingly for all higher meanvalues of products of the deviations $\Delta n_k(t)$), the higher order expansion terms of the Taylor expansion (11.26) can indeed be neglected against those terms which have been taken into account in (11.28), (11.29)).

Because of (11.36) and (11.38) even further terms in (11.28), (11.29) turn out to be very small against the others so that in this case the approximate meanvalue- and variance-equations can be further simplified to assume the form:

$$\frac{d\bar{n}_k(t)}{dt} = \sum_{j=1}^{L}\left(w_{kj}(\bar{\mathbf{n}}(t); t) - w_{jk}(\bar{\mathbf{n}}(t); t)\right) + w_{k+}(\bar{\mathbf{n}}(t); t) - w_{k-}(\bar{\mathbf{n}}(t); t) \qquad (11.39)$$

and

$$\frac{d\bar{v}_{kl}(t)}{dt} = \left\{ \sum_p w_{l|p}^{NM}(\bar{\mathbf{n}}(t); t)\bar{v}_{kp}(t) + \sum_p w_{k|p}^{NM}(\bar{\mathbf{n}}(t); t)\bar{v}_{lp}(t) \right.$$
$$\left. + \delta_{kl}w_k^{SM}(\bar{\mathbf{n}}(t); t) - w_{kl}^{SM}(\bar{\mathbf{n}}(t); t)\right\}$$
$$+ \left\{ \sum_p w_{l|p}^{NBD}(\bar{\mathbf{n}}(t); t)\bar{v}_{kp}(t) + \sum_p w_{k|p}^{NBD}(\bar{\mathbf{n}}(t); t)\bar{v}_{lp}(t)\right.$$
$$\left. + \delta_{kl}w_k^{SBD}(\bar{\mathbf{n}}(t); t)\right\}.$$

$$(11.40)$$

For a sharply peaked unimodal probability distribution the equations (11.39) and (11.40) represent the final form of approximate meanvalue- and variance-equations. Their structure is now the following: Equations (11.39) are a system of coupled, in general nonlinear differential equations for the meanvalues $\bar{n}_i(t)$ only. If they can be solved, the result can be inserted in equations (11.40) which become thereupon a system of inhomogeneous linear differential equations for the variances $\bar{v}_{kl}(t)$ with known time-dependent coefficients.

It depends on the form of the transition rates as functions of $\mathbf{n}$, whether the initially unimodal distribution function remains unimodal for all times or evolves into a multimodal distribution with more than one maximum.

In the first case the equations (11.39) and (11.40) remain valid for all times. If the transition rates do not explicitly depend on time, the meanvalues then approach *unambiguous* stationary values $\bar{n}_k^{st}$ and the variances approach according to (11.40) stationary values $\bar{v}_{kl}^{st}$, too.

A coarse estimation of the magnitude of the stationary variances can be given in the purely migratory case (where the second bracket { } in (11.40) vanishes), if the nondiagonal elements $\bar{v}_{kp}, k \neq p$ are neglected. The stationary variance $\bar{v}_{kk}^{st}$ then obeys the equation

$$\frac{d\bar{v}_{kk}^{st}}{dt} \stackrel{!}{=} 0 = 2w_{k|k}^{NM}(\bar{\mathbf{n}}^{st})\bar{v}_{kk}^{st} + w_k^{SM}(\bar{\mathbf{n}}^{st}) \tag{11.41}$$

or

$$\bar{v}_{kk}^{st} = -\frac{w_k^{SM}(\bar{\mathbf{n}}^{st})}{2w_{k|k}^{NM}(\bar{\mathbf{n}}^{st})}. \tag{11.42}$$

Because $w_k^{SM}(\bar{\mathbf{n}}^{st})$ and $\bar{v}_{kk}^{st}$ are positive definite by definition, equation (11.42) is only consistent, if

$$w_{k|k}^{NM}(\bar{\mathbf{n}}^{st}) < 0 \tag{11.43}$$

holds. Indeed, (11.43) is the condition for a *stable* stationary state $\bar{\mathbf{n}}^{st}$. Only at a stable stationary state a unimodal probability distribution can approach its stationary form with stationary variance. With regard to (11.34) and (11.36) one concludes from (11.42) that the order of magnitude of the stationary variance $\bar{v}_{kk}^{st}$ must then be:

$$O(\bar{v}_{kk}^{st}) = O(N) \tag{11.44}$$

which is in accordance with the conditions for the validity of equations (11.39) and (11.40).

If, alternatively, the distribution function evolves into a *multimodal function* the equations (11.39) and (11.40) are *inadequate* and *fail* in describing the evolution of *meanvalues* and *variances*. This follows from two arguments:

(a) For a multimodal distribution the – always unambiguously defined – mean-value $\bar{\mathbf{n}}(t)$ lies *between* the various maxima $\mathbf{n}_M^{(1)}(t)$, $\mathbf{n}_M^{(2)}(t)$, ... of the distribution function. The distance $d(\mathbf{n}_M, \bar{\mathbf{n}})$ between a maximum $\mathbf{n}_M(t)$ and the meanvalue $\bar{\mathbf{n}}(t)$ is in general of order $O(N)$, i.e.

$$O(d(\mathbf{n}_M, \bar{\mathbf{n}})) \equiv O\left(\sqrt{\sum_{i=1}^{L}(n_{iM} - \bar{n}_i)^2}\right) = O(N) \tag{11.45}$$

which implies that at least some of the expressions $\bar{v}_{pp}$, $\bar{v}_{ppqq}$ are of order $O(N^2)$, $O(N^4)$, respectively:

$$O(\bar{v}_{pp}) = O(N^2); \quad O(\bar{v}_{ppqq}) = O(N^4) \quad \text{for at least one } p \text{ and } q \tag{11.46}$$

These orders of magnitude for *multimodal* distributions contrast with those found in (11.38) for *unimodal* distribution functions of small width σ. The higher terms of the Taylor expansion (11.26) can now no more be neglected in setting up meanvalue- and variance-equations if (11.46) instead of (11.38) holds, because it can easily be checked that they now have the same order of magnitude as the lower terms.

(b)   Furthermore we consider the approximate meanvalue equations (11.39) in the case of pure migration, assuming the explicit form of transition rates (see (10.116)):

$$w_{ji}(\mathbf{n}) = p_{ji}(\mathbf{n}) \cdot n_i = \mu_{ji} \exp[u_j(\mathbf{n}_{ji}) - u_i(\mathbf{n})] \cdot n_i$$
$$\text{with} \quad \mu_{ji} = \mu_{ij}. \tag{11.47}$$

Their stationary form reads

$$0 = \sum_{j=1}^{L} \mu_{ji}\{\exp[u_j(\bar{\mathbf{n}}) - u_i(\bar{\mathbf{n}})]\bar{n}_i - \exp[u_i(\bar{\mathbf{n}}) - u_j(\bar{\mathbf{n}})]\bar{n}_j\}, \tag{11.48}$$

where we have put $\bar{\mathbf{n}}_{ji} \approx \bar{\mathbf{n}}$, which is justified for large numbers $\bar{n}_i$, $\bar{n}_j$. It can easily be seen that its solutions $\bar{\mathbf{n}}$ have to fulfill

$$\bar{n}_i = c \exp[2u_i(\bar{\mathbf{n}})], \tag{11.49}$$

where c is a normalisation constant which is determined by (11.30).

It is remarkable that equation (11.49) coincides with equation (10.141) for the determination of the extrema $\{\hat{\mathbf{n}}\}$ of the stationary probability distribution in cases, where detailed balance holds.

If equation (11.49) has only *one solution*, (which in the case of detailed balance coincides with the maximum of the explicitly constructed unimodal stationary probability distribution) $\bar{\mathbf{n}}$ can be interpreted as the (approximate) meanvalue $\bar{\mathbf{n}}^{st}$ belonging to this distribution $P_{st}(\mathbf{n})$.

If, alternatively, equation (11.49) has more than one solutions, *these solutions cannot at all be interpreted as meanvalues*, not even approximately, because the meanvalue $\bar{\mathbf{n}}$ of a probability distribution $P_{st}(\mathbf{n})$ (whether unimodal or multimodal) is *one unambiguously defined state*. This meanvalue lies *between* the maxima in the case of a multimodal probability distribution.

The structure of equation (11.39) and its stationary version (11.48), (11.49) can therefore be taken as a *criterion* for the interpretability of its solutions $\bar{n}(t)$ as meanvalues. If (11.48) or (11.49) has *more than one solution*, the corresponding probability distribution, even if initially unimodal, has eventually developed a multimodal shape. In this case, the stationary solutions of (11.48) have lost their meaning as meanvalues. Instead they characterize the maxima of the final probability distribution.

Fortunately, the set of equations (11.39) keeps its importance also in the multimodal case. But the interpretation of its solutions must be thoroughly reconsidered. This will be done in Chapter 12.

11.4 An Exactly Solvable Example for Meanvalue- and Variance-Equations

The equations (11.39) and (11.40) for meanvalues and variances have a rather complex structure even if all conditions for their applicability are fulfilled. In most cases they can only be solved numerically. It is therefore instructive to solve them analytically in a very simple case.

We consider a pure migration process in a population consisting of two kinds $i = 1, 2$ only and assume migration rates which are linear in the configuration variables **n**.

The population configuration consists of two variables $\{n_1, n_2\}$ only. Since only pure migration is considered, the total population number (assumed as an even integer)

$$n_1 + n_2 = 2N \tag{11.50}$$

remains constant with time. It is convenient to introduce the difference variable n by

$$n_2 - n_1 = 2n; \quad -N \le n \le +N$$
$$n_1 = N - n; \quad n_2 = N + n. \tag{11.51}$$

All variables n_1, n_2, N, n are integers. The transition rates belonging to the transitions $\{n_1, n_2\} \rightarrow \{(n_1 - 1), (n_2 + 1)\}$ and $\{n_1, n_2\} \rightarrow \{(n_1 + 1), (n_2 - 1)\}$, respectively, are

$$w_{21}(\mathbf{n}) = p_\uparrow n_1 = p_\uparrow (N - n);$$
$$w_{12}(\mathbf{n}) = p_\downarrow n_2 = p_\downarrow (N + n), \tag{11.52}$$

where it is assumed that the individual transition rates $p_\uparrow, p_\downarrow$ do neither depend on time nor depend on $\{n_1, n_2\}$. Furthermore we put for simplicity, since these quantities cancel in all equations of motion:

$$w_{11} = w_{22} \equiv 0. \tag{11.53}$$

The equations (11.39) for the meanvalues

$$\bar{n}_j(t) = \sum_{\mathbf{n}} n_j P(n_1, n_2; t) \quad \text{with} \quad j = 1, 2 \tag{11.54}$$

now assume the form

$$\frac{d\bar{n}_1}{dt} = w_{12}(\bar{\mathbf{n}}) - w_{21}(\bar{\mathbf{n}}) = p_{\downarrow}\bar{n}_2 - p_{\uparrow}\bar{n}_1;$$

$$\frac{d\bar{n}_2}{dt} = w_{21}(\bar{\mathbf{n}}) - w_{12}(\bar{\mathbf{n}}) = p_{\uparrow}\bar{n}_1 - p_{\downarrow}\bar{n}_2 \tag{11.55}$$

or, going over to $\bar{N}$ and $\bar{n}$,

$$\frac{d\bar{N}}{dt} = \frac{1}{2}(\dot{\bar{n}}_1 + \dot{\bar{n}}_2) = 0 \tag{a}$$

$$\frac{d\bar{n}}{dt} = \frac{1}{2}(\dot{\bar{n}}_2 - \dot{\bar{n}}_1) = (p_{\uparrow} - p_{\downarrow})\bar{N} - (p_{\uparrow} + p_{\downarrow})\bar{n} \tag{b}$$
$$\tag{11.56}$$

The equations (11.40) for the variances

$$\bar{v}_{ij}(t) = \sum_{\mathbf{n}} (n_i - \bar{n}_i)(n_j - \bar{n}_j) P(n_1, n_2; t)$$

$$= \overline{n_i n_j} - \bar{n}_i \cdot \bar{n}_j \quad \text{with} \quad i, j = 1, 2 \tag{11.57}$$

now read

$$\frac{d\bar{v}_{11}}{dt} = -p_{\uparrow}\bar{v}_{11} + p_{\downarrow}\bar{v}_{12} - p_{\uparrow}\bar{v}_{11} + p_{\downarrow}\bar{v}_{12} + p_{\downarrow}\bar{n}_2 + p_{\uparrow}\bar{n}_1 \tag{a}$$

$$\frac{d\bar{v}_{12}}{dt} = +p_{\uparrow}\bar{v}_{11} - p_{\downarrow}\bar{v}_{12} - p_{\uparrow}\bar{v}_{21} + p_{\downarrow}\bar{v}_{22} - p_{\uparrow}\bar{n}_1 - p_{\downarrow}\bar{n}_2 \tag{b}$$

$$\frac{d\bar{v}_{21}}{dt} = -p_{\uparrow}\bar{v}_{21} + p_{\downarrow}\bar{v}_{22} + p_{\uparrow}\bar{v}_{11} - p_{\downarrow}\bar{v}_{12} - p_{\uparrow}\bar{n}_1 - p_{\downarrow}\bar{n}_2 \tag{c}$$

$$\frac{d\bar{v}_{22}}{dt} = +p_{\uparrow}\bar{v}_{21} - p_{\downarrow}\bar{v}_{22} + p_{\uparrow}\bar{v}_{21} - p_{\downarrow}\bar{v}_{22} + p_{\uparrow}\bar{n}_1 + p_{\downarrow}\bar{n}_2 \tag{d}$$
$$\tag{11.58}$$

where we have inserted into (11.40) the expressions according to (11.20), (11.21) and (11.22):

$$w_1^{NM}(\mathbf{n}) = p_{\downarrow}n_2 - p_{\uparrow}n_1; \quad w_2^{NM}(\mathbf{n}) = p_{\uparrow}n_1 - p_{\downarrow}n_2;$$

$$w_1^{SM}(\mathbf{n}) = p_{\downarrow}n_2 + p_{\uparrow}n_1; \quad w_2^{SM}(\mathbf{n}) = p_{\uparrow}n_1 + p_{\downarrow}n_2; \tag{11.59}$$

$$w_{11}^{SM} = w_{22}^{SM} = 0; \quad w_{21}^{SM} = w_{12}^{SM} = p_{\uparrow}n_1 + p_{\downarrow}n_2$$

and

$$w_{1|1}^{NM} = -p_\uparrow; \quad w_{1|2}^{NM} = +p_\downarrow;$$
$$w_{2|1}^{NM} = +p_\uparrow; \quad w_{2|2}^{NM} = -p_\downarrow. \tag{11 60}$$

We have assumed a fixed total population number $2N = 2\bar{N} = 2N_0$. This implies that the variances $\bar{v}_{NN}$, $\bar{v}_{Nn}$ and $\bar{v}_{nN}$ are zero:

$$\bar{v}_{NN} = \bar{v}_{Nn} = \bar{v}_{nN} = 0 \tag{11.61}$$

and that the probability distribution has the form (which is consistent with the master equation):

$$P(n_1, n_2; t) = P((N - n), (N + n); t) = \delta_{NN_0} P(n; t), \tag{11.62}$$

where $P(n; t)$ is a distribution over the difference variable n only. Going over to variables $\{N, n\}$ and taking into account (11.61) one obtains:

$$\bar{v}_{11} = \overline{[(N-n)-(\bar{N}-\bar{n})] \cdot [(N-n)-(\bar{N}-\bar{n})]} = +\bar{v}_{nn};$$
$$\bar{v}_{12} = \overline{[(N-n)-(\bar{N}-\bar{n})] \cdot [(N+n)-(\bar{N}+\bar{n})]} = -\bar{v}_{nn};$$
$$\bar{v}_{21} = \overline{[(N+n)-(\bar{N}+\bar{n})] \cdot [(N-n)-(\bar{N}-\bar{n})]} = -\bar{v}_{nn};$$
$$\bar{v}_{22} = \overline{[(N+n)-(\bar{N}+\bar{n})] \cdot [(N+n)-(\bar{N}+\bar{n})]} = +\bar{v}_{nn}. \tag{11.63}$$

That means, the four variances $\bar{v}_{ji}$ can be expressed by the variance $\bar{v}_{nn}$ of the difference variable n only. After inserting (11.63) into (11.58) it turns out that the four equations (11.58a,b,c,d) *coincide* and amount to *one* equation for $\bar{v}_{nn}$ only:

$$\frac{d\bar{v}_{nn}}{dt} = (p_\uparrow \bar{n}_1 + p_\downarrow \bar{n}_2) - 2(p_\uparrow + p_\downarrow)\bar{v}_{nn}. \tag{11.64}$$

Thus the conservation of $N = N_0$ and the vanishing of its variance has led to a considerable simplification: Instead of solving the two equations (11.55) and the four equations (11.58) one has only to solve one meanvalue equation (11.56b) and one variance equation (11.64) for the difference variable.
The solution of (11.56b) is

$$\bar{n}(t) = \bar{n}_{st} + c\exp[-(p_\uparrow + p_\downarrow)t], \tag{11.65}$$

where the stationary value of $\bar{n}$

$$\bar{n}_{st} = \frac{(p_\uparrow - p_\downarrow)}{(p_\uparrow + p_\downarrow)} N_0 \tag{11.66}$$

follows from the stationary version of (11.56b). The integration constant c is determined by the initial value $\bar{n}_0 = \bar{n}(t = 0)$:

$$c = (\bar{n}_0 - \bar{n}_{st}).$$

(11.67)

Expressing $n_1(t)$ and $n_2(t)$ by $n(t)$ via (11.51) one obtains

$$\bar{n}(t) = \bar{n}_{st} + (\bar{n}_0 - \bar{n}_{st}) \exp[-(p_\uparrow + p_\downarrow)t];$$
$$\bar{n}_1(t) = \bar{n}_{1st} + (\bar{n}_{10} - \bar{n}_{1st}) \exp[-(p_\uparrow + p_\downarrow)t];$$
$$\bar{n}_2(t) = \bar{n}_{2st} + (\bar{n}_{20} - \bar{n}_{2st}) \exp[-(p_\uparrow + p_\downarrow)t].$$

(11.68)

The variance equation (11.64) is an inhomogeneous linear differential equation of the type

$$\frac{dy}{dt} = g(t) + f(t)y(t)$$

(11.69)

which can be exactly solved. The solution reads

$$y(t) = y_0 \exp[F(t)] + \int_0^t g(t') \exp[F(t) - F(t')]dt'$$

(11.70)

with

$$y_0 = y(t = 0); \quad F(t) = \int_0^t f(t')dt'.$$

(11.71)

Applying (11.69) to (11.64) one has to identify

$$y(t) = \bar{v}_{nn}(t) \tag{a}$$
$$f(t) = -2(p_\uparrow + p_\downarrow); \quad F(t) = -2(p_\uparrow + p_\downarrow)t \tag{b}$$
$$g(t) = (p_\uparrow \bar{n}_1(t) + p_\downarrow \bar{n}_2(t)) \tag{c}$$
$$= (p_\uparrow(N_0 - \bar{n}(t)) + p_\downarrow(N_0 + \bar{n}(t)))$$
$$= \frac{4 p_\uparrow p_\downarrow}{(p_\uparrow + p_\downarrow)} N_0 - (p_\uparrow - p_\downarrow)(\bar{n}_0 - \bar{n}_{st}) \exp[-(p_\uparrow + p_\downarrow)t].$$

(11.72)

By inserting (11.72) into (11.70) there follows the final result

$$\bar{v}_{nn}(t) = \bar{v}_{nn}(0) \exp[-2(p_\uparrow + p_\downarrow)t] + \bar{v}_{nn}^{st} \left\{ 1 - \exp[-2(p_\uparrow + p_\downarrow)t] \right\}$$
$$- \frac{(p_\uparrow - p_\downarrow)}{(p_\uparrow + p_\downarrow)} (\bar{n}_0 - \bar{n}_{st}) \left\{ \exp[-(p_\uparrow + p_\downarrow)t] - \exp[-2(p_\uparrow + p_\downarrow)t] \right\},$$

(11.73)

where

$$\bar{v}_{nn}^{st} = \bar{v}_{nn}(t = \infty) = \frac{2 p_\uparrow p_\downarrow}{(p_\uparrow + p_\downarrow)^2} N_0.$$

(11.74)

The result (11.73) with (11.74) implies the following conclusions:

(1) If the initial variance $\bar{v}_{nn}(0)$ is of order $O(N_0)$ the variance $\bar{v}_{nn}(t)$ remains of order $O(N_0)$ during the temporal evolution, because also $\bar{v}_{nn}^{st}$ and $\bar{n}_0, \bar{n}_{st}$ are of order $O(N_0)$. The conditions for applying the approximate equations (11.39) and (11.40) are therefore selfconsistently fulfilled. This was of course to be expected, because in our simple case the higher derivatives of the (in n_1, n_2 linear) transition rates vanish exactly, so that equations (11.39) and (11.40) are even exact.

(2) The initial variance $\bar{v}_{nn}(0)$ decays in the course of time and a final stationary variance $\bar{v}_{nn}^{st}$ builds up, which is independent of $\bar{v}_{nn}(0)$.

(3) The evolution of the variance $\bar{v}_{nn}(t)$ accompanies the evolution of the mean-value $\bar{n}(t)$ on its way from $\bar{n}_0$ to $\bar{n}_{st}$.

12. Stochastic Trajectories and Dynamic Equations for Quasi-Meanvalues

In the mathematical theory of stochastic systems two main approaches have been developed. The *one approach* treats a *whole ensemble* of equally structured but probabilistically evolving stochastic systems. The other approach focusses on a *single system* and investigates the properties of its stochastic evolution in which it traverses probabilistically a sequence of system states. This set of probabilistically traversed system states is denoted as a *stochastic trajectory*.

Both approaches are complementary and even in principle equivalent but each of them has methodical and applicational advantages and disadvantages.

Here there appears a specific difference between *natural sciences* and *social sciences*. Whereas in natural science, for instance in nuclear physics, it is often possible to measure the evolution of a *whole ensemble* of millions of equally prepared but probabilistically evolving systems, the social sciences, e.g. economics, politics or sociology, only dispose of *one* or at best of *a few* comparable systems as their objects of investigation. Therefore it is understandable that in natural science the ensemble approach has found widespread application whereas in social science often only the properties of the single system are investigated.

In §10 and §11 we have exhibited some central mathematical concepts of the ensemble approach. Complementary to this we shall focus in this chapter on the properties of stochastic trajectories and their relation to the concepts of the ensemble theory.

12.1 Stochastic Trajectories and their Relation to the Probability Distribution

We consider stochastically evolving systems which can probabilistically traverse a sequence of states belonging to a set of discrete system states. The system states are, as in §10 and §11, either denoted by $\mathbf{i}, \mathbf{j}, \mathbf{k}, \ldots$ or in applications to configuration space by $\mathbf{n} = \{n_1, n_2, \ldots, n_L\}, \mathbf{n}' = \{n_1', n_2', \ldots, n_L'\} \ldots$.

However, for purposes of comparison we begin with a short reminiscence of fully deterministic systems. The classical example of such systems is found in classical mechanics. The (continuous) states of a system are here described by $2f$ canonically conjugate variables $\{\mathbf{q}(t), \mathbf{p}(t)\} = \{q_1(t), \ldots, q_f(t); p_1(t), \ldots, p_f(t)\}$ which are elements of a $2f$-dimensional phase space Γ and obey the Hamiltonian equations:

$$\frac{dq_k(t)}{dt} = \frac{\partial H(\mathbf{q}; \mathbf{p})}{\partial p_k}; \quad \frac{dp_k(t)}{dt} = -\frac{\partial H(\mathbf{q}; \mathbf{p})}{\partial q_k}, \tag{12.1}$$

where $H(\mathbf{q}; \mathbf{p})$ is the Hamilton function. If the system starts from an initial point $\{q_1(0), \ldots, q_f(0); p_1(0), \ldots, p_f(0)\} \in \Gamma$ it traverses in the course of time an unambiguously defined continuous set of states – the orbit in phase space – which is determined by the Hamiltonian equations (12.1). This implies that the trajectory proceeds from each of its state in *one unambiguous direction and velocity only*.

The *stochastic trajectory* of a probabilistically evolving system *behaves in a completely different manner!* Let us consider the short time behavior for an infinitesimally small time interval δt of a stochastic system which is in state i at time $t = 0$. Its further evolution is *not unambiguously defined!* For given probabilistic transition rates per unit of time $w(\mathbf{j}|\mathbf{i})$ from state i to neighboring states j there exists the probability $\delta t w(\mathbf{j}|\mathbf{i})$ that the system may have hopped to a state j in the time interval δt. On the other hand there exists the probability $(1 - \sum_j \delta t w(\mathbf{j}|\mathbf{i}))$ that it may have remained in state i during that time interval δt. If very many, say $S(\mathbf{i})$, equally structured systems – that means systems fitted out with the same transition rates – are present in state i at time $t = 0$, the fraction $\delta t w(\mathbf{j}|\mathbf{i}) S(\mathbf{i})$ of them will have hopped to state j and the fraction $(1 - \sum_j \delta t w(\mathbf{j}|\mathbf{i})) S(\mathbf{i})$ will have remained in state i during the time interval δt. (Thus, the interpretation of the concept "probability" as "relative frequency in the limit of very many samples" necessitates that we come back to an ensemble of systems!)

Now we trace the sequence of states $\mathbf{j}_1, \mathbf{j}_2, \mathbf{j}_3, \ldots$ traversed by probabilistic sequential hopping processes of the system! Because the process is a probabilistic one the series of states $\mathbf{j}_1, \mathbf{j}_2, \mathbf{j}_3$ is – in contrast to the deterministic case – *not uniquely defined*. Nevertheless some sequences can be preferred against others, i.e. they occur more frequently, depending on the form of the transition rates.

We now make the assumption that each state i is connected with each other state j by at least one chain of intermediate states $\mathbf{i}_1, \mathbf{i}_2, \ldots, \mathbf{i}_{n-1}, \mathbf{i}_n = \mathbf{j}$ with finite transition rates $w(\mathbf{i}_1|\mathbf{i}), w(\mathbf{i}_2|\mathbf{i}_1), \ldots, w(\mathbf{j}|\mathbf{i}_{n-1})$ from i to j, and by at least one chain of intermediate states $\mathbf{j}_1', \mathbf{j}_2', \ldots, \mathbf{j}_{m-1}', \mathbf{j}_m' = \mathbf{i}$ with finite transition rates $w(\mathbf{j}_1'|\mathbf{j}), w(\mathbf{j}_2'|\mathbf{j}_1'), \ldots,$ $w(\mathbf{i}|\mathbf{j}_{m-1}')$ from j to i.

This seemingly weak assumption has the farreaching consequence that, starting from an arbitrary initial state i, the stochastic trajectory can "*sooner or later*" reach *any one* of the possible states j with a finite probability and that, complementary to this statement, the probability of completely *avoiding* a given state j in the time interval Δt goes to zero for $\Delta t \to \infty$. Since the same holds for the return from any state j to the initial state i, there exists a finite probability that a stochastic trajectory which has left the initial state i at time $t = 0$ will "sooner or later", i.e. in a given mean time interval, return to the initial state.

These statements for *stochastic trajectories*, which are intuitively clear but involve complicated mathematics if formulated in terms of exact theorems, have their analogy in the case of *deterministic Hamiltonian trajectories* (see above), for which the French mathematician Poincaré could prove the famous *recurrence theorem* stating that Hamiltonian systems obeying equations (12.1) and starting from initial states confined to a small subset $\gamma \subset \Gamma$ of the phase space Γ (with finite total volume $\phi(\Gamma) < \infty$) *must return* to the subset γ "sooner or later", i.e. after a finite mean recurrence time T. It turns out, however, that T is extremely large (compared with the age of the cosmos) for all realistic systems, so that this theoretical statement has no practical consequences.

We are now particularly interested in the relation between a large ensemble of, say, $S \ggg 1$ systems, each of them moving probabilistically along a stochastic trajectory, and the probability distribution $P(\mathbf{j}; t)$.

We begin with the *stationary case*. Then in each state $\mathbf{i}$ (or more illustratively in each "cell" $\mathbf{i}$) we find $S(\mathbf{i})$ systems at each moment of time, so that

$$\sum_{\mathbf{i}} S(\mathbf{i}) = S. \tag{12.2}$$

Writing

$$S(\mathbf{i}) = S \cdot Q(\mathbf{i}) \quad \text{with} \quad \sum_{\mathbf{i}} Q(\mathbf{i}) = 1, \tag{12.3}$$

the quantity $Q(\mathbf{i})$ is the relative frequency to find systems in state $\mathbf{i}$. We will now show that

$$Q(\mathbf{i}) = P_{st}(\mathbf{i}), \tag{12.4}$$

where $P_{st}(\mathbf{i})$ is the stationary probability which satisfies the stationary master equation (10.42).

The proof follows from a simple consideration: Each of the S systems traverses a stochastic trajectory by hopping from state to state. The stationary mean number $S(\mathbf{i})$ of systems in "cell" $\mathbf{i}$ is then produced by the mean number of systems hopping per unit of time into the cell $\mathbf{i}$ from neighboring cells $\mathbf{j}$ *times* the mean staying time $\bar{\tau}_{\mathbf{i}}$ in cell $\mathbf{i}$.

The *first factor* is equal to

$$\text{number of systems per unit time hopping into cell } \mathbf{i} = \sum_{\mathbf{j}} w(\mathbf{i}|\mathbf{j}) S(\mathbf{j}). \tag{12.5}$$

The *second factor*, the *mean staying time* $\bar{\tau}_{\mathbf{i}}$, must now be calculated. For this purpose let us introduce the probability $p_{\mathbf{i}}(\tau)$ of a system, which has arrived in cell $\mathbf{i}$ at a time $t = 0$, to stay in this cell until time τ. Evidently, $p_{\mathbf{i}}(\tau)$ is a monotonously decreasing function with $p_{\mathbf{i}}(0) = 1$. To derive the functional form of $p_{\mathbf{i}}(\tau)$ we state that

$$p_{\mathbf{i}}(\tau + \delta\tau) = p_{\mathbf{i}}(\tau) - \delta p_{\mathbf{i}}(\tau), \tag{12.6}$$

where $\delta p_i(\tau)$ is the probability to haven been in cell $\mathbf{i}$ until time τ times the probability to make a transition into any other cell in the time interval $(\tau, \tau + \delta\tau)$, i.e.

$$\delta p_i(\tau) = p_i(\tau) \cdot \delta\tau w(\mathbf{i})$$

$$\text{with} \quad w(\mathbf{i}) = \sum_j w(\mathbf{j}|\mathbf{i}). \tag{12.7}$$

From (12.6) and (12.7) there follows

$$\frac{dp_i(\tau)}{d\tau} = -w(\mathbf{i}) \cdot p_i(\tau) \tag{12.8}$$

with the solution

$$p_i(\tau) = \exp(-w(\mathbf{i})\tau), \tag{12.9}$$

where the initial condition $p_i(0) = 1$ has been taken into account.

The mean staying time $\bar{\tau}_i$ is then easily calculated starting from its definition:

$$\bar{\tau}_i = \int_0^\infty \tau \cdot \delta p_i(\tau) = -\int_0^\infty \tau \cdot \frac{dp_i}{d\tau} d\tau$$

$$= -[\tau p_i(\tau)]_0^\infty + \int_0^\infty p_i(\tau) d\tau = \frac{1}{w(\mathbf{i})}. \tag{12.10}$$

With (12.5) and (12.10) we now obtain

$$S(\mathbf{i}) = \frac{1}{w(\mathbf{i})} \cdot \sum_j w(\mathbf{i}|\mathbf{j}) S(\mathbf{j}) \tag{12.11}$$

or, inserting (12.3) and (12.7):

$$\sum_j w(\mathbf{j}|\mathbf{i}) Q(\mathbf{i}) = \sum_j w(\mathbf{i}|\mathbf{j}) Q(\mathbf{j}) \tag{12.12}$$

Since the equation (12.12) coincides with the stationary master equation (10.42) and $Q(\mathbf{i})$ is normalized by (12.3), the statement (12.4) is a direct consequence.

The nonstationary equation for

$$S(\mathbf{i}; t) = S \cdot Q(\mathbf{i}; t) \tag{12.13}$$

follows from the formula

$$\text{number of systems per unit time hopping out of cell } \mathbf{i} = \sum_j w(\mathbf{j}|\mathbf{i}) S(\mathbf{i}; t) \tag{12.14}$$

together with (12.5), and the balance consideration, that the increase per unit of time of the number of systems in cell $\mathbf{i}$ is the difference of the number of systems hopping into and hopping out of cell $\mathbf{i}$ per unit of time, i.e.

$$\frac{dS(\mathbf{i}; t)}{dt} = \sum_{\mathbf{j}} w(\mathbf{i}\,|\,\mathbf{j})S(\mathbf{j}; t) - \sum_{\mathbf{j}} w(\mathbf{j}\,|\,\mathbf{i})S(\mathbf{i}; t) \qquad (12.15)$$

which immediately leads to the time-dependent master equation (10.24) for $Q(\mathbf{i}; t)$.

12.2 Quasi-Meanvalues, their Dynamic Equations and their Relation to Stochastic Trajectories

We are now searching for quantities which *characterize the mean behavior of stochastic trajectories* without comprising the full complexity of their random hopping process. We consider this question in the configuration space of states $\mathbf{n} = \{n_1, n_2, \ldots, n_L\}$.

At first sight one might guess that the meanvalues $\bar{\mathbf{n}} = \{\bar{n}_1(t), \bar{n}_2(t), \ldots, \bar{n}_L(t)\}$ over the probability distribution $P(\mathbf{n}; t)$ are these appropriate quantities.

For a *unimodal* probability distribution this is indeed true, since the meanvalues $\bar{\mathbf{n}}(t)$ essentially agree with the states $\mathbf{n}_{max}(t)$ where the probability has its maximum. On the other hand the number of systems being momentarily in state $\mathbf{n}$ is proportional to $P(\mathbf{n}; t)$, so that $\bar{\mathbf{n}}(t) \approx \mathbf{n}_{max}(t)$ characterizes the state where most of the systems are at time t.

However for multimodal probability distributions the situation is different. Now there exist several states $\mathbf{n}_{1, max}(t), \mathbf{n}_{2, max}(t), \ldots$ where $P(\mathbf{n}; t)$ has relative maxima and where a majority of the stochastic trajectories abide at time t. The unambiguously defined meanvalue $\bar{\mathbf{n}}(t)$, on the other hand, lies somewhere *between* the states $\mathbf{n}_{1, max}(t), \mathbf{n}_{2, max}(t), \ldots$ of maximal probability and is therefore *not appropriate* to characterize the mean evolution of trajectories.

In order to find better quantities $\hat{\mathbf{n}}(t) = \{\hat{n}_1(t), \ldots, \hat{n}_L(t)\}$ instead of $\bar{\mathbf{n}}(t)$ which characterize the states along which the clusters of stochastically hopping systems are evolving in the mean, we start with a cluster of, say C, systems at position $\mathbf{n}$ in configuration space at time t. In the interval δt a fraction $\delta t w_{ji}(\mathbf{n})$ of the C systems has made the transition $\mathbf{n} \to \mathbf{n}_{ji} = \{n_1, \ldots, (n_i - 1), \ldots, (n_j + 1), \ldots, n_L\}$.

Let us now consider the position-component n_j: The fraction $\delta t \sum_i w_{ji}(\mathbf{n})$ of the C systems has changed this component from n_j to $(n_j + 1)$ in δt, and the fraction $\delta t \sum_i w_{ij}(\mathbf{n})$ has changed it from n_j to $(n_j - 1)$ in δt, whereas the fraction $[1 - \delta t(\sum_i w_{ji}(\mathbf{n}) + \sum_i w_{ij}(\mathbf{n}))]$ has retained its coordinate n_j. The meanvalue $\hat{n}_j$ of the coordinate n_j in the considered cluster has therefore changed in δt as follows:

$$(\hat{n}_j + d\hat{n}_j) = (\hat{n}_j + 1)\delta t \sum_i w_{ji}(\hat{\mathbf{n}}) + (\hat{n}_j - 1)\delta t \sum_i w_{ij}(\hat{\mathbf{n}})$$

$$+ \hat{n}_j\left[1 - \delta t\left(\sum_i w_{ji}(\hat{\mathbf{n}}) + \sum_i w_{ij}(\hat{\mathbf{n}})\right)\right] \qquad (12.16)$$

or

$$\frac{d\hat{n}_j}{dt} = \sum_i w_{ji}(\hat{\mathbf{n}}) - \sum_i w_{ij}(\hat{\mathbf{n}}).\qquad(12.17)$$

The variables $\hat{\mathbf{n}} = \{\hat{n}_1, \ldots, \hat{n}_L\}$ describing the mean position of a locally concentrated cluster of stochastically evolving systems are denoted as *quasi-meanvalues*. Their *exact equation of motion* is by definition equation (12.17). Only in the case of a *unimodal* probability distribution it agrees with the *approximate meanvalue equation* (11.39). In the case of multimodal probability distributions, equation (12.17) is *no more* an approximation for (true) meanvalues as already explained in detail in Chapter 11. But it *still characterizes* the mean evolution of a localized cluster of stochastic systems!

Evidently the quasi-meanvalue equation (12.17) is much more appropriate to describe this mean evolution behaviour of *individual systems* at point $\hat{\mathbf{n}}$ than the exact meanvalue equation (11.16), in particular if the evolution belongs to a multi-modal probability distribution $P(\mathbf{n}; t)$. The reason is the following: In the quasi-meanvalue equation (12.17) there appear only transition rates depending on the local variables $\hat{\mathbf{n}}(t)$ of the momentary state of the system, whereas in the meanvalue equation (11.16) there appear meanvalues of transition rates taken over the multi-modal distribution $P(\mathbf{n}; t)$. It is well known, however, that the probabilistic behaviour of a stochastic system is *only influenced* by its *momentary local state* and *not* by far distant states which appear in the distribution $P(\mathbf{n}; t)$.

The equations (12.17) are a *system of autonomous nonlinear differential equations for the quasi-meanvalues*. They may have several *attractors*, i.e. solutions into which $\hat{\mathbf{n}}(t)$ evolves for $t \to \infty$. Such attractors can be stationary states, limit cycles or so called strange attractors. Each attractor has a "*basin of attraction*" . That means, initial states lying in the basin of attraction of an attractor will approach this attractor asymptotically.

Whereas the meanvalue $\bar{\mathbf{n}}(t)$ of a probability distribution is unambiguously defined and reaches *one* unambiguous stationary state $\bar{\mathbf{n}}_{st}$, the evolution of quasi-meanvalues in general depends on their *initial state*. This means, the stationary final state reached for $t \to \infty$, if it exists at all, is *path-dependent*. In many cases the quasi-meanvalues do not approach stationary states but limit cycles or strange attractors. This can occur if the condition of detailed balance is not fulfilled.

Quasi-meanvalues and their equations of motion are of special importance for social systems because, as already mentioned, only one or a few stochastic traject-ories are empirically at disposal. The quasi-meanvalue equation then takes (for given transition rates) the average over the flows into the random directions to which the stochastic trajectory may proceed: As long as the "velocity" $\dot{\hat{\mathbf{n}}}$, i.e. the l.h.s. of (12.17) does not vanish, there exists at position $\hat{\mathbf{n}}(t)$ a *preferential direction* into which the probabilistic process drives the systems. If on the other hand $\hat{\mathbf{n}}$ has reached a stationary value $\hat{\mathbf{n}}_{st}$, with vanishing velocity $\dot{\hat{\mathbf{n}}}$, the random motions of the stochastic trajectories do not disappear, but the fluctuations starting from $\hat{\mathbf{n}}_{st}$ go with equal probability into all directions being opposite to each other. In the case of detailed balance it is for individual stochastic trajectories *less probable* to fluctuate *away from* a stable state $\hat{\mathbf{n}}_{st}$ than to fluctuate *towards* this stable state. This follows from the fact that stable stationary states of the quasi-meanvalue equations (12.17) are then simultaneously maxima of the stationary probability distribution $P_{st}(\mathbf{n})$. Furthermore, $P_{st}(\mathbf{n})$ is proportional to the stationary number of stochastic systems in a state $\mathbf{n}$. Because of $P_{st}(\mathbf{n}_{max}) > P_{st}(\mathbf{n})$ and because detailed balance holds it must be more probable to fluctuate from state $\mathbf{n}$ to state $\mathbf{n}_{max}$ than vice versa because otherwise the stationary distribution of systems over states could not be maintained.

Stationary, Stagnating and Transient States

In order to characterize stages of *stationarity*, *stagnation* and *transience* of a stochastic system $\mathbf{n} = \{n_1, n_2, \ldots, n_L\}$ it is useful to introduce the *evolution speed parameter*

$$s(\hat{\mathbf{n}}) = \left[\sum_{i=1}^{L} (\dot{\hat{n}}_i)^2\right]^{1/2} \geq 0$$

$$\text{with} \quad \dot{\hat{n}}_i \equiv \frac{d\hat{n}_i}{dt}.$$

(12.18)

Evidently, the positive semidefinite quantity $s(\hat{\mathbf{n}})$ is a function of the system point $\hat{\mathbf{n}}$, if equations (12.17) are inserted on the r.h.s. of (12.18).

We can now define:

Stationary states $\mathbf{n} = \hat{\mathbf{n}}_{st}$ *by*

$$s(\hat{\mathbf{n}}_{st}) = 0$$

(12.19)

which is equivalent to

$$\dot{\hat{n}}_i(\hat{\mathbf{n}}_{st}) = 0 \quad \text{for} \quad i = 1, 2, \ldots L.$$

(12.20)

Stagnating states $\hat{\mathbf{n}} = \hat{\mathbf{n}}_{stg}$ *by*

$$s(\hat{\mathbf{n}}) = \text{Min} \quad \text{at} \quad \hat{\mathbf{n}} = \hat{\mathbf{n}}_{stg}.$$

(12.21)

Transient states $\hat{\mathbf{n}} = \hat{\mathbf{n}}_{tr}$ *by*

$$s(\hat{\mathbf{n}}) = \text{Max} \quad \text{at} \quad \hat{\mathbf{n}} = \hat{\mathbf{n}}_{tr}.$$

(12.22)

A stationary state is always a stagnating state, since $s(\hat{\mathbf{n}})$ is a positive definite quantity and $s(\hat{\mathbf{n}}) = 0$ is its absolute minimum. However, the inverse is not true! Beneath stationary points $\hat{\mathbf{n}}_{st}$ where $s(\hat{\mathbf{n}})$ assumes its *absolute* minimum, there may exist system points $\hat{\mathbf{n}}_{stg}$ where $s(\hat{\mathbf{n}})$ assumes relative minima.

At stationary or stagnating states the fluctuating hopping processes of an ensemble of stochastic trajectories compensate either *exactly* or *approximately* so that their resulting mean speed described by the quasi-meanvalue equations (12.17) is either zero or very small. This means that the system is more or less trapped at $\hat{\mathbf{n}}_{st}$ or $\hat{\mathbf{n}}_{stg}$. Conversely, it is very probable that a system will *soon leave a transient* state $\hat{\mathbf{n}}_{tr}$, because the hopping processes of the stochastic trajectories have here a large bias towards the preferential direction given by the vector $\hat{\mathbf{n}}$ which has maximal amplitude at $\hat{\mathbf{n}}_{tr}$.

In Chapter 6 examples of stochastic trajectories (see Figure 6.6(d) and Figures 6.7(b) and 6.7(e)) and of stagnation points (see Figure 6.7(d)) have been exhibited and discussed.

References and Related Literature

The references and the literature for further reading are ordered according to the Parts I, II.1, II.2, II.3, II.4 and III of the book:

I   Structures and Modelling Concepts (Chapters 1, 2, 3)

[1] Nicolai Hartmann (1940). *Der Aufbau der realen Welt*, Walter de Gruyter, Berlin.

[2] Nicolai Hartmann (1941). *Zur Grundlegung der Ontologie*, Walter de Gruyter, Berlin.

[3] Ilya Prigogine and Isabelle Stengers (1981). *Dialog mit der Natur – Neue Wege natur- wissenschaftlichen Denkens*, Piper-Verlag, München.

[4] Hermann Haken (1981). *Erfolgsgeheimnisse der Natur*, Deutsche Verlags-Anstalt.

[5] Werner Ebeling and Rainer Feistel (1994). *Chaos und Kosmos-Prinzipien der Evolution*, Spektrum, Akademischer Verlag.

[6] Bernulf Kanitscheider (1993). *Von der mechanistischen Welt zum kreativen Universum – Zu einem neuen philosophischen Verständnis der Natur*, Wissenschaftliche Buchgesell- schaft, Darmstadt.

[7] Klaus Mainzer (1996). *Thinking in Complexity, The Complex Dynamics of Matter, Mind and Mankind*, Springer-Verlag.

[8] Hermann Haken (1977). *Synergetics – An Introduction; Nonequilibrium Phase Transitions and Self-Organization in Physics, Chemistry and Biology*, Springer-Verlag.

[9] Ludwig von Bertalanffy (1971). *General System Theory; Foundations, Development, Applications*, Allen Lane The Penguin Press, London.

[10] Anatol Rapoport (1986). *General System Theory; Essential Concepts & Applications*, Abacus Press, Cambridge, Mass.

[11] Paul Glansdorff and Ilya Prigogine (1971). *Thermodynamic Theory of Structure, Stability and Fluctuations*, Wiley, Interscience, London.

[12] John S. Nicolis (1986). *Dynamics of Hierarchical Systems, an Evolutionary Approach*, Springer-Verlag.

[13] John Casti (1985). *Nonlinear System Theory*, Academic Press, Orlando.

[14] Stuart A. Kauffman (1993). *The Origins of Order; Selforganisation and Selection in Evolution*, Oxford University Press.

[15] Mosekilde, E. and Mouritsen, O. G. (eds) (19..). *Modelling the Dynamics of Biological Systems*, Springer-Verlag.

[16] Werner Ebeling, Manfred Peschel and Wolfgang Weidlich (eds) (1991). *Models of Self- organisation in Complex Systems, MOSES*, Akademie Verlag.

[17] Frank Schweitzer (ed.) (1997). *Self-Organization of Complex Structures – From Individual to Collective Dynamics*, Gordon and Breach Science Publishers.

[18] Jürgen Parisi, Stefan C. Müuller and Walter Zimmermann (eds) (1998). *A Perspective Look at Nonlinear Media – from Physics to Biology and Social Sciences*, Springer-Verlag.

[19] Oswald Spengler (1922). *Der Untergang des Abendlandes*, Beck-Verlag, München.

[20] Hermann Haken (1993). *Advanced Synergetics: Instability Hierarchies of Self-Organizing Systems and Devices*, Springer-Verlag.

[21] Hermann Haken (19..). *Principles of Brain Functioning; A Synergetic Approach to Brain Activity, Behaviour and Cognition*, Springer-Verlag.

[22] Hermann Haken (1970). *Encyclopedia of Physics, Vol. XXV/2c. Light and Matter*, Springer-Verlag.

[23] Hermann Haken (1964). "Statistische nichtlineare Theorie des Laserlichts", *Z. Physik*, **181**, p. 96.

[24] Montroll, E. W. and Badger, W. W. (1974). *Introduction to Quantitative Aspects of Social Phenomena*, Gordon and Breach, New York.

[25] Hermann Haken (1996). "Synergetik und Sozialwissenschaften", pp. 587–675, in: Benseler, F., Blanek, B., Greshoff, R., Keil-Slawik, R. and Loh, W. (eds), *Ethik und Sozialwissenschaften (EuS)*, 7.

[26] Renate Mayntz (1992). "The Influence of Natural Science Theories on Contemporary Social Science", pp. 27–79, in: Dierkes, M. and Biervert, B. (eds), *European Social Science in Transition*, Campus, Frankfurt (M).

[27] Wolfgang Weidlich (1972). "The use of statistical models in sociology", *Collective Phenomena*, **1**, p. 51.

[28] Wolfgang Weidlich and Günter Haag (1983). *Concepts and Models of a Quantitative Sociology*, Springer-Verlag.

[29] Wolfgang Weidlich (1987). "Quantitative Social Science", *Physica Scripta*, **35**, pp. 380–387.

[30] Wolfgang Weidlich (1988). "Stability and Cyclicity in Social Systems", *Behavioral Science*, **33**, pp. 241–256.

[31] Wolfgang Weidlich (1990). "Quantitative Social Science – the Dynamics of Social Processes", pp. 321–338, in: Gladitz, J. and Troitzsch, K. G. (eds), *Computer Aided Sociological Research*, Akademie-Verlag Berlin.

[32] Wolfgang Weidlich (1991). "Physics and Social Science – The Approach of Synergetics", *Physics Reports*, **204**, pp. 1–163.

[33] Dirk Helbing (1995). *Quantitative Sociodynamics, Stochastic Methods and Models of Social Interaction Processes*, Kluwer Academic Publishers.

[34] Wolfgang Weidlich (1998). "The Modelling Concept of Sociodynamics", pp. 140–162, in: Jürgen Parisi *et al.* (eds), *A Perspective Look at Nonlinear Media – from Physics to Biology and Social Science*, Springer-Verlag.

[35] Dirk Helbing and Wolfgang Weidlich (1995). "Quantitative Soziodynamik – Gegenstand, Methodik, Ergebnisse und Perspektiven", *Kölner Zeitschrift für Soziologie und Sozialpsychologie*, **47**, pp. 114–140.

[36] Jakob Burckhardt (1978). *Weltgeschichtliche Betrachtungen*, Alfred Kröner Verlag, Stuttgart.

II.1   Application to Population Dynamics (Chapter 4)

[1] Samuel P. Huntington (1996). *The Clash of Civilisations*, Simon & Schuster, New York.

[2] Franciss Fukuyama (1993). *End of history and the last man*, Penguin.

[3] Ian Kershaw (1995). *Der NS-Staat. Geschichtsinterpretationen und Kontroversen im Überblick*, Reinbek; original English edition (1988).

[4] Daniel Jonah Goldhagen (1997). *Hitlers Willing Executioners*, Abacus.

[5] Victor Klemperer (1998). *I will be witness*, Random House.

[6] Eberhard Jäckel (1988). *Hitlers Herrschaft*, 2nd edition, Deutsche Verlags-Anstalt.

[7] Stéphane Courtois *et al.* (1997). *Le livre noir du communisme*, Editions Robert Laffont, Paris.

[8] Dimitrios S. Dendrinos and Michael Sonis (1990). *Chaos and Socio-Spatial Dynamics*, Springer-Verlag.

[9] Everett S. Lee (1966). "A Theory of Migration", pp. 47–57, *Demography*.

[10] Michael Sonis (1997). "Socio-Ecology, Competition of Elites and Collective Choice: Implication for Culture of Peace", pp. 77–83 in: Lasker, G. E. (ed.), *Advances in Socio-cybernetics and Human Development, Vol. V: Culture of Peace, Human Habitat and Sustainable Living,*.

[11] Martin Munz and Wolfgang Weidlich (1990). "Settlement formation: (I) A dynamic theory", pp. 83–106, and "(II) Numerical simulation", pp. 177–196, *The Annals of Regional Science*, **24**.

[12] Denise Pumain (ed.) (1991). *Spatial analysis and population dynamics*, John Libbey Eurotext Ltd.

[13] Wolfgang Weidlich and Günter Haag (1980). "Migration behaviour of mixed populations in a town", *Collective Phenomena*, **3**, p. 89.

[14] Wolfgang Weidlich and Günter Haag (1980). "Dynamics of interacting groups in society with application to the migration of population", in: Haken H. (ed.), *Dynamics of Synergetic Systems*, Springer-Verlag.

[15] Wolfgang Weidlich and Günter Haag (1983). *Concepts and Models of a Quantitative Sociology*, Springer-Verlag.

[16] Wolfgang Weidlich (1991). "Physics and Social Science – The Approach of Synergetics", *Physics Reports*, **204**, pp. 1–163.

[17] Rolf Reiner, Martin Munz, Günter Haag and Wolfgang Weidlich (1986). "Chaotic evolution of migratory systems", pp. 285–308, *Sistemi Urbani*, **2**.

[18] Rolf Reiner, Martin Munz and Wolfgang Weidlich (1988). "Migratory dynamics of interacting subpopulations: regular and chaotic behaviour", pp. 179–199, *System Dynamics Review*, **4**.

[19] Rolf Reiner and Martin Munz (1990). "Chaotic evolution of migratory systems", pp. 725–736, and "Quantitative analysis of migratory systems", pp. 737–748, in: Fuchs-steiner, B., Lengauer, T. and Skala, H. J. (eds), *Methods of Operation Research 60*, Anton Hain, Paderborn.

[20] Rolf Reiner (1988). *Interregionale Migration – Theoretische und numerische Analyse des Zwei-Populationenfalls*, PhD thesis, Universität Stuttgart.

[21] Wolfgang Weidlich and Günter Haag (eds) (1988). *Interregional Migration – Dynamic Theory and Comparative Analysis*, Springer-Verlag.

[22] Günter Haag and Dimitrios S. Dendrinos "Toward a stochastic dynamical theory of location: (I) A nonlinear migration process", pp. 269–286, *Geographical Analysis*, **15** (1983). "(II) Empirical Evidence", pp. 287–300, *Geographical Analysis*, **16** (1984).

[23] Günter Haag and Wolfgang Weidlich (1986). "A dynamic migration theory and its evaluation for concrete systems", pp. 57–80, *Regional Science and Urban Economics*, **16**.

II.2 Applications to Sociology (Chapters 5 and 6)

[1] Burt, R. S.(1982). *Toward a Structural Theory of Action*, Academic Press, New York.

[2] Homans, G. C. (1950). *The Human Group*, Harcourt Brace, New York.

[3] Homans, G. C. (1974). *Social Behavior: Its Elementary Forms*, Harcourt Brace Jovanovich, New York.

[4] Coleman, J. S. (1990). *Foundations of Social Theory*, Harvard University Press, Cambridge, MA.

[5] Durkheim, E.(1915). *The Elementary Forms of Religious Life*, Free Press, New York.

[6] Bellatz, R. N. (ed.) (1973). *Emile Durkheim on Morality and Society*, University of Chicago Press.

[7] Durkheim, E. (1964). *The Division of Labour in Society*, Mac Millan, New York.

[8] Parsons, T.(1951). *The Social System*, Free Press, New York.

[9] Parsons, T. (1967). *Sociological Theory and Modern Society*, Free Press, New York.

[10] Collins, R. (1981). "On the micro-foundations of macrosociology", *American Journal of Sociology*, **86**, pp. 984–1014.

[11] Collins, R. (1988). *Theoretical Sociology*, Harcourt Brace Jovanovich, San Diego.

[12] Glance, N. S. and Huberman, B. A. (1993). "The outbreak of cooperation", *Journal of Mathematical Sociology*, **17**, pp. 281–302.

[13] Axelrod, R. (1984). *The Evolution of Cooperation*, Basic Books, New York.

[14] Hechter, M. (1987). *Principles of Group Solidarity*, University of California Press, Berkeley.

[15] Patrick Doreian and Thomas Fararo (eds) (1998). *The Problem of Solidarity; Theories and Models*, Gordon and Breach.

[16] Matthias Mikuletz (1996). *Analyse und numerische Simulation eines Modells der Gruppendynamik*, Diplom Thesis, Universität Stuttgart.

[17] Eberhard Jäckel (1996). *Das deutsche Jahrhundert, Eine historische Bilanz*, Deutsche Verlags-Anstalt Stuttgart.

[18] Jan Kershaw(1998). *Hitler 1889–1936: Hubris*, The Penguin Press, London.

[19] Samuel P. Huntington (1996). *The Clash of Civilisations*, Simon & Schuster, New York.

[20] Michael Sonis (1997). "Socio-Ecology, Competition of Elites and Collective Choice: Implication for Culture of Peace", in: Lasker, G. F. (ed.) *Advances in Sociocybernetics and Human Development, Vol. V: Culture of Peace, Human Habitat and Sustainable Living*.

[21] Wolfgang Weidlich (1991). "Physics and Social Science – The Approach of Synergetics", *Physics Reports*, **204**, pp. 1–163.

[22] Ebeling, W., Peschel, M. and Weidlich, W. (eds) (1991). *Models of Selforganisation in Complex Systems*, Akademie-Verlag Berlin.

[23] Wolfgang Weidlich (1994). "Synergetic modelling concepts for sociodynamics with application to collective political opinion formation", *Journal of Mathematical Sociology*, **18**, pp. 267–291.

[24] Wolfgang Weidlich (1971). "The statistical description of polarization phenomena in society", *Math. Br. J., Stat., Psychol.*, **24**, p. 51.

[25] Wolfgang Weidlich and Günter Haag (1983). *Concepts and Models of a Quantitative Sociology*, Springer-Verlag.

[26] Stéphane Courtois *et al.* (1998). *Das Schwarzbuch des Kommunismus*, Piper Verlag, München.

II.3   Applications to Economics (Chapters 7 and 8)

[1] Arrow, K. and Hahn, F. (1971). *General Competitive Analysis*, San Francisco.

[2] James M. Henderson and Richard E. Quandt (1980). *Microeconomic Theory – A Mathematical Approach*, McGraw-Hill Book Company.

[3] Walter Nicholson (1992). *Microeconomic Theory – Basic Principles and Extensions*, The Dryden Press.

[4] Hal R. Varian (1992). *Microeconomic Analysis*, W. W. Norton & Company, New York.
[5] Ulrich Witt (ed.) (1993). *Evolutionary Economics*, Edward Elgar Publishing Company.
[6] Philip W. Anderson, Kenneth J. Arrow, David Pines (eds) (1990). "The Economy as an Evolving Complex System I", *Santa Fe Institute Studies in the Sciences of Complexity*, Vol. V, Addision Wesley, Reading, Mass.
[7] Brian Arthur, W., St. Durlauf, N., David A. Lane (eds) (1997). "The Economy as an Evolving Complex System II", *A Proceedings Volume of the Santa Fe Institute*, Vol. XXVII, Addison Wesley, Reading, Mass.
[8] Schumpeter, J. A. (1934). *The Theory of Economic Development*, Harvard University Press, Cambridge, Mass.
[9] Haag, G., Weidlich, W. and Mensch, G. O. (1987). "The Schumpeter clock", in: Batten, D., Casti, J. and Johansson, B. (eds), *Economic Evolution and Structural Adjustment*, pp. 187–226, Springer-Verlag, and in: Witt, U. (ed.) (1993), *Evolutionary Economics*, Edward Elgar Publ. Comp.
[10] Frank C. Englmann (1994). "A Schumpeterian model of endogenous innovation and growth", *Journal of Evolutionary Economics*, pp. 227–241.
[11] Silverberg, G. (1988). "Modelling Economic Dynamics and Technical Change: Mathematical Approaches to Selforganisation and Evolution", pp. 531–559, in: Dosi, G., Freeman, C., Nelson, R., Silverberg, G. and Soete, L. (eds), *Technical Change and Economic Theory*, Pinter, London.
[12] Vasko, T. (ed.) (1985). *The Long-Wave Debate*, Springer-Verlag.
[13] Hayek, F. A. (1967). "Notes on the Evolution of Systems of Rules of Conduct", pp. 66–81, in: Hayek, F. A., *Studies in Philosophy and Economics*, Routledge and Kegan Paul, London.
[14] Hayek, F. A. (1988). *The Fatal Conceit*, Routledge, London.
[15] Alchian, A. A. (1950). "Uncertainty, Evolution and Economic Theory", *Journal of Political Economy*, 58, pp. 211–221.
[16] Penrose, E. T. (1952). "Biological Analogies in the Theory of the Firm", *American Economic Review*, 42, pp. 804–819.
[17] Nelson, R. R. and Winter, S. G. (1982). *An Evolutionary Theory of Economic Change*, Harvard University Press, Cambridge, Mass.
[18] Matthews, R. C. O. (1984). "Darwinism and Economic Change", pp. 91–117, in: Collard, D. A., Helm, D. R., Scott, M. F. G. and Sen, A. K. (eds), *Economic Theory and Hicksian Themes*, Clarendon Press, Oxford.
[19] Bruckner, E., Ebeling, W., Jimenez, M. A. Montano and Scharnhorst, A. (1996). "Nonlinear stochastic effects of substitution – An evolutionary approach", *Journal of Evolutionary Economics*, pp. 1–30.
[20] Günter Haag (1990). "A master equation formulation of aggregate and disaggegrate economic decision making", *Sistemi Urbani*, 1, pp. 65–81.
[21] Georg Erdmann (1993). *Elemente einer evolutorischen Innovationstheorie*, J. C. B. Mohr (Paul Siebeck), Tübingen.
[22] Masanao Aoki (1996). *New Approaches to Macroeconomic Modeling: Evolutionary Stochastic Dynamics, Multiple Equilibria and Externalities as Field Effects*, Cambridge University Press.
[23] Wei-Bin Zhang (1991). *Synergetic Economics – Time and Change in Nonlinear Economics*, Springer-Verlag.
[24] Tönu Puu (1992). *Nonlinear Economic Dynamics*, Springer-Verlag.
[25] Holyst, J. A., Hagel, T., Haag, G. and Weidlich, W. (1996). "How to control a chaotic economy", *Journal of Evolutionary Economics*, 6, pp. 31–42.
[26] Kauffman, S. A. (1993). *The Origins of Order – Self-Organization and Selection in Evolution*, Oxford University Press.

[27] Wolfgang Weidlich and Martin Braun (1992). "The Master Equation Approach to Nonlinear Economics", *Journal of Evolutionary Economics*, **2**, pp. 233–265.

[28] Ulrich Witt (ed.) (1993). "Evolution in Markets and Institutions", in: Weidlich, W. and Braun, M. *The master equation approach to nonlinear economics*, pp. 85–117, Physica Verlag, Heidelberg.

[29] Wolfgang Weidlich and Thomas Brenner (1995). "Dynamics of Demand including Fashion Effects for Interacting Consumer Groups", in: Wagner, A. and Lorenz, H. W. (eds) *Studien zur Evolutorischen Okonomik III*, pp. 79–115, Duncker & Humblot, Berlin.

[30] Hermann Haken (1977). *Synergetics – An Introduction; Nonequilibrium Phase Transitions and Self-Organization in Physics, Chemistry and Biology*, Springer-Verlag.

[31] Sherif, M. and Sherif, C. W. (1956). *An Outline of Social Psychology*, New York.

[32] Asch, S. E. (1956). "Studies of Independence and Conformity", *Psychological Monographs*, **70**, pp. 1–70.

[33] Simmel, G. (1904). "Fashion", *International Quarterly*, **10**, pp. 130–155.

[34] McCracken, G. D. (1985). "The Trickle-Down Theory Rehabilitated", in: Solomon, M. R. (ed.), *The Psychology of Fashion*, Lexington MA/Toronto.

[35] Blumer, H. (1968). "Fashion: From Class Differentiation to Collective Selection", *Sociological Quarterly*, **10**, pp. 275–291.

[36] Leibenstein, H. (1976). *Beyond Economic Man: A New Foundation for Micro-economics*, Cambridge, MA.

[37] Adams, R. D. and McCormick, K. (1992). "Fashion Dynamics and the Economic Theory of Clubs", *Review of Social Economy*, **50**, pp. 24–39.

[38] Bikhchandani, S., Hirshleifer, D. and Welch, I. (1992). "A Theory of Fads, Fashion, Custom, and Cultural Change as Informational Cascades", *Journal of Political Economy*, **100**, pp. 992–1026.

[39] MacIntegre, S. H. and Miller, C. M. (1992). "Social Utility and Fashion Behaviour", *Marketing Letters*, **3**, pp. 371–382.

[40] Weise, P. (1993). "Eine dynamische Analyse von Konsumptionseffekten", *Jahrbücher für Nationalökonomie und Statistik*, **211**, pp. 159–172.

II.4   Application to Regional Science (Chapter 9)

[1] Yorgiou Papageorgiou (1980). "On Sudden Urban Growth", *Environment and Planning A*, **12**.

[2] Herbert Girardet (1992). *The Age of Cities*, Gaia Books Limited.

[3] Stöckle, S. (1998). *Untersuchungen eines mathematischen Modells der Stadtentwicklung unter Populationsdruck*, Diplomarbeit Universität Stuttgart.

[4] Wolfgang Weidlich (1997). "Sociodynamics applied to the evolution of urban and regional structures", *International Journal of Discrete Chaotic Dynamics* 1, pp. 85–98.

[5] Wolfgang Weidlich (1995). "From fast to slow processes in the evolution of urban and regional settlement structures", in: *Proceedings of the International Conference on Self-Organization of Complex Structures*, Berlin.

[6] Timm Sigg and Wolfgang Weidlich (1998). "A Mathematical Model of Urban Evolution", *Geographical Systems*, **5**, pp. 261–300.

[7] Allen, P. and Sanglier, M. "Dynamic models of urban growth", *Journal of Social and Biological Structures*, **1**, pp. 265–280 (1978), and **2**, pp. 269–298 (1979).

[8] Allen, P. and Sanglier, M. (1979). *A Dynamic Model of growth in a central place system*, *Geographical Analysis*, **11**, pp. 256–277.

[9] Allen, P. and Sanglier, M. (1981). *Urban Evolution, Self-Organisation and Decision Making*, *Environment and Planning*, **13**, pp. 167–183.

[10] White, R. and Engelen, G. (1993). "Cellular automata and fractal urban form: a cellular modelling approach to the evolution of urban land-use patterns", *Environment and Planning A*, **25**, pp. 1175–1199.
[11] White, R. and Engelen, G. (1993). "Complex Dynamics and Fractal Urban Form", Chapter 10 in: Nijkamp, P. and Reggiani, A. (eds), *Nonlinear Evolution of Spatial Economic Systems*, Springer-Verlag.
[12] White, R. and Engelen, G. (1997). "Cellular automata as the basis of integrated dynamic regional modelling", *Environment and Planning B: Planning and Design*, 24, pp. 235–246.
[13] White, R. and Engelen, G. (1997). "The use of constrained cellular automata for high-resolution modelling of urban land-use dynamics", *Environment and Planning B*, 24, pp. 323–343.
[14] Denise Pumain, Lena Sanders et Thérèse Saint-Julien (1989). "Villes et Auto-Organisation", *Economica*, Paris.
[15] Denise Pumain (ed.) (1991). *Spatial analysis and population dynamics*, John Libbey Eurotext Ltd.
[16] Lena Sanders (1992). "Système de Villes et Synergétique", *Anthropos-Economica*.
[17] Bernard Lepetit and Denise Pumain (1993). *Temporalités Urbaines*, Anthropos-Economica.
[18] Wolfgang Weidlich and Günter Haag (1987). "A dynamic phase-transition model for spatial agglomeration processes", *Journal of Regional Science*, **27**, pp. 529–569.
[19] Günter Haag (1989). *Dynamic Decision Theory: Applications to Urban and Regional Topics*, Kluwer Academic Publishers.
[20] Martin Munz and Wolfgang Weidlich (1990). "Settlement formation: (I) A dynamic theory", pp. 83–106, "(II) Numerical Simulation", pp. 177–196, in: *The Annals of Regional Science*, 24.
[21] Wolfgang Weidlich (1994). *Settlement formation at the Meso-scale*, pp. 507–518, in: Dendrinos, D. S. and ElNaschie, M. S. (eds), *Nonlinear Dynamics in Urban and Transportation Analysis, Special Issue of Chaos, Solitons & Fractals*, Elsevier Science.
[22] Wolfgang Weidlich (1994). "Settlement Formation at the Meso-Scale", *Chaos, Solitons & Fractals*, 4, pp. 507–518.
[23] Wolfgang Weidlich (1991). "Spatial Dynamics of Social Processes", *Socio-Spatial Dynamics*, 2, pp. 111–119.
[24] Pierre Frankhauser (1994). "La Fractalité des Structures urbaines", *Anthropos-Economica*.
[25] Denise Pumain and Günter Haag (1991). "Urban and Regional Dynamics – Towards an integrated Approach", *Environment and Planning A*, **23**, pp. 1301–1313.
[26] Haag, G., Pumain, D., Munz, M., Sanders, L. and Saint-Julien, T. (1992). "Inter-Urban Migration and the Dynamics of a System of Cities: The Stochastic Framework with an Application to the French Urban System", *Environment and Planning A*, **24**, pp. 181–198.
[27] Popkov, Y. S., Shvetsov, V. I. and Weidlich, W. (1998). it Settlement formation models with entropy operator, *Annals of Regional Science*, **32**, pp. 267–294.
[28] Juval Portugali (1996). "The Construction of Cognitive Maps", *The Geo-Journal Library*, **32**, Kluwer Academic Publishers.
[29] Timm Sigg (1996). *Ein mathematisches Modell der Stadtentwicklung unter Populationsdruck*, PhD-Thesis, Universität Stuttgart.

III Mathematical Methods (Chapters 10, 11, 12)

[1] Bharucha-Reid, A. T. (1960). *Elements of the Theory of Markov Processes and their Applications*, McGraw Hill, New York.
[2] Stratonovich, R. L. (1963 and 1967). *Topics in the Theory of Random Noise, Vol I and II*, Gordon and Breach.

[3] van Kampen, N. G. (1983). *Stochastic Processes in Physics and Chemistry*, North-Holland Publishing Company.

[4] Hans Risken (1984). *The Fokker-Planck Equation, Methods of Solution and Applications*, Springer-Verlag.

[5] Crispin W. Gardiner (1983). *Handbook of Stochastic Methods for Physics, Chemistry and the Natural Sciences*, Springer-Verlag.

[6] Wolfgang Weidlich and Günter Haag (1983). *Concepts and Models of a Quantitative Sociology*, Springer-Verlag.

[7] Dirk Helbing (1993). "Boltzmann-like and Boltzmann-Fokker-Planck equations as a foundation of behavioral models", *Physica A*, **196**, pp. 546–573.

[8] Dirk Helbing (1995). *Quantitative Sociodynamics, Stochastic Methods and Models of Social Interaction Processes*, Kluwer Academic Publishers.

[9] Robert Rosen (1970). *Dynamic System Theory in Biology: Vol. I: Stability Theory and its Applications*, Wiley-Interscience.

[10] Morris W. Hirsch and Stephen Smale (1974). *Differential Equations, Dynamical Systems and Linear Algebra*, Academic Press.

[11] Marsden, J. E., McCracken, M. (1976). "The Hopf Bifurcation and its Applications", *Appl. Math. Sc.*, **19**, Springer, New York.

[12] Yury, S. Popkov (1995). *Macrosystems Theory and its Applications*, Springer-Verlag.

[13] Stig I. Andersson, Åke E. Andersson, Ulf Ottoson (eds) (1993). *Dynamical Systems – Theory and Applications*, World Scientific Publishing Co.

[14] Heinz G. Schuster (1985). *Deterministic Chaos – An Introduction*, Physik-Verlag Weinheim.

Author Index

The author index firstly indicates the pages where the author is cited by numbers in brackets, and secondly the pages and parts of the references where the full quotations of the author's publications appear.

371

Subject Index

A CATALOG OF SELECTED
DOVER BOOKS
IN SCIENCE AND MATHEMATICS

Mathematics

FUNCTIONAL ANALYSIS (Second Corrected Edition), George Bachman and Lawrence Narici. Excellent treatment of subject geared toward students with background in linear algebra, advanced calculus, physics and engineering. Text covers introduction to inner-product spaces, normed, metric spaces, and topological spaces; complete orthonormal sets, the Hahn-Banach Theorem and its consequences, and many other related subjects. 1966 ed. 544pp. 6⅛ x 9¼.   0-486-40251-7

ASYMPTOTIC EXPANSIONS OF INTEGRALS, Norman Bleistein & Richard A. Handelsman. Best introduction to important field with applications in a variety of scientific disciplines. New preface. Problems. Diagrams. Tables. Bibliography. Index. 448pp. 5⅜ x 8½.   0-486-65082-0

VECTOR AND TENSOR ANALYSIS WITH APPLICATIONS, A. I. Borisenko and I. E. Tarapov. Concise introduction. Worked-out problems, solutions, exercises. 257pp. 5⅜ x 8¼.   0-486-63833-2

AN INTRODUCTION TO ORDINARY DIFFERENTIAL EQUATIONS, Earl A. Coddington. A thorough and systematic first course in elementary differential equations for undergraduates in mathematics and science, with many exercises and problems (with answers). Index. 304pp. 5⅜ x 8½.   0-486-65942-9

FOURIER SERIES AND ORTHOGONAL FUNCTIONS, Harry F. Davis. An incisive text combining theory and practical example to introduce Fourier series, orthogonal functions and applications of the Fourier method to boundary-value problems. 570 exercises. Answers and notes. 416pp. 5⅜ x 8½.   0-486-65973-9

COMPUTABILITY AND UNSOLVABILITY, Martin Davis. Classic graduate-level introduction to theory of computability, usually referred to as theory of recurrent functions. New preface and appendix. 288pp. 5⅜ x 8½.   0-486-61471-9

ASYMPTOTIC METHODS IN ANALYSIS, N. G. de Bruijn. An inexpensive, comprehensive guide to asymptotic methods—the pioneering work that teaches by explaining worked examples in detail. Index. 224pp. 5⅜ x 8½   0-486-64221-6

APPLIED COMPLEX VARIABLES, John W. Dettman. Step-by-step coverage of fundamentals of analytic function theory—plus lucid exposition of five important applications: Potential Theory; Ordinary Differential Equations; Fourier Transforms; Laplace Transforms; Asymptotic Expansions. 66 figures. Exercises at chapter ends. 512pp. 5⅜ x 8½.   0-486-64670-X

INTRODUCTION TO LINEAR ALGEBRA AND DIFFERENTIAL EQUATIONS, John W. Dettman. Excellent text covers complex numbers, determinants, orthonormal bases, Laplace transforms, much more. Exercises with solutions. Undergraduate level. 416pp. 5⅜ x 8½.   0-486-65191-6

RIEMANN'S ZETA FUNCTION, H. M. Edwards. Superb, high-level study of landmark 1859 publication entitled "On the Number of Primes Less Than a Given Magnitude" traces developments in mathematical theory that it inspired. xiv+315pp. 5⅜ x 8½.   0-486-41740-9

CALCULUS OF VARIATIONS WITH APPLICATIONS, George M. Ewing. Applications-oriented introduction to variational theory develops insight and promotes understanding of specialized books, research papers. Suitable for advanced undergraduate/graduate students as primary, supplementary text. 352pp. 5⅜ x 8½.
0-486-64856-7

COMPLEX VARIABLES, Francis J. Flanigan. Unusual approach, delaying complex algebra till harmonic functions have been analyzed from real variable viewpoint. Includes problems with answers. 364pp. 5⅜ x 8½. 0-486-61388-7

AN INTRODUCTION TO THE CALCULUS OF VARIATIONS, Charles Fox. Graduate-level text covers variations of an integral, isoperimetrical problems, least action, special relativity, approximations, more. References. 279pp. 5⅜ x 8½.
0-486-65499-0

COUNTEREXAMPLES IN ANALYSIS, Bernard R. Gelbaum and John M. H. Olmsted. These counterexamples deal mostly with the part of analysis known as "real variables." The first half covers the real number system, and the second half encompasses higher dimensions. 1962 edition. xxiv+198pp. 5⅜ x 8½. 0-486-42875-3

CATASTROPHE THEORY FOR SCIENTISTS AND ENGINEERS, Robert Gilmore. Advanced-level treatment describes mathematics of theory grounded in the work of Poincaré, R. Thom, other mathematicians. Also important applications to problems in mathematics, physics, chemistry and engineering. 1981 edition. References. 28 tables. 397 black-and-white illustrations. xvii + 666pp. 6⅛ x 9¼.
0-486-67539-4

INTRODUCTION TO DIFFERENCE EQUATIONS, Samuel Goldberg. Exceptionally clear exposition of important discipline with applications to sociology, psychology, economics. Many illustrative examples; over 250 problems. 260pp. 5⅜ x 8½.
0-486-65084-7

NUMERICAL METHODS FOR SCIENTISTS AND ENGINEERS, Richard Hamming. Classic text stresses frequency approach in coverage of algorithms, polynomial approximation, Fourier approximation, exponential approximation, other topics. Revised and enlarged 2nd edition. 721pp. 5⅜ x 8½. 0-486-65241-6

INTRODUCTION TO NUMERICAL ANALYSIS (2nd Edition), F. B. Hildebrand. Classic, fundamental treatment covers computation, approximation, interpolation, numerical differentiation and integration, other topics. 150 new problems. 669pp. 5⅜ x 8½. 0-486-65363-3

THREE PEARLS OF NUMBER THEORY, A. Y. Khinchin. Three compelling puzzles require proof of a basic law governing the world of numbers. Challenges concern van der Waerden's theorem, the Landau-Schnirelmann hypothesis and Mann's theorem, and a solution to Waring's problem. Solutions included. 64pp. 5⅜ x 8½.
0-486-40026-3

THE PHILOSOPHY OF MATHEMATICS: AN INTRODUCTORY ESSAY, Stephan Körner. Surveys the views of Plato, Aristotle, Leibniz & Kant concerning propositions and theories of applied and pure mathematics. Introduction. Two appendices. Index. 198pp. 5⅜ x 8½. 0-486-25048-2

Physics

OPTICAL RESONANCE AND TWO-LEVEL ATOMS, L. Allen and J. H. Eberly. Clear, comprehensive introduction to basic principles behind all quantum optical resonance phenomena. 53 illustrations. Preface. Index. 256pp. 5⅜ x 8½. 0-486-65533-4

QUANTUM THEORY, David Bohm. This advanced undergraduate-level text presents the quantum theory in terms of qualitative and imaginative concepts, followed by specific applications worked out in mathematical detail. Preface. Index. 655pp. 5⅜ x 8½. 0-486-65969-0

ATOMIC PHYSICS (8th EDITION), Max Born. Nobel laureate's lucid treatment of kinetic theory of gases, elementary particles, nuclear atom, wave-corpuscles, atomic structure and spectral lines, much more. Over 40 appendices, bibliography. 495pp. 5⅜ x 8½. 0-486-65984-4

A SOPHISTICATE'S PRIMER OF RELATIVITY, P. W. Bridgman. Geared toward readers already acquainted with special relativity, this book transcends the view of theory as a working tool to answer natural questions: What is a frame of reference? What is a "law of nature"? What is the role of the "observer"? Extensive treatment, written in terms accessible to those without a scientific background. 1983 ed. xlviii+172pp. 5⅜ x 8½. 0-486-42549-5

AN INTRODUCTION TO HAMILTONIAN OPTICS, H. A. Buchdahl. Detailed account of the Hamiltonian treatment of aberration theory in geometrical optics. Many classes of optical systems defined in terms of the symmetries they possess. Problems with detailed solutions. 1970 edition. xv + 360pp. 5⅜ x 8½. 0-486-67597-1

PRIMER OF QUANTUM MECHANICS, Marvin Chester. Introductory text examines the classical quantum bead on a track: its state and representations; operator eigenvalues; harmonic oscillator and bound bead in a symmetric force field; and bead in a spherical shell. Other topics include spin, matrices, and the structure of quantum mechanics; the simplest atom; indistinguishable particles; and stationary-state perturbation theory. 1992 ed. xiv+314pp. 6⅛ x 9¼. 0-486-42878-8

LECTURES ON QUANTUM MECHANICS, Paul A. M. Dirac. Four concise, brilliant lectures on mathematical methods in quantum mechanics from Nobel Prize-winning quantum pioneer build on idea of visualizing quantum theory through the use of classical mechanics. 96pp. 5⅜ x 8½. 0-486-41713-1

THIRTY YEARS THAT SHOOK PHYSICS: THE STORY OF QUANTUM THEORY, George Gamow. Lucid, accessible introduction to influential theory of energy and matter. Careful explanations of Dirac's anti-particles, Bohr's model of the atom, much more. 12 plates. Numerous drawings. 240pp. 5⅜ x 8½. 0-486-24895-X

ELECTRONIC STRUCTURE AND THE PROPERTIES OF SOLIDS: THE PHYSICS OF THE CHEMICAL BOND, Walter A. Harrison. Innovative text offers basic understanding of the electronic structure of covalent and ionic solids, simple metals, transition metals and their compounds. Problems. 1980 edition. 582pp. 6⅛ x 9¼. 0-486-66021-4

A TREATISE ON ELECTRICITY AND MAGNETISM, James Clerk Maxwell. Important foundation work of modern physics. Brings to final form Maxwell's theory of electromagnetism and rigorously derives his general equations of field theory. 1,084pp. 5⅜ x 8½. Two-vol. set.   Vol. I: 0-486-60636-8   Vol. II: 0-486-60637-6

QUANTUM MECHANICS: PRINCIPLES AND FORMALISM, Roy McWeeny. Graduate student-oriented volume develops subject as fundamental discipline, opening with review of origins of Schrödinger's equations and vector spaces. Focusing on main principles of quantum mechanics and their immediate consequences, it concludes with final generalizations covering alternative "languages" or representations. 1972 ed. 15 figures. xi+155pp. 5⅜ x 8½.   0-486-42829-X

INTRODUCTION TO QUANTUM MECHANICS With Applications to Chemistry, Linus Pauling & E. Bright Wilson, Jr. Classic undergraduate text by Nobel Prize winner applies quantum mechanics to chemical and physical problems. Numerous tables and figures enhance the text. Chapter bibliographies. Appendices. Index. 468pp. 5⅜ x 8½.   0-486-64871-0

METHODS OF THERMODYNAMICS, Howard Reiss. Outstanding text focuses on physical technique of thermodynamics, typical problem areas of understanding, and significance and use of thermodynamic potential. 1965 edition. 238pp. 5⅜ x 8½.
0-486-69445-3

THE ELECTROMAGNETIC FIELD, Albert Shadowitz. Comprehensive undergraduate text covers basics of electric and magnetic fields, builds up to electromagnetic theory. Also related topics, including relativity. Over 900 problems. 768pp. 5⅜ x 8¼.   0-486-65660-8

GREAT EXPERIMENTS IN PHYSICS: FIRSTHAND ACCOUNTS FROM GALILEO TO EINSTEIN, Morris H. Shamos (ed.). 25 crucial discoveries: Newton's laws of motion, Chadwick's study of the neutron, Hertz on electromagnetic waves, more. Original accounts clearly annotated. 370pp. 5⅜ x 8½.   0-486-25346-5

EINSTEIN'S LEGACY, Julian Schwinger. A Nobel Laureate relates fascinating story of Einstein and development of relativity theory in well-illustrated, nontechnical volume. Subjects include meaning of time, paradoxes of space travel, gravity and its effect on light, non-Euclidean geometry and curving of space-time, impact of radio astronomy and space-age discoveries, and more. 189 b/w illustrations. xiv+250pp. 8⅜ x 9¼.   0-486-41974-6

STATISTICAL PHYSICS, Gregory H. Wannier. Classic text combines thermodynamics, statistical mechanics and kinetic theory in one unified presentation of thermal physics. Problems with solutions. Bibliography. 532pp. 5⅜ x 8½.   0-486-65401-X

Paperbound unless otherwise indicated. Available at your book dealer, online at **www.doverpublications.com**, or by writing to Dept. GI, Dover Publications, Inc., 31 East 2nd Street, Mineola, NY 11501. For current price information or for free catalogues (please indicate field of interest), write to Dover Publications or log on to **www.doverpublications.com** and see every Dover book in print. Dover publishes more than 500 books each year on science, elementary and advanced mathematics, biology, music, art, literary history, social sciences, and other areas.